Lecture Notes in Computer Science   12147

More information about this series at http://www.springer.com/series/7410

Mauro Conti · Jianying Zhou ·
Emiliano Casalicchio · Angelo Spognardi (Eds.)

Applied Cryptography and Network Security

18th International Conference, ACNS 2020
Rome, Italy, October 19–22, 2020
Proceedings, Part II

 Springer

Editors
Mauro Conti (iD)
Department of Mathematics
University of Padua
Padua, Italy

Jianying Zhou
Singapore University of Technology
and Design
Singapore, Singapore

Emiliano Casalicchio (iD)
Dipt di Informatica Sistemi e Produ
Università di Roma "Tor Vergata"
Rome, Roma, Italy

Angelo Spognardi (iD)
Sapienza University of Rome
Rome, Italy

ISSN 0302-9743 ISSN 1611-3349 (electronic)
Lecture Notes in Computer Science
ISBN 978-3-030-57877-0 ISBN 978-3-030-57878-7 (eBook)
https://doi.org/10.1007/978-3-030-57878-7

LNCS Sublibrary: SL4 – Security and Cryptology

This Springer imprint is published by the registered company Springer Nature Switzerland AG
The registered company address is: Gewerbestrasse 11, 6330 Cham, Switzerland

Preface

We are pleased to present the proceedings of the 18th International Conference on Applied Cryptography and Network Security (ACNS 2020).

ACNS 2020 was planned to be held in Rome, Italy, during June 22–25, 2020. Due to the unexpected covid crisis, we first postponed the conference to October 19–22, 2020, but ended up deciding for the safety of all participants to have a virtual conference. The local organization was in the capable hands of Emiliano Casalicchio and Angelo Spognardi (Sapienza University of Rome, Italy) and Giuseppe Bernieri (University of Padua, Italy) as general co-chairs, and Massimo Bernaschi (CNR, Italy) as organizing chair. We are deeply indebted to them for their tireless work to ensure the success of the conference even in such complex conditions.

For the first time, ACNS had two rounds of submission cycles, with deadlines in September 2019 and January 2020, respectively. We received a total of 214 submissions in two rounds from 43 countries. This year's Program Committee (PC) consisted of 77 members with diverse backgrounds and broad research interests. The review process was double-blind and rigorous, and papers were evaluated on the basis of research significance, novelty, and technical quality. Some papers submitted in the first round received a decision of major revision. The revised version of those papers were further evaluated in the second round and most of them were accepted. After the review process concluded, a total of 46 papers were accepted to be presented at the conference and included in the proceedings, representing an acceptance rate of around 21%.

Among those papers, 30 were co-authored and presented by full-time students. From this subset, we awarded the Best Student Paper Award to Joyanta Debnath (co-authored with Sze Yiu Chau and Omar Chowdhury) for the paper "When TLS Meets Proxy on Mobile." The reviewers particularly appreciated its practical contributions in the proxy-based browsers field and the comments were positive overall. The monetary prize of 1,000 euro was generously sponsored by Springer.

We had a rich program including the satellite workshops in parallel with the main event, providing a forum to address specific topics at the forefront of cybersecurity research. The papers presented at those workshops were published in separate proceedings.

This year we had two outstanding keynote talks: "Global communication guarantees in the presence of adversaries" presented by Prof. Adrian Perrig, ETH Zurich, Switzerland, and "Is AI taking over the world? No, but it's making it less private" by Prof. Giuseppe Ateniese, Stevens Institute of Technology, USA. To them, our heartfelt gratitude for their outstanding presentations.

In this very unusual year, the conference was made possible by the untiring joint efforts of many individuals and organizations. We are grateful to all the authors for their submissions. We sincerely appreciate the outstanding work of all the PC members and the external reviewers, who selected the papers after reading, commenting, and debating them. Finally, we would thank all the people who volunteered their time and energy to put together the conference, speakers and session chairs, and everyone who contributed to the success of the conference.

Last, but certainly not least, we are very grateful to Sapienza University of Rome for sponsoring the conference, and Springer, for their help in assembling these proceedings.

June 2020

Mauro Conti
Jianying Zhou

Organization

ACNS 2020

18th International Conference on Applied Cryptography and Network Security
Virtual Conference
October 19–22 2020
Organized by Sapienza University of Rome - Rome, Italy

General Chairs

Emiliano Casalicchio   Sapienza University of Rome, Italy
Angelo Spognardi   Sapienza University of Rome, Italy
Giuseppe Bernieri   University of Padua, Italy

Program Chairs

Mauro Conti   University of Padua, Italy
Jianying Zhou   SUTD, Singapore

Organizing Chair

Massimo Bernaschi   CNR, Italy

Workshop Chairs

Jianying Zhou   SUTD, Singapore
Mauro Conti   University of Padua, Italy

Poster Chair

Joonsang Baek   University of Wollongong, Australia

Publication Chair

Edlira Dushku   Sapienza University of Rome, Italy

Publicity Chair

Chhagan Lal   University of Padua, Italy

Sponsorship Chair

Eleonora Losiouk   University of Padua, Italy

Web Chair

Fabio De Gaspari   Sapienza University of Rome, Italy

Program Committee

Cristina Alcaraz   University of Malaga, Spain
Moreno Ambrosin   Google, USA
Joonsang Baek   University of Wollongong, Australia
Lejla Batina   Radboud University, The Netherlands
Karthikeyan Bhargavan   Inria, France
Alexandra Boldyreva   Georgia Tech, USA
Levente Buttyan   BME, Hungary
Stefano Calzavara   University of Venezia, Italy
Emiliano Casalicchio   Sapienza University of Rome, Italy
Sudipta Chattopadhyay   SUTD, Singapore
Sherman S. M. Chow   Chinese University of Hong Kong, Hong Kong
Bruno Crispo   University of Trento, Italy
Roberto Di Pietro   HBKU, Qatar
Xuhua Ding   SMU, Singapore
Christian Doerr   TU Delft, The Netherlands
F. Betül Durak   Robert Bosch LLC, USA
Zekeriya Erkin   TU Delft, The Netherlands
Sara Foresti   University of Milan, Italy
Olga Gadyatskaya   Leiden University, The Netherlands
Debin Gao   SMU, Singapore
Paolo Gasti   New York Institute of Technology, USA
Manoj S Gaur   IIT Jammu, India
Dieter Gollmann   TUHH, Germany
Mariano Graziano   Cisco, Italy
Stefanos Gritzalis   University of the Aegean, Greece
Jinguang Han   Queen's University Belfast, UK
Ghassan Karame   NEC Laboratories Europe, Germany
Sokratis Katsikas   NTNU, Norway
Riccardo Lazzeretti   Sapienza University of Rome, Italy
Qi Li   Tsinghua University, China
Yingjiu Li   University of Oregon, USA
Zhou Li   UC Irvine, USA
Zhiqiang Lin   Ohio State University, USA
Joseph Liu   Monash University, Australia
Peng Liu   Penn State University, USA
Javier Lopez   University of Malaga, Spain

Additional Reviewers

Acar, Abbas
Ács, Gergely
Al-Kuwari, Saif
Alcaraz, Cristina
Alhebaishi, Nawaf
Aly, Abdelrahaman
Aris, Ahmet
Armknecht, Frederik
Avarikioti, Georgia
Aysen, Miray
Baker, Richard
Banik, Subhadeep
Bay, Asli
Beullens, Ward
Bian, Rui
Bootland, Carl
Braeken, An
Buser, Maxime
Caforio, Andrea
Cao, Chen
Castelblanco, Alejandra
Cebe, Mumin
Chainside, Federico
Chakraborty, Sudip
Chang, Deliang
Chen, Bo
Chen, Joann
Chen, Sanchuan
Chen, Yu-Chi
Chillotti, Ilaria
Cozzo, Daniele
Cui, Hongrui
D'Anvers, Jan-Pieter
da Camara, Jehan
Daemen, Joan
Dargahi, Tooska
Datta, Nilanjan
De Feo, Luca
De Gaspari, Fabio
Delpech de Saint Guilhem, Cyprien
Diamantopoulou, Vasiliki
Ding, Ding
Dobraunig, Christoph

Dong, Xiaoyang
Dragan, Constantin Catalin
Du, Minxin
Duong, Dung Hoang
Dutta, Avijit
Esgin, Muhammed
F. Aranha, Diego
Fang, Song
Friolo, Daniele
Fu, Hao
Fu, Shange
Fuchs, Jonathan
Galbraith, Steven
Gao, Xing
Gardham, Daniel
Giorgi, Giacomo
Granger, Robert
Griffioen, Harm
Gunsing, Aldo
Han, Runchao
Hanisch, Simon
Hartung, Gunnar
He, Xingkang
Hitaj, Dorjan
Horváth, Máté
Huang, Jheng-Jia
Huang, Qiong
Huguenin-Dumittan, Loïs
Iliashenko, Ilia
Jia, Yanxue
Jin, Lin
Jinguang, Han
Kalloniatis, Christos
Karyda, Maria
Ke, Junming
Kim, Intae
Kim, Jongkil
Kokolakis, Spyros
Kuchta, Veronika
Kumar, Manish
Kurt, Ahmet
Lai, Russell W. F.
Lee, Hyunwoo

Li, Yun
Li, Zengpeng
Lin, Yan
Liu, Baojun
Liu, Guannan
Liu, Jia
Liu, Tao
Liu, Zhen
Lopez, Christian
Ma, Haoyu
Ma, Jack P. K.
Majumdar, Suryadipta
Makri, Eleftheria
Mandal, Bimal
Marson, Giorgia Azzurra
Mayer, Rudi
Mazumdar, Subhra
Mercaldo, Francesco
Mohammady, Meisam
Naldurg, Prasad
Ng, Lucien K. L.
Ning, Jianting
Orsini, Emmanuela
Pagnotta, Giulio
Pal, Arindam
Parra-Arnau, Javier
Paul, Souradyuti
Picek, Stjepan
Pirani, Mohammad
Piskozub, Michal
Rabbani, Masoom
Raiber, Markus
Renes, Joost
Rios, Ruben
Rivera, Esteban
Rodríguez Henríquez, Francisco
Rotaru, Dragos
Rotella, Yann
Roy, Partha Sarathi
Rubio, Juan
Saha, Sudip
Samardjiska, Simona
Sardar, Laltu

Saritaş, Serkan
Sasahara, Hampei
Schindler, Philipp
Schulz, Steffen
Sengupta, Binanda
Shaojui Wang, Peter
Sharma, Vishal
Sinha Roy, Sujoy
Solano, Jesús
Soriente, Claudio
Stamatiou, Yannis
Stifter, Nicholas
Sui, Zhimei
Sun, Siwei
Tabiban, Azadeh
Tengana, Lizzy
Ti, Yenwu
Tian, Yangguang
Tiepelt, Kevin Marcel
Tj. Wallas, Amr
Tsabary, Itay
Tseng, Yi-Fan
Tsou, Yao-Tung
Ugwuoke, Chibuike
van Bruggen, Christian
Vaudenay, Serge
Venugopalan, Sarad
Viet Xuan Phuong, Tran
Walther, Paul
Wang, Hongbing
Wang, Liping
Wang, Ming-Hung
Wang, Wubing
Wang, Xiuhua
Wong, Harry W. H.
Xiao, Jidong
Xin, Jin
Xu, Shengmin
Xue, Haiyang
Yang, Shaojun
Yautsiukhin, Artsiom
Yeh, Lo-Yao
Zhang, Lan

Zhang, Xiaoli
Zhang, Yicheng
Zhao, Yongjun
Zhou, Man
Zhou, Wei

Ziemann, Ingvar
Zou, Qingtian
Zucca, Vincent
Zuo, Cong

Contents – Part II

Contents – Part I

Post-Quantum Cryptography

Authentication and Biometrics

A Breach into the Authentication with Built-in Camera (ABC) Protocol

Cezara Benegui and Radu Tudor Ionescu[✉]

Faculty of Mathematics and Computer Science, University of Bucharest,
14 Academiei, Bucharest, Romania
cezara.benegui@fmi.unibuc.ro, raducu.ionescu@gmail.com

Abstract. In this paper, we propose a simple and effective attack on the recently introduced Smartphone Authentication with Built-in Camera Protocol, called ABC. The ABC protocol uses the photo-response non-uniformity (PRNU) as the main authentication factor in combination with anti-forgery detection systems. The ABC protocol interprets the PRNU as a fingerprint of the camera sensor built-in a smartphone device. The protocol works as follows: during the authentication process, the user is challenged with two QR codes (sent by the server) that need to be photographed with a pre-registered device. In each QR code, the server embeds a unique pattern noise (not visible to the naked eye), called probe signal, that is used to identify potential forgeries. The inserted probe signal is very similar to a genuine fingerprint. The photos of QR codes taken by the user are then sent to the server for verification. The server checks (*i*) if the photos contain the user's camera fingerprint (used to authenticate the pre-registered device) and (*ii*) if the photos contain the embedded probe signal.

If an adversary tries to remove (subtract) his own camera fingerprint and replace it with the victim's camera fingerprint (computed from photos shared on social media), then he will implicitly remove the embedded probe signal and the attack will fail. The ABC protocol is able to detect these attacks with a false acceptance rate (FAR) of 0.5%. However, the ABC protocol wrongly assumes that the attacker can only determine his own camera fingerprint from the photos of the presented QR codes. The attack proposed in our work is able to get past the anti-forgery detection system with a FAR of 54.1%, simply by estimating the attacker's camera fingerprint from a different set of photos (e.g. five photos) owned by the attacker. This set of photos can be trivially obtained before the attack, allowing the adversary to compute his camera fingerprint independently of the attack. The key to the success of our attack is that the independently computed adversary's camera fingerprint does not contain the probe signal embedded in the QR codes. Therefore, when we subtract the adversary's camera fingerprint and add the victim's camera fingerprint, the embedded probe signal will remain in place. For this reason, the proposed attack can successfully pass through the anti-forgery detection system of the ABC protocol. In this paper, we also propose a potential fix based on analyzing signals from built-in motion sensors, which are not typically shared on social media.

© Springer Nature Switzerland AG 2020
M. Conti et al. (Eds.): ACNS 2020, LNCS 12147, pp. 3–20, 2020.
https://doi.org/10.1007/978-3-030-57878-7_1

Keywords: ABC protocol · PRNU fingerprint · Camera fingerprint · Impersonation attack · Forgery attack · Authentication with built-in camera

1 Introduction

With the rapid growth of the online environments, e.g. social media platforms, in which users generate content on a daily basis using their smartphones, it becomes easier and easier for attackers to gather information about specific individuals. The information collected can be used in different identity forgery attacks, especially impersonation attacks. Since more than half of the smartphone users are using mobile banking services [8], preventing identity forgery attacks is critical. One possible approach to prevent such impersonation attacks (from different devices) is to determine that the user is actually using a known (pre-registered) device. Typical verification protocols are based on sending a confirmation code by SMS [17], tying the user to his mobile device. An alternative approach is the recently-proposed Smartphone Authentication with Built-in Camera Protocol, called ABC [28], which represents the main focus of our work. The ABC protocol uses the photo-response non-uniformity (PRNU) [21] signal as the main authentication factor. The PRNU is a fixed pattern noise specific to a camera sensor, and it can be estimated using different techniques [3,4,10,18,20,21]. The ABC protocol is mainly based on interpreting the PRNU as a fingerprint of the camera sensor that is usually built-in any smartphone device.

Associating the information available on the Internet to a potential victim can easily offer attackers access to a set of images (or at least an image) taken by the victim, which in the context of PRNU-based verification, can be used to compute the camera fingerprint of the victim. With this information, the attackers can impersonate the victim and pursue transactions or other fraudulent activities in that person's name. As it is generally well known that the PRNU fingerprint is vulnerable to such forgery attacks [24,28], the ABC protocol is equipped an anti-forgery detection mechanism. Indeed, the ABC protocol claims to solve the fingerprint forgery problem along with other possible attacks, such as replay attacks, with a total error rate lower than 0.5% [28]. The ABC authentication process consists in a set of steps that require the user to take two photos of two QR codes displayed on a screen and send the photos to a server for verification. The server processes the images and identifies if the content from the QR codes is legitimate, then it verifies the user's camera fingerprint and checks for forgery attacks. The forgery attack detection process scans the received image for a fixed pattern noise (probe signal) included in the two QR codes, a noise that is very similar to a device fingerprint (not visible to the naked eye). In case of an attack, in which the fingerprint of the attacker is replaced with the victim's fingerprint, the forgery detection system detects that the fixed pattern noise added to the initial QR code images is missing [28]. However, the ABC protocol assumes that the attacker computes the camera fingerprint of his own device, using the photos of the presented QR codes, taken during the authentication. As explained below, this assumption is wrong.

We propose a different approach for the attack, in which the attacker (adversary) uses an external set of photos (even a single photo is enough) to compute his own camera fingerprint. Clearly, an external set of photos can be trivially collected by the attacker before performing the attack, independently. Hence, the adversary's camera fingerprint can also be computed in a completely independent manner from the attack. More importantly, the independently computed adversary's camera fingerprint will no longer contain the fixed pattern noise embedded in the QR codes by the verification system. Therefore, when we subtract the adversary's camera fingerprint and add the victim's camera fingerprint during the attack, the embedded fixed pattern noise will remain in place. For this reason, the proposed attack can successfully pass through the anti-forgery detection system of the ABC protocol. Since our attack requires several changes to the photos sent for verification (subtracting attacker's fingerprint, adding victim's fingerprint), the fixed pattern noise can be deteriorated by these changes. Therefore, our attack succeeds in about 50% of the cases. To estimate the number of successful attempts, we conduct experiments using 630 photos collected from six different smartphone devices. During registration, we use either one or five photos per device to compute the fingerprint of each device. While Zhongjie et al. [28] use one photo during registration, we noticed that our attack has a better success rate when using more photos, e.g. five. Since the attacker can trivially take any number of photos with his own smartphone and the victim is likely to post multiple photos on social media, we believe that using five photos for PRNU estimation is realistic although different from Zhongjie et al. [28]. In the experiments, one by one, each device is considered as being the victim's device in order to be able to simulate attacks. We attack each victim's device with photos from the other devices, using 100 image samples per attacker's device. In total, we perform a set of 3000 attacks, achieving a successful attack rate (false acceptance rate) of 54.1% when using five images for PRNU estimation and a successful attack rate of 47.7% when using one image for PRNU estimation, respectively. Since our attack is successful in about half of the cases, we consider it as a viable threat to the ABC protocol. We thus conclude that the anti-forgery detection system of the ABC protocol needs to be revised. In this paper, we also propose a revised ABC protocol based on using signals captured from built-in motion sensors, which are not typically shared on social media. The false acceptance rate of the revised ABC protocol is 5.3%.

The rest of this paper is organized as follows. Recent related work on authentication protocols and vulnerabilities is presented in Sect. 2. The ABC protocol and our attack scheme are described in Sect. 3. Our comparative experiments and results are presented in Sect. 4. Our revised ABC protocol is described in Sect. 5. Finally, we draw our conclusions in Sect. 6.

2 Related Work

Aghili et al. [1] presented attacks for breaking into a lightweight machine-to-machine (M2M) authentication protocol [12] used for communication in Industrial Internet of Things (IIoT) environments. The authors showed that the

M2M authentication protocol [12] is vulnerable to Denial-of-Service (DoS) and router impersonation attacks. In a different work, Aghili et al. [2] showed that the untraceable and anonymous three-factor authentication scheme [6] for Heterogeneous Wireless Sensor Networks is vulnerable to user impersonation, de-synchronization and traceability attacks. Aghili et al. [2] also proposed an improved protocol that is resilient to these kinds of attacks.

To our knowledge, there are no previous works that study attacks for PRNU-based authentication protocols using the built-in camera of smartphone devices. However, there are previous works that study the implementation of PRNU-based fingerprinting methods as a single authentication protocol [28] or as a component in a multifactor authentication scheme [27]. Different from the approach studied by Zhonjie et al. [28], which implemented the camera's fingerprint as the main component of an authentication protocol, Valsesia et al. [27] employed the PRNU of the built-in camera as a weak physical unclonable function (PUF) [16] in a multifactor authentication scheme. Moreover, there are other works that use multiple device sensor fingerprints, including PRNU, and combine them with machine learning, to build strong authentication systems [5].

In this section, we provide a brief overview of commonly used smartphone authentication approaches and some of their vulnerabilities. The most common approach used in the recent user authentication systems is to employ a multifactor scheme. Systems based on multifactor authentication are composed of a known secret, which is usually a password, that is complemented by one or more hardware or software tokens [9]. One of the most commonly used tokens is the One-Time Password [22], which consists of a token that is sent to the user via e-mail or SMS, in order to better assess the possession of a hardware or software element which identifies the user. Using the PRNU as an authentication system or as a component in a multifactor scheme requires additional security measures. Considering that PRNU fingerprints are vulnerable to forgery attacks [13,15], it is not a secure option to rely on PRNU fingerprint authentication alone. Hence, along with a fingerprint matching technique, other systems such as forgery detection must be implemented [28].

In our paper, we study the vulnerability of the ABC Protocol [28], presenting a simple attack scheme that showcases the weakness of the ABC protocol against forgery attacks and adversary fingerprint removal attacks. We also propose a revised ABC protocol that is based on multi-factor authentication, i.e. it considers the signals captured by the built-in motion sensors, e.g. accelerometer or gyroscope, along with the images captured by the built-in camera.

3   Method

In this section, we present in detail the ABC protocol [28] and the protection methods implemented in this protocol. We then explain in detail our impersonation attack scheme that is able to bypass the ABC protocol.

3.1 ABC Protocol

The ABC protocol [28] is composed of two main phases: **registration** and **authentication**. In the **registration** phase, the user sends a sample image $I_{(r)}$ (taken with the smartphone camera) to the server (verifier) that implements the ABC protocol. The process does not impose any constraint on the reference image $I_{(r)}$. The image is used to register the smartphone device into the system. More exactly, after the image is received, the sever extracts the PRNU fingerprint $\hat{K}_{(c)}$ from the image $I_{(r)}$ and builds a user profile for the specific device. As Zhongjie et al. [28], we use the notation $\hat{K}_{(c)}$ to denote an accurate estimation of the actual PRNU fingerprint $K_{(c)}$. Once the user's device is registered into the system, we can perform one or more authentications.

The **authentication** process is composed of three main steps: Quick Response (QR) codes generation by the server, pictures upload by the user and pictures verification by the server.

In the **first authentication step** (i), in which the QR codes are generated, the system embeds information about the transaction in progress. The transaction details are accompanied by a timestamp T_i and a random string str_i. Along with this information, the QR code images also embed a non-related white Gaussian noise Γ_i, called probe signal, with a variance equal to 5. In this step, the verifier generates two images defined as:

$$I_{i(s)} = QR(str_i, T_i) + \Gamma_i, \forall i \in \{1, 2\}, \tag{1}$$

which are displayed on a screen to the user.

In the **second authentication step** (ii), the user captures the above images $I_{1(s)}$ and $I_{2(s)}$ with the registered smartphone's built-in camera, and sends the captured images securely back to the server. The captured images, denoted by $I_{i(c)}$, should contain a noise residue $W_{i(c)}$ composed of the PRNU fingerprint of the user and the probe signal Γ_i:

$$I_{i(c)} = QR(str_i, T_i) + W_{i(c)}, \forall i \in \{1, 2\}, \tag{2}$$

where the noise residue is formally defined as follows:

$$W_{i(c)} = \Gamma_i + K_{(c)}. \tag{3}$$

We note that $K_{(c)}$ is present in Eq. (3) only if the authentication is performed by the registered user. Otherwise, the noise residue will contain an adversary's camera fingerprint $K_{(a)}$ instead of $K_{(c)}$.

The **third authentication step** (iii) of the protocol is composed of multiple sub-steps: verification of the presented QR codes, fingerprint verification, forgery detection and probe signal verification. The verification of the received QR codes step checks the content of the QR codes to match with the ones generated in the first authentication step (i). Then, the verifier detects if the images $I_{1(c)}$ and $I_{2(c)}$ captured during the second authentication step (ii) contain the same fingerprint $\hat{K}_{(c)}$ as the reference image $I_{(r)}$ provided in the registration stage. Proceeding forward, the forgery detection system tries to identify whether an adversary's camera fingerprint $\hat{K}_{(a)}$ is present in the analyzed image. If an adversary's fingerprint $\hat{K}_{(a)}$ is detected, the system rejects the transaction. In the last sub-step, the protocol verifies if the probe signal Γ_i is present. If the unique pattern noise was removed (subtracted) in the forgery process, or in a counterfeit attempt, then the system rejects the transaction.

3.2   ABC Protocol Defense Systems

Forgery Detection: The anti-forgery detection system implemented in the ABC protocol [28] protects the system from forged images in which an adversary's fingerprint, $K_{(a)}$, might be present. For each of the two images received by the verifier, the noise residue $W_{i(c)}$ is extracted. Next, the noise residue from the first received image is compared with both the noise residue from the second image and the noise residue (PRNU fingerprint) of the image sample provided by the user during registration. The similarity value between the analyzed noise residues $W_{1(c)}$ and $W_{2(c)}$ is given by:

$$PCE(W_{1(c)}, W_{2(c)}),\tag{4}$$

while the similarity value between the analyzed noise residue $W_{1(c)}$ and the registered PRNU fingerprint $\hat{K}_{(c)}$ is given by:

$$PCE(W_{1(c)}, \hat{K}_{(c)}),\tag{5}$$

where PCE is the Peak to Correlation Energy [14].

If the images captured during authentication are forged, they should contain the attacker's fingerprint along with the victim's fingerprint. Therefore, the similarity between $W_{1(c)}$ and $W_{2(c)}$ is higher in comparison with the similarity of the noise residue $W_{1(c)}$ and the registered PRNU fingerprint $\hat{K}_{(c)}$, i.e.:

$$PCE(W_{1(c)}, W_{2(c)}) > PCE(W_{1(c)}, \hat{K}_{(c)}) + t_1,\tag{6}$$

where t_1 is a pre-established threshold. As noted in [28], the forgery detection system can be bypassed if the adversary removes his own PRNU fingerprint $K_{(a)}$ and replaces it with the victim's PRNU fingerprint $K_{(c)}$. The removal detection system proposed by Zhongjie et al. [28] and described below is used to prevent this situation.

Removal Detection: During the authentication procedure, the verifier sends two images that contain a probe signal to the user. When the system receives the verification photos back from the user, subsamples of the received images $I_{i(c)}$ are extracted, obtaining a larger set of images $\hat{I}_{i(c)}$ in which the presence of the unique pattern noise Γ_i is verified. If the captured images $I_{i(c)}$ are forged, the similarity value between the known probe signal Γ_i and the noise residue $W_{i(c)}$ should be substantially lower, falling below a precisely chosen threshold t_2:

$$PCE(W_{i(c)}, \Gamma_i) < t_2. \tag{7}$$

If Eq. (7) holds, then the transaction is rejected. We note that Eq. (7) is based on the supposition that the adversary estimates his own PRNU fingerprint from the captured images $I_{i(c)}$. In this case, the estimated PRNU fingerprint $\hat{K}_{(a)}$ will contain the probe signal Γ_i. Consequently, removing the PRNU fingerprint $\hat{K}_{(a)}$ in order to pass forgery detection will implicitly remove the probe signal. In this case, the attack is successfully stopped by the removal detection system. However, as we are about to discuss in detail next, the ABC protocol does not consider the trivial case in which the adversary estimates his own PRNU fingerprint from a different set of images than those photographed during the authentication. We exploit this vulnerability in our attack described below.

3.3   Proposed Attack Scheme

While the ABC Protocol assumes that the adversary computes his camera fingerprint using the photos $I_{i(c)}$ captured during the authentication phase, we propose a different approach for the attack, in which the adversary uses a pre-computed camera fingerprint $\hat{K}_{(a)}$, obtained from an external set of photos $I_{j(x)}$, captured with the same device used for the attack. In our experiments described in Sect. 4, we used either one or five images, i.e. $j \in \{1\}$ or $j \in \{1, 2, 3, 4, 5\}$. While the decision to use one image during registration is motivated by the fact that Zhongjie et al. [28] do the same, the decision to use five images is motivated by two facts: the attacker can easily take several images with his smartphone and the victim is likely to post multiple images on social media. We thus believe that it is realistic to consider that the attacker might use five images to compute his PRNU fingerprint $\hat{K}_{(a)}$ and another five images from social media to compute the victim's PRNU fingerprint $\hat{K}_{(c)}$. We empirically observed that using five images instead of one during registration increases the success rate of our attack.

When the verifier generates the two verification images defined as in Eq. (1), the attacker takes pictures of those images in order to send them back to the verifier. In this step, the images taken by the attacker are defined as follows:

$$I_{i(c)} = QR(str_i, T_i) + \Gamma_i + K_{(a)}, \forall i \in \{1, 2\}. \tag{8}$$

We note that Eq. (8) is similar to Eq. (2), the only difference being that the captured image contains the PRNU fingerprint $K_{(a)}$ of the attacker instead of the PRNU fingerprint $K_{(c)}$ of the victim. In order to perform the attack, we aim to remove $\hat{K}_{(a)}$ and replace it with $\hat{K}_{(c)}$, assuming (as Zhongjie et al. [28]) that the attacker has access to a very small set of photos (or at least a photo), e.g. shared on social media, that belong to the victim, which allows the attacker to estimate the victim's PRNU fingerprint denoted by $\hat{K}_{(c)}$. At this stage, Zhongjie et al. [28] assume that the attacker estimates the PRNU fingerprint $\hat{K}_{(a)}$ using the images $I_{i(c)}$ defined in Eq. (8), thus including the probe signal Γ_i into the estimation. Hence, the attempt to remove $\hat{K}_{(a)}$ will also remove Γ_i. Since we compute the adversary's camera fingerprint $\hat{K}_{(a)}$ on an independent set of images $I_{j(x)}$, removing $\hat{K}_{(a)}$ from the captured images $I_{i(c)}$ does not imply the removal of the probe signal Γ_i. Hence, the attacker can proceed with the forgery by subtracting the estimated PRNU fingerprint $\hat{K}_{(a)}$ and by adding the victim's fingerprint $\hat{K}_{(c)}$ to the captured images $I_{i(c)}$, resulting in a set of forged images defined by:

$$I_{i(f)} = I_{i(c)} - \hat{K}_{(a)} + \hat{K}_{(c)}, \forall i \in \{1,2\}. \tag{9}$$

By replacing $I_{i(c)}$ in Eq. (9), we obtain:

$$I_{i(f)} = QR(str_i, T_i) + \Gamma_i + K_{(a)} - \hat{K}_{(a)} + \hat{K}_{(c)}, \forall i \in \{1,2\}. \tag{10}$$

We note that $\hat{K}_{(a)}$ and $\hat{K}_{(c)}$ are estimated values of actual PRNU fingerprints of the attacker's and the victim's smartphone built-in cameras, respectively. Through the operations performed in Eq. (9), the probe signal Γ_i can be affected to some small extent. Therefore, the forged images $I_{i(f)}$ are only approximately equal to the results desired by the attacker:

$$I_{i(f)} \approx QR(str_i, T_i) + \Gamma_i + \hat{K}_{(c)}, \forall i \in \{1,2\}. \tag{11}$$

The forged images $I_{i(f)}$, which contain the victim's fingerprint, are sent back to the verifier, easily passing the fingerprint verification process. Then, the forgery detection and removal detection algorithms process the images received by the verifier. The forgery detection algorithm processes the images and computes the similarity values defined in Eqs. (4) and (5). Then, the verifier applies Eq. (6) to determine if the images are forged. Since the forged images do not contain the attacker's fingerprint $K_{(a)}$, the similarity values defined in Eqs. (4) and (5) are roughly equal. Thus, our attack can bypass the forgery detection system.

Since we compute the adversary's camera fingerprint using an external set of images, in the process of removing the attacker's fingerprint $\hat{K}_{(a)}$ and adding the victim's fingerprint $\hat{K}_{(c)}$, the value of the probe signal Γ_i is only slightly altered, but still present in the forged images. When the removal detection algorithm checks for the presence of the probe signal Γ_i using Eq. (7) against a predefined threshold, the algorithm will find that Γ_i is included in the received images. Therefore, our attack can bypass the removal detection system.

With the proposed attack scheme, we can bypass both protection systems of the ABC protocol. Due to the approximation errors involved in the forgery process, the attack only succeeds in about one in every two cases, as detailed in the following experiments.

4 Experiments

4.1 Data Set

In order to test our attack scheme and estimate the number of successful attempts in which the ABC protocol fails to detect our attack, we collect our own data set of images. The data set consists of 630 images gathered from six different smartphone devices: two iPhone X, two Samsung S8, one Huawei P20 Lite and one Huawei P10 Lite. We select the first 1000 × 750 pixels to compute the PRNU fingerprints, as recommended in previous works [24,28]. For each device we collect a number of 105 photos.

In the first set of experiments, we use the first five images to compute the reference PRNU fingerprint of each device, which leaves 100 images to perform authentications on the same device (simulating the actions of a registered user) or attacks on the other devices (simulating the actions of an impersonator). In total, we perform 600 authentications (100 per device) and, considering all possible combinations of device pairs, 3000 attacks (500 per device). The justification for using five images during registration is given by two facts: (1) the attacker can take any number of photos on his device and (2) the victim is likely to post at least five photos on social media platforms.

In the second set of experiments, we use only the first image to compute the reference PRNU fingerprint, as the method [21] used for PRNU estimation can be applied on a single image and this is how Zhongjie et al. [28] conduct their experiments. Our second set of experiments are aimed at demonstrating that our attack can defeat the ABC protocol in the same setting as Zhongjie et al. [28]. As in the first set of experiments, we use the last 100 images to perform authentications on the same device or attacks on the other devices, resulting in the same number of total authentications (600) and attacks (3000).

4.2 Evaluation Details

Evaluation Measures: We report the number of successful attacks (false acceptances) as well as the False Acceptance Rate (FAR), which is typically defined as the ratio of the number of false acceptances divided by the number of authentication attempts. A *false acceptance* is an instance of a security system, in our case the ABC protocol, incorrectly verifying an unauthorized person, e.g. an impersonator. We note that our attack does impact the False Rejection Rate (FRR) of the ABC protocol, i.e. the FRR is similar to that reported in [28]. Therefore, we focus only on reporting the FAR.

Evaluation Protocol: The main goal of the experiments is to validate the attack scheme proposed in this paper. While reporting the FAR values for our attack is necessary, we also have to validate that the forgery detection (FD) system and the removal detection (RD) system of the ABC protocol work properly. For this reason, we need to perform attacks as described in [28]. Our aim is to show that the protection systems of the ABC protocol are indeed able to reject the attacks specified in [28], while not being able to detect our own attack.

One by one, each of the n smartphone devices is considered as being the victim's device. In order to perform attacks, the remaining $n - 1$ devices are considered to belong to adversaries. Each adversary performs 100 attacks. Given that our data set consists of $n = 6$ devices, we obtain a number of 3000 (6 × 5 × 100) attacks. For each attack, we determine if it passes undetected by the Forgery Detection system and by the Removal Detection system. We consider a successful attack only if it succeeds to cross both Forgery Detection and Removal Detection systems. We count the number of successful attacks and compute the corresponding FAR at different PCE thresholds between 10000 and 50000, using a step of 100. We note that the threshold values are generally higher than those used in [28], because we compute the PRNU fingerprints on larger images. We determine the *optimal threshold* as the threshold that provides a FAR of roughly 0.5% for the attack scheme detailed in [28], because Zhongjie et al. [28] report a FAR of 0.5% in their paper. We note that they selected the threshold that corresponds to equal FAR and FRR.

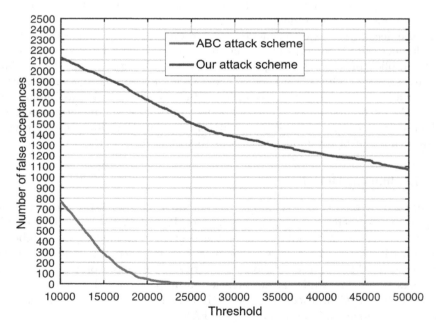

Fig. 1. Number of false acceptances (on the vertical axis) bypassing both Forgery Detection and Removal Detection systems, for the attack scheme proposed in our paper versus the attack scheme detailed in [28], when five images are used for PRNU estimation. False acceptances are counted for multiple PCE thresholds (on the horizontal axis) between 10000 and 50000, with a step of 100. Best viewed in color. (Color figure online)

4.3   Results Using Five Images for PRNU Estimation

Figure 1 illustrates the number of false acceptances for the proposed attack scheme versus the attack scheme considered by Zhongjie et al. [28], using five images for PRNU estimation and multiple PCE thresholds between 10000 and 50000. Threshold values are taken at a step of 100. The false acceptance counts represent attacks that bypass both Forgery Detection and Removal Detection systems of the ABC protocol. Zhongjie et al. [28] reported a FAR of 0.5% for their attack scheme. In our case, we obtain a similar FAR for their attack when the PCE threshold is set to 22500. We thus select this value as the optimal threshold. We note that for each and every threshold between 10000 and 50000, our attack scheme provides significantly more successful attempts.

We present the number of false acceptances for the proposed attack scheme versus the attack scheme considered by Zhongjie et al. [28] in Table 1, using five different PCE thresholds between 10000 and 50000, additionally including results for the optimal threshold (22500). For the optimal threshold, there are 1624 successful attacks from the total of 3000 attacks. Hence, we conclude that more than half of the attacks are successful, rendering the ABC protocol unsafe in scenarios where an impersonator could gain access to the victim's photos.

In Table 2, we provide the false acceptance rates for the proposed attack scheme versus the attack scheme considered by Zhongjie et al. [28]. The values essentially correspond to those presented in Table 1, each number being divided by the total number of attacks (3000). Based on the results presented in Table 2, we conclude that our attack can bypass the Forgery Detection and the Removal Detection systems with a very high FAR (54.1%) at a PCE threshold of 22500. We note that, at the same threshold, the ABC protocol achieves a FAR of 0.5% for the attack scheme described in [28]. In the same time, we computed the False Rejection Rate (FRR) for the ABC protocol, using 600 authentications. At the respective threshold, the FRR is under 0.1%, further proving that the results are consistent with the numbers reported in [28].

We observe that the Forgery Detection and Removal Detection systems perform very well, but only for the attack scheme assumed by the ABC protocol [28]. Considering that in the respective attack scheme the adversary's camera fingerprint is computed from the QR code images which include the probe signal Γ_i, the value Γ_i is removed along with the attacker's fingerprint $\hat{K}_{(a)}$. This leads to a better performance of the Removal Detection system. For instance, the attack scheme considered in [28] is identified by the Removal Detection system with a FAR of 1% at a PCE threshold of 22500.

In our attack scheme, the adversary computes his own PRNU fingerprint by using an external set of five images. Due to the fact that the fingerprint is computed without including the probe signal Γ_i, when the adversary's fingerprint $\hat{K}_{(a)}$ removal (subtraction) and victim's fingerprint $\hat{K}_{(c)}$ addition occurs, the probe signal is mostly unaffected. In this case, the Removal Detection system is not able to identify our attack. For instance, our attack scheme is identified by the Removal Detection system with a FAR of 81.7% at a PCE threshold of 22500.

Table 1. Number of successful attempts (false acceptances) for the attack scheme proposed in our paper versus the attack scheme detailed in [28], when five images are used for PRNU estimation. Successful attempts are counted for five PCE thresholds between 10000 and 50000. Results (highlighted in bold) for the optimal PCE threshold (22500) are also included. For each attack scheme, we report the number of false acceptances for the Forgery Detection (FD) system, the Removal Detection (RD) system, and both (FD+RD).

Threshold	Proposed attack			ABC attack		
	FD bypass count	RD bypass count	FD+RD bypass count	FD bypass count	RD bypass count	FD+RD bypass count
10000	2235	2701	2122	2628	920	776
20000	1879	2517	1726	2487	73	45
22500	**1800**	**2451**	**1624**	**2446**	**31**	**16**
30000	1600	2292	1378	2350	0	0
40000	1444	2184	1219	2234	0	0
50000	1315	2090	1071	2150	0	0

Table 2. False acceptance rates (FAR) for the attack scheme proposed in our paper versus the attack scheme detailed in [28], when five images are used for PRNU estimation. False acceptance rates are computed for five PCE thresholds between 10000 and 50000. Results (highlighted in bold) for the optimal PCE threshold (22500) are also included. For each attack scheme, we report the false acceptance rates for the Forgery Detection (FD) system, the Removal Detection (RD) system, and both (FD+RD).

Threshold	Proposed attack			ABC attack		
	FD FAR	RD FAR	FD+RD FAR	FD FAR	RD FAR	FD+RD FAR
10000	74.5%	90.0%	70.7%	87.6%	30.7%	25.9%
20000	62.6%	83.9%	57.5%	82.9%	2.4%	1.5%
22500	**60.0%**	**81.7%**	**54.1%**	**81.5%**	**1.0%**	**0.5%**
30000	53.3%	76.4%	45.9%	78.3%	0.0%	0.0%
40000	48.1%	72.8%	40.6%	74.5%	0.0%	0.0%
50000	43.8%	69.7%	35.7%	71.7%	0.0%	0.0%

While our attack can bypass the Removal Detection system with a much higher FAR than the attack scheme considered in [28], it gives slightly lower FAR values in trying to bypass the Forgery Detection system, because the attacker's PRNU fingerprint is computed on a different set of images than the two QR code images used during the authentication. In other words, the lower FAR rates are generated by the approximation errors between the PRNU estimation $\hat{K}_{(a)}$ and the actual PRNU fingerprint $K_{(a)}$ in the QR code images. Nevertheless, our attack scheme achieves a much higher false acceptance rate even when the two protection systems, Forgery Detection and Removal Detection, are considered together.

Overall, the results presented in Table 1 and 2 prove that the ABC Protocol is vulnerable to our attack scheme, since about one in every two attacks succeeds.

4.4   Results Using One Image for PRNU Estimation

Figure 2 illustrates the number of false acceptances for the proposed attack scheme versus the attack scheme considered by Zhongjie et al. [28], using one image for PRNU estimation and multiple PCE thresholds between 10000 and 50000. Threshold values are taken at a step of 100. It is important to mention that in this setting, both the victim's and the adversary's PRNU are estimated from single images. Therefore, this setting is slightly more difficult and the attack is less likely to succeed. Although using five images during registration (as in the previous setting) is realistic, we consider the setting with one image for an apples to apples comparison with Zhongjie et al. [28].

Comparing the results presented in Fig. 1 with those presented in Fig. 2, we observe that the number of attacks that bypass the ABC protocol is typically lower when one image is used for PRNU estimation instead of five images. However, there are still enough successful attacks to pose a real problem for the ABC protocol. At the optimal threshold (22500), the number of successful attacks is 1430, which translates to a FAR of 47.7% with respect to the total number of attacks (3000). These empirical results demonstrate that the ABC protocol can still be easily bypassed, even when we use a single image for estimating the PRNU.

Considering both experimental settings (with one or five images for PRNU estimation) and the corresponding results, we conclude that the Removal Detection and Forgery Detection systems of the ABC protocol need to be revised to prevent the attack scheme exposed in our work.

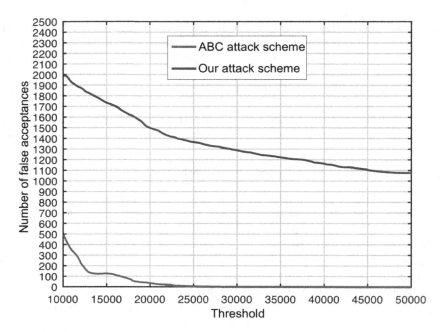

Fig. 2. Number of false acceptances (on the vertical axis) bypassing both Forgery Detection and Removal Detection systems, for the attack scheme proposed in our paper versus the attack scheme detailed in [28], when one image is used for PRNU estimation. False acceptances are counted for multiple PCE thresholds (on the horizontal axis) between 10000 and 50000, with a step of 100. Best viewed in color. (Color figure online)

5   Discussion

In this section, we propose a revised ABC protocol that relies on additional built-in sensors, e.g. the accelerometer and/or the gyroscope. We note that motion sensors contain similar fabrication defects as the camera [19], deeming them recognizable based on the captured signals. The main advantage compared to the camera sensor is that motion signals, unlike photographs, are not typically shared on social media by people. Therefore, attackers cannot easily get their hands on these signals. The only disadvantage of our augmented ABC protocol is that it only works on devices that are equipped with motion sensors. However, most smartphones available nowadays do have built-in motion sensors.

In addition to the PRNU fingerprint check, we employ a machine learning system that classifies an authentication session as legitimate or not based on the signals recorded by the built-in motion sensors, following the approach described in [25]. The user is not required to perform any additional steps during authentication, we just have to record the motion signals while the user is pressing the button to take photos.

5.1 Data Set

In order to validate our revised protocol, we select a subset of motion signals recorded on six devices from the data set provided by Sitova et al. [26]. We record motion sensor values during screen taps (e.g. when the user taps the button to take a photo) for 1.5 s, starting the recording with 0.5 s before the tap event. The accelerometer and the gyroscope each provide 3-axis values at about 100 Hz. For each tap event, we thus have six signals (two sensors × three axes) composed of 150 discrete values (1.5 s at 100 Hz). For each of the six devices, we collect motion signals for 105 tap events. Each tap event is matched with one and only one of the photos used in the experiments presented in Sect. 4. The image and motion signal data sets are mixed and formatted in a way that simulates a realistic scenario, as if the motion signals are recorded during authentication with the ABC protocol.

5.2 Model

Since the signals recorded by the motion sensors contain noise and large variations, a machine learning model will not be able to learn invariant features from raw signal values. In order to obtain invariant features for each signal, we follow the approach proposed by Shen et al. [25], which is based on extracting a set of statistical features such as: the minimum value, the maximum value, the mean, the variance, the skewness (the orientation of the peak), the kurtosis (the width of the peak) and the quantiles (from 30% to 80%, with a step of 10%). The feature vector corresponding to a tap event is thus composed of 72 statistical features (six signals × 12 features). We take the feature vectors corresponding to the first five tap events and use them to train a Support Vector Machines (SVM) classifier [11] based on the Radial Basis Function (RBF) kernel. During optimization, the SVM finds a hyperplane that separates the training samples by a maximum margin. We use the SVM implementation from Scikit-learn [23], setting the regularization parameter $C = 100$ and leaving the RBF parameter γ to the default value (scale). Our motion-based verification system authorizes or rejects sessions based on the positive or negative labels provided by the SVM.

5.3 Results

We conduct experiments to show how our motion-based verification system performs by itself and in conjunction with the ABC protocol. When combining the ABC system with the motion-based verification system, a session must be validated by both systems, i.e. we use the AND operator. This reduces the FAR, but increases the FRR. The corresponding results are presented in Table 3.

First, we notice that our motion-based verification system alone attains a FAR of 12.4% and a FRR of 11.0%. Although the motion-based verification system is able to withstand the attacks better than the ABC protocol, it has a much higher FRR. The higher FRR can be caused by several factors: the number of training samples (five) might not be sufficient to learn a good SVM model, the

Table 3. False acceptance rates (FAR) and false rejection rates (FRR) for the attack scheme proposed in our paper, when five images and/or motion signals are used during registration. For the ABC protocol, the FAR and the FRR measures are computed for the optimal PCE threshold (22500). For the motion-based verification system, the FAR and the FRR measures are computed for the SVM regularization parameter $C = 100$. We report results for the individual as well as the combined systems (i.e. for the revised ABC protocol).

Authentication system	FAR	FRR
ABC protocol	54.1%	0.1%
Motion-based verification	12.4%	11.0%
Revised ABC protocol (ABC + motion-based verification)	5.3%	11.0%

chosen model (SVM based on statistical features) might not be the right choice to capture the defects of motion sensors, the task of recognizing motion sensors based on defects observed in output signals might simply be harder than the task of recognizing camera fingerprints. We leave the search for an explanation in this regard for future work.

By combining the ABC protocol with the motion-based verification system, we obtain the revised ABC protocol, which relies on multi-factor (images and motion signals) authentication. The revised protocol attains a lower FAR (5.3%), since attacks have to bypass both the ABC protocol and the motion-based verification system. However, the FRR stays at the same level as for the motion-based verification system (11.0%).

We note that the revised ABC protocol is able to reduce the FAR from 54.1% to 5.3%. However, we consider that the FAR and the FRR values of the revised ABC protocol are still higher than acceptable. In future work, we aim to improve or completely replace the motion-based verification system in order to further reduce the FAR and the FRR values to acceptable thresholds, e.g. below 1%. A better solution might require more than five training samples and end-to-end training, e.g. by employing deep neural networks [7].

6   Conclusion

In this paper, we have presented a simple and effective attack for the ABC protocol [28]. Our strategy is based on computing the adversary's PRNU fingerprint on an external set of samples, which do not include the fixed probe signal used by the verifier to detect PRNU fingerprint removal. This allowed us to remove the adversary's fingerprint while preserving the probe signal, which led to successful attempts in bypassing the Removal Detection and Forgery Detection systems of the ABC protocol. We have conducted experiments on six mobile devices, performing 3000 attacks, in order to provide an empirical proof and validation of our attack. Our attack scheme provides a FAR of 54.1%, demonstrating that the ABC protocol is not entirely secure. We thus conclude that the ABC protocol is not suited as an authentication measure for high-risk applications, such as applications where financial transactions are involved.

We also took important steps towards revising the ABC protocol. By analyzing and verifying the authenticity of signals recorded by built-in motion sensors, we were able to reduce the FAR from 54.1% to 5.3% when the protocol is exposed to our attack. In future work, we aim to identify other solutions to further reduce the FAR and the FRR values, since we believe that the ABC protocol still has enough potential to become a reliable authentication protocol.

References

1. Aghili, S.F., Mala, H.: Breaking a lightweight M2M authentication protocol for communications in IIoT environment. IACR Cryptol. ePrint Arch. **2018**, 891 (2018)
2. Aghili, S.F., Mala, H., Peris-Lopez, P.: Securing heterogeneous wireless sensor networks: breaking and fixing a three-factor authentication protocol. Sensors **18**(11), 3663 (2018)
3. Akshatha, K., Karunakar, A., Anitha, H., Raghavendra, U., Shetty, D.: Digital camera identification using PRNU: a feature based approach. Digit. Invest. **19**, 69–77 (2016)
4. Altinisik, E., Tasdemir, K., Sencar, H.T.: Extracting PRNU noise from H.264 coded videos. In: Proceedings of European Signal Processing Conference (EUSIPCO), pp. 1367–1371 (2018)
5. Amerini, I., Bestagini, P., Bondi, L., Caldelli, R., Casini, M., Tubaro, S.: Robust smartphone fingerprint by mixing device sensors features for mobile strong authentication. In: Media Watermarking, Security, and Forensics, pp. 1–8. Ingenta (2016)
6. Amin, R., Islam, S.H., Kumar, N., Choo, K.K.R.: An untraceable and anonymous password authentication protocol for heterogeneous wireless sensor networks. J. Netw. Comput. Appl. **104**, 133–144 (2018)
7. Benegui, C., Ionescu, R.T.: Convolutional neural networks for user identification based on motion sensors represented as images. IEEE Access **8**, 61255–61266 (2020)
8. Board of Governors of the Federal Reserve System: Consumers and mobile financial services 2016 (2016). https://www.federalreserve.gov/econresdata/consumers-and-mobile-financial-services-report-201603.pdf. Accessed 01 Apr 2019
9. Burr, W., Dodson, D., Polk, W.: Electronic authentication guideline. Technical report National Institute of Standards and Technology (2004)
10. Cooper, A.J.: Improved photo response non-uniformity (PRNU) based source camera identification. Forensic Sci. Int. **226**(1–3), 132–141 (2013)
11. Cortes, C., Vapnik, V.: Support-vector networks. Mach. Learn. **20**(3), 273–297 (1995)
12. Esfahani, A., et al.: A lightweight authentication mechanism for M2M communications in industrial IoT environment. IEEE Internet Things J. **6**(1), 288–296 (2019)
13. Gloe, T., Kirchner, M., Winkler, A., Böhme, R.: Can we trust digital image forensics? In: Proceedings of the ACM International Conference on Multimedia (ACMMM), pp. 78–86. ACM (2007)
14. Goljan, M.: Digital camera identification from images - estimating false acceptance probability. In: Proceedings of the International Workshop on Digital Watermarking (IWDW), pp. 454–468 (2008)

15. Goljan, M., Fridrich, J., Chen, M.: Defending against fingerprint-copy attack in sensor-based camera identification. IEEE Trans. Inf. Forensics Secur. **6**(1), 227–236 (2011)
16. Herder, C., Yu, M.M., Koushanfar, F., Devadas, S.: Physical unclonable functions and applications: a tutorial. Proc. IEEE **102**(8), 1126–1141 (2014)
17. Jurcut, A.D., Liyanage, M., Chen, J., Gyorodi, C., He, J.: On the security verification of a short message service protocol. In: Proceedings of the IEEE Wireless Communications and Networking Conference (WCNC), pp. 1–6 (2018)
18. Kang, X., Li, Y., Qu, Z., Huang, J.: Enhancing source camera identification performance with a camera reference phase sensor pattern noise. IEEE Trans. Inf. Forensics Secur. **7**(2), 393–402 (2012)
19. Khanna, N., et al.: A survey of forensic characterization methods for physical devices. Digit. Invest. **3**, 17–28 (2006)
20. Li, C.T.: Source camera identification using enhanced sensor pattern noise. IEEE Trans. Inf. Forensics Secur. **5**(2), 280–287 (2010)
21. Lukáš, J., Fridrich, J., Goljan, M.: Digital camera identification from sensor pattern noise. IEEE Trans. Inf. Forensics Secur. **1**(2), 205–214 (2006)
22. M'Raïhi, D., Machani, S., Pei, M., Rydell, J.: TOTP: time-based one-time password algorithm. Internet Eng. Task Force 1–16 (2011)
23. Pedregosa, F., et al.: Scikit-learn: machine learning in python. J. Mach. Learn. Res. **12**, 2825–2830 (2011)
24. Quiring, E., Kirchner, M.: Fragile sensor fingerprint camera identification. In: Proceedings of the IEEE International Workshop on Information Forensics and Security (WIFS), pp. 1–6 (2015)
25. Shen, C., Yu, T., Yuan, S., Li, Y., Guan, X.: Performance analysis of motion-sensor behavior for user authentication on smartphones. Sensors **16**(3), 345 (2016)
26. Sitová, Z., et al.: HMOG: new behavioral biometric features for continuous authentication of smartphone users. IEEE Trans. Inf. Forensics Secur. **11**(5), 877–892 (2016)
27. Valsesia, D., Coluccia, G., Bianchi, T., Magli, E.: User authentication via PRNU-based physical unclonable functions. IEEE Trans. Inf. Forensics Secur. **12**(8), 1941–1956 (2017)
28. Zhongjie, B., Sixu, P., Xinwen, F., Dimitrios, K., Aziz, M., Kui, R.: ABC: enabling smartphone authentication with built-in camera. In: Proceedings of the Network and Distributed Systems Security Symposium (NDSS) (2018)

A Practical System for Privacy-Preserving Video Surveillance

Elmahdi Bentafat, M. Mazhar Rathore, and Spiridon Bakiras[✉]

Division of Information and Computing Technology,
College of Science and Engineering, Hamad Bin Khalifa University, Doha, Qatar
{ebentafat,mrathore,sbakiras}@hbku.edu.qa

Abstract. Video surveillance on a massive scale can be a vital tool for law enforcement agencies. To mitigate the serious privacy concerns of wide-scale video surveillance, researchers have designed secure and privacy-preserving protocols that obliviously match live feeds against a suspects' database. However, existing approaches provide stringent privacy guarantees and, as a result, they do not scale well for ubiquitous deployment. To this end, we introduce a system that relaxes the underlying privacy requirements by giving away some information when a face is compared against the law enforcement's database. Specifically, our protocol reveals a random permutation of obfuscated similarity scores, where each obfuscated score discloses minimal information about the actual similarity score. We show that, despite the relaxed security definitions, our system protects the privacy of the underlying faces, while offering significant improvements in terms of performance. In particular, our protocol necessitates a single round of communication between the camera and the server and, for a database of 100 suspects, the online computation time at the camera and the server is 155 ms and 34 ms, respectively, while the online communication cost is only 12 KB.

Keywords: Video surveillance · Biometric privacy · Homomorphic encryption

1 Introduction

Video surveillance is being deployed in numerous countries around the world. An effective video surveillance system automatically monitors all available data feeds, extracts the individual faces (feature vectors), compares them against a suspects' database, and raises an alarm when a match is found. Nevertheless, this approach raises significant privacy concerns, because all individuals with known feature vectors can be tracked on a daily basis. Analyzing such information-rich datasets has the potential to reveal sensitive personal information, including home and work locations, health issues, religious affiliations, etc. Even if we trust the law enforcement authorities to protect the location privacy of their citizens, the stored location data may still be accessed by malicious users, such as rogue insiders or hackers.

© Springer Nature Switzerland AG 2020
M. Conti et al. (Eds.): ACNS 2020, LNCS 12147, pp. 21–39, 2020.
https://doi.org/10.1007/978-3-030-57878-7_2

As a result, the research community has proposed several methods [9,17,19] that perform privacy-preserving face recognition. In particular, these methods execute a secure two-party protocol between the camera and the database server, which lets the camera learn in zero knowledge whether a captured face matches one of the suspects in the database. If a match is found, the id number of the suspect is revealed; otherwise, the protocol discloses no information to either party. These protocols first compute an encrypted similarity score (Euclidean or Hamming distance) for each suspect in the database, using an additively homomorphic cryptosystem. Then, a variety of techniques are employed to identify the matching suspect, if and only if the underlying similarity distance is below a certain threshold. These techniques involve standard cryptographic primitives for secure computations, such as homomorphic encryption, garbled circuits, and oblivious transfer.

Nevertheless, all the aforementioned systems suffer from high computational and communication costs that render them impractical for wide-scale deployment. For instance, the Eigenfaces implementation by Sadeghi et al. [19] necessitates 40 s of online computations to match a single face against a database of 320 suspects. In addition, the online communication cost is over 5 MB. Similarly, SCiFI [17] reports 31 s of online computations for a database of 100 suspects. Another significant limitation of these protocols is their reliance on offline computation and communication that has to be performed for every face that is captured by the camera. While the offline tasks reduce the overall online cost dramatically, it is not feasible to process and store the underlying data for potentially millions of detected faces on a daily basis.

To this end, our work introduces the first practical system for privacy-preserving video surveillance on a large scale. The efficiency of our approach stems mainly from two design decisions. First, the suspects' database is distributed to all cameras, after it is encrypted with the public key of the law enforcement agency. As such, the expensive operations for computing the encrypted similarity scores are performed at the surveillance cameras, thus alleviating the server's computational load. The local database copy also allows the cameras to precompute most values that are involved in the encrypted distance computations. More importantly, unlike existing approaches, the offline computations are performed only once, during the system's initialization.

Our second decision is to relax the zero knowledge requirement of the face recognition protocol. In particular, for each captured face, the database server will learn a random permutation of *obfuscated* similarity scores between the captured face and all suspects in the database. As a result, the protocol involves a single round of communication for the server to learn the (binary) result of the identification. If a match is found, an additional verification protocol is invoked, where the server learns the suspect's id and optionally receives the image of the potential suspect. The relaxed privacy requirements also facilitate the use of an efficient elliptic curve cryptosystem (ElGamal) that reduces significantly the computational and communication costs. Nevertheless, as we will show, the permuted and obfuscated scores are not sufficient for the server to infer any meaningful information about the underlying individuals.

We built our system on top of the OpenFace [2] platform that implements the face recognition layer. OpenFace is one of the most accurate open-source face recognition systems that employs Google's FaceNet [22] algorithm. Besides its high accuracy, a notable advantage of FaceNet over other approaches is its compact feature vector (just 128 bytes) that speeds up considerably the encrypted distance computations. We performed an extensive experimental evaluation of our system and demonstrated its applicability in a wide-scale video surveillance environment. Specifically, matching one face against a database of 100 suspects entails 190 ms of compute time and 12 KB of communication between the camera and the server. These costs are orders of magnitude lower compared to the current state-of-the-art systems.

The rest of the paper is organized as follows. Section 2 presents a literature review on privacy-preserving video surveillance and face recognition systems, and Sect. 3 discusses the main tools that we utilized in our implementation. Section 4 introduces our problem definition and describes the underlying threat model. Section 5 discusses in detail the operation of our system and Sect. 6 evaluates its security. A performance comparison against other approaches is introduced in Sect. 7, while the implementation details are presented in Sect. 8. Section 9 summarizes our experimental results and Sect. 10 concludes our work.

2   Related Work

2.1   Face Recognition

Face recognition systems face several challenges–such as brightness, face position, and facial expression–that can highly influence the appearance of an individual. The first industrial face recognition applications were based on the Eigenfaces [26] technique. This groundbreaking study by Turk and Pentlandin in 1991 is the milestone for many other methods that have been introduced since then. The original Eigenfaces approach employed Principal Component Analysis (PCA) to generate the eigenvectors. Following that, other transformations were adopted, including Linear Discriminant Analysis (LDA) [23], Independent Component Analysis (ICA) [15], and Support Vector Machines (SVM) [13]. Additionally, some approaches combined multiple classifiers for dimensionality reduction and feature extraction [6,25].

Lately, neural networks have also been employed in the face recognition domain to improve the classification accuracy [8,20]. The current state-of-the-art algorithms are Facebook's DeepFace [24] and Google's FaceNet [22], both of which are based on Convolutional Neural Networks (CNNs). OpenFace [2] is a face recognition library written in Python that leverages the aforementioned CNN systems to provide better accuracy. In 2018, Tadas et al. introduced Open-Face 2.0 [3] as a C++ toolkit for facial behavior analysis. The implementation targets a real-time environment and is, therefore, optimized in terms of computational cost. OpenFace 2.0 presents a more accurate facial landmark detection, head pose estimation, facial action unit recognition, and eye-gaze estimation.

2.2 Privacy-Preserving Video Surveillance

The first privacy-preserving face recognition protocol is due to Erkin et al. [9] in 2009. It leverages the Eigenfaces algorithm for face recognition, but is very inefficient in terms of online performance. Specifically, the protocol requires $O(\log M)$ rounds of online communication (M is the number of suspects in the database) and heavy public key homomorphic operations over the ciphertexts. Sadeghi et al. [19] improved the performance of Erkin's work by shifting some computations into a precomputation phase, and using garbled circuits [28] to compute the *Minimum* function. In a recent work, Xiang et al. [27] further improved upon the aforementioned protocols [9,19] by outsourcing the expensive server computations to the cloud.

SCiFI [17] is the only protocol in the literature that is not based on the Eigenfaces representation. Instead, the authors proposed a novel face recognition method that takes into account the appearance of certain facial features. In SCiFI, each face is represented with a 900-bit vector, while the similarity score is simply the Hamming distance between two vectors. After the Hamming distance is computed, the result of the suspect identification is revealed through a 1-out-of-$d_{max} + 1$ oblivious transfer protocol [16], where d_{max} is the maximum theoretical Hamming distance. One advantage of this approach is that Hamming distance computations on the ciphertext space are significantly faster than the Euclidean ones. Finally, various studies have used similar cryptographic tools, mainly garbled circuits and oblivious transfer, in the context of biometric identification. In particular, researchers have proposed several efficient protocols to compute the similarity scores, including Hamming distance, Euclidean distance, Mahalanobis distance, and scalar product [5,10,11,14,29].

3 Tools

3.1 OpenFace

OpenFace [2] is an open-source face verification and recognition system that maps face images to a compact Euclidean space. It is a deep convolutional network trained method for face recognition that achieves an accuracy of 92.95% on the Labeled Faces in the Wild (LFW) benchmark, one of the largest publicly-available datasets. OpenFace matches very well the performance of FaceNet [22] and DeepFace [24], despite the small size of the trained network. The advantage of OpenFace is the face representation efficiency that consists of 128 features. This vector can be reduced to just 128 bytes with a very small loss in recognition accuracy. The similarity score between two faces is represented by the Euclidean distance of the two feature vectors, and ranges between 0 (for the same image) and 4. A threshold $t = 0.9$ has been set empirically by the system developers of OpenFace, such that a distance less than t indicates a positive match.

3.2   Homomorphic Encryption

Homomorphic cryptosystems [1] allow for the evaluation of certain arithmetic operations directly on the ciphertext domain. Fully homomorphic encryption (FHE) [12] supports both addition and multiplication operations and can, thus, be used to evaluate any circuit over encrypted data. Nevertheless, FHE schemes are still very inefficient to be used in real-time applications, such as video surveillance. Instead, similar to previous work, we built our protocol on top of additively homomorphic cryptosystems, such as Paillier [18] or ElGamal [7]. More specifically, we opted for an implementation of ElGamal's cryptosystem over elliptic curves, due to its computational efficiency and compact ciphertexts (128 bytes). The cryptosystem consists of the following functions:

- **Key generation**: Instantiate an elliptic curve group of prime order q with generator P. Choose a *private* key x uniformly at random from $\mathbb{Z}_q^*$ and set the *public* key $Q = x \cdot P$.
- **Encrypt**: Let m be the secret message. Choose r uniformly at random from $\mathbb{Z}_q^*$ and compute ciphertext $\mathsf{Enc}(m) = \langle r \cdot P, (m + r) \cdot Q \rangle$.
- **Decrypt**: Compute $m \cdot Q = (m + r) \cdot Q - x \cdot r \cdot P$ and solve the discrete log to recover m.

ElGamal's scheme is semantically secure and its security is based on the decisional Diffie-Hellman assumption. Note that, in our implementation, we utilized a look-up table of precomputed $m \cdot Q$ values (for all theoretically possible values of m) in order to speed up the discrete log computations at the database server.

4   Problem Definition and Threat Model

We assume a wide-scale surveillance environment, where a large number of cameras, equipped with moderate computational, storage, and communication capabilities, are deployed throughout a city. The database server (law enforcement) holds a database $\mathbb{S} = \{S_1, S_2, \ldots, S_M\}$ of M suspects, where each suspect S_i is represented by an N-th dimensional feature vector x_i. More specifically, the feature vectors are generated from OpenFace's deep learning model and consist of $N = 128$ values. During the system initialization, the database server shares an encrypted version of $\mathbb{S}$ (to be discussed later) with all cameras, using its own public key Q that is also known to all cameras. Every camera will then capture all passing-by faces and, for each candidate face C_j, compute its feature vector y_j using OpenFace's model. What follows, is a two-party protocol between the camera and the database server, where

- The server learns a random permutation π_j of obfuscated similarity scores between y_j and $x_i, \forall i \in \{1, 2, \ldots, M\}$.
- The camera learns nothing.

When the protocol's output is revealed to the server, it will immediately disclose the identification result. In particular, if all similarity scores are positive, then the candidate face does not match any suspect in the database; otherwise, a negative score is a potential match for a suspect, whose identity is unknown due to the underlying permutation. In that case, the camera and the server invoke a separate two-party protocol, where the camera verifies that the similarity score is indeed negative. During that protocol,

- The server learns the actual id of the matching suspect and (optionally) receives the captured image from the camera.
- The camera learns the actual similarity score and id of the matching suspect.

We assume that the server and all cameras are semi-honest players. In other words, they will follow the protocols correctly, but try to infer some non-trivial information about the other party's input from the communication transcript. For example, the camera might want to learn the plaintext content of the suspects' database, while the server might want to infer some information about the captured faces that do not produce a database match. We also allow the server to act maliciously after the initial identification result, by falsely claiming that a certain similarity score is negative. Such behavior will be discovered during the subsequent verification protocol. Finally, we should note that our protocol cannot protect against illegitimate inputs from any of the parties. For instance, the server can insert into their database $\mathbb{S}$ an innocent civilian that it wants to track, while the camera can test whether a specific individual is part of $\mathbb{S}$ by using their feature vector in the identification protocol. However, none of the existing privacy-preserving protocols can protect against such attacks, since they are not cryptographic in nature.

5   System Description

In this section, we present in detail the operation of our privacy-preserving video surveillance system. We begin by introducing the offline/initialization phase of the protocol, and then proceed to describe the various elements involved in the online face identification process.

5.1   Offline Phase

The server first instantiates an elliptic curve group of prime order q (as described in Sect. 3) and generates its public and private keys. The public key is distributed securely to all surveillance cameras in the city. Next, the server employs Open-Face to generate the feature vectors x_i for every suspect $S_i \in \mathbb{S}$. By default, OpenFace operates over floating point numbers, so we first had to convert the vectors into integers before applying any homomorphic operations. We empirically computed the normalization parameters for a floating point representation f as follows: $\lfloor f \times 400 + 128 \rfloor$, where $f \in \mathbb{Q} : -0.32 < f < 0.32$. With this transformation, every element in a feature vector is an integer in the range $[0, 256)$, thus allowing us to represent a vector with just 128 bytes. Furthermore, the transformation does not result in a significant loss of accuracy, as illustrated in

Table 1. Specifically, the table depicts the accuracy results from various state-of-the-art face recognition algorithms, and also quantifies the loss of accuracy due to the normalization of the features values. For our system, we trained the CNN model using integers in the range $[0, 256)$ instead of floats and, out of 13,233 images, we had only one misidentification compared to the original OpenFace implementation. Note that FaceNet and DeepFace are more accurate than OpenFace because they are trained on much larger datasets.

Table 1. Accuracy results on the LFW benchmark [2]

Model	Accuracy
Human	97.53%
EigenFaces	60.02% ± 0.79
FaceNet	99.64% ± 0.9
DeepFace	97.35% ± 0.25
OpenFace	92.95% ± 1.34
OpenFace, normalized	92.92% ± 1.36

Given suspect S_i's feature vector x_i and a potential candidate's vector y_i, the first step of FaceNet's face recognition algorithm is to compute the Euclidean distance between the two feature vectors. In the ciphertext domain, it is only feasible to compute the squared Euclidean distance, i.e.,

$$d_i^2 = \sum_{j=1}^{N}(x_{i,j} - y_{i,j})^2 = \sum_{j=1}^{N}(x_{i,j}^2 + y_{i,j}^2 - 2x_{i,j}y_{i,j}) \tag{1}$$

where $N = 128$ is the vector dimensionality. In the ciphertext domain over elliptic curves, this is equivalent to

$$\mathsf{Enc}(d_i^2) = \sum_{j=1}^{N}\mathsf{Enc}(x_{i,j}^2) + \sum_{j=1}^{N}\mathsf{Enc}(y_{i,j}^2) + \sum_{j=1}^{N} y_{i,j} \cdot \mathsf{Enc}(-2x_{i,j}) \tag{2}$$

Therefore, for the cameras to correctly compute $\mathsf{Enc}(d_i^2)$, the server will send them an encrypted version of the database $\mathbb{S}$, consisting of

- $\sum_{j=1}^{N} \mathsf{Enc}(x_{i,j}^2), \forall i \in \{1, 2, \dots, M\}$.
- $\mathsf{Enc}(-2x_{i,j}), \forall i \in \{1, 2, \dots, M\}, j \in \{1, 2, \dots, N\}$.

As such, the offline communication cost of our protocol is $(N+1) \times M \times T$ bytes, where T is the size of an ElGamal ciphertext (typically 128 bytes). Due to the semantic security of the cryptosystem, the cameras cannot infer any information regarding the feature vectors of the suspects.

After a camera receives the encrypted database, it performs a series of offline precomputations, in order to speed up the online computation of the similarity

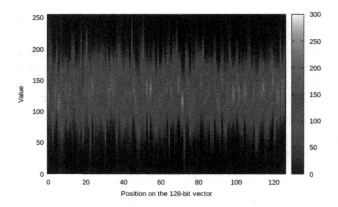

Fig. 1. Heat map of feature vector coefficients for 13095 faces

scores. In particular, the camera will precompute all possible values for the second and third terms of Eq. 2, which is feasible due to the limited range of $y_{i,j}$ (just 256 distinct values). The computational cost involves $256 \times N \times M$ elliptic curve point multiplications and 256 encryption operations. Additionally, the storage requirements at the camera (for the database and all precomputed values) is $(256 + M + 256 \times N \times M) \times T$ bytes. Even for large databases (e.g., $M = 1000$), the storage cost is approximately $4\,\mathrm{GB}$, which is very reasonable for a low-cost camera.

Nevertheless, if a camera does not possess the storage capacity to hold the entire set of precomputed values, we may still gain a lot in performance if we store partial information. (We will illustrate this in our experimental results.) As shown in Fig. 1, the coefficients of a feature vector are not uniformly distributed over the entire range, but instead, values ranging from 64 to 191 tend to occur more frequently. As such, the camera may only precompute, say, 50% of the values (for $y_{i,j} \in [64, 191]$) and perform the remaining elliptic point multiplications, i.e., $y_{i,j} \cdot \mathsf{Enc}(-2x_{i,j})$, on the spot.

At the server side, the offline cost to compute the encrypted database is $2 \times N \times M$ encryption operations plus $N \times M$ elliptic curve point additions, which is trivial for a powerful multi-core server. On the other hand, in order to speed up the decryption operations that constitute the bottleneck of the online identification protocol, we need to precompute a large number of elliptic curve points (lookup table), as explained in Sect. 3. Assuming a maximum bit-length of k bits for the obfuscated similarity scores, the server will precompute and store 2^k 32-byte values with a computational cost of 2^k additions (that are relatively cheap). In our implementation, we set $k = 30$, which necessitates $32\,\mathrm{GB}$ of main memory.

Finally, it is worth noting that, unlike existing approaches, the offline costs of our method are incurred only once and are independent of the number of faces that are captured by the camera.

5.2 Similarity Score Computation

Following the offline phase, our system is ready for real-time video surveillance. A camera will capture all passing-by faces and, for each face C_i, it will generate the plaintext feature vector y_i. Based on the generated $y_{i,j}$, the camera selects the corresponding ciphertexts from the precomputed values and evaluates the encrypted squared Euclidean distances $\mathsf{Enc}(d_i^2)$ for every suspect i, as given in Eq. 2. This task entails, for all M suspects, $(2 \times N + 1) \times M$ elliptic curve point additions. Each distance is then adjusted by subtracting the normalized similarity threshold t, thus generating an encrypted similarity score s_i that is (i) positive for a non-match or (ii) negative for a match. Therefore, the encrypted similarity score for suspect i is computed as

$$\mathsf{Enc}(s_i) = \mathsf{Enc}(d_i^2 - t) = \mathsf{Enc}(d_i^2) + \mathsf{Enc}(-t) \tag{3}$$

By precomputing the encrypted threshold value (constant), the computational cost of this step is M point additions. To summarize, the overall cost for computing the similarity score is $2 \times (N + 1) \times M$ point additions. Finally, we should mention that, based on the normalization parameters given is Sect. 5.1, the normalized similarity threshold is set to $t = (0.9 \times 400)^2 = 129,600$.

5.3 Similarity Score Obfuscation

To further strengthen the privacy of our system, each similarity score is obfuscated, in order to increase the uncertainty at the database server. In particular, for every similarity score s_i, the camera selects two uniformly random numbers $r_1, r_2 \in [0, 2^\ell)$ and masks the score as $\delta_i = s_i \cdot r_1 + r_2$. In the ciphertext domain this is computed as

$$\mathsf{Enc}(\delta_i) = r_1 \cdot \mathsf{Enc}(s_i) + \mathsf{Enc}(r_2) \tag{4}$$

To avoid reversing the sign of the similarity score, we always choose $r_1 > r_2$. The exact value of ℓ depends on the main memory specifications of the server. In our experiments, we empirically determined the max value for the similarity score to be $< 2^{19}$ and set $\ell = 11$, which limits the obfuscated scores to values $< 2^{30}$. Note that, since $r_2 < 2048$, we may precompute all possible encryptions of r_2 and reduce the computational cost of this step to M point multiplications and M point additions.

5.4 Matching

When all obfuscated scores δ_i are computed for a captured face C_j, the camera applies a random permutation π_j and sends the permuted score vector to the database server. The server then decrypts all ciphertexts with its private key and, if all M are positive, it infers that C_j is not a potential suspect. On the other hand, if a score is negative, a verification protocol is invoked in order for the server to learn the id of the potential suspect and (optionally) receive the image of the captured face. This step is necessary to prevent a malicious server

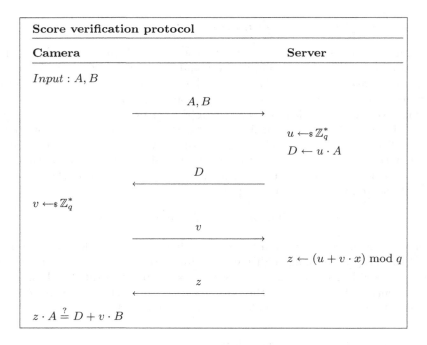

Fig. 2. Score verification protocol

from requesting footage of random individuals that did not actually produce a database match.

The verification protocol works as follows. The server first informs the camera of the suspect's position and score on the permuted vector, and the camera then looks up the suspect's real id and encrypted score in the permutation π_j that is temporarily stored in its local storage. Assume that the stored copy of the encrypted score is equal to $\mathsf{Enc}(s) = \langle r_1 \cdot P, (s + r_1) \cdot Q \rangle$. The camera will then generate an encryption of the score s' that the server claims to be true: $\mathsf{Enc}(s') = \langle r_2 \cdot P, (s' + r_2) \cdot Q \rangle$. If $s = s'$, then a subtraction of the two ciphertexts will produce an encryption of the value zero. Therefore, the camera will compute

$$\mathsf{Enc}(s) - \mathsf{Enc}(s') = \langle (r_1 - r_2) \cdot P, (s - s' + r_1 - r_2) \cdot Q \rangle \tag{5}$$

which is supposedly equal to $\langle A, B \rangle = \langle r \cdot P, r \cdot Q \rangle$ for some unknown random r. As such, it suffices to prove that $x \cdot A = B$, where x is the server's private key. Essentially, the server has to prove to the camera that it knows the value x that satisfies the above equation. This is trivially done with Schnorr's identification protocol [21], as shown in Fig. 2. D represents the server's commitment in the protocol, while v is the challenge posed by the camera. The server's response z can only be computed by the party who knows x, and the camera accepts the result if and only if the last equation holds.

Under normal conditions, the overwhelming majority of captured faces will not produce a database match, so the cost of the matching protocol is dominated by the M decryption operations, each requiring one point multiplication and one point addition (due to the stored lookup table). The communication cost involves the transmission of M ciphertexts and is, thus, equal to $M \times T$ bytes.

6   Security

We consider two types of attacks against our system. The first one is a complete privacy break, where the server is able to retrieve the plaintext version of the feature vector for some captured face. This is only possible if the server is able to correctly inverse the camera's permutation and obfuscation steps and solve the underlying non-linear equations with N unknowns (assuming $M \geq N$). Nevertheless, this is infeasible due to (i) the exponential number $M!$ of possible permutation outcomes and (ii) the unpredictability of FaceNet's deep learning approach to feature vector generation that makes it very difficult to link a similarity score to a specific face-suspect pair.

To illustrate the second point above, we analyzed the similarity scores generated by our system for four random faces from the LFW dataset. We selected 500 images from person P_1 and computed the (non-obfuscated) similarity scores against one image of P_1, P_2, P_3, P_4. The results are shown in Fig. 3, where it is evident that the obtained scores follow a Gaussian-like distribution with a large overlap among the different faces. In particular, for the non-matching faces, the large majority of similarity scores lie within the interval $[50K, 200K]$, thus preventing the server from inferring any non-trivial information about the underlying permutation.

The second type of attack is less severe and pertains to the ability of the database server to distinguish an unknown individual across multiple cameras. For example, suppose that a captured face generates an identical feature vector across a series of cameras. While the probability of that event is negligible, it is worth investigating the effect of the obfuscation step on the generated score distribution. Figure 4 depicts the probability distribution of the obfuscated score bit-lengths against a database of 1000 suspects. P_1 is indistinguishable across two different obfuscations (for an identical feature vector) and all four distributions are very similar to each other with large overlaps. Note that, we are not interested in the distribution of negative scores, since a match will trigger the verification protocol that reveals the suspect's identity.

7   Performance Comparison

Compared to the current state-of-the-art approaches, such as Eigenfaces [19] and SCiFI [17], our system offers tremendous improvements (multiple orders of magnitude) in terms of online cost, while still maintaining strong privacy guarantees. We were able to obtain these results because of (i) the efficiency of FaceNet's

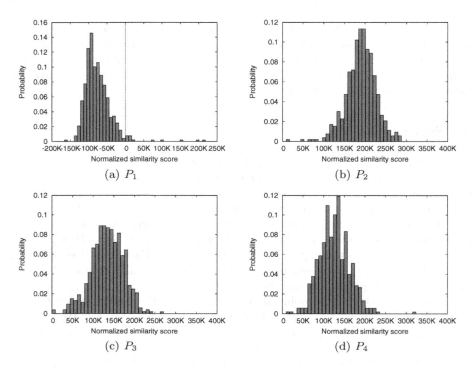

Fig. 3. Distribution of non-obfuscated similarity scores for 500 images of P_1 against one image of P_1, P_2, P_3, P_4

feature vectors and (ii) the storage of the suspects' database at the surveillance cameras. Indeed, the feature vector of Eigenfaces is equal to the number of image pixels, which cannot be less than 10,000; SCiFI also suffers from high vector dimensionality, as it utilizes 900-bit vectors. On the other hand, FaceNet achieves very accurate image classification with only 128 features. Feature vector dimensionality is a major factor that affects the online cost, since every feature has to be encrypted at the camera and transmitted to the database server (for Eigenfaces and SCiFI). These methods utilize precomputations to reduce that cost, but they do not come for free, as they have to be performed for every captured face, potentially millions per day.

This brings us to our major contribution, i.e., the distribution the suspects' encrypted database to the entire network of cameras. There are significant advantages with this approach. First, the cameras do not need to encrypt the feature vectors, thus alleviating the computational burden at these low-cost devices. Second, the static database facilitates the (one-time) precomputation of all intermediate results that reduces the computation of the encrypted similarity scores to a series of cheap elliptic curve point additions. Finally, the server is no longer involved in the expensive homomorphic operations that compute the similarity

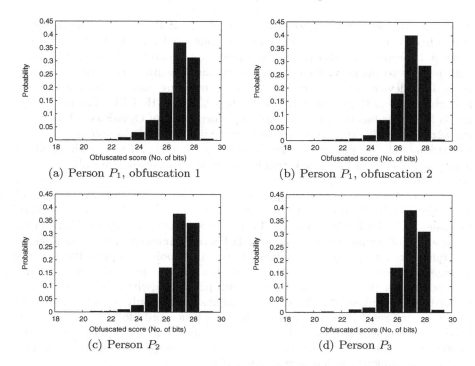

Fig. 4. Distribution of obfuscated score bit-lengths against a database of 1000 suspects $(r_1, r_2 < 2048)$

scores (as in Eigenfaces and SCiFI), which is a much more scalable approach for wide-scale video surveillance.

Our final contribution towards practical privacy-preserving video surveillance is the relaxation of the strict privacy guarantees of previous methods without any measurable consequences on user privacy. This eliminates an expensive zero knowledge protocol that reveals the id of the potential suspect only if the similarity score is below a certain threshold. Such protocols include garbled circuits [19] and oblivious transfers [17], which incur a lot of overhead, especially in terms of communication. Precomputations certainly improve the online costs, but they have to be performed for every captured face. On the other hand, our protocol necessitates a single communication round (with the exception of infrequent positive matches) and a few KB of communication cost.

8   Implementation Details

We implemented our system on two machines, one to emulate the law enforcement server and the other to simulate the camera operations. The server is a Ubuntu desktop machine equipped with Intel Xeon CPU E5-2620 2.10 GHz × 16, 64 GB of RAM, and a 512 GB SSD. The other machine is a Ubuntu laptop with

Intel Core i7-6500U CPU 2.50 GHz× 4 and 8 GB of RAM (it is also equipped with a front camera). The two machines are connected via a TCP/IP4 LAN over Gigabit Ethernet. We also tested our system on a more realistic environment, with regards to the surveillance cameras, by implementing our code on a Raspberry Pi 3 device. This device has limited computing and storage capabilities, featuring 1 GB of RAM and a 4ARM Cortex-A53 1.2 GHz CPU. The face recognition layer was based on the original implementation of OpenFace[1]. It employs *shape_predictor_68_face_landmarks* as face predictor and *nn4.small2.v1.t7* as the network model. The package is written in Python version 2.7 and, with the aforementioned configuration, face recognition and normalization takes about 600 ms on the laptop.

The cryptographic layer (elliptic curve ElGamal) was implemented in C, using the BIGNUM library of OpenSSL (version 1.1.0 g). We also used SWIG to connect C with Python (version 4.0.1). We set the order of the elliptic curve to be a 256-bit prime number, as per NIST's recommendations [4]. As a result, all ciphertexts, which consist of two elliptic curve points, require 128 bytes of storage/communication. Under this C/Python environment, the average time for encryption, decryption, and point multiplication (with 256-bit scalars) is about 0.3 ms. On the other hand, point addition takes only about 0.02 ms. For each reported result, we run the experiment 4 times and plot the average time. Finally, our implementation leverages the parallel computing abilities of the two multi-core machines, since all our algorithms are easily parallelizable. The source code of our implementation is available online[2].

9   Experimental Results

In this section, we present the results of our experimental evaluation. The reported times correspond to actual measurements collected from the two implementations on the separate devices (laptop and workstation). Starting with the offline phase, we first evaluate the computation and communication/storage costs at both the camera and the server, as a function of the database size M. To this end, Fig. 5 illustrates the CPU time at all parties. G represents the database of precomputed values, so the bottom curve of the plot corresponds to the cost where only 50% of the precomputations are actually performed. The cost at the camera is clearly linear in M and is dominated by the computation of the terms $y_{i,j} \cdot \mathsf{Enc}(-2x_{i,j})$, as explained in Sect. 5.1. This is, by any means, an acceptable cost, as it is incurred only once and can terminate within a few minutes.

At the server-side, the offline cost includes the generation of the suspects' feature vectors from the corresponding images (OpenFace), the normalization of their representations (our algorithm), and the generation of the encrypted database that is sent to the cameras. Nevertheless, these costs are not evident in Fig. 5, as they are dominated by the cost of the precomputations for the discrete log lookup table. This operation necessitates over an hour of compute time, but is

---

[1] https://github.com/cmusatyalab/openface.
[2] https://github.com/mahdihbku/BlindGuardian.

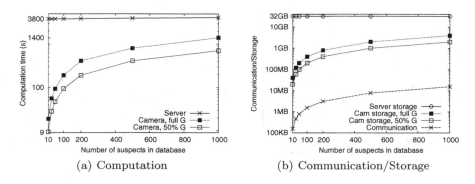

(a) Computation   (b) Communication/Storage

Fig. 5. Offline cost

crucial in our system because it speeds up considerably the decryption operations
at the server. More importantly, this is a one-time cost that is incurred before
the system becomes operational.

Figure 5(b) depicts the offline communication/storage cost at the two devices.
The compact representation of elliptic curve points makes it feasible to store
the entire database G at the camera with only 4 GB of main memory. On the
other hand, the cost at the server is again dominated by the discrete log lookup
table, whose size is equal to 32 GB. However, this is a trivial requirement for
today's state-of-the-art servers. Finally, the offline communication cost entails
the transmission of the encrypted database and remains under 10 MB, even for
a database of 1000 suspects.

In the next set of experiments, we evaluate the online cost of our approach,
as a function of the database size M. First, Fig. 6(a) shows the online CPU time
at all parties. Clearly, the cameras absorb most of the computational cost, since
they have to compute the encrypted similarity scores for every suspect in the
database. Nevertheless, the online cost is order of magnitudes lower compared to
existing approaches, and remains below 1 s for databases of up to 500 suspects.
A notable observation that motivates the partial storage of G (as explained
in Sect. 5.1) is that the performance penalty from storing 50% of G is not
significant. In particular, for $M = 100$, the CPU time at the camera when the
full G is available is 155 ms, and it only increases by 35% (to 210 ms) when
50% is available. Finally, a very promising result of our implementation is the
online computation cost at the database server. For $M = 100$ the cost is just
34 ms, while for $M = 1000$ it only raises to 50 ms. As mentioned previously,
the database server is the bottleneck in a wide-scale video surveillance system,
because it may potentially process thousands of captured faces every second.

Figure 6(b) illustrates the online communication cost for our system. It
involves a single round of communication, where the camera transmits M
encrypted similarity scores to the server. For a database of 1000 suspects, this
entails a communication cost of just 128 KB.

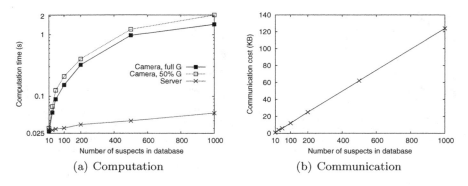

(a) Computation   (b) Communication

Fig. 6. Online cost

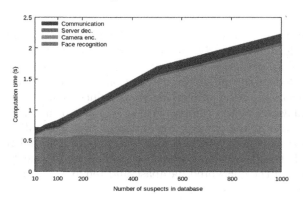

Fig. 7. Round Trip Time to detect a suspect

Our previous experiments focused only on the cryptographic overhead of the privacy-preserving face recognition system. Alternatively, Fig. 7 illustrates the true Round Trip Time (RTT) for detecting a suspect. It includes face recognition and detection at the camera, all the cryptographic operations at both the camera and the server, and the required communication that includes sending the suspect's image from the camera to the server. For a database of 100 suspects, the RTT is less than 0.8 s (with a precomputation of the entire database G), while for $M = 1000$ the RTT is approximately 2.2 s. Nevertheless, a large portion of the RTT (around 0.6 s) is consumed on non-cryptographic operations, namely the face recognition and detection by the OpenFace software. A better combination of hardware/software at the surveillance cameras could improve that cost considerably.

Finally, Fig. 8 shows the computational costs of our Raspberry Pi 3 implementation. As we can see, the CPU time on the Raspberry device is around $10\times$ slower than the laptop. Even so, by storing the entire table of precomputations, we can match a face against a database with 100 suspects in under 2 s. There-

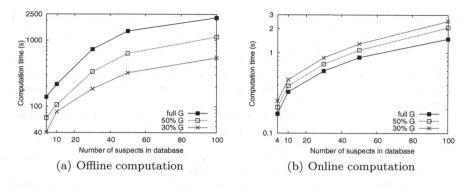

(a) Offline computation   (b) Online computation

Fig. 8. Raspberry Pi 3 computational costs

fore, we argue that our system can be featured in a real-life implementation of privacy-preserving video surveillance, using cameras with moderate computational capabilities.

10   Conclusions

In this paper, we proposed the first near real-time privacy-preserving video-surveillance system that is based on the state-of-the-art face recognition algorithm. Our protocol diverges from the standard techniques employed by existing approaches by (i) replicating the suspects' database at the surveillance cameras and (ii) relaxing the stringent privacy requirements by disclosing some trivial information during the identification process. These design decisions facilitate the use of extensive precomputations that reduce significantly the computation of encrypted similarity scores. As a result, our system is able to match a single person against a database of 100 suspects in under 200 ms, while incurring a network transfer of just 12 KB of data. In our future work, we plan to incorporate specialized hardware (like GPUs) to further speed up the server computations, given the fact that our algorithms are highly parallelizable. We also plan to extend our framework to other domains as well, including biometric authentication and traffic surveillance.

References

1. Acar, A., Aksu, H., Uluagac, A.S., Conti, M.: A survey on homomorphic encryption schemes: theory and implementation. ACM Comput. Surv. (CSUR) **51**(4), 79 (2018)
2. Amos, B., Ludwiczuk, B., Satyanarayanan, M.: Openface: a general-purpose face recognition library with mobile applications. CMU School Comput. Sci. **6**, 1–18 (2016)
3. Baltrusaitis, T., Zadeh, A., Lim, Y.C., Morency, L.P.: Openface 2.0: facial behavior analysis toolkit. In: Proceedings of IEEE International Conference on Automatic Face & Gesture Recognition (FG), pp. 59–66 (2018)

4. Barker, E., Barker, W., Burr, W., Polk, W., Smid, M.: NIST special publication 800–57. NIST Special publication, Recommendation for Key Management-Part 1: General (Revision 3), vol. 800, no. 57, pp. 1–142 (2012)
5. Bringer, J., Chabanne, H., Favre, M., Patey, A., Schneider, T., Zohner, M.: GSHADE: faster privacy-preserving distance computation and biometric identification. In: Proceedings of ACM Workshop on Information Hiding and Multimedia Security, pp. 187–198 (2014)
6. Dagher, I.: Incremental PCA-LDA algorithm. In: Proceedings of IEEE International Conference on Computational Intelligence for Measurement Systems and Applications, pp. 97–101 (2010)
7. ElGamal, T.: A public key cryptosystem and a signature scheme based on discrete logarithms. IEEE Trans. Inf. Theory $31(4)$, 469–472 (1985)
8. Er, M.J., Wu, S., Lu, J., Toh, H.L.: Face recognition with radial basis function (RBF) neural networks. IEEE Trans. Neural Netw. $13(3)$, 697–710 (2002)
9. Erkin, Z., Franz, M., Guajardo, J., Katzenbeisser, S., Lagendijk, I., Toft, T.: Privacy-preserving face recognition. In: Proceedings of International Symposium on Privacy Enhancing Technologies (PETS), pp. 235–253 (2009)
10. Evans, D., Huang, Y., Katz, J., Malka, L.: Efficient privacy-preserving biometric identification. In: Proceedings of Network and Distributed System Security Symposium (NDSS), vol. 68 (2011)
11. Gasti, P., Šeděnka, J., Yang, Q., Zhou, G., Balagani, K.S.: Secure, fast, and energy-efficient outsourced authentication for smartphones. IEEE Trans. Inf. Forensics Secur. $11(11)$, 2556–2571 (2016)
12. Gentry, C.: Fully homomorphic encryption using ideal lattices. In: Proceedings ACM Symposium on Theory of Computing (STOC), pp. 169–178 (2009)
13. Heisele, B., Ho, P., Poggio, T.: Face recognition with support vector machines: global versus component-based approach. In: Proceedings of IEEE International Conference on Computer Vision (ICCV), vol. 2, pp. 688–694 (2001)
14. Karabat, C., Kiraz, M.S., Erdogan, H., Savas, E.: THRIVE: threshold homomorphic encryption based secure and privacy preserving biometric verification system. EURASIP J. Adv. Signal Process. $2015(1)$, 1–18 (2015). https://doi.org/10.1186/s13634-015-0255-5
15. Liu, C., Wechsler, H.: Comparative assessment of independent component analysis (ICA) for face recognition. In: Proceedings of International Conference on Audio and Video Based Biometric Person Authentication (1999)
16. Naor, M., Pinkas, B.: Computationally secure oblivious transfer. J. Cryptol. $18(1)$, 1–35 (2005)
17. Osadchy, M., Pinkas, B., Jarrous, A., Moskovich, B.: Scifi - a system for secure face identification. In: Proceedings of IEEE Symposium on Security and Privacy (SP), pp. 239–254 (2010)
18. Paillier, P.: Public-key cryptosystems based on composite degree residuosity classes. In: Proceedings of International Conference on the Theory and Applications of Cryptographic Techniques, pp. 223–238 (1999)
19. Sadeghi, A.R., Schneider, T., Wehrenberg, I.: Efficient privacy-preserving face recognition. In: Proceedings of International Conference on Information Security and Cryptology, pp. 229–244 (2009)
20. Sahoolizadeh, A.H., Heidari, B.Z., Dehghani, C.H.: A new face recognition method using PCA, LDA and neural network. Int. J. Comput. Sci. Eng. $2(4)$, 218–223 (2008)
21. Schnorr, C.P.: Efficient signature generation by smart cards. J. Cryptol. $4(3)$, 161–174 (1991). https://doi.org/10.1007/BF00196725

22. Schroff, F., Kalenichenko, D., Philbin, J.: Facenet: a unified embedding for face recognition and clustering. In: Proceedings of IEEE Conference on Computer Vision and Pattern Recognition (CVPR), pp. 815–823 (2015)
23. Swets, D.L., Weng, J.J.: Using discriminant eigenfeatures for image retrieval. IEEE Trans. Pattern Anal. Mach. Intell. (TPAMI) **18**(8), 831–836 (1996)
24. Taigman, Y., Yang, M., Ranzato, M., Wolf, L.: Deepface: closing the gap to human-level performance in face verification. In: Proceedings of IEEE Conference on Computer Vision and Pattern Recognition (CVPR), pp. 1701–1708 (2014)
25. Toygar, Ö., Adnan, A.: Face recognition using PCA, LDA and ICA approaches on colored images. Istanbul Univ.-J. Electr. Electron. Eng. **3**(1), 735–743 (2003)
26. Turk, M., Pentland, A.: Eigenfaces for recognition. J. Cognit. Neurosci. **3**(1), 71–86 (1991)
27. Xiang, C., Tang, C., Cai, Y., Xu, Q.: Privacy-preserving face recognition with outsourced computation. Soft Comput. **20**(9), 3735–3744 (2015). https://doi.org/10.1007/s00500-015-1759-5
28. Yao, A.C.C.: How to generate and exchange secrets. In: Proceedings of Symposium on Foundations of Computer Science (FOCS), pp. 162–167 (1986)
29. Zhou, K., Ren, J.: PassBio: privacy-preserving user-centric biometric authentication. IEEE Trans. Inf. Forensics Secur. **13**(12), 3050–3063 (2018)

Biometric-Authenticated Searchable Encryption

Daniel Gardham[⊠], Mark Manulis, and Constantin Cătălin Drăgan

Surrey Centre for Cyber Security, University of Surrey, Guildford, UK
{d.gardham,c.dragan}@surrey.ac.uk,
mark@manulis.eu

Abstract. We introduce *Biometric-Authenticated Keyword Search (BAKS)*, a novel searchable encryption scheme that relieves clients from managing cryptographic keys and relies purely on client's biometric data for authenticated outsourcing and retrieval of files indexed by encrypted keywords.

BAKS utilises *distributed trust* across two servers and the *liveness assumption* which models physical presence of the client; in particular, BAKS security is guaranteed even if clients' biometric data, which often has low entropy, becomes public. We formalise two security properties, Authentication and Indistinguishability against Chosen Keyword Attacks, which ensure that only a client with a biometric input sufficiently close to the registered template is considered legitimate and that neither of the two servers involved can learn any information about the encrypted keywords.

Our BAKS construction further supports outsourcing and retrieval of files using multiple keywords and flexible search queries (e.g., conjunction, disjunction and subset-type queries). An additional update mechanism allows clients to replace their registered biometrics without requiring re-encryption of outsourced keywords, which enables smooth user migration across devices supporting different types of biometrics.

Keywords: Searchable encryption · Biometric authentication · Secret sharing

1 Introduction

Searchable Encryption. *Searchable Encryption* addresses the need for clients with computation or storage limitations to outsource encrypted data to (potentially multiple) servers. Retrieval processes typically operate on encrypted keywords that preserve the privacy of search queries of the client from malicious servers. Most of existing solutions can be generally split into two approaches: *Symmetric Searchable Encryption (SSE)*, e.g., [4,17,37], where a high-entropy key is shared between the client and the server, and *Public Key Encryption with Keyword Search (PEKS)*, e.g., [2,7,8,11,16,32,37,38].

© Springer Nature Switzerland AG 2020
M. Conti et al. (Eds.): ACNS 2020, LNCS 12147, pp. 40–61, 2020.
https://doi.org/10.1007/978-3-030-57878-7_3

From the practical perspective, both of these approaches require the client to store and manage cryptographic keys, which can be generally considered error-prone and brings further limitations for users who wish to use multiple devices to outsource and perform search over encrypted data. *Password-Authenticated Keyword Search (PAKS)* [26] was recently introduced to alleviate this problem by basing security of searchable encryption on a human-memorisable password and adopting a two-server architecture [12,45] to account for dictionary attacks on low-entropy passwords and keywords which arise in such case. The high-level idea used in [26] is to use a password-authenticated key-recovery protocol in combination with an SSE scheme.

Precisely due to their nature of being memorable, passwords are often re-used, in different contexts than their initial purpose [36]. Moreover, strict policies that require the user to frequently update his password, can further exacerbate this problem. A security breach on a particular server may impact all other servers for which the user has re-used some form of his password. The current trend, observed in the domain of web authentication (e.g. [21]), is to move away from passwords to other forms of usable authentication factors. In this context, biometric data (e.g., fingerprints, iris recognition, facial imagery, etc.) can be seen as an alternative to passwords, especially since support for different types of biometrics on commodity user devices such as laptops, smartphones, and wearables is on the rise.

Challenges for Biometric-Based Searchable Encryption. Crucially, biometric data used for authentication is inherently noisy (e.g., as opposed to passwords), which introduces unique challenges for the design and security analysis of biometric-based protocols. In the context of searchable encryption, a general approach for a purely biometric-based solution could be to adopt fuzzy extractors [9,13,19,20] and combine them with SSE schemes [4,17,37], i.e., user's biometric input would be processed by a fuzzy extractor to obtain a symmetric key, which will then be used to outsource encrypted keywords to the server and perform the search. However, to practically use fuzzy extractors to source high-entropy (symmetric) keys, the biometric data needs to be of a certain "quality" (i.e., the min-entropy greater than a fixed threshold). Techniques to utilize distributions with low-entropy have been studied in [13], but require some additional structure, in particular, that random subsequences of the biometric data source still have sufficient min-entropy. It is shown that this property is necessary to support low-entropy source material [13]. Finding biometric data that satisfies these requirements is particularly challenging, as even the best source of biometric data, i.e., iris recognition [41], ran by the state-of-the-art iris recognition protocol IrisCode [18] falls short of the minimum bound [6]. Additionally, it is unclear how to apply the techniques in [13] to arbitrarily type biometric data, and enforce the structure required by low entropy source distributions. Therefore, the use of fuzzy extractors imposes restrictions over the selection of biometric data, that makes them unsuitable for our construction.

Another aspect for the unsuitability of fuzzy-extractors for our model relates to their security assumptions. The security of this general approach would rely on the secrecy of the biometric data, which often has low entropy (i.e., comparable to 32 bits security [23]), and if this data is leaked the server would be able to break the privacy of the outsourced keywords. However, the assumption that biometric data is secret, although widely used in academia [10, 19, 29], is often too strong for the real world. Indeed, in many practical applications biometric authentication often relies on mechanisms ensuring physical presence of the user, e.g., in applications of e-passports and in recent FIDO standards for web authentication [21], etc. This so-called *liveness assumption* is also part of industrial standardization efforts, e.g., ISO/IEC WD 30107 [1], to detect and prevent impersonation attacks based on digital copies of biometric data or other fake artefacts, and has been also considered in the academic literature [22, 40]. Under this assumption biometric data used as input to the cryptographic protocol can be considered public as long as it remains fresh and stems from a living subject, in which case security of the protocol can still be guaranteed. The liveness assumption, however, is only valid and enforced on the client side, and does not prevent malicious servers from running brute-force attacks against the biometric template, thus enabling dictionary-type attacks on the outsourced (low-entropy) keywords [16]. Hence, designing a searchable encryption scheme that would rely only on biometric data and remain secure is particularly challenging and requires a new approach.

We note that access pattern attacks, when paired with auxiliary information about the files in the database, could allow an adversary to recover the keyword of a search query (e.g. [27]). A variety of works [14, 30, 35, 46] have shown that it may also be impossible to protect against access pattern leakage attacks, and that SSE as a primitive leaks too much information to feasibly mitigate against these attacks. Some of these known attacks [14, 46] require an adversary to perform active insertion of files, which could be mitigated against by enforcing an authentication property for at least the outsourcing protocol. We briefly note that oblivious RAM (ORAM), or other techniques [33], can be used to achieve minimal information leakage, that is, the server only learns the number of files in the database. However, ORAM typically requires high bandwidth, but where low bandwidth is sufficient, much more client storage is needed [44]. With this in mind, understanding when pattern leakage is acceptable is an important direction for future research, but is not considered further in this work.

Our Contribution: Biometric-Authenticated Keyword Search (BAKS). We propose a novel searchable encryption scheme, BAKS, that relies purely on a client's biometric data for authenticated outsourcing and retrieval of files indexed by encrypted keywords and relieves clients from managing cryptographic keys. The scheme relies on the two-server architecture and the liveness assumption on the biometric inputs. BAKS makes use of symmetric searchable encryption techniques with the symmetric key being linked to the biometric data and protected by secret-sharing techniques involving both servers. BAKS accounts for the noise in biometric measurements and consists of a protocol that allows the client to reconstruct this key following an interaction with both servers as long as the measured biometric input is "similar" to the template that was used during the initial registration phase. The degree of similarity, potentially influenced by the accuracy of the measuring device, is defined by the client during the registration. The use of a two-server architecture not only is crucial for the secrecy of the keywords but also improves the availability of outsourced files, since each server stores a copy. Our security model for BAKS defines two main security properties: (i) indistinguishability against chosen keyword attacks guaranteeing that keywords remain secret against an active adversary in control of at most one server and (ii) authentication ensuring that only legitimate clients can outsource the encrypted keywords. Security of our construction is proven under standard cryptographic assumptions and its efficiency analysis shows that the scheme has linear overhead in the length of the biometric template. In addition, BAKS supports update of the registered biometric without requiring any re-encryption of the outsourced keywords, thus making it easier for the users to migrate across devices.

2   Preliminaries and Building Blocks

We introduce the assumptions and building blocks underlying our BAKS scheme.

2.1   Cryptographic Building Blocks

Pedersen Commitment [39]. Let $\mathbb{G}$ be a multiplicative cyclic group of order q, with $g, h \leftarrow_\$ \mathbb{G}$ two generators such that $\log_g h$ is unknown. A Pedersen commitment is computed as $c \leftarrow g^r h^m$, for some message m, with $r \leftarrow_\$ \mathbb{Z}_q$. It can be opened by providing (r, m). Pedersen commitments provide perfect hiding and computational binding of the message under the Discrete Logarithm (DL) assumption in $\mathbb{G}$.

Pseudorandom Function [25,34]. A pseudorandom function (PRF) takes as input a high entropy key k and a message m, and produces an output $\mathsf{PRF}(k, m)$ that should be indistinguishable from a uniformly random bit string of the same length, for any efficient adversary $\mathcal{A}$. In this paper, we restrict the key space, message space, and output to be a cyclic group $\mathbb{G}$ of order q, $\mathsf{PRF} : \mathbb{G} \times \mathbb{G} \to \mathbb{G}$.

Key Derivation Function [31]. A key derivation function (KDF) takes as input a source of key material σ and a context variable c, to produce a key k. Any efficient adversary $\mathcal{A}$ can distinguish with a negligible probability between the output of $\mathsf{KDF}(\sigma, c)$ and a uniformly sampled binary string of the same length, for some σ, c. Let $\mathbb{G}$ be a cyclic group of order q, we consider $\mathsf{KDF} : \mathbb{G} \times \{0, 1\}^* \to \mathbb{G}$.

Message Authentication Code [5]. A message authentication code (MAC) is defined as $(\mathsf{KGen}, \mathsf{Tag}, \mathsf{Ver})$, where the secret key $\mathsf{mk} \leftarrow \mathsf{KGen}(1^\lambda)$, for some security parameter λ. Algorithm $\mathsf{Tag}(\mathsf{mk}, m)$ outputs a code (or a tag) μ, for any key mk and any message m. The verification algorithm $\mathsf{Ver}(\mathsf{mk}, m, \mu)$ evaluates if the tag μ is valid w.r.t. mk and a message m. The MAC satisfies a *correctness* property: $\mathsf{true} \leftarrow \mathsf{Ver}(\mathsf{mk}, m, \mathsf{Tag}(\mathsf{mk}, m))$, for some m and any $\mathsf{mk} \leftarrow \mathsf{KGen}(1^\lambda)$. The MAC is *unforgeable* if any efficient adversary $\mathcal{A}$ has a negligible advantage to create a tag μ^* for a message m^*, without access to the key mk. The adversary has access to an oracle $\mathcal{O}_{\text{tag}}(\cdot)$ that outputs $\mu \leftarrow \text{Tag}(\text{mk}, m)$ for any message $m \neq m^*$. In this paper, we use the output of KDF as the key space, and consider messages of arbitrary length $\{0,1\}^*$. There is no restriction on the code space, but for uniformity with the previous cryptographic primitives we take it as $\mathbb{G}$.

Secret Sharing of Group Elements [39,42,43]**.** We consider a threshold secret-sharing scheme $\text{SS} = (\text{Setup}, \text{Shr}, \text{Rec})$ that shares group elements in $\mathbb{G}$ for which we know the discrete logarithm. The setup algorithm $\text{Setup}(1^\lambda)$ sets the public parameters $\text{pp} = (t, N, g, \mathbb{G}, q)$, with N as the number of shares, $0 < t \leq N$ as the threshold, the group $\mathbb{G}$ of order q as the secret space and share space, and $g \in \mathbb{G}$ as the generator. Algorithm $\text{Shr}(\text{pp}, k)$ shares the secret $K = g^k$ by returning the shares $\{K_i\}_{i=1}^N$. This is done by first applying Shamir's threshold secret sharing scheme [43] to create the shares $k_1, \ldots, k_N \in \mathbb{Z}_q$ from k, before returning $\{K_i\}_{i=1}^N$ with $K_i = g^{k_i}$. The reconstruction $\text{Rec}(\text{pp}, T)$ returns K for any set of shares $|T| \geq t$, by replicating Shamir's reconstruction in the exponent [39]. The scheme SS is *private*, if any efficient adversary $\mathcal{A}$ has an negligible advantage to distinguish between given shares of $K \in \mathbb{G}$ or shares of $K' \in \mathbb{G}$, when he can see at most $(t-1)$ shares [42], for any $\text{pp} = (t, N, g, \mathbb{G}, q)$. This scheme trivially satisfies privacy, as the underlying Shamir scheme is perfect [43].

2.2 Biometric Sampling and Liveness Assumption

A user's biometric data is modelled as a distribution $\mathcal{D}$, and an instance of a user submitting a biometric reading is captured by sampling $\mathcal{W} \leftarrow_{\$} \mathcal{D}$. Let M be a metric space with distance function $d : M \times M \rightarrow \mathbb{R}^+$. Our protocol is constructed for d being the Hamming distance over $M := \{0,1\}^N$, however, we note that the *model* fits a generic instance to encompass other metrics suitable for different types of biometric data. To relate the biometric sampling to the security properties, it is necessary to define two error-probabilities.

The first error we consider is *false rejection*. That is, the distance between any two samples from the same biometric distribution is bounded by a constant τ_1 with probability $1 - \varepsilon_{fr}$. Here we capture the event a legitimate user submits a biometric sample that is sufficiently noisy and is therefore rejected. This probability will be necessary in the definition for the correctness of the protocol. Formally, we have:

$$\Pr[\mathcal{W} \leftarrow \mathcal{D}, \mathcal{W}' \leftarrow \mathcal{D} : d(\mathcal{W}, \mathcal{W}') \leq \tau_1] \geq 1 - \varepsilon_{fr}$$

Secondly, we introduce *false acceptance*. This states that any two biometrics sampled from two different distributions (which corresponds to different users submitting biometric data) have a minimum distance τ_2 with probability $1 - \varepsilon_{fa}$. We use this to model an adversary, who cannot sample from the user's biometric distribution, that is able to falsely authenticate himself as that user. We define false acceptance formally as:

$$\Pr[\mathcal{W} \leftarrow \mathcal{D}, \mathcal{W}' \leftarrow \mathcal{D}' : d(\mathcal{W}, \mathcal{W}') > \tau_2] \geq 1 - \varepsilon_{fa}$$

Finally, we assume that the biometric distribution $\mathcal{D}$ for user U is public and consequently rely on the *liveness assumption* [1,18] which states that any input of biometric data is sampled fresh from a user. It ensures the physical presence of the user and thus prevents an attacker from mounting replay attacks, or altering the output of the biometric sensor. We model it through an oracle $\mathcal{O}_{\text{bio}}$ that takes as input some biometric distribution $\mathcal{D}$, chosen by the adversary, and outputs results of the computation using a fresh sample $\mathcal{W} \leftarrow_{\$} \mathcal{D}$. Any step that involves computation on the biometric sample directly must be computed and output by the oracle.

An implementation of liveness assumption in practice would require some form of trusted processing of biometric measurements, which is not in the focus of this paper. We note, however, there exist a number of methods for enforcing liveness detection such as *software enhancement* (e.g. pupil and eye movement for iris recognition), *hardware enhancement* (e.g. temperature sensing, pulse, electrical conductivity, ECG for fingerprints) and *challenge-response techniques* (e.g. expressions in face recognition) [3].

3 Biometric-Authenticated Keyword Search: Syntax and Definitions

In this section we model BAKS and its security properties. Our model is inspired by the recent model for password-authenticated keyword search from [26], which in turn addresses main security requirements that have been previously formulated for other flavours of searchable encryption, e.g. [2,7,16]. The main differences to [26] is that we need to account for the inherent errors in the imperfectness of the measurement process, and also application of the liveness assumption to this protocol.

3.1 Syntax of BAKS

Definition 1 (BAKS). *The* BAKS $=$ (Setup, Register, Outsource, Retrieve) *protocol consists of the following algorithms:*

- Setup(1^λ) : pp, takes as input a security parameter λ and outputs public parameters pp, that include a description for the structure of the biometric data.

  - Register(pp, U, t, $\mathcal{W}$, S_0, S_1) is executed between user U and two servers S_0 and S_1, and consists of the following two interactive algorithms:

- RegisterU(pp, t, $\mathcal{W}$, S_0, S_1) : {succ, fail} performed by U, takes an input a description of the biometric data $\mathcal{W}$, public parameters pp, and the identities of the two servers S_0 and S_1. It interacts with RegisterS$_d$ for $d \in \{0,1\}$ and outputs succ if registration was successful and fail otherwise.

- RegisterS$_d$(pp, U, S_{1-d}) : info$_d$, performed by S_d, $d \in \{0,1\}$, takes as input the users identity U and the identity of the other server S_{1-d}. It interacts with RegisterU and RegisterS$_{1-d}$. At the end of the protocol, it stores info$_d$ associated with user U on S_d.

- Outsource(pp, U, $\mathcal{W}'$, w, f, S_0, info$_0$, S_1, info$_1$) is executed between a user U and two servers S_0 and S_1 that follow the interactive algorithms:

  - OutsourceU(pp, U, $\mathcal{W}'$, w, f, S_0, S_1) : {succ, fail} executed by U, takes as input a sampled biometric $\mathcal{W}'$, a keyword w, and a file descriptor f, and finally the identity of two servers S_0 and S_1. The algorithm interacts with OutsourceS$_d$ for $d \in \{0, 1\}$, it outputs succ if successful, and fail otherwise.
  - OutsourceS$_d$(pp, U, S_{1-d}, info$_d$) : (C, f) is performed by server S_d for $d \in \{0, 1\}$. It takes as input the identity of the user U, identity of the other server S_{1-d} and information info$_d$. This protocol interacts with OutsourceU and OutsourceS$_{1-d}$, and upon completion, stores (C, f) in a database $\boldsymbol{C}_d$.

- Retrieve(pp, U, $\mathcal{W}'$, w, S_0, info$_0$, S_1, info$_1$) is executed between user U and the servers S_0 and S_1 that follow the two interactive algorithms below.

  - RetrieveU(pp, $\mathcal{W}'$, w, S_0, S_1) : $\boldsymbol{F}$, executed by the user U, takes as input a sampled biometric $\mathcal{W}'$, a keyword w, and the identity of the servers S_0 and S_1. It interacts with RetrieveS$_d$ for $d \in \{0, 1\}$. It outputs a set $\boldsymbol{F}$ containing all file descriptors f associated with keyword w.
  - RetrieveS$_d$(pp, U, S_{1-d}, info$_d$) : {succ, fail}, executed by server S_d for $d \in \{0, 1\}$. It takes as input user identity U, server identity S_{1-d} and information info$_d$, it interacts with RetrieveU and RetrieveS$_{1-d}$, and outputs a flag in {succ, fail}.

We store the outsourced data on both servers for redundancy and increased availability. In particular, a user suffers minimal data loss in the event a server is compromised and mounts a denial of service attack.

Correctness. Intuitively, correctness ensures that a file $f \in \mathcal{F}$ outsourced under a keyword w will be retrieved (i.e., $f \in \boldsymbol{F}$) with probability of $1 - \varepsilon_{fr}$, where ε_{fr} is the probability of false rejection, provided the user presents a biometric sample $\mathcal{W}'$ which is sufficiently close to the registered template $\mathcal{W}$. Formally, we say that the BAKS scheme is *correct* if $\forall \lambda \in \mathbb{N}, f \in \mathcal{F}, w \in wd, \mathcal{W}, \mathcal{W}' \in \mathcal{D}$, pp $\leftarrow$ Setup(1^λ) we get $\Pr[f \in \boldsymbol{F}] = 1 - \varepsilon_{fr}$ iff:

$$\langle \text{succ}, \text{info}_0, \text{info}_1 \rangle \leftarrow \text{Register}(\text{pp}, \text{U}, t, \mathcal{W}, S_0, S_1)$$
$$\langle \text{succ}, (C, f), (C, f) \rangle \leftarrow \text{Outsource}(\text{pp}, \text{U}, \mathcal{W}', w, f, S_0, \text{info}_0, S_1, \text{info}_1)$$
$$\langle \boldsymbol{F}, \text{succ}, \text{succ} \rangle \leftarrow \text{Retrieve}(\text{pp}, \text{U}, \mathcal{W}', w, S_0, \text{info}_0, S_1, \text{info}_1)$$

3.2 Security Definitions

We define two notions of security for BAKS, *Indistinguishability against Chosen Keyword Attacks* (IND-CKA) and *Authentication* (Auth), inspired by the recent model from [26]. We model the adversary $\mathcal{A}$ as a probabilistic polynomial-time algorithm (PPT), and we define security through experiments in Fig. 1.

Oracles. We consider a PPT adversary $\mathcal{A}$ that interacts with the BAKS functionality through the following set of oracles and can possibly corrupt one of the two servers, S_0 or S_1, involved in the protocol. During each user registration, the adversary gets access to the information assigned to server S_{1-d}, for any one d of his choice. Then, the adversary can *only* play an active role in the retrieval and outsourcing protocols by assuming the role of server S_{1-d}, for d fixed during registration. We further give the adversary the capability to impersonate the user, together with his control over server S_{1-d}, and interact with an honest server S_d either during retrieval or outsourcing.

To manage multiple registration sessions, even for the same user (with potentially different biometric distributions), we use a unique session identifier j. For simplicity, this session identifier starts at 0, and with each registration it is incremented. Each time the adversary wants to retrieve or outsource files for a particular user, he needs to provide the corresponding session identifier i, s.t. $0 \le i < j$. Due to the *liveness assumption* each oracle call that handles (adversarial given) biometric distributions must first call the biometric sampling oracle to extract a biometric sample.

Internal to the oracles, we use a table E (initially empty) to store and access the tuples $(d, \mathcal{D}, \mathtt{info}_d)$ assigned to the honest servers S_d during registration, i.e. $E[j] \leftarrow (d, \mathcal{D}, \mathtt{info}_d)$. We store all biometric distributions for which the adversary has requested a sample in a list B; that is initially empty. We also log all keyword requests by the adversary in the sets $\mathtt{ASet}$ (during outsourcing) and $\mathtt{ISet}$ (during retrieval); that are initialised at the beginning of both security experiments. The variables $i^* \in \mathbb{Z}, \mathtt{f}^* \in \boldsymbol{F}$ and user distribution $\mathcal{D}^*$ are used to store the challenge values during the challenge outsource oracle in the IND-CKA experiment.

- $\mathcal{O}_{\mathrm{ch}}(b, \cdot)$ is a challenge oracle, which on input $(\cdot) = (i, w_0, w_1, \mathtt{f})$ aborts if $((i^* \ge 0) \vee (i \ge j) \vee ((i, w_0) \in \mathtt{ISet}) \vee ((i, w_1) \in \mathtt{ISet}))$. Otherwise, it sets $i^* \leftarrow i$, $\mathtt{f}^* \leftarrow \mathtt{f}$, and takes $\mathcal{D}^* \leftarrow \mathcal{D}$ from $E[i] \leftarrow (d, \mathcal{D}, \mathtt{info}_d)$. Then, it invokes oracle $\mathcal{O}_{\mathrm{outU}}(i^*, w_b, \mathtt{f}^*)$. It is used as the indistinguishably challenge in the IND-CKA proof for BAKS, where bit b is defined.
- $\mathcal{O}_{\mathrm{reg}}(\cdot)$, with $(\cdot) = (d, \mathcal{D})$, is the oracle that registers user U and its biometric distribution $\mathcal{D}$. First, a biometric sample $\mathcal{W}$ is obtained from the $\mathcal{O}_{\mathrm{bio}}(\mathcal{D})$. The registration protocol Register is run between the adversary $\mathcal{A}$ playing the role of server S_{1-d}, and the oracle running RegisterU and RegisterS$_d$. Then, the map E gets updated for the current session identifier j as $E[j] \leftarrow (d, \mathcal{D}, \mathtt{info}_d)$, and j is incremented $j \leftarrow j + 1$.
- $\mathcal{O}_{\mathrm{outU}}(\cdot)$ on input $(\cdot) = (i, w, \mathtt{f})$ the oracle aborts if $(i \ge j)$, otherwise it obtains $(d, \mathcal{D}, \mathtt{info}_d) \leftarrow E[i]$. The biometric sample is taken from $\mathcal{W} \leftarrow \mathcal{O}_{\mathrm{bio}}(\mathcal{D})$. Then, the protocol Outsource is then executed, with the oracle running OutsourceU and OutsourceS$_d$, and the adversary $\mathcal{A}$ playing as S_{1-d}. During the authentication game, the oracle performs an additional step $\mathtt{ASet} \leftarrow \mathtt{ASet} \cup (i, w, \mathtt{f})$.
- $\mathcal{O}_{\mathrm{outS}}(\cdot)$ on input $(\cdot) = (i)$. If $i < j$ the oracle parses list E and obtains $(d, \mathcal{D}, \mathtt{info}_d)$; otherwise it aborts. Then, the protocol Outsource is executed with $\mathcal{A}$ playing the roles of S_{1-d} and U, and the oracle running OutsourceS$_d$. This oracle is used in the AUTH experiment for BAKS.

– $\mathcal{O}_{\mathrm{retU}}(\cdot)$ on input $(\cdot) = (i, w)$. If $i \geq j$ and $((i = i^*) \wedge (w \in \{w_0, w_1\}))$ the oracle aborts; otherwise it parses list E and obtains $(d, \mathcal{D}, \mathtt{info}_d)$. A biometric sample is taken from $\mathcal{W} \leftarrow \mathcal{O}_{\mathrm{bio}}(\mathcal{D})$. Then, the protocol $\mathtt{Retrieve}$ is then executed with the adversary $\mathcal{A}$ in role of S_{1-d}, and the oracle honestly running $\mathtt{RetrieveU}$ and $\mathtt{RetrieveS}_d$. If $(i^* = -1)$ then the oracle further computes $\mathtt{ISet} \leftarrow \mathtt{ISet} \cup (i, w)$.

– $\mathcal{O}_{\mathrm{retS}}(\cdot)$ takes as input $(\cdot) = (i)$, and aborts only if $i \geq j$. Otherwise, it obtains $(d, \mathcal{D}, \mathtt{info}_d) \leftarrow E[i]$. The retrieve protocol $\mathtt{Retrieve}$ is then executed, with the oracle running $\mathtt{RetrieveS}_d$ honestly, and the adversary $\mathcal{A}$ playing the roles of user U and server S_{1-d}. This oracle is used in the IND-CKA property of BAKS.

– $\mathcal{O}_{\mathrm{bio}}(\cdot)$ takes as input a biometric distribution $(\cdot) = (\mathcal{D})$. It samples $\mathcal{W} \leftarrow_{\$} \mathcal{D}$, possibly performs computations on $\mathcal{W}$ and outputs the result. Additionally, it updates the list of all queried biometric distributions $B \leftarrow B \cup \{\mathcal{D}\}$.

Indistinguishability Against Chosen Keyword Attacks (IND-CKA). This security property is closely related to [4] and [26], with the extension that our definition considers authentication with regard to the retrieval phase based on a user's biometric data. It is formally defined through the experiment $\mathbf{Exp}_{\mathsf{BAKS},\mathcal{A}}^{\mathrm{IND-CKA}-b}$ in Fig. 1. The experiment is initialised and the public parameters $\mathtt{pp}$ are set, the adversary is given access to the oracles $\mathcal{O}_{\mathrm{ch}}$, $\mathcal{O}_{\mathrm{reg}}$, $\mathcal{O}_{\mathrm{out}}$, $\mathcal{O}_{\mathrm{retU}}$, $\mathcal{O}_{\mathrm{retS}}$ and $\mathcal{O}_{\mathrm{bio}}$ where it makes $1, q_r, q_o, q_t, q_s$ and q_b queries respectively. The adversary wins the game if, when presented with a challenge, is unable to distinguish which keyword w_b was used in the execution of the protocol except in the case an (illegitimate) biometric sample is falsely accepted. We capture the two scenarios for $\mathcal{A}$ in the IND-CKA experiment. Firstly, an adversary who has control of a corrupt server S_{1-d} interacts with the honest user U and server S_d, or secondly, where the adversary controls an illegitimate user communicating with the honest servers S_d and S_{1-d}. We must also consider the case $\mathcal{A}$ samples a biometric sufficiently close to the registered template of a user. This is incorporated by utilising the false acceptance probability ε_{fa} defined in Sect. 2.2. We say that a BAKS scheme is IND-CKA-secure if the following advantage is bounded by $\varepsilon_{fa} + \mathtt{negl}$, where $\mathtt{negl}$ is negligible in λ:

$$\mathbf{Adv}_{\mathsf{BAKS},\mathcal{A}}^{\mathrm{IND-CKA}}(1^\lambda) := \big| \Pr[\mathbf{Exp}_{\mathsf{BAKS},\mathcal{A}}^{\mathrm{IND-CKA}-1}(1^\lambda) = 1] - \Pr[\mathbf{Exp}_{\mathsf{BAKS},\mathcal{A}}^{\mathrm{IND-CKA}-0}(1^\lambda) = 1] \big|$$

Authentication (AUTH). Motivated by a similar property in the password-based setting [26], the authentication property of BAKS captures two attack scenarios for an adversary. In the first case, $\mathcal{A}$ wins if he is able to outsource a file on behalf of some user without sampling the user's biometric. Secondly, if it is able to retrieve an honestly outsourced, file again without sampling a biometric from the user's biometric distribution. We define this property with the experiment $\mathbf{Exp}_{\mathsf{BAKS},\mathcal{A}}^{\mathrm{AUTH}}$ in Fig. 1. In the game, variables are initialised, and the adversary is given access to the oracles $\mathcal{O}_{\mathrm{reg}}$, $\mathcal{O}_{\mathrm{outU}}$, $\mathcal{O}_{\mathrm{outS}}$, $\mathcal{O}_{\mathrm{retU}}$ and $\mathcal{O}_{\mathrm{bio}}$ where each oracle is queried q_r, q_o, q_s, q_t and q_b times, respectively. The adversary is allowed to interact with the user U with biometric distribution $\mathcal{D}$, as well as an honest server S_d. We allow the adversary to control server S_{1-d} as well as interrupt and

$\mathrm{Exp}_{\mathrm{BAKS},\mathcal{A}}^{\mathrm{AUTH}}$	$\mathrm{Exp}_{\mathrm{BAKS},\mathcal{A}}^{\mathrm{IND\text{-}CKA}-b}$
$E \leftarrow \emptyset; B \leftarrow \emptyset; j \leftarrow 0;$	$E \leftarrow \emptyset; B \leftarrow \emptyset; i^* \leftarrow (-1); j \leftarrow 0;$
$\mathrm{ASet} \leftarrow \emptyset; \mathrm{pp} \leftarrow \mathrm{Setup}(1^\lambda);$	$\mathrm{ISet} \leftarrow \emptyset; \mathrm{pp} \leftarrow \mathrm{Setup}(1^\lambda);$
$(i^*, w^*, \mathtt{f}^*, \mathcal{D}^*) \leftarrow \mathcal{A}^{\mathcal{O}_{\mathrm{reg}}, \mathcal{O}_{\mathrm{outU}}, \mathcal{O}_{\mathrm{outS}}, \mathcal{O}_{\mathrm{retU}}, \mathcal{O}_{\mathrm{bio}}}(\mathrm{pp})$	$b' \leftarrow \mathcal{A}^{\mathcal{O}_{\mathrm{ch}}, \mathcal{O}_{\mathrm{reg}}, \mathcal{O}_{\mathrm{outU}}, \mathcal{O}_{\mathrm{retU}}, \mathcal{O}_{\mathrm{retS}}, \mathcal{O}_{\mathrm{bio}}}(\mathrm{pp})$
$\mathcal{W}' \leftarrow_\$ \mathcal{D}^*$	$\mathbf{return}\ b' \wedge (\mathcal{D}^* \notin B)$
$\langle \boldsymbol{F}, \mathrm{succ}, \mathrm{succ} \rangle \leftarrow \mathrm{Retrieve}(\mathrm{pp}, \mathrm{U}, \mathcal{W}', w^*, \hat{S})$	
$\mathbf{return}\ (((i^*, w^*, \mathtt{f}^*) \notin \mathrm{ASet}) \wedge$	
$\qquad (\mathtt{f}^* \in \boldsymbol{F}) \wedge (\mathcal{D}^* \notin B))$	

Fig. 1. Security Experiments for BAKS, where $\hat{S} = (S_0, \mathrm{info}_0, S_1, \mathrm{info}_1)$.

alter all communication in sessions between the honest server S_d and the user U. The probability the adversary samples a biometric (from a distinct distribution $\mathcal{D}' \neq \mathcal{D}$) sufficiently close to the registered template and thus is able to trivially break security by including the false acceptance probability ε_{fa} from Sect. 2.2. The adversary loses the game if it invokes the $\mathcal{O}_{\mathrm{bio}}$ on the user's U distribution $\mathcal{D}$.

A BAKS scheme provides *authentication* if the following advantage is bounded by $\varepsilon_{fa} + \mathtt{negl}$, where $\mathtt{negl}$ is negligible in λ:

$$\mathbf{Adv}_{\mathrm{BAKS},\mathcal{A}}^{\mathrm{AUTH}}(1^\lambda) := \big| \Pr[\mathbf{Exp}_{\mathrm{BAKS},\mathcal{A}}^{\mathrm{AUTH}}(1^\lambda) = 1] \big|$$

4 Construction

In this section we present our Biometric-Authenticated Keyword Search (BAKS) protocol. We start with a high-level description of the protocol, and emphasise the functionality for the users. Then, we detail the protocol, and provide explicit description for the setup and registration algorithm, and refer to Figs. 3 and 4 for the outsource and retrieval algorithms. To ease presentation, we illustrate in Fig. 2 the method for key reconstruction that both outsource and retrieval algorithms use. Additionally, we provide an efficiency analysis and show how our protocol can be extended to handle multiple keywords and update of user's biometric data.

High-Level Overview. Our construction is based on the password-authenticated keyword search [26], that we modify significantly to work with (noisy) biometric templates. We account for the imperfections of biometric data, where at each scan some bits may differ from the initial template, by considering a threshold secret-sharing scheme [43]. We fix as N the total number of bits that can be extracted and used by users, but trivial extension can consider an arbitrary number, dependingent the user's biometric device.

When each user U registers in our protocol, he calls **Register** and creates a high entropy key $K = g^k$, for $k \leftarrow_\$ \mathbb{Z}_q^*$. All future computations between the

---

Key reconstruction sub-routine `KRec`

User $\mathtt{U}(\mathrm{pp}, \mathcal{W})$ **Server** $\mathtt{S}_d(\mathrm{pp}, \mathtt{info}_d)$, with $\mathtt{info}_d = (x_d,$

     with $\mathcal{W} = \{W_i\}_{i=1}^N$ $g^{r_1}, g^{r_2}, \{C_W^{(i)}, K_d^{(i)}, \mathtt{mk}_d^{(i)}\}_{i=1}^N, \mathtt{mk}_d)$

$1:$ **for** $1 \le i \le N$ **do**

     $a_i \leftarrow_\$ \mathbb{Z}_q^*, \ A_i \leftarrow g^{a_i} h_i^{W_i}$

$2:$ $\xrightarrow{\{A_i\}_{i=1}^N}$ $s_d, y_d \leftarrow_\$ \mathbb{Z}_q^*, \ Y_d \leftarrow g^{y_d}$ 3

                               $R_d \leftarrow (g^{r_2})^{y_d}, \ \mathtt{c}_d \leftarrow g^{s_d} h^{H(Y_d, R_d)}$ 4

                               $(\mathtt{c}_{1-d}, s_{1-d}, Y_{1-d}, R_{1-d}) \xleftrightarrow{\ \mathtt{StS}\ }$ 5

                               if $\mathtt{c}_{1-d} \ne g^{s_{1-d}} h^{H(Y_{1-d}, R_{1-d})}$ **then abort**   6

                               $Y \leftarrow Y_0 Y_1, \ R \leftarrow R_0 R_1$ 7

                               for $1 \le i \le N$ **do**   8

                                 $Z_d^{(i)} \leftarrow K_d^{(i)} (C_W^{(i)} A_i^{-1})^{y_d} (g^{r_1} R)^{-x_d}$

                                 $\mu_d^{(i)} \leftarrow \mathtt{Tag}(\mathtt{mk}_d^{(i)}, (A_i, Y, Z_d^{(i)}))$

$9:$ $\xleftarrow{Y, \{Z_d^{(i)}, \mu_d^{(i)}\}_{i=1}^N}$ **return** $(\{A_i\}_{i=1}^N, Y)$

$10: T \leftarrow \emptyset$ $\xleftarrow{Y, \{Z_{1-d}^{(i)}, \mu_{1-d}^{(i)}\}_{i=1}^N}$

$11:$ **for** $1 \le i \le N$ **do**

     $T_i \leftarrow Z_0^{(i)} Z_1^{(i)} Y^{a_i}$

     $\mathtt{mk}_0^{(i)} \leftarrow \mathtt{KDF}_1(T_i, \mathtt{S}_0, \text{`1'}), \ \mathtt{mk}_1^{(i)} \leftarrow \mathtt{KDF}_1(T_i, \mathtt{S}_1, \text{`1'})$

     if $\mathtt{Ver}(\mathtt{mk}_0^{(i)}, (A_i, Y, Z_0^{(i)}), \mu_0^{(i)}) \wedge \mathtt{Ver}(\mathtt{mk}_1^{(i)}, (A_i, Y, Z_1^{(i)}), \mu_1^{(i)})$ **then**

         $T \leftarrow T \cup \{T_i\}$

$12: K \leftarrow \mathtt{SS.Rec}(T)$, **return** $(K, \{A_i\}_{i=1}^N, Y)$

Fig. 2. This is a partial view of subroutine `KRec` that construct the key K from the biometric input W. The complete routine `KRec` involves the user $\mathtt{U}$ sending the message in Step 2 to both servers $\mathtt{S}_0$ and $\mathtt{S}_1$, then at Steps 9 and 10 receiving messages from both servers. We illustrate only the computation done by $\mathtt{S}_d$, as $\mathtt{S}_{1-d}$ performs the exact same steps. Moreover, we use $\xleftrightarrow{\mathtt{StS}}$ to model the communication between $\mathtt{S}_d$ and $\mathtt{S}_{1-d}$; at a high level $\mathtt{S}_d$ sends the commitment $\mathtt{c}_d$, waits for $\mathtt{c}_{1-d}$, then sends the opening s_d, Y_d, R_d and receives $s_{1-d}, Y_{1-d}, R_{1-d}$. $\mathtt{SS.Rec}$ returns either a valid key or an error symbol $\perp$.

user $\mathtt{U}$ and the servers $\mathtt{S}_0$ and $\mathtt{S}_1$ are done with respect to this key K. One core property of our protocol is that we do not require the user to store this key, and devise a method where the user's biometric data $\mathcal{W} = \{W_i\}_{i=1}^N$ is used to reconstruct this key. More precisely, the user applies $\mathtt{SS.Shr}(t, N, g, \mathbb{G}, q, K)$ to create the shares $\{K^{(i)}\}_{i=1}^N$ that can later be used to directly recover K (See Remark 1). Further, each share $K^{(i)}$ is split into $K_0^{(i)}$ and $K_1^{(i)}$, such that the reconstruction of $K^{(i)}$ can done only when the shares $K_0^{(i)}, K_1^{(i)}$ are processed

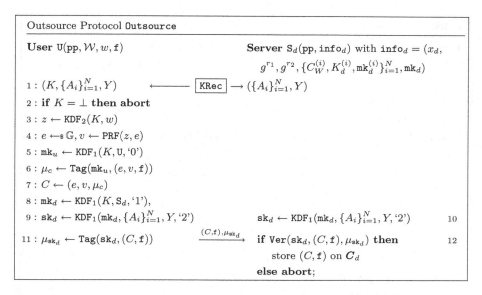

Fig. 3. This is a partial view of the interactive protocol Outsource, and captures only the interactions between user U that outsources file f with keyword w and biometric data W to server S_d. The complete algorithm requires U to replicate Steps 9 and 11 for S_{1-d}, and send $((C, f), \mu_{sk_{1-d}})$ to S_{1-d}. Step 1 executes the routine KRec from Fig. 2.

together with an encryption $C_W^{(i)}$ of the bit W_i. The value $K_d^{(i)}$ is sent to S_d, for $d \in \{0, 1\}$ and all $1 \leq i \leq N$. We also account for the fact that some of the inputs W_i the user is submitting at later stage may differ from the ones in the initial template W that has used when sharing K. As pointed by the steps in the subroutine KRec in Fig. 2 we use MAC tags $\mu_d^{(i)}$ to identify the shares $T_i = K^{(i)}$ that have been correctly recovered before applying SS.Rec to reconstruct K.

Whenever the user U wants to outsource a file f characterized by the keyword w, he does so by calling Outsource. The first step is for the user to recover the key K using his current scanned biometric data W, and establish some session identifiers $(\{A_i\}_{i=1}^N, Y)$ with the two servers S_0, S_1. Then, the user constructs a ciphertext C that should be stored together with the file f by both servers. The ciphertext C plays a fundamental role during retrieval, as it contains a MAC tag μ_c that can be used to authenticate the file provenance, as could have been produced only by the user with the knowledge of K and w. We assume the communication between U and server S_d during outsourcing and retrieval is performed over insecure channels, and in addition to (C, f) it contains a MAC that uses a fresh KDF key composed of the long term key mk_d and the current session identifiers. If the MAC tag verifies, server S_d stores (C, f) in an internal database C_d. Notice, that each S_d stores a copy of the file f to achieve better availability.

At any point of time, the user U can retrieve all outsourced files that match the keyword w, by running Retrieve with servers S_0, S_1. Similar to the outsource

---

Retrieve Protocol Retrieve

User $U(\mathrm{pp}, \mathcal{W}, w)$ **Server** $S_d(\mathrm{pp}, \mathrm{info}_d)$ with $\mathrm{info}_d = (x_d,$

$$g^{r_1}, g^{r_2}, \{C_W^{(i)}, K_d^{(i)}, \mathrm{mk}_d^{(i)}\}_{i=1}^N, \mathrm{mk}_d)$$

$1 : (K, \{A_i\}_{i=1}^N, Y) \quad\longleftarrow\quad \boxed{\text{KRec}} \longrightarrow (\{A_i\}_{i=1}^N, Y)$

$2 :$ **if** $K = \bot$ **then abort** $L_d \leftarrow \emptyset$ 3

$4 : \mathrm{mk}_d \leftarrow \mathrm{KDF}_1(K, S_d, \text{'1'})$

$5 : \mathrm{sk}_d \leftarrow \mathrm{KDF}_1(\mathrm{mk}_d, \{A_i\}_{i=1}^N, Y, \text{'2'})$ $\mathrm{sk}_d \leftarrow \mathrm{KDF}_1(\mathrm{mk}_d, \{A_i\}_{i=1}^N, Y, \text{'2'})$ 6

$7 : z \leftarrow \mathrm{KDF}_2(K, w), \mu_{\mathrm{sk}_d} \leftarrow \mathrm{Tag}(\mathrm{sk}_d, z) \xrightarrow{z, \mu_{\mathrm{sk}_d}}$ **if** $\mathrm{Ver}(\mathrm{sk}_d, z, \mu_{\mathrm{sk}_d})$ **then**   8

                                                  for $(C, \mathtt{f}) \in C_d$ **do**

                                                    $(e, v, \mu_c) \leftarrow C$

                                                    if $v = \mathrm{PRF}(z, e)$ **then**

$9 : \mathrm{mk}_u \leftarrow \mathrm{KDF}_1(K, U, \text{'0'})$ $L_d \leftarrow L_d \cup (C, \mathtt{f})$

                                                 else abort;

$10 : \quad\xleftarrow{\quad L_d \quad}$

$11 : L \leftarrow L_0 \cup L_1, \mathbf{F} \leftarrow \emptyset \quad\xleftarrow{\quad L_{1-d} \quad}$

$12 :$ **for** $(C, \mathtt{f}) \in L$ with $C = (e, v, \mu_c)$ **do**

     if $(v = \mathrm{PRF}(z, e) \wedge \mathrm{Ver}(\mathrm{mk}_u, (e, v, \mathtt{f}), \mu_c))$ **then**

         $\mathbf{F} \leftarrow \mathbf{F} \cup \mathtt{f}$

$13 :$ **return** F

Fig. 4. This is a partial view of the interactive protocol Retrieve, and captures the interaction between user U, authenticated by the biometric data W, and server S_d, such that the user retrieves all files $\mathtt{f}$ that have keyword w. The complete algorithm requires U to replicate Steps 5 and 7 for S_{1-d}, then send $(t, \mu_{\mathrm{sk}_{1-d}})$ to S_{1-d}. The set $\mathbf{L}$ does not contain duplicate elements.

algorithm, the user inputs his biometric data $\mathcal{W}$, recovers the key K, and creates the session identifiers $(\{A_i\}_{i=1}^N, Y)$. Then, the user defines a search query $z \leftarrow \mathrm{KDF}(K, w)$ that depends on the key K and keyword w. As the communication between U and S_d is over an insecure channel, z is sent together with a MAC that is built and verified using the knowledge of mk_d and the session identifiers $(\{A_i\}_{i=1}^N, Y)$. Finally, the user collects the responses from the two servers in the list $\mathbf{L}$, and discards the responses that do not match his query or have an invalid MAC tag μ_c to produce the final output list $\mathbf{F}$.

Detailed Description. We provide the complete specification of our protocol only for the setup and registration algorithms, and illustrate the outsource and retrieval steps in Figs. 3 and 4. Both algorithms contain a key reconstruction phase, that for simplicity is presented separately in Fig. 2.

- Setup(1^λ). Based on the type of biometric data considered, we define the number of bits N that can be extracted. For simplicity, we provide a uniform value for all users, but trivial extensions of our protocol can allow users to define their own number of bits during registration. Moreover, we generate a cyclic group $\mathbb{G}$ of order q with the following $(N+2)$ random generators: $g, h, \{h_i\}_{i=1}^N \leftarrow_\$ \mathbb{G}$. Additionally, we introduce the building blocks $\mathsf{SS}, \mathsf{MAC}, \mathsf{KDF}_1, \mathsf{KDF}_2$, and PRF using the notations from Sect. 2. The algorithm outputs $\mathsf{pp} = (N, \mathbb{G}, q, g, h, \{h_i\}_{i=1}^N, \mathsf{SS}, \mathsf{MAC}, \mathsf{KDF}_1, \mathsf{KDF}_2, \mathsf{PRF})$.

- $\mathsf{Register}(\mathsf{pp}, \mathsf{U}, t, \mathcal{W}, \mathsf{S}_0, \mathsf{S}_1)$. Let $\mathcal{W} = \{W_i\}_{i=1}^N$. User U randomly selects a secret key $k \leftarrow_\$ \mathbb{Z}_q^*$, sets $K = g^k$, and builds the shares $\{K^{(i)}\}_{i=1}^N \leftarrow \mathsf{SS.Shr}(t, N, g, \mathbb{G}, q, k)$. Additionally, the user generates $r_1, r_2, x_0, x_1 \leftarrow_\$ \mathbb{Z}_q^*$ and $\{K_0^{(i)}\}_{i=1}^N \leftarrow_\$ \mathbb{G}$, then sets $X = g^{x_0+x_1}$, $K_1^{(i)} = X^{r_1} K^{(i)} (K_0^{(i)})^{-1}$ and $C_W^{(i)} = X^{r_2} h_i^{W_i}$ for all $1 \leq i \leq N$. For each server $\mathsf{S}_d \in \{\mathsf{S}_0, \mathsf{S}_1\}$, the values $\mathsf{mk}_d \leftarrow \mathsf{KDF}_1(K, \mathsf{S}_d, \text{'1'})$ and $\mathsf{mk}_d^{(i)} \leftarrow \mathsf{KDF}_1(K^{(i)}, \mathsf{S}_d, \text{'1'})$ for all $1 \leq i \leq N$, are derived and used to define $\mathsf{info}_d = (x_d, g^{r_1}, g^{r_2}, \{C_W^{(i)}, K_d^{(i)}, \mathsf{mk}_d^{(i)}\}_{i=1}^N, \mathsf{mk}_d)$ before info_d is sent over an authenticated and secure channel to S_d.

Correctness. Correctness of each key share $K^{(i)}$ can be observed by computing the following:

$$
\begin{aligned}
Z_0^{(i)} Z_1^{(i)} Y^{a_i} &= K_0^{(i)} (C_W^{(i)} A_i^{-1})^{y_0} (g^{r_1} R)^{-x_0} \cdot K_1^{(i)} (C_W^{(i)} A_i^{-1})^{y_1} (g^{r_1} R)^{-x_1} \cdot g^{a_i(y_0+y_1)} \\
&= K_0^{(i)} K_1^{(i)} (C_W^{(i)} A_i^{-1} g^{a_i})^{(y_0+y_1)} (g^{r_1} R)^{-(x_0+x_1)} \\
&= X^{r_1} K^{(i)} (X^{r_2} h_i^{W_i} (g^{a_i} h_i^{W_i})^{-1} g^{a_i})^{(y_0+y_1)} (g^{r_1} g^{r_2(y_0+y_1)})^{-(x_0+x_1)} \\
&= g^{(x_0+x_1)r_1} K^{(i)} g^{(x_0+x_1)r_2(y_0+y_1)} (g^{r_1} g^{r_2(y_0+y_1)})^{-(x_0+x_1)} = K^{(i)}
\end{aligned}
$$

The correctness of SS ensures that they key K can be recovered from t or more correct shares.

Remark 1. The desired level of accuracy for the biometric measurement is defined by the SS threshold $t \leq N$, such that any t bits W_i that are correct would lead to the recovery of the key K. In particular, the false rejection parameter τ_1 is proportional to the value of t and similarly τ_2, the false accept parameter is inversely proportional to t. However, the true values for τ_1 and τ_2 cannot be derived from the threshold parameter alone, as they also depend on the accuracy of the biometric sensor. We assume that selection of t can be made based on the sensors used such that the scheme adheres to appropriate security guarantees.

4.1 Efficiency Analysis and Improvements

We compare the efficiency of our BAKS scheme with the PAKS construction from [26], which relies on a password and by this also supports searchable encryption without requiring users to store and manage private keys. We immediately note that BAKS has the same number of rounds for the outsourcing and retrieval as PAKS. This leads to BAKS having the same server-side storage $\mathcal{O}(D)$ as PAKS, for a database of size D, but without any user-side storage. The computational cost of PAKS for the user and each server is 3, resp. 8, exponentiations, while in our BAKS scheme it amounts to $3N$, resp. $6 + 2N$, exponentiations, for the noisy biometric sample of N bits. During the key reconstruction phase, the communication overheads are 8 group elements, and 2 MACs for PAKS, and $2 + 6N$ group elements along with 2 MAC tags for BAKS. The linear growth in BAKS complexity is unavoidable due to existence of noise and hence bitwise processing of the biometric template.

We remark that it is possible to reduce the value of N by splitting the biometric sample W into k blocks of N/k bits, which would reduce the computational and communication costs to $O(N/k)$. This could be used, for example, where the biometric is a fingerprint, the data stored represents k features (or *minutiae* [28]) and the data stored in each block is the feature-type and location. While we would not loose security by supporting this mechanism, the corresponding false-rejection rate would be significantly affected by the accuracy of the biometric scanner. In particular, even one bit difference in the feature description would render the share invalid, whereas the presented BAKS scheme offers more flexible tolerance to errors.

BAKS with Sublinear Search Complexities. BAKS achieves $\mathcal{O}(D)$ search complexity (as highlighted in Step. 7 of Fig. 4), for a database DB of size D, whilst state-of-the-art schemes achieve a bound of $\mathcal{O}(\log D)$. We can improve BAKS search complexity by employing some of the general ideas from [15, 17, 44]. However, this would introduce security and/or functionality limitations. One first approach would be to restrict only to static databases [15, 17], and loose the dynamic aspect of our solution. Another approach would be to use ORAM and maintain the dynamic aspects of our database, but at the cost of requiring periodic (costly, i.e., $\mathcal{O}(D \log D)$ comparisons) oblivious sorting [44]. The final method, and the one we highlight in the rest of this section, is to consider dynamic databases with limited update (i.e., handles only adding entries) [17].

At a high level, [17] does each outsourcing over batches of documents, and treats each update as an outsource of a static database DB. Their optimisation relies on a look-up table T that stores pointers to location of documents in DB, such that the table inputs depend on the document keyword. In the setup phase, the look-up table T is initialized to empty. We extend the outsource protocol from Fig. 3 to upload the database $DB = \{(w_i, f_i)|1 \leq i \leq N\}$ instead of a single file f and keyword w. First, for all unique keywords w_i, we create the list $L_i = \{(w_i, \mathsf{ind}(f_{i_j}), f_{i_j})|(w_i, f_{i_j}) \in DB\}$ with $\mathsf{ind}(f_{i_j})$ the index in DB where file f_{i_j} can be found. Then, for each entry $(w_i, \mathsf{ind}(f_{i_j}), f_{i_j})$ steps 1–9 are performed, followed by the generation of the key $o_{i_j} \leftarrow \mathsf{KDF}_2(z_i, j)$ and setting the look-up table $T[o_{i_j}] = \mathsf{ind}(f_{i_j})$. Finally, Step 11 is executed for all entries and the entire encrypted database C_d is sent with the look-up table. Notice that C_d preserves the same order of elements from DB, and $\mathsf{ind}(\cdot)$ should give the same location for both C_d and DB. The retrieval protocol is performed in the same way as in Fig. 4, except the server receives $(z, \mu_{\mathsf{sk}_d}, \{o_{i_j}\}_{j=1}^{n_i})$ in step 7, for $|L_i| = n_i$. Then, the values $\{o_{i_j}\}_{j=1}^{n_i}$ are used to identify the entries $\{(C_{i_j}, f_{i_j})\}_{j=1}^{n_i}$ from C_d, based on $\mathsf{ind}(f_{i_j})$ from the look-up table T. To stop adversaries from trivially differentiating based on the list size, we can use the techniques in [17] to extend DB to DB^* with dummy files, such that all lists have the same size $|L_i| = n$, for $n = \max_i\{n_i\}$. This version of BAKS with sublinear search complexity would satisfy the same security guarantees as the initial version. The main limitation is that now we are restricted to dynamic databases that only allow addition of entries, and not removal. The security intuition is based on the fact that each outsource operation is treated as an outsource of a new independent static database.

4.2 Extensions with Multiple Keywords

The construction we have presented in this paper is limited to only allowing a user to search for a single keyword. In practise, it is likely that a user would want to outsource a file with multiple keywords in a single execution, or search for multiple keywords in one running of the retrieve protocol. We briefly show that our BAKS construction allows for a natural extension to support this functionality.

Outsourcing with Multiple Keywords. Here, we allow a user to outsource a file f with keywords $\overline{w} := (w_1, ..., w_k)$. This can be achieved by computing $t_j \leftarrow \text{KDF}_2(K, w_j), v_j \leftarrow \text{PRF}(t_j, e)$ and finally $\mu_c \leftarrow \text{tag}(\text{mk}_u(e, \overline{v}))$ as part of out. Each server receives the ciphertext $C = (e, \overline{v}, \mu_c)$ where $\overline{v} = (v_1, ..., v_k)$.

Retrieval Based on Complex Queries. A user submits the keywords $\overline{w} = (w_1, ..., w_k)$ to a single execution of the retrieve protocol. It computes search queries $t_j \leftarrow \text{KDF}_2(K, w_j)$ for each keyword. Then for every entry $(e, \overline{v}, \mu_c, f)$ in the database $\boldsymbol{C}_d$, the server computes $v'_j = \text{PRF}(t_j, e)$ $(j = 1, ..., k)$ and updates the output list $\mathcal{A}_d$ according to the search query. We note this approach supports conjunctive, disjunctive and subset type queries which can be enforced by line 7 in the retrieve protocol.

4.3 Biometric Update

Our BAKS construction supports a user who may wish to update their registered biometric template $\mathcal{W}$ to a new biometric template $\mathcal{W}^*$. This could be the case when a user changes their biometric device (e.g., from fingerprint to iris recognition), or does not have access to the initial biometric feature they registered (e.g., vision loss). To prevent the need for re-encryption of all keywords for all outsourced files, we do not change the key K and simply update only the commitments to the biometric template. If the user cannot use their already registered biometric template for authentication, we can use an alternative authenticated channel to each of the servers S_0 and S_1 to update the biometric sample. This process is executed independent of the previous biometric sample, and has the following steps:

- Servers S_d, for $d \in \{0, 1\}$, compute $X_d \leftarrow g^{x_d}$ and send this to the user U over a secure and authenticated channel.
- User U then samples $r_2^* \leftarrow_\$ \mathbb{Z}_q^*$, computes $C_{W^*}^{(i)} \leftarrow (X_0 X_1)^{r_2^*} h_i^{W_i^*}$ for each bit W_i^* in the new biometric, and forwards $(g^{r_2^*}, \{C_{W^*}^{(i)}\}_{i=1}^N)$ to both servers, on the same authenticated channel.

– Each server S_d updates their information $\mathtt{info}_d$ to reflect the new biometric sample, from $(g^{r_2}, \{C_W^{(i)}\}_{i=1}^N)$ to $(g^{r_2^*}, \{C_{W^*}^{(i)}\}_{i=1}^N)$, for $d \in \{0,1\}$.

5   Security Analysis

In this section, we give proof that our construction for BAKS in Figs. 2, 3 and 4 meets the security definitions from Sect. 3.2. We extend the table E to also include some secret values, s.t. $E[j] \leftarrow (d, \mathcal{D}, \mathtt{info}_d, r_2, r_1, x_{1-d})$ for some session identifier j. This is possible due to the oracle playing the role of the user and generating the values r_2, r_1, x_{1-d}.

Theorem 1. *Our BAKS construction is IND-CKA secure given KDF$_1$ and KDF$_2$ are secure, PRF is pseudorandom, MAC is unforgeable, SS offers privacy, the discrete logarithm (DL) assumption is hard in $\mathbb{G}$ and the liveness assumption holds.*

Proof. $\mathcal{G}_0$: Game $\mathcal{G}_0$ is defined exactly by the experiment $\mathbf{Exp}_{\mathsf{BAKS},\mathcal{A}}^{\mathtt{IND-CKA}-b}$. Thus:

$$\Pr[\mathcal{G}_0 = 1] = \Pr[\mathbf{Exp}_{\mathsf{BAKS},\mathcal{A}}^{\mathtt{IND-CKA}-b} = 1].$$

$\mathcal{G}_1$: This game is obtained from $\mathcal{G}_0$ by aborting if y_d is used in more than one protocol session in oracles $\mathcal{O}_{\mathrm{out}}$, $\mathcal{O}_{\mathrm{retU}}$ or $\mathcal{O}_{\mathrm{retS}}$, the rest remains the same. The probability of winning $\mathcal{G}_1$ over $\mathcal{G}_0$ is bounded by the probability of sampling y_d twice or more from j samples of a uniform distribution over $\mathbb{Z}_q^*$. Thus we have:

$$\left| \Pr[\mathcal{G}_1 = 1] - \Pr[\mathcal{G}_0 = 1] \right| \leq \frac{j^2}{q}$$

$\mathcal{G}_2$: This game is identical to $\mathcal{G}_1$ except that the game aborts if Y appears in two different protocol sessions through oracles $\mathcal{O}_{\mathrm{out}}$, $\mathcal{O}_{\mathrm{retU}}$ or $\mathcal{O}_{\mathrm{retS}}$. We note because the Pedersen commitment c_d is perfectly hiding, Y_{1-d} must be independent of Y_d. Additionally, the binding property (based on the DL assumption) ensures that it is computationally hard to open c_{1-d} to a $Y'_d \neq Y_d$. Hence, since Y_d and Y_{1-d} are fresh and independent, Y is also fresh based on the hardness of DL assumption. Thus we have:

$$\left| \Pr[\mathcal{G}_2 = 1] - \Pr[\mathcal{G}_1 = 1] \right| \leq \mathbf{Adv}_{\mathcal{B}}^{DL}$$

$\mathcal{G}_3$: This game is defined by $\mathcal{G}_2$ where PRF is replaced with a function. In the outsourcing protocol, when the adversary has control of U, it is able to provide a μ'_c such that $\mathsf{Ver}(\mathtt{mk}_d, (e, v, \mathtt{f}), \mu'_c) = 1$. If $\mathcal{A}$ is able to do so without knowledge of $\mathtt{mk}_d$, he breaks the unforgeability of MAC.

Hence, the games are bounded by:

$$\left| \Pr[\mathcal{G}_3 = 1] - \Pr[\mathcal{G}_2 = 1] \right| \leq \mathbf{Adv}_{\mathcal{B}}^{unforge}$$

We now split the games conditioned on the value of some components. In $\mathcal{G}_4$, the adversary does not have knowledge of $\mathtt{mk}_d$ and is therefore forced to try to break unforgeability of the message authentication code. We let prime-counterpart mk'_d denote the adversary's guess at mk_d and capture the case the adversary *does* know mk_d in game $\mathcal{G}_5$ by letting $\text{mk}'_d = \text{mk}_d$. The law of total probability gives us:

$$\Pr[\mathcal{G}_3 = 1] = \underbrace{(\Pr[\mathcal{G}_3 = 1] \wedge \text{mk}'_u \neq \text{mk}_u)}_{\mathcal{G}_4} + \underbrace{(\Pr[\mathcal{G}_3 = 1] \wedge \text{mk}'_u = \text{mk}_u)}_{\mathcal{G}_5}$$

$\mathcal{G}_4$: This game is defined by $\mathcal{G}_3$ where PRF is replaced with a function. In the outsourcing protocol, when the adversary has control of U, it is able to provide a μ'_c such that $\text{Ver}(\text{mk}_d, (e, v, \mathbf{f}), \mu'_c) = 1$. If $\mathcal{A}$ is able to do so without knowledge of mk_d, he breaks the unforgeability of MAC. Hence, the game is bounded by:

$$\Pr[\mathcal{G}_4 = 1] \leq (q_o + q_t)\mathbf{Adv}_{\mathcal{B}}^{PRF}$$

$\mathcal{G}_5$: We now split the games conditioned on the value of some components. In $\mathcal{G}_6$, the adversary does not have knowledge of K and is therefore forced to try to break the security of KDF, we capture the case the adversary *does* know K in game $\mathcal{G}_7$. The law of total probability gives:

$$\Pr[\mathcal{G}_5 = 1] = \underbrace{(\Pr[\mathcal{G}_5 = 1] \wedge K' \neq K)}_{\mathcal{G}_6} + \underbrace{(\Pr[\mathcal{G}_5 = 1] \wedge K' = K)}_{\mathcal{G}_7}$$

$\mathcal{G}_6$: In this game, the adversary does not know the key which we denote $K' \neq K$, where K' is his guess at the key. Thus, the adversary is only able to win this game if he can break the security of the key derivation function. Hence we have the following bound its success probability:

$$\Pr[\mathcal{G}_6 = 1] \leq \mathbf{Adv}_{\mathcal{B}}^{KDF}$$

$\mathcal{G}_7$: In this game, we necessarily have $K' = K$ and we analyse the adversary's probability of being able to compute K. We define game $\mathcal{G}_7$ to be $\mathcal{G}_5$ except that SS.share and SS.rec are replaced with functions F_s and F_r. T_s is initialised as an empty table at the beginning of the experiment, on input K, and returns $\{K_i\}_{i=1}^{N}$ if $\exists (K, \{K_i\}_{i=1}^{N}) \in T_s$.

We aim to show that the success probability of this game is bounded by an adversary against the secret sharing scheme. To start, the adversary to SS, $\mathcal{B}$, guesses a user i for which $\mathcal{A}$ is going to break the authentication property, he does with probability $1/U$ for U total users. For U_j where $j \neq i$, he runs the protocol honestly. Upon registration and when $j = 1$, he invokes his challenge oracle from the privacy game against SS by inputting two challenge secrets S_0 and S_1, the game returns the shares $\{S_b^{(i)}\}_{i=1}^{N}$ for some $b \in \{0, 1\}$. The adversary $\mathcal{B}$ wins the game if he can correctly guess the challenge bit b. It invokes $\mathcal{G}_5$ with $\mathcal{A}$ in the role of U and S_{1-d}.

If $\mathcal{A}$ submits his biometric reading via the $\mathcal{O}_{\text{bio}}$ oracle, with probability ε_{fa}, for a sampled biometric $\mathcal{W}'$ (sampled from a distribution $\mathcal{D}'$) we have $d(\mathcal{W}', \mathcal{W}) \leq \tau_2$ (equivalent to more than $t - 1$ bits matching). Thus, with probability $1 - \varepsilon_{fa}$, $\mathcal{A}$ is only able to compute at most $t - 1$ correct shares of K (for biometric $\mathcal{W}$) given $\{Z_0^{(i)'}, Z_1^{(i)'}, Y^{a_i'}\}_{i=1}^N$ from $\mathcal{W}'$. The adversary has a negligible probability of reconstructing the tth share by either guessing $Z_d^{(t)}$ such that $T_t = Z_0^{(t)} Z_1^{(t)} Y^{a_t}$, or finding another user (in a different session) with common features to the challenge user, breaking liveness assumption. In particular, the liveness assumption prevents an adversary from submitting $\mathcal{W}'$ sampled from the user's distribution $\mathcal{D}$. The SS adversary $\mathcal{B}$ waits for $\mathcal{A}$ to finish the run of the user. If it outputs a response (t, μ_{sk_d}) then adversary $\mathcal{B}$ answers its SS challenge with $b = 0$. We note that if $b = 1$, then $\mathcal{A}$ would not have been able to complete the protocol due to the security properties of KDF and MAC that we have ruled out in games $\mathcal{G}_3$ and $\mathcal{G}_4$, respectively. Thus, any correct response from $\mathcal{A}$ implies the challenge bit $b = 0$. Hence, the probability of winning game $\mathcal{G}_5$ is bound by the probability that $\mathcal{B}$ can break the privacy property of the secret sharing scheme.

$$\Pr[\mathcal{G}_7 = 1] \leq \frac{1}{|U|} \mathbf{Adv}_{\mathcal{B}}^{priv} + \varepsilon_{fa}$$

By the sequence of games $\mathcal{G}_0$ to $\mathcal{G}_7$, we have shown that the probability of a BAKS adversary against the IND-CKA property is bounded by $\varepsilon_{fa} + \mathtt{negl}$ where $\mathtt{negl}$ is negligible in the security parameter λ. $\qquad\square$

Theorem 2. *Our* BAKS *construction provides authentication given* KDF$_1$ *and* KDF$_2$ *are secure,* MAC *is unforgeable,* SS *offers privacy, the discrete logarithm (DL) assumption is hard in* $\mathbb{G}$ *and the liveness assumption holds.*

Proof. See Full Version.

6 Conclusion

We introduced Biometric-Authenticated Keyword Search (BAKS), a novel searchable encryption scheme that uses biometric data as authentication mechanism for outsourcing and retrieval of files indexed by encrypted keywords. We accounted for the imperfections in the biometric measurements, and designed BAKS such that users can authenticate via biometric data that is "similar" to their template. This degree of similarity is modeled using threshold secret sharing techniques, and selecting the threshold involves at least considering the accuracy of the measuring device and the nature of used biometric factors, e.g. fingerprint, iris, face, voice.

BAKS employs a two-server architecture together with the liveness assumption to provide security guarantees and doesn't assume that biometric data remains private. Moreover, BAKS allows users to update their biometric template without the need to re-encrypt the outsourced keywords and provides support for multi-keyword outsourcing and search. BAKS ensures that only legitimate users can outsource and retrieve files (via authentication property) and confidentiality of the outsourced keywords (via indistinguishability against chosen keyword attacks) in presence of at most one compromised server.

References

1. Biometric presentation attack detection: Standard ISO/IEC WD 30107–3:2017. International Organization for Standardization, Geneva, CH (2017)
2. Abdalla, M., et al.: Searchable encryption revisited: consistency properties, relation to anonymous IBE, and extensions. J. Cryptol. **21**(3), 350–391 (2007). https://doi.org/10.1007/s00145-007-9006-6
3. Akhtar, Z., Micheloni, C., Foresti, G.L.: Biometric liveness detection: challenges and research opportunities. IEEE Secur. Priv. **13**(5), 63–72 (2015)
4. Ballard, L., Kamara, S., Monrose, F.: Achieving efficient conjunctive keyword searches over encrypted data. In: Qing, S., Mao, W., López, J., Wang, G. (eds.) ICICS 2005. LNCS, vol. 3783, pp. 414–426. Springer, Heidelberg (2005). https://doi.org/10.1007/11602897_35
5. Bellare, M., Canetti, R., Krawczyk, H.: Keying hash functions for message authentication. In: Koblitz, N. (ed.) CRYPTO 1996. LNCS, vol. 1109, pp. 1–15. Springer, Heidelberg (1996). https://doi.org/10.1007/3-540-68697-5_1
6. Blanton, M., Hudelson, W.M.P.: Biometric-based non-transferable anonymous credentials. In: Qing, S., Mitchell, C.J., Wang, G. (eds.) ICICS 2009. LNCS, vol. 5927, pp. 165–180. Springer, Heidelberg (2009). https://doi.org/10.1007/978-3-642-11145-7_14
7. Boneh, D., Di Crescenzo, G., Ostrovsky, R., Persiano, G.: Public key encryption with keyword search. In: Cachin, C., Camenisch, J.L. (eds.) EUROCRYPT 2004. LNCS, vol. 3027, pp. 506–522. Springer, Heidelberg (2004). https://doi.org/10.1007/978-3-540-24676-3_30
8. Boneh, D., Waters, B.: Conjunctive, subset, and range queries on encrypted data. In: Vadhan, S.P. (ed.) TCC 2007. LNCS, vol. 4392, pp. 535–554. Springer, Heidelberg (2007). https://doi.org/10.1007/978-3-540-70936-7_29
9. Boyen, X.: Reusable cryptographic fuzzy extractors. In: ACM CCS 2004, pp. 82–91. ACM (2004)
10. Boyen, X., Dodis, Y., Katz, J., Ostrovsky, R., Smith, A.: Secure remote authentication using biometric data. In: Cramer, R. (ed.) EUROCRYPT 2005. LNCS, vol. 3494, pp. 147–163. Springer, Heidelberg (2005). https://doi.org/10.1007/11426639_9
11. Bringer, J., Chabanne, H., Kindarji, B.: Error-tolerant searchable encryption. In: IEEE ICC 2009, pp. 1–6 (2009)
12. Camenisch, J., Lehmann, A., Lysyanskaya, A., Neven, G.: Memento: how to reconstruct your secrets from a single password in a hostile environment. In: Garay, J.A., Gennaro, R. (eds.) CRYPTO 2014. LNCS, vol. 8617, pp. 256–275. Springer, Heidelberg (2014). https://doi.org/10.1007/978-3-662-44381-1_15
13. Canetti, R., Fuller, B., Paneth, O., Reyzin, L., Smith, A.: Reusable fuzzy extractors for low-entropy distributions. In: Fischlin, M., Coron, J.-S. (eds.) EUROCRYPT 2016. LNCS, vol. 9665, pp. 117–146. Springer, Heidelberg (2016). https://doi.org/10.1007/978-3-662-49890-3_5
14. Cash, D., Grubbs, P., Perry, J., Ristenpart, T.: Leakage-abuse attacks against searchable encryption. In: Proceedings of the 22Nd ACM SIGSAC Conference on Computer and Communications Security, CCS 2015, pp. 668–679. ACM (2015)
15. Cash, D., Jarecki, S., Jutla, C., Krawczyk, H., Roşu, M.-C., Steiner, M.: Highly-scalable searchable symmetric encryption with support for boolean queries. In: Canetti, R., Garay, J.A. (eds.) CRYPTO 2013. LNCS, vol. 8042, pp. 353–373. Springer, Heidelberg (2013). https://doi.org/10.1007/978-3-642-40041-4_20

16. Chen, R., Mu, Y., Yang, G., Guo, F., Wang, X.: Dual-server public-key encryption with keyword search for secure cloud storage. Trans. Inf. Forensics Secur. **11**(4), 789–798 (2016)
17. Curtmola, R., Garay, J.A., Kamara, S., Ostrovsky, R.: Searchable symmetric encryption: improved definitions and efficient constructions. J. Comput. Secur. **19**(5), 895–934 (2011). A preliminary version appeared in ACM CCS 2006
18. Daugman, J.: How iris recognition works. IEEE Trans. Circ. Syst. Video Technol. **14**(1), 21–30 (2004)
19. Dodis, Y., Katz, J., Reyzin, L., Smith, A.: Robust fuzzy extractors and authenticated key agreement from close secrets. In: Dwork, C. (ed.) CRYPTO 2006. LNCS, vol. 4117, pp. 232–250. Springer, Heidelberg (2006). https://doi.org/10.1007/11818175_14
20. Dodis, Y., Reyzin, L., Smith, A.: Fuzzy extractors: how to generate strong keys from biometrics and other noisy data. In: Cachin, C., Camenisch, J.L. (eds.) EUROCRYPT 2004. LNCS, vol. 3027, pp. 523–540. Springer, Heidelberg (2004). https://doi.org/10.1007/978-3-540-24676-3_31
21. FIDO Alliance: FIDO 2.0. Technical report (2015). https://fidoalliance.org/specifications. Accessed 03 Mar 2019
22. Fleischhacker, N., Manulis, M., Azodi, A.: A modular framework for multi-factor authentication and key exchange. In: Chen, L., Mitchell, C. (eds.) SSR 2014. LNCS, vol. 8893, pp. 190–214. Springer, Cham (2014). https://doi.org/10.1007/978-3-319-14054-4_12
23. Fuller, B., Simhadri, S., Steel, J.: Reusable authentication from the iris. Cryptology ePrint Archive, Report 2017/1177 (2017). https://eprint.iacr.org/2017/1177
24. Gardham, D., Drăgan, C-C., Manulis, M.: Biometric Authenticated Searchable Encryption. Cryptology ePrint Archive, Report 2020/017 (2020). https://eprint.iacr.org/2020/017
25. Håstad, J., Impagliazzo, R., Levin, L.A., Luby, M.: A pseudorandom generator from any one-way function. SIAM J. Comput. **28**(4), 1364–1396 (1999)
26. Huang, K., Manulis, M., Chen, L.: Password authenticated keyword search. In: PAC 2017, pp. 129–140 (2017)
27. Islam, M.S., Kuzu, M., Kantarcioglu, M.: Access pattern disclosure on searchable encryption: Ramification, attack and mitigation. In: NDSS 2012 (2012)
28. Jain, A.K., Ross, A., Prabhakar, S.: Fingerprint matching using minutiae and texture features. In: ICIP 2001, pp. 282–285 (2001)
29. Juels, A., Wattenberg, M.: A fuzzy commitment scheme. In: ACM CCS 1999, pp. 28–36 (1999)
30. Kellaris, G., Kollios, G., Nissim, K., O'Neill, A.: Generic attacks on secure outsourced databases. In: ACM CCS 2016, pp. 1329–1340 (2016)
31. Krawczyk, H.: Cryptographic extraction and key derivation: the HKDF scheme. In: Rabin, T. (ed.) CRYPTO 2010. LNCS, vol. 6223, pp. 631–648. Springer, Heidelberg (2010). https://doi.org/10.1007/978-3-642-14623-7_34
32. Kuchta, V., Manulis, M.: Public key encryption with distributed keyword search. In: Yung, M., Zhang, J., Yang, Z. (eds.) INTRUST 2015. LNCS, vol. 9565, pp. 62–83. Springer, Cham (2016). https://doi.org/10.1007/978-3-319-31550-8_5
33. Liu, C., Zhu, L., Wang, M., Tan, Y.: Search pattern leakage in searchable encryption: attacks and new construction. Inf. Sci. **265**, 176–188 (2014)
34. Luby, M., Rackoff, C.: How to construct pseudorandom permutations from pseudorandom functions. SIAM J. Comput. **17**(2), 373–386 (1988)
35. Naveed, M., Kamara, S., Wright, C.V.: Inference attacks on property-preserving encrypted databases. In: ACM SIGSAC 2015, pp. 644–655 (2015)

36. O'Gorman, L.: Comparing passwords, tokens, and biometrics for user authentication. Proc. IEEE **91**(12), 2021–2040 (2003)
37. Örencik, C., Selcuk, A., Savas, E., Kantarcioglu, M.: Multi-keyword search over encrypted data with scoring and search pattern obfuscation. Int. J. Inf. Secur. **15**(3), 251–269 (2016)
38. Park, D.J., Kim, K., Lee, P.J.: Public key encryption with conjunctive field keyword search. In: Lim, C.H., Yung, M. (eds.) WISA 2004. LNCS, vol. 3325, pp. 73–86. Springer, Heidelberg (2005). https://doi.org/10.1007/978-3-540-31815-6_7
39. Pedersen, T.P.: Non-interactive and information-theoretic secure verifiable secret sharing. In: Feigenbaum, J. (ed.) CRYPTO 1991. LNCS, vol. 576, pp. 129–140. Springer, Heidelberg (1992). https://doi.org/10.1007/3-540-46766-1_9
40. Pointcheval, D., Zimmer, S.: Multi-factor authenticated key exchange. In: Bellovin, S.M., Gennaro, R., Keromytis, A., Yung, M. (eds.) ACNS 2008. LNCS, vol. 5037, pp. 277–295. Springer, Heidelberg (2008). https://doi.org/10.1007/978-3-540-68914-0_17
41. Prabhakar, S., Pankanti, S., Jain, A.K.: Biometric recognition: security and privacy concerns. IEEE Secur. Priv. **1**(2), 33–42 (2003)
42. Rogaway, P., Bellare, M.: Robust computational secret sharing and a unified account of classical secret-sharing goals. In: ACM CCS 2007, pp. 172–184 (2007)
43. Shamir, A.: How to share a secret. Commun. ACM **22**(11), 612–613 (1979)
44. Stefanov, E., Papamanthou, C., Shi, E.: Practical dynamic searchable encryption with small leakage. In: NDSS 2014. The Internet Society (2014)
45. Yi, X., Hao, F., Chen, L., Liu, J.K.: Practical threshold password-authenticated secret sharing protocol. In: Pernul, G., Ryan, P.Y.A., Weippl, E. (eds.) ESORICS 2015. LNCS, vol. 9326, pp. 347–365. Springer, Cham (2015). https://doi.org/10.1007/978-3-319-24174-6_18
46. Zhang, Y., Katz, J., Papamanthou, C.: All your queries are belong to us: the power of file-injection attacks on searchable encryption. USENIX Secur. **2016**, 707–720 (2016)

BioLocker: A Practical Biometric Authentication Mechanism Based on 3D Fingervein

F. Betül Durak[1], Loïs Huguenin-Dumittan[2], and Serge Vaudenay[2(✉)]

[1] Robert Bosch LLC - Research and Technology Center, Pittsburgh, PA, USA
[2] Ecole Polytechnique Fédérale de Lausanne (EPFL), Lausanne, Switzerland
serge.vaudenay@epfl.ch

Abstract. We design a consecution of protocols which allows organizations to have secure strong access control of their users to their desktop machines based on biometry. It provides both strong secure authentication and privacy. Moreover, our mechanism allows the system admins to grant a various level of access to their end-users by fine tuning access control policy. Our system implements privacy-by-design. It separates biometric data from identity information. It is practical: we fully implemented our protocols as a proof of concept for a hospital. We use a 3D fingervein scanner to capture the biometric data of the user on a Raspberry Pi. For the biometry part, we developed an optimal way to aggregate scores using sequential distinguishers. It trades desired FAR and FRR against an average number of biometric captures.

1 Introduction

Biometric access control provides a mechanism to authenticate users. It has been an interesting research domain throughout the years. Several secure and privacy-preserving biometric protocols have been proposed with different techniques. We take a traditional approach to develop a biometric access control with strong security guarantees. By assuming a secured server storing a database of biometric templates, we develop a mechanism called BioLocker for strong access control (AC) using end-to-end encryption and fingervein recognition.

Motivated from the real-world use cases, we focus on users aiming to log in desktops/laptops **D** under a large network in an organization using a biometric scanner **B**. In such an organization, a directory **L** is used to identify them through passwords. In the present work, to add an extra layer of secure authentication, a server **S** which is responsible for the biometric recognition is introduced. For such a structure, we design two bodies: an enrollment station that lets admins enroll users with their biometric data and a laptop login control that lets the user authenticate themselves through biometric scanner before logging in to their devices. The high-level overview of BioLocker is given in Fig. 1.

F. Betül Durak—The work was done when the author was in LASEC/EPFL.

© Springer Nature Switzerland AG 2020
M. Conti et al. (Eds.): ACNS 2020, LNCS 12147, pp. 62–80, 2020.
https://doi.org/10.1007/978-3-030-57878-7_4

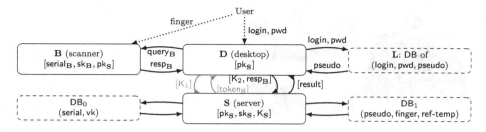

Fig. 1. Full BioLocker mechanism. Enrollment is shown with fully black figures and Biometric AC Method is same as Enrollment in addition to added gray arrows/queries between **D** and **S**. Solid rectangles are the machines whereas dashed rectangles are the databases on the corresponding machines. Dashed arrow indicates the inputs from the user to the specified machines. Solid arrows indicate the exchanges between the machines over the network.

As depicted in Fig. 1, **D** serves as an intermediate machine between the biometric scanner **B** and server **S** to make them communicate. The idea is to use this "intermediary" in a secure way by encrypting the exchange of messages between **B** and **S** in an authenticated manner.

The goal of our construction is to add strong AC to an existing password-based AC system deployed between **D** and **L**. We assume that the password-based protocol between **D** and **L** is already secure by default. And, we focus on adding a biometric AC following the existing password-based protocol. Our constraints are to add no software on **L** and to make as little changes as possible on **D**. More importantly, for privacy reasons, nobody but **B** and **S** sees biometric templates. The maintenance and security of the server **S** must be high. Nobody but **L** and **D** sees the identity of the user. Hence, we only allow **S** to associate biometric data to a pseudo. Nobody but **L**, **D**, and **S** see the pseudo of the user. Unless there is any collusion with any of these participants, BioLocker offers privacy by design.

We make sure, in BioLocker, that the server **S** will only treat information coming from a legitimate scanner. We design the mechanism in a way that **D** only forwards messages and does two encryptions for **S**. Hence, the overhead on **D** is minimal. This makes our protocol feasible to deploy on already existing systems.

For our system, we adopted fingervein biometry. To defeat spoofing attacks [21], we use what we call *3D fingervein* by capturing fingervein through several angles. In cooperation with Global ID, IDIAP, HES-SO Valais-Wallis, and EPFL, we built a biometric scanner to scan 3D fingerveins, algorithms, and security protocols.[1] It is shown in Fig. 2.

---

[1] https://www.global-id.ch
   https://www.idiap.ch
   https://www.hevs.ch
   https://www.epfl.ch.

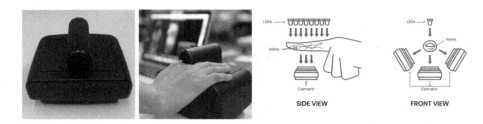

Fig. 2. Current version of the scanner.

Previous Work. While not as widely deployed as fingerprint authentication, fingervein recognition has been a hot topic in recent years and many systems have been proposed [5,18,20]. In 2015, Wang et al. [24] showed how hand-vein recognition can be used to build a practical physical access control system. In 2018, Yang et al. [25] presented a system providing authentication and encryption of healthcare data via a smartcard storing finger-vein biometric templates. Finally, Kang et al. [10] studied real 3D fingervein algorithms.

Multimodal biometric (or multi-biometric) systems combine several biometric sources (e.g. face, fingervein, and voice) or techniques (e.g. matching algorithms) to obtain a highly reliable authentication. The design of such systems has thus led to the study of biometric score aggregation (also called *score fusion*, i.e. how one can combine the different scores obtained to get the best performance). The NIST surveyed many proposals for biometric score fusion in 2006 [23] and another study was published by Lumini and Nanni [12] in 2017. A popular technique for score aggregation is the maximum likelihood ratio test [16]. Recently, Ni et al. [17] proposed a scheme based on the maximum decision reliability ratio and weighted voting. In 2018, Kabir et al. [9] introduced an algorithm that relies on normalization and a weighted sum of the different scores. Finally, another common approach for score fusion is the use of classifiers (e.g. based on random forests [13] and SVM [7]).

There exist few products deploying access control with biometry. However, to the best of our knowledge, there is no known publicly available protocol.

In BioID [3], a previous project, we developed a suite of protocols to design a privacy-preserving identity document based on biometric recognition. Our scanners and protocols can host BioID.

Our Contribution. We design a practical biometric authentication mechanism called BioLocker that is integrated into an already existing authentication system such as password-based systems. Our construction makes no changes to the existing system and only extends security integrating 3D fingervein recognition. Our algorithms optimally use biometry. Since the matching algorithm runs with three images of the same finger from different angles, we needed to come up with a way to aggregate the matching scores to grant access. We developed our aggregation of matching scores to reach a desired FAR and FRR.[2] To do this, we use the theory of sequential distinguishers: at every capture, our algorithm decides if the recognition succeeded, failed, or requires more biometric samples to conclude. Hence, a user may be required to be scanned several times, although in most cases, one capture is enough. To the best of our knowledge, such an AC mechanism with biometric algorithm is a novel design in many ways: 1. it is easy to integrate on existing weakly private systems where strong privacy is required; 2. its policy-based methods run AC in fine-grained iterative mode and can accommodate other modalities; 3. it uses 3D fingervein image recognition.

Designing a biometric mechanism in a secure manner may be very tedious and requires a lot of crafting. Nevertheless, we prove the security of our mechanism and support the practicality with implementation results.

Structure of the Paper. We start with introducing our infrastructure in Sect. 2. Then, we detail the AC protocol and enrollment station in Sects. 3.1 and 3.2 respectively. Then, we detail the biometric algorithms in Sect. 4. We analyze the security of our system in Sect. 5. Finally, we present implementation results from a proof-of-concept in Sect. 6.

Notation. We will use a few cryptographic primitives for our protocols. In what follows, $\perp$ denotes an error message or a dummy value (e.g. a null pointer, an empty string, or an empty list). We use a public-key cryptosystem PKC, a digital signature scheme DSS, an authenticated encryption with associated data AEAD, and a hash function H. Given a key pair (pk, sk), PKC encrypts a plaintext pt into a ciphertext ct using pk and decrypts it back using sk. Dec is a deterministic function. Given a key pair (vk, sk), DSS signs data data using sk and verify the signature using vk. Given a key $K \in$ AEAD.$\mathcal{K}$, AEAD encrypts a plaintext pt with associated data ad and a nonce $N \in$ AEAD.$\mathcal{N}$ and decrypts it back with the same K. Given a bitstring x, H computes a digest with $H(x)$. Typically, PKC provides INDCCA security, DSS is EFCMA-secure, AEAD is secure as a MAC and as an encryption against chosen plaintext/ciphertext attacks, and we consider a collision-resistant hash function H. These primitives work with the following notations:

$$\text{PKC.Gen} \rightarrow (\text{pk,sk}) \qquad \text{PKC.Enc}_{\text{pk}}(\text{pt}) \rightarrow \text{ct} \qquad \text{PKC.Dec}_{\text{sk}}(\text{ct}) \rightarrow \text{pt}$$
$$\text{DSS.Gen} \rightarrow (\text{vk,sk}) \qquad \text{DSS.Sign}_{\text{sk}}(\text{data}) \rightarrow \sigma \qquad \text{DSS.Verify}_{\text{vk}}(\text{data},\sigma) \rightarrow 0/1$$
$$\text{AEAD.Enc}_K(N,\text{ad,pt}) \rightarrow \text{ct} \qquad \text{AEAD.Dec}_K(N,\text{ad,ct}) \rightarrow \text{pt}$$

2   Infrastructure Specification

In this work, we focus on an organization which has its own network and file system. Most of the organizations offer a system to authenticate its users with passwords, such as Active Directory implemented with LDAP-like protocol. For

---

[2] FAR is the *false acceptance rate*, i.e. the probability that a wrong finger is accepted, FRR is the *false rejection rate*, i.e. the probability that the right finger is rejected.

instance, the organization could be a hospital with many different departments. Each department has a set of doctors who can access the files of their assigned patients and nothing else.

The mechanism BioLocker has an infrastructure with different entities: some machines and human users. The machines are of several types.

Biometric Scanner: **B**. Scanners capture biometric information of users and do necessary computations by following the protocol honestly. In our settings, scanners take three images of a finger from different angles, which we call 3D fingervein. A malicious biometric scanner can clearly store and reuse some biometric templates as will. Hence, we assume that **B** is honest in AC. Scanners will be considered as malicious when studying the privacy of the user identity or pseudo.

Organization Server: **L**. This server belongs to the organization and contains the directory of its users, their names and passwords (or their hash). We extend it with a pseudo for privacy reasons. The pseudo is not required to be remembered (or even known) by the user. The server **L** has a unique identifier serial$_L$. A user name login is assumed to be unique to each **L**, meaning that the (serial$_L$, login) pair is unique. In AC, the organization server is assumed to be honest. When studying the privacy of biometric templates, **L** can be malicious.

Desktops: **D**. These desktop computers belong to the information network of the organization. The goal is to control access of users to desktops. Each desktop is set up with the address of its server **L** and the address addr$_B$ of a close-by biometric scanner **B**. We assume that only **D** has access to **B** (e.g. **B** is connected to **D** by a USB cable). Since the purpose of AC is to grant access to **D**, we assume that **D** is honest. When studying the privacy of biometric templates, **D** can be malicious.

Enrollment Station: **E**. It consists of a *security-sensitive* computer in order to enroll users with their biometric templates scanned through **B**. The sensitive computer communicates with **B** to capture templates and communicates with **S** to add, remove, or modify entries in the database on the server. The enroller is assumed to be honest in AC. When studying the privacy of biometric templates, **E** can be malicious.

Biometric Server: **S**. There is only one biometric server. It contains two databases: one stores the reference biometric templates of users along with their associated pseudo and the other stores identifiers of the enrollment stations and biometric scanners. The former is used for matching the reference templates to the claimed users for the AC. The latter is used during the authentication of data coming through legitimate **E** and **B**. The server **S** can be outside of the organization, but high security is provided. As the server gives the final result of AC to **D**, **S** is assumed to be honest. Servers will be considered as malicious when studying the privacy of the user identity or pseudo.

Communication between **D**, **E**, and **S** is going through an insecure network. Communication between **D** and **B** is assumed to be authenticated. Communication between **D** and **L** is assumed to be fully secure, and outside of the scope of the present construction.

Since the organization may consist of many departments, all elements except **S** belong to a department. We identify each department with "domain" which is referred by a unique string domain. The server **L** is unique for each domain, that is **L** stores users data for this specific department. We assume that each pseudo is unique. The biometric server **S** is unique (cross-domain). We assume secure communication between **D** and **L**.

Setup. We give the list of parameters that each elements of the infrastructure hold in Table 1. More specifically, the server **S** generates its PKC key pair (pk_S, sk_S) and a symmetric key $K_S \in$ AEAD.$\mathcal{K}$. Each biometric scanner **B** is configured with its own DSS key pair (vk_B, sk_B) and a unique serial number $serial_B$. It keeps a copy of pk_S, as well.

In each enrollment station, **E** is configured with its own DSS key pair (vk_E, sk_E) and a unique serial number $serial_E$. It stores pk_S, as well. The server **S** maintains a directory DB_0 of the public keys vk (vk_B or vk_E) of each **B** and **E** by their serial numbers ($serial_B$ or $serial_E$). The server **S** holds one database DB_1 of (pseudo, finger, ref-temp, policy) and (pseudo, policy) entries which is populated by enrollment station through a protocol which we will describe in Sect. 3.2.

We let each desktop **D** hold the public key pk_S of the server **S**. The server **L** holds a database of (login, pwd, pseudo) entries for first layer authentication with passwords.

Table 1. The elements of the infrastructure and their configuration parameters.

D	B	L	E	S
pk_S	pk_S		pk_S	(pk_S, sk_S)
$serial_L$	(vk_B, sk_B)		(vk_E, sk_E)	K_S
$addr_B$	$serial_B$	$serial_L$	$serial_E$	
		$DB = \{(login, pwd, pseudo)\}$		$DB_0 = \{(serial, vk)\}$
				$DB_1 = \{(pseudo, finger_i, ref\text{-}temp, policy)\}$

3 Protocols

3.1 Access Control Protocols

For this section, we will focus on the communication between devices in AC without giving the details about the biometric algorithms. We start defining a (straightforward) prior AC with login credentials and then continue with extended AC mechanisms. Prior AC is the password authentication between **E** and **L**. We assume that there is an already existing secure protocol for this. More precisely, the prior AC works as follows.

1. The user types his identifier login and his password pwd on **D**.
2. The desktop **D** queries the server **L** with $query_L = (login, pwd)$ and gets the response $resp_L$. Then, the server **L** computes the response by $resp_L = pseudo$, where $(login, pwd, pseudo)$ is a valid record in the database. Otherwise, $resp_L = \perp$.
3. If the response by **L** is $\perp$, access is denied and the protocol ends. Otherwise, **D** proceeds with our protocol.

$finger_{I,n}$	Represents a set I of fingers to be scanned n times. The access is granted conditioned that the user's corresponding finger matches with the reference template stored in the database. The method may include a message to display on the scanner.
"always"	The desktop **D** always grants access.
"never"	The desktop **D** always denies access.
"sms"	A verification code is sent by SMS to the user who types it on **D**.
"securitas"	An alert is sent to the security officer who may call the user.

Fig. 3. Various methods the protocol sets with method variable.

To be able to follow the description in the present section, we need some back story about the biometry. The AC heavily depends on the biometric matching. That is, upon inviting the user to the scanner to provide a fingervein image, it will be used to match it to the user's reference templates stored in DB_0 during enrollment (described in Sect. 3.2). The matching algorithm returns a score denoted by score which may be insufficient to decide to accept or reject. The decision in that case is to ask for another trial. The final decision is based on all collected trials. Therefore, the extended AC works in a succession of iterations which are defined by a *method* which we denote by method. The method can be to prompt the capture of one specific finger or any other mean/modality. Some special methods are used to terminate the iteration cycle: the method which accepts and the method which rejects. In Fig. 3, we give the list of methods for extended AC along with their descriptions. We need to define both the method of the first iteration and then the algorithm to decide on the next method based on the collected results (i.e. aggregated scores). These two elements form the *policy*: policy.initmethod and policy.method. More precisely, the initial method to be used is policy.initmethod and after having collected a list hist of scores, the next method is policy.method(hist). If hist is enough, we have policy.method(hist) = "always" (access granted) or policy.method(hist) = "never" (access denied). The method could repeatedly be $finger_{\{i\},1}$ (meaning to scan finger i once), change fingers, or try other modalities. We specify the policy for each user at enrollment, as one record of DB_1. We give the extended AC in three stages in Figs. 4, 5, and 6.

The first iteration of extended AC starts with a protocol called "Stage 1" with the server **S** who sets the initial method (line 4–6 on the right in Fig. 4). Then, it

Desktop D (Stage 1)
input: $\mathsf{pseudo}, \mathsf{addr}_B, \mathsf{serial}_B$
stored: pk_S
  1: $K_1 \leftarrow\!\!\$\, \mathsf{AEAD}.\mathcal{K}$
  2: $\mathsf{query}_S \leftarrow \mathsf{PKC.Enc}_{\mathsf{pk}_S}(\text{"Request"}, K_1, \mathsf{pseudo}, \mathsf{serial}_B)$
  3: send query_S to **S**
  4: get resp_S
  5: parse $\mathsf{resp}_S = [N_{12}, \mathsf{ct}_1]$
  6: $(\mathsf{token}_S, K) \leftarrow \mathsf{AEAD.Dec}_{K_1}(N_{12}, \perp, \mathsf{ct}_1)$
  7: erase K_1
  8: continue to Stage 2

Biometric server S ("Request" query)
stored: sk_S, K_S
  1: receive query_S
  2: **if** anything fails below **then return** $\mathsf{resp}_S = \perp$
  3: $\mathsf{PKC.Dec}_{\mathsf{sk}_S}(\mathsf{query}_S) \rightarrow (\text{"Request"}, K_1, \mathsf{pseudo}, \mathsf{serial}_B)$
  4: retrieve policy with pseudo from DB_1
  5: $\mathsf{hist} \leftarrow \perp$
  6: $\mathsf{method} \leftarrow \mathsf{policy.method}(\mathsf{hist})$
  7: set T as current time
  8: $\mathsf{ad} \leftarrow \mathsf{method}$
  9: $K \xleftarrow{\$} \mathsf{AEAD}.\mathcal{K}$
 10: $\mathsf{pt} \leftarrow (T, \mathsf{pseudo}, \mathsf{hist}, \mathsf{serial}_B, K)$
 11: $N_{11}, N_{12} \leftarrow\!\!\$\, \mathsf{AEAD}.\mathcal{N}$
 12: $\mathsf{token}_S \leftarrow [N_{11}, \mathsf{ad}, \mathsf{AEAD.Enc}_{K_S}(N_{11}, \mathsf{ad}, \mathsf{pt})]$
 13: $\mathsf{resp}_S \leftarrow [N_{12}, \mathsf{AEAD.Enc}_{K_1}(N_{12}, \perp, \mathsf{token}_S, K)]$
 14: **return** resp_S

Fig. 4. Access control Stage 1 (between **D** and **S**).

continues like in every other iteration. That is, it goes through a protocol called "Stage 2" using method (line 2–8 on the left and line 7 on the left in Fig. 5). In Stage 2, **D** may decide to end (by granting access or denying access) or interact with **B**. After that, it goes through a protocol with **S** called "Stage 3". In this stage, we determine the next method to use (line 24 in Fig. 6). Then, AC goes back to Stage 2. Note that whenever there is a failure in verification in a protocol, the protocol aborts immediately. Otherwise, they continue in the flow.

Our scanner is a stateless device. When it receives a request, it takes pictures, sends its response, then sleeps back.

As the server is stateless as well, state information is carried inside a *token* that **S** encrypts for himself. The token works like a cookie in a browser: **S** gives token in the response to **D** and **D** must provide it in the next query to **S**. The token also contains method which is in clear and which can be parsed by **D** and **B**.

Desktop D (Stage 2)
1: parse $\mathsf{token_S} = [\mathsf{N_{11}}, \mathsf{ad}, \mathsf{ct_2}]$
2: parse $\mathsf{ad} = \mathsf{method}$
3: **if** method $\in$ { "sms", "securitas"} **then**
4:      method $\leftarrow$ treat(method,hist,serial$_B$,login,host)
5: **end if**
6: **if** method = "always" **then** grant access
7: **if** method = "never" **then** deny access
8: **if** method is not biometric **then** abort
9: display "scan finger in scanner serial$_\mathsf{B}$"
10: $\mathsf{query_B} \leftarrow (\mathsf{serial_B}, \mathsf{token_S})$
11: send $\mathsf{query_B}$ to B at $\mathsf{addr_B}$
12: get $\mathsf{resp_B}$
13: continue to Stage 3

Biometric scanner B
stored: $\mathsf{sk_B}$, $\mathsf{pk_S}$, $\mathsf{serial_B}$
1: receive $\mathsf{query_B}$
2: **if** anything fails below **then return** $\mathsf{resp_B} = \perp$
3: parse $\mathsf{query_B} = (\mathsf{serial_B}, \mathsf{token})$
4: check that $\mathsf{serial_B}$ is correct
5: parse token = $[\mathsf{N}, \mathsf{ad}, \mathsf{ct}]$
6: parse $\mathsf{ad} = \mathsf{method}$
7: parse method = $(\mathsf{finger}_{I,n}, \mathsf{message})$
8: display message
9: extract I, n from $\mathsf{finger}_{I,n}$
10: **for** $i \in I, j = 1, \ldots, n$ **do**
11:      invite finger_i
12:      capture $\mathsf{temp}_{i,j}$
13: **end for**
14: temp $\leftarrow$ list of all $(\mathsf{finger}_i, \mathsf{temp}_{i,j})$
15: $\mathsf{data_0} \leftarrow (\mathsf{query_B}, \mathsf{temp})$
16: $\mathsf{sign_0} \leftarrow \mathsf{DSS.Sign}_{\mathsf{sk_B}}(\mathsf{data_0})$
17: $\mathsf{resp_B} \leftarrow \mathsf{PKC.Enc}_{\mathsf{pk_S}}(\mathsf{data_0}, \mathsf{sign_0})$
18: **return** $\mathsf{resp_B}$

Fig. 5. Access control Stage 2 (between **D** and **B**).

3.2   Enrollment Protocol

The enrollment protocol is given in Fig. 7. The input to the enrollment protocol (on **E**) is a string pseudo associated to a user to register, and the address $\mathsf{addr_B}$ of the scanner **B**. In practice, operating the enrollment station **E** is restricted to an administrator or a security officer who checks the identity of the enrolling user and retrieves his/her pseudo securely before enrollment. Specifically, **E** goes through two stages: Stage 1 with **B** and Stage 2 with **S**. In Stage 2, **S** receives a query of type "Enroll". Both stages are defined in Fig. 7. In communication with **B**, only $\mathsf{serial_B}$, N, and ad = method are in clear. All the rest is end-to-end encrypted. More importantly, we design both the server **S** and the scanner **B** as stateless (both in enrollment and AC phase). **E** (and later **D**) acts as a master

Desktop D (Stage 3)

1: $K_2 \xleftarrow{\$} AEAD.\mathcal{K}$
2: $query_S \leftarrow PKC.Enc_{pk_S}(\text{"Match"}, K_2, K)$
3: send $query_S$ and $resp_B$ to **S**
4: get $resp_S$
5: parse $resp_S \leftarrow (N_{12}, ct_2)$
6: $(token_S, \bar{K}) \leftarrow AEAD.Dec_{K_2}(N, H(query_B), ct_2)$
7: erase K_2
8: continue to Stage 2

Biometric server S ("Match" query)

stored: sk_S, K_S

1: receive $query_S$ and $resp_B$
2: **if** anything fails below **then return** $resp_S = \bot$
3: parse $(\text{"Match"}, K_2, \bar{K}) = PKC.Dec_{sk_S}(query_S)$
4: $(data, sign) \leftarrow PKC.Dec_{sk_S}(resp_B)$
5: parse $data$ as $(query_B, temp)$
6: parse $query_B$ as $(serial_B, token_S)$
7: retrieve vk_B form DB_0 with $serial_B$
8: $DSS.Verify_{vk_B}(data, sign)$
9: parse $token_S$ as (N, ad, ct)
10: $pt \leftarrow AEAD.Dec_{K_S}(N, ad, ct)$
11: parse $ad = finger_{I,n}$
12: parse $pt = (T, pseudo, hist, serial_B, K)$
13: check $K = \bar{K}$
14: check $serial_B$ is correct
15: verify T not too early/late
16: $x \leftarrow \bot$
17: **for all** $(finger_i, temp_{i,j}) \in temp$ **do**
18:     retrieve $ref\text{-}temp_i$ from DB_1 with $(pseudo, finger_i)$
19:     compute $score$ with the matching algorithm
20:     $x \leftarrow (x, (i, score))$
21: **end for**
22: $hist' \leftarrow (hist, x)$
23: retrieve $policy$ from DB_1 with $pseudo$
24: determine $method = policy.method(hist')$
25: set T' as current time
26: $ad \leftarrow method$
27: $K' \xleftarrow{\$} AEAD.\mathcal{K}$
28: $pt \leftarrow (T', pseudo, hist', serial_B, K')$
29: $N_{11}, N_{12} \xleftarrow{\$} AEAD.\mathcal{N}$
30: $token'_S \leftarrow [N_{11}, ad, AEAD.Enc_{K_S}(N_{11}, ad, pt)]$
31: $resp_S \leftarrow (N_{12}, AEAD.Enc_{K_2}(N_{12}, H(query_B), token'_S, K'))$
32: **return** $resp_S$

Fig. 6. Access control Stage 3 (between **D** and **S**).

in the communication with **S** and **B**. Interestingly, the scanner **B** answers to queries in a unique way, so there in no difference between access control and enrollment for **B**.

Enrollment station on device E
input: pseudo, policy, addr_B, serial_B
stored: sk_E, pk_S, serial_E

Stage 1:
1: set T as current time
2: $K_0 \leftarrow\!\!\$\ \text{AEAD}.\mathcal{K}$, $N \xleftarrow{\text{cte}} \text{AEAD}.\mathcal{N}$
3: $\text{finger}_{I,n} \leftarrow \text{policy.initmethod}$
4: $\text{ad} \leftarrow \text{finger}_{I,n}$
5: $\text{pt} \leftarrow (T, \text{pseudo}, \text{policy})$
6: $\text{token}_E \leftarrow \left[N, \text{ad}, \text{AEAD}.\text{Enc}_{K_0}(N, \text{ad}, \text{pt}) \right]$
7: $\text{query}_B \leftarrow (\text{serial}_B, \text{token}_E)$
8: send query_B to B at addr_B ┄┄┄┄┄► ⌐┄┄┄┐
9: get resp_B ◄┄┄┄┄┄┄┄┄┄┄┄┄┄┄   **B**
                                        └┄┄┄┘

Stage 2:
10: $\text{data}_1 \leftarrow (\text{"Enroll"}, K_0, \text{serial}_E, H(\text{query}_B), \text{resp}_B)$
11: $\text{sign}_1 \leftarrow \text{DSS}.\text{Sign}_{\text{sk}_E}(\text{data}_1)$
12: $\text{query}_S \leftarrow \text{PKC}.\text{Enc}_{\text{pk}_S}(\text{data}_1, \text{sign}_1)$
13: send query_S to S
14: get resp_S
15: parse $\text{resp}_S = [N', \text{ct}']$
16: check "ok" $= \text{AEAD}.\text{Dec}_{K_0}(N', \perp, \text{ct}')$
17: erase K_0

Biometric server S ("Enroll" query)
stored: sk_S
18: receive query_S
19: **if** anything fails below **then return** $\text{resp}_S = \perp$
20: $(\text{data}_1, \text{sign}_1) \leftarrow \text{PKC}.\text{Dec}_{\text{sk}_S}(\text{query}_S)$
21: parse $\text{data}_1 = (\text{"Enroll"}, K_0, \text{serial}_E, h, \text{resp}_B)$
22: retrieve vk_E from DB_0 with serial_E
23: $\text{DSS}.\text{Verify}_{\text{vk}_E}(\text{data}_1, \text{sign}_1)$
24: $(\text{data}_0, \text{sign}_0) \leftarrow \text{PKC}.\text{Dec}_{\text{sk}_S}(\text{resp}_B)$
25: parse $\text{data}_0 = (\text{query}_B, \text{temp})$
26: check $h = H(\text{query}_B)$
27: parse $\text{query}_B = (\text{serial}_B, \text{token}_E)$
28: retrieve vk_B from DB_0 with serial_B
29: $\text{DSS}.\text{Verify}_{\text{vk}_B}(\text{data}_0, \text{sign}_0)$
30: parse $\text{token}_E = (N, \text{ad}, \text{ct})$
31: $\text{pt} \leftarrow \text{AEAD}.\text{Dec}_{K_0}(N, \text{ad}, \text{ct})$
32: parse $\text{ad} = \text{finger}_{I,n}$
33: parse $\text{pt} = (T, \text{pseudo}, \text{policy})$
34: verify T not too early/late
35: store $(\text{pseudo}, \text{policy})$ in DB_1
36: parse $\text{temp} = (\text{finger}_i, \text{temp}_{i,j})_{i \in I, j=1,\ldots,n}$
37: **for** each $i \in I$ **do**
38:     decide which j defines $\text{ref-temp}_i = \text{temp}_{i,j}$
39:     store $(\text{pseudo}, \text{finger}_i, \text{ref-temp}_i)$ in DB_1
40: **end for**
41: pick $N' \in \text{AEAD}.\mathcal{N}$
42: $\text{resp}_S \leftarrow [N', \text{AEAD}.\text{Enc}_{K_0}(N', \perp, \text{"ok"})]$
43: **return** resp_S

Fig. 7. Enrollment protocol. The dashed square represents the steps run by **B** same as in Fig. 5.

4   Biometric Algorithms

Image Processing on Fingervein Images (See Fig. 8). The image from the scanner is first cleaned up using image processing algorithms. After the contour of the finger is identified, the image is cropped. A linear regression is performed to determine the angle of the finger and to correct it. Finally, the biometric feature is extracted using the algorithm of Miura et al. [14,15,22] with Lee mask preprocessing [11]. The final feature extraction is a black-and-white image which takes about 2 KB. This is the image which is stored in the database. Since we have three images, a record takes less than 10 KB.

Matching Algorithm. We use the matching algorithm from Miura et al. [14, 15,22]. Given two images, the biometric matching algorithm runs with the two images as input and returns a score between 0 and 0.5.

Score Algorithms with Aggregation. Since we have three pairs of images, we obtain three scores. We design an optimal way to aggregate the scores. Namely, we consider the following problem. After m iterations, we have a list hist $=$ (score$_1$, ..., score$_m$) where each score$_i$ is a triplet of numbers. Hence, hist $= (s_1, ..., s_n)$ with $n = 3m$. We model the s_i by *independent* random variables. If the templates correspond to the same random finger, we assume that every s_i follows one distribution same$_c$, depending on the used camera c (left, center, or right) to scan the templates. If they correspond to different random fingers, we assume that every s_i follows one distribution diff$_c$. More precisely, we let ref-temp(finger) be the reference template of a random finger and capture$_i$(finger$_i$) be a captured template of a finger finger$_i$. We let match$_{C(i)}$(ref-temp(finger), capture$_i$(finger$_i$)) $=$ score$_i$ be the score obtained by the matching algorithm based on Camera $C(i)$. We define the events AUTH (authentic) and IMP (impersonation) by

$$\text{AUTH : finger} = \text{finger}_1 = \cdots = \text{finger}_m$$
$$\text{IMP : finger} \neq \text{finger}_1, \ldots, \text{finger} \neq \text{finger}_m$$

The distributions same and diff are defined by

$$\Pr_{\text{same}}[\text{score}_1, \ldots, \text{score}_m] = \Pr[\text{score}_1, \ldots, \text{score}_m | \text{AUTH}]$$
$$\Pr_{\text{diff}}[\text{score}_1, \ldots, \text{score}_m] = \Pr[\text{score}_1, \ldots, \text{score}_m | \text{IMP}]$$

We design a sequential distinguisher such that given hist, the output is either "same", or "diff", or $\perp$, meaning that no decision is reached, hence more samples are needed. We define FAR $= \Pr_{\text{diff}}[\textbf{output} = \textbf{same}]$, FRR $= \Pr_{\text{same}}[\textbf{output} = \textbf{diff}]$. Our goal is to make a distinguisher reaching a target FAR$_{\text{target}}$ and FRR$_{\text{target}}$, and requiring as few samples as possible.

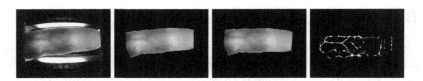

Fig. 8. Image processing: raw capture, background elimination, angle correction, and feature extraction.

We use the theory of *sequential distinguishers*. This theory is described in Siegmund [19]. It was first used in block cipher cryptanalysis [8], then in the side-channel attack against SSL [4]. Given a tuple of m scores $(\mathsf{score}_1, \ldots, \mathsf{score}_m)$, we compute the likelihood ratio

$$\mathsf{lr} = \frac{\Pr_{\mathsf{same}}[\mathsf{score}_1, \ldots, \mathsf{score}_m]}{\Pr_{\mathsf{diff}}[\mathsf{score}_1, \ldots, \mathsf{score}_m]}$$

The best sequential distinguisher accepts the hypothesis that the scores comes from same if $\mathsf{lr} \geq \tau_+$, for some parameter τ_+. It accepts the hypothesis that the score comes from diff if $\mathsf{lr} \leq \tau_-$, for some parameter τ_-. In between, the distinguisher waits for more samples. Using the Wald approximation, if we want to obtain $\mathsf{FAR}_{\mathsf{target}}$ and $\mathsf{FRR}_{\mathsf{target}}$, we should use $\tau_+ \approx 1/\mathsf{FAR}_{\mathsf{target}}$ and $\tau_- \approx \mathsf{FRR}_{\mathsf{target}}$.

We make the approximation that the scores are normally distributed, which is well supported by experiment. Namely, matching from the camera c follows either $\mathcal{N}(\mu_c^{\mathsf{same}}, (\sigma_c^{\mathsf{same}})^2)$ or $\mathcal{N}(\mu_c^{\mathsf{diff}}, (\sigma_c^{\mathsf{diff}})^2)$. We let c_i be the camera used to compute s_i. Hence, $\ln \mathsf{lr}$ can be computed by summing all $\ln \frac{\Pr_{\mathsf{same}}[s_i]}{\Pr_{\mathsf{diff}}[s_i]} = \Delta \mathsf{lpdf}_{c_i}(s_i)$. Using the probability density function of the normal distribution, we obtain

$$\Delta \mathsf{lpdf}_c(s) = \frac{\left(s - \mu_c^{\mathsf{diff}}\right)^2}{2(\sigma_c^{\mathsf{diff}})^2} - \frac{\left(s - \mu_c^{\mathsf{same}}\right)^2}{2(\sigma_c^{\mathsf{same}})^2} + \ln \frac{\sigma_c^{\mathsf{diff}}}{\sigma_c^{\mathsf{same}}}$$

The expected value of $\ln \mathsf{lr}$ with same distribution is

$$E_{\mathsf{same}}(\ln \mathsf{lr}) = \sum_i \left(\frac{(\sigma_{c_i}^{\mathsf{same}})^2}{2(\sigma_{c_i}^{\mathsf{diff}})^2} + \frac{(\mu_{c_i}^{\mathsf{same}} - \mu_{c_i}^{\mathsf{diff}})^2}{2(\sigma_{c_i}^{\mathsf{diff}})^2} - \frac{1}{2} + \ln \frac{\sigma_{c_i}^{\mathsf{diff}}}{\sigma_{c_i}^{\mathsf{same}}} \right)$$

Given that we have m iterations for each camera c, we deduce that the complexity to reach a good decision with same is approximately

$$m_{\mathsf{same}} \approx \frac{\ln \tau_+}{\sum_c \left(\frac{(\sigma_c^{\mathsf{same}})^2}{2(\sigma_c^{\mathsf{diff}})^2} + \frac{(\mu_c^{\mathsf{same}} - \mu_c^{\mathsf{diff}})^2}{2(\sigma_c^{\mathsf{diff}})^2} - \frac{1}{2} + \ln \frac{\sigma_c^{\mathsf{diff}}}{\sigma_c^{\mathsf{same}}} \right)}$$

As an application, we assume that we have scores coming from three cameras with the following experimental parameters:

same	left	center	right	diff	left	center	right
μ	0.141	0.148	0.151	μ	0.112	0.111	0.129
σ	0.037	0.032	0.043	σ	0.020	0.014	0.026

In Fig. 9, we plotted the pdf for the central camera. We obtain $m_{\mathsf{same}} \approx \frac{-\ln \mathsf{FAR}_{\mathsf{target}}}{7.5}$. For $\mathsf{FAR}_{\mathsf{target}} = 0.1\%$, this is $m_{\mathsf{same}} \approx 0.9$. In Fig. 9, we can see the curve of $\varDelta\mathsf{lpdf}$ for the central camera. Cumulated with the two others, we easily reach $-\ln 0.1\% \approx 6.9$.

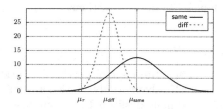
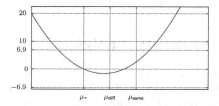

Fig. 9. Probability density (left) and $\varDelta\mathsf{lpdf}$ (right) of the score from the central camera.eps

This theory has one limitation though: it assumes a bad distribution coming from taking the biometric features of two random different persons. If an adversary tries another distribution of pictures (like a totally white picture), he may have better chances than what our analysis shows. It is typically a problem when the score is very low. In Fig. 9, we can see that for very low scores, the same distribution becomes more likely than the diff one. We let μ_τ be the lower crossing point on the two probability density functions. We decide to skip score_i whenever $(\mathsf{score}_i)_{\mathsf{center}} < \mu_\tau$. It does not deny access. It only declares this capture unusable. Hence, its effect is to divide m_{same} by $\mathrm{Pr}_{\mathsf{same}}[\mu > \mu_\tau]$. In our case, $\mu_t = 0.0739$ and this increases m_{same} by only 1.04%. Finally, our decision algorithm works as on Fig. 10.

Given n samples $\mathsf{temp}_1, \ldots, \mathsf{temp}_n$ (typically, $n = 3$), we use the algorithm on Fig. 10 to select the best temp_i as the reference one.

Decision Algorithm

input: hist

1: acc ← 0
2: **for** $i = 1$ to |hist| **do**
3:     **if** $(\text{score}_i)_\text{center} \geq \mu_\tau$ **then**
4:         **for** $c \in \{\text{left}, \text{center}, \text{right}\}$ **do**
5:             acc ← acc + $\Delta\text{lpdf}_c((\text{score}_i)_c)$
6:         **end for**
7:     **end if**
8: **end for**
9: **if** acc $\geq$ $-\ln \text{FAR}_\text{target}$ **then return** "accept"
10: **if** acc $\leq \ln \text{FRR}_\text{target}$ **then return** "reject"
11: **return** "undecided"

Reference Template Selection Algorithm

Input $(\text{temp}_1, \ldots, \text{temp}_n)$:

1:     $L = \{\text{temp}_1, \ldots, \text{temp}_n\}$
2: **while** $\#L > 1$ **do**
3:     find $x \in L$ such that $\sum_{y \in L - \{x\}} \text{score}(x, y)$ is minimal
4:     remove x from L
5: **end while**
6: output L

Fig. 10. Decision and reference template selection algorithms.

5   Security Analysis

The security model assumes that the adversary has full control on the network and can make participants launch protocols with adversarially chosen inputs. Desktops **D**, scanner **B**, the server **S**, and enrollment desktop **E** are supposed to be honest in AC. The **D** ↔ **L** link is assumed to be secure and out of the scope of this security analysis. As discussed below, **B** is accessible to only one **D** but communication may leak. That is, in our security games, the adversary plays with every **D**, **E**, **B**, **S** with chosen input and sits in the middle of communication between them. He can also require a chosen user to have his finger scanned on a chosen **B**.

We list our security results. Due to lack of space, we only informally state our security results here. Formal models, results, and proofs are provided in the full version of this article [6].

We assume that PKC is INDCCA-secure, DSS is EFCMA-secure, AEAD is indistinguishable from an ideal primitive against chosen plaintext and ciphertext attacks, and H is collision-resistant. We prove that

- (enrollment) if **E** says that pseudo was successfully enrolled with **B**, it must be the case that **S** did so, and if **S** enrolls pseudo from **B**, it must be because **E** asked for it and **B** followed (however, **E** may fail before announcing a success);
- (AC) if **D** granted access to pseudo from **B**, it is certainly the case that its policy in DB_1 validated a sequence of captures from **B**;
- (privacy of templates) the adversary cannot extract information about the biometric templates taken from **B**, even if **E** is malicious;
- (privacy of pseudo) a semi-passive adversary cannot distinguish the pseudo of a user from a random one (however, an active adversary could simulate **D** and test a pseudo for a user).

Note that even though the biometric template could be known by the adversary (for instance, from another organization who enrolled the same user and who is malicious), the security of **B** prevents this template to be used.

One limitation of our model is that **D** does not authenticate to **B**. Hence, a user scanning on **B** is not sure it is in context of a request from **D**. We could have made it more secure, either by adding a PKI for **D** (which we did not want), or by using the help of the user to check that a random number selected by **D** displays the same on **D** and **B**. Eventually, **B** is connected to **D** by a unique (USB) cable so we concluded it was not worth making the protocol heavier.

6 Implementation Results

We implemented the entire BioLocker mechanism from enrollment to the biometric AC for a hospital. The IT department of the hospital has run the proof of concept to test the reliability, performance, and security of BioLocker with its employees. Our implementation choices were made to be compatible with the infrastructure of the hospital. They use Active Directory for password authentication on Windows 7/10 computers. We did not change any settings of their password authentication and integrated our protocols on top of the Windows password authentication. This means that in the login session to access the desktops, we implemented another layer of authentication through biometric scanners that run when password authentication succeeds.

The current prototype of our scanner (which is shown in Fig. 2) is based on a Raspberry Pi PI3.[3] The communication with the scanner happens through Ethernet, USB or WiFi. The scanning of the finger is made via infrared lights and three cameras placed with different angles. It happens when the user inserts her finger in a hole where the top is filled with a rack of infrared LEDs and the bottom has the cameras. The scanner interacts with its user through color LEDs and a small color display. The infrared LEDs illuminate a finger and three cameras take QVGA images of the finger from three different angles.

When prompted to scan a finger, the scanner waits until a presence sensor detects a finger. As each LED corresponds to a region of the picture, we dynamically adjust by software the power of each LED so that the histogram of the corresponding region is optimal. Then, the cameras take a picture. Images are in gray-scale of size 320×240. They are stored in png format with a file size of one image being around 70 KB in total.

We implemented the enrollment station in pure python. For communications, we chose REST POST requests with JSON payload. We chose the Flask python framework to handle these requests on **D**, **B**, and **S**.

For the AC protocol, we implemented **S** in python and the code on **B** for enrollment was reusable. The choice we made for the authentication on **D** which is a Windows machine is a tool called pGina. It is a credential provider that supports custom plugins. The code is in C#. Alternatively, one could create a custom credential provider.

For PKC, we use 2048-bits RSA-OAEP and AES-GCM. AES-GCM is implemented with 128-bit key size, 128-bit Mac/Tag size, and 128- bit IV/Nonce. The

---

[3] A new version is currently under development.

additional data is either empty, 6 bytes or a hash. For hash, we use SHA256. For DSS, we use 2048-bits RSA-PSS.

For the biometric algorithms, we use the Bob library [1,2].

The performance of both enrollment station and AC is fairly fast. Except the time for users to type information and insert fingers, enrollment takes about 3 s when we take 3 fingervein images triplets. (Roughly, time is evenly split between Stage 1 and Stage 2.) AC is very fast running under 2 s after the user has inserted her finger. (Stage 1 is negligible as it takes 2 ms. Stage 2 takes about 500 ms. Stage 3 is the bottleneck part taking 1225 ms.) Given that more optimization can be done, we find these figures very practical.

The correct fingers are always accepted, almost all the time at the very first capture. Hence, the experimental FRR is close to 0%, with good complexity. Incorrect fingers are always rejected, typically after 1, 2, or 3 captures (but it is reasonable if the complexity is high when we scan incorrect fingers). Hence, the experimental FAR is close to 0% as well.

7 Conclusion

We designed a secure access control mechanism with biometry integration with privacy protection. We implemented a proof of concept with 3D fingervein biometry and demonstrated that this technique can be deployed in a hospital. As future work, we aim at making a systematic survey on a big scale to measure the effective FAR and FRR. We also want to study the evolution of biometry on a long time-scale. We should also revisit the spoofing attacks on fingervein [21] to see how effective is our 3D technique. Finally, we plan to strengthen privacy on the server side by having a distributed database and multiparty matching.

Acknowledgement. The authors are grateful to Lambert Sonna and the Global ID SA company for having sponsored this project. We also thank Dóra Neubrandt for her contribution in biometric acquisition and extraction.

References

1. Anjos, A., Günther, M., de Freitas Pereira, T., Korshunov, P., Mohammadi, A., Marcel, S.: Continuously reproducing toolchains in pattern recognition and machine learning experiments. In: International Conference on Machine Learning (ICML), August 2017
2. Anjos, A., El Shafey, L., Wallace, R., Günther, M., McCool, C., Marcel, S.: Bob: a free signal processing and machine learning toolbox for researchers. In: 20th ACM Conference on Multimedia Systems (ACMMM), Nara, Japan, October 2012
3. Balli, F., Durak, F.B., Vaudenay, S.: BioID: a privacy-friendly identity document. In: Mauw, S., Conti, M. (eds.) STM 2019. LNCS, vol. 11738, pp. 53–70. Springer, Cham (2019). https://doi.org/10.1007/978-3-030-31511-5_4
4. Canvel, B., Hiltgen, A., Vaudenay, S., Vuagnoux, M.: Password interception in a SSL/TLS channel. In: Boneh, D. (ed.) CRYPTO 2003. LNCS, vol. 2729, pp. 583–599. Springer, Heidelberg (2003). https://doi.org/10.1007/978-3-540-45146-4_34

5. Daas, S., Boughazi, M., Sedhane, M., Bouledjfane, B.: A review of finger vein biometrics authentication system. In: 2018 International Conference on Applied Smart Systems (ICASS), pp. 1–6, November 2018

6. Durak, F.B., Huguenin-Dumittan, L., Vaudenay, S.: BioLocker: a practical biometric authentication mechanism based on 3D fingervein. Cryptology ePrint Archive, Report 2020/453 (2020). https://eprint.iacr.org/2020/453

7. Fahmy, M.S., Atyia, A.F., Elfouly, R.S.: Biometric fusion using enhanced SVM classification. In: 2008 International Conference on Intelligent Information Hiding and Multimedia Signal Processing, pp. 1043–1048, August 2008

8. Junod, P.: On the optimality of linear, differential, and sequential Distinguishers. In: Biham, E. (ed.) EUROCRYPT 2003. LNCS, vol. 2656, pp. 17–32. Springer, Heidelberg (2003). https://doi.org/10.1007/3-540-39200-9_2

9. Kabir, W., Ahmad, M.O., Swamy, M.N.S.: Normalization and weighting techniques based on genuine-impostor score fusion in multi-biometric systems. IEEE Trans. Inf. Forensics Secur. **13**(8), 1989–2000 (2018)

10. Kang, W., Liu, H., Luo, W., Deng, F.: Study of a full-view 3D finger vein verification technique. IEEE Trans. Inf. Forensics Secur. **15**, 1175–1189 (2020)

11. Lee, E.C., Lee, H.C., Park, K.R.: Finger vein recognition using minutia-based alignment and local binary pattern-based feature extraction. Int. J. Imag. Syst. Technol. **19**(3), 179–186 (2009)

12. Lumini, A., Nanni, L.: Overview of the combination of biometric matchers. Inf. Fusion **33**, 71–85 (2017)

13. Ma, Y., Cukic, B., Singh, H.: A classification approach to multi-biometric score fusion. In: Kanade, T., Jain, A., Ratha, N.K. (eds.) AVBPA 2005. LNCS, vol. 3546, pp. 484–493. Springer, Heidelberg (2005). https://doi.org/10.1007/11527923_50

14. Miura, N., Nagasaka, A., Miyatake, T.: Feature extraction of finger-vein patterns based on repeated line tracking and its application to personal identification. Mach. Vision Appl. **15**(4), 194–203 (2004)

15. Miura, N., Nagasaka, A., Miyatake, T.: Extraction of finger-vein patterns using maximum curvature points in image profiles. IEICE Trans. **90-D**(8), 1185–1194 (2007)

16. Nandakumar, K., Chen, Y., Dass, S.C., Jain, A.: Likelihood ratio-based biometric score fusion. IEEE Trans. Pattern Anal. Mach. Intell. **30**(2), 342–347 (2008)

17. Ni, L., Zhang, Y., Liu, S., Huang, H., Li, W.: A decision reliability ratio based fusion scheme for biometric verification. In: Proceedings of the 9th International Conference on Bioinformatics and Biomedical Technology, ICBBT 2017, New York, NY, USA, pp. 16–21. ACM (2017)

18. Shaheed, K., Liu, H., Yang, G., Qureshi, I., Gou, J., Yin, Y.: A systematic review of finger vein recognition techniques. Information **9**(9), 213 (2018)

19. Siegmund, D.: Sequential Analysis: Tests and Confidence Intervals. Springer Series in Statistics. Springer, New York (1985). https://doi.org/10.1007/978-1-4757-1862-1

20. Syazana-Itqan, K., Syafeeza, A.R., Saad, N.M., Hamid, N.A., Saad, W.H.B.M.: A review of finger-vein biometrics identification approaches. Indian J. Sci. Technol. **9**(32), 1–9 (2016)

21. Tome, P., Vanoni, M., Marcel, S.: On the vulnerability of finger vein recognition to spoofing. In: Brömme, A., Busch, C. (eds.) Proceedings of the 13th International Conference of the Biometrics Special Interest Group, BIOSIG 2014, Volume 230 of Lecture Notes in Informatics, Darmstadt, Germany, 10–12 September 2014, pp. 111–120. Gesellschaft für Informatik (2014)

22. Ton, B.T., Veldhuis, R.N.J.: A high quality finger vascular pattern dataset collected using a custom designed capturing device. In: Fiérrez, J., Kumar, A., Vatsa, M., Veldhuis, R.N.J., Ortega-Garcia, J. (eds.) International Conference on Biometrics, ICB 2013, 4–7 June 2013, Madrid, Spain, pp. 1–5. IEEE (2013)
23. Ulery, B., Hicklin, A., Watson, C., Fellner, W., Hallinan, P.: Studies of biometric fusion. NIST Interagency Report, 7346 (2006)
24. Wang, Y., Xie, W., Xiaojie, Yu., Shark, L.-K.: An automatic physical access control system based on hand vein biometric identification. IEEE Trans. Consum. Electron. **61**(3), 320–327 (2015)
25. Yang, W., et al.: Securing mobile healthcare data: a smart card based cancelable finger-vein bio-cryptosystem. IEEE Access **6**, 36939–36947 (2018)

Privacy and Anonymity

Accelerating Forward and Backward Private Searchable Encryption Using Trusted Execution

Viet Vo[1,2(✉)], Shangqi Lai[1,2], Xingliang Yuan[1(✉)], Shi-Feng Sun[1],
Surya Nepal[2], and Joseph K. Liu[1]

[1] Monash University, Melbourne, Australia
{Viet.Vo,Shangqi.Lai,Xingliang.Yuan,Shifeng.Sun,Joseph.Liu}@monash.edu
[2] Data61, CSIRO, Sydney, Australia
Surya.Nepal@data61.csiro.au

Abstract. Searchable encryption (SE) is one of the key enablers for building encrypted databases. It allows a cloud server to search over encrypted data without decryption. Dynamic SE additionally includes data addition and deletion operations to enrich the functions of encrypted databases. Recent attacks exploiting the leakage in dynamic operations drive the rapid development of SE schemes revealing less information while performing updates; they are also known as forward and backward private SE. Newly added data is no longer linkable to queries issued before, and deleted data is no longer searchable in queries issued later. However, those advanced SE schemes reduce the efficiency of SE, especially in the communication cost between the client and server. In this paper, we resort to the hardware-assisted solution, aka Intel SGX, to ease the above bottleneck. Our key idea is to leverage SGX to take over most tasks of the client, i.e., tracking keyword states along with data addition and caching deleted data. However, handling large datasets is non-trivial due to the I/O and memory constraints of SGX. We further develop batch data processing and state compression techniques to reduce the communication overhead between the SGX and untrusted server and minimise the memory footprint within the enclave. We conduct a comprehensive set of evaluations on both synthetic and real-world datasets, which confirm that our designs outperform the prior art.

1 Introduction

Searchable encryption (SE) [10,20] is designed to enable a user to outsource her data to remote servers (i.e., cloud) securely while preserving search functionalities. It is considered as the most promising solution to build encrypted databases defending against data breaches. Generic solutions like fully homomorphic encryption, multi-party computation, and oblivious RAM (ORAM) achieve strong security but introducing considerable computational and communication overhead. Property-preserving encryption like deterministic encryption and order-preserving/revealing encryption is efficient and legacy compatible in

© Springer Nature Switzerland AG 2020
M. Conti et al. (Eds.): ACNS 2020, LNCS 12147, pp. 83–103, 2020.
https://doi.org/10.1007/978-3-030-57878-7_5

databases, but those solutions are not secure in practice [2]. The reasonable security and performance tradeoff brought by SE continuously drives the rapid development of new SE schemes with more functionalities [27], and improved security [4,5,15].

In [7], Cash et al. introduced the concept of active attacks against dynamic SE; the leakage in data update operations can be exploited to compromise the claimed security of SE. After that, Zhang et al. [25] proposed the first instantiation of active attacks called file-injection attacks through the exploitation of the leakage in data addition. This work raises a natural question: whether a dynamic SE scheme with less leakage can be designed to mitigate existing and even prevent prospective active attacks. To address this question, forward and backward private SE schemes [4,5,13,22] have drawn much attention recently.

In dynamic SE, the notion of forward privacy means that the linkability between newly added data and previously issued search queries should be hidden against the server, and the notion of backward privacy means that the linkability between deleted data and search queries after deletion should be hidden. To achieve higher security for SE, the efficiency of SE is compromised. Existing forward and backward private SE schemes [5,13,22] introduce large overhead in storage and computation at both client and server, and/or increase the client-server interaction. In order to maintain the efficiency of SE, an alternative approach is to employ the hardware-assisted solution, i.e., Intel SGX, where native code and data can be executed in a trusted and isolated execution environment. Recent work in ORAM powered by SGX [16] demonstrates that SGX can be treated as a delegate of clients, so as to ease the overhead of client storage and computation, and reduce the communication cost between the client and server.

Amjad et al. [1] proposed the first forward and backward private SE schemes using SGX. As generic ORAM or ORAM-like data structures can natively be adapted to achieve the strongest forward and backward privacy in SE (i.e., Type-I backward privacy [5]), one of their schemes is built from ORAM, where data addition and deletion are completely oblivious to the server [1]. It is noteworthy that such an approach could still be inefficient due to the high I/O complexity between the SGX and server. Like prior forward and backward private SE studies, Amjad et al. also proposed an efficient scheme (i.e., Type-II [5]) that trades security for higher efficiency named Bunker-B [1]. Timestamps of update operations will not be exposed, while the rounds of interaction between the SGX and server can be reduced. In this work, we are interested in designs with forward and Type-II backward privacy due to its practical balance between security and efficiency.

Unfortunately, only the theoretical construction of Bunker-B is given in [1], and we observe that it is not scalable, especially when handling large datasets. First, deletion operations are realised via insertion operations, which will (a) incur large communication costs between the SGX and server, i.e., the number of *ocalls* scales with the number of deletions, and (b) increase search latency, because all deleted data needs to be retrieved, decrypted, and filtered out from the search results. Second, re-encryption is adopted after each search for forward and backward privacy, which will also incur long search latency and affect the performance of concurrent queries. The reason is that if deleted documents are only a small portion of the matched results, most of the results (non-deleted ones) need to be re-encrypted and re-inserted to the database. More detailed analysis can be found in Sect. 5.

To avoid the potential performance bottleneck introduced by SGX, in this paper, we devise forward and backward private SE schemes from a simple yet effective approach. Our idea is to leverage the SGX enclave to fully act as the client. The enclave will cache both the keyword state and the deletions, so as to reduce the communication cost and roundtrips between the SGX and server in search, addition, and deletion operations, and make the client almost free in computation and storage. Furthermore, we propose several optimisations to accelerate the performance, including batch document processing, state compression via Bloom filter, and memory efficient implementation.

Contributions: Our contributions in this paper can be summarised as follows:

- We design and implement two forward and backward private SE schemes, named SGX-SE1 and SGX-SE2. By using SGX, the communication cost between the client and server of achieving forward and backward privacy in SE is significantly reduced.
- Both SGX-SE1 and SGX-SE2 leverage the SGX enclave to carefully track keyword states and document deletions, in order to minimise the communication overhead between the SGX and untrusted memory. In particular, SGX-SE2 is an optimised version of SGX-SE1 by employing Bloom filter to compress the information of deletions, which speeds up the search operations and boosts the capacity of batch processing in addition and deletion.
- We formalise the security model of our schemes and perform security analysis accordingly.
- We conduct comprehensive evaluations on both synthetic and real-world datasets. Our experiments show that the latest art Bunker-B takes $10\times$ more *ecall/ocalls* than our schemes SGX-SE1 and SGX-SE2 when inserting 10^6 documents. Even more, Bunker-B needs $30\times$ *ecall/ocalls* when deleting 25% of the above documents. W.r.t. search latency, SGX-SE1 and SGX-SE2 are 30% and $2\times$ faster than Bunker-B, respectively.

2   Related Work

Searchable Encryption: Song et al. [20] presented the first searchable encryption (SE) to enable search over encrypted documents. After that, Curtmola et al. [10] and Kamara et al. [14] formalised the security definitions for static and dynamic SE, respectively, and proposed schemes with sublinear search time. Since SSE was formalised, a long line of studies has been proposed to improve query efficiency [8] and support expressive queries [27].

Forward and Backward Privacy in SE: In dynamic SE, forward privacy means data additions do not reveal their associations to any query made in the past, and deleted documents cannot be accessed via any post queries. Forward privacy has been studied widely to mitigate file-injection attacks [4, 21, 25]. Backward privacy has received less attention [5, 13, 22, 26]. There are three types of backward privacy from Type-I to Type-III in the descending order of security. However, strong backward private (Type-I and Type-II) schemes are known to be inefficient in computation and communication overhead, as shown in [5, 13].

Encrypted Search with Trusted Execution: Another line of research in this field [1, 9, 12, 16] enabling search over encrypted data is to leverage hardware-assisted trusted execution environment (TEE). In general, TEE such as Intel SGX can reduce the network roundtrips between the client and server and enrich the database functions in the encrypted domain. Fuhry et al. [12] proposed HardIDX that organises database index in a B^+-tree structure and utilises enclave to traverse a subset of the tree nodes to do searches. Later, Mishra et al. [16] designed a doubly-oblivious SE scheme that supports inserts and deletes, named Oblix. In this scheme, one oblivious data index resides in the enclave to map the search index of each keyword to a location in another oblivious structure located in untrusted memory. However, the performance of their implementation on large databases is less efficient due to the fact of using ORAM. Regarding SE, Borges et al. [3] migrated secure computation to the enclave to improve the search efficiency of SE boolean queries. When two or more keywords are queried, the result set can be unionised or intersected within the enclave. Note that this work focuses on a different problem with ours. Very recently, Amjad et al. [1] proposed three schemes to enable single-keyword query with different search leakage (i.e., information that the server can learn about the query and data). However, the practical performance of these schemes has not been investigated. Meanwhile, Ren et al. [18] proposed a volume-hiding range query scheme via SGX.

3   Background

3.1   Intel SGX

Intel SGX is a set of x86 instructions designed for improving the security of application code and data. On SGX-enabled platforms, ones need to partition the application into both trusted part and untrusted part. The trusted part, dubbed enclave, is located in a dedicated memory portion of physical RAM with strong protection enforced by SGX. The untrusted part is executed as an ordinary process and can invoke the enclave only through the well-defined interface, named *ecall*, while the enclave can encrypt clear data and send to untrusted code via the interface named *ocall*. Furthermore, decryption and integrity checks are performed when the data is loaded inside the enclave. All other software, including OS, privileged software, hypervisor, and firmware cannot access the enclave's memory. The actual memory for storing data in the enclave is only up to 96 MB. Above that, SGX will automatically apply page swapping. SGX also has a remote attestation feature that allows to verify the creation of enclaves on a remote server and to create a secure communication channel to the enclaves.

There has been a lot of existing SGX side-channel attacks such as hardware side-channels attacks [19,24]. However, we are also aware that the security in future SGX versions will be improved [6].

3.2   Dynamic Searchable Symmetric Encryption

In this section, we briefly overview dynamic SE and the notion of forward and backward privacy in dynamic SE. Following the verbatim in [4,5], let DB represent a database of documents, and each document doc with a unique identifier id is a variable-length set of unique keywords. We use $DB(w)$ to present the set of documents where keyword w occurs. The total number of keyword-document pairs is denoted by N, W is the total number of distinct keywords in DB. All N keyword-document pairs are stored in an index M_I, which is a dictionary structure mapping each unique keyword w to a list of matching documents in $DB(w)$. The encrypted database, named EDB is a collection of encrypted documents. A dynamic SE scheme $\Sigma = (\mathsf{Setup}, \mathsf{Search}, \mathsf{Update})$ consists of three protocols between a client and a server as follows:

$\mathsf{Setup}(1^\lambda, DB)$: The protocol inputs a security parameter λ and outputs a secret key K, a state ST for the client, and an encrypted database EDB.

$\mathsf{Search}(K, w, ST; EDB)$: The protocol allows to query w based on the state ST, the secret key K and the state ST from the client, and the encrypted database EDB from the server. After that, it outputs the search result Res.

$\mathsf{Update}(K, (\mathsf{op}, \mathsf{in}), ST; EDB)$: The protocol takes K, ST, an input in associated with an operation op from the client, and EDB, where $\mathsf{op} \in \{add, del\}$ and in consists of a document identifier id and a set of keywords in that document. Then, the protocol inserts or removes in from EDB upon op.

Giving a list of queries Q sent by the client, the server records the timestamps u for every query with $Q = \{q : q = (u, w) \text{ or } (u, \mathsf{op}, \mathsf{in})\}$. Following the verbatim from [4,5], we let $\mathsf{TimeDB}(w)$ be the access pattern which consists of the non-deleted documents *currently* matching w and the timestamps of inserting them to the database. Formally,

$$\mathsf{TimeDB}(w) = \{(u, id) : (u, add, (w, id)) \in Q \\ \text{and } \forall u', (u', del, (w, id)) \notin Q\}$$

and let $\mathsf{Updates}(w)$ be the list of timestamps of updates:

$$\mathsf{Updates}(w) = \{u : (u, \mathsf{op}, (w, id)) \in Q\}$$

There are two security properties based on the leakage function of dynamic SE [5]. The *forward privacy* ensures that each update leaks no information about the keyword that was queried in the past and currently is in the document to be updated. The *backward privacy* guarantees that when a keyword-document pair (w, id) is added and then deleted, subsequent searches on w do not reveal *id.* There are three types of *backward privacy* with varying levels of leakages from Type-I to Type-III introduced in [5]. Type-I backward privacy is the most secure. It only reveals what time the current (non-deleted) documents matching to w added (i.e., TimeDB(w)). Type-II additionally leaks what time updates on w made, presented as $\{\mathsf{TimeDB}(w), \mathsf{Updates}(w)\}$. In a less secure manner, Type-III inherits the leakage of Type-II and additionally reveals which addition updates cancel which deletion updates.

Current Type-II schemes Fides [5] and Mitra [13] require multiple roundtrips and high communication cost, while Horus [13] relies on Path-ORAM. Until recently, Amjad et al. [1] proposed three SGX-supported schemes, including the Type-I scheme Fort, Type-II scheme Bunker-B, and Type-III scheme Bunker-A. However, Fort requires an oblivious map (OMAP) similar to the one in Orion [13] to do the update, causing high computation overhead. Bunker-A [1] improves the update computation, but it downgrades the security guarantees. In contrast, Bunker-B is designed with a good tradeoff in computation/communication cost and security guarantees. We will later compare the performance of Bunker-B with our schemes in Sect. 5.

4   Our Proposed Schemes

We present the overview of our proposed schemes, as shown in Fig. 1. After that, we detail our scheme design intuition by analysing previous SGX-supported schemes [1] in terms of communication/computation overhead and then highlight our technical solution. Finally, we present SGX-SE1 and SGX-SE2 with corresponding protocols.

4.1   System Overview

The design involves three entities: the client (who is the data owner and therefore trusted), the untrusted server, and the trusted SGX enclave within the server. The system flow involves 9 steps.

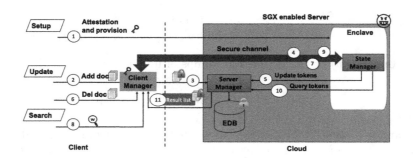

Fig. 1. High level design

At step 1, the client uses the SGX attestation feature to authenticate the enclave and establish a secure channel with the enclave. The client then provisions a secret key K to the enclave through this channel. This completes the Setup protocol of our proposed protocol. Note that this operation does not deploy any EDB to the server as in dynamic SE schemes [5]. Instead, we consider that the client outsources documents to the server via Update operations later.

At step 2, giving a document with a unique identifier id, the *Client Manager* encrypts the document with the key K and sends the encrypted version of the document to the *Server Manager* (see step 3). The encrypted version with its id is then inserted to EDB. After that, the *Client Manager* sends the original document to the *State Manager* located in the enclave via the secure channel (see step 4). At this step, the *State Manager* performs cryptographic operations to generate update tokens that will be sent to *Server Manager* (see step 5). The tokens are used to update the encrypted index of dynamic SE located in the *Server Manager*. Note that traditional dynamic SE schemes [5,8,22] often consider EDB as the underlying encrypted index of dynamic SE, and omit the data structure storing encrypted documents. Here, we locate them separately to avoid that ambiguity, i.e., the index of dynamic SE M_I is located in *Server Manager*, and encrypted documents reside in EDB as an encrypted document repository, respectively. To delete a document with a given id (step 6), the *Client Manager* directly sends the document id to the *State Manager* (see step 7).

At step 8, the client wants to search documents matching a given query keyword w. The *Client Manager* will send the keyword w to the *State Manager* (see step 9). Then, the *State Manager* computes query tokens and excludes the tokens for deleted documents according to the deletion information from step 6. Later, the *State Manager* sends them to the *Server Manager* (in step 10). The *Server Manager* will search over the received tokens and return the list of encrypted matching documents back to the *Client Manager*. At that stage, the encrypted documents are decrypted with K.

4.2 Assumptions and Threat Models

Our Assumptions with Intel SGX: We assume that SGX behaves correctly, (i.e., there are no hardware bugs or backdoors), and the preset code and data inside the enclave are protected. Also, the communication between the client and the enclave relies on the secure channel created during SGX attestation. Like many other SGX applications [11,16], side-channel attacks [19,24] against SGX are out of our scope. Denial-of-service (DoS) attacks are also out of our focus, i.e., the enclave is always available whenever the client invokes or queries. Finally, we assume that all the used cryptographic primitives and libraries of SGX are trusted.

Threat Models: Like existing work [1,12], we consider a semi-honest but powerful attacker at the server-side. Although the attacker will not deviate from the protocol, he/she can gain full access over software stack outside of the enclave, OS and hypervisor, as well as hardware components in the server except for the processor package. In particular, the attacker can observe memory addresses and (encrypted) data on the memory bus, in memory, or in EDB to generate data access patterns. Additionally, the attacker can log the time when these memory manipulations happen. The goal of the attacker is to learn extra information about the encrypted database from the leakage both revealed by hardware and the leakage function defined in SSE. See our full version for security analysis [23].

4.3   Design Intuition

As mentioned, Amjad et al. [1] proposed three backward private SGX-supported schemes: the Type-I scheme Fort, Type-II scheme Bunker-B, and Type-III scheme Bunker-A. The performance and security overview of these schemes can be found in our full version [23]. Fort is the most secure while still relying on ORAM and thus we exclude it in this work due to its overhead. Bunker-A does not perform re-encryption and re-insertion after search and thus only achieves Type-III backward privacy. However, it still treats deletion as insertion, just like Bunker-B. Therefore, we only analyse the limitations of Bunker-B as follows.

Performance Analysis of Prior Work: The Update and Search protocols of Bunker-B are summarily presented in our full version [23]. Bunker-B only requires $O(1)$ update computation complexity and a_w update *ocalls*. For each (w, id), Bunker-B lets the enclave follow the same routine to generate tokens for addition and deletion and uses the generated tokens to update M_I on the server. However, it causes high computation complexity $O(a_w)$ and involves a large number of roundtrips (i.e., a_w) during the search. In the Search protocol, the core idea of Bunker-B is to let the enclave read all records (associated with *add* or *del*) in M_I corresponding to the keyword. Then, the enclave decrypts them and filters deleted *ids* based on the operation. After query, the enclave re-encrypts non-deleted ids and sends the newly generated tokens to the server for updates. We have implemented Bunker-B (see Sect. 5) and found that the scheme also has other limitations in practice as follows:

Intensive Ecall/Ocall Usage: Giving a document doc with an identifier id and M unique keywords to the server, Bunker-B repeatedly performs the Update protocol by using M *ecalls* and then the same number of *ocalls* to insert tokens to the index map M_I. It indicates that the number of *ecall/ocall* for Bunker-B is linear to the keyword-document pairs for updates. In practice, a dataset can include a large number of keyword-document pairs ($>10^7$). As a result, Bunker-B takes $12\,\mu s$ to insert one (w, id) pair, and 2.36×10^7 *ecall/ocalls* to insert 10^6 documents to the database. Similarly, deleting a doc in Bunker-B is the same as the addition, with the exception that the tokens contain $op = del$. Experimentally, Bunker-B takes 1.98×10^8 *ecall/ocalls* to delete 2.5×10^5 documents. The practical performance of Bunker-B can be found in Sect. 5. We also note that Bunker-B only supports deletion updates on the index map M_I without considering deleting real documents [1].

Search Latency: The re-encryption on non-deleted *id*s per search makes Bunker-B inefficient. In particular, when the number of those *id*s is large and the deleted ones is a small portion (adding 10^6 documents and deleting 25% documents), Bunker-B takes 3.2 s to query a keyword (see Sect. 5).

Technical Highlights: Motivated by the limitations of Bunker-B, we design SGX-SE1 and SGX-SE2 that are Type-II backward private schemes with: (1) reduced number of *ecall/ocall* when the client wants to add/delete a document, (2) reduced search roundtrips, and (3) accelerated enclave's computation in search.

We achieve (1) by allowing the client to transfer the document to the enclave for document addition, instead of transferring (w, id) pairs. This design reduces the number of *ecall*s to 1. We then use the enclave to store the latest states ST of all keywords, where the state of a keyword w is $ST[w] = count$. As a result, the enclave is able to generate addition tokens based on ST. Our experiments (see Sect. 5) show that this design improves 2× the addition throughput compared to Bunker-B. We note that it is negligible to store ST in the enclave since it costs less than 6 MB to store the states of all keywords in the American dictionary of English[1] (assuming each keyword state item can take up 18 bytes in a dictionary map). Additionally, our scheme only requires 1 *ecall* if the client deletes a document, by transferring that document id to the enclave.

W.r.t. (2), the SGX-SE1 scheme reduces the search roundtrips between the enclave and the server to $(d + d_w)$. The basic idea behind SGX-SE1 is to let the enclave cache the mapping between w and the deleted document *id*s. In particular, the enclave loads and decrypts d deleted documents to extract the mapping (w, id). It cleans the memory after loading each deleted document to avoid the memory bottleneck. After that, the enclave needs d_w roundtrips to retrieve the *counters* when the enclave filters those deleted *id*s. SGX-SE2 is more optimal by requiring only d_w roundtrips without the need for loading d deleted documents. To do this, SGX-SE2 uses a Bloom filter BF to store the mapping (w, id) within the enclave. Note that the BF can track 1.18×10^7 (w, id) pairs with the storage cost of 34 MB enclave memory[2] with the false positive probability $P_e = 10^{-4}$. Our experiments (see Sect. 5) show that the search latency of SGX-SE1 is 30% faster than Bunker-B after inserting 10^6 documents and caching 2.5×10^5 deleted documents. Moreover, SGX-SE2 is 2× faster than Bunker-B for the query after deleting 25% documents.

W.r.t. (3), the proposed SGX-SE1 scheme improves the search computation complexity to $O(n_w + d)$. We note that the complexity is even amortised if there is no deletion updates between a sequence of queries. The reason is that the enclave only loads d document for the first query to update the mapping of all keywords in ST with the deleted documents. Furthermore, the search computation complexity of SGX-SE2 is only $O(n_w)$. We note that testing the membership of d documents in the BF is v_d where v is the vector of BF. Our experiments (see Sect. 5) show that Bunker-B takes 3.2s for queries after inserting

---

[1] The dictionary contains about 300,000 common and obsolete keywords.
[2] 1.18×10^7 pairs $\approx 386×$ `Hamlet` tragedy written by William Shakespeare.

Setup(1^λ)		14:	$k_{id} \leftarrow H_1(k_w, c)$;		6:	$doc_i \leftarrow$ Dec(k_f, f_i);
Client:		15:	$(u,v) \leftarrow (H_2(k_w,c),$ Enc(k_{id}, id))	7:	if w in doc_i then
1: $k_\Sigma, k_f \xleftarrow{\$} \{0,1\}^\lambda$;		16:	add (u,v) to T_1;		8:	$D[w] \leftarrow id_i \cup D[w]$;
2: Launch a remote attestation;		17:	$(u',v') \leftarrow (H_3(k_w, id),$ Enc(k_c, c))	9:	delete $R[id_i]$;
3: Establish a secure channel;		18:	add (u',v') to T_2;		10:	end if
4: Send $K = (k_\Sigma, k_f)$ to *Enclave*;		19:	$ST[w] \leftarrow c$;		11:	end foreach
Enclave:		20:	end foreach		12:	foreach id in $D[w]$ do
5: Initialise maps ST and D;		21:	send (T_1, T_2) to *Server*;		13:	$u' \leftarrow H_3(k_w, id)$;
6: Initialise a list d;		22:	reset T_1 and T_2;		14:	$v' \leftarrow M_c[u']$;
7: Initialise tuples T_1 and T_2;		23:	else // op = del		15:	$c \leftarrow$ Dec(k_c, v');
8: Receive $K = (k_\Sigma, k_f)$;		24:	add id to d;		16:	$st_{w_c} \leftarrow \{c\} \cup st_{w_c}$;
Server:		25:	end if		17:	delete $M_c[u']$;
9: Initialise maps M_I and M_c;		*Server:*		18:	end foreach
10: Initialise a repository R;		26:	// if op = add		19:	$st_{w_c} \leftarrow \{0,\ldots, ST[w]\} \setminus st_{w_c}$
Update(op,in)		27:	receive (id, f) from *Client*;		20:	foreach c in st_{w_c} do
Client:		28:	$R[id] \leftarrow f$;		21:	$u \leftarrow H_2(k_w, c)$;
1: if op = add then		29:	receive (T_1,T_2) from *Enclave*;		22:	$k_{id} \leftarrow H_1(k_w, c)$;
2: $f \leftarrow$ Enc(k_f,doc);		30:	foreach (u,v) in T_1 do		23:	$Q_w \leftarrow \{(u, k_{id})\} \cup Q_w$;
3: send (id, f) to *Server*;		31:	$M_I[u] \leftarrow v$;		24:	end foreach
4: end if		32:	end foreach		25:	send Q_w to *Server*;
5: send (op,id) to *Enclave*		33:	foreach (u',v') in T_2 do		26:	delete $D[w]$;
Enclave:		34:	$M_c[u'] \leftarrow v'$;		*Server:*
6: if op = add then		35:	end foreach		27:	receive Q_w from *Enclave*;
7: $f \leftarrow R[id]$;		36:	// if op = del then do nothing		28:	$Res \leftarrow \emptyset$; // file collection
8: $\{(w,id)\} \leftarrow Parse($Dec($k_f, f$));		Search(w)		29:	foreach (u_i, k_{id_i}) in Q_w do
9: foreach (w,id) do		*Client:*		30:	$id_i \leftarrow$ Dec($k_{id_i}, M_I[u_i]$);
10: $k_w \| k_c \leftarrow F(k_\Sigma, w)$;		1: send w to *Enclave*;		31:	$doc_i \leftarrow R[id_i]$;
11: $c \leftarrow ST[w]$;		*Enclave:*		32:	add doc_i to Res;
12: if $c = \perp$ then $c = -1$;		2: $st_{w_c} \leftarrow \{\emptyset\}, Q_w \leftarrow \{\emptyset\}$;		33:	end foreach
13: $c \leftarrow c + 1$;		3: $k_w \| k_c \leftarrow F(k_\Sigma, w)$;		34:	send Res to *Client*;
		4: foreach id_i in d do		*Client:*
		5: $f_i \leftarrow R[id_i]$;		35:	decrypt Res with k_f;

Fig. 2. Protocols in SGX-SE1. In Update, weak backward privacy (i.e., type-III) can be achieved by letting the enclave queries the deleted document from S to update D. If there are no deletion updates between two searches, the enclave records the deleted id to other keywords in $D[w]$.

10^6 documents and deleting 25% documents while SGX-SE1 only takes 2.4s after caching those deleted documents. In addition, SGX-SE2 spends the least time 1.4s, i.e., 2× faster than Bunker-B.

4.4   SGX-SE1 Construction

The basic idea behind SGX-SE1 is to let the enclave store the latest states ST of keywords and keeps the list d of deleted document ids, in order to facilitate searches. Then, the enclave only loads the deleted documents for the first search between two deletion updates to update the mapping between deleted ids and tracked keywords. Subsequent searches between the two deletion updates do not require loading the deleted documents again. We note that the enclave clearly needs to remove d after retrieving them in the first query to save the enclave's storage. Once the enclave knows the mapping between the query keyword and deleted documents, it infers the mapping of the query keyword with the rest non-deleted documents, in order to generate query tokens. After that, the server retrieves documents based on the received tokens and returns the document result list to the client. The detail protocols of SGX-SE1 can be found in Fig. 2. We explain the protocols further as follows:

In setup, client communicates with enclave upon an established secure channel to provision $K = (k_\Sigma, k_f)$ where k_Σ enables enclave to generate update/query tokens and k_f is the symmetric key for document encryption/decryption. The enclave maintains the maps ST and D, and the list d, where ST stores the states of keywords, D presents the mapping between keywords and deleted documents, and d is the array of deleted ids. The server holds an encrypted index M_I, the map of encrypted state M_c, and the repository R with $R[id]$ stores the encrypted document of document identifier id.

In update, the client receives a tuple $(\mathsf{op}, \mathsf{in})$, where it could be ($\mathsf{op} = add, \mathsf{in} = (\mathsf{doc}, id)$) or ($\mathsf{op} = del, \mathsf{in} = id$). If the update is addition, the client encrypts doc by using k_f and sends that encrypted document to server. After that, the client sends $(\mathsf{op}, \mathsf{in})$ to the enclave. The enclave will then parse doc to retrieve the list L of $\{(w, id)\}$. For each w, the enclave generates k_w and k_c from k_Σ, and retrieves the latest state $c \leftarrow ST[w]$. The enclave will then generate k_{id} from c by using $H_1(k_w, c)$ with H_1 is a hash function. After that, the enclave uses k_w, k_c, and k_{id} to generate encrypted entries (u, v) and (u', v') for w. In particular, the first encrypted entry, with $(u, v) \leftarrow (H_2(k_w, c), \mathsf{Enc}(k_{id}, id))$, holds the mapping between c and id to allows the server retrieves id based on given u and k_{id}. The second encrypted entry, with $(u', v') \leftarrow (H_3(k_w, id), \mathsf{Enc}(k_c, c))$, hides the state c of documents. In this way, the client can retrieve the state c of deleted documents upon sending u' in search operation. In our protocols, H_1 and H_2 are hash functions, and Enc is a symmetric encryption cipher. We note that enclave only sends a batch of (T_1, T_2) to the server within one *ocall* per a document addition, where $T1 = \{(u_{w_1}, v_{w_1}), \ldots, (u_{w_{|L|}}, v_{w_{|L|}})\}$ and $T2 = \{(u'_{w_1}, v'_{w_1}), \ldots, (u'_{w_{|L|}}, v'_{w_{|L|}})\}\}$. Then, the server will update T_1 and T_2 to M_I and M_c, respectively. If the update is deletion, the enclave simply updates d by the deleted id without further computation or communication to the server.

In search, the client sends a query q containing w to the enclave via the secure channel and expects to receive all the *current* (non-deleted) documents matching w from the server. The enclave begins loading deleted encrypted documents in d from the server in a sequential manner. By using k_f, the enclave decrypts those documents for checking the existence of w, and updating $D[w]$ if applicable. By leveraging $D[w]$, the enclave can retrieve the state list $st_{w_c} = \{c_{id}^{del}\}$, where c_{id}^{del} is the state used when the enclave added the deleted document id for w. After that, the enclave simply infers the states of non-deleted documents by excluding st_{w_c} from the set of $\{0, \ldots, ST[w]\}$. Finally, the enclave will compute the query token u and k_{id} for these non-deleted documents, and send the list $Q_w = \{(u, k_{id})\}$ to the server. At the server, upon receiving Q_w, it can retrieve id_i when decrypting $M_I[u_i]$ with k_{id_i}. Finally, the server returns the encrypted documents $Res = \{R[id_i]\}$ to the client.

Efficiency of SGX-SE1: In update, SGX-SE1 only takes n_w *ocalls* to add all n documents containing w to the server, and no *ocall* for deletion due to the

Setup(1^λ)	5: $h_j'(w,id) \stackrel{\Delta}{=} H_j'(k_{BF}, w \parallel id);$
1: Performs the same Setup in SGX-SE1;	6: $BF[h_j'(w,id)] \leftarrow 1;$
2: Client inits $k_{BF} \xleftarrow{\$} \{0,1\}^\lambda;$	**Search(w)**
3: Client sets integers $b, h;$	Replacing lines 4-18 in Search in SGX-SE1 with:
4: Provisions (k_{BF}, b, h) to Enclave;	1: **foreach** id **in** d **do**
5: Enclave selects $\{H_j'\}_{j\in[h]}$ for $BF;$	2: **if** $BF[H_j'(k_{BF}, w \parallel id)]_{j\in[h]} = 1$
5: Enclave does not maintain $D;$	3: $u' \leftarrow H_3(k_w, id);$
Update(op,in)	4: $v' \leftarrow M_c[u'];$
1: Performs the same Update in SGX-SE2;	5: $c \leftarrow \text{Dec}(k_c, v');$
2: **if** op $= add$ **then**	6: $st_{w_c} \leftarrow \{c\} \cup st_{w_c};$
3: **foreach** (w, id) **do**	7: delete $M_c[u'];$
4: **for** $j = 1 : h$ **do**	8: delete $R[id];$ // delete doc

Fig. 3. Protocols in SGX-SE2. The new instructions of SGX-SE2 is in blue (Color figure online)

caching of deleted documents within the enclave. That efficiency outperforms Bunker-B since the latter requires an additional *ocall* per a deletion. However, we note that the asymptotic performance of SGX-SE1 is affected by $(d + d_w)$ search roundtrips. In particular, the enclave needs to load and decrypt deleted documents within the enclave. Thus, the search performance really depends on how large the number of deleted documents is at the query time. We will later compare our search latency with Bunker-B in Sect. 5.

4.5 SGX-SE2 Construction

SGX-SE1 has $(d + d_w)$ search roundtrips and non-trivial $O(n_w + d)$ computation. One downside is that the enclave needs to spend time on decrypting deleted documents. Here, we present SGX-SE2, an advanced version of SGX-SE1, that reduces search roundtrips to d_w and achieves better asymptotic and concrete search time $O(n_w + v_d)$. The main solution we make to SGX-SE2 is that we use a Bloom filter BF within the enclave to verify the mapping between query keyword w and deleted document ids. In this way, SGX-SE2 avoids loading them from the server. Since BF is a probabilistic data structure, we can configure it to achieve a negligible false positive rate P_e (see Sect. 5). In Fig. 3, we highlight the solution of SGX-SE2. We summarily introduce SGX-SE2 as follows:

In setup, SGX-SE2 is almost the same with that one in SGX-SE1 with the exception that the client also requires to initialise the parameters of BF. They are, k_{BF}, b and h, where k_{BF} is the key for computing the hashed value of $(w \| id)$, and b is the number of bits in the BF vector (i.e, vector size), and h is the number of hash functions. Upon receiving the BF setting, the enclave initialises the BF vector and the set of hash functions $\{H_j'\}_{j\in[h]}$. In SGX-SE2, the mapping D between keywords and deleted ids is no longer needed within the enclave like that one in SGX-SE1.

In update, SGX-SE2 is also similar with SGX-SE1. However, if the update is addition, the enclave computes a new member $H_j'(k_{BF}, w \| id)$ to update BF.

In search, SGX-SE2 verifies the mapping between query keyword w and deleted ids by checking the membership of $(w \| id)$ with BF. If the mapping is valid, SGX-SE2 performs the same as SGX-SE1 to retrieve the state list $st_{w_c} = \{c_{id}^{del}\}$, where c_{id}^{del} is the state used for deleted ids. After that, the enclave infers the states of non-deleted documents and computes query tokens to send to the server.

Efficiency of SGX-SE2: The scheme clearly outperforms SGX-SE1 in terms of search computation and communication roundtrips due to the usage of the Bloom filter. It avoids loading d deleted documents into the enclave, making the search roundtrip only d_w. The scheme is even more efficient when $|d|$ is large. The reason is that the cost of verifying a membership $(w||id)$ is always $O(1)$ under the fixed BF setting. We note that checking d members in the BF is still more efficient than loading/decrypting their real documents. BF is also memory-efficiently; therefore, one can configure its size to balance the enclave memory with the demand of large datasets.

Remark: Note that deleting a document doc with identifier id in Bunker-B requires deletion entries of all keywords in that doc with $(w_i, id, \mathsf{op} = del)$ have been inserted in the encrypted index M_I beforehand. That would require M *ocalls* for the doc of M keywords. Then, Bunker-B takes extra one *ocall* to physically delete the doc. This physical deletion cost is the same with SGX-SE1 and SGX-SE2 (i.e., one *ocall*) except that these two schemes do not require any deletion entries to be inserted in M_I. Clearly, Bunker-B, SGX-SE1, and SGX-SE2 can do batch processing to delete d documents in one *ocall*. With SGX-SE1, deleting a doc can be done right after all keywords in the deleted document have been cached in $D[w]$ (see Fig. 2). With SGX-SE2, a doc can be deleted at the earliest time when any keyword in the doc is being searched (see Fig. 3).

4.6   Security Analysis

SGX-SE1 and SGX-SE2 contain the leakage of search and updates, because the server can observe the interaction between its memory and the enclave. In setup, the schemes leak nothing due to the remote attestation and secure data communication channel between the client and the enclave. If update is addition, the server is able to track the time and memory access when new entries are inserted into data structures M_I, M_c, and R (see Fig. 2 for their definitions). If update is deletion, the enclave does not communicate with the server during deletion. Hence, there is no leakage in the operation. In search, the access patterns on M_I, M_c, and R are revealed to the server. We formulate the detail leakage and define the $\mathbf{Real}_\mathcal{A}(\lambda)$ and a $\mathbf{Ideal}_{\mathcal{A},\mathcal{S}}(\lambda)$ game for an adaptive adversary $\mathcal{A}$ and a polynomial time simulator $\mathcal{S}$ with the security parameter λ in [23].

We prove the schemes are secure if they achieve both forward privacy and Type-II backward privacy. We note that the client issues a query on w to the enclave via an established secure channel. Hence, $\mathcal{A}$ has to generate a query token by itself in the game. Regarding forward privacy, the increasing state $ST[w]$ (see Fig. 2) when adding a new document containing w ensures that $\mathcal{A}$ cannot generate a query token to retrieve a newly added document. W.r.t. backward privacy, $\mathcal{A}$ statistically knows the timestamps when the deleted states of w added in M_c when the enclave requests the server to access to M_c during search. However, $\mathcal{A}$ does not know when they were requested for deletion by the client. The reason for that is because SGX-SE1 and SGX-SE2 cache these deletion requests in the enclave and only access them during search. As a result, $\mathcal{A}$ does not know which delete updates occur and have cancelled addition updates [23].

5   Implementation and Evaluation

Experiment Setup and Implementation: We choose two datasets: One is a synthesis dataset (3.2 GB) generated from the English keyword frequency data based on the Zipf's law distribution, and the other one is the Enron email dataset[3] (1.4 GB). A summary of the datasets is given in Table 1.

We build the prototype of SGX-SE1 and SGX-SE2 using C++ and the Intel SGX SDK[4]. In addition, we implement the prototype of Bunker-B as the baseline for comparisons, since its implementation is not publicly available. The prototype leverages the built-in cryptographic primitives in the SGX SDK to support the required cryptographic operations. It also uses the settings and APIs from the SDK to create, manage and access the application (enclave) designed for SGX. Recall that the SGX can only handle 96 MB memory within the enclave. Access to the extra memory space triggers the paging mechanism of the SGX, which brings an extra cost to the system. To avoid paging in our prototype, our prototypes are implemented with batch processing to tackle with the keyword-document pairs, which splits a huge memory demand into multiple batches with smaller resource requests. The batch processing enables our prototypes to handle queries with large memory demands. Moreover, the prototype should avoid

Table 1. Statistics of the datasets used in the evaluation.

Name	# of keyword s	# of docs	# of keyword-doc pairs
Synthesis	1,000	1,000,000	$11,879,100$
Enron	29,627	517,401	$37,219,800$

Table 2. Avg. (μs) for adding a keyword-doc pair under different schemes.

# of docs	# of keyword-doc pairs	BunkerB	SGX-SE1	SGX-SE2
2.5×10^5	2.5×10^5	21	23	26
5×10^5	6.5×10^5	19	19	21
7.5×10^5	1.9×10^6	15	12	14
1×10^6	1.18×10^7	12	7	8

$\star$: The average time decreases since the average I/O cost of loading keywords from the file decreases

[3] Enron email dataset: https://www.cs.cmu.edu/~./enron/.
[4] Source code: https://github.com/MonashCybersecurityLab/SGXSSE.

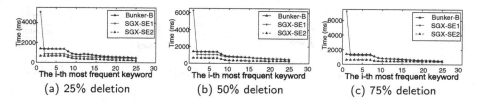

Fig. 4. The query delay of querying the i-th most frequent keyword in the synthesis dataset under different schemes (insert 2.5×10^5 docs and delete a portion).

too many *ecalls/ocalls* as it incurs the I/O communication cost between the untrusted and the trusted application (enclave). Hence, in the following experiments, we set the batch size to 1×10^5 for all schemes, which can avoid triggering paging while minimising the number of *ecall/ocalls*. The prototypes are deployed in a workstation equipped SGX-enabled Intel i7 2.6 GHz and 32 GB RAM.

5.1 Performance Evaluation on the Synthesis Dataset

Insertion and Deletion: First, we evaluate the time for insertion and deletion under three different schemes. We follow a reversed Zipf's law distribution to generate the encrypted database of our synthesis dataset, and we measure the runtime for adding one keyword-document pair into the encrypted database of different schemes. As shown in Table 2, Bunker-B takes 21 μs to insert one pair, which is faster than our schemes (23 μs and 26 μs) when the number of keyword-document pairs equals the number of documents. The reason is that the insertion time of the above three schemes is bounded by the I/O (*ecall/ocall*) between the untrusted application and the enclave. For Bunker-B, the I/O cost is linear to the number of keyword-document pairs (see Sect. 4.3 for details), while the one for our schemes is linear to the number of documents. Also, our schemes involve more computations (PRF, Hash) and maintain more data structures (Bloom filter), which require more time to be processed. Nonetheless, when inserting 1×10^6 documents, our schemes only require 7 μs and 8 μs respectively to insert one keyword-document pair, which is 2× faster than Bunker-B (12 μs). In the above case, the number of keyword-document pairs is 10× larger than the number of documents, which implies that Bunker-B needs 10× more I/O operations (*ecall/ocall*) to insert the whole dataset comparing to our schemes (see Table 3 for details). Note that the real-world document typically consists of more than one keyword. Hence, our schemes are more efficient than Bunker-B when dealing with a real-world dataset (see Sect. 5.2).

For deletion, the performance of Bunker-B is identical to that for insertion (12 μs), because deletion runs the same algorithm with different operations. For our schemes, the deletion process only inserts the document *id* into a list, and the deletion operation is executed by excluding the deleted *id* during the query phase. Thus, our schemes only need 4 μs to process one doc in deletion phase.

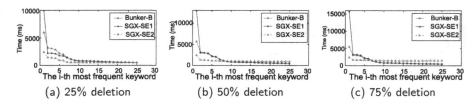

(a) 25% deletion   (b) 50% deletion   (c) 75% deletion

Fig. 5. The query delay of querying the i-th most frequent keyword in the synthesis dataset (insert 1×10^6 documents and delete a portion of them).

Table 3. Number of *ecall*/*ocall* for adding 1×10^6 documents for different schemes.

# of calls	BunkerB	SGX1	SGX2
ecall	1.18×10^7	1×10^6	1×10^6
ocall	1.18×10^7	1×10^6	1×10^6

Table 4. Number of *ecall*/*ocall* for deleting a portion of documents after adding 1×10^6 documents.

Deletion %	BunkerB		SGX1		SGX2	
	ecall	*ocall*	*ecall*	*ocall*	*ecall*	*ocall*
25%	9.9×10^6	9.9×10^6	2.5×10^5	0	2.5×10^5	0
50%	1.12×10^7	1.1×10^7	5×10^5	0	5×10^5	0
75%	1.16×10^7	1.16×10^7	7.5×10^5	0	7.5×10^5	0

Query Delay: Next, we report the query delay comparison between Bunker-B and our schemes to show the advantage of using SGX-SE1 and SGX-SE2. To measure the query delay introduced by keyword frequency and the deletion operation, we choose to query the top-25 keywords after deleting a portion of documents. In our first evaluation, we insert 2.5×10^5 documents and delete 25%, 50% and 75% of the documents, respectively. Fig. 4a illustrates the query delays when deleting 25% of documents: For the most frequent keyword, Bunker-B needs 1.3 s to query while SGX-SE2 only needs 654 ms. Although SGX-SE1 takes 5 s to perform the first search, it also caches the deleted keyword-document pairs inside the enclave and performs deletion on documents during the first query. As a result, the rest of the queries are much faster, as the number of *ocall*s is significantly reduced (900 μs if we query the most frequent keyword again). Even for the 25-th most frequent keyword, SGX-SE1 (159 ms) and SGX-SE2 (155 ms) are still 40% faster than Bunker-B (221 ms). Bunker-B is always slower than SGX-SE1 and SGX-SE2 in the above case as it requires to re-encrypt the remaining 75% documents after each query. Compared to Bunker-B, SGX-SE1 and SGX-SE2 only access the deleted 25% files and exclude the corresponding token of deleted files before sending the token list (see Sect. 4.5). With the increase of the deletion portion, the difference of the query delay between our schemes and Bunker-

Table 5. Number of *ecall*/*ocall* when querying the most frequent keyword after adding 1×10^6 documents and deleting a portion of them.

Deletion %	BunkerB		SGX1		SGX2	
	ecall	*ocall*	*ecall*	*ocall*	*ecall*	*ocall*
25%	1	21	1	$250,011^*/11$	1	11
50%	1	20	1	$500,010^*/10$	1	10
75%	1	21	1	$750,011^*/11$	1	11

*: It includes the *ocall* for caching and deleting the encrypted documents.

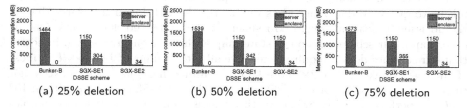

(a) 25% deletion   (b) 50% deletion   (c) 75% deletion

Fig. 6. The memory consumption in the synthesis dataset (inserted 1×10^6 documents and deleted a portion of them).

B becomes smaller as Bunker-B has fewer documents to be re-encrypted after queries. When 75% of the documents are deleted, our schemes still outperform Bunker-B when querying the keywords with a higher occurrence rate (see Fig. 4c). However, their performances are almost the same when querying the 25-th most frequent keyword, i.e., about 400 ms for three schemes, because Bunker-B only re-encrypts a tiny amount of document id (almost 0).

The second evaluation shows the query delay when inserting all 1×10^6 documents into the encrypted database. The major difference between this experiment and the previous one is that SGX-SE1 scheme requires more than 128 MB to cache the deleted documents, which triggers paging. As shown in Fig. 5a, SGX-SE1 needs 10 s to cache the deleted documents. When processing the query that contains a large number of documents (e.g., the second most frequent keyword), SGX-SE1 (2.4 s) is almost 2× slower than SGX-SE2 (1.4 s). Nonetheless, their query performance is still better than Bunker-B, which takes 3.2 s to answer the above query. When our schemes delete a larger portion of documents (see Figs. 5b and 5c), the query delay of SGX-SE1 and SGX-SE2 is very close, since SGX-SE1 only refers to the small deletion information cached in the enclave while SGX-SE2 requires to check the Bloom filter for each deleted document.

Communication Cost: The next evaluation demonstrates the impact of I/O operation (*ecall*/*ocall*) on the performance of different schemes. As shown in Table 3, Bunker-B needs 10× more *ecall*/*ocall* operations than our schemes. Consequently, although both Bunker-B and our schemes generate and store the encrypted keyword-document pairs at the end, our schemes can achieve a better performance for insertion, because our schemes rely on less I/O operations. This result is consistent with the average insertion time reported in the insertion and deletion part. In terms of the deletion operation, Bunker-B needs almost $30\times$ more I/O operation than ours (see Table 4). Moreover, the deletion in our schemes only requires to insert the deleted id, which does not involve any cryptographic operation, whereas Bunker-B executes the same procedure as insertion. This indicates that our schemes also have less communication cost than Bunker-B. We further present the number of *ecall/ocall* involved during the query process in Table 5. Note that we implement batch processing for all schemes, so each *ocall* can process 10^5 query tokens at the same time. The result shows that Bunker-B has more *ocall* during the query process because it needs to issue tokens to query all document id as well as the deleted document. After that, it should issue additional tokens to re-encrypt the undeleted documents. On the other hand, our schemes keep the state map within the enclave, which indicates that our schemes do not require to retrieve all the document id via *ocall*. In most of the case, Bunker-B has $2\times$ more I/O operations than our schemes except for the cache stage of SGX-SE1. Despite the fact that SGX-SE1 takes more than 10^5 *ocall*s to perform caching, we stress that this is a one-time cost; it also enables our scheme to remove the document physically, whereas Bunker-B only can delete the document from the encrypted index.

Memory Consumption: Finally, we present the memory consumption of three different schemes. Since the memory consumption on the client is negligible comparing to that for the server and enclave (i.e., less than 1 MB). As shown in Fig. 6, the encrypted database always keeps unchanged for SGX-SE1 and SGX-SE2 because they keep the same keyword-document pairs after adding 1×10^6 documents. On the other hand, the memory usage of Bunker-B keeps increasing when we delete more documents as it should maintain the deleted keyword-document pairs on the server. Within the enclave, Bunker-B does not maintain any persistent data structure while SGX-SE1 and SGX-SE2 need to store the necessary information for deletion. For SGX-SE1, it caches all the document *id* in the enclave, which leads to notably high memory usage (e.g., 304 MB when deleting 25% documents, and 355 MB when deleting 75%). The memory resource requests in SGX-SE1 triggers the paging mechanism of the SGX, resulting in a larger query delay as presented above. SGX-SE2 successfully prevents the paging by using the Bloom filter. After applying a Bloom filter with the false positive rate 10^{-4}, SGX-SE2 only needs 34 MB to store all keyword-document pairs (1.18×10^7 pairs) and maintains a low query delay over the dataset.

5.2 Performance Evaluation on the Enron Dataset

We use a real world dataset to illustrate the practicality of the proposed scheme. Since the bulk deletion (e.g. delete 50%) is rare in real world, we only focus on the setting with a small deletion portion. Therefore, in the following experiments, we insert the whole Enron dataset and test the average runtime for insertion/deletion as well as the query delay with a small deletion portion (25%).

Table 6. Average time (μs) for adding a keyword-doc pair from Enron dataset and removing 25% documents under different schemes.

Operation	BunkerB	SGX-SE1	SGX-SE2
Insertion	12	7	8
Deletion (25%, 129,305 documents)	12	4	4

Insertion and Deletion: As described in Sect. 5.1, our schemes are more efficient for the insertion and deletion if the number of keyword-document pairs is larger than the number of documents. The evaluation result on the Enron dataset further verifies our observation: as shown in Table 6, our schemes only need 7 μs and 8 μs respectively to insert one keyword-document pair while Bunker-B needs 12 μs to do that. Besides, both of SGX-SE1 and SGX-SE2 only take 4 μs to delete one document, but Bunker-B still requires 12 μs to execute the same algorithm as the insertion.

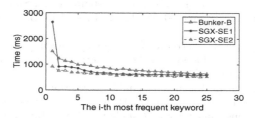

Fig. 7. The query delay of querying the i-th most frequent keyword in the Enron dataset under different schemes (insert all documents and delete 25% of them).

Query Delay: Finally, we present the query delay when using the Enron dataset. As the Enron dataset has more keyword-document pairs than our synthesis dataset, deleting 25% documents still triggers paging, as it includes more keyword-document pairs than the whole synthesis dataset. In Fig. 7, we present the query delay when querying the top-25 frequent keywords in the Enron dataset. The result shows that SGX-SE2 maintains a relative low query delay (530 ms to 900 ms) while SGX-SE1 needs 580 ms to 2.6 s and Bunker-B requires 645 ms to 1.5 s. This above result further illustrates that SGX-SE2 can both prevent the paging within the SGX enclave and eliminate the cost of re-encryption. Note that using *exit-less* system calls can further improve the performance in the enclave by eliminating the overheads of enclave exits and optimising *enclave page cache* accesses [17]. Hence, we will evaluate this performance in the future work.

6   Conclusion

In this paper, we leverage the advance of Intel SGX to design and implement forward and backward private dynamic searchable encryption schemes. We carefully analyse the limitations of the recent theoretical constructions and propose new designs to avoid the bottleneck of the SGX enclave. We present a basic scheme and then further optimise it for better performance. We implement prior work and our schemes, and conduct a detailed performance comparison. The results show that our designs are more efficient in query latency and data deletion.

Acknowledgement. This work was supported by the Australian Research Council (ARC) Discovery Project grant DP200103308.

References

1. Amjad, G., Kamara, S., Moataz, T.: Forward and backward private searchable encryption with SGX. In: EuroSec 2019 (2019)
2. Bindschaedler, V., Grubbs, P., Cash, D., Ristenpart, T., Shmatikov, V.: The tao of inference in privacy-protected databases. Proc. VLDB Endow. **11**, 1715–1728 (2018)
3. Borges, G., Domingos, H., Ferreira, B., Leitão, J., Oliveira, T., Portela, B.: BISEN: efficient Boolean searchable symmetric encryption with verifiability and minimal leakage. In: SRDS 2019 (2019)
4. Bost, R.: Sophos - forward secure searchable encryption. In: ACM CCS 2016 (2016)
5. Bost, R., Minaud, B., Ohrimenko, O.: Forward and backward private searchable encryption from constrained cryptographic primitives. In: ACM CCS 2017 (2017)
6. Brasser, F., Capkun, S., Dmitrienko, A., Frassetto, T., Kostiainen, K., Sadeghi, A.R.: DR.SGX: automated and adjustable side-channel protection for SGX using data location randomization. In: ACSAC 2019 (2019)
7. Cash, D., Grubbs, P., Perry, J., Ristenpart, T.: Leakage-abuse attacks against searchable encryption. In: ACM CCS 2015 (2015)
8. Cash, D., Jaeger, J., Jarecki, S., Jutla, C.: Dynamic searchable encryption in very large databases: data structures and implementation. In: NDSS 2014 (2014)
9. Christian, P., Kapil, V., Manuel, C.: EnclaveDB: a secure database using SGX. In: IEEE S&P 2018 (2018)
10. Curtmola, R., Garay, J., Kamara, S., Ostrovsky, R.: Searchable symmetric encryption: improved definitions and efficient constructions. In: ACM CCS 2006 (2006)
11. Duan, H., Wang, C., Yuan, X., Zhou, Y., Wang, Q., Ren, K.: LightBox: full-stack protected stateful middlebox at lightning speed. In: ACM CCS 2019 (2019)
12. Fuhry, B., Bahmani, R., Brasser, F., Hahn, F., Kerschbaum, F., Sadeghi, A.-R.: HardIDX: practical and secure index with SGX. In: Livraga, G., Zhu, S. (eds.) DBSec 2017. LNCS, vol. 10359, pp. 386–408. Springer, Cham (2017). https://doi.org/10.1007/978-3-319-61176-1_22
13. Ghareh Chamani, J., Papadopoulos, D., Papamanthou, C., Jalili, R.: New constructions for forward and backward private symmetric searchable encryption. In: ACM CCS 2018 (2018)
14. Kamara, S., Papamanthou, C., Roeder, T.: Dynamic searchable symmetric encryption. In: ACM CCS 2012 (2012)

15. Lai, S., Patranabis, S., Sakzad, A., Liu, J.K., Mukhopadhyay, D., Steinfeld, R., et al.: Result pattern hiding searchable encryption for conjunctive queries. In: ACM CCS 2018 (2018)
16. Mishra, P., Poddar, R., Chen, J., Chiesa, A., Popa, R.A.: Oblix: an efficient oblivious search index. In: IEEE S&P 2018 (2018)
17. Orenbach, M., Lifshits, P., Minkin, M., Silberstein, M.: Eleos: exitless OS services for SGX enclaves. In: EuroSys 2017 (2017)
18. Ren, K., et al.: Hybridx: new hybrid index for volume-hiding range queries in data outsourcing services. In: ICDCS 2020 (2020)
19. Shinde, S., Chua, Z.L., Narayanan, V., Saxena, P.: Preventing page faults from telling your secrets. In: ACM AsiaCCS 2016 (2016)
20. Song, D., Wagner, D., Perrig, A.: Practical techniques for searches on encrypted data. In: IEEE S&P 2000 (2000)
21. Stefanov, E., Papamanthou, C., Shi, E.: Practical dynamic searchable symmetric encryption with small leakage. In: NDSS 2014 (2014)
22. Sun, S.F., et al.: Practical backward-secure searchable encryption from symmetric puncturable encryption. In: ACM CCS 2018 (2018)
23. Vo, V., Lai, S., Yuan, X., Sun, S.F., Nepal, S., Liu, J.K.: Accelerating forward and backward private searchable encryption using trusted execution (2020). http://arxiv.org/abs/2001.03743
24. Yarom, Y., Falkner, K.: FLUSH+RELOAD: a high resolution, low noise, L3 cache side-channel attack. In: USENIX Security 2014 (2014)
25. Zhang, Y., Katz, J., Papamanthou, C.: All your queries are belong to us: the power of file-injection attacks on searchable encryption. In: USENIX Security 2016 (2016)
26. Zuo, C., Sun, S.-F., Liu, J.K., Shao, J., Pieprzyk, J.: Dynamic searchable symmetric encryption with forward and stronger backward privacy. In: Sako, K., Schneider, S., Ryan, P.Y.A. (eds.) ESORICS 2019. LNCS, vol. 11736, pp. 283–303. Springer, Cham (2019). https://doi.org/10.1007/978-3-030-29962-0_14
27. Zuo, C., Sun, S.-F., Liu, J.K., Shao, J., Pieprzyk, J.: Dynamic searchable symmetric encryption schemes supporting range queries with forward (and backward) security. In: Lopez, J., Zhou, J., Soriano, M. (eds.) ESORICS 2018. LNCS, vol. 11099, pp. 228–246. Springer, Cham (2018). https://doi.org/10.1007/978-3-319-98989-1_12

Cluster-Based Anonymization
of Knowledge Graphs

Anh-Tu Hoang$^{(\boxtimes)}$, Barbara Carminati, and Elena Ferrari

DiSTA, University of Insubria, Varese, Italy
{ahoang,barbara.carminati,elena.ferrari}@uninsubria.it

Abstract. While knowledge graphs (KGs) are getting popular as they can formalize many types of users' data in social networks, sharing these data may reveal users' identities. Although many protection models have been presented to protect users in anonymized data, they are unsuitable to protect the users in KGs. To cope with this problem, we propose k-AttributeDegree (k-ad), a model to protect users' identities in anonymized KGs. We further present information loss metrics tailored to KGs and a cluster-based anonymization algorithm to generate anonymized KGs satisfying k-ad. Finally, we conduct experiments on five real-life data sets to evaluate our algorithm and compare it with previous work.

Keywords: k-anonymity · Knowledge graphs · Privacy

1 Introduction

More and more data providers share users' data by using knowledge graphs (KGs) as these graphs can represent many types of users' attributes and relationships. For instance, in 2012, Google published its API to find entities in the Google KGs. In 2015, Wikipedia Foundation also released their Wikidata Query Service to run queries on Wikidata. Even though providers protect users' identities by removing explicit identifiers (e.g., *name*, *address*) in the published KGs, adversaries can still re-identify them by exploiting users' attributes (e.g., *gender*, *age*) or their relationships (e.g., the number of *neighbors*) [3,7,8,14]. To protect user identities, providers must anonymize KGs before sharing them.

Many studies have been presented to protect users from being re-identified in published data. Since the well-known k-anonymity principle for relation data has been proposed, many other protection models (e.g., k-degree, k-neighborhood, k-automorphism) extend it to protect users in anonymized undirected graphs [8]. As an example, Yuan et al. [8] combine k-anonymity and k-degree to protect users in anonymized undirected graphs containing users' attributes and relationship. The Paired k-degree [3] and K-In&Out-Degree Anonymity [14] protect users in anonymized directed graphs by requiring that, for every user in the graph, there are at least $k-1$ other users having the same out- and in-degree. As the Paired k-degree's algorithm does not always generate anonymized directed

© Springer Nature Switzerland AG 2020
M. Conti et al. (Eds.): ACNS 2020, LNCS 12147, pp. 104–123, 2020.
https://doi.org/10.1007/978-3-030-57878-7_6

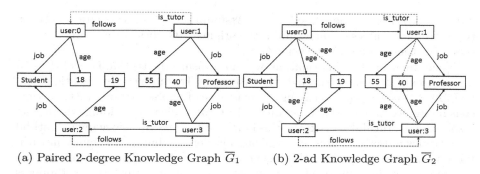

(a) Paired 2-degree Knowledge Graph $\overline{G}_1$ (b) 2-ad Knowledge Graph $\overline{G}_2$

Fig. 1. Knowledge graphs satisfying paired k-degree and k-ad.

graphs, Hoang et al. [7] present a cluster-based algorithm to anonymize the graphs providing strong privacy guarantees. However, these models are insufficient to protect users in KGs as adversaries can exploit both users' attributes and different types of relationships [12,13] as the following example shows.

Example 1. Let $\overline{G}_1$ in Fig. 1a be a KG anonymized according to the Paired k-degree. For all types of relationships (e.g., *follows*, *is_tutor*), *user:0* and *user:1*'s out- and in-degrees are equal to those of *user:2* and *user:3*, respectively. Therefore, $\overline{G}_1$ satisfies the Paired 2-degree. However, as the values of nodes (e.g., *18*, *19*, *Student*) representing attributes' values are not replaced by random numbers, adversaries can re-identify users by their attributes.

In this paper, we present k-AttributeDegree (k-ad). Different from previous models, k-ad requires that, for each user, his/her attributes and the out-/in-degree of any type of his/her relationships are indistinguishable from those of $k-1$ other users. Therefore, an adversary cannot re-identify any user in k-ad KGs with a confidence higher than $\frac{1}{k}$. Figure 1b illustrates the 2-ad version of $\overline{G}_1$. As we add fake edges to make both the attributes (e.g., *age*, *job*) and the relationships out-/in-degree (e.g., *follows*, *is_tutor*) of *user:0* and *user:1* equal to those of *user:2* and *user:3*, respectively, all of them cannot be re-identified with a confidence higher than $\frac{1}{2}$.

The modifications performed to generate k-ad KGs decrease the amount of information the anonymized KGs have. To cope with this, we present the Attribute and Degree Information Loss (ADM) to measure the information loss of anonymized KGs. Moreover, as k-ad requires modifying values of users' attributes, we have to consider whether the new values are truthful or not. As an example, we cannot associate to *age* attribute the value *18* if user's *job* is *Professor*, because an adversary can easily detect these untruthful associations and try to remove them to infer real values. For instance, the adversary can figure out that either the user' *age* or *job* is fake. As such, we have to measure the truthfulness of attributes' values in anonymized KGs. To estimate this, we propose to consider how truthful are associations between attributes' values.

Indeed, according to the Closed-World Assumption [9], an association between two attributes' values is untruthful if the original KG does not contain any user that have these values at the same time.[1]

Then, by using this information, we can measure the truthfulness of the values of users' attributes, through the Attribute Truthfulness Information Loss (ATM). Moreover, since verifying the existence of an association in KGs is time consuming, we use bilinear functions to learn an indicator deciding whether an association is truthful. We exploit this indicator to measure how many untruthful associations a user has after anonymizing his/her attributes. The more untruthful associations he/she has, the higher his/her ATM is. Then, by minimizing the number of these untruthful associations, we can maximize the truthfulness of users' attributes.

In this paper, we present a Cluster-Based Knowledge Graph Anonymization Algorithm (CKGA) allowing data providers to use any type of clustering algorithm (e.g., k-means [4]) to anonymize KGs. First, we turn users into data points in Euclidean space such that their information loss is almost equal to the Euclidean distance of their corresponding points. By minimizing the distances between points in the same cluster, we minimize the information loss of users in these clusters. Also, we present strategies to make the sizes of the generated clusters in between k and $2 \times k - 1$. Finally, we extend the Directed Graph Generalization algorithm (DGG) [7] to make the attributes' values and out-/in-degrees of users in the same cluster identical. We conduct experiments on five real-life data sets to evaluate the quality of anonymized KGs generated by our algorithm and compare it with previous work [3,7].

The remaining sections of this paper are organized as follows. Section 2 illustrates the adversaries' attack model. We introduce our information loss metrics in Sect. 3 and our algorithms in Sect. 4. In Sect. 5, we evaluate the efficiency of our approach, whereas Sect. 6 concludes the paper.

2   Anonymizing Knowledge Graphs

We model a knowledge graph (KG) as a graph $G(V, E, R)$, where V is the set of nodes, E is the set of edges connecting these nodes, and R is the set of relationship types. Since a node can be used to represent a user or the value of an attribute, there are two subsets of nodes: the set $V^U \subseteq V$, modelling users (e.g., *user:0*, *user:1*), and the set $V^A \subseteq V$, representing attributes' values (e.g., *18*, *Student*). Thus, $V = V^U \cup V^A$. Different from previous work [8], users can have more than one value for each attribute.

Relationship types in R are categorized into two subsets: user-to-user relationship types R^{UU}, representing users' relationships (e.g., *follows*), and user-to-attribute relationship types R^{UA}, modelling users' attributes (e.g., *age*, *gender*, *job*). Then, $R = R^{UU} \cup R^{UA}$. Each edge $e \in E$ is defined as a triple (u, r, v),

---

[1] In case the truthful associations are absent in the original KG, our work can be extended easily by checking whether these associations exist in completed KGs containing more truthful data.

where $u, v \in V$ and $r \in R$. We denote with $E^{UA} \subseteq E$ those $e = (u, r_a, v_a)$, such that $r_a \in R^{UA}$. Similarly, we denote with E^{UU} those $e = (u, r_u, v_u)$, such that $r_u \in R^{UU}$. Figure 1 shows an example of using KGs to model users' data.

2.1 Adversary Background Knowledge

Let $G(V, E, R)$ be a KG and $\overline{G}(\overline{V}, \overline{E}, \overline{R})$ be an anonymized version of G created by modifying V, E, and R. Let u be a user in $\overline{V}^U$. As KGs contain values of many attributes, adversaries can re-identify u by using all of his/her attributes' values in $\overline{G}$, denoted as $I_a^{\overline{G}}(u) = \{(r_a, v_a) | (u, r_a, v_a) \in \overline{E}^{UA}\}$. Additionally, adversaries can also re-identify u if they know his/her out- and in-degree. However, as $\overline{G}$ represents many types of relationships, adversaries can exploit the out- and in-degree from any type of these relationships to re-identify u. More precisely, given a relationship type $r_u \in \overline{R}^{UU}$, we denote with $I_o^{\overline{G}}(u, r_u) = |\{(u, r_u, v_u) \in \overline{E}^{UU}\}|$ and $I_i^{\overline{G}}(u, r_u) = |\{(v_u, r_u, u) \in \overline{E}^{UU}\}|$ the u's out- and in-degree of the relationship type r_u, respectively. Then, the out- and in-degree from all relationship types of u in $\overline{G}$ are $I_o^{\overline{G}}(u) = \{(r_u, I_o^{\overline{G}}(u, r_u)) | r_u \in \overline{R}^{UU}\}$ and $I_i^{\overline{G}}(u) = \{(r_u, I_i^{\overline{G}}(u, r_u)) | r_u \in \overline{R}^{UU}\}$, respectively.

The adversaries' background knowledge about a user $u \in \overline{V}^U$ is the combination of attributes, out- and in- background knowledge. More formally, we define it as follows:

Definition 1 (Adversary Background Knowledge). *Let u be a user in $\overline{G}$. The background knowledge that an adversary can use to re-identify u is $\mathcal{BK}^{\overline{G}}(u) = \{\mathcal{BK}_a^{\overline{G}}(u), \mathcal{BK}_o^{\overline{G}}(u), \mathcal{BK}_i^{\overline{G}}(u)\}$, where $\mathcal{BK}_a^{\overline{G}}(u) \subseteq I_a^{\overline{G}}(u)$, $\mathcal{BK}_o^{\overline{G}} \subseteq I_o^{\overline{G}}(u)$, and $\mathcal{BK}_i^{\overline{G}}(u) \subseteq I_i^{\overline{G}}(u)$ are the background knowledge about u's attributes, out- , and in-degrees and $I_a^{\overline{G}}$, $I_o^{\overline{G}}$, and $I_i^{\overline{G}}$ are u's attributes', out-, and in-degrees extracted from $\overline{G}$.*

Example 2. In Fig. 1b, the attributes, out-, and in-degrees about user *user:0* that can be extracted from the anonymized KG $\overline{G}_2$ is $I_a^{\overline{G}_2}$ (*user:0*) = {(*age*, 18), (*age*, 19), (*job*, *Student*)}; $I_o^{\overline{G}_2}$(*user:0*) = {(*follows*, 1), (*is_tutor*, 0)}; $I_i^{\overline{G}_2}$(*user:0*) = {(*follows*, 0), (*is_tutor*, 1)}. Thus, the background knowledge about *user:0* is $\mathcal{BK}^{\overline{G}_2}$ (*user:0*) = {$\mathcal{BK}_a^{\overline{G}_2}$ (*user:0*), $\mathcal{BK}_o^{\overline{G}_2}$ (*user:0*), $\mathcal{BK}_i^{\overline{G}_2}$ (*user:0*)}, where $\mathcal{BK}_a^{\overline{G}_2}$ (*user:0*), $\mathcal{BK}_o^{\overline{G}_2}$ (*user:0*), and $\mathcal{BK}_i^{\overline{G}_2}$ (*user:0*) are subsets of $I_a^{\overline{G}_2}$(*user:0*), $I_o^{\overline{G}_2}$(*user:0*), $I_i^{\overline{G}_2}$(*user:0*), respectively.

2.2 Anonymity of Knowledge Graphs

We present k-AttributeDegree (k-ad), a privacy protection model to protect users in anonymized KGs. In particular, let $\overline{G}(\overline{V}, \overline{E}, \overline{R})$ be an anonymized version of G. For each user u in $\overline{V}^U$, we have to ensure that his attributes' values, out-, and in-degrees extracted from $\overline{G}$ are indistinguishable from those of at least $k - 1$ other ones in $\overline{V}^U$. More formally, k-AttributeDegree (k-ad) is defined as follows:

Definition 2 (k-AttributeDegree). *Let $\overline{G}(\overline{V}, \overline{E}, \overline{R})$ be an anonymized KG. $\overline{G}$ satisfies k-AttributeDegree (k-ad), if and only if, for every user u in $\overline{V}^U$, there exists a set of users, denoted $\zeta^{\overline{G}}(u)$, such that $\zeta^{\overline{G}}(u) = \{v \in \overline{V}^U | I_a^{\overline{G}}(u) = I_a^{\overline{G}}(v) \wedge I_o^{\overline{G}}(u) = I_o^{\overline{G}}(v) \wedge I_i^{\overline{G}}(u) = I_i^{\overline{G}}(v)\}$ and $|\zeta^{\overline{G}}(u)| \geq k$.*

As the values of all attributes and the out- and-in degree of all relationship types of every user in the k-ad anonymized KGs are indistinguishable from those of $k - 1$ other users, it can be easily proved that these KGs also satisfy the previous protection models: k-anonymity [8], the Paired k-degree [3], and K-In&Out-Degree Anonymity [14].

Theorem 1. *Let $\overline{G}(\overline{V}, \overline{E}, \overline{R})$ be an anonymized KG. If $\overline{G}$ satisfies k-ad, $\overline{G}$ satisfies k-anonymity, the Paired k-degree, and K-In&Out-Degree Anonymity.*

Proof. Suppose $\overline{G}(\overline{V}, \overline{E}, \overline{R})$ satisfies k-ad. Then, according to Definition 1, for every user $u \in \overline{V}^U$, $|\zeta^{\overline{G}}(u)| \geq k$, where $\zeta^{\overline{G}}(u) = \{I_a^{\overline{G}}(u), I_o^{\overline{G}}(u), I_i^{\overline{G}}(u)\}$. Suppose that $\overline{G}$ does not satisfy k-anonymity, the Paired k-degree, or K-In&Out-Degree Anonymity. Then, there is at least one user $u \in \overline{V}^U$, such that there are less than $k - 1$ other users whose values of all attributes (i.e., $I_a^{\overline{G}}$), out-, and in-degree of all types of relationships (i.e., $I_o^{\overline{G}}$ and $I_i^{\overline{G}}$, respectively) are identical to those of u. Thus, $|\zeta^{\overline{G}}(u)| < k$. But, this contradicts the fact that $|\zeta^{\overline{G}}(u)| \geq k$ for every user $u \in \overline{V}^U$. Thus, we can conclude that if $\overline{G}$ satisfies k-ad, it also satisfies k-anonymity, the Paired k-degree, and K-In&Out-Degree Anonymity.

3   Information Loss Metrics

In what follows, we describe the information loss metrics we use to evaluate the quality of anonymized KGs.

3.1   Attribute and Degree Information Loss

As KGs contain both users' attributes and relationships, our information loss metrics consider the loss on all of these types of information. We present the Attribute Information Loss Metric (AM') to evaluate the loss of attributes' information on a user in anonymized KGs. In what follows, we denote with $G(V, E, R)$ and with $\overline{G}(\overline{V}, \overline{E}, \overline{R})$ the original KG and one of its anonymized version. Let u be a user in G and r_a be an attribute in R^{UA}. We denote with $I_a^G(u, r_a) = \{v_a | (u, r_a, v_a) \in E^{UA}\}$ and $I_a^{\overline{G}}(u, r_a) = \{v_a | (u, r_a, v_a) \in \overline{E}^{UA}\}$ the values of attribute r_a of user u in G and $\overline{G}$, respectively. If r_a is a categorical attribute, AM' measures the differences of values of u's r_a attribute in $\overline{G}$ and G: $I_a^{\overline{G}}(u, r_a) \setminus I_a^G(u, r_a)$. In contrast, if r_a is a numerical attribute, the value of u's attribute r_a in $\overline{G}$ and G can be represented as a range $[\min I_a^{\overline{G}}(u, r_a), \max I_a^{\overline{G}}(u, r_a)]$ and $[\min I_a^G(u, r_a), \max I_a^G(u, r_a)]$, respectively. Then, AM' measures the changes of these ranges: $|\min I_a^{\overline{G}}(u, r_a) - \min I_a^G(u, r_a)| + |\max I_a^{\overline{G}}(u, r_a) - \max I_a^G(u, r_a)|$. Therefore, we define AM' as follows:

Definition 3 (AM'). *Let u be a user in G. The Attribute Information Loss Metric (AM') of anonymizing user u in $\overline{G}$ is:*

$$AM_c'^{\overline{G}}(u, r_a) = \frac{|I_a^{\overline{G}}(u, r_a) \setminus I_a^{G}(u, r)|}{|dom_a^{G}(r_a) \setminus I_a^{G}(u, r_a)| + 1}$$

$$AM_n'^{\overline{G}}(u, r_a) = \frac{|\min I_a^{\overline{G}}(u, r_a) - \min I_a^{G}(u, r_a)| + |\max I_a^{\overline{G}}(u, r_a) - \max I_a^{G}(u, r_a)|}{|\min dom_a^{G}(r_a) - \min I_a^{G}(u, r_a)| + |\max dom_a^{G}(r_a) - \max I_a^{G}(u, r_a)| + 1}$$

$$AM'^{\overline{G}}(u) = \frac{1}{|R^{UA}|} \times \sum_{r_a}^{R^{UA}} \begin{cases} AM_c'^{\overline{G}}(u, r_a), \textit{if } r_a \textit{ is a categorical attribute} \\ AM_n'^{\overline{G}}(u, r_a), \textit{if } r_a \textit{ is a numerical attribute} \end{cases}$$

where $dom_a^{G}(r_a) = \{v_a | (u, r_a, v_a) \in E^{UA}\}$.

Then, we exploit this metric to evaluate the information loss of making identical the attributes' values of two users by introducing this further definition:

Definition 4 (AM). *Let u, v be two users in G. The Attribute Information Loss (AM) of making u and v having the same values for all of their attributes in $\overline{G}$ is:*

$$AM^{\overline{G}}(u, v) = \frac{AM'^{\overline{G}}(u) + AM'^{\overline{G}}(v)}{2}$$

Example 3. Let $\overline{G}_2$ be the KG showed in Fig. 1b and G be its original version. $R^{UA} = \{age, \ job\}$, $dom_a^{G}(age) = \{18, 19, 40, 50\}$ and $dom_a^{G}(job) = \{Student, Professor\}$. Let assume we make the values of all attributes of *user:0* and *user:2* identical, $I_a^{\overline{G}_2}(user{:}0, age) = I_a^{\overline{G}_2}(user{:}2, age) = \{18, 19\}$, and $I_a^{\overline{G}_2}(user{:}0, job) = I_a^{\overline{G}_2}(user{:}2, job) = \{Student\}$. The information loss of anonymizing *user:0*'s *job* and *age* are $AM_c'^{\overline{G}_2}(user{:}0, job) = \frac{|\{Student\} \setminus \{Student\}|}{|\{Student, Professor\} \setminus \{Student\}| + 1} = \frac{0}{2}$ $= 0$, $AM_n'^{\overline{G}_2}(user{:}0, age) = \frac{|\min\{18,19\} - \min\{18\}| + |\max\{18,19\} - \max\{18\}|}{|\min\{18,19,40,50\} - \min\{18\}| + |\max\{18,19,40,50\} - \max\{18\}| + 1}$ $= \frac{0+1}{0+32+1} = 0.03$. The information loss of anonymizing *user:2*'s *job* is $AM_c'^{\overline{G}_2}(user{:}2, job) = \frac{0}{2} = 0$, $AM_n'^{\overline{G}_2}(user{:}2, age) = \frac{1+0}{1+31+1} = 0.03$. The information loss of anonymizing all attributes of *user:0* and *user:2* are: $AM'^{\overline{G}_2}(user{:}0) = AM'^{\overline{G}_2}(user{:}2) = \frac{0+0.03}{2} = 0.015$. The information loss of making *user:0* and *user:2* having the same values for their attributes is: $AM^{\overline{G}_2}(user{:}0, \ user{:}2) = \frac{0.015 + 0.015}{2} = 0.015$.

To measure the loss of out- and in-degree information on a user u, we calculate the difference between the out- and in-degree of u in the original and anonymized KG. At this purpose, we extend metrics proposed in [7] to consider also multiple relationship types.

Definition 5 (DM_o'). *Let u be a user in G. The out-degree loss metric (DM_o') of anonymizing user u in $\overline{G}$ is:*

$$DM_o'^{\overline{G}}(u) = \frac{1}{|R^{UU}|} \times \sum_{r}^{R^{UU}} \frac{I_o^{\overline{G}}(u, r) - I_o^{G}(u, r)}{|V^{U}|}$$

where $I_o^G(u, r)$ and $I_o^{\overline{G}}(u, r)$ are the out-degree of the relationship type $r \in R^{UU}$ of user u in G and $\overline{G}$, respectively.

Similarly, we define the in-degree information loss (DM'_i) of anonymizing a user u in KG as follows:

Definition 6 (DM'_i). *Let u be a user in G. The in-degree loss metric (DM'_i) of anonymizing user u in $\overline{G}$ is:*

$$DM'^{\overline{G}}_i(u) = \frac{1}{|R^{UU}|} \times \sum_r^{R^{UU}} \frac{I_i^{\overline{G}}(u, r) - I_i^G(u, r)}{|V^U|}$$

where $I_i^G(u, r)$ and $I_i^{\overline{G}}(u, r)$ are the in-degree of the relationship type $r \in R^{UU}$ of user u in G and $\overline{G}$, resp.

By exploiting these metrics, we define the Out- and In-Degree Information Loss (DM) of making identical the out- and in-degree on all types of relationships of two users.

Definition 7. *Let u, v be two users in G. The Out- and In-Degree Information Loss Metric (DM) of making u and v having the same out- and in-degree on all types of relationships in $\overline{G}$ is defined as follows:*

$$DM^{\overline{G}}(u, v) = \frac{DM'^{\overline{G}}_o(u) + DM'^{\overline{G}}_o(v) + DM'^{\overline{G}}_i(u) + DM'^{\overline{G}}_i(v)}{4}$$

Example 4. Let $\overline{G}_2$ be the KG showed in Fig. 1b and G be its original version. $R^{UU} = \{follows, is\_tutor\}$ and $|V^U| = 4$. If we make *user:0* and *user:2* have the same out- and in-degree on all types of relationships: $I_o^{\overline{G}_2}$ (*user:0, follows*) $= I_o^{\overline{G}_2}$ (*user:2, follows*) $= 1$, $I_o^{\overline{G}_2}(user:0, is\_tutor) = I_o^{\overline{G}_2}(user:2, is\_tutor) = 0$; $I_i^{\overline{G}_2}$ (*user:0, follows*) $= I_i^{\overline{G}_2}(user:2, follows) = 0$, $I_i^{\overline{G}_2}(user:0, is\_tutor) = I_i^{\overline{G}_2}$ (*user:2, is_tutor*) $= 1$. Then, $DM'^{\overline{G}_2}_o(user:0) = \frac{1}{2} \times (\frac{1-1}{4} + \frac{0-0}{4}) = 0$ and $DM'^{\overline{G}_2}_i(user:0) = \frac{1}{2} \times (\frac{0-0}{4} + \frac{1-0}{4}) = 0.125$. Similarly, $DM'^{\overline{G}_2}_o$ (*user:2*) $= \frac{1}{2} \times (\frac{1-0}{4} + \frac{0-0}{4}) = 0.125$ and $DM'^{\overline{G}_2}_i(user:2) = \frac{1}{2} \times (\frac{0-0}{4} + \frac{1-1}{4}) = 0$. Out- and In-Degree Information Loss of anonymizing *user:0* and *user:2* is $DM^{\overline{G}_2}(user:0, user:2) = \frac{0+0.125+0.125+0}{4} = 0.0615$.

Finally, we combine AM and DM in the Attribute and Degree Information Loss Metric (ADM).

Definition 8 (ADM). *Let u, v be two users in G. The Attribute and Degree Information Loss Metric (ADM) of making u and v having the same values on all attributes, and the same out- and in-degree on all types of relationships in $\overline{G}$ is as follows:*

$$ADM^{\overline{G}}(u, v) = \alpha^{AM} \times AM^{\overline{G}}(u, v) + (1 - \alpha^{AM}) \times DM^{\overline{G}}(u, v)$$

where α^{AM} is a number between 0 and 1.

As anonymizing KGs modifies both users' attributes and relationships, we use α^{AM} to control the information loss on these two categories of information. If data providers want to preserve users' attributes more than their relationships, they can assign α^{AM} a value greater than 0.5. They can also assign α^{AM} a values less than 0.5 if they want to preserve more users' relationships. Otherwise, they can assign α^{AM} to 0.5.

Example 5. With $\alpha^{AM} = 0.5$, the information loss of making values of all attributes and the out- and in-degrees of all types of relationships of *user:0* and *user:2* in $\overline{G}_2$ (Fig.1b) identical is: $ADM^{\overline{G}_2}(user{:}0, user{:}2) = \alpha^{AM} \times AM^{\overline{G}_2}(user{:}0, user{:}2) + (1 - \alpha^{AM}) \times DM^{\overline{G}_2}(user{:}0, user{:}2) = 0.5 \times 0.015 + (1 - 0.5) \times 0.0615 = 0.03825$.

3.2 The Attribute Truthfulness Information Loss

AM measures the information loss of users' attribute independently, whereas it does not consider the associations between values of different attributes. In particular, let u be a user. We denote with $h \leftrightarrow t$, where $h, t \in I_a^{\overline{G}}(u)$, the association between his/her values in $\overline{G}$. These associations can be extracted by finding all combinations of size 2 in $I_a^{\overline{G}}(u)$. By using the original KG G as the knowledge base, we assume an association is truthful if it can be extracted from the attributes of any user in G. In addition, if two associations $h_1 \leftrightarrow t_1$ and $h_2 \leftrightarrow t_2$ are truthful, $h_1 \leftrightarrow t_2$ and $h_2 \leftrightarrow t_1$ are truthful as well. Conversely, any association that cannot be extracted from G is untruthful. Then, the truthfulness of u's attributes in $\overline{G}$ can be measured as the number of truthful associations that can be extracted from $I^{\overline{G}}(u)$.

Example 6. Let $\overline{G}_2$ be the KG showed in Fig. 1b and G be its original version. $I_a^G(user{:}0) = \{(job, Student), (age, 18)\}$, $I_a^G(user{:}2) = \{(job, Student), (age, 19)\}$. As we make values of *user:0* and *user:2*'s attributes in $\overline{G}_2$ identical, $I_a^{\overline{G}_2}(user{:}0) = I_a^{\overline{G}_2}(user{:}2) = \{(job, Student), (age, 18), (age, 19)\}$. We can extract the following associations $(job, Student) \leftrightarrow (age, 18)$, $(job, Student) \leftrightarrow (age, 19)$, $(age, 19) \leftrightarrow (age, 18)$. $(job, Student) \leftrightarrow (age, 18)$ and $(job, Student) \leftrightarrow (age, 19)$ are truthful as they can be extracted from $I_a^G(user{:}0)$ and $I_a^G(user{:}2)$ while $(age, 18) \leftrightarrow (age, 19)$ is truthful as $(job, Student) \leftrightarrow (age, 18)$ and $(job, Student) \leftrightarrow (age, 19)$ are truthful.

Let D^+ and D^- be the set of truthful and untruthful associations, respectively. The naive solution to check whether an association $(r_a, v_a) \leftrightarrow (r'_a, v'_a)$ is truthful or not is to check if it exists in D^+ or D^-. However, this solution is time consuming and impractical due to the high number of associations in D^+ and D^-. Therefore, we implement a bilinear function $f((r_a, v_a), (r'_a, v'_a))$ to measure the probability that the association $(r_a, v_a) \leftrightarrow (r'_a, v'_a)$ is truthful. We define f as follows:

$$g(r_a, v_a) = \tanh(e_{r_a} * W_g * e_{v_a} + b_g)$$
$$f((r_a, v_a), (r'_a, v'_a)) = \text{sigmoid}(g(r_a, v_a) * W_f * g(r'_a, v'_a) + b_f)$$

where $e_{r_a}, e_{v_a} \in \mathbb{R}^{d_1}$ are d_1-dimensional vectors illustrating r_a, v_a. $W_g \in \mathbb{R}^{d_1 \times d_1 \times d_1}$, $W_f \in \mathbb{R}^{d_1 \times d_1}$, $b_g, b_f \in \mathbb{R}^{d_1}$ are the parameters of f and g. Here, we use tanh and sigmoid to normalize the outputs of g and f to $[-1, 1]$ and $[0, 1]$, respectively, as they are showed to achieve good results in previous work [5].

We train f in the set of all associations $D = D^+ \cup D^-$. Each association $h \leftrightarrow t \in D$ is assigned a positive label $y = 1$, if $h \leftrightarrow t \in D^+$, and $y = 0$, otherwise. Let θ be the set of all parameters of f and g. We learn f by minimizing the Cross Entropy Loss function:

$$\mathcal{J}_1(\theta) = -\sum_x^D y \log(f(h, t)) + (1 - y) \log(1 - f(h, t)) \tag{1}$$

By using the learned function f, we implement an indicator $\mathcal{R}$ deciding whether the association $h \leftrightarrow t$ is truthful or not as follows:

$$\mathcal{R}(h, t) = \begin{cases} 1, \text{if } f(h, t) \geq 0.5 \\ 0, \text{otherwise} \end{cases}$$

We therefore introduce the Attribute Truthfulness Information Loss Metric (ATM) to minimize the number of untruthful associations in the anonymized KGs.

Definition 9 (ATM). *Let u, v be two users in G, and $\mathcal{R}$ be the indicator deciding whether an association is truthful. ATM is defined as follows:*

$$ATM'^{\overline{G}}(u) = \frac{1}{|I_a^{\overline{G}}(u)|^2} \sum_{(r,v)}^{I_a^{\overline{G}}(u)} \sum_{(r',v')}^{I_a^{\overline{G}}(u)} 1 - \mathcal{R}((r_a, v_a), (r'_a, v'_a))$$

$$ATM^{\overline{G}}(u, v) = \frac{ATM'^{\overline{G}}(u) + ATM'^{\overline{G}}(v)}{2}$$

Furthermore, we define the Attribute Truthfulness and Degree Information Loss Metric $(ATDM)$ by combining ATM and DM to minimize the untruthfulness of users' attributes and the degree information loss:

Definition 10 (ATDM). *Let u, v be two users in G. The Attribute Truthfulness and Degree Information Loss (ATDM) of making u and v having the same values on all attributes, and the same out- and in-degree on all types of relationships in $\overline{G}$ identical is:*

$$ATDM^{\overline{G}}(u, v) = \alpha^{ATM} \times ATM^{\overline{G}}(u, v) + (1 - \alpha^{ATM}) \times DM^{\overline{G}}(u, v)$$

where α^{ATM} is a number between 0 and 1.

Similar to ADM, $ATDM$ uses α^{ATM} to control the contribution of ATM and DM to $ATDM$.

4   Cluster-Based Knowledge Graph Anonymization

Our Cluster-Based Knowledge Graph Anonymization Algorithm (CKGA) is designed to modify the structure of the original KG such that users' identities in the anonymized KG are protected according to k-ad while maximizing its quality. Given a KG $G(V, E, R)$ and a positive number k, CKGA generates G's k-ad anonymized version $\overline{G}(\overline{V}, \overline{E}, \overline{R})$ according to three main steps:

1. **Users' points generation.** This step generates a point $e_u \in \mathbb{R}^{d_2}$ for each user $u \in V^U$ such that the Euclidean distance between two points e_u, e_v is nearly equal to the information loss, measured by using ADM and $ATDM$, of their corresponding users u, v.[2]
2. **Clusters generation.** The goal of this step is to construct a set of user clusters $C^{\overline{G}} = \{c \subseteq \overline{V}^U || c| >= k\}$ that minimizes the Euclidean distances between the points of users who are in the same cluster.
3. **Knowledge graph generalization.** In this step, we add and remove edges such that all users in the same cluster have the same values for all of their attributes and the same out- and in-degrees for all relationships.

4.1   Users' Points Generation

Given a KG G and a positive number d_2. We denote with $InfoLoss(u, v)$ the information loss of two users u, v in V^U, measured by using either ADM or $ATDM$. To generate users' points, we first generate a random point $e_u \in \mathbb{R}^{d_2}$ for every user $u \in V^U$. Then, given two users $u, v \in V^U$, we calculate the Squared Euclidean distance between their points e_u, e_v: $d^2(e_u, e_v) = \sum_{i=1}^{d_2}(e_u[i] - e_v[i])^2$.

Then, for every pair of users u, v in V^U, we minimize the differences between the squared information loss of u, v: $InfoLoss(u, v)^2$ and the Squared Euclidean distance between their corresponding points e_u, e_v: $d^2(u, v)$ by using the Mean Squared Error loss function:

$$\mathcal{J}_2(\theta) = \sum_{u, v \in V^U \times V^U} (d^2(e_u, e_v) - InfoLoss(u, v)^2)^2 \tag{2}$$

After minimizing $\mathcal{J}_2$, we obtain points such that for every pair of users $u, v \in V^U$, their squared $InfoLoss(u, v)^2$ is almost equal to the Squared Euclidean distance between their points e_u, e_v:$d^2(e_u, e_v)$. In other words, $InfoLoss(u, v)$ is almost equal to $d(e_u, e_v)$.

4.2   Clusters Generation

Given a KG G, a positive number k, the generated points $\mathcal{U}$ representing users in G, and a clustering algorithm $\mathcal{A}$, we aim at generating a set of clusters that have

---

[2] Although we use ADM and $ATDM$ in this work, our algorithm can be easily extended by using other information loss metrics as well.

Algorithm 1. k-Means Partition$(C, \mathcal{U}, k, \tau)$

Input: C: the set of clusters generated by the clustering algorithm $\mathcal{A}$; $\mathcal{U}$: points of users; k: a positive number; and τ: a number in $[0, 1]$.

Output: The set of clusters $C^{\overline{G}}$.

1: Let Δ be the set of users whose clusters have less than k users.
2: $C^{\overline{G}} \leftarrow \{c | c \in C \wedge |c| \geq k\}$
3: $assign\_new\_clusters(\Delta, C^{\overline{G}}, \mathcal{U}, k, \tau)$
4: **while** $C^{\overline{G}} \neq \varnothing$ **do**
5:     Let c be the first cluster in C
6:     **if** $|c| \geq 2 * k$ **then**
7:         $C^{\overline{G}} \leftarrow C^{\overline{G}} \setminus \{c\}$
8:         Let $\mathcal{U}_c$ be the points in $\mathcal{U}$ representing users in c.
9:         $C_{new} = run\_balanced\_kmeans(\mathcal{U}_c, |c|/k)$
10:        $C^{\overline{G}} \leftarrow C^{\overline{G}} \cup C_{new}$
11:    **end if**
12: **end while**
13: **return** $C^{\overline{G}}$

---

at least k users such that the average Euclidean distances between the points of the users in the same cluster are minimized. As we represent users by using points in Euclidean space, most of the state-of-the-art clustering algorithms (e.g., k-means, DBSCAN [4], and HDBSCAN [2]) can be used.

As the clustering algorithm $\mathcal{A}$ can generate clusters that have less than k users, we use two strategies to make all clusters having at least k users. The first one is the Invalid Removal strategy (IR), which removes all clusters that have less than k users. However, this approach can remove too many users since some clustering algorithms (e.g., k-means) do not consider how many users each cluster has. Furthermore, the more users each cluster has, the more information we lose [7]. To cope with these issues, we present the k-Means Partition strategy (KP). Instead of removing users whose clusters have less than k users, KP adds these users to their nearest clusters that have at least k users. To prevent the resulting clusters from having too many users, KP splits clusters that have at least $2 \times k$ users such that the number of users in all of these clusters is between k and $2 \times k - 1$.

However, adding all users whose clusters have less than k users to new clusters can make the resulting clusters containing outliers whose distances to remaining users in the merged clusters are too big. Therefore, our algorithm uses a parameter $\tau \in [0, 1]$ to prevent merging these outliers. We denote with d_{min}, d_{max} the minimum and maximum Euclidean distance between all users' points in $\mathcal{U}$. Then, $\tau_d = \tau \times (d_{max} - d_{min}) + d_{min}$. We only merge a user to a cluster if the maximum distance between this user and all users in the cluster is less than or equal to τ_d.

Procedure 1 $assign\_new\_clusters$ $(\Delta, C^{\overline{G}}, \mathcal{U}, k, \tau)$

1: Let d_{max}, d_{min} be the maximum and minimum distance between all users' points in $\mathcal{U}$.
2: $\tau_d = \tau \times (d_{max} - d_{min}) + d_{min}$.
3: **for** $u \in \Delta$ **do**
4:     Let $e_u \in \mathcal{U}$ be the point of user u.
5:     $d^c_{min} \leftarrow +\infty$
6:     **for** $c \in C^{\overline{G}}$ **do**
7:         $d_c \leftarrow 0$
8:         **for** $v \in c$ **do**
9:             Let $e_v \in \mathcal{U}$ be the point of user v.
10:            $d_c \leftarrow \max\{d_c, d(e_u, e_v)\}$
11:        **end for**
12:        **if** $d_c < d^c_{min}$ **and** $d_c \leq \tau_d$ **then**
13:            $d^c_{min} \leftarrow d_c$
14:            $c_{selected} \leftarrow c$
15:        **end if**
16:    **end for**
17:    **if** $d^c_{min} \neq +\infty$ **then**
18:        $c_{selected} \leftarrow c_{selected} \cup \{u\}$
19:    **end if**
20: **end for**

Algorithm 1 takes as input the clusters of users generated by the selected clustering algorithm $\mathcal{A}$, C, the set of points representing users $\mathcal{U}$, a positive number k, and the threshold τ. At the beginning, it finds the set of users Δ whose clusters have less than k users (line 1) and the set $C^{\overline{G}}$ containing clusters that have at least k users (line 2). Then, it calls function $assign\_new\_clusters()$ to assign a cluster in $C^{\overline{G}}$ to each user in Δ (line 3). Then, for each cluster $c \in C^{\overline{G}}$ that has more than $2 \times k$ users, it removes this cluster from $C^{\overline{G}}$ (line 7), finds points $\mathcal{U}_c$ corresponding to users in c (line 8), and uses the Balanced k-Means algorithm [11] to split c to $|c|/k$ smaller clusters C_{new} which have at least k users (line 9). This algorithm finds $|c|/k$ centers, each of which represents a cluster in C_{new}. Then, it assigns users in c to these clusters such that all clusters in C_{new} have at least k users and the average squared Euclidean distances of user's points the same cluster is minimized. C_{new} is then added to $C^{\overline{G}}$ (line 10). Finally, it returns $C^{\overline{G}}$ (line 13).

Procedure $assign\_new\_clusters()$. Given a set of users Δ, a set of clusters $C^{\overline{G}}$, a set of users' points $\mathcal{U}$, a positive number k, and the parameter τ, it assigns a cluster in $C^{\overline{G}}$ for each user in Δ. At the beginning it calculates τ_d (line 2). Then, for each user u in Δ, it finds u's point: e_u and calculates the maximum Euclidean distance between e_u and points of users in c: d_c (lines 7–11). If d_c is less than d^c_{min} and less than or equal to τ_d, it updates d^c_{min} and $c_{selected}$ with d_c and c, respectively (lines 13–14). Next, if d^c_{min} is not equal to $+\infty$, it adds u to $c_{selected}$ (line 18).

Algorithm 2. Attributes Generalization $(G, C^{\overline{G}})$

Input: Graph $G(V, E, R)$; clusters of users $C^{\overline{G}}$.
Output: The set of edges representing users' attributes $\overline{E}^{UA}$.

1: $\overline{E}^{UA} \leftarrow \varnothing$
2: **for** $c \in C^{\overline{G}}$ **do**
3:     $\Im_c^G \leftarrow \bigcup_{u \in c} I_a^G(u)$
4:     **for** $u \in c$ **do**
5:         **for** $(r_a, v_a) \in \Im_c^G$ **do**
6:             $\overline{E}^{UA} \leftarrow \overline{E}^{UA} \cup \{(u, r_a, v_a)\}$
7:         **end for**
8:     **end for**
9: **end for**
10: **return** $\overline{E}^{UA}$

It is straightforward to show that, given a set of clusters C and denoting with $C^{\overline{G}}$ the set of clusters returned by Algorithm 1, executed with a positive number k and the parameter τ, all clusters in $C^{\overline{G}}$ have at least k users. Indeed, let c be an arbitrary cluster in $C^{\overline{G}}$. Suppose that c has less than k users. As Algorithm 1 only adds clusters that have at least k users to $C^{\overline{G}}$ (lines 2 and 10), $C^{\overline{G}}$ cannot contain c.

4.3 Knowledge Graph Generalization

Given a KG $G(V, E, R)$ and the set of clusters $C^{\overline{G}}$ returned by Algorithm 1, we aim at generating the anonymized KG $\overline{G}(\overline{V}, \overline{E}, \overline{R})$ such that all users in the same cluster have the same information (i.e., $I^{\overline{G}}$). At this purpose, we present the Knowledge Graph Generalization algorithm (KGG) to add and remove edges such that the values of all attributes and the out- and in-degree of all types of relationships of users in the same cluster are identical. KGG contains two steps:

1) **Attributes generalization.** The goal of this step is to generate values of users' attributes such that all users in the same cluster have the same values for all of their attributes. Formally, $\forall c \in C^{\overline{G}} \wedge \forall u, v \in c \wedge I_a^{\overline{G}}(u) = I_a^{\overline{G}}(v)$;

2) **Out- and in-degree generalization.** In this step, we aim at adding and removing users' relationships such that every user in the same cluster has the same out- and in-degree for all types of his/her relationships. More precisely, $\forall c \in C^{\overline{G}} \wedge \forall u, v \in c \wedge I_o^{\overline{G}}(u) = I_o^{\overline{G}}(v) \wedge I_i^{\overline{G}}(u) = I_i^{\overline{G}}(v)$.

For step 1, we have defined Algorithm 2. It takes as input the original KG G and the set of clusters $C^{\overline{G}}$ generated by Algorithm 1. First, the algorithm initializes empty the set of edges describing users' attributes $\overline{E}^{UA}$ (line 1). Then, for every cluster c in $C^{\overline{G}}$, it calculates the union of attributes' values in G (i.e., I_a^G) of all users $u \in c$: $\Im_c^G$ (line 3). For each user u in c, it adds edge (u, r_a, v_a) to represent that u has value v_a for attribute r_a for all pairs (r_a, v_a) in $\Im_c^G$ (line 6).

Finally, it returns $\overline{E}^{UA}$ (line 10). Therefore, attributes' values of users in the same clusters are identical.

Theorem 2. *Given a KG G and the set of clusters $C^{\overline{G}}$ generated by Algorithm 1. Let $\overline{E}^{UA}$ be set of edges representing users' attributes in $\overline{G}$ created by Algorithm 2. For every cluster c in $C^{\overline{G}}$, for every user u and v in c, $I_a^{\overline{G}}(u) = I_a^{\overline{G}}(v)$.*

Proof. Suppose that there is a cluster $c \in C^{\overline{G}}$ containing two users u, v such that $I_a^{\overline{G}}(u) \neq I_a^{\overline{G}}(v)$. However, if u, v are in the same cluster c, $I_a^{\overline{G}}(u) = I_a^{\overline{G}}(v)$ as Algorithm 2 initializes $\overline{E}^{UA}$ to the empty set (line 1) and adds the same attributes' values to u and v (lines 4–8). Therefore, we can conclude that, for every cluster c in $C^{\overline{G}}$, for every user u and v in c, $I_a^{\overline{G}}(u) = I_a^{\overline{G}}(v)$.

The Out- and In-Degree Generalization algorithm takes as input the original KG G and the set of clusters $C^{\overline{G}}$. For every relationship type $r_u \in R^{UU}$, it uses the Directed Graph Generalization algorithm (DGG) [7] to make the out- and in-degree for r_u of all users in the same cluster identical. Therefore, the out- and in-degrees for every relationship types of users in the same cluster are identical.

As attributes' values and out- and in-degrees in the anonymized KG $\overline{G}$ of users in the same cluster are identical, $\overline{G}$ satisfy k-ad.

Theorem 3. *Given a KG $G(V, E, R)$ and the set of clusters $C^{\overline{G}}$ created by Algorithm 1. Let $\overline{G}(\overline{V}, \overline{E}, \overline{R})$ be the anonymized version of G created by the Knowledge Graph Generalization algorithm. $\overline{G}$ satisfies k-ad.*

Proof. As $C^{\overline{G}}$ is generated by Algorithm 1, all clusters in $C^{\overline{G}}$ have at least k users. Then, for every user, there is a cluster $\zeta^{\overline{G}}(u) \in C^{\overline{G}}$ such that $|\zeta^{\overline{G}}(u)| \geq k$. Additionally, for every user $u, v \in \overline{V}^U$, if u and v are in the same cluster, $I_a^{\overline{G}}(u) = I_a^{\overline{G}}(v)$ (according to Theorem 2), $I_o^{\overline{G}}(u) = I_o^{\overline{G}}(v)$, and $I_i^{\overline{G}}(u) = I_i^{\overline{G}}(v)$ [7]. Then, for every user $u \in \overline{V}^U$, there is a set of users $\zeta^{\overline{G}}(u) = \{v | v \in \overline{V}^U \wedge I_a^{\overline{G}}(u) = I_a^{\overline{G}}(v) \wedge I_o^{\overline{G}}(u) = I_o^{\overline{G}}(v) \wedge I_i^{\overline{G}}(u) = I_i^{\overline{G}}(v)\}$ and $|\zeta^{\overline{G}}(u)| \geq k$. Therefore, we can conclude that $\overline{G}$ satisfies k-ad.

5   Experiments

In this section, we evaluate the quality of anonymized KGs generated by the proposed anonymization algorithm.

5.1   Data Sets

Due to the flexibility of KGs in illustrating users' data, we use different kinds of real-world data sets (see Table 1) to evaluate the capabilities of the proposed technique, namely *Email-Eu-core*, *Google+*, and *Freebase* data sets. Also, we use *Email-temp* and *DBLP* to compare our work with previous algorithms: DGA [3] and CDGA [7].

Table 1. Properties of data sets used for experiments.

Data set	$|V^U|$	$|V^A|$	$|R^{UA}|$	$|R^{UU}|$	$|E^{UA}|$	$|E^{UU}|$
Email-Eu-core [10]	1,005	42	1	1	1,005	25,571
Google+ [6]	7,805	1,962	6	1	20,780	321,268
Freebase [1]	5,000	7,338	10	3	41,067	2,713
Email-temp [10]	986	0	0	1	0	24,929
DBLP [10]	12,591	0	0	1	0	49,743

5.2 Evaluating Users' Points

In this experiment, we evaluate the impact of d_2 to the difference of the Euclidean distance between data points in Euclidean space representing users and the information loss of making their information identical. We generate these points by minimizing the loss function $\mathcal{J}_2$ (Eq. 2) until the mean of these differences has stopped decreasing for 50 epochs. The initial learning rate is 0.1 and we decrease it by multiplying it with 0.5 if the mean of these differences does not decrease for 10 epochs. We implement this step by using PyTorch.

Table 2 illustrates mean and standard deviation of the differences between ADM of users and the Euclidean distance of their points in all data sets. Here, we use ADM with $\alpha^{ADM} = 0.5$ and $\alpha^{DM} = 0.5$. In all data sets, the higher d_2 is, the lower the differences are. In *Email-Eu-core*, by increasing d_2 from 2 to 50, the mean and standard deviation of these differences decreases from 0.0046 to 0.0005 and from 0.0038 to 0.0009, respectively. At $d_2 = 50$, these differences are very small in all data sets.

Therefore, our approach is efficient enough to find points representing users such that the differences between the Euclidean distances of these points are almost similar to the information loss of their corresponding users.

5.3 Tuning CKGA

In this experiment, we aim at evaluating the effects of the adopted clustering algorithm $\mathcal{A}$; of the strategies IR, KP; and k to the average information loss.

Table 2. The mean ($\pm$ standard deviation) of the differences between the Euclidean distance of the learned points and the ADM of the corresponding users.

Data set	$d_2 = 2$	$d_2 = 10$	$d_2 = 50$
Email-Eu-core	0.0046 ($\pm$0.0038)	0.0012 ($\pm$0.0015)	**0.0005 ($\pm$0.0009)**
Google+	0.0099 ($\pm$0.0083)	0.0054 ($\pm$0.0040)	**0.0008 ($\pm$0.0012)**
Freebase	0.0072 ($\pm$0.0073)	0.0036 ($\pm$0.0032)	**0.0003 ($\pm$0.0010)**
Email-temp	0.0030 ($\pm$0.0030)	0.0019 ($\pm$0.0012)	**0.0001 ($\pm$0.0002)**
DBLP	0.0073 ($\pm$0.0021)	0.0031 ($\pm$0.0011)	**0.0002 ($\pm$0.0001)**

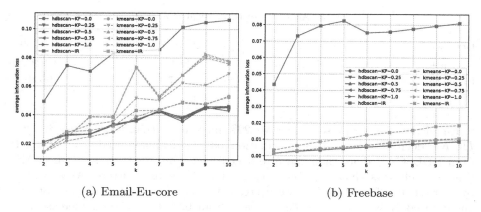

(a) Email-Eu-core   (b) Freebase

Fig. 2. Average information loss of users with varying clustering algorithms and IR/KP strategies.

The average information loss is calculated by taking the average of the loss of users' attributes (i.e., $AM'^{\overline{G}}$), the out- and in-degrees (i.e., $DM'^{\overline{G}}_o$, and $DM'^{\overline{G}}_i$).

Effects of $\mathcal{A}$. Figure 2 shows the average information loss in two data sets: *Email-Eu-core* and *Freebase*, where k-means [4] and HDBSCAN [2] are chosen. We choose these algorithms as they are the state-of-the-art algorithms of two most popular clustering approaches: centroid-based and density-based clustering. With k-means, we assign the number of resulting clusters to $\frac{|V^U|}{k}$. Also, we assign the minimum size of all resulting clusters to k, when running HDBSCAN. We keep default values for all of the remaining parameters of these algorithms. Also, we use IR to show the effects of $\mathcal{A}$ as it only removes clusters that have less than k users. k-means returns anonymized KGs with the information loss lower than those returned from HDBSCAN in both data sets (about 0.06 at $k = 10$). The reason is that HDBSCAN's clusters have more users than those of k-means. At $k = 10$, the average number of users in clusters returned from HDBSCAN and k-means are 36.89 and 22.33 in *Email-Eu-core*, and 76.40 and 21.17 in *Freebase*, respectively. However, IR removes about 30% and 25% of users returned from HDBSCAN and k-means, respectively, in the *Email-Eu-core* data set, whereas about 20% and 27% of users returned from HDBSCAN and k-means, respectively, are removed by IR in the *Freebase* data set. IR only removes users returned from k-means as all clusters returned from HDBSCAN have at least k users. Therefore, k-means is better than HDBSCAN as it returns clusters that have less users than those returned from HDBSCAN.

Effects of IR and KP. KP ensures that the resulting clusters have a number of users from k to $2 \times k - 1$. Thus, we can decrease the average information loss of anonymized KGs returned from HDBSCAN by 0.06 and 0.07 in the *Email-Eu-core* and *Freebase* data set, respectively. Although we increase the average information loss of the anonymized KGs returned from k-means by at least 0.02

Table 3. Accuracy of the indicator $\mathcal{R}$ (%).

Data set	$d_1 = 2$	$d_1 = 10$	$d_1 = 50$
Google+	97.91	99.43	**99.91**
Freebase	95.7	95.7	**96.9**

in Email-Eu-core, we preserve at least 22% more users than those generated by IR. KP decreases the average information loss of the anonymized KGs returned from HDBSCAN more than those returned from k-means because HDBSCAN generates clusters that have more users than k-means' clusters. At $k = 10$, by increasing τ from 0 to 1.0, we decrease the average information loss of the anonymized KGs returned from k-means from 0.08 to 0.05 and increase the ratio of remaining users from about 74% to 100% in both data sets. Here, τ does not affect the ratio of remaining users of the anonymized KGs returned from HDBSCAN as HDBSCAN does not return any cluster that have less than k users. The anonymized KGs executed with HDBSCAN and KP have lower average information loss than those executed with k-means in both data sets as they contain less users than the other ones. Therefore, KP is more effective than IR in improving the quality of anonymized KGs.

Effects of k. The results of these experiments show that the quality of the anonymized KGs decreases by increasing k in all data sets.

5.4 Evaluating the Truthfulness of Anonymized KGs

In this experiment, we investigate the impact of using ADM and $ATDM$ on minimizing the number of untruthful associations.

We first analyze the impact of d_1 on the accuracy of the indicator $\mathcal{R}$. The accuracy is evaluated in truthful/untruthful associations extracted from the $Google+$ and $Freebase$ data sets. We optimize $\mathcal{J}_1$ (Eq. 1) as in the previous experiment in Sect. 5.2. Table 3 shows the accuracy of the trained models on varying values of d_1. The accuracy is higher than 95%. In both data sets, the accuracy is increased by increasing d_1 from 5 to 50 (2% in $Google+$ and 1.2% in $Freebase$). We achieve the highest accuracy with $d = 50$ on both the $Google+$ and $Freebase$ data sets.

We use the trained models with $d_1 = 50$ to evaluate the impacts of $ATDM$ and ADM on the ratio of the untruthful associations in anonymized KGs. We normalize the number of untruthful associations by the number of maximum untruthful associations in the original KG: $\frac{D^+(\overline{G}) \setminus D^+(G)}{D^-(G)}$. Figure 3 illustrates the ratio of untruthful associations of anonymized KGs by considering with ADM and $ATDM$ in: $Google+$ (Fig. 3a) and $Freebase$ (Fig. 3b). We use k-means and KP strategy with $\tau = 1.0$ to generate the anonymized KGs in this experiment. The anonymized KGs generated by using $ATDM$ contain less untruthful associations than those generated by using ADM in both data sets. At $k = 10$, $ATDM$ decreases the ratio of untruthful associations by 0.04% compared to

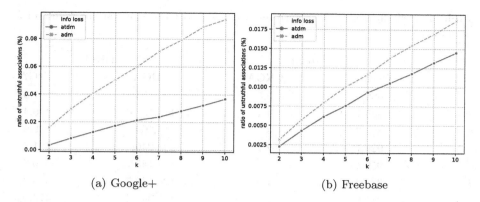

(a) Google+   (b) Freebase

Fig. 3. Ratio of untruthful associations by using ADM and $ATDM$.

those generated by ADM in the *Google+* data set. We achieve similar results for the *Freebase* data set. The anonymized KGs of *Freebase* contain less untruthful associations than those of *Google+* as *Freebase* contains less untruthful associations than *Google+* does. Therefore, $ATDM$ is better than ADM in making users' attributes truthful.

5.5 Comparative Analysis

In this experiment, we compare the quality of anonymized KGs generated by our algorithm and those generated by DGA [3] and CDGA [7] on two data sets: *DBLP* and *Email-temp*. Furthermore, we compare the efficiency of our algorithm and CDGA as we have their implementation. We generate users' points with $d_2 = 50$ and use $\mathcal{A} = k\text{-}means$ and KP strategy with $\tau = 0.5$ to anonymize both data sets (Table 4).

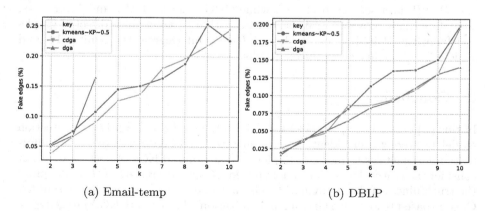

(a) Email-temp   (b) DBLP

Fig. 4. Ratio of fake edges of anonymized graphs returned by DGA, CDGA, and our algorithm on varying values of k.

Table 4. Performance of our algorithm (CKGA) and CDGA on varying values of k (seconds).

k	Email-temp		DBLP	
	CDGA	CKGA	CDGA	CKGA
2	680.8	6.5	91,855.4	607.9
3	825.7	4.4	111,181.6	420.4
4	893.3	3.2	118,269.7	629.9
5	929.7	2.7	122,246.1	581.5
6	950.4	2.3	124,145.7	540.3
7	977.4	1.9	126,542.7	483.3
8	987.9	1.8	127,343.4	474.9
9	1,000.7	1.5	128,254.3	457.6
10	1,007.1	1.5	128,727.9	398.9

As our algorithm removes some users to reduce the number of fake edges of the anonymized KGs, we use the number of fake edges of the remaining users in the anonymized KGs to compare our works with DGA and CDGA. Figure 4 illustrates the results. We take results of DGA and CDGA from the respective papers [3,7]. For both data sets, the anonymized KGs returned by our algorithm contain a number of fake edges similar to that of those returned from CDGA and DGA while preserving more than 99% of users in the original KG. Furthermore, the execution time of our algorithm is extremely lower than that of CDGA. Although our algorithm needs 408 and 40,415 s to train users' points for the *Email-temp* and *DBLP* data sets, the trained points can be reused to anonymize users at any values of k as well as tune the quality of anonymized KGs under different values of our parameters. After obtaining the trained points, it only needs 1.5 s and 398.9 s to anonymize KGs that have at least $k = 10$ users for the *Email-temp* and *DBLP* data sets, respectively, while CDGA needs 1007.1 and 128,727.9 s. Therefore, data providers can use our algorithm to anonymize directed graphs satisfying the Paired k-degree [3] and K-In&Out-Degree Anonymity [14] and achieve good quality anonymized graphs.

6 Conclusion

In this paper, we have presented k-AttributeDegree (k-ad), a privacy protection model, to protect users' identities in anonymized KGs. Also, we present two information loss metrics to measure the loss in anonymized KGs. As *ADM* does not consider the truthfulness of the anonymized KGs, we design *ATDM* to maximize the truthfulness of the anonymized KGs' attributes. Furthermore, we present the Cluster-based Knowledge Graph Anonymization Algorithm (CKGA) to generate the anonymized KGs on k-ad. Our algorithm allows using most of the state-of-the-art clustering algorithms to anonymize KGs. We conduct experiments on five real-life data sets. The experimental results show that our algorithm can generate high-quality anonymized KGs. Moreover, our work is the starting point of anonymization solutions for KG and it can be extended to overcome limitations of k-anonymity model. Firstly, it can be extended to protect not only users' identities but also their sensitive information by adopting l-diversity [8]. Secondly, we also consider extending this work for sequential publishing scenarios, when a data provider publishes a new version of the anonymized data when users update their data. Furthermore, we intend to investigate how differential privacy approaches can also be used to protect KGs.

Acknowledgements. This work has received funding from CONCORDIA, the Cybersecurity Competence Network supported by the European Union's Horizon 2020 research and innovation programme under grant agreement No 830927.

References

1. Bollacker, K., Evans, C., et al.: Freebase: a collaboratively created graph database for structuring human knowledge. In: Proceedings of SIGMOD, pp. 1247–1250 (2008)
2. Campello, R.J., Moulavi, D., et al.: Hierarchical density estimates for data clustering, visualization, and outlier detection. In: ACM TKDD, pp. 1–51 (2015)
3. Casas-Roma, J., Salas, J., et al.: k-degree anonymity on directed networks. Knowl. Inf. Syst. **61**, 1743–1768 (2019)
4. Fahad, A., et al.: A survey of clustering algorithms for big data: taxonomy and empirical analysis. IEEE TETC **2**, 267–279 (2014)
5. Goyal, P., Ferrara, E.: Graph embedding techniques, applications, and performance: a survey. Knowl.-Based Syst. **151**, 78–94 (2018)
6. He, T., Chan, K.C.C.: Discovering fuzzy structural patterns for graph analytics. IEEE Trans. Fuzzy Syst. **26**, 2785–2796 (2018)
7. Hoang, A., Carminati, B., Ferrari, E.: Cluster-based anonymization of directed graphs. In: 5th IEEE International Conference on Collaboration and Internet Computing (CIC), pp. 91–100 (2019)
8. Ji, S., Mittal, P., et al.: Graph data anonymization, de-anonymization attacks, and de-anonymizability quantification: a survey. IEEE Commun. Surv. Tutorials **19**, 1305–1326 (2017)
9. Keet, C.M.: Closed world assumption. In: Dubitzky, W., Wolkenhauer, O., Cho, K.H., Yokota, H. (eds.) Encyclopedia of Systems Biology, p. 415. Springer, New York (2013). https://doi.org/10.1007/978-1-4419-9863-7_731
10. Leskovec, J., Krevl, A.: SNAP datasets: Stanford large network dataset collection (2014). http://snap.stanford.edu/data
11. Malinen, M.I., Fränti, P.: Balanced K-means for clustering. In: Fränti, P., Brown, G., Loog, M., Escolano, F., Pelillo, M. (eds.) S+SSPR 2014. LNCS, vol. 8621, pp. 32–41. Springer, Heidelberg (2014). https://doi.org/10.1007/978-3-662-44415-3_4
12. Qian, J., Li, X.Y., et al.: Social network de-anonymization and privacy inference with knowledge graph model. IEEE TDSC **16**, 679–692 (2017)
13. Qian, J., Li, X.Y., et al.: Social network de-anonymization: more adversarial knowledge, more users re-identified? ACM Trans. Internet Technol. **19**, 1–22 (2019)
14. Zhang, X., Liu, J., et al.: Large-scale dynamic social network directed graph k-in&out-degree anonymity algorithm for protecting community structure. IEEE Access **7**, 108371–108383 (2019)

Same Point Composable and Nonmalleable Obfuscated Point Functions

Peter Fenteany and Benjamin Fuller[✉]

University of Connecticut, Mansfield, CT, USA
{peter.fenteany,benjamin.fuller}@uconn.edu

Abstract. A point obfuscator is an obfuscated program that indicates if a user enters a previously stored password. A digital locker is stronger: outputting a key if a user enters a previously stored password. The real-or-random transform allows one to build a digital locker from a composable point obfuscator (Canetti and Dakdouk, Eurocrypt 2008).

Ideally, both objects would be nonmalleable, detecting adversarial tampering. Appending a non-interactive zero knowledge proof of knowledge adds nonmalleability in the common random string (CRS) model.

Komargodski and Yogev (Eurocrypt, 2018) built a nonmalleable point obfuscator without a CRS. We show a lemma in their proof is false, leaving security of their construction unclear. Bartusek, Ma, and Zhandry (Crypto, 2019) used similar techniques and introduced another nonmalleable point function; their obfuscator is not secure if the same point is obfuscated twice. Thus, there was no composable and nonmalleable point function to instantiate the real-or-random construction.

Our primary contribution is a nonmalleable point obfuscator that can be composed any polynomial number of times with the same point (which must be known ahead of time). Security relies on the assumption used in Bartusek, Ma, and Zhandry. This construction enables a digital locker that is nonmalleable with respect to the input password.

As a secondary contribution, we introduce a key encoding step to detect tampering on the key. This step combines nonmalleable codes and seed-dependent condensers. The seed for the condenser must be public and not tampered, so this can be achieved in the CRS model. The password distribution may depend on the condenser's seed as long as it is efficiently sampleable. This construction is black box in the underlying point obfuscation.

Nonmalleability for the password is ensured for functions that can be represented as low degree polynomials. Key nonmalleability is inherited from the class of functions prevented by the nonmalleable code.

Keywords: Digital lockers · Point obfuscation · Virtual black-box obfuscation · Nonmalleable codes · Seed-dependent condensers · Nonmalleability

© Springer Nature Switzerland AG 2020
M. Conti et al. (Eds.): ACNS 2020, LNCS 12147, pp. 124–144, 2020.
https://doi.org/10.1007/978-3-030-57878-7_7

1   Introduction

Obfuscation hides the implementation of a program from all users of the program. This work is concerned with *virtual black-box obfuscation*, where an obfuscator creates a program that reveals nothing about the program other than its input and output behavior [BGI+01, BGI+12]. Barak et al. showed that a virtual black-box obfuscator cannot exist for all polynomial time circuits [BGI+01]. However, this leaves open the possibility of virtual black-box obfuscators for interesting classes of programs [CD08, BC10, CRV10, WZ17, BR17].[1]

We focus on *obfuscated point functions* [Can97] and *digital lockers* [CD08] [BC10]. A *point function obfuscator* is an algorithm lockP(val) which outputs a circuit ulockP$_{val}(\cdot)$. The circuit ulockP$_{val}(\cdot)$ stores val and indicates when val is inputted to it. An obfuscated point function needs to hide all partial information about val [Can97].

A digital locker obfuscator inputs a value, val, and key, key. The output is a program ulock$_{val,key}(\cdot)$ which outputs key if and only if the input is val. Soundness says ulock$_{val,key}$ should reveal nothing about val or key if the adversary cannot guess val. Digital lockers have applications in password [Can97] and biometric authentication [CFP+16, ABC+18].

The *real-or-random* construction composes point functions to build a digital locker [CD08]. It works as so: sample a random point r. For each bit of the key, either r (corresponding to a 0 in key) or val (corresponding to a 1) is obfuscated. An obfuscation of val is prepended as a check value. When running the program, if the check obfuscation opens, the user runs the other programs: failures to open correspond to a key bit 0 and successes correspond to a key bit of 1. The point function must retain security when val is obfuscated multiple times.

Nonmalleability. A desirable property of an obfuscated program is nonmalleability. A *nonmalleable* obfuscator detects if an adversary attempts to tamper the obfuscation into a related program [CV09], where being related is defined by some family of functions $\mathcal{F}$. For example, it is desirable to prevent ulock$_{val,key}$ from being mauled to ulock$_{f(val),f'(key)}$ for $f, f' \in \mathcal{F}$.

In the random oracle model, designing nonmalleable digital lockers and point functions is easy: For a random oracle RO one outputs the program RO(val) $\oplus$ (key$||$RO$'$(key)), where RO and RO$'$ are two independent random oracles of different output length. Similarly, using general non-interactive zero-knowledge proofs of knowledge (NIZKPoKs) in the common random string (CRS) model one can achieve nonmalleability. For ulock$_{val,key}(\cdot)$, appending a NIZKPoK of key and val would prevent the adversary from creating a valid obfuscation for any point related to the inputs.[2]

Komargodski and Yogev constructed a nonmalleable point obfuscator without resorting to these tools [KY18a]. Their construction follows. Let g be a fixed

---

[1] We do not consider indistinguishability obfuscation in this work [GGH+13, GGH+16, SW14, PST14, GLSW15, AJ15].

[2] The adversary can always substitute an obfuscation on an unrelated point. Thus, it is possible to create obfuscations for functions f where $f(val)$ is easy to guess.

group generator. To obfuscate the point val, the obfuscator computes a random r and outputs

$$\mathsf{lockP}(\mathsf{val}) = \left(r, r^{g^{\sum_{i=1}^{4} \mathsf{val}^i}} \right).$$

We observe that nonmalleability of Komargodski and Yogev's scheme relies on an incorrect lemma in a way that is not apparently repairable. We discuss this in detail below.

Bartusek, Ma, and Zhandry [BMZ19] using similar mathematical structure showed a nonmalleable point function using random a, b, c:

$$\mathsf{lockP}(\mathsf{val}) = a, g^{a\cdot\mathsf{val}+(\mathsf{val})^2+(\mathsf{val})^3+(\mathsf{val})^4+(\mathsf{val})^5}, b, g^{b\cdot\mathsf{val}+(\mathsf{val})^6}, c, g^{c\cdot\mathsf{val}+(\mathsf{val})^7}.$$

The structure of the group element is similar to Komargodski and Yogev's construction, but with a random scalar in place of "double exponentiation". The terms involving b and c ensure no incorrect point causes the obfuscation to unlock. In both constructions, g is assumed to be fixed; this means the distribution of val may depend on generator g. Bartusek, Ma, and Zhandry [BMZ19] show security based on new Diffie-Hellman variants and show these variants hold in the generic group model, using tools from the auxiliary input generic group model [CDG18].

The natural nonmalleability definition is that, given $\mathsf{ulockP_{val}}$, an adversary can only output the same obfuscation or obfuscations of independent points. The above constructions use a weaker definition. Given an obfuscation $\mathsf{lockP_{val}}$, the adversary is required to output a function f and an obfuscation $\mathsf{lockP}_{f(\mathsf{val})}$. That is, the definition requires the adversary to *know* what tampering function they are applying. Both constructions consider f as a polynomial of bounded degree related to the assumed hardness in the DDH assumptions. The definition considers the tampering functions prevented, not what operations are performed by the adversary.

The goal of this work is to construct nonmalleable digital lockers. The real-or-random construction instantiated with nonmalleable point functions would provide nonmalleability over val. Crucially, this construction requires security to hold when the nonmalleable point functions are *composed* though only with the same val. Both previous constructions have issues that prevent incorporation. The proof of nonmalleability for [KY18a] relies on an untrue lemma and the proof does not seem easily repairable, and the construction of [BMZ19] cannot be composed twice or more. We discuss these issues and then introduce our contribution.

[KY18b, **Lemma 4.6**] **is not true.** Let g be a fixed generator of a group. The version of Komargodski and Yogev published in Eurocrypt 2018 [KY18a] relied on a *fixed generator* power DDH assumption which says for any distribution x with super logarithmic entropy (here the distribution of x can depend on generator g) that

$$g, g^x, g^{x^2}, ..., g^{x^t} \approx_c g, g^{u_1}, g^{u_2}, ..., g^{u_t},$$

for a truly random set of elements $u_1, ..., u_t$. This assumption is used in the proof by assuming that the adversary sees $\sum_{i=1}^{4} u_i$ and arguing they can't predict any linear combinations other than $c \sum_{i=1}^{4} u_i$ for some constant c. However, Bartusek, Ma, and Zhandry [BMZ19] showed that for a fixed generator this assumption cannot be true: x can be drawn from points where most bits of g^x are fixed. As a result, a revised version [KY18b] proposes a revised assumption called entropic power where

$$g, g^x, g^{x^2}, ..., g^{x^t} \approx_c g, g^{z_1}, g^{z_2}, ..., g^{z_t}.$$

where z_i are independent and have some super logarithmic min-entropy. This assumption does not appear to suffice. In particular, [KY18b, Lemma 4.6] is incorrect as stated. The lemma states it is hard to predict linear combinations of z_i other than $c \sum_{i=1}^{4} z_i$ for any constant c, even knowing $\sum_{i=1}^{4} z_i$. However, even if each z_i has entropy, the value $\sum_{i=1}^{4} z_i$ may uniquely determine each z_i: let z_i vary in the ith quarter of bits and fix the rest of bits to be 0. The attack of [BMZ19] prevents arguing that z_i has any greater amount of entropy.

This does not seem to be an issue of just the proof technique. The point of the entropic power assumption is to switch to an information-theoretic setting where the adversary cannot predict new powers from a linear combination, but bounding the entropy of each z_i may cause all powers to be predictable. Repairing this scheme seems to require a new Diffie-Hellman assumption or a major change in analysis.

[BMZ19] **is not composable.** One might try to compose the construction of Bartusek et al. [BMZ19]. However, this scheme is not secure even when used twice for the same val. The hardness of finding g^x is the underlying assumption used to show nonmalleability [BMZ19, Assumption 4]. Since the distribution of x may depend on g, one can construct distributions x where g^x is distinguishable from a random group element g^r. If one can find g^x, the scheme can not be secure. If one tries to obfuscate the same point x twice, all the higher order terms can be removed by dividing two instances. That is, given

$$a_1, g_1 = g^{a_1 x + x^2 + x^3 + x^4 + x^5}$$
$$a_2, g_2 = g^{a_2 x + x^2 + x^3 + x^4 + x^5}$$

one can easily compute $g^{(a_1 - a_2)x} = g_1/g_2$, and recover $g^x = (g_1/g_2)^{(a_1-a_2)^{-1}}$.

1.1 Our Contribution

The primary contribution of this work is the first same-point composable nonmalleable point function. The composable, nonmalleable point function can instantiate the real-or-random construction providing a nonmalleable digital locker that prevents tampering over val only. This construction is in the standard model.

As a secondary contribution, we introduce a key encoding step to detect tampering on key. The key encoding step allows us to achieve a digital locker that is nonmalleable over both val and key. However, our key encoding step requires a public value that all distributions can depend on. This can be achieved in the common random string (CRS) model. In our construction the distribution of val can depend on the public value. In the CRS model, one can achieve nonmalleability in a non-black box way using non-interactive zero knowledge proofs of knowledge [CV09].

Composable Same Point Nonmalleable Point Function Obfuscation. We introduce a new nonmalleable point function that can be safely composed τ times as long as the *same point* is obfuscated each time. The construction builds on the one-time scheme of Bartusek et al. [BMZ19]. We include additional randomized powers to prevent the above attack. The construction needs to know the desired composition parameter τ ahead of time. The value τ would be known in the case when a point function is being used to construct a digital locker. Let a, b, c be uniform vectors of length τ. The construction is as follows:

$$\mathsf{lockP}(x; a, b, c) \overset{def}{=} \begin{bmatrix} a, & g^{\sum_{i=1}^{\tau} a_i x^i + \sum_{i=\tau+1}^{\tau+5} x^i}, \\ b, & g^{b_1 x + \sum_{i=2}^{\tau} b_i x^{i+\tau+4} + x^{2\tau+5}}, \\ c, & g^{c_1 x + \sum_{i=2}^{\tau} c_i x^{i+2\tau+4} + x^{3\tau+5}}. \end{bmatrix}$$

The intuition for the formation of the first group element is that we need to randomize more powers to prevent the adversary from removing the higher order powers and being able to linear solve for g^x. Since the adversary can create $\tau - 1$ linearly independent pairs, τ randomized powers are necessary. We add a fifth non-randomized power in the a term to deal with the additional flexibility created by τ. The crucial step in the proof is showing that some linear system has no interesting solutions, the extra power is to counteract the degree of freedom introduced by τ (see Theorem 2).

The intuition for the b and c terms is similar. Due to our proof technique, we need to randomize different powers for the a term, the b term, and the c term, resulting in the above construction. All terms have a randomized x^1 coefficient so we can reduce to [BMZ19, Assumption 4].

We can instantiate the real-or-random construction with this construction to yield a nonmalleable digital locker that only provides nonmalleability over the locked val. As mentioned above, one could prove knowledge (using a NIZKPoK) of just key to prevent modification of this value. Such a method would inherently depend on the underlying point function. Our goal is to avoid general NIZKPoKs.

Detecting Key Tampering. Our strategy is to use nonmalleable codes [DPW10]. We use nonmalleable codes in a nonstandard way: the adversary sees obfuscations that are correlated to the codeword before choosing how to tamper. This seems okay at first glance, correlated obfuscations shouldn't be distinguishable from random obfuscations. If a tampering adversary performs differently in the presence of correlated obfuscations or random obfuscations, if one can check success probability it be turned into a distinguisher.

However, nonmalleable codes don't yield such a check because nonmalleable codes allow the adversary to tamper to an independent value. When using nonmalleable codes in the reduction, one needs to know if the value is independent. Rather than just encoding key we include the output of a seed-dependent condense [DRV12] applied to val, cond(val), as part of the encoded value. This allows us to argue that an adversary that succeeds in mauling the nonmalleable code more frequently when presented with correlated obfuscations breaks soundness of the obfuscation. However, this change necessitates that the seed of the condenser is public and not tampered. This can be achieved in the CRS model.

Our construction does not assume independence of distributions from the random object. The CRS is only necessary for preventing tampering of key, the real-or-random construction prevents tampering of val in the standard model. We discuss alternative tools in Sect. 4.

Organization. In Sect. 2, we present definitions. In Sect. 3, we introduce the composable nonmalleable point function. In Sect. 4, we present the real-or-random digital locker construction and add checks for key tampering.

2   Preliminaries

For random variables X_i over some alphabet $\mathcal{Z}$ we denote by $X = X_1, ..., X_n$ the tuple $(X_1, ..., X_n)$. For a set of indices J, X_J is the restriction of X to the indices in J. The *minentropy* of X is $\mathrm{H}_\infty(X) = -\log(\max_x \Pr[X = x])$, and the *average (conditional) minentropy* [DORS08, Section 2.4] of X given Y is $\tilde{\mathrm{H}}_\infty(X|Y) = -\log\left(\mathbb{E}_{y \in Y} \max_x \Pr[X = x|Y = y]\right)$. For a distinguisher D, the *computational distance* between X and Y is $\delta^D(X, Y) = |\mathbb{E}[D(X)] - \mathbb{E}[D(Y)]|$ (we extend it to a class of distinguishers $\mathcal{D}$ by taking the maximum over all distinguishers $D \in \mathcal{D}$). We denote by $\mathcal{D}_s$ the class of randomized circuits which output a single bit and have size at most s. Logarithms are base 2. In general, capitalized letters are used for random variables and the corresponding lowercase letters for their samples. We say that two circuits, C and C', with inputs in $\{0, 1\}^\lambda$ are equivalent if $\forall x \in \{0, 1\}^\lambda, C(x) = C'(x)$. We denote this as $C \equiv C'$. For a matrix $\mathbf{A}$ let $\mathbf{A}_{i,j}$ denote the entry in the ith row and the jth column. Let $\mathbf{A}_{(\cdot,j)}$ represent the jth column and $\mathbf{A}_{(i,\cdot)}$ represent the ith row.

Definition 1. *An ensemble of distributions $\mathcal{X} = \{X_\lambda\}_{\lambda \in \mathbb{N}}$, where $\mathcal{X}_\lambda$ is over $\{0, 1\}^\lambda$, is* well-spread *if*

1. *It is efficiently and uniformly samplable. That is, there exists a PPT algorithm given 1^λ as input whose output is identically distributed as X_λ.*
2. *For all large enough $\lambda \in \mathbb{N}$, it has super-logarithmic minentropy. Namely, $\mathrm{H}_\infty(X_\lambda) = \omega(\log \lambda)$.*

Obfuscation Definitions. All obfuscation definitions include a requirement of *polynomial slowdown*, which says the running time should be at most a polynomial factor larger than the original program. Running time of our constructions can be easily verified. For all definitions, we include a tampering function $\mathcal{F}$. The traditional definition can be achieved by taking $\mathcal{F} = \emptyset$. We adapt nonmalleability definitions from Komargodski and Yogev [KY18a]. See Komargodski and Yogev for definitional considerations [KY18a].

Our constructions require that the challenger can recognize a legitimate
obfuscation. We call this object a value verifier or V_{val}. It was called a verifier
(without the word value) in [KY18a].

Definition 2 (Value Verifier). *Let $\lambda \in \mathbb{N}$ be a security parameter. Let $\mathcal{O}$ be a
program that takes inputs $x \in \{0,1\}^\lambda$ and outputs a program $\mathcal{P}$. A PPT algorithm
V_{val} is called a* value verifier *if for all $x \in \{0,1\}^\lambda$, it holds that $\Pr[V_{val}(\mathcal{P}) =
1|\mathcal{P} \leftarrow \mathcal{O}(x)] = 1$, (prob. over the randomness of V_{val} and $\mathcal{O}$).*

Our constructions consist of tuples of group elements and strings. The obvious
value verifier suffices as long as group elements are recognizable. A point function
is a function $I_{val}: \{0,1\}^n \mapsto \{0,1\}$ that outputs 1 on input val and 0 elsewhere.
An obfuscator preserves functionality while hiding the point val if val is not
provided as input to the program. In this work we consider a version that allows
for the same point to be obfuscated multiple times while retaining security.

Definition 3 (τ-Same Point Nonmalleable Point Function). *For security
parameter $\lambda \in \mathbb{N}$, let $\mathcal{F} : \{0,1\}^\lambda \rightarrow \{0,1\}^\lambda$ be a family of functions, let $\mathcal{X}$ be
a family of distributions over $\{0,1\}^\lambda$. A $(\mathcal{F}, \mathcal{X})$-non malleable point function
obfuscation* lockP *is a PPT algorithm that inputs a point* val $\in \{0,1\}^\lambda$, *and
outputs a circuit* ulockP. *Let V_{val} be a value verifier for* lockP *as defined in
Definition 2. The following properties must hold:*

1. **Completeness:** *For all* val $\in \{0,1\}^\lambda$, *it holds that*
$$\Pr[\text{ulockP}(\cdot) \equiv I_{val}(\cdot)|\text{ulockP} \leftarrow \text{lockP}(val)] \geq 1 - \text{ngl}(\lambda),$$
   where the probability is over the randomness of lockP.
2. **Soundness:** *For every PPT $\mathcal{A}$ and any polynomial function p, there exists a
simulator $\mathcal{S}$ and a polynomial $q(\lambda)$ such that, for all large enough $\lambda \in \mathbb{N}$, all*
val $\in \{0,1\}^\lambda$ *and for any predicate $\mathcal{P} : \{0,1\}^\lambda \mapsto \{0,1\}$,*
$$|\Pr[\mathcal{A}(\{\text{ulockP}_i\}_{i=1}^\tau) = \mathcal{P}(val)|\{\text{ulockP}_i\}_{i=1}^\tau \leftarrow \text{lockP}(val)]$$
$$- \Pr[\mathcal{S}^{I_{val}(\cdot)}(1^\lambda) = \mathcal{P}(val)]| \leq \frac{1}{p(\lambda)},$$
   *where S is allowed $q(\lambda)$ oracle queries to I_{val} and the probabilities are over
the internal randomness of $\mathcal{A}$ and* lockP, *and of $\mathcal{S}$, respectively. Here $I_{val}(\cdot)$
is an oracle that returns 1 when provided input* val *and 0 otherwise.*
3. **Nonmalleability:** *For any $X \in \mathcal{X}$, for any PPT $\mathcal{A}$, there exists $\epsilon = \text{ngl}(\lambda)$,
such that:*
$$\Pr_{val \leftarrow X} \left[V_{val}(C) = 1, f \in \mathcal{F}, (I_{f(val)} \equiv C) \middle| \begin{array}{l} \{\text{ulockP}_i\}_{i=1}^\tau \leftarrow \text{lockP}(val) \\ (C, f) \leftarrow \mathcal{A}(\{\text{ulockP}_i\}_{i=1}^\tau) \end{array} \right] \leq \epsilon.$$

In the above ulockP$_i$ are τ outputs of lockP on the same input point val and
independent randomness. Note that the simulator is still only provided with a
single oracle. In usual composition definitions the simulator has τ oracles. Since

we consider the same point being obfuscated multiple times, all of these oracles would have the same functionality and can be reduced to a single oracle.

In addition to the above traditional definition of soundness, in the full version [FF18, Section 2.1] we introduce two auxiliary definitions of privacy for nonmalleable point functions. These are known as distributional indistinguishability and oracle indistinguishability (both first defined in [Can97]). We show those definitions are equivalent to soundness. We use these two auxiliary definitions in the proof of Theorem 1. We now present our definition of a nonmalleable digital locker. Our notation for digital lockers adds a key verifier which checks if the key should be accepted. This is analogous to the value verifier in the previous subsection:

Definition 4 (Key Verifier). *Let* $\lambda \in \mathbb{N}$ *be a security parameter and let* $n = n(\lambda)$ *be a parameter. Let* $\mathcal{O}$ *be a program that takes inputs* $x \in \{0,1\}^{\lambda}, y \in \{0,1\}^{k}$ *and outputs a program* $\mathcal{P}$. *A PPT algorithm* $\mathsf{V}_{\mathsf{key}}$ *(with inputs in* $\{0,1\}^{\lambda+n}$ *and outputs in* $\{0,1\}^{k} \cup \bot$*) for program class* $\mathcal{O}$ *is called a* key verifier *if it holds that* $\Pr[\mathsf{V}_{\mathsf{key}}(x,z) \neq \bot \mid \mathcal{P} \leftarrow \mathcal{O}(x,y), z \leftarrow \mathcal{P}(x)] = 1$, *where the probability is over the randomness of* $\mathsf{V}_{\mathsf{key}}$ *and* $\mathcal{O}$*).*

Note the three different values x, y, z. The value x is the input value, y is the input key, and z as an encoded version of the key. The output of the locker is z which is then checked. There must be an independent algorithm that checks z otherwise no manipulation detection is possible. A definition for traditional digital lockers is found in Canetti and Dakdouk [CD08]. Our definition considers tampering on both key and val.

Definition 5 (Nonmalleable Digital Locker). *For security parameter* $\lambda \in \mathbb{N}$, *Let* $\mathcal{F} : \{0,1\}^{\lambda} \rightarrow \{0,1\}^{\lambda}, \mathcal{G} : \{0,1\}^{n} \rightarrow \{0,1\}^{n}$ *be families of functions and* $\mathcal{X}$ *be a family of distributions over* $\{0,1\}^{\lambda}$. *A* $(\mathcal{F}, \mathcal{G}, \mathcal{X})$-nonmalleable *digital locker* lock *is a PPT algorithm that inputs a point* val $\in \{0,1\}^{\lambda}$ *and string* key $\in \{0,1\}^{n}$. *Let* $\mathsf{V}_{\mathsf{val}}$ *be a value verifier for* lock *and let* $\mathsf{V}_{\mathsf{key}}$ *be a key verifier for* lock. *The following conditions must be met:*

1. *Completeness: For a circuit* ulock *define the circuit* ulock$'(x) = \mathsf{V}_{\mathsf{key}}(x,$ ulock$(x))$. *For all* val $\in \{0,1\}^{\lambda}$, key $\in \{0,1\}^{n}$ *it holds that*

$$\Pr[\mathsf{ulock}'(\cdot) \equiv I_{\mathsf{val,key}}(\cdot) \mid \mathsf{ulock} \leftarrow \mathsf{lock}(\mathsf{val,key})] \geq 1 - \mathsf{ngl}(\lambda),$$

where the probability is over the randomness of lock.

2. *Soundness: For every PPT* $\mathcal{A}$ *and any polynomial function* p, *there exists a simulator* $\mathcal{S}$ *and a polynomial* $q(\lambda)$ *such that, for all large enough* $\lambda \in \mathbb{N}$, *all* val $\in \{0,1\}^{\lambda}$, *all* key $\in \{0,1\}^{k}$, *and for any* $\mathcal{P} : \{0,1\}^{\lambda+k} \mapsto \{0,1\}$,

$$\left| \Pr[\mathcal{A}(\mathsf{lock}(\mathsf{val,key})) = \mathcal{P}(\mathsf{val,key})] - \Pr[\mathcal{S}^{I_{\mathsf{val,key}}}(1^{\lambda}) = \mathcal{P}(\mathsf{val,key})] \right| \leq \frac{1}{p(\lambda)},$$

where S *is allowed* $q(\lambda)$ *oracle queries to* $I_{\mathsf{val,key}}$ *and the probabilities are over the internal randomness of* $\mathcal{A}$ *and* lock, *and of* $\mathcal{S}$, *respectively. Here* $I_{\mathsf{val,key}}$ *is an oracle that returns* key *when provided input* val, *otherwise* $I_{\mathsf{val,key}}$ *returns* $\bot$.

3. **Nonmalleability:** *For any distribution $X \in \mathcal{X}$, for any PPT $\mathcal{A}$, for any key $\in \{0,1\}^n$, there exists $\epsilon = \texttt{ngl}(\lambda)$ such that:*

$$
\Pr_{\text{val} \leftarrow X}
\left[
\begin{array}{l|l}
V_{\text{val}}(C) = 1, f \in \mathcal{F}, g \in \mathcal{G}, & \\
\quad y = C(f(\text{val})), & \\
\quad y = g(\text{ulock}_{\text{val},\text{key}}(\text{val})), & \text{ulock}_{\text{val},\text{key}} \leftarrow \text{lock}(\text{val}, \text{key}) \\
\quad V_{\text{key}}(f(\text{val}), y) \neq \perp, & (C, f, g) \leftarrow \mathcal{A}(\text{ulock}_{\text{val},\text{key}}) \\
\quad \exists \alpha \ s.t. \ I_{f(\text{val}),\alpha} \equiv C &
\end{array}
\right] \leq \epsilon.
$$

where at most one of f and g may be the identity function.

If nonmalleability is not a requirement a traditional digital locker can be obtained by outputting $\text{ulock}'(x) = V_{\text{key}}(x, \text{ulock}(x))$ instead of $\text{ulock}(x)$.

3   A Composable Nonmalleable Point Function

In this section, we introduce a new construction of a nonmalleable point function that can be composed as long as the same point is used each time. Our construction draws on ideas from [BMZ19] and is secure under the same assumptions. Their construction is as follows for randomly sampled a, b, c:

$$
\text{lockP}(\text{val}) = a, g^{a \cdot \text{val} + (\text{val})^2 + (\text{val})^3 + (\text{val})^4 + (\text{val})^5}, b, g^{b \cdot \text{val} + (\text{val})^6}, c, g^{c \cdot \text{val} + (\text{val})^7}.
$$

The first group element is the key to nonmalleability, the second two group elements are there to provide correctness. Security of their construction and ours relies on two assumptions (they showed security of these assumptions in the generic group model even if the distribution of val depends on the chosen generator of the group).

Assumption 1 *[BMZ19, Assumption 3].* *Let $\mathcal{G} = \{\mathbb{G}_\lambda\}_{\lambda \in \mathbb{N}}$ be a group ensemble with efficient representation and operations where each $\mathbb{G}_\lambda$ is a group of prime order $p \in (2^\lambda, 2^{\lambda+1})$. We assume that for every $\lambda \in \mathbb{N}$ there is a canonical group (and efficiently computable) and canonical and efficient mapping between the elements of $\{0,1\}^\lambda$ to $\mathbb{G}_\lambda$. Let $\{\mathcal{X}_\lambda\}$ be a family of well-spread distributions over $\{0,1\}^\lambda$. Then for any $\ell = \texttt{poly}(\lambda)$ for any PPT $\mathcal{A}$:*

$$
\left| \Pr[\mathcal{A}(\{k_i, g^{k_i x + x^i}\}_{i \in [2,\ldots,\ell]}) = 1] - \Pr[\mathcal{A}(\{k_i, g^{k_i r + r^i}\}_{i \in [2,\ldots,\ell]})] \right| = \texttt{ngl}(\lambda).
$$

where $x \leftarrow \mathcal{X}_\lambda, r \leftarrow \mathbb{Z}_{p(\lambda)}, k_i \leftarrow \mathbb{Z}_{p(\lambda)}$.

The second assumption can be proved from Assumption 1, see [BMZ19, Lemma 8], and is useful for arguing nonmalleability:

Assumption 2 *[BMZ19, Assumption 4].* *Let $\mathcal{G}$ and $\mathcal{X}_\lambda$ be defined as in Assumption 1. Then for any $\ell = \texttt{poly}(\lambda)$ for any PPT $\mathcal{A}$:*

$$
\Pr[g^x \leftarrow \mathcal{A}(\{k_i, g^{k_i x + x^i}\}_{i \in [2,..,\ell]}] = \texttt{ngl}(\lambda).
$$

where $x \leftarrow \mathcal{X}_\lambda$ and $k_i \leftarrow \mathbb{Z}_{p(\lambda)}$.

We now introduce our main construction. The intuition behind the construction is to increase the number of randomized powers to deal with the additional constraints on val that the adversary gains by seeing multiple copies; it will be proved secure under Assumptions 1 and 2.

Construction 1. *Let $\lambda \in \mathbb{N}$ be a security parameter. Let $\mathcal{G} = \{\mathbb{G}_\lambda\}_{\lambda \in \mathbb{N}}$ be a group ensemble with efficient representation and operations where each $\mathbb{G}_\lambda$ is a group of prime order $p \in (2^\lambda, 2^{\lambda+1})$. We assume that for every $\lambda \in \mathbb{N}$ there is a canonical and efficient mapping between the elements of $\{0,1\}^\lambda$ to $\mathbb{G}_\lambda$. Let g be a generator of the group $\mathbb{G}_\lambda$. For some parameter $\tau \in \mathbb{Z}^+$, let $\boldsymbol{a}, \boldsymbol{b}, \boldsymbol{c} \xleftarrow{\$} \mathbb{G}_\lambda$ be input randomness and define the algorithm* lockP *as:*

$$\mathsf{lockP}(\mathsf{val}; \boldsymbol{a}, \boldsymbol{b}, \boldsymbol{c}) \overset{def}{=} \begin{bmatrix} \boldsymbol{a}, & g^{\sum_{i=1}^{\tau} a_i x^i + \sum_{i=\tau+1}^{\tau+5} x^i} \\ \boldsymbol{b}, & g^{b_1 x + \sum_{i=2}^{\tau} b_i x^{i+\tau+4} + x^{2\tau+5}} \\ \boldsymbol{c}, & g^{c_1 x + \sum_{i=2}^{\tau} c_i x^{i+2\tau+4} + x^{3\tau+5}} \end{bmatrix},$$

Given a program ulockP *consisting of three vectors $\boldsymbol{a}, \boldsymbol{b}, \boldsymbol{c}$ and group elements g_1, g_2, g_3 and input* val *compute:*

$$g^{\sum_{i=1}^{\tau} a_i \mathsf{val}^i + \sum_{i=\tau+1}^{\tau+5} \mathsf{val}^i} \overset{?}{=} g_1$$

$$g^{b_1 \mathsf{val} + \sum_{i=2}^{\tau} b_i \mathsf{val}^{i+\tau+4} + \mathsf{val}^{2\tau+5}} \overset{?}{=} g_2$$

$$g^{c_1 \mathsf{val} + \sum_{i=2}^{\tau} c_i \mathsf{val}^{i+2\tau+4} + \mathsf{val}^{3\tau+5}} \overset{?}{=} g_3.$$

If all of these checks pass, output 1. Otherwise, output 0.

In order to add same point composability, we extend from three scalars to 3τ scalars (while keeping 3 group elements). We note that this scheme is that of [BMZ19] if we let $\tau = 1$.

Lemma 1. *For any $\tau = \mathtt{poly}(\lambda)$ Construction 1 satisfies completeness.*

Proof. This argument is analogous to the functionality preservation argument in [BMZ19]. The only difference is that polynomials are higher degree due to composition. Fix some point $x \in \mathbb{Z}_{p(\lambda)}$. It suffices to argue that over the randomness of ulockP $\leftarrow$ lockP(x) that the probability that there exists some y such that ulockP$(y) = 1$ is $\mathtt{ngl}(\lambda)$.

Recall that the randomness used to construct ulockP is the vectors $\boldsymbol{a}, \boldsymbol{b}, \boldsymbol{c}$. Fix some $x \in \mathbb{Z}_{p(\lambda)}$. Fix some value $\boldsymbol{a}$ and define $\alpha \overset{def}{=} \sum_{i=1}^{\tau} x^i + \sum_{i=\tau+1}^{\tau+5} x^i$. For some other value y, since $\mathcal{G}$ is prime order the only way for the first element to match is for $\alpha = \sum_{i=1}^{\tau} y^i + \sum_{i=\tau+1}^{\tau+5} y^i$. Since this is a polynomial of degree $\tau + 5$ there are at most $\tau + 4$ such values y (excluding the original value x). Consider one such value y. Then, consider the polynomial $P(\boldsymbol{b}) \overset{def}{=} b_1(x - y) + \sum_{i=2}^{\tau} b_i(x^{i+\tau+4} - y^{i+\tau+4}) + (x^{2\tau+5} - y^{2\tau+5})$. Fix some values of b_i for $i = 2, ..., \tau$. Then this is a linear polynomial in b_1 that is zero with probability at most $1/p(\lambda)$. A similar argument holds for the second check value. Thus, a candidate y is a solution to both equations with probability $1/p(\lambda)^2$. Thus means for a fixed x the probability of one of the y's working is at most $(\tau+5)/p(\lambda)^2$ by union bound. With a second application of union bound, the probability across all x of some y existing is at most $(\tau+5)/p(\lambda) = \mathtt{ngl}(\lambda)$ as desired.

Theorem 1. *Suppose that Assumption 1 holds. Then for any $\tau = \mathtt{poly}(\lambda)$, Construction 1 satisfies virtual black box security (when composed up to τ times).*

Proof. We show that Construction 1 satisfies distributional indistinguishability [FF18, Definition 2.4]. Virtual black box security then follows by [FF18, Theorem 2.1].

Suppose for the aim of arriving at a contradiction that there exists some well-spread distribution $\mathcal{X}_\lambda$ such that there exists a PPT adversary $\mathcal{A}$ and a polynomial $q(\cdot)$ such that

$$\left|\Pr[\mathcal{A}(\{\mathsf{lockP}(x)\}_{i=1}^{\tau}) = 1] - \Pr[\mathcal{A}(\{\mathsf{lockP}(r)\}_{i=1}^{\tau}) = 1]\right| > \frac{1}{q(\lambda)},$$

where $x \leftarrow X_\lambda$ and $r \leftarrow \mathbb{Z}_{p(\lambda)}$. We then show how to build an adversary $\mathcal{B}$ that breaks Assumption 1 (with respect to distribution family $\mathcal{X}_\lambda$) receiving $\ell = 3\tau+4$ elements (corresponding to a maximum power of $3\tau + 5$). That is, $\mathcal{B}$ will receive $3\tau + 4$ pairs of the form

$$\{k_i, g^{k_i z + z^i}\}_{i \in \{2,\ldots,3\tau+5\}},$$

where z is either distributed according to $\mathcal{X}_\lambda$ or uniformly in $\mathbb{Z}_{p(\lambda)}$. Denote by $\{k_i, g^{h_i}\}_{i=2,\ldots,3\tau+5}$ the received values, defining $h_i = k_i z + z^i$. Then, $\mathcal{B}$ samples three matrices $\mathbf{A}, \mathbf{B}, \mathbf{C}$ uniformly in $\mathbb{Z}_{p(\lambda)}^{\tau \times (\tau-1)}$.

Our goal is to produce τ obfuscations (either of x or r). $\mathcal{B}$ compute the matrices $\mathbf{A}', \mathbf{B}', \mathbf{C}' \in \mathbb{Z}_{p(\lambda)}^{\tau \times \tau}$ as follows:

$$\mathbf{A}'_{i,j} = \begin{cases} \sum_{\alpha=1}^{\tau-1} \mathbf{A}_{i,\alpha} k_{\alpha+1} + \sum_{\alpha=\tau}^{\tau+4} k_{\alpha+1} & j = 1 \\ \mathbf{A}_{i,j-1} & \text{otherwise.} \end{cases}$$

$$\mathbf{B}'_{i,j} = \begin{cases} \sum_{\alpha=1}^{\tau-1} \mathbf{B}_{i,\alpha} k_{\alpha+\tau+5} + k_{2\tau+5} & j = 1 \\ \mathbf{B}_{i,\alpha-1} & \text{otherwise.} \end{cases}$$

$$\mathbf{C}'_{i,j} = \begin{cases} \sum_{\alpha=1}^{\tau-1} \mathbf{C}_{i,\alpha} k_{\alpha+2\tau+5} + k_{3\tau+5} & j = 1 \\ \mathbf{C}_{i,j-1} & \text{otherwise.} \end{cases}$$

Then $\mathcal{B}$ computes the ith value to be fed into $\mathcal{A}$ as:

$$\mathsf{lockP}_i = \begin{cases} \mathbf{A}'_{(i,\cdot)}, & g^{\sum_{j=1}^{\tau-1} \mathbf{A}_{i,j} h_{j+1} + \sum_{j=t}^{\tau+5} h_{j+1}}, \\ \mathbf{B}'_{(i,\cdot)}, & g^{\sum_{j=1}^{\tau-1} \mathbf{B}_{i,j} h_{j+\tau+4} + h_{2\tau+5}}, \\ \mathbf{C}'_{(i,\cdot)}, & g^{\sum_{j=1}^{\tau-1} \mathbf{C}_{i,j} h_{j+2\tau+4} + h_{3\tau+5}}. \end{cases}$$

The above group elements can be formed linearly from the received values $\{k_i, g^{h_i}\}_{i\in[2,\dots,3\tau+5]}$ and $\mathbf{A}, \mathbf{B}, \mathbf{C}$. For the ith obfuscation, the values produced in the exponent are (omitting the exponential notation):

$$\sum_{j=1}^{\tau-1} \mathbf{A}_{i,j} h_{j+1} + \sum_{j=\tau+1}^{\tau+5} h_j = \left(\sum_{j=1}^{\tau-1} \mathbf{A}_{i,j} k_{j+1} + \sum_{j=\tau}^{\tau+4} k_{j+1}\right) z + \sum_{j=1}^{\tau-1} \mathbf{A}_{i,j} z^{j+1} + \sum_{j=\tau+1}^{\tau+5} z^j,$$

$$\sum_{j=1}^{\tau-1} \mathbf{B}_{i,j} h_{j+\tau+5} + h_{2\tau+5} = \left(\sum_{j=1}^{\tau-1} \mathbf{B}_{i,j} k_{i+\tau+5} + k_{2\tau+5}\right) z + \sum_{j=1}^{\tau-1} \mathbf{B}_{i,j} z^{j+\tau+5} + z^{2\tau+5},$$

$$\sum_{j=1}^{t-1} \mathbf{C}_{i,j} h_{j+2\tau+5} + h_{3\tau+5} = \left(\sum_{j=1}^{\tau-1} \mathbf{C}_{i,j} k_{i+2\tau+5} + k_{3\tau+5}\right) z + \sum_{j=1}^{\tau-1} \mathbf{C}_{i,j} z^{j+2\tau+5} + z^{3\tau+5}.$$

From the above equations, it is apparent that the matrices $\mathbf{A}', \mathbf{B}', \mathbf{C}'$ are consistent with the group elements. Furthermore it is clear for $j > 1$ that the coefficients for z^j are appropriately formed. It remains to show that the 3τ coefficients of z are uniformly random. Denote by ζ_i for $i = 1, \dots, 3\tau$ coefficients of z respectively. Let $\mathbf{1}^{i,j}$ represent an all 1 matrix of dimension $i \times j$ and define $\mathbf{0}^{i\times j}$ similarly. Define the matrix of coefficients:

$$\mathbf{D} \stackrel{def}{=} \left(\begin{array}{c|c|c|c|c|c|c|c} \mathbf{A}_{(\cdot,1)} & \mathbf{A}_{(\cdot,2,\dots,t-1)} & \mathbf{1}^{\tau\times 5} & \mathbf{0}^{\tau\times\tau-5} & \mathbf{0}^{\tau\times 1} & \mathbf{0}^{\tau\times\tau-1} & \mathbf{0}^{\tau\times 1} \\ \hline \mathbf{B}_{(\cdot,1)} & \mathbf{0}^{\tau\times\tau-1} & \mathbf{0}^{\tau\times 5} & \mathbf{B}_{(\cdot,2,\dots,t-1)} & \mathbf{1}^{\tau\times 1} & \mathbf{0}^{\tau\times\tau-1} & \mathbf{0}^{\tau\times 1} \\ \hline \mathbf{C}_{(\cdot,1)} & \mathbf{0}^{\tau\times\tau-1} & \mathbf{0}^{\tau\times 5} & \mathbf{0}^{\tau\times\tau-5} & \mathbf{0}^{\tau\times 1} & \mathbf{C}_{(\cdot,2,\dots,t-1)} & \mathbf{1}^{\tau\times 1} \end{array}\right).$$

The set of values received by the adversary can be described by:

$$\mathbf{D}\begin{bmatrix} k_2 \\ k_2 \\ \dots \\ k_{3t+5} \end{bmatrix} = \begin{bmatrix} \zeta_1 \\ \zeta_2 \\ \dots \\ \zeta_{3t} \end{bmatrix}$$

The matrix $\mathbf{D}$ has dimension $3\tau \times 3\tau + 5$. For each coefficient ζ_j to be random it suffices for the matrix $\mathbf{D}$ to have row rank of 3τ. For $\mathbf{D}$ to have rank 3τ it suffices for each $\mathbf{A}||\mathbf{1}, \mathbf{B}|\mathbf{1}, \mathbf{C}||\mathbf{1}$ to have rank of τ. Since each matrix is random this occurs with probability at most $\tau/p = \mathtt{ngl}(\lambda)$. If one these matrices is not full rank, $\mathcal{B}$ aborts and outputs a random value. Conditioning on these matrices being full rank the obfuscation are properly prepared for $\mathcal{A}$. Denote by

$$\mathtt{Disting}_\mathcal{A} \stackrel{def}{=} |\Pr[\mathcal{A}(\{\mathsf{lockP}(x)\}_{i=1}^\tau) = 1] - \Pr[\mathcal{A}(\{\mathsf{lockP}(r)\}_{i=1}^\tau) = 1]|.$$

Then one has that

$$\left|\Pr[\mathcal{B}(\{k_i, g^{k_i x + x^i}\}_{i\in[2,\dots,3\tau+4]} = 1] - \Pr[\mathcal{B}(\{k_i, g^{k_i r + r^i}\}_{i\in[2,\dots,3\tau+4]}]\right| =$$

$$\Pr[\mathbf{A} \vee \mathbf{B} \vee \mathbf{C} \text{ not full rank}] + \Pr[\mathbf{A} \wedge \mathbf{B} \wedge \mathbf{C} \text{ full rank}] \cdot \mathtt{Disting}_\mathcal{A} =$$

$$\mathtt{ngl}(\lambda) + (1 - \mathtt{ngl}(\lambda))\frac{1}{q(\lambda)} = \frac{1}{q'(\lambda)}$$

for some polynomial function $q'(\lambda)$. This completes the proof of Theorem 1.

Theorem 2. *Let λ be a security parameter Let $\{\mathcal{X}_\lambda\}$ be a well-spread distribution ensemble and let $m, \tau \in \mathbb{Z}^+$ be parameters that are both* $\texttt{poly}(\lambda)$. *Let $\mathcal{F}_{poly}$ be the ensemble of functions f_λ where f_λ is the set of non-constant, non-identity polynomials in $\mathbb{Z}_{p(\lambda)}[x]$ with degree at most m. Suppose that Assumption 1 holds for $\ell = m(3\tau+5)$. Then, the above obfuscator is non-malleable for τ-compositions for $\mathcal{F}_{poly}$ and distribution ensemble $\{\mathcal{X}_\lambda\}$.*

Proof. We look to contradict Assumption 2, which follows from Assumption 1. Consider a mauling adversary $\mathcal{A}$ that, given τ obfuscations of a point x, can output a new obfuscation of $f(x)$ for $f \in \mathcal{F}_{poly}$. Consider m to be the degree of f. We build an adversary $\mathcal{B}$ which given the ensemble $\{k_i, g^{k_i x + x^i}\}_{i=2\ldots,m(3\tau+5)}$ and access to $\mathcal{A}$ recovers g^x with noticeable probability.

First, we consider the case when $m > 1$. We set up the reduction as so: upon receiving the ensemble $\{k_i, g^{k_i x + x^i}\}_{i=2\ldots,m(3\tau+5)}$, we create τ obfuscations of x as detailed in Theorem 1. We send these to $\mathcal{A}$, which returns $(f, \boldsymbol{a}, \boldsymbol{b}, \boldsymbol{c}, j_a, j_b, j_c)$ where $\boldsymbol{a}, \boldsymbol{b}, \boldsymbol{c} \in \mathbb{Z}_{p(\lambda)}^\tau$ and $j_a, j_b, j_c \in \mathbb{G}_\lambda$. Define the vector $\boldsymbol{l}$ as the coefficients of:

$$c_1(f(x)) + \sum_{i=2}^{\tau} c_i(f(x))^{i+2\tau+4} + (f(x))^{3\tau+5} = \sum_{i=0}^{m(3\tau+5)} l_i x^i.$$

In order for the adversary to succeed, this value must equal the exponent of j_c with noticeable probability. $\mathcal{B}$ computes and returns

$$\left(j_c \left(g^{l_0} \cdot \prod_{i=2}^{m(3\tau+5)} h_i^{l_i} \right)^{-1} \right)^{1/(l_1 - \sum_{i=2}^{m(3\tau+5)} k_i l_i)}.$$

Since $\mathcal{B}$ has properly prepared the set of obfuscations to $\mathcal{A}$, $\mathcal{A}$ returns a valid obfuscation of $f(x)$ with probability at least $1/\texttt{poly}(\lambda)$. In this case then $j_c = g^{l_0 + l_1 x + \ldots + l_{m(3\tau+3)} x^{m(3\tau+5)}}$ with the same probability. In this case, we see that the value in parenthesis is

$$g^{x\left(l_1 - \sum_{i=2}^{m(3\tau+5)} k_i l_i \right)}.$$

Since all l_i, k_i are known, this can be computed unless $l_1 - \sum_{i=2}^{m(3\tau+5)} k_i l_i = 0$. Since $f(x)$ is of degree m, $l_{m(3\tau+5)}$ must be nonzero. $\mathcal{A}$'s view is independent of $k_{m(3\tau+5)}$. So, the probability that the sum is equal to l_1 is $1/(p(\lambda) - 1)$. So, $\mathcal{B}$ returns the correct value with probability $1/\texttt{poly}(\lambda) - 1/(p(\lambda) - 1) = 1/\texttt{poly}(\lambda)$ contradicting Assumption 2.

We now consider the case where $m = 1$, or for linear functions f. In this case, we are given the ensemble $\{k_i, g^{k_i x + x^i}\}_{i=2,\ldots,3\tau+5}$. This time, upon receiving $(f, \boldsymbol{a}, \boldsymbol{b}, \boldsymbol{c}, j_a, j_b, j_c)$ from $\mathcal{A}$, $\mathcal{B}$ instead computes the coefficients $\boldsymbol{l}$ of

$$\sum_{i=1}^{\tau} a_i f(x)^i + \sum_{i=\tau}^{\tau+5} f(x)^i = \sum_{i=0}^{\tau+5} l_i x^i$$

as in the nonlinear case. In this case, $\mathcal{B}$ computes and outputs:

$$\left(j_a\left(g^{l_0}\cdot\prod_{i=2}^{\tau+5}h_i^{l_i}\right)^{-1}\right)^{1/(l_1-\sum_{i=2}^{\tau+5}k_il_i)}.$$

Because $\mathcal{A}$ outputs the value $g^{\sum_{i=1}^{\tau}a_if(x)^{\tau}+(f(x))^{\tau+1}+...+(f(x))^{\tau+5}}$ with noticeable probability, $\mathcal{B}$'s computation evaluates to g^x unless $l_1-\sum_{i=2}^{\tau+5}k_il_i=0$. Let $\mathbf{R}$ be a random $\mathbb{Z}_{p(\lambda)}^{\tau\times\tau-1}$ and let $\mathbf{1}^{\tau\times5}$ be a $\tau\times5$ matrix of all 1s. To see that this happens with negligible probability, for the first group element of each obfuscation received the coefficient of x^1 are as follows: $a_1=[\mathbf{R}|\mathbf{1}^{\tau\times5}]\cdot(k_2\ k_3\ ...\ k_{\tau+5})^{\mathsf{T}}$.

As shown in the proof of Theorem 1 the values of R are uniformly random conditioned on the other values seen by the adversary. We note that, as all k_i are uniformly chosen, the only information $\mathcal{A}$ learns about $k_{\tau+1},...,k_{\tau+5}$ is in the vector a_1 Furthermore $\mathbf{R}$ is independent of these values. Thus, we can see that $\mathcal{A}$ receives items of the form

$$a_{1,j}=\sum_{i=2}^{\tau}k_i\mathbf{R}_{i,j}+\sum_{i=\tau+1}^{\tau+5}k_i.$$

Without loss of generality, we assume that an adversary knows the values $k_2,...,k_\tau$. To change the obfuscated point they will also need to change the higher order powers $x^{\tau+1},...,x^{\delta+5}$. The only value they have seen that involves the values $k_{\tau+1},...,k_{\tau+5}$ are terms of the form $c+\left(\sum_{i=1}^5k_{\tau+i}\right)x$ for some value c. Since the function is linear, we can represent $f(x)=\alpha x+\beta$. So, the adversary must find α,β,γ such that

$$\sum_{i=0}^4(\alpha x+\beta)^{i+\tau+1}=\gamma\sum_{i=0}^4 x^{i+\tau+1}.$$

Define $\delta=\tau+1$. We can write the desired linear combination as follows:

$$\begin{bmatrix}\alpha^{4+\delta}\\\alpha^{3+\delta}\left(\binom{\delta+4}{1}\beta+\binom{\delta+3}{0}\right)\\\alpha^{2+\delta}\left(\binom{\delta+4}{2}\beta^2+\binom{\delta+3}{1}\beta+\binom{\delta+2}{0}\right)\\\alpha^{1+\delta}\left(\sum_{i=0}^3\left(\binom{\delta+4-i}{3-i}\beta^{3-i}\right)\right)\\\alpha^{\delta}\left(\sum_{i=0}^4\left(\binom{\delta+4-i}{4-i}\beta^{4-i}\right)\right)\end{bmatrix}^{\mathsf{T}}\begin{bmatrix}k_{4+\delta}&0&0&0&0\\0&k_{3+\delta}&0&0&0\\0&0&k_{2+\delta}&0&0\\0&0&0&k_{1+\delta}&0\\0&0&0&0&k_\delta\end{bmatrix}=\gamma\begin{bmatrix}k_{4+\delta}\\k_{3+\delta}\\k_{2+\delta}\\k_{1+\delta}\\k_\delta\end{bmatrix}$$

Substituting, one has that

1. If $\beta=0$ then this implies $\alpha^{\delta+4}=\alpha^{\delta+3}=\alpha^{\delta+2}=\alpha^{\delta+1}=\alpha^\delta$ which only has solutions if $\alpha=0$ or $\alpha=1$. These are both considered trivial solutions.
2. Otherwise, $\gamma=\alpha^{\delta+4}$ (using first equation),

3. $(\delta + 4)\beta + 1 = \alpha$ (using second equation),
4. $(\delta + 4)\beta + 2 = 0$ or $\delta = -5$ (using third equation, relying on $\beta \neq 0$).
5. Assume that $\delta \neq -5$, then $\alpha = -1$ (substitution of third constraint into second equation)
6. $\gamma = (-1)^{\delta}$ (substitution of α in first equation). Note that $\gamma = 1$ corresponds to no tampering. Thus, we consider $\gamma = -1$.
7. $\delta \equiv -5$ or $\delta \equiv -6$ (solving fourth equation using prior constraints) and thus $\tau \equiv -6$ or $\tau \equiv -7$.

We note that since $\tau = \mathtt{poly}(\lambda)$ for large enough λ one can be sure that $\tau \not\equiv \{-6, -7\} \mod |\mathbb{G}_\lambda|$. So, the only functions that $\mathcal{A}$ can maul to are the constant and identity functions, neither of which are in $\mathcal{F}_{poly}$. This means that $\mathcal{A}$ returns a solution where $l_1 - \sum_{i=2}^{\tau+5} k_i l_i = 0$. with negligible probability. So, with non-negligible probability, $\mathcal{B}$ can break Assumption 2.

4   Nonmalleable Digital Lockers

We now use the nonmalleable point function from Construction 1 to construct a nonmalleable digital locker that does not prevent any tampering over the stored key. We use the well known real-or-random construction of digital-lockers [CD08]. The basic real or random construction is in Fig. 1. We do not argue security of this basic construction, as long as lockP is $n+1$ same point composable then this construction provides a digital locker that provides nonmalleability over val. The argument is the same as in [CD08] with the worst case for nonmalleability being when all of key is 1 since this provides the adversary with $n + 1$ obfuscations of val.

---

lock(val, key) :

1. Sample $r \leftarrow \mathbb{Z}_{p(\lambda)}$.
2. Compute $z_1 = \mathsf{lockP}(\mathsf{val})$.
3. For $i = 1$ to n:
   (a) If $\mathsf{key}_i = 1$,
       set $\mathsf{ulockP}_{i+1} = \mathsf{lockP}(\mathsf{val})$.
   (b) Else, set $z_{i+1} = \mathsf{lockP}(r)$.
4. Output z.

ulock($\{z_i\}_{i=1}^{n+1}$, val):

1. If $\mathsf{ulockP}_1(\mathsf{val}) = \perp$ output $\perp$.
2. Initialize $\mathsf{key} = \mathbf{0}$.
3. For $i = 1$ to n:
   (a) If $\mathsf{ulockP}_{i+1}(\mathsf{val}) \neq \perp$
       set $\mathsf{key}_i = 1$.
4. Output key.

Fig. 1. Nonmalleable digital locker preventing tampering over only val

4.1 Detecting Tampering over key

With the ability to instantiate the real or random construction with nonmalleable point functions, we turn to detecting tampering over the encoded key. As mentioned in the introduction, this construction requires a public object that all parties can depend on (as long as the distribution is efficiently sampleable) which can be achieved in the CRS model. However, the construction is black box in the underlying digital locker (unlike a construction from NIZKs).

We combine nonmalleable codes and seed-dependent condensers to check if the adversary tampers over the key value. We use the locked point val as input to a seed-dependent condenser as part of the value encoded in the nonmalleable code. If the adversary tampers to an *independent value*, they are unlikely to match the output of the condenser on the real val. We introduce these tools and then our construction. We first present the notion of nonmalleable codes, introduced by Dziembowski, Pietrzak, and Wichs [DPW10].

Definition 6. *A pair of algorithms* (Enc, Dec) *is called a* coding scheme *if* Enc : $\{0,1\}^k \to \{0,1\}^n$ *is randomized and* Dec : $\{0,1\}^n \to \{0,1\}^k \cup \bot$ *is deterministic and for each* $s \in \{0,1\}^k$ *it holds that* $\Pr[\text{Dec}(\text{Enc}(s)) = s] = 1$.

Definition 7. *A coding scheme* (Enc, Dec) *is called* $(\epsilon_{nmc}, s_{nmc}, \mathcal{F})$-*nonmalleable if for each* $f \in \mathcal{F}$ *and each* $s \in \{0,1\}^k$, *there exists a distribution* $D_f()$ *over* $\{\{0,1\}^k, \text{same}\}$ *that is efficiently sampleable given oracle access to* f *such that the following holds:*

$$\delta^{s_{nmc}}(\{c \leftarrow \text{Enc}(s); \overline{c} \leftarrow f(c), \overline{s} = \text{Dec}(\overline{c}) : Output\ \overline{s}\},$$
$$\{\tilde{s} \leftarrow D_f,\ Output\ s\ if\ \tilde{s} = \text{same}\ else\ \tilde{s}\}) \leq \epsilon_{nmc}.$$

Seed-dependent condensers were introduced by Dodis, Ristenpart, and Vadhan [DRV12]. Their goal is similar to a traditional randomness extractor, except the output only has to be statistically close to a distribution with minentropy. Importantly, it is possible to construct condensers where the adversary is allowed to output the chosen distribution after seeing the seed.

Definition 8. *Let* cond : $\{0,1\}^\lambda \times \{0,1\}^d \to \{0,1\}^\alpha$ *be a* (k, k', s, ϵ) *seed-dependent condenser if for all probabilistic adversaries of size at most* s *who take a random seed* seed $\leftarrow U_d$ *and output a distribution* $X_{\text{seed}} \leftarrow \mathcal{A}(\text{seed})$ *of entropy* $H_\infty(X|\text{seed}) \geq k$, *then for the joint distribution* (X, U_d) *over* X_{seed} *arising from a random* seed $\leftarrow U_d$, *there exists a distribution* Y *such that* $\tilde{H}_\infty(Y|U_d) \geq k'$ *such that* $\Delta((Y, U_d), (\text{cond}(X; U_d), U_d)) \leq \epsilon$.

Dodis, Ristenpart, and Vadhan showed that seed-dependent condensers can be constructed using collision resistant hash functions. Furthermore, this construction works for $\epsilon = 0$. That is, the output has entropy instead of being close to a distribution with entropy. For our construction, we will require $k' = \omega(\log \lambda)$.

We now present the construction. Instead of directly *locking* the value key we instead lock the value $c = \text{Enc}(\text{key}||\text{cond}(\text{val}; \text{seed}))$, where Enc is the encoding function for a nonmalleable code and cond is a seed dependent condenser.

Notionally, the nonmalleable code prevents tampering to *independent* points and the condenser detects if the adversary tampers to an independent point.

Construction 2. *Let* (lock', ulock') *be defined as in Fig. 1. Let* (Enc, Dec) *be a coding scheme where* Enc $: \{0,1\}^{k+\alpha} \to \{0,1\}^n$. *Let* cond $: \{0,1\}^\lambda \times \{0,1\}^d \to \{0,1\}^\alpha$ *be a seed-dependent condenser. Define the algorithms* (lock', ulock', V_{key}) *as in Fig. 2.*

---

lock'(val, key),
input in $\{0,1\}^{\lambda+k}$:

1. Compute $z = $ cond(val, seed).
2. Compute $y = $ Enc(key$\|z$).
3. Output lock(val, y).

ulock'(val') $\overset{def}{=}$ ulock(val')

V_{key}(val', y),
input in $\{0,1\}^{\lambda+n}$:

1. Compute $z = $ cond(val', seed).
2. Run decode key' = Dec(y).
3. If key'$_{k...k+n} \neq z$ output $\perp$.
   Else output key'$_{0,...,k-1}$.

Fig. 2. Nonmalleable digital locker preventing tampering over both val and key. A seed of a seed-dependent condenser must be public and global.

However, security of this construction is not straightforward as we are using nonmalleable codes in a nonstandard way. In a nonmalleable code, the adversary specifies the tampering function before seeing any information about c. In our setting, the adversary sees obfuscations that have c embedded before deciding how to tamper. The crucial part to our argument is that the set of obfuscations is pseudorandom condition on c and $s \overset{def}{=}$ cond(val; seed). If an adversary is able to tamper substantially better given obfuscations of val from some entropic distribution than with uniformly random val we can check whether they tampered properly and use this to break distributional indistinguishability. The proof of Theorem 3 is deferred to the full version [FF18, Section 4.2].

Theorem 3. *Let* $\lambda \in \mathbb{N}$ *be a security parameter and let* $\{0,1\}^\lambda$ *be the domain. Let* (lockP, ulockP) *be a* $(n+1)$-*same point composable and* $\mathcal{F}_{single}$-*nonmalleable.*

1. *Suppose for any* $s = \text{poly}(\lambda)$ *there exists* $\mu, \beta = \omega(\log \lambda)$ *such* cond $: \{0,1\}^\lambda \times \{0,1\}^d \to \{0,1\}^\alpha$ *is a* $(\mu, \beta, s, 0)$-*seed-dependent condenser.*
2. *Let* seed $\leftarrow \{0,1\}^d$ *be a public parameter.*
3. $X \overset{def}{=} X(\text{seed})$ *be an* s-*samplable distribution so* $\tilde{H}_\infty(X|\text{seed}, \text{cond}(\text{seed}, X)) \geq \beta$.[3]

---

[3] In the previous sections, we consider X that have worst case min-entropy. However, if $\tilde{H}_\infty(X|\text{seed}, \text{cond}(\text{seed}, X)) \geq \beta$ for some $\beta = \omega(\log \lambda)$ then there exists some $\beta' = \omega(\log \lambda)$ such that with $\text{Pr}_{\text{seed}}[H_\infty(X|\text{seed}, \text{cond}(\text{seed}, X)) \geq \beta'] \geq 1 - \text{ngl}(\lambda)$. Thus, this change does not effect the set of distributions assumed to be secure in Assumption 1.

4. Let a description of $\mathbb{G}_\lambda$, a generator g for $\mathbb{G}_\lambda$ and seed $\leftarrow \{0,1\}^d$ be system parameters.
5. Let $\mathcal{F}_{nmc}$ be a function class. Suppose for any $s_{nmc} = \texttt{poly}(\lambda)$ there exists $\epsilon_{nmc} = \texttt{ngl}(\lambda)$ such that (Enc, Dec) is an $(\epsilon_{nmc}, s_{nmc}, \mathcal{F}_{nmc})$ nonmalleable code.

Then (lock', ulock') in Construction 2 and Fig. 2 is point nonmalleable for $\mathcal{F}_{single}$ and key nonmallable for $\mathcal{F}_{nmc}$. In particular, (lock', ulock') is a $(\mathcal{F}_{single}, \mathcal{F}_{nmc}, \mathcal{X})$-nonmalleable digital locker.

We recommend using a nonmalleable code that detects at least permutations and $1 \rightarrow 0$ bit tampers, such as [AGM+15a, AGM+15b], as these transforms are otherwise computable in polynomial time.

Constructions using nonmalleable extractors [DW09, CRS14] or one-way hashes [BCFW09, BFS11, CQZ+16] may be possible. However, they are not immediate, we use the primitive of nonmalleable hashes to illustrate. A nonmalleable hash function is a family of functions $h \in \mathcal{H}$ such that an adversary given $h(x)$ (sampled $h \leftarrow \mathcal{H}$ and x from some distribution) cannot find $h(f(x))$ for f in some function class $\mathcal{F}$. Several of these works claim to be "standard model" but all require h is random and not tampered by the adversary. One could append a nonmalleable hash, obfuscating key' = key$||h($key$||$val$)$. However, this approach assumes that the function instance h is assumed to be independently sampled from key and val. In our approach, the public randomness required is for seed of the condenser, and the distribution of val (and key) can depend on this value. Furthermore, non malleable hashes are analyzed with the adversary only knowing the output value $h(x)$. It is not clear that security would hold in the presence of multiple correlated obfuscations. Similar issues arise with nonmalleable extractors [DW09, CRS14].

Acknowledgements. This work was funded in part by a grant from Comcast Inc, by NSF Grant CNS 1849904, and ONR Grant N00014-19-1-2327. This research is based upon work supported in part by the Office of the Director of National Intelligence (ODNI), Intelligence Advanced Research Projects Activity (IARPA), via Contract No. 2019-19020700008. The views and conclusions contained herein are those of the authors and should not be interpreted as necessarily representing the official policies, either expressed or implied, of ODNI, IARPA, or the U.S. Government. The U.S. Government is authorized to reproduce and distribute reprints for governmental purposes notwithstanding any copyright annotation therein.

The authors thank Luke Demarest, Pratyay Mukherjee, Alex Russell, and Mayank Varia for their helpful feedback. Special thanks to James Bartusek, Fermi Ma, and Mark Zhandry for discussing their work and its compositional properties.

References

[ABC+18] Alamélou, Q., et al.: Pseudoentropic isometries: a new framework for fuzzy extractor reusability. In: AsiaCCS (2018)

[AGM+15a] Agrawal, S., Gupta, D., Maji, H.K., Pandey, O., Prabhakaran, M.: Explicit non-malleable codes against bit-wise tampering and permutations. In: Gennaro, R., Robshaw, M. (eds.) CRYPTO 2015. LNCS, vol. 9215, pp. 538–557. Springer, Heidelberg (2015). https://doi.org/10.1007/978-3-662-47989-6_26

[AGM+15b] Agrawal, S., Gupta, D., Maji, H.K., Pandey, O., Prabhakaran, M.: A rate-optimizing compiler for non-malleable codes against bit-wise tampering and permutations. In: Dodis, Y., Nielsen, J.B. (eds.) TCC 2015. LNCS, vol. 9014, pp. 375–397. Springer, Heidelberg (2015). https://doi.org/10.1007/978-3-662-46494-6_16

[AJ15] Ananth, P., Jain, A.: Indistinguishability obfuscation from compact functional encryption. In: Gennaro, R., Robshaw, M. (eds.) CRYPTO 2015. LNCS, vol. 9215, pp. 308–326. Springer, Heidelberg (2015). https://doi.org/10.1007/978-3-662-47989-6_15

[BC10] Bitansky, N., Canetti, R.: On strong simulation and composable point obfuscation. In: Rabin, T. (ed.) CRYPTO 2010. LNCS, vol. 6223, pp. 520–537. Springer, Heidelberg (2010). https://doi.org/10.1007/978-3-642-14623-7_28

[BCFW09] Boldyreva, A., Cash, D., Fischlin, M., Warinschi, B.: Foundations of non-malleable hash and one-way functions. In: Matsui, M. (ed.) ASIACRYPT 2009. LNCS, vol. 5912, pp. 524–541. Springer, Heidelberg (2009). https://doi.org/10.1007/978-3-642-10366-7_31

[BFS11] Baecher, P., Fischlin, M., Schröder, D.: Expedient non-malleability notions for hash functions. In: Kiayias, A. (ed.) CT-RSA 2011. LNCS, vol. 6558, pp. 268–283. Springer, Heidelberg (2011). https://doi.org/10.1007/978-3-642-19074-2_18

[BGI+01] Barak, B., et al.: On the (im)possibility of obfuscating programs. In: Kilian, J. (ed.) CRYPTO 2001. LNCS, vol. 2139, pp. 1–18. Springer, Heidelberg (2001). https://doi.org/10.1007/3-540-44647-8_1

[BGI+12] Barak, B., et al.: On the (im) possibility of obfuscating programs. J. ACM (JACM) **59**(2), 6 (2012)

[BMZ19] Bartusek, J., Ma, F., Zhandry, M.: The distinction between fixed and random generators in group-based assumptions. In: Advances in Cryptology - CRYPTO (2019)

[BR17] Brakerski, Z., Rothblum, G.N.: Obfuscating conjunctions. J. Cryptol. **30**(1), 289–320 (2017)

[Can97] Canetti, R.: Towards realizing random oracles: hash functions that hide all partial information. In: Kaliski, B.S. (ed.) CRYPTO 1997. LNCS, vol. 1294, pp. 455–469. Springer, Heidelberg (1997). https://doi.org/10.1007/BFb0052255

[CD08] Canetti, R., Dakdouk, R.R.: Obfuscating point functions with multi-bit output. In: Smart, N. (ed.) EUROCRYPT 2008. LNCS, vol. 4965, pp. 489–508. Springer, Heidelberg (2008). https://doi.org/10.1007/978-3-540-78967-3_28

[CDG18]   Coretti, S., Dodis, Y., Guo, S.: Non-uniform bounds in the random-permutation, ideal-cipher, and generic-group models. In: Shacham, H., Boldyreva, A. (eds.) CRYPTO 2018. LNCS, vol. 10991, pp. 693–721. Springer, Cham (2018). https://doi.org/10.1007/978-3-319-96884-1_23

[CFP+16] Canetti, R., Fuller, B., Paneth, O., Reyzin, L., Smith, A.: Reusable fuzzy extractors for low-entropy distributions. In: Fischlin, M., Coron, J.-S. (eds.) EUROCRYPT 2016. LNCS, vol. 9665, pp. 117–146. Springer, Heidelberg (2016). https://doi.org/10.1007/978-3-662-49890-3_5

[CQZ+16] Chen, Yu., Qin, B., Zhang, J., Deng, Y., Chow, S.S.M.: Non-malleable functions and their applications. In: Cheng, C.-M., Chung, K.-M., Persiano, G., Yang, B.-Y. (eds.) PKC 2016. LNCS, vol. 9615, pp. 386–416. Springer, Heidelberg (2016). https://doi.org/10.1007/978-3-662-49387-8_15

[CRS14]   Cohen, G., Raz, R., Segev, G.: Nonmalleable extractors with short seeds and applications to privacy amplification. SIAM J. Comput. **43**(2), 450–476 (2014)

[CRV10]   Canetti, R., Rothblum, G.N., Varia, M.: Obfuscation of hyperplane membership. In: Micciancio, D. (ed.) TCC 2010. LNCS, vol. 5978, pp. 72–89. Springer, Heidelberg (2010). https://doi.org/10.1007/978-3-642-11799-2_5

[CV09]   Canetti, R., Varia, M.: Non-malleable obfuscation. In: Reingold, O. (ed.) TCC 2009. LNCS, vol. 5444, pp. 73–90. Springer, Heidelberg (2009). https://doi.org/10.1007/978-3-642-00457-5_6

[DORS08] Dodis, Y., Ostrovsky, R., Reyzin, L., Smith, A.: Fuzzy extractors: how to generate strong keys from biometrics and other noisy data. SIAM J. Comput. **38**(1), 97–139 (2008)

[DPW10]   Dziembowski, S., Pietrzak, K., Wichs, D.: Non-malleable codes. In: ICS, vol. 2010, p. 1st. Citeseer (2010)

[DRV12]   Dodis, Y., Ristenpart, T., Vadhan, S.: Randomness condensers for efficiently samplable, seed-dependent sources. In: Cramer, R. (ed.) TCC 2012. LNCS, vol. 7194, pp. 618–635. Springer, Heidelberg (2012). https://doi.org/10.1007/978-3-642-28914-9_35

[DW09]   Dodis, Y., Wichs, D.: Non-malleable extractors and symmetric key cryptography from weak secrets. In: Proceedings of the forty-first annual ACM symposium on Theory of computing, pp. 601–610. ACM (2009)

[FF18]   Fenteany, P., Fuller, B.: Same point composable and nonmalleable obfuscated point functions. Cryptology ePrint Archive, Report 2018/957 (2018). https://eprint.iacr.org/2018/957

[GGH+13] Garg, S., Gentry, C., Halevi, S., Raykova, M., Sahai, A., Waters, B.: Candidate indistinguishability obfuscation and functional encryption for all circuits. In: 2013 IEEE 54th Annual Symposium on Foundations of Computer Science, pp. 40–49. IEEE (2013)

[GGH+16] Garg, S., Gentry, C., Halevi, S., Raykova, M., Sahai, A., Waters, B.: Candidate indistinguishability obfuscation and functional encryption for all circuits. SIAM J. Comput. **45**(3), 882–929 (2016)

[GLSW15] Craig, G., Lewko, A.B., Sahai, A., Waters, B.: Indistinguishability obfuscation from the multilinear subgroup elimination assumption. In: 2015 IEEE 56th Annual Symposium on Foundations of Computer Science (FOCS), pp. 151–170. IEEE (2015)

[KY18a] Komargodski, I., Yogev, E.: Another step towards realizing random oracles: non-malleable point obfuscation. In: Nielsen, J.B., Rijmen, V. (eds.) EUROCRYPT 2018. LNCS, vol. 10820, pp. 259–279. Springer, Cham (2018). https://doi.org/10.1007/978-3-319-78381-9_10

[KY18b] Komargodski, I., Yogev, E.: Another step towards realizing random oracles: Non-malleable point obfuscation. Cryptology ePrint Archive, Report 2018/149 (2018). Version 20190226:074205. https://eprint.iacr.org/2018/149

[PST14] Pass, R., Seth, K., Telang, S.: Indistinguishability obfuscation from semantically-secure multilinear encodings. In: Garay, J.A., Gennaro, R. (eds.) CRYPTO 2014. LNCS, vol. 8616, pp. 500–517. Springer, Heidelberg (2014). https://doi.org/10.1007/978-3-662-44371-2_28

[SW14] Sahai, A., Waters, B.: How to use indistinguishability obfuscation: deniable encryption, and more. In: Proceedings of the forty-sixth annual ACM symposium on Theory of computing, pp. 475–484. ACM (2014)

[WZ17] Wichs, D., Zirdelis, G.: Obfuscating compute-and-compare programs under LWE. In: 2017 IEEE 58th Annual Symposium on Foundations of Computer Science (FOCS), pp. 600–611. IEEE (2017)

A Concise Bounded Anonymous Broadcast Yielding Combinatorial Trace-and-Revoke Schemes

Xuan Thanh Do[1,2(✉)], Duong Hieu Phan[2], and Moti Yung[3]

[1] Vietnam National University, Hanoi, Vietnam
[2] XLIM, University of Limoges, Limoges, France
{xuan-thanh.do,duong-hieu.phan}@unilim.fr
[3] Google Research and Columbia University, New York, USA
motiyung@google.com

Abstract. This work is about constructing methods for simultaneously broadcasting multimedia data privately to a set of subscribers, and on various connections among important efficient variants of the general paradigm. Broadcast Encryption is such a fundamental primitive supporting sending a secure message to any chosen target set of N users. While many efficient constructions are known, understanding the efficiency possible for an "Anonymous Broadcast Encryption" (AnoBE), i.e., one which can hide the target set itself, is quite open. The best solutions by Barth, Boneh, and Waters ('06) and Libert, Paterson, and Quaglia ('12) are built on public key encryption (PKE) and their ciphertext sizes are, in fact, N times that of the underlying PKE (rate=N). Kiayias and Samary ('12), in turn, showed a lower bound showing that such rate is the best possible if N is an independent unbounded parameter. However, when considering certain user set size bounded by a system parameter (e.g., the security parameter), the problem remains interesting. We consider the problem of comparing AnoBE with PKE under the same assumption. We call such schemes *Anonymous Broadcast Encryption for Bounded Universe* – AnoBEB.

We first present an AnoBEB construction for up to k users from LWE assumption, where k is bounded by the scheme security parameter. The scheme does not grow with the parameter and beat the PKE method. Actually, our scheme is as efficient as the underlying LWE public-key encryption; namely, the rate is, in fact, 1 and thus optimal.

More interestingly, we move on to employ the new AnoBEB in other multimedia broadcasting methods and as a second contribution, we introduce a new approach to construct an efficient "Trace and Revoke scheme" which combines the functionalites of revocation and of tracing people (called traitors) who in a broadcasting schemes share their keys with the adversary which, in turn, generates a pirate receiver. Note that, as was put forth by Kiayias and Yung (EUROCRYPT '02), combinatorial traitor tracing schemes can be constructed by combining a system for small universe, integrated via an outer traceability codes (collusion-secure code or identifying parent property (IPP) code). There were many efficient traitor tracing schemes from traceability codes, but no known

© Springer Nature Switzerland AG 2020
M. Conti et al. (Eds.): ACNS 2020, LNCS 12147, pp. 145–164, 2020.
https://doi.org/10.1007/978-3-030-57878-7_8

scheme supports revocation as well. Our new approach integrates our AnoBEB system with a Robust IPP code, introduced by Barg and Kabatiansky (IEEE IT '13). This shows an interesting use for robust IPP in cryptography. The robust IPP codes were only implicitly shown by an existence proof. In order to make our technique concrete, we propose two explicit instantiations of robust IPP codes. Our final construction gives the most efficient trace and revoke scheme in the bounded collusion model.

Keywords: Secure multimedia broadcasting · Anonymous broadcast encryption · Robust IPP code · Trace and revoke system

1   Introduction

Broadcast encryption (BE) is designed to efficiently distribute an encrypted content via a public channel to a designated set of users so that only privileged users can decrypt while the other users learn nothing about the content. The first constructions of BE were proposed by Berkovits [5], and most notably by Fiat-Naor [14] who advocated that an efficient scheme should be more efficient than just repeating a single ciphertext per user. Thereafter, many interesting schemes were proposed, in particular Boneh, Gentry and Waters [6] introduced a scheme with a constant size ciphertext.

Privacy, and anonymity of receivers, in particular, are important in numerous real-life applications. Unfortunately, it turned out to be extremely difficult to hide the target set in broadcast encryption and no concise anonymous broadcast encryption has been constructed, while being considered by many, see: [4,13,23,24,29]. The state of the art constructions by Barth et $al.$ and Libert et $al.$ [4,24] start from a public-key encryption (PKE) and result in schemes with ciphertext size which is N times the ciphertext size of the underlying PKE scheme. Moreover, justifying the above results, Kiayias and Samari [21] proved lower bounds: ciphertext size of any anonymous broadcast encryption is $\Omega(s \cdot n)$, where s is the cardinality of the set of enabled users and n is security parameter, and $\Omega(r + n)$ for any set of r revoked users. Note that it can be that $s = O(N)$ and $r = O(N)$. Hence, unfortunately, sub-linear complexity in the number of users is impossible.

However, in practice, the case where N is a constant has been largely employed. In fact, all combinatorial traitor tracing schemes start with a scheme of small bounded size (say 2-user for collusion-secure codes in Boneh-Shaw scheme [7] and in Kiayias and Yung scheme [22] and q-user for q-IPP codes in Chor-Fiat-Naor scheme [11] and in Phan-Safavi-To scheme [28]), and then combine these schemes to achieve a general one. So we ask here: What can be done for a user set whose size is not an unbounded independent parameter? does the ciphertext size of such an anonymous broadcast encryption scheme still grows linearly in the number of users, comparing to the single-user encryption, namely the corresponding public-key encryption from the same assumption? For $N = 2$, Phan et

al. [29] provided a construction of anonymous broadcast encryption scheme in which the ciphertext length is about 1.5 times the ciphertext size of its underlying ElGamal encryption scheme. Here, we will consider the case where N is much larger but is bounded by another system parameter (namely the security parameter). We call this case "anonymous broadcast encryption for bounded universe," or for short (AnoBEB). We will then employ the scheme to combinatorially build a traitor tracing scheme (a broadcast scheme where rogue devices are traceable to participants who helped building them) [11] and the scheme is in fact a "trace and revoke" allowing tracing and also revoking of bad participants [26] and as our main result.

1.1   Our Contributions

We present three main results:

1. First note that it was not known how to generalize a PKE to an anonymous BE scheme for, say, a bounded universe of N users (AnoBEB for short) with a ciphertext rate (between the anonymous BE scheme and the underlying PKE) strictly less than N, for any $N \neq 2$. We show a purpose transformation from LWE PKE into an AnoBEB with an optimal rate. The security of our proposed schemes for k users relies on the k-LWE problem [25].
2. We then propose a new efficient method for achieving a trace and revoke system from an AnoBEB, a secret sharing scheme, and a robust IPP code. It is worth remarking that robust IPP code, introduced by Barg *et al.* [3], is an interesting generalization of IPP code, but to the best of our knowledge, till today it has not found any application in cryptography.
3. We, finally, give a concrete construction of a trace and revoke system. In [3], only a proof of existence of robust IPP codes was given. We propose two explicit instantiations of such codes, while adding a condition to deal with the revocation aspects. Our final trace and revoke system (TR) also enjoys the more demanding "public traceability" property as in [8, 10, 28].

1.2   Techniques

LWE-*based anonymous broadcast encryption for bounded universe.* In [25], Ling *et al.* introduced the first lattice-based traitor tracing scheme (LPSS) based on the $k - \text{LWE}$ assumption (parameter k is bounded by the underlying lattice dimension). They showed a polynomial-time reduction from $k - \text{LWE}$ to LWE, so their scheme is as efficient as the LWE encryption. Our construction of an AnoBEB scheme comes from a basic "tweaking purpose" idea: switching the tracing procedure LPSS to be functional as a broadcast encryption. We first recall that in the LPSS traitor tracing scheme, the linear tracing technique [11] was applied to detect a traitor in a group of suspect users, they first create a ciphertext so that every user in this group can decrypt successfully. In the subsequent steps, the tracer will disable, one by one, users in the group, preventing them from decrypting the ciphertext. We observe that if we switch the suspected users in

LPSS scheme to be the legitimate users, and the removed users in the suspected set to the revoked users, then, in fact, in principle we get a broadcast encryption. Because the LPSS traitor tracing can deal with a bounded number of traitors, we actually get a broadcast encryption for a bounded number of users, that we call broadcast encryption for bounded universe.

The main remaining technical difficulty is to prove the anonymity property of this broadcast encryption. Anonymity requires that an adversary cannot distinguish between encryptions for two targets S_0, S_1 of its choice. If we consider an outsider adversary, defined in [13], which only corrupts users outside both S_0 and S_1, then the proof is direct because from the k-LWE assumption, the encryption for S_0 and for S_1, both, look like random ciphertexts to the adversary. It is more challenging to consider a general adversary which can also corrupt the keys in the intersection of S_0 and S_1. Fortunately, we can exploit an intermediate theorem in [25] which informally states that the encryptions for a set S and for a set $S \cup \{i\}$ are indistinguishable if the adversary does not corrupt the user i, even if the adversary corrupts users in S. Thanks to this result, our technique applies a hybrid argument which moves an encryption for the set S_0 (or S_1) to an encryption for the set $S_0 \cup S_1$ by adding one by one users in $S_1 \setminus S_0$ (or in $S_1 \setminus S_0$, respectively).

Revocation from robust IPP *code.* We next explain why it is difficult to get revocation with code-based schemes and how we can overcome the problem. We recall that the binary collusion secure code is well suitable for traitor tracing. Its shortcoming is the incapacity to support revocation. In a revoke system, each user will be assigned to a codeword and its decryption key is a set of sub-keys are given respectively for each symbol in the codeword. In fact, to revoke a group of users, the authority has to disable the ability to decrypt with sub-keys in each position of the revoked group. In using the binary collusion secure code scenario, there are only two possibilities for sub-key of each position. Whenever the authority executes the revocation procedure, a large number of legitimate non-revoked users will be affected, and will not be able to decrypt anymore. A non-trivial remedy is for the system's designer to choose a code with big alphabet for example $q-$ary IPP code instead of a binary collusion secure code with alphabet size two. Revocation will decrease the number of valid keys slightly. Certainly, in this case, the possibility that legitimate users will be excluded from the system with revoked users must also be taken into account. A secret sharing scheme, in turn, is the mechanism that allows us to think about a solution: a legitimate user only needs to have a certain fraction (over the threshold) of the sub-keys to be able to recover the original message. However, this reduced requirement gives an advantage to the pirates as well: they become stronger as they do not need to put all sub-keys in the pirate decoder; namely, they are permitted to delete sub-keys. The introduction of robust IPP of Barg *et al.* [3] which allows the identification of parents even if some positions are intentionally erased, allows for a tool dealing with the above problem. We propose here a new generic method for designing a trace and revoke system from robust IPP codes and AnoBEB. As in previous code-based methods, the ciphertext size of the trace and revoke system is proportional to the length of the code and the ciphertext size of the AnoBEB.

Finally, because robust IPP codes were only implicitly shown in [3], we propose two explicit instantiations of robust IPP codes. Our final construction results in the most efficient trace and revoke scheme in the bounded collusion model.

2 Preliminaries

2.1 Trace and Revoke Systems

We next recall the standard definition of a trace and revoke scheme. Let $\mathcal{PT}$ and $\mathcal{CT}$ denote the plaintext and ciphertext spaces, respectively. We also let $U(\mathcal{PT})$ denote the uniform distribution over plaintext space $\mathcal{PT}$.

Adapted from the definition of the trace and revoke system in [1], we will present a trace and revoke system for a universe $\mathcal{U} = \{1, \ldots, N\}$ in the black-box model. A Trace and Revoke (TR) system, in turn, consists of the following algorithms:

Setup($1^n, t, r$): Takes as input the security parameter n, a maximum malicious coalition size t and the bound r on the number of revoked users. It outputs the global parameters param of the system, a public key ek and a master secret key MSK.

Extract(ek, MSK, i): Takes as input the public key ek, the master secret key MSK and a user index $i \in \mathcal{U}$, the algorithm extracts the decryption keys dk_i which is sent to the corresponding user i.

Encrypt(ek, $M, \mathcal{R}$): Takes as input the public key ek, a message $M \in \mathcal{PT}$ and a set of revoked users $\mathcal{R} \subset \mathcal{U}$ (cardinality $\leq r$), outputs a ciphertext $c \in \mathcal{CT}$.

Decrypt(ek, dk_i, c): Takes as input the public key ek, the decryption key dk_i of user i and a ciphertext $c \in \mathcal{CT}$. The algorithm outputs the message $M \in \mathcal{PT}$ or an invalid symbol $\perp$.

Tracing($\mathcal{D}, \mathcal{R}$, ek): is a black-box tracing algorithm which takes as input a set $\mathcal{R}$ of $\leq r$ revoked users, public key ek and has access to a pirate decoder $\mathcal{D}$. The tracing algorithm outputs the identity of at least one user who participated in building $\mathcal{D}$ or an invalid symbol $\perp$.

The correctness requirement is that, with overwhelming probability over the randomness used by the algorithms, we have:

$$\forall M \in \mathcal{PT}, \forall i \notin \mathcal{R} : \mathsf{Decrypt}(\mathsf{ek}, dk_i, \mathsf{Encrypt}(\mathsf{ek}, M, \mathcal{R})) = M,$$

for any set $\mathcal{R}$ of $\leq r$ revoked users.

Requirement on the pirate decoder

- The classical requirement is that the pirate decoder $\mathcal{D}$ is a device that is able to decrypt successfully any ciphertext with overwhelming probability and the pirate device is resettable, meaning that it should not maintain state during the tracing process. In [25], a strong model of pirate decoder was considered where the tracing algorithm is executing in minimal access black-box model and the pirate decoder is only required to have a non-negligible probability of success. More formally, the tracer is allowed to access $\mathcal{D}$ via an oracle $\mathcal{O}^{\mathcal{D}}$. It means that the oracle $\mathcal{O}^{\mathcal{D}}$ will be fed the input which has the form $(\mathbf{c}, M) \in (\mathcal{CT}, \mathcal{PT})$. The tracer will get 1 from the output $\mathcal{O}^{\mathcal{D}}$ in the case that the decoder decrypts correctly the ciphertext c, i.e. $\mathcal{D}(\mathbf{c}) = M$ and will get 0 in the other case. It requires that the pirate device $\mathcal{D}$ decrypts correctly with a non-negligible probability (ϵ) in the security parameter n, namely:

$$\Pr_{\substack{M \hookleftarrow U(\mathcal{PT}) \\ \mathbf{c} \hookleftarrow \mathsf{Encrypt}(M)}} [\mathcal{O}^{\mathcal{D}}(\mathbf{c}, M) = 1] \geq \epsilon = \frac{1}{|\mathcal{PT}|} + \frac{1}{n^{\alpha}},$$

for some constant $\alpha > 0$.

- In [19], the authors show a flaw in the transformation of an augmented broadcast encryption into traitor tracing and proposed a fix in which a very strong notion of Pirate Distinguisher [19,27] was put forth, in place of the classical notion of pirate decoder. The Pirate Distinguisher is not required to output entire message (or an indicator bit as in minimal access model) nor to decrypt with high probability every ciphertexts which are taken from random messages. Instead, it is enough that the pirate decoder can distinguish the encryption of two different messages M_0, M_1 of its choice. We call $\mathcal{D}$ is a ϵ-useful Pirate Distinguisher if

$$\left| \Pr \left[\mathcal{D}(\mathbf{c}_b) = b : \begin{array}{l} T \leftarrow \mathcal{A}(1^n); (\mathsf{MSK}, \mathsf{ek}) \leftarrow \mathsf{Setup}(\cdot); \\ \{\mathsf{dk}_i \leftarrow \mathsf{Extract}(\mathsf{ek}, \mathsf{MSK}, i)\}_{i \in T}; \\ (\mathcal{D}, M_0, M_1) \leftarrow \mathcal{A}(\mathsf{ek}, \{\mathsf{dk}_i\}_{i \in T}); \\ b \hookleftarrow \{0, 1\}; \mathbf{c}_b \hookleftarrow \mathsf{Encrypt}(\mathsf{ek}, M_b, \mathcal{R}) \end{array} \right] - \frac{1}{2} \right| \geq \epsilon,$$

In this work, we will deal with this notion of pirate distinguisher which is actually the strongest notion about the usefulness of pirate decoders.

Interestingly, in the case of bit encryption like in LPSS scheme [25] and in our scheme, the notion of pirate distinguisher is equivalent to the pirate decoder in the minimal access black-box model. Indeed, as there are only two messages 0 and 1, the requirement that the oracle $\mathcal{O}^{\mathcal{D}}$ (in the definiton of pirate decoder) can correctly decrypt ciphertexts of one of these two messages with non-negligible probability is equivalent to a pirate distinguisher that can distinguish the encryption of the two messages 0 and 1. Therefore, the LPSS scheme is also secure when considering the notion of pirate distinguisher. Inherently, our tracing algorithm can also deal with pirate distinguishers.

Semantic Security. The CPA security of a trace-and-revoke scheme TR is defined based on the following game.

- The challenger runs $\mathsf{Setup}(1^n, t, r)$ and gives the produced public key ek to the adversary $\mathcal{A}$.

- The adversary (adaptively) chooses a set $\mathcal{R} \subset \mathcal{U}$ of $\leq r$ revoked users. The challenger gives $\mathcal{A}$ all the dk_i for all $i \in \mathcal{R}$.
- The adversary then chooses two messages $M_0, M_1 \in \mathcal{PT}$ of equal length and gives them to the challenger.
- The challenger samples $b \leftarrow \{0,1\}$ and provides $c \leftarrow \mathsf{Encrypt}(\mathsf{ek}, M_b, \mathcal{R})$ to $\mathcal{A}$.
- Finally, the adversary returns its guess $b' \in \{0,1\}$ for the b chosen by the challenger. The adversary wins this game if $b = b'$.

We define $\mathsf{Succ}^{\mathtt{IND}}(\mathcal{A}) = \Pr[b' = b]$, the probability that $\mathcal{A}$ wins the game. We say that a TR system is semantically secure ($\mathtt{IND}$) if all polynomial time adaptive adversaries $\mathcal{A}$ have at most negligible advantage in the above game, where $\mathcal{A}$'s advantage is defined as $\mathsf{Adv}^{\mathtt{IND}}(\mathcal{A}) = |\mathsf{Succ}^{\mathtt{IND}}(\mathcal{A}) - \frac{1}{2}| = |\Pr[b' = b] - \frac{1}{2}|$.

Traceability. The tracing game between an attacker $\mathcal{A}$ and a challenger $\mathcal{B}$ is defined as following:

1. The challenger runs $\mathsf{Setup}(1^n, t, r)$ and gives ek to $\mathcal{A}$.
2. The adversary $\mathcal{A}$ outputs a set $\mathcal{T} \subset \{u_1, u_2, \ldots, u_t\} \subset \{1, \ldots, N\}$ of colluding users. We assume that $\mathcal{T} \cap \mathcal{R} = \emptyset$. The adversary sends t arbitrary key queries in an adaptive way to $\mathcal{B}$.
3. The challenger $\mathcal{B}$ responds to $\mathcal{A}$ decryption keys $\mathsf{dk}_1, \ldots, \mathsf{dk}_t$.
4. The adversary $\mathcal{A}$ outputs two messages M_0, M_1 and creates a pirate distinguishser $\mathcal{D}$ so that it can distinguishable correctly the encryptions of M_0, M_1 with probability at least ϵ.
5. The challenger $\mathcal{B}$ executes the procedure $\mathsf{Tracing}(\mathcal{D}, \mathcal{R}, \mathsf{ek})$. The adversary wins the game if $\mathcal{B}$ outputs $\bot$ or a user index that does not belong to $\mathcal{T}$.

2.2   Anonymous Broadcast Encryption

A broadcast system is called anonymous (AnoBE for short) if it allows addressing a message to a subset of the users, without revealing this privileged set even to users who successfully decrypt the message. When the number of users in our system is bounded by the security parameter, we have the notion of *anonymous broadcast encryption for bounded universe* – AnoBEB. We follow the definition in [24]:

Let $\mathcal{PT}$ and $\mathcal{CT}$ denote the plaintext and ciphertext spaces, respectively. Let $\mathcal{U} = \{1, \ldots, N\}$ be the universe of users, where $N \leq k$ for some k bounded by a security parameter n. An anonymous broadcast encryption for bounded universe (AnoBEB) consists of the following algorithms:

$\mathsf{Setup}(1^n, N)$: Takes as input the security parameter n and the maximal number of users N. It outputs a public key ek and a master secret key MSK.

$\mathsf{Extract}(\mathsf{ek}, \mathsf{MSK}, i)$: Takes as input the public key ek, the master secret key MSK and a user index $i \in \mathcal{U}$, the algorithm extracts the decryption keys dk_i which is sent to the corresponding user i.

$\mathsf{Encrypt}(\mathsf{ek}, M, \mathcal{S})$: Takes as input the public key ek, a message $M \in \mathcal{PT}$ and a set of target users $\mathcal{S} \subset \mathcal{U}$, outputs a ciphertext $c \in \mathcal{CT}$.

Decrypt(ek, dk_i, c): Takes as input the public key ek, the decryption key dk_i of user i and a ciphertext $c \in \mathcal{CT}$. The algorithm outputs the message $M \in \mathcal{PT}$ or an invalid symbol $\perp$.

The correctness requirement is that, with overwhelming probability over the randomness used by the algorithms, we have:

$$\forall M \in \mathcal{PT}, \forall i \in \mathcal{S} : \mathsf{Decrypt}(\mathsf{ek}, \mathsf{dk}_i, \mathsf{Encrypt}(\mathsf{ek}, M, \mathcal{S})) = M.$$

The CPA security of AnoBEB defined based on the following game between an adversary $\mathcal{A}$ and a challenger $\mathcal{B}$

- The challenger runs $\mathsf{Setup}(1^n, N)$ and gives the produced public key ek to the adversary $\mathcal{A}$.
- The adversary (adaptively) chooses indices $i \in \mathcal{U}$ to ask decryption keys. The challenger gives $\mathcal{A}$ all the dk_i for all required indices.
- The adversary then chooses two messages $M_0, M_1 \in \mathcal{PT}$ of equal length and a set $\mathcal{S} \subset \mathcal{U}$ of users with restriction that no index $i \in \mathcal{S}$ required decryption key before. It then gives M_0, M_1 and $\mathcal{S}$ to the challenger.
- The challenger samples $b \hookleftarrow \{0,1\}$ and provides $c \hookleftarrow \mathsf{Encrypt}(\mathsf{ek}, M_b, \mathcal{S})$ to $\mathcal{A}$.
- The adversary $\mathcal{A}$ continues asking for decryption keys for any index i outside $\mathcal{S}$.
- Finally, the adversary returns its guess $b' \in \{0,1\}$ for the b chosen by the challenger. The adversary wins this game if $b = b'$.

We define $\mathsf{Succ}^{\mathrm{IND}}(\mathcal{A}) = \Pr[b' = b]$, the probability that $\mathcal{A}$ wins the game. We say that AnoBEB is semantically secure (IND) if all polynomial time adaptive adversaries $\mathcal{A}$ have at most negligible advantage in the above game, where $\mathcal{A}$'s advantage is defined as $\mathsf{Adv}^{\mathrm{IND}}(\mathcal{A}) = |\mathsf{Succ}^{\mathrm{IND}}(\mathcal{A}) - \frac{1}{2}| = |\Pr[b' = b] - \frac{1}{2}|$.

For anonymous game, the challenger $\mathcal{B}$ runs $\mathsf{Setup}(1^n, N)$ to obtain a public key ek and a master secret key MSK and sends ek to adversary $\mathcal{A}$.

Phase 1. The adversary $\mathcal{A}$ adaptively issues decryption key extraction queries for any index $i \in \mathcal{U}$. The challenger runs Extract algorithm on index i and returns to $\mathcal{A}$ the decryption key $dk_i = \mathsf{Extract}(\mathsf{ek}, \mathsf{MSK}, i)$.

Challenger. The adversary chooses a message $M \in \mathcal{PT}$ and two distinct subsets $\mathcal{S}_0, \mathcal{S}_1 \subset \mathcal{U}$ of users. We require that $\mathcal{A}$ has not issued key queries for any index $i \in \mathcal{S}_0 \triangle \mathcal{S}_1 = (\mathcal{S}_0 \setminus \mathcal{S}_1) \cup (\mathcal{S}_1 \setminus \mathcal{S}_0)$. The adversary $\mathcal{A}$ passes M and $\mathcal{S}_0, \mathcal{S}_1$ to the challenger $\mathcal{B}$. The challenger $\mathcal{B}$ randomly chooses a bit $b \in \{0,1\}$, computes $c = \mathsf{Encrypt}(\mathsf{ek}, M, \mathcal{S}_b)$ and sends c to $\mathcal{A}$.

Phase 2. $\mathcal{A}$ adaptively issues decryption key extraction queries on indices $i \notin \mathcal{S}_0 \triangle \mathcal{S}_1$ and obtains decryption keys dk_i.

Guess. The adversary outputs a guess $b' \in \{0,1\}$ and wins the game if $b' = b$.

We denote by $\mathsf{Succ}^{\mathrm{ANO}}(\mathcal{A}) = \Pr[b' = b]$ the probability that $\mathcal{A}$ wins the game, and its advantage is $\mathsf{Adv}^{\mathrm{ANO}}(\mathcal{A}) = |\mathsf{Succ}^{\mathrm{ANO}}(\mathcal{A}) - \frac{1}{2}| = |\Pr[b' = b] - \frac{1}{2}|$. We say that a scheme Π is *anonymous against chosen plaintext attacks* – ANO if all polynomial-time adversaries $\mathcal{A}$ have a negligible advantage in the above game.

2.3   Lattice and k-LWE Problem

For two matrices A, B of compatible dimensions, let $(A \| B)$ (or sometimes $\left(\frac{A}{B}\right)$) denote vertical concatenations of A and B. For $A \in \mathbb{Z}_q^{m \times n}$, define $\text{Im}(A) = \{As \mid s \in \mathbb{Z}_q^n\} \subseteq \mathbb{Z}_q^m$. For $X \subseteq \mathbb{Z}_q^m$, let $\text{Span}(X)$ denote the set of all linear combinations of elements of X and define $X^\perp$ to be $\{b \in \mathbb{Z}_q^m \mid \forall c \in X, \langle b, c \rangle = 0\}$.

Assume that D_1 and D_2 are distributions over a countable set X, their statistical distance is defined to be $\frac{1}{2} \sum_{x \in X} |D_1(x) - D_2(x)|$. We say that two distributions D_1 and D_2 (two ensembles of distributions indexed by n) are statistically close if their statistical distance is negligible in n. We use the notation $x \hookleftarrow D$ to refer that the element x is sampled from the distribution D. We also let $U(X)$ denote the uniform distribution over X. Let $\mathbf{B} = \{b_1, b_2, \ldots, b_n\} \subset \mathbb{R}^n$ consists of n linearly independent vectors. The n-dimensional lattice Λ generated by the basis $\mathbf{B}$ is $\Lambda = L(\mathbf{B}) = \{\mathbf{B}c = \sum_{i \in [n]} c_i \cdot b_i \mid c \in \mathbb{Z}^n\}$. The length of a matrix $\mathbf{B}$ is defined as the norm of its longest column: $\|\mathbf{B}\| = \max_{1 \leq i \leq n} \|b_i\|$. Here we view a matrix as simply the set of its column vectors.

For a lattice $L \subseteq \mathbb{R}^m$ and an invertible matrix $S \in \mathbb{R}^{m \times m}$, we define the Gaussian distribution of parameters L and S by $D_{L,S}(\mathbf{b}) = \exp(-\pi \|S^{-1}\mathbf{b}\|^2)$ for all $\mathbf{b} \in L$.

The q-ary lattice associated with a matrix $A \in \mathbb{Z}_q^{m \times n}$ is defined as $\Lambda^\perp(A) = \{\mathbf{x} \in \mathbb{Z}^m \mid \mathbf{x}^t \cdot A = \mathbf{0} \bmod q\}$. It has dimension m, and a basis can be computed in polynomial-time from A. For $\mathbf{u} \in \mathbb{Z}_q^m$, we define $\Lambda_{\mathbf{u}}^\perp(A)$ as the coset $\{\mathbf{x} \in \mathbb{Z}^m \mid \mathbf{x}^t \cdot A = \mathbf{u}^t \bmod q\}$ of $\Lambda^\perp(A)$.

Lemma 1 (Theorem 3.1, [2]). *There is a probabilistic polynomial-time algorithm that, on input positive integers $n, m, q \geq 2$, outputs two matrices $A \in \mathbb{Z}_q^{m \times n}$ and $T \in \mathbb{Z}^{m \times m}$ such that the distribution of A is within statistical distance $2^{-\Omega(n)}$ from $U(\mathbb{Z}_q^{m \times n})$; the rows of T form a basis of $\Lambda^\perp(A)$; each row of T has norm $\leq 3mq^{n/m}$.*

Lemma 2 (GPV algorithm, [15]). *There exists a probabilistic polynomial-time algorithm that given a basis $\mathbf{B}$ of an n-dimensional lattice $\Lambda = L(\mathbf{B})$, a parameter $s \geq \|\tilde{\mathbf{B}}\| \cdot \omega\left(\sqrt{\log n}\right)$ [1], outputs a sample from a distribution that is statistically close to $D_{\Lambda,s}$.*

Definition 3 (k-LWE problem, [25]). *Let $S \in \mathbb{R}^{m \times m}$ be an invertible matrix and denote $\mathbb{T}^{m+1} = (\mathbb{R}/\mathbb{Z})^{m+1}$. The $(k, S) - \text{LWE}$ problem is: given $A \hookleftarrow U(\mathbb{Z}_q^{m \times n})$, $\mathbf{u} \hookleftarrow U(\mathbb{Z}_q^n)$ and $\mathbf{x}_i \hookleftarrow D_{\Lambda_{-\mathbf{u}}^\perp(A),S}$ for $i \leq k \leq m$, the goal is to distinguish between the distributions (over $\mathbb{T}^{m+1}$)*

$$\frac{1}{q} \cdot U\left(\text{Im}\left(\frac{\mathbf{u}^t}{A}\right)\right) + \nu_\alpha^{m+1} \quad \text{and} \quad \frac{1}{q} \cdot U\left(\text{Span}_{i \leq k}(1 \| \mathbf{x}_i)^\perp\right) + \nu_\alpha^{m+1},$$

where ν_α denotes the one-dimensional Gaussian distribution with standard deviation $\alpha > 0$.

---

[1] $\tilde{\mathbf{B}}$ is Gram-Schmidt orthogonalization of $\mathbf{B}$.

In [25], it was shown that this problem can be reduced to LWE problem for a specific class of diagonal matrices S. In our work, we only need any such S where (k, S)-LWE is hard, and thus the use of S is implicit. For simplicity, we will use k-LWE and (k, S)-LWE interchangeably in this paper.

2.4 Projective Sampling

Inspired by the notion of projective hash family [12], Ling *et al.* [25] proposed a new concept called projective sampling family. A construction of projective sampling family from $k - \mathsf{LWE}$ problem was built as well. The major purpose of their construction is to switch a secret key traitor tracing scheme into a public key one, where tracing signals are sampled from a distribution of spanned spaces by secret keys $\mathbf{x}_j$. In their scheme, each secret key $\mathbf{x}_j \in \mathbb{Z}_q^m$ is associated with a public matrix H_j (projective key). Given the projective keys H_j, any entity in the system can simulate the tracing signal in a computationally indistinguishable way (under the k-LWE assumption) in the sense that the simulated signal $U(\cap_j \mathrm{Im}(H_j))$ is indistinguishable from original tracing signal $U\left(\mathrm{Span}_j(\mathbf{x}_j^+)^\perp\right)$ even for entities who know the secret keys $\mathbf{x}_j$. This implies that anyone in the system is allowed to execute the tracing procedure.

We recall the construction of H_j [25] as following:

1. Given a matrix $A \in \mathbb{Z}_q^{m \times n}$ and an invertible matrix $A \in \mathbb{Z}_q^{m \times m}$, sampling signals are taken from a spanned space $U\left(\mathrm{Span}_{j \leq k}(\mathbf{x}_j^+)^\perp\right) + \lfloor \nu_{\alpha q} \rceil^{m+1}$, where $\mathbf{x}_j \hookleftarrow D_{\Lambda_{-\mathbf{u}}^\perp(A), S}$. We call vectors $\mathbf{x}_j \in \mathbb{Z}_q^m$ secret keys.
2. Sample $H \hookleftarrow U\left(\mathbb{Z}_q^{m \times (m-n)}\right)$, conditioned on $\mathrm{Im}(H) \subset \mathrm{Im}(A)$. Define the public projected value of $\mathbf{x}_j$ on H as $\mathbf{h}_j = -H^t \cdot \mathbf{x}_j$.
3. Define $H_j = (\mathbf{h}_j^t \parallel H) \in \mathbb{Z}_q^{(m+1) \times (m-n)}$ as the public projected key of $\mathbf{x}_j$.

Simulated signals are now sampled from the distribution $U(\cap_{j \leq k} \mathrm{Im}(H_j)) + \lfloor \nu_{\alpha q} \rceil^{m+1}$. Under the (k, S)-LWE hardness assumptions, the following two distributions:

$$U\left(\mathrm{Span}_{j \leq k}(\mathbf{x}_j^+)^\perp\right) + \lfloor \nu_{\alpha q} \rceil^{m+1} \text{ and } U\left(\cap_{j \leq k} \mathrm{Im}(H_j)\right) + \lfloor \nu_{\alpha q} \rceil^{m+1}$$

are indistinguishable. This implies that given projected keys H_j, anyone can take samples from the distribution $U\left(\mathrm{Span}_{j \leq k}(\mathbf{x}_j^+)^\perp\right) + \lfloor \nu_{\alpha q} \rceil^{m+1}$ although he does not have the secret keys $\mathbf{x}_j$.

We restate an important result that is frequently used in our proofs. This result comes directly from Theorem 25 and Theorem 27 in [25].

Lemma 4. *We denote by* $[t] = \{1, \ldots, t\}$ *the set of the t first positive integers. Under the k-LWE assumption, for $k > t$, given t secret keys $\mathbf{x}_1, \mathbf{x}_2, \ldots, \mathbf{x}_t$, for any $j \notin [t]$, the distrisbutions*

$$U\left(\mathrm{Span}_{i \in [t]}(\mathbf{x}_i^+)^\perp\right) + \lfloor \nu_{\alpha q} \rceil^{m+1}, \ U\left(\mathrm{Span}_{i \in [t] \cup \{j\}}(\mathbf{x}_i^+)^\perp\right) + \lfloor \nu_{\alpha q} \rceil^{m+1},$$

are indistinguishable (from Theorem 25 in [25]), and the distributions

$$U\left(\cap_{i\in[t]}\mathrm{Im}(H_i)\right) + \lfloor\nu_{\alpha q}\rceil^{m+1}, \ U\left(\cap_{i\in[t]\cup\{j\}}\mathrm{Im}(H_i)\right) + \lfloor\nu_{\alpha q}\rceil^{m+1},$$

are indistinguishable as well (from Theorem 27 in [25]).

3 Anonymous Broadcast Encryption for Bounded Universe

We now construct an anonymous broadcast encryption for bounded universe scheme (AnoBEB) from k-LWE problem. Let N be the maximal number of users (receivers are implicitly represented by integers in $\mathcal{U} = \{1, \ldots, N\}$). Given a security parameter n, we assert that parameters q, m, α, S are chosen so that the (k, S)-LWE problem is hard to solve as presented in [25]. Since the adversary can corrupt any user, we require that $N \le k$ (the system's bounded universe constraint).

Setup($1^n, N$): Takes as input the security parameter n and maximal number of users N. It uses Lemma 1 to generate 2 matrices $(A, T) \in \mathbb{Z}_q^{m\times n} \times \mathbb{Z}^{m\times m}$ and picks $\mathbf{u}$ uniformly in $\mathbb{Z}_q^n$. We set a master secret key $\mathsf{MSK} = (A, T)$ and a public key $\mathsf{ek} = \{A^+, (H_j)_{j\le N}\}$, where $A^+ = (\mathbf{u}^t \| A)$ and the projected keys H_j (corresponding to the secret keys $\mathbf{x}_j$, defined in Sect. 2.4) are added each time a secret key $\mathbf{x}_j$ is generated by the Extract. For a system of N users, one can run N times Extract inside the Setup to generate N secret keys.

Extract($\mathsf{ek}, \mathsf{MSK}, j$): Takes as input the public key ek, the master secret key MSK and a user index $j \in \mathcal{U}$, the algorithm calls the GPV algorithm (Lemma 2) using the basis $\Lambda^\perp(A)$ consisting of the rows of T and the standard deviation matrix S. It obtains a sample $\mathbf{x}_j$ from $D_{\Lambda_{-\mathbf{u}}^\perp(A), S}$. The algorithm outputs decryption key $\mathsf{dk}_j = \mathbf{x}_j^+ := (1 \| \mathbf{x}_j) \in \mathbb{Z}^{m+1}$ for user j.

Encrypt($\mathsf{ek}, M, \mathcal{S}$): Takes as input the public key ek, a message $M \in \mathcal{PT} = \{0, 1\}$ and a set of users $\mathcal{S} \subseteq \mathcal{U}$. To encrypt M, one chooses a vector $\mathbf{y} \in \mathbb{Z}_q^{m+1}$ from the distribution $U(\cap_{i\in\mathcal{S}}\mathrm{Im}(H_i))$, $\mathbf{e} \hookleftarrow \lfloor\nu_{\alpha q}\rceil^{m+1}$ and outputs $\mathbf{c} \in \mathcal{CT}$, which is broadcasted to every member of $\mathcal{S}$ as follows:

$$\mathbf{c} = \mathbf{y} + \mathbf{e} + \begin{pmatrix} M\lfloor q/2 \rfloor \\ 0 \end{pmatrix},$$

whereas $\lfloor x \rfloor$ denotes the greatest integer less than or equal to x.

Decrypt($\mathsf{ek}, \mathsf{dk}_j, \mathbf{c}$): Takes as input the public key ek, a decryption key $\mathsf{dk}_j = \mathbf{x}_j^+$ of user j and a ciphertext $\mathbf{c} \in \mathcal{CT}$. The function Decrypt will return 0 if $\langle\mathbf{x}_j^+, \mathbf{c}\rangle$ is closer 0 than to $\lfloor q/2 \rfloor$ modulo q, otherwise return 1.

Correctness. We require that for a given subset $\mathcal{S} \subseteq \mathcal{U}$ and all $j \in \mathcal{S}$, if $\mathbf{c} = \mathsf{Encrypt}(\mathsf{ek}, m, \mathcal{S})$ and dk_j is the decryption key for user $j \in \mathcal{S}$, we then recover $M = \mathsf{Decrypt}(\mathsf{ek}, \mathsf{dk}_j, \mathbf{c})$ with overwhelming probability. Indeed, since

$\cap_{i \in S} \text{Im}(H_i) \subseteq \text{Span}_{i \in S}(\mathbf{x}_i^+)^\perp$, for each user $j \in S$ and $\mathbf{y} \hookleftarrow U(\cap_{i \in S}\text{Im}(H_i))$, we have $\langle \mathbf{x}_j^+, \mathbf{y} \rangle = 0$. Therefore,

$$\langle \mathbf{x}_j^+, \mathbf{c} \rangle = \langle \mathbf{x}_j^+, \mathbf{y} \rangle + \langle \mathbf{x}_j^+, \mathbf{e} \rangle + \langle \mathbf{x}_j^+, \left(\frac{M\lfloor q/2 \rfloor}{0}\right)\rangle \mod q$$
$$= \langle \mathbf{x}_j^+, \mathbf{e} \rangle + M\lfloor q/2 \rfloor \mod q,$$

where $\mathbf{e} \hookleftarrow \lfloor \nu_{\alpha q} \rceil^{m+1}$. According to [25], the quantity $\langle \mathbf{x}_j^+, \mathbf{e} \rangle$ is relatively small modulo q with overwhelming probability. The procedure Decrypt returns the original message with overwhelming probability. Therefore, every user in S can decrypt successfully.

We now consider the security of the scheme, essentially showing that an adversary which is allowed to corrupt any user outside S, cannot break the semantic security of the scheme.

Theorem 5. *Under the k-LWE hardness assumption, for any $N \leq k$, the AnoBEB scheme Π constructed as above is IND-secure.*

Proof. The proof of this theorem can be found in the full version. ∎

We next consider the anonymity of the AnoBEB scheme (our main result in this section):

Theorem 6. *Under the k-LWE hardness, for any $N \leq k$, our scheme is ANO-secure.*

Proof. The proof of this theorem can be found in the full version. ∎

Finally, we also note that, as shown in [25], example parameters are $k = m/10$, $\sigma = \widetilde{\Theta}(n)$, $q = \widetilde{\Theta}(n^5)$ and $m = \Theta(n \log n)$. We can therefore set our parameters to: $N = k$ and the efficiency of the AnoBEB scheme is approximately as efficient as the underlying LWE-PKE, inherently from the fact the LPSS k-LWE traitor tracing has approximately the same efficiency as the underlying LWE-PKE, as shown in [25].

4   Trace and Revoke System from **AnoBEB** and Robust IPP Codes

Our goal now is to construct a Trace and Revoke (TR) scheme from AnoBEB. The formal definition of a TR scheme is provided in Sect. 2.1. In our approach, we combine a robust t-IPP code with an AnoBEB scheme. We will start this section by recalling the notion of robust IPP code [3].

4.1   Robust IPP Codes

Let $\mathcal{C} = \{w_1, \ldots, w_N\} \subset \Sigma^\ell$ be a $q-$ary code of size N and length ℓ, mimimum Hamming distance Δ over alphabet $\Sigma = \{1, \ldots, q\}$. We assume that $w_i = (w_{i,1}, \ldots, w_{i,\ell})$. Given a positive integer t, a subset of codewords $X = \{w_1, w_2, \ldots, w_t\} \subset \mathcal{C}$ is called a coalition of size t. Let $X_i = \{w_{1,i}, \ldots, w_{t,i}\}$ be the set of the $i-$th coordinates of the coalition X. If the cardinality of X_i is equal to 1, say $|X_i| = 1$, the coordinate i is called undetectable, else it is called detectable. The set of detectable coordinates for the coalition X is denoted by $D(X)$. The set of descendants of X, denoted $\mathsf{desc}(X)$, is defined by

$$\mathsf{desc}(X) = \Big\{ x = (x_1, \ldots, x_\ell) \in \Sigma^\ell \mid x_j \in X_j, 1 \leq j \leq \ell \Big\}.$$

We call codewords in the coalition X are parents of the set $\mathsf{desc}(X)$. Define a $t-$descendant of the code $\mathcal{C}$, denoted $\mathsf{desc}_t(\mathcal{C})$, $\mathsf{desc}_t(\mathcal{C}) = \bigcup_{X \subset \mathcal{C}, |X| \leq t} \mathsf{desc}(X)$.

The $\mathsf{desc}_t(\mathcal{C})$ consists of all $\ell-$tuples that could be generated by some coalition of size at most t. Codes with identifiable parent property (IPP codes) are defined next.

Definition 7. *Given a code $\mathcal{C} = (\ell, N, q)$, let $t \geq 2$ be an integer. The code $\mathcal{C}$ is called a t-IPP code if for all $x \in \mathsf{desc}_t(\mathcal{C})$, it holds that* $\bigcap_{x \in \mathsf{desc}(X), X \subset \mathcal{C}, |X| \leq t} X \neq \emptyset.$

Then, in a t-IPP code, given a descendant $x \in \mathsf{desc}_t(\mathcal{C})$, we can always identify at least one of its parent codewords.

In [7], Boneh and Shaw considered a more general coalition, called wide-sense envelope of the coalition X. The set of descendants in their fingerprinting code is $\Big\{ x = (x_1, \ldots, x_\ell) \in (\Sigma \cup \{*\})^\ell \mid$ if $j \notin D(X)$ then $x_j \in X_j \Big\}$, where $D(X)$ consists of detectable coordinates of the coalition X. This means that any symbol of Σ or erased symbols $*$ are allowed in the detectable coordinates. Only detectable coordinates of descendant are allowed to modify the values (*marking assumption*). The notion Robust IPP code is a concept that allows a limited number of coordinates to not follow their parents. These coordinates are allowed to deviate by breaking the marking assumption.

Let $X \subset \Sigma^\ell, |X| \leq t$ be a coalition. For $i = 1, \ldots, \ell$, let X_i be the set of the $i-$th coordinates of the elements of a coalition X. Assume that there is a descendant x in the set $\mathsf{desc}(X)$, following the marking assumption rule except εn coordinates that can deviate from this rule. Call a coordinate i of $x \in \mathsf{desc}(X)$ a mutation if $x_i \notin X_i$ and consider mutations of two types: erasures, where x_i is replaced by an erasure symbol $*$, and one replaced by an arbitrary symbol $y_i \in \Sigma - X_i$.

Denote by $\mathsf{desc}(X)_\varepsilon$ the set of all vectors x formed from the vectors in the coalition X so that $x_i \in X_i$ for $\ell(1 - \varepsilon)$ coordinates i and x_i is a mutation in at most $\varepsilon\ell$ coordinates. Codes with robust identifiable parent property (Robust IPP codes) are defined below:

Definition 8. *Code* $\mathcal{C} \subset \Sigma^\ell$ *is a* (t, ε)-IPP *code (robust* t-IPP *code) if for all* $x \in \mathsf{desc}(X)_\varepsilon$, *where* $X \subset \mathcal{C}$ *and* $|X| \leq t$, *it holds that* $\bigcap\limits_{X \subset \mathcal{C}, |X| \leq t, x \in \mathsf{desc}(X)_\varepsilon} X \neq \emptyset$.

In words: the code $\mathcal{C}$ guarantees exact identification of at least one member of the coalition X of size at most t for any collusion with at most $\varepsilon\ell$ mutations. In the case $\varepsilon = 0$, a robust IPP becomes an IPP code.

A robust IPP code is said to have the traceability property if for any $x \in \mathsf{desc}_\varepsilon(X)$, the codeword $c \in \mathcal{C}$ closest to x by the Hamming distance is always one of the parents of x, i.e., $c \in \bigcap\limits_{X \subset \mathcal{C}, |X| \leq t, x \in \mathsf{desc}(X)_\varepsilon} X$. This implies that a pirate can be provably identified by finding any vector $c \in \mathcal{C}$ such that the distance from c to x is the shortest. A robust IPP code with traceability property is called robust TA code. We shall use robust IPP with traceability property.

4.2   Construction of a TR Scheme

We first choose a $(\rho\ell, \ell)$-secret sharing scheme, where $\rho = 1 - \varepsilon$. A secret sharing scheme will consist of 2 algorithms: Share which splits a secret into ℓ shares and Combine, where any user who keeps at least $\rho\ell$ shares will recover the secret by using the algorithm Combine.

Let r be maximum number of revoked users. We require that the distance Δ is set to verify the condition: $\Delta > \ell\left(1 - \frac{1-\rho}{r}\right)$. We denote by $[N] = \{1, \ldots, N\}$ the set of N users. We define a *mixture* $S = (S_1, \ldots, S_\ell)$ over Σ^ℓ to be a sequence of ℓ subsets of Σ, i.e. $S_i \subseteq \Sigma$. Given a vector $\omega = (\omega_1, \ldots, \omega_\ell) \in \Sigma^\ell$, the *agreement* between ω and a mixture S is defined to be the number of positions $i \in [\ell]$ for which $\omega_i \in S_i$: $\mathrm{AGR}(\omega, S) = \sum_{i=1}^{\ell} \mathbf{1}_{\omega_i \in S_i}$, where $\mathbf{1}_{\omega_i \in S_i} = 1$ if $\omega_i \in S_i$ and $\mathbf{1}_{\omega_i \in S_i} = 0$ if otherwise.

We will construct a TR system Γ for the set $[N]$ as follows: we identify each user $i \in [N]$ with the codeword $w_i = (w_{i,1}, \ldots, w_{i,\ell})$ in $\mathcal{C}$, whereas $w_{i,j}$ is the j-th coordinate of the codeword $w_i \in \mathcal{C}$. By assigning each user i in Γ to a set with ℓ sub-keys, the decryption key for the user i has form $\mathsf{dk}_i = (\mathsf{sk}_{1,w_{i,1}}, \ldots, \mathsf{sk}_{j,w_{i,j}}, \ldots, \mathsf{sk}_{\ell,w_{i,\ell}})$, where each sub-key is generated by the Extract algorithm of AnoBEB.

We consider an arbitrary group of decryption keys. At any coordinate component of the group, there are at most q sub-keys. We have a one-to-one correspondence between the set of q sub-keys and the set of decryption keys of q users in AnoBEB system. Consequently, to broadcast a message K (will be splitted into ℓ shares $K_1, \ldots, K_\ell$) to the set of N users, we apply the Share($K, \rho\ell, \ell$) of $(\rho\ell, \ell)$−secret sharing scheme and we encrypt each jth-share K_j with AnoBEB. Note that the message K is then often used as a session key to encrypt the data via a data encapsulation mechanism.

Formally, to build a TR system for N users, we concatenate ℓ instantiations of the scheme AnoBEB (for q users) according to an q−ary code $\mathcal{C}$. In particular, we will combine AnoBEB with robust IPP code $\mathcal{C}$. Our construction consists of 5 algorithms: Setup, Extract, Encrypt, Decrypt and Tracing.

Setup($1^n, t, r$): Takes as input the security parameter n, a maximum malicious coalition size t and the bound r on the number of revoked users. Let $\mathcal{C}$ be a t-IPP robust code size N over alphabet $\Sigma = [q]$. By calling ℓ times the procedure AnoBEB.Setup($1^n, q$), where ℓ is the length of the code $\mathcal{C}$, we obtain public keys ek_j and master secret keys MSK_j, $j = 1, \ldots, \ell$. We set $\mathsf{ek} = (\mathsf{ek}_1, \ldots, \mathsf{ek}_\ell)$ and $\mathsf{MSK} = (\mathsf{MSK}_1, \ldots, \mathsf{MSK}_\ell)$.

Extract($\mathsf{ek}, \mathsf{MSK}, i$): Takes as index $i \in [N]$ for each user, we use MSK to extract ℓ decryption keys for user i: $\mathsf{dk}_i = (\mathsf{sk}_{1, w_{i,1}}, \ldots, \mathsf{sk}_{j, w_{i,j}}, \ldots, \mathsf{sk}_{\ell, w_{i,\ell}})$, where $w_{i,j}$ is the value at position j of codeword w_i. Here,

$$\mathsf{sk}_{j, w_{i,j}} = \mathsf{AnoBEB.Extract}(\mathsf{ek}_j, \mathsf{MSK}_j, w_{i,j}), j \in [\ell].$$

Encrypt($\mathsf{ek}, K, \mathcal{R}$): Takes as input a set of revoked users $\mathcal{R} \subset \mathcal{C}$, where the cardinality of $\mathcal{R}$ is at most r. The message $K \in \mathcal{PT}$, where $\mathcal{PT}$ is the plaintext domain, will be broadcasted to the target set $\mathcal{C} \setminus \mathcal{R}$. We call the procedure Share($K, \rho\ell, \ell$) of ($\rho\ell, \ell$)-secret sharing scheme and obtain ℓ shares $K_1, \ldots, K_\ell$ in which at least $\rho\ell$ of the shares are needed to recover the message K. We consider the following mixture $\mathcal{M} = (\mathcal{M}_1, \ldots, \mathcal{M}_\ell) = (\Sigma \setminus \mathcal{R}[1], \ldots, \Sigma \setminus \mathcal{R}[\ell])$, where $\mathcal{R}[j] = \cup_{i \in \mathcal{R}} w_{i,j}$. Set $c_i = \Big(\mathsf{AnoBEB.Encrypt}(\mathsf{ek}_i, K_i, \mathcal{M}_i)\Big)$ for each $i = 1, \ldots, \ell$. The ciphertext is $\mathbf{c} = (c_1, \ldots, c_\ell) \in \mathcal{CT}^\ell$, where $\mathcal{CT}$ is the ciphertext domain of AnoBEB.

Decrypt($\mathsf{ek}, \mathsf{dk}_i, \mathbf{c}$): Takes as input ciphertext $\mathbf{c} \in \mathcal{CT}^\ell$ and a decryption key dk_i of user i. The user i calls the decryption function $\mathsf{AnoBEB.Decrypt}(\mathsf{ek}_j, \mathsf{sk}_{j, w_{i,j}}, c_j)$ of the AnoBEB scheme on sub-keys $\mathsf{sk}_{j, w_{i,j}}$ for each $j = 1, \ldots, \ell$. If $i \in \mathcal{R}$ then i cannot decrypt any c_i and cannot recover K (will be proved in the part of semantic security of Theorem 9). Otherwise, $i \notin \mathcal{R}$, the user obtains at least $\rho\ell$ values among the shared values K_j (as will be proved in the correctness). By calling the function Combine of the secret sharing scheme over pairs $\{(j, K_j)\}$, the user recovers the original message K.

Tracing($\mathcal{D}, \mathcal{R}, \mathsf{ek}$): Takes as input a set $\mathcal{R}$ of $\leq r$ revoked users, a public key ek and has access to a pirate distinguisher $\mathcal{D}$. We consider the mixture $\mathcal{M}$ as in Encrypt procedure. Let $\mathcal{T}$ be the subset of $\mathcal{U} \setminus \mathcal{R}$ with at most t elements (traitors). The pirate distinguisher outputs two messages K^0 and K^1 and then sends to the Tracer. We assume that the pirate distinguisher is an ϵ-useful in the sense that it can distinguish, with a non-negligible probability ϵ, ciphertexts in the form $\mathbf{c} = (c_1, \ldots, c_\ell)$, where $c_i = \Big(\mathsf{AnoBEB.Encrypt}(\mathsf{ek}_i, K_i^b, \mathcal{M}_i)\Big)$ for each K_i^b is i-th component of the message K^b, $b \leftarrow \{0, 1\}$. We denote here $\mathcal{M}_j = \{j_\iota\}_{\iota \in Q}$, $Q \subseteq [q]$ or $\mathcal{M}_j = \emptyset$ for all $j = 1, \ldots, \ell$. We consider the tracing procedure as follows:

For $j = 1$ to ℓ, do the following:
  1. While $\mathcal{M}_j \neq \emptyset$, do the following:
     (a) Let $\mathsf{cnt} \leftarrow 0$.
     (b) Repeat the following steps $W \leftarrow 8n(q/\epsilon)^2$ times:
         i. $c_j = \mathsf{AnoBEB.Encrypt}(\mathsf{ek}_j, K_j^b, \mathcal{M}_j)$.

      ii. Call the pirate distinguisher $\mathcal{D}$ on input
          $\mathbf{c} = (c_1, \ldots, c_j, \ldots, c_\ell)$. If $\mathcal{D}(\mathbf{c}) = b$ then cnt $\leftarrow$ cnt $+ 1$.
    (c) Let $\tilde{p}_{j,j_\iota}$ be the fraction of times that $\mathcal{D}$ outputs b correctly. We
       have $\tilde{p}_{j,j_\iota} = \mathsf{cnt}/W$.
    (d) $\mathcal{M}_j = \mathcal{M}_j \setminus \{j_\iota\}$.
  2. If there exists an index $j_\iota \in \mathcal{M}_j$ for which $\tilde{p}_{j,j_\iota} - \tilde{p}_{j,j_{\iota'}} \geq \epsilon/4q\ell$ for all
    $j_{\iota'} \in \mathcal{M}_j$ then
    (a) the key j_ι is accused and $\omega_j = j_\iota$,
    (b) $c_j = \mathsf{AnoBEB.Encrypt}(\mathsf{ek}_j, K_j^b, \mathcal{M}_j)$
    else $c_j = $ random and $\omega_j = *$.
End for.
From the pirate word $\omega = (\omega_1, \ldots, \omega_\ell)$ found after the Loop finished, call
tracing procedure in robust IPP code on input ω. The Tracing returns a
traitor.

We next present the main result of this Section.

Theorem 9. *Given*

- $\mathcal{C} = (\ell, N, q)$, *a robust* t-IPP *code of Hamming distance* Δ *and* $0 < \varepsilon < (t+1)^{-1}$;
- *a* $(\rho\ell, \ell)-$*secret sharing scheme, where* $\rho = 1 - \varepsilon$;
- *an anonymous broadcast encryption for* q *users* AnoBEB;

satisfying the following condition

$$\Delta/\ell > 1 - \min\left\{\frac{1-\rho}{r}, \frac{1-\varepsilon}{t^2} - \frac{\varepsilon}{t}\right\}. \tag{1}$$

Then Γ, *constructed as above, is a* TR *scheme for* N *users in which we can revoke up to* r *users and trace successfully at least one traitor from any coalition of up to* t *traitors. Moreover, assume that the scheme* AnoBEB *is IND-secure, then the scheme* Γ *is also an IND-secure scheme.*

Proof. The proof of this theorem can be found in the full version. ∎

Two explicit instantiations of Robust IPP. Let us pick $1 - 1/d < \delta \leq 1 - \frac{1}{q}$, where $d = \max\left\{\dfrac{r}{1-\rho}, \dfrac{t^2}{(1-\varepsilon) - \varepsilon t}\right\}$. We briefly present two explicit instantiations of robust IPP codes verifying the condition (1). More detailed descriptions of these constructions can be found in the full version.

Construction 1. The relative distance of the code $\mathcal{C}$ is defined by $\delta := \Delta/\ell$. According to Gilbert-Varshamov bound Theorem in [31], there exists a $q-$ary code $\mathcal{C}$ with rate $R(\mathcal{C}) = \frac{1}{\ell} \log_q N$ satisfying $R(\mathcal{C}) \geq 1 - H_q(\delta) - o(1)$, where $H_q(\delta)$ is some q-ary entropy function. We would like to ensure the obtained code is not a random code, we apply the derandomization procedure of Porat-Rothschild [30] and we finally obtain parameters of the code: the size of alphabet is $q = \Theta(d)$ and the length is $\ell = O(d \log N)$.

Construction 2. In this second construction, we rely on the Reed-Solomon code, and thus obtain a polynomial-time decoding. The efficiency is not as optimal as the Construction 1 but the cost is only $\log N$. Finally we obtain parameters of the code: the size of alphabet and the length are $q = \ell = O\left(\frac{2d \log N}{\log(d \log N)}\right)$.

Ciphertext size of the TR System. We now consider the ciphertext size of scheme Γ, which is the size of an AnoBEB ciphertext times the length of the Robust IPP code. By relying on the Construction 2 of the IPP robust code, our trace and revoke achieves the ciphertext size complexity of $\widetilde{O}((r + t^2)(n^2) \log N)$ which is the code length multiplied by the LWE ciphertext size. This is an LWE-based scheme and thus a bit-encryption, as in [25].

From bit encryption to multi-bit encryption. As we want to encrypt an n-bit size session key, we need to repeat our scheme n times and therefore, the ciphertext size becomes $\widetilde{O}((r + t^2)(n^3) \log N)$, which is still the most efficient trace and revoke scheme for standard black-box tracing in the bounded collusion model.

Efficiency Comparison with other TR Systems in Bounded Collusion Model. For bounded schemes where the number of traitors is small, the Agrawal et al.'s scheme [1], relying on learning with errors, is very efficient with ciphertext size $\widetilde{O}(r + t + n)$ where r is the maximum number of revoked users, t the maximum number of traitors, and n the security parameter. But they only support a weak level of tracing: black-box confirmation with the assumption that the tracer gets a suspect set that contains all the traitors. Converting black-box confirmation into black-box tracing requires an exponential time complexity in the number of traitors. Concerning black-box trace and revoke in bounded collusion model, up to now, the instantiation of the NWZ scheme gives the most efficient construction. However, as stated in [1], the generic nature of their construction results in loss of concrete efficiency: when based on the bounded collusion FE of [17], the resulting scheme has a ciphertext size growing at least as $\widetilde{O}((r + t)^5 \mathcal{P}oly(n))$; by relying on learning with errors, this blowup can be improved to $\widetilde{O}((r + t)^4 \mathcal{P}oly(n))$, but at the cost of relying on heavy machinery such as attribute based encryption [18] and fully homomorphic encryption [16]. Our trace and revoke result, in contrast, achieves ciphertext size $\widetilde{O}((r + t^2)(n^3) \log N)$ with black-box tracing like in [27], which is the prevalent standard model for tracing and is by far more realistic than the black-box confirmation as in [1]. The following Table 1 resumes the comparison between Trace and Revoke schemes in bounded collusion model.

5   Discussion and Conclusion

Let us discuss a few points of interest.

- In trace and revoke systems, there are two main approaches to tackle the problem:

Table 1. Comparison between Trace and Revoke schemes in bounded collusion model. n is the security parameter, N is the total number of recipients and r, t are respectively the bounds on the number of revoked users and traitors

Trace & revoke schemes	Ciphertext size	Type of tracing algorithm	Type of pirate
ABPSY [1]	$\tilde{O}(r + t + n)$	Black-box confirmation	Decoder
NWZ [27]	$\tilde{O}\left((r + t)^4\mathsf{Poly}(N)\right)$	Black-box tracing	Distinguisher
Ours	$\tilde{O}\left((r + t^2)n^3\log N\right)$	Black-box tracing	Distinguisher

- restrict to bounded collusion model (motivated by the fact that this is a practical scenario) and give efficient solutions;
- consider the full collusion setting (all users can become traitors) and improve theoretical results as there are actually no efficient scheme, say, of ciphertext size which depends on $polylog(N)$, from the standard assumptions without relying on general iO or multi-linear maps [9] or positional witness encryption [20] (for which there are currently no algebraic implementations that are widely accepted as secure).

Recently, at STOC '18, Goyal, Koppula and Waters [19], relying on Mixed Functional Encryption with Attribute-Based Encryption, gave a traitor tracing scheme for full collusion from the LWE assumption with $polylog(N)$ ciphertext size. This avoids the use of iO or multi-linear maps in Boneh-Zhandry scheme from CRYPTO '14 [9]. However, this scheme support traitor tracing only. It is an interesting open question to construct a polylog size trace and revoke scheme for full collusion from a standard assumption, since combining tracing and revoking functionalities is always a difficult problem.

- In this paper we provided an LWE-based construction of AnoBEB which is as efficient as the underlying LWE PKE. We raise an open question of constructing AnoBEB schemes from other standard and well established encryptions, namely ElGamal, RSA, Paillier encryptions, without a significant loss in efficiency. This seems to us to suggest an interesting and a challenging problem, even for the simplest case of a system of $N = 2$ users. The solution will directly give the most efficient trace and revoke systems for bounded collusion model (by instantiating our trace and revoke scheme of Sect. 4) from DDH, RSA and DCR assumptions, respectively.

Acknowledgments. This work was supported in part by the ANR ALAMBIC (ANR16-CE39-0006).

References

1. Agrawal, S., Bhattacherjee, S., Phan, D.H., Stehlé, D.H., Yamada, S.: Efficient public trace and revoke from standard assumptions: extended abstract. In: Thuraisingham, B.M., Evans, D., Malkin, T., Xu, D. (eds.) ACM CCS 2017, pp. 2277–2293. ACM Press, October/November 2017
2. Alwen, J., Peikert, C.: Generating shorter bases for hard random lattices. Theor. Comput. Sci. **48**(3), 535–553 (2011)

3. Barg, A., Kabatiansky, G.: Robust parent-identifying codes and combinatorial arrays. IEEE Trans. Inf. Theory **59**(2), 994–1003 (2013)
4. Barth, A., Boneh, D., Waters, B.: Privacy in encrypted content distribution using private broadcast encryption. In: Di Crescenzo, G., Rubin, A. (eds.) FC 2006. LNCS, vol. 4107, pp. 52–64. Springer, Heidelberg (2006). https://doi.org/10.1007/11889663_4
5. Berkovits, S.: How to broadcast a secret. In: Davies, D.W. (ed.) EUROCRYPT 1991. LNCS, vol. 547, pp. 535–541. Springer, Heidelberg (1991). https://doi.org/10.1007/3-540-46416-6_50
6. Boneh, D., Gentry, C., Waters, B.: Collusion resistant broadcast encryption with short ciphertexts and private keys. In: Shoup, V. (ed.) CRYPTO 2005. LNCS, vol. 3621, pp. 258–275. Springer, Heidelberg (2005). https://doi.org/10.1007/11535218_16
7. Boneh, D., Shaw, J.: Collusion-secure fingerprinting for digital data. In: Coppersmith, D. (ed.) CRYPTO 1995. LNCS, vol. 963, pp. 452–465. Springer, Heidelberg (1995). https://doi.org/10.1007/3-540-44750-4_36
8. Boneh, D., Waters, B.: A fully collusion resistant broadcast, trace, and revoke system. In: Juels, A., Wright, R.N., De Capitani di Vimercati, S. (eds.) ACM CCS 2006, pp. 211–220. ACM Press, October/November 2006
9. Boneh, D., Zhandry, M.: Multiparty key exchange, efficient traitor tracing, and more from indistinguishability obfuscation. In: Garay, J.A., Gennaro, R. (eds.) CRYPTO 2014. LNCS, vol. 8616, pp. 480–499. Springer, Heidelberg (2014). https://doi.org/10.1007/978-3-662-44371-2_27
10. Chabanne, H., Phan, D.H., Pointcheval, D.: Public traceability in traitor tracing schemes. In: Cramer, R. (ed.) EUROCRYPT 2005. LNCS, vol. 3494, pp. 542–558. Springer, Heidelberg (2005). https://doi.org/10.1007/11426639_32
11. Chor, B., Fiat, A., Naor, M.: Tracing traitors. In: Desmedt, Y.G. (ed.) CRYPTO 1994. LNCS, vol. 839, pp. 257–270. Springer, Heidelberg (1994). https://doi.org/10.1007/3-540-48658-5_25
12. Cramer, R., Shoup, V.: Universal hash proofs and a paradigm for adaptive chosen ciphertext secure public-key encryption. In: Knudsen, L.R. (ed.) EUROCRYPT 2002. LNCS, vol. 2332, pp. 45–64. Springer, Heidelberg (2002). https://doi.org/10.1007/3-540-46035-7_4
13. Fazio, N., Perera, I.M.: Outsider-anonymous broadcast encryption with sublinear ciphertexts. In: Fischlin, M., Buchmann, J., Manulis, M. (eds.) PKC 2012. LNCS, vol. 7293, pp. 225–242. Springer, Heidelberg (2012). https://doi.org/10.1007/978-3-642-30057-8_14
14. Fiat, A., Naor, M.: Broadcast encryption. In: Stinson, D.R. (ed.) CRYPTO 1993. LNCS, vol. 773, pp. 480–491. Springer, Heidelberg (1994). https://doi.org/10.1007/3-540-48329-2_40
15. Gentry, C., Peikert, C., Vaikuntanathan, V.: Trapdoors for hard lattices and new cryptographic constructions. In Proceedings of STOC, pp. 197–206. ACM (2008)
16. Goldwasser, S., Kalai, Y.T., Popa, R.A., Vaikuntanathan, V., Zeldovich, N.: Reusable garbled circuits and succinct functional encryption. In: Boneh, D., Roughgarden, T., Feigenbaum, J. (eds.) 45th ACM STOC, pp. 555–564. ACM Press, June 2013
17. Gorbunov, S., Vaikuntanathan, V., Wee, H.: Functional encryption with bounded collusions via multi-party computation. In: Safavi-Naini, R., Canetti, R. (eds.) CRYPTO 2012. LNCS, vol. 7417, pp. 162–179. Springer, Heidelberg (2012). https://doi.org/10.1007/978-3-642-32009-5_11

18. Gorbunov, S., Vaikuntanathan, V., Wee, H.: Attribute-based encryption for circuits. In: Boneh, D., Roughgarden, T., Feigenbaum, J. (eds.) 45th ACM STOC, pp. 545–554. ACM Press, June 2013

19. Goyal, R., Koppula, V., Waters, B.: Collusion resistant traitor tracing from learning with errors. In: Diakonikolas, I., Kempe, D., Henzinger, M. (eds.) 50th ACM STOC, pp. 660–670. ACM Press, June 2018

20. Goyal, R., Vusirikala, S., Waters, B.: Collusion resistant broadcast and trace from positional witness encryption. In: Lin, D., Sako, K. (eds.) PKC 2019. LNCS, vol. 11443, pp. 3–33. Springer, Cham (2019). https://doi.org/10.1007/978-3-030-17259-6_1

21. Kiayias, A., Samari, K.: Lower bounds for private broadcast encryption. In: Kirchner, M., Ghosal, D. (eds.) IH 2012. LNCS, vol. 7692, pp. 176–190. Springer, Heidelberg (2013). https://doi.org/10.1007/978-3-642-36373-3_12

22. Kiayias, A., Yung, M.: Traitor tracing with constant transmission rate. In: Knudsen, L.R. (ed.) EUROCRYPT 2002. LNCS, vol. 2332, pp. 450–465. Springer, Heidelberg (2002). https://doi.org/10.1007/3-540-46035-7_30

23. Li, J., Gong, J.: Improved anonymous broadcast encryptions. In: Preneel, B., Vercauteren, F. (eds.) ACNS 2018. LNCS, vol. 10892, pp. 497–515. Springer, Cham (2018). https://doi.org/10.1007/978-3-319-93387-0_26

24. Libert, B., Paterson, K.G., Quaglia, E.A.: Anonymous broadcast encryption: adaptive security and efficient constructions in the standard model. In: Fischlin, M., Buchmann, J., Manulis, M. (eds.) PKC 2012. LNCS, vol. 7293, pp. 206–224. Springer, Heidelberg (2012). https://doi.org/10.1007/978-3-642-30057-8_13

25. Ling, S., Phan, D.H., Stehlé, D., Steinfeld, R.: Hardness of k-LWE and Applications in Traitor Tracing. In: Garay, J.A., Gennaro, R. (eds.) CRYPTO 2014. LNCS, vol. 8616, pp. 315–334. Springer, Heidelberg (2014). https://doi.org/10.1007/978-3-662-44371-2_18

26. Naor, M., Pinkas, B.: Efficient trace and revoke schemes. Int. J. Inf. Secur. **9**, 411–424 (2010). https://doi.org/10.1007/s10207-010-0121-2

27. Nishimaki, R., Wichs, D., Zhandry, M.: Anonymous traitor tracing: how to embed arbitrary information in a key. In: Fischlin, M., Coron, J.-S. (eds.) EUROCRYPT 2016. LNCS, vol. 9666, pp. 388–419. Springer, Heidelberg (2016). https://doi.org/10.1007/978-3-662-49896-5_14

28. Phan, D.H., Safavi-Naini, R., Tonien, D.: Generic construction of hybrid public key traitor tracing with full-public-traceability. In: Bugliesi, M., Preneel, B., Sassone, V., Wegener, I. (eds.) ICALP 2006. LNCS, vol. 4052, pp. 264–275. Springer, Heidelberg (2006). https://doi.org/10.1007/11787006_23

29. Phan, D.H., Pointcheval, D., Strefler, M.: Message-based traitor tracing with optimal ciphertext rate. In: Hevia, A., Neven, G. (eds.) LATINCRYPT 2012. LNCS, vol. 7533, pp. 56–77. Springer, Heidelberg (2012). https://doi.org/10.1007/978-3-642-33481-8_4

30. Porat, E., Rothschild, A.: Explicit non-adaptive combinatorial group testing schemes. In: Aceto, L., Damgård, I., Goldberg, L.A., Halldórsson, M.M., Ingólfsdóttir, A., Walukiewicz, I. (eds.) ICALP 2008. LNCS, vol. 5125, pp. 748–759. Springer, Heidelberg (2008). https://doi.org/10.1007/978-3-540-70575-8_61

31. Roth, R.: Introduction to Coding Theory. Cambridge University Press, New York (2006)

Secure Communication

Multi-Device for Signal

Sébastien Campion[1], Julien Devigne[2], Céline Duguey[2,3(✉)],
and Pierre-Alain Fouque[3]

[1] Inria, Rennes, France
`sebastien.campion@inria.fr`
[2] DGA Maîtrise de l'information, Bruz, France
`julien.devigne@intradef.gouv.fr`
[3] Irisa, Rennes, France
{`celine.duguey,pierre-alain.fouque`}`@irisa.fr`

Abstract. Nowadays, we spend our life juggling with many devices such as smartphones, tablets or laptops, and we expect to easily and efficiently switch between them without losing time or security. However, most applications have been designed for single device usage. This is the case for secure instant messaging (SIM) services based on the Signal protocol, that implements the Double Ratchet key exchange algorithm. While some adaptations, like the Sesame protocol released by the developers of Signal, have been proposed to fix this usability issue, they have not been designed as specific multi-device solutions and no security model has been formally defined either. In addition, even though the group key exchange problematic appears related to the multi-device case, group solutions are too generic and do not take into account some properties of the multi-device setting. Indeed, the fact that all devices belong to a single user can be exploited to build more efficient solutions.

In this paper, we propose a Multi-Device Instant Messaging protocol based on Signal, ensuring all the security properties of the original Signal.

Keywords: Cryptography · Secure instant messaging · Ratchet · Multi-device

1 Introduction

1.1 Context

Over the last years, secure instant messaging has become a key application accessible on smartphones. In parallel, more and more people started using several devices - a smartphone, a tablet or a laptop - to communicate. They need to be able to frequently and rapidly switch between them. Security protocols such as SIM have to be adapted to this ever-changing multi-device setting. However, the modifications have to be as light as possible for the users and efficient so that it will be the same if we use this or that device.

M. Conti et al. (Eds.): ACNS 2020, LNCS 12147, pp. 167–187, 2020.
https://doi.org/10.1007/978-3-030-57878-7_9

The Double Ratchtet algorithm, implemented in the Signal protocol, is currently the leading key management algorithm for SIM. It is implemented in WhatsApp (1.5 billion of users, for 60 billions of messages sent each day[1]), in Facebook Messenger as an optional secret conversation mode (1,3 billion of users[2]), in Wire, Viber, Google Allo and, of course, in the Signal app itself. It has been released in 2016 by its designers Perrin and Marlinspike [22]. The idea of the Double Ratchet, and of other ratcheted key exchanges (RKE), is to propose a continuous update of session keys. The interesting property of this protocol is that the confidentiality of past and future messages is still guaranteed even after an exposure of long-term keys or even of state secrets by a passive adversary. This forces the adversary to expose keys regularly. Those features are often identified as forward secrecy and healing (or future secrecy, post-compromise security). Regrettably, the Double Ratchet algorithm has been designed for device to device interaction and its use in a multi device context is more difficult. Consequently, each SIM application has developed its own strategy to solve this problem.

1.2   Existing Solutions

WhatsApp. The most widely used SIM is designed to be used on a single phone. However, in order to enable its users to communicate from a computer, WhatsApp developers released WhatsApp web. This interface establishes a secure channel between the "master phone" and the computer, with the former just pushing data from the server to the latter, and conversely. Thus, a user can use WhatsApp from its computer only if his phone is also connected.

Facebook Messenger. This SIM enables end-to-end encryption as an option, called secret conversation. A technical white paper issued in May 2017 [14] explains that "Secret conversations with more than two devices use the Signal Protocol's group Messaging Protocol". In this solution, called Sender's Key, each device sends (through a Signal Channel unused afterward) a same symmetric key: the Sender's key. This key is ratcheted through a key derivation function (KDF), without additional key exchange information. This protocol does not achieve future secrecy and does not offer the security we are looking for.

Signal. In April 2017, Open Whisper Systems (the company who developed Signal) released Sesame, a new protocol dedicated to multi-device secure messaging [24]. Sesame consists in establishing Signal sessions between all devices, as shown in Fig. 1. If Alice has n_A devices and Bob n_B, it requires for Alice $(n_A - 1) \cdot n_B$ encryptions for each message she sends, and as many ratchet executions. Adding or removing a device from a user's pool of devices is possible through opening/closing the corresponding pairwise channel. In Sesame as in Facebook Messenger, Alice knows that Bob communicates from several devices. She can even identify which channel - hence which device - sent the message.

---

[1] http://techcrunch.com - Facebook Q4 2017 earnings announcement.
[2] https://www.socialmediatoday.com/newsFacebookMessenferbythenumbers2019.

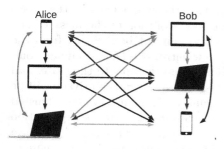

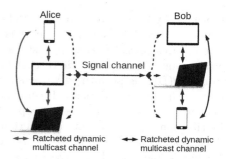

Fig. 1. Sesame multi-device protocol. Each array corresponds to pairwise Signal channel.

Fig. 2. Our Multi-Device Dynamic Ratcheted Key Exchange protocol. Only one Signal channel is needed between Alice and Bob.

Messaging Layer Security. In a related area, Cohn-Gordon *et al.* proposed in [9] a solution for groups, based on Diffie-Hellman trees. This solution could be adapted to the multi-device context, by considering each device as a single user. However, secure group messaging tries to tackle a broader and more complicated problem than secure multi-device messaging. We detail below some particularities of multi-device messaging that we take advantage of. More generally, we believe that designing a solution for the multi-device case is of prime importance, given the evolution of users' practices, and that such a solution, besides being secure, must also be efficient and easy to use in order to be widespread.

Multi-Device Messaging vs. Group Messaging. In multi-device messaging, a single user controls the different devices, while in group messaging, multiple users discuss using a single device each. Passive authentication is therefore easier to achieve in the multi-device case: received messages are authenticated as coming from a valid device but the identity of the sending device does not need to be revealed - the sender knows this information. Moreover, in order to authenticate a new device to another one of the same user, one can easily assume that the devices will be physically close at some point. This means that a QR code can be used to exchange data between them (as it is the case in Sesame) for instance. Finally, assuming average usage, we will not take into account concurrent actions, such as revoking one's phone from one's tablet and conversely, at the same time. This also exclude the case when one honest device and a malicious one try to revoke each other at the same time. This could be handled at an application level by requiring a password or some personal data before revoking, what we consider out of the scope of this paper.

1.3 The Signal Protocol

Here we briefly describe Signal and its Double Ratchet algorithm. Signal is a non interactive key exchange that proposes a continuous update of the message key used to encrypt the messages. To achieve this, parties have to store many intermediary keys. There are two kinds of update: the symmetric and the asymmetric ratchet. The symmetric part is a one-way evolution of the message key that ensures *forward secrecy*: past message keys can not be deduced from the current one. The asymmetric ratchet brings new entropy: a Diffie-Hellman computation (DH) is performed with new random values to update the state, and ensures the *healing* property. If some past keys are revealed, the privacy will be recovered thanks to this new entropy. The security of Signal relies on a trusted distribution server, to avoid interactivity between users. During the registration phase, each user U sends to the server some public credentials: a long term (unchangeable) user key upk_U and some ephemeral initialization keys $ephpk_U$. When Alice wants to open a session with Bob, she asks the server for Bob's credentials. Then she can execute the non interactive key exchange protocol X3DH specified in [23]: Alice and Bob compute a shared root secret, even if they are not on-line at the same time. From then, Alice and Bob store a common root key (rk_x), a chain key ($ck_{x,y}$), a DH ratchet secret key (their own $rchsk_A$, $rchsk_B$), a DH ratchet public key ($rchpk_B$, respectively $rchpk_A$, corresponding to the other's secret key). Those ratchet keys will be regularly renewed - this is how new entropy is injected in the protocol. From a chain key $ck_{x,y}$ are derived a new chain key $ck_{x,y+1}$ and a message key $mk_{x,y+1}$ - that will be used to encrypt messages - with a key derivation function as: $KDF\_CK(ck_{x,y}) \to ck_{x,y+1}, mk_{x,y+1}$. This is the symmetric ratchet.

As long as Alice sends messages, she updates her chain and message keys with this symmetric ratchet procedure. Bob does the same on its side to obtain the same message keys so that he can decrypt the messages he receives. Once Bob wants to answer, he updates the root key rk_x with an asymmetric ratchet. He generates a new ratchet key pair: $DHKeyGen(1^n) \to rchsk'_B, rchpk'_B$. He performs a DH between this new secret key and the ratchet public key of Alice ($rchpk_A$), obtaining a value E: $DH(rchsk'_B, rchpk_A) \to E$.

Then using a second KDF, he updates his rootkey and his chain key as follow: $KDF\_RK(rk_x, E) \to rk_{x+1}, ck_{x+1,0}$. The chain key $ck_{x+1,0}$ initiates a new chain of (chain key, message key) pairs. Bob sends his new ratchet public key $rchpk'_B$ as an associated authenticated data with its message m: $AEAD(mk_{x+1,1}, m, rchpk'_B)$, so that Alice updates the root key the same way. An asymmetric ratchet is performed each time Alice or Bob sends a first response to the other. The following messages sent by the same sender only require the symmetric ratchet.

1.4   Our Contributions

We propose a multi-device protocol, based on the classical two users Signal, in which a user does not need to know how many devices his correspondent has or which one he uses. This represents a notable improvement in terms of privacy. The idea is to open a specific multicast channel between a user's devices to broadcast the one Signal secret essential to perform the protocol: the ratchet secret key ($rchsk_A$ in Sect. 1.3). As illustrated in Fig. 2, each time one device of Alice sends a Signal message to Bob, it also sends a specific message to Alice other devices, containing the new Signal ratchet secret key. Thanks to this non interactive synchronization, all Alice devices have the same voice in the Signal conversation: they speak through the same Signal channel to Bob. On the way back, when Bob answers Alice through the unique Signal channel, his message is duplicated by the Server to all of Alice devices. A multicast channel is created for each Signal's session. To keep the security properties offered by the two-users ratchet, the multicast must guarantee these properties.

We propose as a first step a new primitive: a **Ratcheted dynamic multicast (RDM).** As for a traditional multicast, our RDM establishes a secure channel shared between several participants (in our case devices). It is dynamic since one can add or revoke devices during the execution of the protocol. The novelty is that the keys used to secure this channel are regularly updated, so as to obtain the forward secrecy and healing properties. This is the ratchet feature. The update can be done independently by any party. It is of utmost importance that each device remains independent in its ratcheting process, because in real life, one does not want to wait for all - or even a small part - of its devices to interact together before sending a message. For a similar reason, it is essential that our RDM is decentralized, as we want to avoid having a master device that one cannot afford to lose, have corrupted, or run out of battery. We propose a security model in Sect. 2.1 for this new primitive, as well as a construction in Sect. 2.2, that we prove secure. Our construction is based on standard well known primitives: an authenticated asymmetric encryption and a MAC scheme.

In a second step, we instantiate the integration of our multicast with Signal, to obtain **a Multi-Device version of Signal.** Figure 3 represents a high level view of our solution, with Alice sending messages to Bob. Alice sends messages from any devices and Bob receives them on all of its devices. The square box numbers highlight some of our design particularities that we motivate hereafter. We consider the sending device is $d_{A,i}$.

1. When Alice sends a message from any of her devices, this message is identically duplicated by the server and distributed to each of Bob's device. This can be done through mailboxes handled by the Server, who needs to know about Bob's devices (at least about how many he owns). This mailbox system is already offered by the Sesame solution in [24].
2. When the other devices receive a message corresponding to a symmetric Signal step performed by $d_{A,i}$, they have to perform the symmetric ratchet on their own to maintain their chain key up-to-date.
3. When the other devices receive a message corresponding to an asymmetric Signal step performed by $d_{A,i}$, they receive the corresponding ratchet secret key $rchsk_A$. From this key, they can perform the asymmetric ratchet, to derive the needed keys and maintain their state up-to-date.
4. As devices now share the ratchet secret, we need to change this secret when a device is revoked. A revocation hence induces an extra ratchet in the Signal conversation between Alice and Bob. As we do not want a newcomer to be able to read past messages, an additional ratchet also comes up with the joining process. Bob needs to know about this ratchet, otherwise the next message he sends would correspond to old keys, that the revoked device knows. An update message is sent to Bob, to let him know about the ratchet. Bob knows

there has been a ratchet, but he can not know if it corresponds to an addition or a revocation, and he has no clues about which devices are concerned. We take those extra ratchets into account in our security analysis.

We detail the above description in Sect. 3. We explain in Sect. 3.1 how we mix our RDM model with the Signal security model, to obtain a valid security model for our Multi-Device Signal protocol. We introduce some important definitions and we detail how the freshness conditions in Signal's model need to be updated to take into account the multi-device feature, in particular the dynamic aspects. Our model is based on the one issued from the first analysis of the Signal protocol in [10]. However, one could plug our RDM on another RKE security model, with the same adaptations on the freshness conditions, obtaining a flavor of Multi-Device Ratcheted Key Exchange (MDRKE). We implement our solution over the Signal library libsignal-protocol-java accessible on Signal GitHub account. We give details and results in the full version [8].

How Do We Deviate from Signal. One of our goal is to upgrade the existing Signal protocol in a transparent way. However, one modification was unavoidable: the introduction of a device key, that every device generates for itself, before registering to the Signal server. This key is used to initiate the RDM channels between devices, and to add a new device. This key also plays a main part during the revocation process. In this precise case, we allow the renewal of the Signal ephemeral keys $(ephpk, ephsk)$ and user keys (upk, usk). In the original Signal, the user keys cannot be modified without unregistering then registering again and thus closing all current conversations. In our solution, the server accepts a new user key for Alice if it is authenticated with one of Alice's device key. On Bob's side, this will be exactly as if Alice had registered a new account (as it is now in Signal). The main advantage is for Alice to keep her current conversations when revoking a device. If she had registered again, she also would have to add her devices again. Another deviation from the original Signal is that we make it possible to achieve several ratchets in a row on Alice's side (instead of the ping-pong pattern adopted by the original Double Ratchet). We show that this has no consequence on the security, nor on the possibility to deal with out-of-order messages. However, it implied for us a small patch in the Signal library.

Our Choices vs. Signal's Sesame Solution. In our construction, a user is ignorant about his correspondent's devices. This has a positive impact on the number of encryption needed for a single message. A message sent by Bob is only encrypted once for Alice, instead of being encrypted for each device of Alice. This message is also encrypted only once for all of Bob's other devices, instead of once per device. The server will be in charge of broadcasting the message to the devices, as it is proposed by Sesame. The authentication of a new device is also different. The Sesame protocol offers two options: the first requires all the devices of Alice to share a common IDkey. When a new device is added, it obtains this IDkey. Bob recognizes the new device as a device of Alice since it has the same IDkey. This makes the IDkey a very sensitive data. In [11],

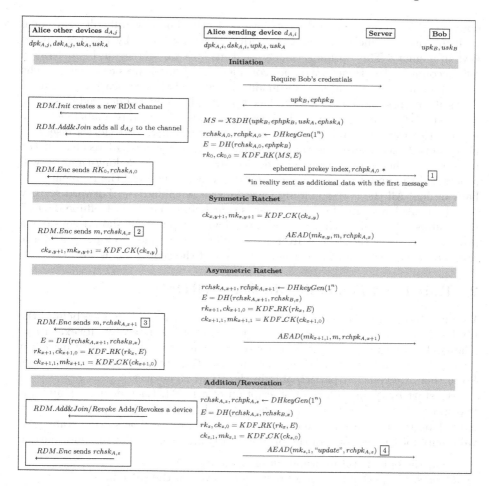

Fig. 3. Multi-Device Signal protocol. Signal procedures $KDF\_RK, KDF\_CK, X3DH,$ $AEAD$ are defined in Sect. 1.3. Boxed messages are sent between Alice devices. The figure without them corresponds to Signal. Boxed numbers 1 to 4 are justified in Sect. 1.4.

authors clearly stipulate that this feature prevented the TextSecure messaging app (the ancestor of Signal) from achieving post-compromise security. In the second option, when Alice adds a device, Bob should physically authenticate it to be sure it is honest and belongs to Alice. In our solution, we only require a new device of Alice to be authenticated by another device of hers.

1.5 PFS, Revocation and Out-of-Order Messages

Forward secrecy ensures that a leakage of secret keys at some time does not compromise the confidentiality of past exchanges. When confronted to reality however, this property is hard to achieve perfectly. The first difficulty is to deal with out-of-order messages. Signal handles those messages by keeping unused keys in memory. This option seriously weakens forward secrecy and is not taken into account in [10]. Hence we do not consider out-of-order messages neither. The other fundamental reason why we made this choice is the revocation feature. If Bob still accepts unused old keys to face up with the arrival of delayed messages, a revoked device of Alice can also use these keys to infiltrate maliciously the session. Revocation would not be efficient. The second obstacle to forward secrecy in a multi-device context is that we consider each device shall receive all the messages in the conversation. If a device stays offline for a long-time, it will process all the updates from the moment he went offline until the moment he is back online. All the corresponding keys are still sensible data. Forward secrecy is to be considered only for the messages sent before the "oldest offline device" went offline. This highlights that a multi-device application should consider a process to prevent the devices from being offline for a time too long (automatic revocation for instance). We consider this out of the scope of this work.

2   Ratcheted Dynamic Multicast (RDM)

We introduce a new protocol for multicast communication. The idea behind the ratchet feature is that the protocol is stateful and the state evolves its execution. The goal is to strengthen the security of the channel. In the security model, it means that the adversary is given more abilities than in a non-ratcheted version. From then, we consider participants in the RDM as devices.

We start by giving a formal description of a RDM. Each device i maintains two states. The device state, π_i, is valid for all the sessions of the protocol. It registers long-term private key and public key: $\pi_i.sk$, $\pi_i.pk$. The session state π_i^s is valid only for the session s of the protocol. It contains the following information:

- $rand$, the ephemeral information of the state.
- $devices$, the public keys of all devices involved in the session.
- PK, the current session public key for the group $\pi_i^s.devices$.

Protocol Description. A RDM is defined by nine algorithms:

- $\mathsf{SetUp}(1^n, i) \rightarrow \pi_i$. Generates secret and public keys (sk_i, pk_i) and creates a device state π_i.
- $\mathsf{Init}(\pi_i, s) \rightarrow \pi_i^s$. Initiates a new session s of the protocol. Generates a session state π_i^s for this session.
- $\mathsf{Enc}(m, \pi_i^s) \rightarrow C_{enc}, \pi_i^s$. On input a message m and a session state π_i^s, returns a ciphertext C_{enc} and the updated state π_i^s.
- $\mathsf{Dec}(C_{enc}, \pi_j^r) \rightarrow m, \pi_j^r$. On input a ciphertext C_{enc} and a session state π_j^r, returns a message m and the updated state π_j^r.
- $\mathsf{Add\&Join}(\{pk_{j_\ell}\}_{\ell \in [1,z]}, \pi_i^s) \rightarrow C_{add}, C_{join}, \pi_i^s$. On input a set of public keys $\{pk_{j_\ell}\}_{\ell \in [1,z]}$ and a session state π_i^s (of the device that adds), returns information C_{join} for the new devices, C_{add} for the already enrolled devices and the updated state π_i^s.

- $\mathsf{DecJoin}(C_{join}, \pi_j, r) \to \pi_j^r$. On input a ciphertext C_{join}, a device state π_j, and a session identifier r, returns a new session state π_j^r.
- $\mathsf{DecAdd}(C_{add}, \pi_k^o) \to \pi_k^o$. On input a ciphertext C_{add} and a session state π_k^o, returns the updated session state π_k^o.
- $\mathsf{Revoke}(pk, \pi_i^s) \to C_{rev}, \pi_i^s$. On input a public key pk and a session state π_i^s, returns a ciphertext C_{rev} and the updated state π_i^s.
- $\mathsf{DecRevoke}(C_{rev}, \pi_k^o) \to \pi_k^o$. On input a ciphertext C_{rev} and a session state π_k^o, returns the updated state π_k^o.

2.1   RDM Security Model

In this section we give an intuition of the security expected from a RDM primitive. A more formal and detailed description is given in the full version [8]. We expect a RDM to provide indistinguishability under chosen-ciphertext attacks, as well as forward secrecy and healing. We define our security model by starting from an ideal case where the adversary has full powers, and then excluding the attacks that we consider as unavoidable. The adversary controls the execution of s sessions of the protocol and he can obtain all the secret information he wishes. At some point, he can query an indistinguishability challenge on one session. He then has to distinguish between a real ciphertext honestly produced by this session or some randomness. We exclude the cases where he could trivially win, or the attacks that we consider as unavoidable by defining some freshness conditions. We introduce three necessary definitions. Firstly, we formalize the notion of step of a protocol. A session can live for a long life time (weeks, months) and some secret data may evolve during this period. Steps are meant to follow this evolution. Secondly, we define matching sessions, based on [5]. This is necessary because we consider a multi-session context. Our definition helps us to define the correctness of our protocol: if two participants are involved in a same execution and have reached corresponding steps - $i.e.$ if they are matching, they should be able to communicate together. Moreover, as matching sessions may share common secret data, the adversary's powers are also defined "matching-session" wise. Finally, because of the dynamic feature, several sessions that correspond to a same execution of the RDM may not be present at the same time, and so do not match. They are however related. We introduce the notion of chained sessions, to take this relationship into account.

Let $\{\mathsf{d}_1, \ldots, \mathsf{d}_{n_d}\}$ be the devices participating in the protocol. Each device d_i is modeled by an oracle π_i and each session s executed by a device d_i (session (i, s)) is modeled by an oracle π_i^s. Oracles maintain states as defined in Sect. 2. In the following, the oracles and their state will be considered as equal.

Protocol Steps. Data registered in a device state for a session will change during the execution of the protocol. To model this phenomenon, we consider steps of the protocol. Each Enc, $\mathsf{Add\&Join}$, Revoke or corresponding decryption algorithm advances the protocol to a new step. Steps are formalized through a counter t, set to 0 at initiation and incremented by oracle queries. This counter is included in the oracle session state with π_i^s.step. It is not necessary in an implementation but needed by the model. (In a general way, we use the typewriter typo for model specific elements). Going from one step to another indicates that the algorithm has processed without error. Intuitively, steps will embody the healing and forward secrecy properties: some restrictions can be needed at some step t and released at step $t + 1$ (or reversely), meaning that the confidence is back (is still there for past steps). We refer with (i, s, t) to the session (i, s) at step t. We note $\pi_i^s[t]$ when we refer to oracle's state π_i^s as it was at step t. We note $\pi_i^s[t].X$ the access to item X at step t.

Matching Sessions. We now define the notion of matching sessions. We denote π_i^s.sid the transcript of the protocol executed in session (i, s), that is, the concatenation of all messages C_i sent or received by π_i^s. We write $\pi_i^s[t_s].\text{sid} = C_i[0]\|C_i[1]\| \ldots \|C_i[t_s]$. As no message is sent or received for the initiation, the first component of a sid for a session running the Init procedure is set to INIT. We refer to a session created by an Init algorithm as an initial session. As all devices are playing similar roles, we do not consider roles in our definition of the matching sessions. Since devices can join and leave during the protocol, we define a matching that is step-wise.

Definition 1 *(Matching sessions at some step). One says (i, s, t_s) and (j, r, t_r), $t_s \geq t_r$ ((i, s) joined first), are matching if $\exists$ sid' substring of $\pi_i^s[t_s]$.sid such that $\pi_i^s[t_s].\text{sid} \stackrel{.}{=} \text{sid}'\|\pi_j^r[t_r].\text{sid}$ (sid' eventually empty). The symbol $\stackrel{.}{=}$ stands for the following definition.*

$\pi_i^s[t_s].\text{sid} \stackrel{.}{=} \text{sid}'\|\pi_j^r[t_r].\text{sid}$ *if,* $\forall t \in [0; t_r]$:

· *either* $C_i[t_s - t_r + t] = C_j[t]$,
· *either* $C_k[t_s - t_r + t] = (C_{add}, C_{join})$ *or* C_{add} *and* $C_\ell[t] = C_{add}$, $k, \ell \in \{i, j\}, k \neq \ell$,
· *or* $t = 0$ *and* $C_i[t_s - t_r] = (C_{add}, C_{join})$ *or* C_{add} *and* $C_j[0] = C_{join}$ *with* (C_{add}, C_{join}) *having been produced by the same* Add&Join *call.*

As devices can join the protocol at any moment, we define a way to link sessions that corresponds to a same execution but were not present at the same time. This composes chains of sessions, as illustrated in Fig. 4.

Definition 2 *(Chained sessions). A session (j, r, t_r) is chained with (i, s, t_s) if t_r is maximal and there exists n sessions (i_α, s_α), and n couples (t'_α, t_α), $t'_\alpha \leq t_\alpha$, $\alpha \in [0, n - 1]$ such that:*

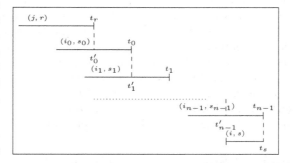

Fig. 4. A chain of sessions between (i, s, t_s) and (j, r, t_r).

· (j, r, t_r) and (i_0, s_0, t_0') are matching,
· $\forall \alpha \in [0, n-2]$, $(i_\alpha, s_\alpha, t_\alpha)$ and $(i_{\alpha+1}, s_{\alpha+1}, t_{\alpha+1}')$ are matching,
· $(i_{n-1}, s_{n-1}, t_{n-1})$ and (i, s, t_s) are matching.

$\{(i_\alpha, s_\alpha, t_\alpha)\}_{\alpha \in [0, n-1]}$ is called a chain of sessions between (i, s, t_s) and (j, r, t_r).

Definition 3 *(Correctness). Suppose a passive adversary that sees communications and may only disturb their delivery. A RDM is said to be correct if, for all matching sessions (i, s, t_s) and (j, r, t_r), for all messages m,*

$$\mathsf{Dec}(\mathsf{Enc}(m, \pi_i^s[t_s]), \pi_j^r[t_r])) = m.$$

RDM Indistinguishability. As in the original IND-CCA experiment, the adversary $\mathcal{A}$ can query for one Challenge of indistinguishability. He is given access to oracles that enables him to perform the whole protocol: OInit, OEnc, ODec, OAdd&Join, ODecAdd, ODecJoin, ORevoke, ODecRevoke. The oracle OInit defines the experiment in a multi-session context. Finally, the adversary can Corrupt a device to obtain its long term secret key, and he can choose to Reveal the state secrets of any device.

Freshness. The natural restrictions defined here are meant to exclude unavoidable attacks or cases where the adversary could win trivially. These restrictions are often valid for a session and all the corresponding chained sessions (not only matching sessions). This expresses the fact that a device has to participate regularly to the protocol to update its state. This is inherent to the ratchet process: the participants have to be actively involved for the ratchet to be operational. One of the direct consequence of this remark, is that we consider that the session specific data are equal to the long term data until a participant is active. This gives the adversary two ways of accessing long-term data, Corrupt and Reveal. We carefully take into account these two paths for the adversary to trivially win the Game.

1. $\mathcal{A}$ shall not Reveal state secrets just before the challenge.
2. $\mathcal{A}$ shall not Reveal a device concerned with the challenge. The sequels of a Reveal are canceled by a OEnc. This ensures the security is back for d_i's secret after d_i performs an encryption. A Reveal on a device only threatens the steps from the last encryption and until the next. This corresponds to the healing property. It also means that forward secrecy depends on devices regularly sending messages, as discussed in Sect. 1.5.
3. $\mathcal{A}$ shall not Corrupt a non active device before/after the challenge. A device is active (enters the ratcheting process) as soon as it performs an encryption.
4. $\mathcal{A}$ shall not Reveal random secrets and use them to maliciously send an encrypted message with its own new random, revoke someone, or join a non authorized corrupted device. There is nothing we can do against this kind of impersonation attack, and the two user ratchet is also vulnerable to it.

5. We prevent $\mathcal{A}$ from sending a joining message with its own data, or after an exposure. This models a physical authentication procedure between the device that adds and the new device.

Definition 4 *(Secure Ratcheted Dynamic Multicast). A RDM running with n_d devices is a secure Ratcheted Dynamic Multicast if it is correct and for all adversaries $\mathcal{A}$, running in polynomial time, making at most q queries to the oracles, there exists a negligible function $\mathsf{negl}\,(n)$ such that:*

$$\mathsf{Adv}^{\mathsf{RDM-IND}}_{\mathcal{A},RDM,n_d,q}(n) = \left| \Pr\left[\mathsf{Exp}^{\mathsf{RDM-IND}}_{\mathcal{A},RDM,n_d,q} \right] - \frac{1}{2} \right| \le \mathsf{negl}\,(n).$$

We denote $\epsilon_{\mathsf{RDM-IND}}$ this advantage.

2.2 RDM Construction

We give a high-level view of our construction in Fig. 5. The detailed pseudocode description is given in the full version [8]. The main idea is that the keys used to encrypt the multicast messages are updated regularly. We base our solution on parallel asymmetric encryption, as studied in [2] or [3]. The authenticated asymmetric encryption scheme is used as a multicast in an obvious manner: PK is the set of public keys of all devices d_i concerned with the encryption. $\mathsf{EncAsym}(m, PK)$ stands for $\{\mathsf{EncAsym}(m, pk)\}_{\forall pk \in PK}$. We consider that the number of devices remains reasonable: around ten for each user does not seem so restrictive. This design allows us to choose among well-known and proven secure primitives. To give some examples, RSA-OAEP is proven IND-CCA secure in [16]. In [12], Cramer and Shoup also propose an IND-CCA secure scheme. Another IND-CCA secure solution based on Elliptic Curve (known as $ECIES$) is defined in [28]. Decentralized broadcast solutions, as studied in [25], either do not offer dynamism properties or do not enable regular key resetting and offer fewer implementation evaluations.

An Asymmetric Ratchet. The Diffie-Hellman ratchet implemented in Signal is only possible for two users. With more than two parties, multiparty computation could be thought of as an option, but we do not want to wait for all, or even a minimum number of devices to be present before sending a message: each device has to be autonomous in its ratcheting process. Our ratchet consists in generating new ephemeral asymmetric keys epk, esk for the device which sends a message. The multicast public key is updated with the new ephemeral public key epk. Here, we take advantage of the multi-device context. As all the devices belong to a single person, we consider that no honest device will try to exclude another device maliciously (by mis-updating the multicast public key). When any device updates its ephemeral key pair, the others only receive the updated common public key. They do not need to know about who updated it. However, when a device wants to revoke another device, it has to know which ephemeral public key to erase from PK. We deal with this by considering there

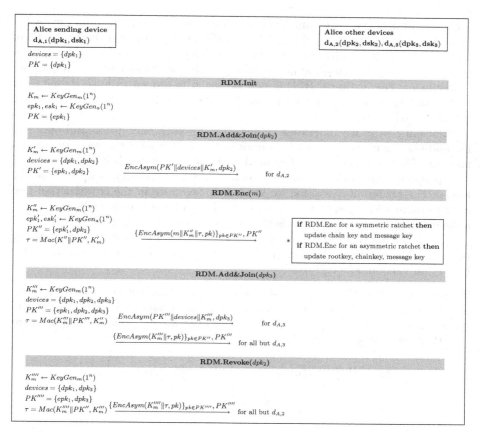

Fig. 5. Our RDM protocol. The sending device can change for each procedure. $KeyGen_{m/a}$ are Key Generation algorithm for the $MAC/EncAsym$ schemes. The instructions * detail the integration of our RDM with Signal.

exists a correspondence between the list *devices* of long term keys recorded in each device state and the list PK of ephemeral public keys. Requirements in the Add&Join algorithm prevent a device from being present in the group several times. In such a case, revoking this device once would not be enough to be sure it is definitively out of the protocol.

Passive Authentication. Another important point is that the messages have to be identified as coming from an honest device, but again, its identity does not matter. Our solution provides passive authentication thanks to a MAC key K_m shared between the devices. A new MAC key is generated with every action: sending a message, joining, or revoking a device. Otherwise, an adversary who could access the MAC key at some step could impersonate any device at any step further. This new MAC key is authenticated under the previous one, creating an authentication chain. This solution is less expensive than generating new signature key pairs regularly. We consider Strong UnForgeability (SUF) of a MAC scheme in a multi-instance setting as defined in [26]. The reduction from multi-instance to the classical unforgeability induces a loss factor in the number of instances. For instance, HMAC defined in [4] is proven to have strong existential unforgeability. Its security can then be extended to the multi instance setting as explained in [26].

Efficiency-wise, we generate two new keys for each encryption and only one for additions and revocations. Maintaining several Signal channels requires a number of key generations that grows linearly with the number of devices.

Ephemeral data esk, epk and K_m constitute the randomness $\pi_i^s.rand$ of the model. For readability reasons, we keep them separate in the construction and refer to them with $\pi_i^s.esk$, $\pi_i^s.epk$, and $\pi_i^s.PK$. To be able to initialize a session, a device must have processed a SetUp to generate its global state π_i.

The following theorem enunciates the security of our construction relatively to the RDM security model described in Sect. 2.1. A complete proof is accessible in the full version [8].

Theorem 1. *If* ENC *is an* IND-CCA *secure asymmetric encryption scheme, and* MAC *is secure under multi-instance strong unforgeability, the above construction is a secure ratcheted dynamic multicast for* n_d *devices, such that, for any PPT adversary making at most* q *queries to the oracles:*

$$\mathsf{Adv}_{RDM,n_d,q,\mathcal{A}}^{\mathsf{RDM-IND}}(n) = \left| \Pr\left[Exp_{RDM,n_d,q,\mathcal{A}}^{\mathsf{RDM-IND}}(n) \right] - \frac{1}{2} \right|$$
$$\leq q \cdot \epsilon_{\mathsf{SUF}} + (q+1) \cdot n_d \cdot \epsilon_{\mathsf{IND\text{-}CCA}}.$$

In practice, one would use hybrid encryption instead of a single asymmetric encryption scheme in this construction. It means that the asymmetric encryption is used to transmit a common symmetric key to all devices and that data are then encrypted with this key. This would modify the security argument only by a negligible term due to the symmetric encryption. We decide to present our construction with the asymmetric part so as not to add extra lines in an already complex construction.

3 Multi-Device Signal

We detail our Multi-Device Signal solution, depicted in Fig. 3. It is built from the Signal protocol and our RDM protocol described in Sect. 2.2. The RDM enables us to share the DH secrets, for all devices to perform the operation. It is also used to share the message's "body". Every Signal sending is doubled with a RDM sending. This way, any device can follow the conversation, can speak for itself, and can directly receive messages sent by Bob. For each Signal session, a specific RDM channel is opened between Alice's devices. Addition and revocation induce extra ratchets, for the joining/revoked device not to access previous/future conversations. We introduce a new procedure, ExtraRatchet. When a device receives a ratchet secret through the RDM channel, he has to update its Signal state accordingly. This is done in an Update procedure. The complete pseudocode description is given in the full version [8]. We recall that our user key is equivalent to the traditional Signal longterm key. It is shared among devices, as well as Signal's ephemeral keys, through the joining process. This is necessary for each device to be able to send or receive an initiation message. The device key never changes.

To execute the protocol, a device has to record some information. To do so, a device state $\pi_{u,i}$ aggregates all non session-specific elements, and a session state $\pi_{u,i}^s$ records all the session-specific ones. A device state $\pi_{u,i}$ is composed of:

- dID, the device identifier.
- uID, the user identifier.
- dsk, the device's secret key.
- $sprekeys$, the user's secret keys registered in Signal. This comprises the user key and the ephemeral keying material needed for initialization (detailed in MedTerm and One-Time prekeys in Signal).
- $Devices$, the public keys of the owner other devices.
- $Sessions$, a list of all sessions the device i is engaged in.

A session state $\pi_{u,i}^s$ gathers a Signal part:

- $role$, the role of the user u: initiator or receiver,
- $peer$, the intended peer user of this session,
- $rand$, the current ratchet secret,
- $rand_{peer}$, the current public ratchet value of the intended peer,
- $sessionkey$, the current messaging session key,
- $state$, all other secret information needed,

and a RDM part (the $device$ item is already in the global state):

- $devrand$, the RDM randomness,
- PK the common public key.

A session state $\pi_{u,i}^s$ has access to general information of the device state $\pi_{u,i}$. Conversely, a device state $\pi_{u,i}$ gives implicit access to every session state $\pi_{u,i}^s$. We describe Signal as a multi-stage key exchange as in [10], except that we split the algorithm Run defined in into Sig.Send and Sig.Receive. We detail Sig.Register to take into account the device key in addition to the user key and the ephemeral keys usually used by Signal. A device shall perform a RDM.SetUp to obtain its devices keys before he registers. We gather Sig.KeyGen and Sig.MedTermKeyGen in a UserKeyGen procedure that returns a set of prekeys $prekeys$. Those keys are registered to the server with the device key. We obtain a Multi-Device Instant Messaging (MDIM) protocol.

3.1 Security Model

We build a security model for a MDIM by mixing our RDM model with Signal security model described in [10]. A formal description can be found in the full version. The joint between the two models is highly related to the way the two primitives overlap in practice. As said before, the present model is there to ensure that we keep the Signal security when adding our RDM. Let $\{\mathcal{P}_1, \ldots, \mathcal{P}_{n_U}\}$ be the set of users in the protocol and $\{d_{u,1}, \ldots, d_{u,n_d}\}$ the set of devices of the user $\mathcal{P}_u$. Each device $d_{u,i}$ is modeled by an oracle $\pi_{u,i}$ and each session s executed by a device $d_{u,i}$ is modeled by an oracle $\pi_{u,i}^s$. Device oracles maintain device states and session oracles maintain session states as defined in Sect. 3. In the following, device or session oracles and their state will be considered as equal. We identify sessions that were present during the initial step of the protocol as initial sessions.

Matching Sessions. In order to define the matching between sessions run by different users, we first need to consider the relationship between devices belonging to a single user. We introduce the notion of partnered sessions. Partnered sessions correspond to devices of a single user that are online at the same moment. Steps are defined as in Sect. 2.1.

Definition 5 *(Partnered sessions at some step). Two sessions (u, i, s, t_s) and (u, j, r, t_r) are partnered if:*

- $\pi_{u,i}^s.role = \pi_{u,j}^r.role$,
- $\pi_{u,i}^s.peer = \pi_{u,j}^r.peer$,
- $\pi_{u,i}^s.uID = \pi_{u,j}^r.uID$,
- (i, s, t_s) and (j, r, t_r) are matching in the sense of RDM.

Chains of partnered sessions are defined as for matching sessions in Sect. 2.1, to connect sessions that are active on different devices that were present at different steps.

   We consider matching sessions relatively to Signal conversation gathered in $\pi_{u,i}^s.sid_2$. The matching is defined between two sessions (u, i, s) and (v, ℓ, o). One session (u, i, s) can match several other sessions (v, ℓ_z, o_z). Our definition is recursive: a matching is well-defined if one can trace the conversations from the very beginning on u and v's side. This is done by calling chains of sessions, and each chain element should match an element in the other chain.

Definition 6 *(Matching sessions at some step). Two sessions (u, i, s, t_s) and (v, ℓ, p, t_p), $t_s \geq t_p$ are matching if:*

- $\pi_{u,i}^s.role \neq \pi_{v,\ell}^p.role$,
- $\pi_{u,i}^s.peer = \pi_{v,\ell}^p.user$ and $\pi_{u,i}^s.user = \pi_{v,\ell}^p.peer$,
- (u, i, s, t_s) and (v, ℓ, p, t_p) are chained with respective initial sessions (u, i_0, s_0, t_{s_0}), (v, l_0, p_0, t_{p_0}), through respective chains $\{(u, i_\alpha, s_\alpha, t_\alpha)\}_{\alpha \in [1,n]}$, $\{(v, \ell_\beta, p_\beta, t_\beta)\}_{\beta \in [1,m]}$,

- $\exists$ sid *subset of* $\pi^s_{u,i}[t_s].\mathtt{sid}_2$ *such that* $\pi^s_{u,i}[t_s].\mathtt{sid}_2 = \mathtt{sid}\|\pi^p_{v,\ell}[t_p].\mathtt{sid}_2$,
- *if* (u, i, s, t_s) *is an initial session, then* $\forall\ \beta \in [0, m]$, $\exists\ \tilde{t}_\beta$ *and* $\mathtt{sid}_\beta$ *such that* $\pi^s_{u,i}[\tilde{t}_\beta].\mathtt{sid}_2 = \mathtt{sid}_\beta\|\pi^{p_\beta}_{v,\ell_\beta}[\tilde{t}_\beta].\mathtt{sid}_2$,
- *else* (u, i, s, t_s) *and* (v, ℓ_m, p_m, t_m) *are matching.*

Definition 7 *(Correctness of MDIM). A Multi-Device Instant Messaging is said to be correct if:*

- *for all users u, all devices i, j, all session identifiers s, r, and all t_s, t_r such that (u, i, s, t_s) and (u, j, r, t_r) are partnered,*
  $\pi^s_{u,i}[t_s].rand = \pi^r_{u,j}[t_r].rand$ *and* $\pi^s_{u,i}[t_s].sessionkey = \pi^r_{u,j}[t_r].sessionkey.$
- *For all users u, v, all devices i, ℓ, all session identifiers s, p, and all t_s, t_p such that (u, i, s, t_s) and (v, ℓ, p, t_p) are matching, $\pi^s_{u,i}[t_s].sessionkey = \pi^p_{v,\ell}[t_p].sessionkey.$*

MDIM Indistinguishability. We will consider an adversary $\mathcal{A}$ that has access to a pool of registered devices. He controls communications through oracles corresponding to the protocol algorithms. $\mathcal{A}$ has access to the oracles corresponding to RDM corruptions (`CorruptDevice`, `RevealDevRand`) and to those corresponding to the Signal security model we consider (`RevealSessionKey`, `CorruptUser`, `CorruptOpt`, `RevealState`, `RevealRandom`).

Freshness. Freshness conditions are obtained by considering the RDM freshness conditions and upgrading the original Signal freshness in the following way: each time an element of a session was concerned in the original freshness, the same element has now to be considered for this session and all the partnered and chained sessions. More precisely, we try to stipulate clearly all the ways that an element can leak to the adversary: directly from the targeted device or a partnering or matching one, or through the communication between devices. For the latter, data of a session (u, i, s) at step t can leak if a device (u, i)'s randomness (or device keys if it has not been active in the ratcheting process yet) is compromised, or if the device randomness of a partnered session is compromised or if there exists a session chained with (u, i, s) whose device randomness is compromised (if it is chained, it means it will not perform any action until it matches (u, i, s, t) - if not revoked - it just has not received all of its messages).

Initial Freshness. As in the original model for Signal, we treat separately the initiation phase, and it has to be treated very carefully. As written in the definition, Signal prekeys (including user key) are renewed with every revocation. On the one hand, this restricts the consequences of a user corruption to the period between two revocations. On the other hand, it means that the prekeys have to be shared with the other devices. Hence the security of a session initiation is now related to the security of the communication between the devices since the last renewal of prekeys, that is, since the last revocation.

Definition 8 *(Secure Multi-Device Instant Messaging). A MDIM executed with n_p users, each having n_d devices is said to be secure in the above model if it is correct and for all adversary $\mathcal{A}$ running in polynomial time, the following advantage is negligible:*

$$\mathsf{Adv}^{\mathsf{MDIM-IND}}_{\mathcal{A},MDIM,n_p,n_d}(n) = \left| \Pr \left[\mathsf{Exp}^{\mathsf{MDIM-IND}}_{\mathcal{A},MDIM,n_p,n_d}(n) \right] - \frac{1}{2} \right|.$$

Theorem 2. *Let Signal be a secure multi-stage key-exchange protocol with advantage ϵ_{sig} and RDM a $\mathsf{RDM-IND}$ secure ratcheted dynamic multicast with advantage $\epsilon_{\mathsf{RDM-IND}}$, the above construction is a secure MDIM such that, for any PPT adversary running n_s sessions from n_d devices of n_p users, making at most q queries to the oracles:*

$$\mathsf{Adv}^{\mathsf{MDIM-IND}}_{\mathcal{A}}(n) \leq n_p^2 \cdot (2 \cdot \epsilon_{\mathsf{RDM-IND}} + \epsilon_{sig}).$$

A detailed proof can be found in the full version [8].

4 Related Work

The first ideas for ratcheting appeared in protocol such as Off-the-Record or TextSecure (the predecessor of Signal) and were studied respectively in [7] and [15]. In [18], Green and Miers studied the interest of puncturable encryption instead of using ratchet to achieve forward security in messaging. The first formal analysis of the Signal protocol has been given by Cohn-Gordon *et al.* in [10]. The same year, Kobeissi *et al.* proposed in [21] a formal verification of a variant of the Signal protocol with ProVerif and CryptoVerif. Later, Bellare *et al.* formalized in [6] the idea of ratcheting, and proposed a security model, as well as constructions, for a single unilateral ratchet key exchange, and the corresponding communication channel. The authors target the already identified security offered by the ratchet: forward secrecy and healing. They clearly stipulate that an active attack after exposure can lead to a continued violation of integrity. At Crypto'18, [27] and [19] extended Bellare *et al.*'s work to define and evaluate the optimal security of bilateral ratcheted key exchanges (messaging channels respectively). Their models define the best security one can expect from such protocols. The drawback is that the associated constructions require less efficient primitives like hierarchical identity-based encryption (HIBE, [17]). One remarkable point of the first paper is that the model allows for concurrent actions. However, in both cases messages still need to be received in the right order.

Recently, Durak and Vaudenay in [13] proposed a solution using standard public key cryptography. They assume the order of transmitted messages is preserved and their model does not allow for exposure of randomness. They also introduced the Recover security to prevent from being safe again after a trivial impersonation. They claim that this kind of recovery not only is not reached by RKE, but also undesirable. Another recent work concerning the two-user ratcheted key exchange setting is the paper by Jost *et al.*, [20]. They introduce a security model that considers suboptimal security. This includes forward secrecy and healing, but they also consider post-impersonation security, under some condition. They claim their model is a bit less permissive than the ones of [27] and [19] but the constructions they propose only require standard public-key cryptography. In [1] Alwen *et al.* proposed their own definition for secure messaging, introducing a continuous key agreement primitive to cover the ratcheting process. They consider a new security notion: the immediate decryption. This property requires that any incoming message can be decrypted, even if some previous messages were lost or arrive out-of-order. According to the authors, Signal achieves this property, but all recent RKE propositions do not. In fact, we discussed this out-of-order problematic in our introduction. Finally, the recent papers [6,13,19,20,27] and [1] concern the ratcheting process and do not analyze the initial non-interactive key exchange.

5   Conclusion

In this paper, we provide a solution to address the multi-device issue. We pay much attention in our model to delegating as little as possible to the system (for instance the physical authentication when adding a device). For the first time, this work introduces some questions that we think can provide great motivation for future work. Studying how recently proposed RKE or messaging schemes as [19,20,27] or [13] could be adapted to the multi-device context with our multicast solution, seems a legitimate follow-up. In addition, the out-of-order message, revocation, and PFS problematics, formally introduced in [1] and detailed in Sect. 1.5 are definitely worth considering.

References

1. Alwen, J., Coretti, S., Dodis, Y.: The double ratchet: security notions, proofs, and modularization for the signal protocol. In: Ishai, Y., Rijmen, V. (eds.) EURO-CRYPT 2019. LNCS, vol. 11476, pp. 129–158. Springer, Cham (2019). https://doi.org/10.1007/978-3-030-17653-2_5
2. Baudron, O., Pointcheval, D., Stern, J.: Extended notions of security for multicast public key cryptosystems. In: Montanari, U., Rolim, J.D.P., Welzl, E. (eds.) ICALP 2000. LNCS, vol. 1853, pp. 499–511. Springer, Heidelberg (2000). https://doi.org/10.1007/3-540-45022-X_42
3. Bellare, M., Boldyreva, A., Micali, S.: Public-key encryption in a multi-user setting: security proofs and improvements. In: Preneel, B. (ed.) EUROCRYPT 2000. LNCS, vol. 1807, pp. 259–274. Springer, Heidelberg (2000). https://doi.org/10.1007/3-540-45539-6_18
4. Bellare, M., Canetti, R., Krawczyk, H.: Keying hash functions for message authentication. In: Koblitz, N. (ed.) CRYPTO 1996. LNCS, vol. 1109, pp. 1–15. Springer, Heidelberg (1996). https://doi.org/10.1007/3-540-68697-5_1

5. Bellare, M., Rogaway, P.: Entity authentication and key distribution. In: Stinson, D.R. (ed.) CRYPTO 1993. LNCS, vol. 773, pp. 232–249. Springer, Heidelberg (1994). https://doi.org/10.1007/3-540-48329-2_21

6. Bellare, M., Singh, A.C., Jaeger, J., Nyayapati, M., Stepanovs, I.: Ratcheted encryption and key exchange: the security of messaging. In: Katz, J., Shacham, H. (eds.) CRYPTO 2017. LNCS, vol. 10403, pp. 619–650. Springer, Cham (2017). https://doi.org/10.1007/978-3-319-63697-9_21

7. Borisov, N., Goldberg, I., Brewer, E.A.: Off-the-record communication, or, why not to use PGP. In: Proceedings of the 2004 ACM Workshop on Privacy in the Electronic Society, WPES 2004, Washington, DC, USA, 28 October 2004, pp. 77–84 (2004)

8. Campion, S., Devigne, J., Duguey, C., Fouque, P.A.: Multi-device for signal. Cryptology ePrint Archive, Report 2019/1363 (2019)

9. Cohn-Gordon, K., Cremers, C., Garratt, L., Millican, J., Milner, K.: On ends-to-ends encryption: asynchronous group messaging with strong security guarantees. In: Proceedings of the 2018 ACM SIGSAC Conference on Computer and Communications Security, CCS 2018 (2018)

10. Cohn-Gordon, K., Cremers, C.J.F., Dowling, B., Garratt, L., Stebila, D.: A formal security analysis of the signal messaging protocol. In: 2017 IEEE European Symposium on Security and Privacy, EuroS&P 2017, Paris, France, 26–28 April 2017, pp. 451–466 (2017)

11. Cohn-Gordon, K., Cremers, C.J.F., Garratt, L.: On post-compromise security. In: IEEE 29th Computer Security Foundations Symposium, CSF 2016, Lisbon, Portugal, 27 June–1 July 2016, pp. 164–178 (2016)

12. Cramer, R., Shoup, V.: A practical public key cryptosystem provably secure against adaptive chosen ciphertext attack. In: Krawczyk, H. (ed.) CRYPTO 1998. LNCS, vol. 1462, pp. 13–25. Springer, Heidelberg (1998). https://doi.org/10.1007/BFb0055717

13. Durak, F.B., Vaudenay, S.: Bidirectional asynchronous ratcheted key agreement without key-update primitives. Cryptology ePrint Archive, Report 2018/889 (2018)

14. Facebook: Messenger secret conversation. Technical whitepaper, version 2.0, May 2017

15. Frosch, T., Mainka, C., Bader, C., Bergsma, F., Schwenk, J., Holz, T.: How secure is TextSecure? Cryptology ePrint Archive, Report 2014/904 (2014)

16. Fujisaki, E., Okamoto, T., Pointcheval, D., Stern, J.: RSA-OAEP is secure under the RSA assumption. J. Cryptol. **17**(2), 81–104 (2002). https://doi.org/10.1007/s00145-002-0204-y

17. Gentry, C., Silverberg, A.: Hierarchical ID-based cryptography. In: Zheng, Y. (ed.) ASIACRYPT 2002. LNCS, vol. 2501, pp. 548–566. Springer, Heidelberg (2002). https://doi.org/10.1007/3-540-36178-2_34

18. Green, M.D., Miers, I.: Forward secure asynchronous messaging from puncturable encryption. In: Proceedings of 2015 IEEE Symposium on Security and Privacy, pp. 305–320 (2015)

19. Jaeger, J., Stepanovs, I.: Optimal channel security against fine-grained state compromise: the safety of messaging. In: Shacham, H., Boldyreva, A. (eds.) CRYPTO 2018. LNCS, vol. 10991, pp. 33–62. Springer, Cham (2018). https://doi.org/10.1007/978-3-319-96884-1_2

20. Jost, D., Maurer, U., Mularczyk, M.: Efficient ratcheting: almost-optimal guarantees for secure messaging. IACR Cryptology ePrint Archive 2018, 954 (2018)

21. Kobeissi, N., Bhargavan, K., Blanchet, B.: Automated verification for secure messaging protocols and their implementations: a symbolic and computational approach. In: Proceedings of 2017 IEEE European Symposium on Security and Privacy (EuroS&P), pp. 435–450, April 2017
22. Marlinspike, M., Perrin, T.: The double ratchet algorithm. Signal's web site (2016)
23. Marlinspike, M., Perrin, T.: The x3dh key agreement protocol. Signal's web site (2016)
24. Marlinspike, M., Perrin, T.: The sesame algorithm: session management for asynchronous message encryption. Signal's web site (2017)
25. Phan, D.H., Pointcheval, D., Strefler, M.: Decentralized dynamic broadcast encryption. In: Visconti, I., De Prisco, R. (eds.) SCN 2012. LNCS, vol. 7485, pp. 166–183. Springer, Heidelberg (2012). https://doi.org/10.1007/978-3-642-32928-9_10
26. Poettering, B., Rösler, P.: Asynchronous ratcheted key exchange. Cryptology ePrint Archive, Report 2018/296 (2018)
27. Poettering, B., Rösler, P.: Towards bidirectional ratcheted key exchange. In: Shacham, H., Boldyreva, A. (eds.) CRYPTO 2018. LNCS, vol. 10991, pp. 3–32. Springer, Cham (2018). https://doi.org/10.1007/978-3-319-96884-1_1
28. Shoup, V.: A proposal for an ISO standard for public key encryption. Cryptology ePrint Archive, Report 2001/112 (2001)

On the Cryptographic Deniability
of the Signal Protocol

Nihal Vatandas[1(✉)], Rosario Gennaro[1], Bertrand Ithurburn[1],
and Hugo Krawczyk[2]

[1] Center for Algorithms and Interactive Scientific Software,
The City College of New York, New York City, USA
nihal.vatandas@gmail.com, rosario@ccny.cuny.edu, bithurburn@gmail.com
[2] Algorand Foundation, New York City, USA
hugo@ee.technion.ac.il

Abstract. *Offline deniability* is the ability to *a posteriori* deny having participated in a particular communication session. This property has been widely assumed for the Signal messaging application, yet no formal proof has appeared in the literature. In this paper, we present what we believe is the first formal study of the offline deniability of the Signal protocol. Our analysis shows that building a deniability proof for Signal is non-trivial and requires very strong assumptions on the underlying mathematical groups where the protocol is run.

1 Introduction

The ever growing privacy concerns and vulnerabilities behind online interactions have made the *deniability of communications* a prime privacy requirement. The goal is to ensure that the transcript of an online communication between two peers cannot be used as a proof to a third party that the communication took place. This property should hold even if one of the parties is willing to deviate from the protocol, just to generate a proof that reveals the identity of the peer to a third party. A well-known fact is that communications protected by a shared symmetric key do not allow one of the peers to frame the other: Any information Bob claims to have been authenticated by Alice could have been produced by Bob himself since he also knows the key.

However, usually shared keys are generated via an online authenticated key exchange (AKE) protocol, where the parties authenticate using their own private/public keys. Then, the question is whether the shared key computed in that protocol can itself be denied. This gives rise to the notion of *deniable authenticated key exchange*. As above, the transcript of the AKE protocol should leave no proof that can convince a third party. Bob should not be able to convince a *judge* that Alice communicated with him, even if Bob is malicious and departs from the prescribed protocol just to generate such proof.

Deniability of AKE was first formally defined in [14] in terms of simulatability (following an approach set forth by [17] in the context of deniable authentication). Roughly, an AKE protocol π between peers Alice and Bob is *deniable for*

© Springer Nature Switzerland AG 2020
M. Conti et al. (Eds.): ACNS 2020, LNCS 12147, pp. 188–209, 2020.
https://doi.org/10.1007/978-3-030-57878-7_10

Alice if the communication transcript generated in an interaction between Alice and Bob in executions of π can be simulated by Bob without Alice's participation. That is, one requires the existence of a simulator that in interactions with Bob generates transcripts that are computationally indistinguishable from real transcripts between Alice and Bob. Here, Alice's actions are those of an honest AKE participant but Bob can deviate from the protocol in arbitrary ways (if that helps him frame Alice as discussed above). Moreover, and crucially, the simulator needs to output a session key under a distribution that is indistinguishable from that of the session key in a real protocol between Alice and (possibly malicious) Bob.

Different flavors of AKE deniability are obtained by considering the type of judge to which a proof is presented. The basic case is that of *offline deniability* that assumes a judge who is not present during the communication between the peers. In this case, the judge examines a transcript presented by Bob to decide whether Alice knowingly communicated with Bob. If we let the judge be an active participant in the protocol, ensuring deniability is harder, or even impossible. In particular, if Bob provides his private keys to the judge, the latter can interact with Alice masquerading as Bob and get convinced directly of Alice's participation. The notion of *online deniability* [42] refers to a judge who participates in the protocol but is not given Bob's private keys. The offline case is of more practical relevance since a protocol that is *not deniable* in this sense can leave proofs of communication that *anyone* can verify later (possibly with Bob's help).

Deniability has been a consideration for AKE protocols for the last 25 years (at least) since the design of the Internet Key Exchange (IKEv1) protocol [21,24], through the influential *off-the-record* protocol [4]. Yet, designing deniable AKE protocols has proven to be a delicate matter and is still an active area of research (see the related work section below), due to the popularity, and privacy concerns, of internet and messaging communications.

1.1   The Case of Signal

Deniability was the central focus in the design of the Signal protocol [9]. The latter has become the de-facto standard in the area of secure messaging protocols, having been adopted in widely deployed protocols such as WhatsApp and Facebook messenger.

However in [39,40] it has already been shown that online deniability does not hold for Signal. Still, offline deniability is widely believed to hold, and yet no formal proof has ever appeared in the literature.

In this paper, we discuss the reasons why a proof for the offline deniability of Signal has been difficult to construct, and analyze ways to overcome this problem. As far as we know, this is the first formal study of the offline deniability of the Signal protocol.

For this, we focus on the offline deniability properties of a particular family of AKE protocols, namely, *implicitly authenticated* protocols. These are characterized by the property that the transcript of the protocol is *independent of the private keys of the peers.* That is, anyone can generate the transcript messages. Authentication is provided *implicitly* by involving the peers' private keys in the derivation of the session key. Implicitly authenticated protocols seem to be perfectly suited to provide deniability. In their minimal form, all the peers exchange are Diffie-Hellman (DH) values $X = g^x, Y = g^y$ with the key being computed as a function of X, Y, the public keys of the parties and their corresponding private keys. There is little one can learn about the participants from these transcripts, hence, *intuitively,* they "must be deniable".

The above intuition, however, has been insufficient to prove these protocols deniable, in particular due to the need to simulate the session key. Thus, the question of deniability of implicitly authenticated protocols has not been settled to this day. This is not just a challenging theoretical question, but one of practical significance. Indeed, prime examples of this family are MQV [27,31], HMQV [26], and 3DH [29] (see Sect. 3 for the description of these protocols). Implicitly authenticated protocols are preferred because of their higher efficiency (since no additional signatures or encryptions are computed/sent together with the basic DH ephemeral keys). Very importantly, 3DH is the basis of the AKE underlying the Signal protocol and a main source of "intuition" regarding Signal's deniability properties.

1.2 Our Contribution

We make progress in the study of deniability of implicitly authenticated key exchange protocols in several ways:

- We demonstrate the insufficiency of implicit authentication as a way to ensure deniability. We present settings, in terms of properties of groups and assumptions, where the original MQV protocol [31] (that does not use a random oracle for key derivation) fails deniability.
- We discuss how the counter-example built around MQV illuminates the difficulties one encounters in attempting to prove deniability for any of the other implicitly authenticated AKEs we consider, including 3DH.
- Using the above result and proof technique, we are able to *characterize the non-deniability* of MQV in terms of the feasibility of the following problem: Given a random group element $A = g^a$, sample $Y = g^y$ in G (with any chosen efficient distribution), so that it is hard to compute the Diffie-Hellman value $DH(A, Y) = g^{ay}$ while it is easy to decide correctness of $DH(A, Y)$. In other words, if such a Y can be feasibly sampled in G, then MQV is non-deniable and an adversary can always prove that he communicated with a particular honest peer.
- We formulate a general "extractability assumption", termed *Knowledge of DH Assumption*, which essentially implies that the above sampling is infeasible. Therefore, under such an assumption and other variations we define, we can prove the (offline) deniability of the three studied protocols (MQV, HMQV, 3DH) in the random oracle model. The assumption can be seen as a plausible strengthening of the related knowledge of exponent assumptions [2]. Because

our result is a characterization of deniability, this assumption, although very strong, is needed to prove deniability of the protocols. An interesting open problem is to formulate a simpler and more intuitive assumption that implies it.

– We prove a general theorem showing that any two-party protocol, whose transcript can be generated from a shared symmetric key and public information, is deniable (namely, simulatable without access to the shared key) if the symmetric key is the product of a deniable AKE. This result yields the deniability of the full Signal protocol under the assumption that its underlying AKE, 3DH, is deniable.

Due to lack of space, all the proofs are omitted and can be found in the full version of this paper [41].

1.3   Related Work

Readers are referred to [3,6,8,37] for the formal definition of secure AKE. These formal treatments provide robust justifications for the security of AKE but do not deal with the issue of deniability. Informal discussions of deniability began to appear in [4,5,13,22,25,28]. Offline Deniable AKE were defined in [14] based on the work on deniable authentication in [17]. Definitions of deniable AKE that offer composability and online deniability were presented in [16,42]. Provably offline deniable AKEs are presented in [14,43], while online deniable ones are presented in [16,39,40,42]. None of these protocols is implicitly authenticated.

There are alternative, relaxed definitions of deniability that work for less expansive purposes [10,18,44]. Each of these alternative definitions involve giving the simulator access to an oracle to perform the simulation. The oracle represent the "deniability loss" with respect to the standard strict definition of simulatability.

Other works in the context of deniability include [12,23,32], and we remark on the work by Pass [33] which stresses the important differences between a deniability simulator and a zero-knowledge one (as defined in [20]).

A full specification of the Signal protocol can be found in [38]. As mentioned above it uses the Extended Triple Diffie-Hellman (X3DH) key agreement protocol [30] (built on the 3DH AKE [29]) followed by a communication session which include a *ratcheting* mechanism to refresh keys [34]. Security analyses of these protocols that do not include deniability can be found in [1,9].

The MQV protocol was presented in [27,31]. It inspired several other protocols including HMQV by Krawczyk in [26] and the OAKE family of AKEs by Yao and Zhao [44]. No formal deniability proof of these protocols has appeared anywhere. In [44], one protocol in the OAKE family is claimed to have the weaker notion of reasonable deniability. Our full deniability results extend to the OAKE family as well. We will present those in the full version.

2   Preliminaries

In the following, we denote with G a cyclic group of prime order q generated by g. For every element $X \in G$ there exist an integer $x \in \mathbb{Z}_q$ such that $X = g^x$. We say that x is the discrete log of X with respect to g and denote it with $x = \log_g X$. Given two elements $A = g^a$ and $B = g^b$ we denote with $DH(A, B) = g^{ab} = A^b = B^a$, the Diffie-Hellman transform of A, B, [15].

With $a \leftarrow S$ we denote the process of sampling a uniformly at random in the set S.

The following definition states that computing the discrete log is hard.

Definition 1. *Let G be a cyclic group of prime order q generated by g. We say that the (T, ϵ) Discrete Log Assumption holds in G if for every probabilistic Turing Machine $\mathcal{A}$ running in time T we have that*

$$Prob[x \leftarrow \mathbb{Z}_q \; ; \; \mathcal{A}(g^x) = x] \leq \epsilon$$

The following definition states that computing the Diffie-Hellman transform is hard.

Definition 2. *Let G be a cyclic group of prime order q generated by g. We say that the (T, ϵ) Computational Diffie-Hellman (CDH) Assumption holds in G if for every probabilistic Turing Machine $\mathcal{A}$ running in time T we have that*

$$Prob[A, B \leftarrow G \; ; \; \mathcal{A}(A, B) = DH(A, B)] \leq \epsilon$$

Consider the set $G^3 = G \times G \times G$ and the following two probability distributions over it:

$$\mathcal{R}_G = \{(g^a, g^b, g^c) \text{ for } a, b, c \in_R [0..q]\}$$

and

$$\mathcal{DH}_G = \{(g^a, g^b, g^{ab}) \text{ for } a, b, \in_R [0..q]\}$$

We use these distributions in the following definition:

Definition 3. *We say that the (T, ϵ) Decisional Diffie-Hellman (DDH) Assumption holds over $G = \langle g \rangle$ if the two distributions $\mathcal{R}_G$ and $\mathcal{DH}_G$ are (T, ϵ)-indistinguishable.*

For Definition 3, we use Goldwasser and Micali's classical definition of computational indistinguishability [19].

Definition 4. *Let $\mathcal{X}, \mathcal{Y}$ be two probability distributions over A. Given a circuit D, the distinguisher, consider the following quantities*

$$\delta_{D,\mathcal{X}} = Prob_{x \in \mathcal{X}}[D(x) = 1]$$

$$\delta_{D,\mathcal{Y}} = Prob_{y \in \mathcal{Y}}[D(y) = 1]$$

We say that the probability distributions $\mathcal{X}$ and $\mathcal{Y}$ are (T, ϵ)-indistinguishable if for every probabilistic Turing Machine D running in time T we have that $|\delta_{D,\mathcal{X}} - \delta_{D,\mathcal{Y}}| \leq \epsilon$.

3   Implicitly Authenticated Key Exchange

In this section, we denote the peers as Alice and Bob. They each hold long-term public keys $A = g^a, B = g^b \leftarrow G$ respectively. The values $a, b \leftarrow \mathbb{Z}_q$ are their respective long-term private keys. In all the protocols we describe in this Section, Alice is the initiator and sends an ephemeral value $X = g^x \leftarrow G$ while keeping $x \leftarrow \mathbb{Z}_q$ secret. Bob is the responder and he answers with $Y = g^y \leftarrow G$ while keeping $y \leftarrow \mathbb{Z}_q$ secret. The protocols differ on how the resulting session key is computed.

MQV and HMQV: The MQV [27,31] and HMQV [26] protocols are described in Fig. 1. Note that in MQV the session key is defined as the group element $\tilde{K}$ (with the use of a hash function left as optional), while HMQV mandates the use of a hash function H to derive the session key from the secret value $\tilde{K}$ shared by Alice and Bob.

Triple Diffie-Hellman. Figure 2 describes the 3DH protocol [29]. The "three Diffie-Hellman" part refers to three separate Diffie-Hellman operators concatenated together and then passed to a hash function to derive a key.

We postpone discussions about how 3DH is used inside Signal to Sect. 9. Here, we simply describe 3DH as a basic key exchange protocol where both parties are alive and communicating with each other.

Key Registration. In the following, MQV [resp. HMQV or X3DH] with Key Registration denotes the MQV [resp. HMQV or X3DH] protocol where participants are required to prove knowledge of their long-term secret keys via an extractable

---

MQV and HMQV Protocols

Public Input: $A = g^a, B = g^b$ public keys of Alice and Bob respectively.
Secret Input of Alice: a; Secret Input of Bob: b;

Alice   Bob

$x \leftarrow \{1, \ldots, q\}$ $\xrightarrow{\quad X = g^x \quad}$

$\xleftarrow{\quad Y = g^y \quad}$ $y \leftarrow \{1, \ldots, q\}$
                                          $\tilde{K} = (XA^d)^{y+eb}$

$\tilde{K} = (YB^e)^{x+da}$

MQV: $K = \tilde{K}$, $d = 2^{\ell} + (X \bmod 2^{\ell})$, $e = 2^{\ell} + (Y \bmod 2^{\ell})$, $\ell = |q|/2$.
HMQV: $K = H(\tilde{K})$, $d = h(X, id_{\text{Bob}})$, $e = h(Y, id_{\text{Alice}})$,

where $h(\cdot), H(\cdot)$ are suitable hash functions.

Fig. 1. Computation of the session key K in MQV and HMQV protocols

---

3DH Protocol

Public Input: $A = g^a$, $B = g^b$ public keys of Alice and Bob respectively.

Secret Input of Alice: a; Secret Input of Bob: b;

Alice   Bob

$x \leftarrow \{1, \ldots, q\}$ $\qquad \xrightarrow{\quad X = g^x \quad}$

$\qquad\qquad\qquad\qquad\quad Y = g^y \qquad\qquad y \leftarrow \{1, \ldots, q\}$

$\qquad\qquad\qquad\xleftarrow{\hspace{3cm}} \qquad K = H(A^y || X^y || X^b)$

$K = H(Y^a || Y^x || B^x)$

where $||$ denotes concatenation and $H(\cdot)$ is a suitable hash function.

Fig. 2. Triple Diffie-Hellman key exchange protocol

proof of knowledge. This step is usually performed when players register their keys with a Public Key Infrastructure (PKI).

For the case of MQV/HMQV/X3DH, this step can be achieved by running the classic Schnorr proof [35].

4 Deniable Key Exchange

We recall the definition of deniable Authenticated Key Exchange (AKE in the rest) from [14, 16, 42].

An AKE protocol works with two parties, A and B, who want to agree on a secret key K. Each party has a long-term public/secret key pair which is associated to the party through a trusted registry. These key pairs are generated via a key generation phase. For notation purposes, A has public key $\mathsf{pk_A}$ and secret key $\mathsf{sk_A}$ – B has $\mathsf{pk_B}$ and $\mathsf{sk_B}$.

One of A and B acts as the initiator and the other acts as the responder. The protocol results in session key K. Informally, security for AKE requires that if an honest party A outputs key K and associates it to an honest party B, then no party other than B may know anything about K. Additional security properties can be enforced, such as perfect forward secrecy (past session keys remain secure, even if long-term keys are compromised), security against state compromise (ephemeral values are revealed to the adversary), etc. A formal treatment of AKE security can be found in [3,6,8,37].

Informally, we say that an AKE is *deniable* if it prevents A or B from proving to a third party (which we will call the *judge*) that an AKE occurred with a particular party. A weaker goal is to be able to deny just the contents of communication protected by the AKE's resulting key.

Recall that a KE protocol involves two communicating parties: the initiator, who sends the first message, and the responder. Let Σ denote an AKE protocol with key generation algorithm KG and interactive machines Σ_I and Σ_R, which respectively denote the roles of the initiator and responder. Both Σ_I and Σ_R take as input their own secret and public keys. In most cases, they also take in the identity and public key of their peer, but other AKE protocols specify that the parties learn this information during the session [7]. The term *session* denotes an individual run of a KE protocol. When the protocol finishes, it outputs either an error or a session key.

ADVERSARY. Let $\mathcal{M}$ denote an adversary that runs on an arbitrary number of randomly chosen public keys $\mathbf{pk} = (\mathsf{pk}_1, \dots, \mathsf{pk}_l)$ generated by KG. The algorithm associates the keys to honest users in the network. $\mathcal{M}$'s input also includes some arbitrary auxiliary information $aux \in AUX$. The adversary runs Σ with an arbitrary number of honest users. Sometimes $\mathcal{M}$ acts as the initiator, and other times $\mathcal{M}$ acts as the responder. The individual sessions run in a concurrent setting, so $\mathcal{M}$ may schedule and interleave them arbitrarily.

VIEW. We define the view of the adversary $\mathcal{M}$ as its internal coin tosses, the transcript of the entire interaction, and the session keys from each session that $\mathcal{M}$ participates either as an initiator or responder. Sessions that do not produce keys result in a key defined by an error value. We denote this view by $\mathsf{View}_{\mathcal{M}}(\mathbf{pk}, aux)$.

SIMULATOR. In order to demonstrate deniability with respect to initiator (*resp.*, responder), the simulator takes the role of the initiator I (*resp.*, responder R) and imitates I (*resp.*, R) without having the long-term secret key sk_I (*resp.*, sk_R).

As input, the simulator receives some random coins, the public keys $\mathbf{pk}$ of all parties and any auxiliary input aux available to the adversary. It generates $\mathsf{Sim}_{\mathcal{M}}(\mathbf{pk}, aux)$ by interacting with the adversary $\mathcal{M}$ as its peer. $\mathsf{Sim}_{\mathcal{M}}(\mathbf{pk}, aux)$ includes the transcript and the resulting shared key of the session.

The simulator provides the inputs to the adversary $\mathcal{M}$ prior to the protocol execution and observes all communication $\mathcal{M}$ has with its environment (such as AKE sessions $\mathcal{M}$ holds with other honest parties and the random oracle queries). The random oracle (RO) queries made by the adversary are visible to the simulator. However, the simulator might not be able to freely tamper with the RO input-output pairs (program the RO), because the judge is granted access to the random oracles, too. Therefore the RO queries involved in the simulation are expected to be consistent with the possible queries made by the judge and other honest parties running a session with the adversary.

Definition 5. *[14] An AKE protocol* $(\mathsf{KG}, \Sigma_I, \Sigma_R)$ *is* $(T_{\mathcal{M}}, T_{\mathcal{S}}, T_{\mathcal{D}}, \epsilon)$ *concurrently deniable with respect to the class of auxiliary Inputs AUX if for any adversary* $\mathcal{M}$ *running in time* $T_{\mathcal{M}}$, *on input honest parties' public keys* $\mathbf{pk} = (\mathsf{pk}_1, \dots, \mathsf{pk}_l)$ *generated by KG and any auxiliary input* $aux \in AUX$, *there exists a simulator SIM running in time* $T_{\mathcal{S}}$ *on the same inputs as* $\mathcal{M}$ *which produces a simulated view* $\mathcal{S}im(\mathsf{pk}, aux)$ *such that the following two distributions are* $(T_{\mathcal{D}}, \epsilon)$*-indistinguishable:*

$$\mathcal{R}eal(aux) = [(\mathsf{sk}, \mathsf{pk})_{I,R} \leftarrow \mathsf{KG}; (aux, \mathbf{pk}, \mathsf{View}_{\mathcal{M}}(\mathbf{pk}, aux))]$$

$$\mathcal{S}im(aux) = [(\mathsf{sk}, \mathsf{pk})_{I,R} \leftarrow \mathsf{KG}; (aux, \mathbf{pk}, \mathsf{Sim}_{\mathcal{M}}(\mathbf{pk}, aux))]$$

The definition follows the usual simulation paradigm which guarantees that the judge cannot decide if anything that the adversary presents (the view) is the result of an interaction with a real party or the product of a simulation. As pointed out by Pass in [33], the simulation requirements for deniability are much stronger than for Zero-Knowledge simulation. Indeed while a ZK simulator can be interpreted as a "thought experiment", a deniability simulator is a real algorithm that must exist in real life, to give a plausible explanation of the adversary view which does not include an honest party. In particular this means that standard simulation techniques for ZK, such as rewinding, random oracle programmability or common parameters are not available to a deniability simulator.

Why the session key is included in the view: Note how we include the session key in the view of the adversary. This guarantees that the contents of the session authenticated by the key can also be denied. Intuitively, since we do not know how the key will be used in the session following the AKE, we must include it in the view. Theorem 1 formalizes this intuition.

5   Deniable Sessions

As we noted above the definition of deniability of an AKE explicitly includes the session key in the view in order for us to claim that any deniability is preserved in any subsequent use of the key in the session that follows the AKE. We now formally prove this statement[1]. First we define deniability for an arbitrary interactive protocol between two parties, and then we show that any communication structured as an AKE, followed by messages where the two parties only use the session key (but not their long-term secret keys) is deniable.

Consider an adversary $\mathcal{M}$ that on input $\mathbf{pk}$ interacts with the parties holding the public keys. The adversary also may have auxiliary input aux drawn from distribution AUX.

$\mathcal{M}$ initiates several concurrent interactions with the parties and we define the adversary's *view* of the interaction as $\mathcal{M}$'s coin tosses together with the transcript of the full interactions. We denote the view as $\mathsf{View}(\mathbf{pk}, aux)$.

Definition 6. *We say that an interactive protocol $\mathcal{P}$ (KG, I, R) is $(T_{\mathcal{M}}, T_{\mathcal{S}}, T_{\mathcal{D}}, \epsilon)$-concurrently deniable with respect to the class of auxiliary inputs AUX if for any adversary $\mathcal{M}$ running in time $T_{\mathcal{M}}$, on input honest parties' public keys $\mathbf{pk} = (\mathsf{pk}_1, \ldots, \mathsf{pk}_l)$ generated by KG and any auxiliary input $aux \in AUX$,*

---

[1] This was claimed informally and without proof in [14]; here, we use this result in essential way in Sect. 9 to show how deniability of 3DH carries to deniability of the whole Signal protocol.

there exists a simulator $SIM_{\mathcal{M}}$ running in time T_S on the same inputs as $\mathcal{M}$, such that the following two distributions are $(T_{\mathcal{D}}, \epsilon)$-indistinguishable

$$\mathcal{R}eal(aux) = [(\mathsf{sk}_i, \mathsf{pk}_i) \leftarrow \mathsf{KG}; (aux, \mathbf{pk}, \mathsf{View}(\mathbf{pk}, aux))]$$

$$\mathcal{S}im(aux) = [(\mathsf{sk}_i, \mathsf{pk}_i) \leftarrow \mathsf{KG}; (aux, \mathbf{pk}, SIM(\mathbf{pk}, aux))]$$

We now define a *session*. Consider two parties Alice and Bob with associated public keys pk_A, pk_B. They also hold private keys sk_A, sk_B respectively, and also additional inputs x_A, x_B. We say that an interactive protocol P between Alice and Bob is a *session* if

- $P = [P_1, P_2]$ where P_1 is an AKE. Let K be the session key resulting from the execution of P_1
- every message sent by Alice (resp. Bob) in P_2 is a function only of the transcript so far, the private input x_A (resp. x_B), and the session key K, but *not* of the private keys sk_A (resp. sk_B)

Theorem 1. *Let $P = [P_1, P_2]$ be a session, where P_1 is a deniable authenticated key exchange according to Definition 5, which includes the session key in the view. Then P is deniable according to Definition 6.*

6   Negative Examples

In this section, we present a strategy that (on certain groups) allows an adversary to prove that an interaction took place for the MQV protocol. This negative result will then point the way to what type of assumption about the underlying group we need to make to guarantee deniability in a provable way.

Consider the MQV protocol in Fig. 1 and let us try to prove that the protocol is deniable for Alice. In other words we need to construct a simulator SIM who plays the role of Alice while talking to Bob. SIM is given the public key of Alice, $A = g^a$, but not the corresponding secret key, a.

SIM runs Bob to simulate the conversation and observes all of Bob's communication in his environment. SIM starts by providing the random coins r, and, if available, the auxiliary information to Bob. SIM then chooses a random x and sends out $X = g^x$ to Bob. In return it receives a group member $Y \in G$ from Bob. SIM's final output must be indistinguishable from Bob's view (r, X, Y, K) and the only thing that SIM does not know is K. Recall that in MQV

$$K = g^{xy} g^{ayd} g^{xbe} g^{abde}$$

where e, d are values computed from the transcript.

When Bob is honestly executing the protocol, the simulator is easy to construct. If Bob follows the protocol and computes Y as g^y for $y \in_R \mathbb{Z}_q$, the simulator can do exactly the same thing and compute the session key $K = g^{xy} A^{yd} (XA^d)^{be}$. Here, we assume that the key generation phase requires an additional key *registration* step where parties prove in ZK knowledge of their secret key[2]. This allows the simulator to have knowledge of b.

However, a malicious Bob can deviate from the protocol at will and having Bob's random coins provides SIM no information about how Y is actually sampled. In the simulation above, SIM can compute two of the DH values $g^{xy} = Y^x$ and $(XA^d)^{be}$ since b and x are known. But $DH(A, Y) = g^{ay}$ cannot be computed because neither a (secret key of Alice) nor $y = \log_g Y$ is known to SIM(maybe not even to Bob).

The only option for SIM would be putting a random string as the simulated key, hoping that a random value is indistinguishable from the actual key. Such strategy would work if we could invoke the DDH assumption to claim the two distributions are indistinguishable. However, a random string does not necessarily substitute for g^{ay}, because though a is uniformly selected, DDH does not apply for an adversarially chosen Y.

6.1   When MQV Is Provably *Non-deniable*

The discussion above shows that an adversarially chosen Y is a barrier to prove deniability for MQV. We now prove that over some groups, it is actually impossible to prove that MQV is deniable, because there is a strategy for Bob to prove that he interacted with Alice.

Assume we are running the protocol over a cyclic group G setting where:

1. The DDH problem is easy
2. The following experiment succeed with negligible probability for every efficient adversary Adv and any efficiently samplable distribution $\mathcal{Y}$
    - Adv runs on input $A, B \in G$ chosen uniformly at random and outputs $X \in G$
    - Adv receives $Y \in G$ chosen according to $\mathcal{Y}$
    - Adv succeeds if it outputs $K_A = (XA^d)^y (XA^d)^{be} = DH(XA^d, Y)DH(XA^d, B^e)$ where d, e are defined as in the MQV protocol

We note that point (2) is necessary for the security of the MQV protocol: in fact a successful adversary Adv could easily impersonate Alice. Point (1) can be guaranteed if for example the group G supports a bilinear map.

ON ASSUMING THAT THE DDH IS EASY. Before we proceed with our counterexample, let us discuss our assumption that the DDH problem is easy in G. Note that the MQV protocol stops being provably secure in a model where security is defined as the indistinguishability of the session key from a random value (i.e., from a random group element in the case of MQV). So it would seem that we are proving a deniability counter-example for an insecure protocol, and one could wonder what's the value in that. There are several answers to this point:

---

[2]   For showing the failure of (proofs of) deniability, assuming a key registration step makes our negative result stronger as it implies that *even if* we allow key registration we do not know how to simulate, and in some cases simulation is actually impossible.

- First of all, one could consider a weaker security notion for key exchange to say that the session key should have "enough" computational entropy rather than being indistinguishable from random. This would be a much weaker but still useful security definition as a full entropy key could be derived via a randomness extractor. It is conceivable that MQV is a secure protocol under this definition (one would have to prove it) but provably non-deniable because of our counter-example.
- Deniability is an orthogonal property to that of security. Our counter-example is designed to illuminate the difficulties of proving deniability for MQV and similar protocols, and demonstrating the failure of the intuition that the sole lack of explicit authentication methods (such as digital signatures) is sufficient to assume that deniability holds.
- Additionally, we point out that there are so-called *trapdoor DDH* groups [11, 36], where the DDH problem is conjectured to be hard unless one is in possession of a trapdoor. In this case, the protocol is secure for anybody who does not possess the trapdoor but non-deniable for a judge who holds the trapdoor.

THE COUNTER-EXAMPLE. We now show a strategy that incriminates Alice. A malicious Bob samples Y uniformly at random in the group but in a way in which he can demonstrate that he does not know $y = \log_g Y$, for example by hashing a publicly known string (e.g. today's copy of the NY Times) into a group element via a sufficiently complicated hash function (which could be modeled as a random oracle[3]).

We now prove by contradiction that there cannot be a simulator. If there is a simulator SIM, let K_S be the key provided by the simulator, while $K = (XA^d)^y(XA^e)^b = DH(XA^d, Y)DH(XA^e, B)$ is the real key. We assume that Bob is willing to reveal b to the judge in order to prove that an interaction took place.

The knowledge of b allows the judge to compute $z = DH(XA^d, B^e) = (XA^d)^{be}$. Since the DDH is easy, the judge can decide if $K = K_S$ by checking if $K_S \cdot z^{-1} = DH(XA^d, Y)$. Therefore, anything other than the authentic key is detected by the judge. So the only possible successful simulator is the one that outputs $K_S = K$. But that means that SIM contradicts assumption (2) above.

3DH without hashing. It is not hard to see that a similar reasoning applies to an "unhashed" version of 3DH where the session key is set as $K = DH(A, Y) || DH(X, Y) || DH(X, B)$. Therefore such a version of 3DH would also be provably non-deniable under the above conditions.

---

[3] It is not necessary to model this hash as a random oracle, as long as we assume that computing g^{ay} is hard when $A = g^a$ is sampled uniformly at random and $Y = g^y$ is sampled according to the procedure used by Bob.

6.2   Does the Random Oracle Help?

In HMQV and 3DH the session key is computed by hashing the secret shared value, i.e.

$$K = H[DH(XA^d, Y)DH(XA^d, B^e)]$$

in HMQV and

$$K = H[DH(A, Y)\|DH(X, Y)\|DH(X, B)]$$

in 3DH. If we model H as a random oracle, would this help in solving the problems described in the previous section?

The question is still how can the simulator provide a session key which is indistinguishable from the real one. In this case, one would hope that the use of the random oracle will allow the simulator to identify the key. Assume Bob is the malicious party and can deviate from the honest execution of the protocol. Every time Bob makes a random oracle query, SIM sees it (even though it is not allowed to choose the answer for it [33]).

If Bob computes the real session key K that matches A, B, X, Y, then he must have queried $DH(XA^d, Y)DH(XA^d, B^e)$ (resp. $DH(A, Y)\|DH(X, Y)\|DH(X, B)$ for 3DH) to the random oracle.

First of all there is no guarantee that Bob will actually query the random oracle on those points. But even if he did, it is not clear how the simulator can identify the correct query that corresponds to the computation of the session key. Indeed, the simulator SIM is able to compute g^{bx} and g^{xy}, but cannot compute g^{ay} since a and y are not known. If Y is uniformly distributed and the DDH holds, SIM cannot *provably* detect which query corresponds to the session key[4].

The only option is to choose a random key, but this is distinguishable from the real view if Bob presents to the judge the correct input to the random oracle (e.g. Bob knows $y = \log_g Y$ and can convince the judge that the session key was computed using the correct input).

Note that if this is the case, Bob still cannot convince the judge that he spoke to Alice. In fact if Bob knows y, then the entire transcript could be his own creation without ever interacting with Alice.

In other words, we have one of two possible cases: either Bob does not know y (and the input to the random oracle) in which case the simulator should be able to put a random key in the view, or Bob knows y (and the correct input to the random oracle) in which case the simulator should be able to identify the correct key from the knowledge of Bob. The problem is that we do not know which case we are in, and therefore we cannot complete the simulation successfully.

The way out of this problem is described in the next section and relies on an appropriate "knowledge extraction" from Bob, which will address also the issues related to the previous counter-example.

---

[4]   One could use a Gap-DDH Assumption, which states that the CDH Assumption holds even in the presence of an oracle that decides the DDH. Then such oracle could be provided to the simulator to detect the query. Yet this simulator would not be a legitimate *deniability* simulator unless the oracle could be implemented in real-life.

7 A Characterization for Non-deniability

In this section, we show that the sampling strategy shown above to make MQV non-deniable is essentially the *only* one. More specifically we prove that if an adversary is able to "frame" one of the parties in the MQV protocol and prove that an interaction took place, then we have a way to sample a group element Y in G in a way that it is hard to compute $DH(A, Y)$ for a fixed group element A, but it must be easy to detect that $DH(A, Y)$ is correct.

The consequence is that if we assume that such a task is computationally infeasible then we can prove (albeit non-constructively) that the MQV protocol is deniable. Details follows.

NON-DENIABLE AKE. First we define what a non-deniable or *incriminating* AKE is, as the logical negation of deniability.

We call a key exchange protocol (KG, I, R) as $(T_{\mathcal{M}}, T_{\mathsf{SIM}}, T_{\mathsf{J}}, \varepsilon_{\mathsf{J}})$-*incriminating* if there is an adversary $\mathcal{M}$ running in time $T_{\mathcal{M}}$ for which, all simulators SIM running in time T_{SIM}, there exists a judge J running in time T_{J} which distinguishes the uniformly selected samples from the following distributions with probability at least ε_{J}.

$$\mathcal{R}eal = \{\mathsf{View}_{\mathcal{M}}(pk_i)\}_{(sk_i, pk_i) \leftarrow KG}$$
$$\mathcal{S}im = \{\mathsf{SIM}_{\mathcal{M}}(pk_i)\}_{(sk_i, pk_i) \leftarrow KG}$$

$$|Pr_{x \in \mathcal{R}eal}[\mathsf{J}(x) = 1] - Pr_{x \in \mathcal{S}im}[\mathsf{J}(x) = 1]| \geq \varepsilon_{\mathsf{J}}$$

$\mathsf{View}_{\mathcal{M}}$ includes the public keys, the transcript, the session key and random coins r given to $\mathcal{M}$. (sk_i, pk_i) denotes long-term key pairs of parties for $i \in \{I, R\}$ (I for initializer, R for responder).

7.1 Bad Sampler

We now define a particular type of sampling algorithm for G which we call a *Bad Sampler*. We will prove that the existence of a bad sampler is equivalent to MQV being incriminating.

We say that a sampling algorithm for G is $(T_{\mathsf{Samp}}, T_{\mathsf{Solv}}, T_{\mathsf{D}}, \varepsilon_{\mathsf{Solv}}, \varepsilon_{\mathsf{D}})$-Bad if the following conditions are satisfied:

There exists a sampling algorithm Sample which satisfies the following

1. Sample takes as input A (uniformly picked from G) and the random coins r to generate $Y = \mathsf{Sample}(A, r)$ running in time $\leq T_{\mathsf{Samp}}$.

2. $\forall$ Solve running in T_{Solv}

$$Pr_{\mathsf{Solve}, A, r}[\mathsf{Solve}(A, Y, r) = g^{ay} \mid Y = \mathsf{Sample}(A, r)] \leq \varepsilon_{\mathsf{Solv}}$$

Probability is over the randomness of Solve, uniform choice of $A = g^a$ and random coins r.

3. There exists a distinguisher D running in time $\leq T_D$ which tells apart g^{ay} from a random group member $\hat{g} \leftarrow G$ for a uniformly chosen A and random coins r.

$$|Pr_{D, A, r}[D(A, Y, r, g^{ay}) = 1 \mid Y = \mathsf{Sample}(A, r)] -$$
$$Pr_{D, A, r}[D(A, Y, r, \hat{g}) = 1 \mid Y = \mathsf{Sample}(A, r)]| \geq \varepsilon_D$$

7.2   Equivalence Between Bad Sampling and Incrimination

In the following Theorem, if T is the running time of an algorithm then the notation $\tilde{T}$ means T plus a constant number of exponentiations in G.

Theorem 2. *If there is a $(T_{\mathsf{Samp}}, T_{\mathsf{Solv}}, T_D, \varepsilon_{\mathsf{Solv}}, \varepsilon_D)$-bad sampler in G then the MQV protocol is $(\tilde{T}_{\mathcal{M}}, \tilde{T}_{\mathsf{SIM}}, \tilde{T}_J, \varepsilon_J)$-incriminating with $\varepsilon_J = \varepsilon_D(1 - \varepsilon_{\mathsf{Solv}})$.*

Conversely if the MQV protocol run over G is $(T_{\mathcal{M}}, T_{\mathsf{SIM}}, T_J, \varepsilon_J)$-incriminating then there exists a $(\tilde{T}_{\mathsf{Samp}}, \tilde{T}_{\mathsf{Solv}}, \tilde{T}_D, \varepsilon_{\mathsf{Solv}}, \varepsilon_D)$-bad sampler for G, with $\varepsilon_{\mathsf{Solv}} = (1 - \varepsilon_J)$ and $\varepsilon_D = \varepsilon_J$.

MALICIOUS INITIATOR. The theorem above proves the equivalence of bad sampling with the non-deniability of MQV for the initiator when interacting with a malicious responder. It is also not hard to see that a similar theorem holds for the case of a malicious initiator who is trying to incriminate the responder. In this case also, the only possible strategy for a malicious initiator will be to run a bad sampler.

THEOREM INTERPRETATION. The above theorem characterizes the strategy that the adversary needs to follow to be able to incriminate one of the parties: the only way to do it is to be able to sample elements Y in G such that for every element $A \leftarrow G$ it is easy to decide if $DH(A, Y)$ is correct while it is still hard to compute it. If we assume that such "bad" sampling is infeasible, then we immediately have a proof that the protocols are deniable. Yet such proof is a 'non-constructive' one, as we are not able to show how the simulator works, but just that it must exist. The significance of such a statement in real-life is not clear, as plausible deniability requires the judge to actually run a simulator to counter Bob's statement that he spoke to Alice. In the absence of such real simulator, there is no way to argue that the conversation was not generated by Alice, even if we assume that bad sampling is impossible.

As before we are stuck on the fact that when we are trying to simulate a malicious Bob we do not know if he did sample $Y = g^y$ with or without knowledge of y (or more precisely with or without knowledge of $DH(A, Y)$). The above theorem says that if bad sampling is impossible then either Bob must know $DH(A, Y)$ or the value is indistinguishable from random: in either case we would be able to successfully complete the simulation if we knew which case we were in (and in the former be able to "extract" $DH(A, Y)$). But the mere assumption that bad sampling is impossible does not give us this knowledge, and therefore leaves us stuck in the construction of a simulator.

The next section shows how to define an appropriate "knowledge extractor" for Bob, that will allow us to build a simulator.

8 Deniability Proof

As we discussed in the previous section, the roadblock in the construction of a deniability simulator is that the simulator does not know if a malicious Bob knows the value $DH(A, Y)$ or not, at the moment he sends Y out. We also showed that the only way a malicious Bob can frame Alice is if he samples a Y for which he does *not* know $DH(A, Y)$, but such value can be efficiently recognized as correct (i.e. distinguished from a random value).

8.1 The Case of MQV

The above discussion therefore points out to the natural definition of a "knowledge extractor" which allows us to build a simulator for MQV. If we assume that given a malicious responder Bob, we can either (i) extract the value $DH(A, Y)$ or (ii) assume that $DH(A, Y)$ is indistinguishable from random, then the simulator immediately follows as the output of the extractor will be the simulated key.

We call this the **Strong Knowledge of DH (SKDH) Assumption** and it is defined below. In the next section we define a weaker version of this assumption which will be sufficient to prove HMQV and 3DH.

Definition 7. *Let G be a cyclic group and AUX a class of auxiliary inputs. Let M be a probabilistic Turing Machine running in time T_M on input (U, aux) where $U \in_R G$, and $aux \in AUX$, and outputs $Z \in G$; we denote with $Z = M(U, aux, r)$ the output of running M on input U, aux with coin tosses r. We say that the $(T_M, T_{\hat{M}}, T_D, \varepsilon_D)$-SKDH Assumption holds over group G and class AUX, if for every such M, there exists a companion probabilistic Turing Machine $\hat{M}$ (called the extractor for M) such that: $\hat{M}$ runs on input U, aux, r in time $T_{\hat{M}}$ and outputs $\hat{Z} \in G$ such that the distributions*

$$[U, aux, r, DH(U, Z)] \quad and \quad [U, aux, r, \hat{Z}]$$

are (T_D, ε_D)-indistinguishable.

Remark: Basically the assumption says that for every sampler M of a value Z, there is an extractor that either computes $DH(U, Z)$ or produces an output distribution that is computationally indistinguishable from $DH(U, Z)$ even when given the internal coin tosses of M. The assumption is written generically: when Bob [resp. Alice] is the adversary $U = A$ [resp. $U = B$] the peer's long-term public key, and $Z = Y$ [resp. $Z = X$] the adversary's ephemeral value.

Theorem 3. *Under the $(T_M, T_{\hat{M}}, T_D, \varepsilon_D)$ SKDH Assumption, MQV with Key Registration is a $(\tilde{T}_M, \tilde{T}_{\hat{M}}, \tilde{T}_D, \varepsilon_D)$ deniable AKE.*

8.2   The Case of HMQV and 3DH

For HMQV and 3DH we can use a weaker assumption. In this case, when the extractor fails to produce $DH(A, Y)$ we do not need to establish that $DH(A, Y)$ is indistinguishable from random, but simply that it cannot be computed by anybody. This is sufficient because the session key (in both HMQV and 3DH) is the result of a random oracle call over a function of $DH(A, Y)$. If nobody (except Alice) knows the input to the random oracle call that produces the session key, then the session key can be simulated with a random value.

Definition 8. *Let G be a cyclic group and AUX a class of auxiliary inputs. Let M be a probabilistic Turing Machine running in time T_M which runs on input (U, aux) where $U \in_R G$, and $aux \in AUX$, and outputs $Z \in G$; we denote with $Z = M(U, aux, r)$ the output of running M on input U, aux with coin tosses r.*

We say that the $(T_M, T_{\hat{M}}, T_C, \varepsilon_C)$ Knowledge of DH (KDH) Assumption holds over group G and class AUX, if for every such M, there exists a companion probabilistic Turing Machine $\hat{M}$ (called the extractor for M) such that: $\hat{M}$ runs on on input U, aux, r in time $T_{\hat{M}}$ and outputs $\hat{Z} \in G$ or $\hat{Z} = \bot$ such that

- *If $\hat{M}(U, aux, r) = \hat{Z} \neq \bot$ then $\hat{Z} = DH(U, Z)$*
- *If $\hat{M}(U, aux, r) = \bot$ then for every probabilistic Turing Machine C running in time T_C we have that*

$$Prob[C(U, Z, r, aux) = DH(U, Z)] \leq \varepsilon_C$$

where the probabilities are taken over $U \leftarrow G$, r and the coin tosses of $\hat{M}$ and C, conditioned on $\hat{M}(U, aux, r) = \bot$.

The first condition says that if the extractor outputs a group element, this element must be $DH(U, Z)$, otherwise no algorithm C can compute the value $DH(U, Z)$ even if C is given the coin tosses of M.

REMARK. Another way to look at the KDH Assumption is as follows. The adversary M samples an element Z in G. For this particular sampling algorithm the extractor $\hat{M}$ tells us if computing $DH(U, Z)$, given the random coins of M, is feasible or not, and if it is feasible it actually gives us the value $DH(U, Z)$.

Theorem 4. *Under the $(T_M, T_{\hat{M}}, T_C, \varepsilon_C)$ KDHA, HMQV with Key Registration is a $(\tilde{T}_M, \tilde{T}_{\hat{M}}, \tilde{T}_C, \varepsilon_C)$ deniable AKE in the random oracle model.*

For the case of 3DH the Key Registration step is not necessary since the value g^{ab} (the Diffie-Hellman transform of the long-term secret keys) is not included in the session key.

Theorem 5. *Under the $(T_M, T_{\hat{M}}, T_C, \varepsilon_C)$ KDHA, 3DH is a $(\tilde{T}_M, \tilde{T}_{\hat{M}}, \tilde{T}_C, \varepsilon_C)$ deniable AKE in the random oracle model.*

9   3DH vs Signal

We refer the reader to [9] for a full description of the Signal protocol and its security analysis. Informally, we can describe Signal as an initial AKE which establishes a *root key*, followed by a secure session where messages are exchanged. However each message exchange is accompanied by a *ratcheting* step, which generates new session key. These sequence of keys, creates a *key chain* where keys are authenticated by their predecessor in the chain. In a *symmetric ratcheting* step the current chain key K is fed to a KDF function to generate two keys, the new chain key K_1 and the key K_2 used to encrypt/authenticate the message at this round. In a *asymmetric* ratcheting the parties perform a new Diffie-Hellman exchange over two ephemeral keys and feed the result to a KDF together with the current chain key, also outputting K_1, K_2 as above.

Note how, in the above description, after the initial AKE which establishes a session key K, the messages exchanged in the protocol do *not* use the long-term secret keys of the parties. Therefore, if the initial AKE is deniable, we can apply Theorem 1 and claim the deniability of Signal.

THE X3DH PROTOCOL. If the initial AKE protocol in Signal were 3DH, we would be done. However to enable asynchronous communication (where Bob, the responder, could be offline at the moment in which Alice, the initiator, sends him a message), the Signal protocol uses the X3DH variant of 3DH. This variant allows Bob to load his ephemeral key Y onto a key distribution server (a *pre-key* in Signal jargon). To prevent impersonation attacks by the server, Bob will *sign* Y with his long term secret key. When Alice wants to talk to Bob she queries the key distribution server for Bob's ephemeral key and runs the 3DH protocol to establish a root chain key K_1 and a message key K_2 used to secure the first message she sends to Bob. At this point Alice and Bob will continue with the ratcheting mechanism described above. We now move to establish the deniability of X3DH.

It is not hard to see that the proof of deniability of 3DH extends to X3DH in the case of the initiator. Indeed, the deniability argument for Alice in X3DH is the same as for the responder in 3DH since here Alice acts on the ephemeral value Y chosen by Bob. In contrast, deniability with respect to Bob in X3DH is complicated by the fact that Bob signs the value Y. But note that Bob places Y and its signature on a public server that anyone can access. Thus, Y is not bound to any specific peer, and cannot be used as a proof that Bob communicated with anyone.

Formally, we can consider Y and its signature as "auxiliary information" that an adversarial Alice has when initiating the protocol, and can therefore be provided to the simulator as well. While this is the intuition behind the simulation argument, there is another technical twist at this point. In the 3DH simulation of Bob against a malicious Alice, the simulator is allowed to choose $y \leftarrow \mathbb{Z}_q$ and set $Y = g^y$; the knowledge of y helps the simulator in the computation of the correct key. In the X3DH simulation, however, Y is part of the auxiliary input and the simulator has no access to y. Intuitively, because Bob signs Y, the latter can be seen as another public key associated with him and the simulator cannot be given its secret key.

The problem boils down to the computation of g^{xy}. In the 3DH simulation, we simply computed it through the knowledge of y. Here, we need to extract it from Alice, and this requires an additional assumption that says we can extract both g^{xy} and g^{bx}.

Definition 9. *Let G be a cyclic group and AUX a class of auxiliary inputs. Let M be a probabilistic Turing Machine running in time T_M which runs on input (U, W, aux) where $U, W \in_R G$, and $aux \in AUX$, and outputs $Z \in G$; we denote with $Z = M(U, W, aux, r)$ the output of running M on input U, W, aux with coin tosses r.*

We say that the $(T_M, T_{\hat{M}}, T_C, \varepsilon_C)$ Knowledge of 2DH (K2DH) Assumption holds over group G and class AUX, if for every such M, there exists a companion probabilistic Turing Machine $\hat{M}$ (called the extractor for M) such that: $\hat{M}$ runs on input U, W, aux, r in time $T_{\hat{M}}$ and outputs $\hat{Z}_1, \hat{Z}_2 \in G$ or $\bot$ such that

- *If $\hat{M}(U, aux, r) \neq \bot$ then $\hat{Z}_1 = DH(U, Z)$ and $\hat{Z}_2 = DH(W, Z)$*
- *If $\hat{M}(U, aux, r) = \bot$ then for every probabilistic Turing Machine C running in time T_C we have that*

$$Prob[C(U, Z, r, aux) \in \{DH(U, Z), DH(W, Z)\}] \leq \varepsilon_C$$

where the probabilities are taken over $U \leftarrow G$, W, r and the coin tosses of $\hat{M}$ and C, conditioned on $\hat{M}(U, aux, r) = \bot$.

Theorem 6. *Under the $(T_M, T_{\hat{M}}, T_C, \varepsilon_C)$ K2DHA, X3DH with Key Registration is a $(\tilde{T}_M, \tilde{T}_{\hat{M}}, \tilde{T}_C, \varepsilon_C)$ deniable AKE in the random oracle model.*

10   On the Need to Extract the Long-Term Private Keys

The simulation arguments of Theorems 4 and 6 assume the ability to extract the incriminating party's (Bob in our examples) private key, for example via key registration. This simplified the proofs and intuition. We note, however, that such extraction is not needed. Instead, we can generalize our extraction assumptions to prevent Bob from sampling either B or Y in a way that he does not know the discrete logs and yet *both g^{ab} and g^{ay}* are distinguishable from random. Indeed, what happens (in either HMQV, 3DH and X3DH) is that Bob will be able to incriminate Alice if (and only if) he is able to sample either B or Y under the above conditions. Formally, we achieve this by adding one extra "knowledge" assumption about the way parties generate their long-term keys; arguably, this additional assumption is not essentially stronger than the previous ones. Details follow.

Definition 10. *Let G be a cyclic group and AUX a class of auxiliary inputs. Let M be a probabilistic Turing Machine running in time T_M which runs on input*

$aux \in AUX$, and outputs $Z \in G$; we denote with $Z = M(aux, r)$ the output of running M on input aux with coin tosses r.

We say that the $(T_M, T_{\hat{M}}, T_C, \varepsilon_C)$ Extended Knowledge of DH (EKDH) Assumption holds over group G and class AUX, if for every such M, there exists a companion probabilistic Turing Machine $\hat{M}$ (called the extractor for M) such that: $\hat{M}$ runs on on input aux, r and an additional input $U \in G$, in time $T_{\hat{M}}$ and outputs $\hat{Z}$ or $\perp$ such that

- *If $\hat{M}(U, aux, r) = \hat{Z} \neq \perp$ then $\hat{Z} = DH(U, Z)$*
- *If $\hat{M}(U, aux, r) = \perp$ then for every probabilistic Turing Machine C running in time T_C we have that*

$$Prob[C(U, Z, r, aux) = DH(U, Z)] \leq \varepsilon_C$$

where the probabilities are taken over r and the coin tosses of $\hat{M}$ and C, conditioned on $\hat{M}(U, aux, r) = \perp$.

Note the difference between the KDH and the EKDH Assumption. In the latter, the group element $U \in G$ is not known to the machine M, but is fed to the extractor as input. This is because we need to model a machine M that generates Z as its long-term public key *before* seeing any of the keys of the parties it will interact with.

Theorem 7. *Under the $(T_M, T_{\hat{M}}, T_C, \varepsilon_C)$ EKDHA, protocols HMQV is $(\tilde{T}_M, \tilde{T}_{\hat{M}}, \tilde{T}_C, \varepsilon_C)$ deniable AKE in the random oracle model, even without registration of long-term public keys.*

A similar theorem holds for X3DH.

Acknowledgment. The authors thank the anonymous reviewer whose excellent comments greatly improved the presentation of this paper.

References

1. Alwen, J., Coretti, S., Dodis, Y.: The double ratchet: security notions, proofs, and modularization for the signal protocol. IACR Cryptology ePrint Archive **2018**, 1037 (2018)
2. Bellare, M., Palacio, A.: The knowledge-of-exponent assumptions and 3-round zero-knowledge protocols. In: Franklin, M. (ed.) CRYPTO 2004. LNCS, vol. 3152, pp. 273–289. Springer, Heidelberg (2004). https://doi.org/10.1007/978-3-540-28628-8_17
3. Bellare, M., Rogaway, P.: Entity authentication and key distribution. In: Stinson, D.R. (ed.) CRYPTO 1993. LNCS, vol. 773, pp. 232–249. Springer, Heidelberg (1994). https://doi.org/10.1007/3-540-48329-2_21
4. Borisov, N., Goldberg, I., Brewer, E.: Off-the-record communication, or, why not to use PGP. In Proceedings of the 2004 ACM Workshop on Privacy in the Electronic Society WPES 2004, pp. 77–84. ACM, New York (2004)

5. Boyd, C., Mao, W., Paterson, K.G.: Key agreement using statically keyed authenticators. In: Jakobsson, M., Yung, M., Zhou, J. (eds.) ACNS 2004. LNCS, vol. 3089, pp. 248–262. Springer, Heidelberg (2004). https://doi.org/10.1007/978-3-540-24852-1_18

6. Canetti, R., Krawczyk, H.: Analysis of key-exchange protocols and their use for building secure channels. In: Pfitzmann, B. (ed.) EUROCRYPT 2001. LNCS, vol. 2045, pp. 453–474. Springer, Heidelberg (2001). https://doi.org/10.1007/3-540-44987-6_28

7. Canetti, R., Krawczyk, H.: Security analysis of IKE's signature-based key-exchange protocol. In: Yung, M. (ed.) CRYPTO 2002. LNCS, vol. 2442, pp. 143–161. Springer, Heidelberg (2002). https://doi.org/10.1007/3-540-45708-9_10

8. Canetti, R., Krawczyk, H.: Universally composable notions of key exchange and secure channels. In: Knudsen, L.R. (ed.) EUROCRYPT 2002. LNCS, vol. 2332, pp. 337–351. Springer, Heidelberg (2002). https://doi.org/10.1007/3-540-46035-7_22

9. Cohn-Gordon, K., Cremers, C., Dowling, B., Garratt, L., Stebila, D.: A formal security analysis of the signal messaging protocol. In: 2017 IEEE European Symposium on Security and Privacy (EuroS P), pp. 451–466, April 2017

10. Cremers, C., Feltz, M.: One-round strongly secure key exchange with perfect forward secrecy and deniability. Cryptology ePrint Archive, Report 2011/300 (2011). https://eprint.iacr.org/2011/300

11. Dent, A.W., Galbraith, S.D.: Hidden pairings and trapdoor DDH groups. In: Hess, F., Pauli, S., Pohst, M. (eds.) ANTS 2006. LNCS, vol. 4076, pp. 436–451. Springer, Heidelberg (2006). https://doi.org/10.1007/11792086_31

12. Di Raimondo, M., Gennaro, R.: New approaches for deniable authentication. J. Cryptol. **22**(4), 572–615 (2009). https://doi.org/10.1007/s00145-009-9044-3

13. Di Raimondo, M., Gennaro, R., Krawczyk, H.: Secure off-the-record messaging. In: Proceedings of the 2005 ACM Workshop on Privacy in the Electronic Society WPES 2005, pp. 81–89. ACM, New York (2005)

14. Di Raimondo, M., Gennaro, R., Krawczyk, H.: Deniable authentication and key exchange. In: Proceedings of the 13th ACM Conference on Computer and Communications Security CCS 2006, pp. 400–409. ACM, New York (2006)

15. Diffie, W., Hellman, M.: New directions in cryptography. IEEE Trans. Inf. Theor. **22**(6), 644–654 (2006)

16. Dodis, Y., Katz, J., Smith, A., Walfish, S.: Composability and on-line deniability of authentication. In: Reingold, O. (ed.) TCC 2009. LNCS, vol. 5444, pp. 146–162. Springer, Heidelberg (2009). https://doi.org/10.1007/978-3-642-00457-5_10

17. Dwork, C., Naor, M., Sahai, A.: Concurrent zero-knowledge. In: Proceedings of the Thirtieth Annual ACM Symposium on Theory of Computing STOC 1998, pp. 409–418. ACM, New York (1998)

18. Fischlin, M., Mazaheri, S.: Notions of deniable message authentication. In: Proceedings of the 14th ACM Workshop on Privacy in the Electronic Society WPES 2015, pp. 55–64. ACM, New York (2015)

19. Goldwasser, S., Micali, S.: Probabilistic encryption. JCSS **28**(2), 270–299 (1984)

20. Goldwasser, S., Micali, S., Rackoff, C.: The knowledge complexity of interactive proof systems. SIAM J. Comput. **18**(1), 186–208 (1989)

21. Harkins, D., Carrel, D.: The internet key exchange (IKE). RFC 2409, RFC Editor, November 1998

22. Harkins, D., Carrel, D.: The internet key exchange (IKE) (1998)

23. Katz, J.: Efficient and non-malleable proofs of plaintext knowledge and applications. In: Biham, E. (ed.) EUROCRYPT 2003. LNCS, vol. 2656, pp. 211–228. Springer, Heidelberg (2003). https://doi.org/10.1007/3-540-39200-9_13

24. Kaufman, C.: Internet key exchange (IKEv2) protocol. RFC 4306, RFC Editor, December 2005
25. Krawczyk, H.: Skeme: a versatile secure key exchange mechanism for internet. In: Proceedings of Internet Society Symposium on Network and Distributed Systems Security, pp. 114–127, February 1996
26. Krawczyk, H.: HMQV: a high-performance secure Diffie-Hellman protocol. In: Shoup, V. (ed.) CRYPTO 2005. LNCS, vol. 3621, pp. 546–566. Springer, Heidelberg (2005). https://doi.org/10.1007/11535218_33
27. Law, L., Menezes, A., Qu, M., Solinas, J., Vanstone, S.: An efficient protocol for authenticated key agreement. Des. Codes Crypt. **28**(2), 119–134 (2003)
28. Mao, W., Paterson, K.: On the plausible deniability feature of internet protocols. Manuscript (2002)
29. Marlinspike, M.: Simplifying OTR deniability (2013). https://signal.org/blog/simplifying-otr-deniability/
30. Marlinspike, M., Perrin, T.: The x3dh key agreement protocol, Rev. 1, November 2016
31. Menezes, A., Qu, M., Vanstone, S.: Some new key agreement protocols providing implicit authentication. In: Workshop on Selected Area in Cryptography (SAC 1995), pp. 22–32 (1995)
32. Naor, M.: Deniable ring authentication. In: Yung, M. (ed.) CRYPTO 2002. LNCS, vol. 2442, pp. 481–498. Springer, Heidelberg (2002). https://doi.org/10.1007/3-540-45708-9_31
33. Pass, R.: On deniability in the common reference string and random oracle model. In: Boneh, D. (ed.) CRYPTO 2003. LNCS, vol. 2729, pp. 316–337. Springer, Heidelberg (2003). https://doi.org/10.1007/978-3-540-45146-4_19
34. Perrin, T., Marlinspike, M.: The double ratchet algorithm, Rev. 1, November 2016
35. Schnorr, C.P.: Efficient signature generation by smart cards. J. Cryptol. **4**(3), 161–174 (1991). https://doi.org/10.1007/BF00196725
36. Seurin, Y.: New constructions and applications of trapdoor DDH groups. In: Kurosawa, K., Hanaoka, G. (eds.) PKC 2013. LNCS, vol. 7778, pp. 443–460. Springer, Heidelberg (2013). https://doi.org/10.1007/978-3-642-36362-7_27
37. Shoup, V.: On formal models for secure key exchange. Technical report RZ 3120, IBM, April 1999
38. Signal technical information. https://signal.org/docs/
39. Unger, N., Goldberg, I.: Deniable key exchanges for secure messaging. In: Proceedings on 22nd ACM SIGSAC Conference on Computer and Communications Security, pp. 1211–1223 (2015)
40. Unger, N., Goldberg, I.: Improved strongly deniable authenticated key exchanges for secure messaging. Proc. Priv. Enhancing Technol. **2018**(1), 21–66 (2018)
41. Vatandas, N., Gennaro, R., Ithurburn, B., Krawczyk, H.: On the deniability of signal communications. Cryptology ePrint Archive (2020). https://eprint.iacr.org/
42. Walfish, S.: Enhanced security models for network protocols. Ph.D thesis (2008)
43. Yao, A.C., Zhao, Y.: Deniable internet key exchange. In: Zhou, J., Yung, M. (eds.) ACNS 2010. LNCS, vol. 6123, pp. 329–348. Springer, Heidelberg (2010). https://doi.org/10.1007/978-3-642-13708-2_20
44. Yao, A.C., Zhao, Y., OAKE: a new family of implicitly authenticated diffie-hellman protocols. In: Proceedings of the 2013 ACM SIGSAC Conference on Computer and Communications Security CCS 2013, pp. 1113–1128. ACM, New York (2013)

Security Analysis

Powerless Security

A Security Analysis of In-Home Power Line Communications Based on HomePlug AV2

Stefan Hoffmann[1][✉], Jens Müller[2][✉], Jörg Schwenk[2][✉],
and Gerd Bumiller[1][✉]

[1] University of Applied Sciences Ruhr West, Bottrop, Germany
{stefan.hoffmann,gerd.bumiller}@hs-ruhrwest.de
[2] Ruhr University Bochum, Bochum, Germany
{jens.a.mueller,joerg.schwenk}@rub.de

Abstract. Power line communication (PLC) allows home users and industries to transfer data over power cables. Protection of transmitted data is crucial because signals are not limited to "one's own four walls". We provide a detailed and structured security analysis of the currently most widely used in-Home PLC standard, namely the Broadband-PLC specification HomePlug AV2 (part of IEEE 1901), and present a design weakness in the pairing process as well as a new offline dictionary attack that can be used to compute the main network key efficiently. We evaluated our attacks on 13 widely used PLC devices and found all of them be vulnerable. We provide different countermeasures and discuss their advantages and disadvantages. We responsibly disclosed the vulnerabilities and are currently supporting the vendors in fixing these issues.

Keywords: Power line communications · PLC · Security · HomePlug

1 Introduction

Power line communication (PLC) is an approach to transfer data over power cables. Its main advantage is that already installed cables with a primary use case (power supply) can be used simultaneously for the purpose of data transmission.

PLC can be separated into two classes: narrowband and broadband PLC. Narrowband PLC works on lower frequencies with small data rates and is typically used for industrial approaches, such as reading out meter counts in smart metering systems. Broadband-PLC is used in the industry as well, but is also an interesting alternative to WiFi for in-home communication, especially with the ongoing development of smart home applications.

The most important standard for in-home broadband-PLC is HomePlug. A first version of this standard was introduced in 2001 with a maximum data rate

---

The research was supported by the German state of North Rhine-Westphalia sponsoring the research training group *Human Centered System Security*.

M. Conti et al. (Eds.): ACNS 2020, LNCS 12147, pp. 213–232, 2020.
https://doi.org/10.1007/978-3-030-57878-7_11

of 14 Mbit/s. In 2005, HomePlug AV ("Audio/Video") was published, offering a data rate of up to 200 Mbit/s. The latest version, HomePlug AV2, was developed in cooperation with the standard IEEE 1901 (together with HD-PLC [3], another broadband-PLC approach that is mainly used in Asia) and published in 2010. HomePlug AV2 is widely-used with over 220 million devices deployed worldwide in 2016 [4]. While there is a new specification called HomeGrid (G.hn, ITU-T G.9960),[1] the number of deployed devices is yet still limited and it can be assumed that HomePlug devices will remain to be the most important PLC implementation for the next 5 years.

The power cable network must be considered as a shared medium, especially in larger buildings where many different parties share the same power supply. HomePlug AV2 therefore supports key management and encryption to protect the privacy and confidentiality of each party's data. The encryption algorithm is discussed in Sect. 3.4. We concentrate on the security of the key management procedures, which offer a greater attack surface because by acquiring the network membership key, which is shared between all devices in a logical HomePlug network, an adversary can get access to *all* data shared over this network.

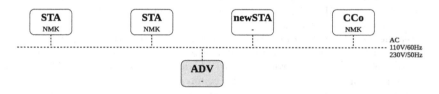

Fig. 1. Simplified architecture of a HomePlug AV2 network. All stations (STA) and the central coordinator (CCo) of a logical network share the same network membership key (NMK). The goal of the adversary (ADV) is to learn the content of the encrypted messages sent over the shared power line cable.

HomePlug stations are typically embedded devices with no or very limited input/output capabilities (e.g., a single pairing button used in one of the key management schemes). This does not impose any restrictions on how to implement symmetric encryption once a key has been established. However, key management techniques are affected by this limitation. Moreover, HomePlug does not use any public key cryptography during key establishment. These limitations imply either the use of trust-on-first-use (TOFU) protocols (method 1 in Sect. 3.2), or connecting one of the embedded devices with a PC/laptop to manually enter configuration data (methods 2 and 3 in Sect. 3.2). Security guarantees can not go beyond these limitations. However, we show that current key management protocols have weaknesses even compared to these limited goals, and could be improved.

It can be expected that the trend towards Smart Home networks will also accelerate the adoption of power line communication, where PLC units are being

---

[1] For the certification status, see https://homegridforum.org/certification-overview/.

directly built into more and more devices such as smart meters, thermostats, smart TVs or in-house surveillance cameras. This enhances the need for robust techniques guaranteeing confidentiality, since in-house communications typically lack the TLS protection used, for example, by modern websites.

Contributions. We make the following contributions:

- We provide technical insights on how confidentiality is defined in the Home-Plug AV2, the most widely used PLC specification (Sect. 3).
- We present the first comprehensive analysis on the security of HomePlug AV2 and show various methods to break confidentiality (Sect. 5).
- We present a novel attack, resulting in efficient offline-cracking and dictionary attacks based on HomePlug AV2 frames captured on the power line up to 500 metres away, whenever a new device enters the network (Sect. 5.2).
- We show that a design flaw in pairing based HomePlug AV2 key exchange can be practically exploited by eavesdroppers and adapt a previously discovered implementation weakness to modern devices (Sect. 5.1 and Sect. 5.3).
- We evaluate the attacks on popular HomePlug AV2 devices and show that all of them are, indeed, vulnerable (Sect. 6).
- We discuss countermeasures and mitigations for HomePlug AV2 implementations as well as the specification (Sect. 7).

Responsible Disclosure. We are working together closely with manufacturers of HomePlug AV2 devices. We reported our findings to the affected vendors and proposed appropriate countermeasures.

2   Related Work

We separated existing research into three categories: description of PLC security standards, actual attacks on HomePlug as well as physical layer countermeasures.

Standards. Regulations and standardization efforts for power line applications in narrowband and broadband systems are provided in [12]. Paruchuri et al. [27] discuss security requirements for power line communications in general. The full specification for HomePlug AV2, including its cryptographic schemes, is given in [18]. The security mechanisms of the predecessing PLC standard, HomePlug AV, are discussed in [24,25,32]. Suomalainen et al. [33] compare HomePlug AV to other standards such as Bluetooth or Wi-Fi Protected Setup (WPS) by presenting a taxonomy of protocols for key establishment. In contrast to our contributions, none of the works mentioned above discuss potential vulnerabilities in the encryption standards such as weaknesses by-design when using the UKE authentication method, leading to attack 1 (see Sect. 5.1).

Attacks. Attacks on HomePlug AV have been proposed in 2010 by Puppe et al. [28] who implemented an online brute-force attack on the (deprecated) DES-based NEK of HomePlug AV devices which allows them to guess 65 keys per second. They conclude that it takes 8.9 billions years to crack the NEK, which is randomly generated and only changes every hour. In contrast to them, we perform an offline dictionary attack against the AES-based NMK of the recent HomePlug AV2 standard (attack 2, see Sect. 5.1). Attacking the NMK instead of the NEK has certain advantages: 1. The NMK is a long-term key (and does not change frequently). 2. The NMK is derived from the NPW in a deterministic way. 3. The NMK has a low entropy in case the user does not choose a strong NPW. In 2014, Tasker [34] discovered that for many HomePlug AV2 devices the DAK is derived from the device's MAC address allowing them to enrol existing STAs into the attacker's network. This attack was found in parallel by Dudek [14] and can be considered as the first practical attack on HomePlug AV2 cryptography – even though it is based on implementation issues. Our third attack (see Sect. 5.3) is based on their work. Our contribution is a re-evaluation on current devices. In 2015, Alves [6] showed a firmware modification attack on a HomePlug AV2 device made by Devolo. Their original goal was to perform a passive sniffing attack on MAC packets containing UKE data in order to obtain the NMK; however, this was not successful. Our attacks instead use firmware modification to sniff the NMK-encrypted management frames, leading to our second attack. Recently Scholz et al. [30] published a security analysis of Devolo HomePlug AV2 devices by reverse engineering their firmware. They do however focus on the application level vulnerabilities such as cross-site scripting (XSS) and DNS rebinding, not on cryptographic issues.

Countermeasures. In 2017, Salem et al. [29] proposed the application of physical layer security within PLC networks by employing a jamming technique to protect against eavesdroppers. In 2018, Baker et al. [7] showed how to use a commercial off-the-shelf (COTS) radio receiver to detect and locate a hidden malicious SAT on the power line based on its leaked radiated emissions.

3   Architecture

The specification of HomePlug AV2 [5] was developed in cooperation with the standardization of IEEE 1901 and first published in 2010 [18], which is the latest version, except for an amendment for Internet of Things (IoT) applications [19].

HomePlug AV2 describes two network layers, a lower physical (PHY) layer and a higher medium access control (MAC) layer. The PHY layer is not relevant for the security analysis in this paper and thus not further described. The security functions of HomePlug AV2 are located within the MAC layer, cryptographic functions (like authentication and encryption) are managed and applied in this layer. A HomePlug device implements both layers. The MAC layer receives payload data from higher layers (e.g., TCP/IP), encapsulates it in MAC frames and sends it over the power line network to another HomePlug device, which in turn processes the data, decapsulates it and forwards it to the higher layers.

3.1 Roles, Passwords and Keys

Figure 1 shows a simplified HomePlug network structure including all roles needed to describe the three key management variants.

HomePlug Network. A HomePlug network is formed by a set of devices (so-called stations, denoted STA) that share the same network membership key (NMK). A station authenticates itself to the other stations in the network by proving knowledge of the NMK (see Sect. 3.2). One of the stations in the network takes on the role of the central coordinator (CCo), which is responsible for certain management tasks, like distributing network encryption keys (NEK) to the other stations, or to provide a new station (newSTA) with the NMK. Authentication is *implicit* using encryption: newSTAs *actively* authenticate themselves to the CCo by the ability to encrypt a randomly chosen value embedded into a known data frame – the authentication results from the correct decryption of this frame, not from the random nonce. All stations *passively* authenticate themselves by being able to decrypt the actual NEK from management messages encrypted with the NMK.

Keys and Passwords. Within a HomePlug AV2 network, different keys and passwords are used. A summary is given in Table 1.

- The network membership key (NMK) is the defining element of any Home-Plug network. It can be established/extended to new stations (newSTA) using three different methods which are described in Sect. 3.2.
- The network encryption key (NEK) is used to encrypt the payload provided by higher layers and applications and is chosen randomly by the CCo. It is valid for roughly one hour (see [18]) and is always distributed by the CCo to all STAs, encrypted with the NMK. Compare Sect. 3.4 for details on the encryption and authentication methods.

Table 1. Passwords, keys and identifiers in HomePlug AV2.

Key/Password	Length	Comment
NPW (network password)	64–512 bit	Chosen by the user
NMK (network membership key)	128 bit	Derived from NPW or chosen by CCo
NID (network ID)	54 bit	Derived from NMK
NEK (network encryption key)	128 bit	Randomly chosen by CCo
TEK (temporary encryption key)	128 bit	Derived during key management
DPW (device password)	128–512 bit	Printed on device
DAK (device access key)	128 bit	Derived from DPW
TEI (terminal equipment id)	8 bit	HomePlug network address

- A temporary encryption key (TEK) is only used in the different authentication methods. The TEK is valid only until the authentication is finished.
- Each station STA has a device access key (DAK) that is directly derived from the device password (DPW). Both DAK and DPW are persistent and should be unique for every STA. According to the HomePlug specification, the DPW shall be chosen randomly for each unique device during the manufacturing process. However, in [14, 34] it was shown that early generations of HomePlug AV devices derived their DAK directly from the MAC address of the device (because the MAC address was used as the DPW). In Sect. 5.3, we discuss resulting attacks based on non-random $DAKs$ which are evaluated for current HomePlug AV2 devices in Sect. 6.3.

NMK Derivation. The NMK can be derived in three different ways.

- The NMK can be derived from a network password (NPW) entered by the user via a user interface station (UIS), a PC which is directly connected to the station via ethernet. The NMK derivation is done using the password-based key derivation function PBKDF1 defined by PKCS #5 v2.0 [21] on the NPW and a constant defined in the IEEE 1901 standard (Sect. 3.2, method 2). See Fig. 2 for the derivation chain of NPW, NMK and NID.
- The NMK can be chosen randomly by the CCo when an initial network is set up by two unassociated devices.

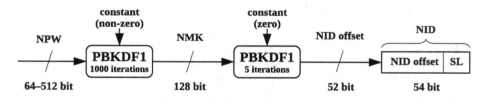

Fig. 2. Derivation of the NMK and a public network identifier (NID). The NID is built by deriving a 52-bit length NID offset from the NMK by using PBKDF1 and applying a 2-bit length security layer (SL), which is zero for HomePlug AV2.

3.2   NMK Key Management

A new station newSTA which intends to join a HomePlug network needs to obtain the NMK. There are three basic methods that can be used by a newSTA to authenticate onto an existing network in order to retrieve this key.

1. Method 1: User pushes the pairing button on the newSTA device and on one of the STA devices within the existing HomePlug network.
2. Method 2: User provides the NPW/NMK of the network to the newSTA.
3. Method 3: User provides the DPW/DAK of the newSTA to the CCo.

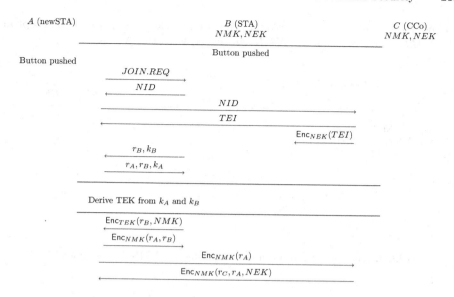

Fig. 3. Authentication method 1: pairing button.

Method 1: Pairing Button. To run authentication method 1 (compare Fig. 3), the user first needs to push the pairing button of a STA B within the existing HomePlug network and the pairing button on the newSTA A. A then starts broadcasting joining requests $JOIN.REQ$ which are ignored by all STAs expect by B. B sends a joining confirmation, including the network identifier NID back to A. The newSTA A can now broadcast an association request which includes the NID. The CCo C responds and includes a network address called terminal equipment identifier (TEI) for newSTA A in cleartext. The CCo informs B about the TEI by sending it encrypted with the NEK.

The STA B now starts the so-called unicast key exchange (UKE) by randomly generating a hash key k_B and a nonce r_B. The newSTA A also generates a different hash key k_A and a nonce r_A. From k_A and k_B, a temporary encryption key TEK is derived. This implements a trust-on-first-use (TOFU) approach to ensure confidentiality of key—clearly an attacker who observes these messages can compromise the security of the HomePlug network. However, an implementation-optional channel estimation can be executed before exchanging the hash keys. Here, the two devices agree on a "tone map" which consists of a unique set of modulation methods and other PHY layer parameters. This approach is used as hash key protection on the signal level; it is expected to be hard to capture the hash keys when implemented.

The TEK is used only once, to protect the confidentiality of the NMK sent by B. Reception of the NMK by A is proven by sending a ciphertext of the two nonces to B. Finally, A requests the current NEK from the CCo C by sending an encrypted nonce (in order to avoid that an attacker convinces A to accept an old NMK), and receives the NEK encrypted with the NMK.

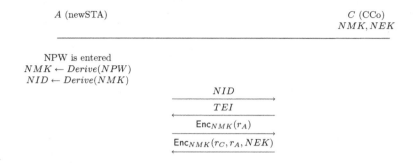

Fig. 4. Authentication method 2: entering the NMK at the newSTA.

Method 2: NPW/NMK. In method 2, a user provides the NPW of the HomePlug network to a newSTA. The newSTA must be connected via Ethernet to a PC where the NPW is entered. After receiving the NPW, the newSTA derives the NMK and the NID, and performs the protocol depicted in Fig. 4.

When the newSTA receives a beacon including a NID that matches the one the newSTA possesses, it broadcasts an association request containing the matching NID. The CCo receives this request and responds with an association confirmation that includes a TEI for the newSTA. The newSTA can now send a get-key request to the CCo, which contains a nonce r_A encrypted with the NMK. If the CCo is able to decrypt this message the authentication of newSTA was successful. The CCo sends a get-key confirmation back to the newSTA, which is encrypted with the NMK and contains the current NEK.

Method 3: DPW/DAK. Method 3 (see Fig. 5) starts with the user entering the DPW of a newSTA via a user interface station (UIS), which is a STA connected to a user interface (typically PC connected via ethernet or Wi-Fi). The UIS derives the DAK from the DPW and broadcasts a set-key request encrypted with the DAK containing the NID and a TEK. Each STA that receives this message shall try to decrypt it with its own DAK, but only the newSTA possesses the entered DAK and thus is able to decrypt the message correctly. The newSTA then sends a set-key confirmation back to the UIS, encrypted with the TEK. The newSTA also sends an association request to the CCo (including the NID) and receives an association confirmation including a TEI. The CCo informs the UIS on the TEI of the newSTA, encrypted with the NEK. The UIS sends another set-key request to the newSTA, again encrypted with the DAK, but this time using the TEI as the network address and containing the NMK and a nonce r_B.

The newSTA confirms this by sending a set-key confirmation, containing the two nonces r_A, r_B encrypted with the NMK. Finally, to obtain the NEK, the newSTA sends a get-key request to the CCo, which in turn sends a get-key confirmation back to the newSTA, including the NEK. Both messages are encrypted with the NMK.

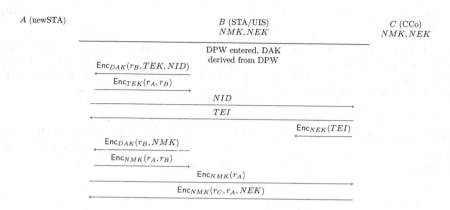

Fig. 5. Authentication method 3: entering the DAK of newSTA.

In method 3, not only unassociated devices must try to decrypt the first message encrypted with a DAK, but also devices that are already part of a Home-Plug network. Using this scheme, an attacker can use authentication method 3 to capture a STA from another HomePlug network in case the attacker is able to discover the DAK of the STA. In Sect. 5.3 we describe an attack discovered by [14,34] who exploited the fact that older generations of HomePlug AV devices derived the DAK directly from the MAC address.

3.3 MAC Frames

All management messages that are relevant for our attacks and all data from higher layers are embedded in MAC frames. Figure 6 describes this frame format. A MAC frame consists of a MAC header and payload data, which embeds either content from higher layers or (encrypted or unencrypted) MAC management messages. Each payload has a payload header and a CRC checksum, which are never encrypted at this layer. Besides cryptographic metadata like the initialization vector, the encrypted payload contains a type field which indicates the type of the data, the data itself, and padding bytes to align the plaintext with the block cipher boundaries.

3.4 MAC Layer Encryption

To encrypt the payload of the frames, HomePlug AV2 uses the Advanced Encryption Standard (AES) in cipher block chaining mode (CBC) with a key size of

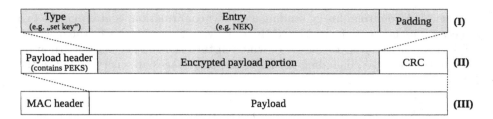

Fig. 6. Structure of a MAC management frame. (I) shows the inner structure of the encrypted payload part containing a frame type, an entry and a padding. This is embedded in (II) in encrypted form with an additional header and a checksum. (III) shows the complete MAC frame given to/by the PHY layer.

128 bits. The used key depends on the purpose of the MAC frame. If the MAC frame transports data from higher layers, the data is encrypted using the NEK. A new NEK is sent as payload encrypted with the NMK.

3.5 PHY Level Encryption

Additionally, another encryption layer at the level of PHY frames is used. If these PHY frames contain data from upper network layers, a constant, known key is used – this key is specified in the HomePlug standard. When a new NEK is sent to a device that is already part of the network (key update), the old NEK is used instead of this constant value.

4   Attacker Model

The main goal of an attacker is to join the HomePlug AV2 network of a victim using the attacker's own device. This can either be achieved by successfully registering the attacker's device as an additional device to the victim's network, or by pulling a device (or all devices) of the victim into the attacker's network.

The attacker's device needs to be plugged into the power grid within a certain physical distance to the HomePlug devices of the victim. Two devices can communicate with each other over the power line up to 500 m away [23].[2] The electric circuit of a house or apartment is typically terminated by an electricity meter. Certain types of meters of older generations (like electromechanical Ferraris meters) implement a choke coil to perform the metering task. Such coils are highly inductive and work as low-pass filters that prevent the high frequencies used by HomePlug to pass them [14]. In such a case, an attacker needs to be able to access the circuit within the victim's household. In some cases however, high frequencies are induced from one power line circuit to another (and therefore into the neighbour's household), for example, if the power cables of two circuits run in parallel (see [9]). Even worse, measurement equipment

---

[2] Note that each STA can act as a repeater, allowing longer distances.

deployed in newer generations of meters, such as electronic meters and modern smart meters, are much less inductive and thus pass high frequencies as used by HomePlug. Thus, with the ongoing smart meter rollout,[3] physical barriers for attackers are strongly decreasing. Compare [35] for a classification of existing metering devices and their properties.

Figure 7 shows a scenario with two houses of which one contains the Home-Plug network of the victim with two devices. The attacker is in a different circuit than the victim. This could be a neighbour in a different apartment within the same house as the victim, an external attacker who has access to a plug socket outside the house (e.g., in the garden), or someone in a neighborhood building.

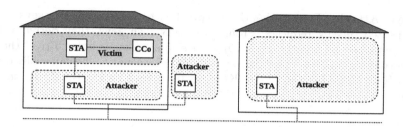

Fig. 7. Attack scenario.

Methodology. We run the attacks on two non-manipulated HomePlug AV2 devices to simulate the HomePlug network of the victim. A third device is used for the attacks themselves. A test setup with only two victims' devices is sufficient because each device in a HomePlug network is authorized to run the authorization methods described in Sect. 3.2 and therefore can act as an entry point for larger networks. The basic requirement of all our attacks is to collect and analyze certain kinds of MAC frames. We achieve this as follows.

- **Sniffer Mode.** On HomePlug devices based on Qualcomm Atheros chipsets, a sniffer mode can be activated [16]. When this mode is enabled, the device encapsulates all received MAC frames within Ethernet frames and makes them available to its own Ethernet interface, such that these frames can be captured (e.g., by using tools like "tcpdump"). However, the payload content of these frames is not revealed, only the header information can be extracted.
- **Device with Root Access.** Following the approach of [6], we were able to get root/superuser access to a HomePlug AV2 device. This allows us to connect to the device via Telnet and run the "tcpdump" command directly on the PLC interface of the device in order to capture MAC frames.

Note that our attacks do *not* require any professional debugging hardware, but instead can be performed by anyone with low-cost equipment (approx. $50).

---

[3] According to a study conducted by GlobalData [17] the global smart meter market is expected to roll out over 588 million units by 2022.

5   Attacks

In this section we present three attacks against the three authentication methods. Attack 1 and 2 target the HomePlug AV2 standard itself, while attack 3 relies on implementation weaknesses.

5.1   Attack 1: Breaking UKE (Pairing Button)

The goal of this attack is to break the pairing-button authentication (method 1, see Sect. 3.2), either by utilizing a passive or an active attack strategy.

Passive Attack. During the UKE, two devices exchange hash keys within unencrypted set-key requests. From these two hash keys, they derive a TEK that is used to encrypt the NMK. If a passive attacker is able to read the two frames that contain both hash keys in this TOFU scenario, she can easily obtain the TEK by applying the public KDF on both keys. Using the TEK, she can also obtain the NMK by decrypting the third frame.

Active Attack. In order to perform an active attack on authentication method 3, the attacker needs to keep her device constantly in pairing mode. This can either be achieved by pushing the button every two minutes manually, or by connecting the device to a UIS and repeatedly sending a MAC management frame which puts the device into pairing mode. This functionality is even implemented in some power line toolkits provided by the PLC device vendors.

5.2   Attack 2: Offline Dictionary Attack on NPW/NMK

The default NPW is "HomePlugAV" for every standard-compatible device [18]. This results in an obviously insecure configuration, because default passwords are publicly known and common to the attacker. In the following part, we assume that the victim is aware of this fact and chooses an individual password. However, studies have shown that users tend to choose weak passwords of which the majority is vulnerable to brute-force attacks in offline cracking scenarios [10,36]. In case a non-random NPW is used, the NMK has a strongly reduced entropy, and thus a dictionary attack on the NPW can be used to determine the NMK.

Our offline attack on the NPW/NMK works as follows. The attacker collects at least one MAC frame containing a set-key request, which is encrypted under the NMK, sent to a device that newly enters the network. The attacker can easily determine if a frame is encrypted under an NMK (and not, e.g., under an NEK) by checking the unencrypted key type field which precedes the encrypted payload (see Fig. 6). The attacker iterates over a dictionary, derives the NMK for each entry and tries to decrypt the MAC frame.

To identify if the correct NMK was found, the attacker can check against 16 bits of known plaintext. A valid decrypted payload has the structure described in Fig. 6. The field "type" contains the type of MAC management frame. The attacker needs to check if it corresponds to a set-key request (value 0x6008). If this is the case, the dictionary entry used for decryption is a candidate for the correct NMK. As the field "type" is 16 bits long (and can occur on four different positions), the probability to find a wrong NMK (i.e., a false positive) by this means is $4 \cdot 2^{-16}$. Hence, with a dictionary size of N entries, a number of $N \cdot 2^{-14}$ false positives is expected after decrypting one frame with the NMKs derived by all dictionary entries. If another frame (encrypted by the same NMK) is collected, the remaining candidates can either be tested and reduced by the same means again (offline) or by trying to authenticate to the network by using the determined candidates. If l frames are collected, an expected number of false positives of $N \cdot 2^{-14l}$ remains. Thus, five frames (i.e., five hours) are sufficient to eliminate false positives for any dictionary of a practically feasible size ($N < 2^{70}$).

5.3   Attack 3: DAK Derived from MAC Address

The DPW must be chosen randomly during the manufacturing process in order to achieve high cryptographic quality of the DAK used for encryption. However, some manufacturers generated the DPW by deriving it from the Ethernet-MAC address allocated to the HomePlug device. By design, Ethernet-MAC addresses are broadcasted unencrypted over the power line and can be obtained using the sniffer mode described in Sect. 4. This weakness was first identified in [34]. An attacker who is able to obtain the Ethernet-MAC address of one or more devices from the victim can derive the DPW on her own and make these device(s) join the attacker's network by using authentication method 3.

6   Evaluation

To evaluate the proposed attacks, we obtained recent in-home PLC devices for all major manufacturers. Evaluation results for the three attacks on 13 HomePlug AV2 devices are given in this section. An overview is depicted in Table 2.

6.1   Attack 1 (UKE)

We were not able to run a passive attack on UKE because with both the sniffer mode and the rooted device it was not possible to record the necessary frames that include the hash keys. The sniffer mode only reveals header information, and on the rooted device, certain types of frames are not captured (cf. [6]).

In order to evaluate the active attack, we used a HomePlug toolkit to constantly keep the attacker's device in pairing mode. We asked a test person to simulate the victim's behavior by starting the pairing mode on one associated and one unassociated device at a randomly chosen point in time. The test person also had to write down on which of the two devices the first button push occurred. We ran the described test ten times for both cases each.

In the case that the button was first pushed on the already *associated* device, our success probability was 1, in all cases we were able to join the victim's

Table 2. Our evaluation shows that all devices are vulnerable to attacks 1 and 2 (i.e., a standard-based vulnerability) while four devices are vulnerable to attack 3 (i.e., an implementation-based vulnerability).

Device	Attack 1	Attack 2	Attack 3
7inova 7HP150	●	●	●
Cudy PL600P	●	●	●
Devolo dLAN 500 WIFI	●	●	○
D-Link DHP-P601AV	●	●	○
FRITZ!Powerline 510E	●	●	○
Intellinet 506564	●	●	●
Netgear PLW1000	●	●	○
Renkforce PL500D	●	●	○
STRONG Powerline 500	●	●	●
Tenda P200	●	●	○
TP-Link TL-PA4010P	●	●	○
TRENDnet Powerline 500 AV	●	●	○
WAVLINK AV500	●	●	○

● vulnerable ○ not vulnerable

network. The reason is that an associated device in pairing mode waits for join requests. During the time until the victim pushes the button of the second device, the first device already received the join request from the attacker's device.

In case the victim (i.e., the test person) pushed the button of the unassociated device first, we achieved a success probability of 1 as well. An unassociated device in pairing mode also listens for join requests of other devices that want to build a new network or join an existing one. After all trials, the attacker's device and the victim's unassociated device built a new network disjoint from the victim's network. Note that at this point the attack is already successful (i.e., the attacker part of the victim's network). However, all further STAs of the victim's existing network are excluded from the new network. It can however be assumed that a user typically will start a new pairing attempt after the user recognizes that the first one apparently did not succeed.

6.2 Attack 2 (NPW)

We generated various dictionaries of different sizes and instructed a test person to: (1) choose an entry from each dictionary; (2) set it as the NPW of a HomePlug network; and (3) register a new device to the network. We captured MAC frames that contain set-key requests (encrypted by the NMK) from this network by using the rooted device, which was not associated to this or any other network. For all different dictionaries, we were successfully able to determine the correct NPW chosen by the test person. Since our rooted device does not capture MAC frames for key updates (because they are encrypted on PHY level individually), we found the NPW by trying to authenticate with each candidate to the network.

The runtime of verifying a single dictionary entry is dominated by the 1000 iterations of the PBKDF1 function used to derive the NMK. Thus, to compute the NMKs of a dictionary with N entries, $1000N$ SHA-1 computations and N AES-128 decryptions need to be performed. On a general-purpose computer 1 000 000 SHA-1 iterations can be computed in less than one second [22]. A dictionary of N entries can thus be (pre-)computed in around $0.001N$ seconds, which is consistent with our experimental results. Performance could further be significantly increased using a GPU-based implementation or FPGA-clusters [15]. Note that the NMKs for all entries of a dictionary can also be precomputed, because HomePlug AV2 uses a constant instead of a salt for PBKDF1.

6.3   Attack 3 (DAK)

We applied the techniques discussed in Sect. 5.3 using the device's sniffer mode. Four of the tested devices were vulnerable to the previously known weaknesses (known since 2014, see [14,34]) in the DAK key derivation. We reviewed to the source code for Qualcomm Atheros based PLC chipsets[4] and noticed counter-measures being implemented in 2015. The DAK derivation was changed from a deterministic algorithm based on the device's Ethernet-MAC address to an algorithm based on /dev/urandom, which can be considered as more secure. It is remarkable that several devices on the market today still use the old algorithm.

7   Countermeasures

In this section we discuss countermeasures and mitigations for the three attacks on HomePlug AV2 on the implementation layer as well as in the specification.

7.1   Attack 1 (UKE)

The only countermeasure against this attack is to avoid using the pairing button method at all. For future implementations of HomePlug AV2 or new standards, an improved pairing method requires a secure channel between the two devices in order to perform the authentication using the pairing button. A secure channel could be established by plugging the devices into each other or by connecting them with an Ethernet cable. A drawback is that devices in operation might not have any unused plug socket or Ethernet interfaces and thus ongoing network operations must be stopped temporarily in order to perform this method.

---

[4] Atheros, *Open Powerline Toolkit*, https://github.com/qca/open-plc-utils.

7.2 Attack 2 (NPW)

Dictionary attacks do not work if a *secure random password* is applied (e.g., by using a password generator). To achieve the full entropy of a 128-bit key, a password of 22 symbols including uppercase letters, lowercase letters and decimal numbers is sufficient (because $(26 + 26 + 10)^{22} = 62^{22} > 2^{128}$).

In order to allocate an NPW for the PLC devices, the user needs to install a HomePlug AV2 toolkit first. If the user wants to build a new HomePlug network with n devices, the user first generates a secure password as described above. Afterwards they plug the first device into a plug socket and connect it via Ethernet cable to the computer where the toolkit is installed. Then the user can utilize the toolkit to set the NPW of the single device to the generated password and plugs off the device. The user then repeats this approach for the remaining $n - 1$ devices each.

Note that the user does not need to remember the password. In case a new device shall join the existing network, the user generates a new password and sets it to the existing HomePlug network by connecting his computer to only one of the devices in the network and using the toolkit to allocate the NPW to all n devices at once. Afterwards he connects the computer using an Ethernet cable with the new device and sets the new password here. Now all $n + 1$ devices possess the same NMK and form a HomePlug network.

On the implementation level of the HomePlug AV2 toolkit, protection could be achieved by integrating a password generator and only allowing the user to set NPWs generated in this manner.

7.3 Attack 3 (DAK)

Because this attack is based on implementation weaknesses, countermeasures are on the implementation level. The DPW must be chosen randomly and independently from the Ethernet-MAC address during the manufacturing process. Note that this attack is even successful if authentication methods 1 or 2 are used, because it allows to pull the victim's device out of an existing network and into the attacker's network. In other words: if the victim's devices are vulnerable to attack 3, there is no way for the victim to establish a secure network.

8 Additional Findings

During our security analysis we discovered further weaknesses which do not target the cryptography of HomePlug AV2 itself but are noteworthy to mention because they affect the real-world security of PLC implementations in the wild.

8.1 Firmware Modification

The dangers of malicious firmware updates are well known and have been discussed, for example, in [1,13]. Of the 13 tested PLC devices, eight allow users to perform firmware updates. As already discovered by [6], the *Devolo dLAN 500 WIFI* does not use digital signatures to verify integrity and authenticity of firmware images, but instead applies a simple cyclic redundancy check (CRC) check. This vulnerability allowed us to modify the firmware to run a Telnet daemon with an empty root password once the device had been rebooted. Getting root access to a PLC device is critical as it allows an attacker to completely take over the device and establish a persistent threat within the victims internal network which can be used, for example, to act as a packet sniffer or to escalate to other network components. Such attacks are a common attack vector and this specific attack was already found by [6]. However, they assume that the attacker has been within the victim's internal network to upload malicious firmware and, thereby, able to compromise the device. We extend this attack to the scenario of a web attacker (i.e., any malicious website visited by the victim) using CSRF, as explained below. Further PLC devices may also be vulnerable to firmware modification attacks; their analysis can be considered as future work.

8.2 NMK Change via CSRF

Of the 13 tested PLC devices, only two run an embedded web server, which allows to configure the device over HTTP: The *FRITZ!Powerline 510E* and the *Devolo dLAN 500 WIFI*. We tested both devices for cross-site request forgery (CSRF)—a well-known weakness which allows an attacker's website to trigger a HTTP request to a target website using JavaScript, HTML forms or image tags, resulting in certain actions being performed on the target website [31]. While none of the devices applied CSRF tokens – the most popular countermeasure against CSRF [8] – the *FRITZ!Powerline 510E* passed the session ID as a URL query parameter, which is generally considered as a bad security practice (see [26]), but in this case also prevents against CSRF. However, the *Devolo dLAN 500 WIFI* allows to set the NPW/NMK via the web interface without any CSRF protection, leaving the PLC network open to exploitation by a web attacker [2]. The attack is outlined as follows: 1. The attacker sets an NPW/NMK for her own PCL device plugged into the power line; 2. The attacker lures the victim onto her malicious website – the typical web attacker scenario; and 3. Using JavaScript (see Listing 1), a POST request to the victim's internal PLC device is triggered, which changes the device's NPW/NMK to the attacker's key. Note that the new NMK is automatically spread to all other associated PLC devices, resulting in the victim's devices now sharing a HomePlug network with the attacker.

```
1  var req = new XMLHttpRequest();
2  req.open('POST', 'http://devolo-123/cgi-bin/htmlmgr');
3  req.withCredentials = true;
4  req.setRequestHeader('Content-Type','application/x-www-form-urlencoded');
5  req.send(':sys:HomePlug.Local.Device{Index=1}.Commands.AVLNPassword=AttackerPasswd');
```

Listing 1. CSRF attack setting a new NPW for the HomePlug network.

Obtaining the correct IP address or hostname for the device is not an obstacle. First, the hostname is always "`devolo-nnn`" (with **n** being a numeric value), so an attacker can simply send up to 1000 requests to guess the correct hostname. Second, using WebRTC [20], which is supported by all modern browsers, the victim's internal IP address can be obtained using JavaScript and based on this knowledge, requests can be send to all remaining 253 IP addresses in the victim's subnet. We tested both propagation variants and found them to take only a few seconds in modern browsers.

Once part of the same network, the attacker can upload her modified firmware to compromise the device, as previously described. However, she can also directly send the malicious firmware via CSRF. This is important to note, as it allows arbitrary websites to gain root access and install persistent malware on the PLC device, without being in the internal network or on the same power line.

Devolo has confirmed the issue and is working on a fix to be applied.

9   Future Work

A security analysis as we performed in this work needs to be conducted for all relevant narrowband-PLC standards. One problem is that devices that work according to these specifications are not as easy to obtain as PLC devices for the purpose of in-home communication. The same holds for devices which follow the IEEE 1901 standard but are designed for industrial purposes.

An important upcoming standard for broadband-PLC is ITU-T G.9960 ("HomeGrid", "G.hn"). Its security layer (ITU-T G.9961) is separated because it is also used for other communication technologies (e.g., Visual Light Communications, VLC). This security layer offers pairing-button authentication as well, but uses the Diffie-Hellman key exchange based on password authentication (password-authenticated key exchange, PAK [11]). A security analysis of this standard will thus become more important soon.

10   Conclusion

Given that: 1. the increasing popularity of LAN-over-power-line and 2. the power line as a shared medium it is important to gain insights into security and privacy aspects of power line communication. In this work we presented the results of our structured analysis of HomePlug AV2 – currently the most widely used PLC standard. We systematically analyzed and evaluated attacks against all three authentication methods provided by HomePlug AV2. Especially, we presented a novel attack which allows for efficiently running an offline-dictionary attack on the main key of the power line network. We show effective countermeasures to protect against our attacks. We provided methods for end-users to securely set up HomePlug AV2 networks despite the described security flaws of the specification. Additionally, our results provide recommendations to PLC device manufacturers and standardization bodies on how to mitigate the attacks, both on the implementation layer as well as in future PLC standards.

References

1. Adelstein, F., Stillerman, M., Kozen, D.: Malicious code detection for open firmware. In: Proceedings of 18th Annual Computer Security Applications Conference, pp. 403–412. IEEE (2002)
2. Akhawe, D., Barth, A., Lam, P., Mitchell, J., Song, D.: Towards a formal foundation of web security. In: 2010 23rd IEEE Computer Security Foundations Symposium, pp. 290–304. IEEE (2010)
3. Alliance, H.P.: IEEE 1901 HD-PLC Complete technical overview (2012). http://www.hd-plc.org/modules/about/hdplc.html
4. Alliance, H.P.: HomePlug AV Specification (2014)
5. Alliance, H.P.: HomePlug Powerline Networking Technology Hits Maturation as Global Broadband Standard (2016)
6. Alves, F.: Vulnerability discovery in power line communications. Ph.D. thesis, Universidade de Lisboa (2015)
7. Baker, R., Martinovic, I.: EMPower: detecting malicious power line networks from EM emissions. In: Janczewski, L.J., Kutylowski, M. (eds.) SEC 2018. IAICT, vol. 529, pp. 108–121. Springer, Cham (2018). https://doi.org/10.1007/978-3-319-99828-2_8
8. Barth, A., Jackson, C., Mitchell, J.: Robust defenses for cross-site request forgery. In: Proceedings of the 15th ACM Conference on Computer and Communications Security, pp. 75–88. ACM (2008)
9. Berger, L.T., Schwager, A., Pagani, P., Schneider, D.: MIMO Power Line Communications: Narrow and Broadband Standards, EMC, and Advanced Processing. CRC Press Inc., Boca Raton (2014)
10. Bonneau, J.: The science of guessing: analyzing an anonymized corpus of 70 million passwords. In: 2012 IEEE Symposium on Security and Privacy, pp. 538–552. IEEE (2012)
11. Boyko, V., MacKenzie, P., Patel, S.: Provably secure password-authenticated key exchange using Diffie-Hellman. In: Preneel, B. (ed.) EUROCRYPT 2000. LNCS, vol. 1807, pp. 156–171. Springer, Heidelberg (2000). https://doi.org/10.1007/3-540-45539-6_12
12. Cano, C., Pittolo, A., Malone, D., Lampe, L., Tonello, A., Dabak, A.: State of the art in power line communications: from the applications to the medium. IEEE J. Sel. Areas Commun. 34(7), 1935–1952 (2016)
13. Cui, A., Costello, M., Stolfo, S.: When firmware modifications attack: a case study of embedded exploitation. In: 20th Annual Network and Distributed System Security Symposium, NDSS 2013, San Diego, California, USA, 24–27 February 2013. The Internet Society (2013)
14. Dudek, S.: HomePlugAV PLC: practical attacks and backdooring (2015)
15. Dürmuth, M., Güneysu, T., Kasper, M., Paar, C., Yalcin, T., Zimmermann, R.: Evaluation of standardized password-based key derivation against parallel processing platforms. In: Foresti, S., Yung, M., Martinelli, F. (eds.) ESORICS 2012. LNCS, vol. 7459, pp. 716–733. Springer, Heidelberg (2012). https://doi.org/10.1007/978-3-642-33167-1_41
16. Qualcomm Atheros via Github: Qualcomm Atheros Open Powerline Toolkit (2018). https://github.com/qca/open-plc-utils
17. GlobalData: Smart Meters, Update 2018 - Global Market Size, Competitive Landscape, Key Country Analysis, and Forecast to 2022 (2018)

18. IEEE Standards Association and Others: IEEE standard for broadband over power line networks: medium access control and physical layer specifications. IEEE Std (2010), 1–1586 (2010)
19. IEEE Standards Association and Others: IEEE standard for broadband over power line networks: medium access control and physical layer specifications - amendment 1: enhancement for internet of things applications. IEEE Std (2010), 1–118 (2019)
20. Jennings, C., Narayanan, A., Burnett, D., Bergkvist, A.: WebRTC 1.0: Real-time Communication Between Browsers (2014)
21. Kaliski, B.: PKCS #5: password-based cryptography specification version 2.0, September 2000. http://tools.ietf.org/rfc/rfc2898.txt, rFC2898
22. Latinov, L.: MD5, SHA-1, SHA-256 and SHA-512 speed performance (2018)
23. Matchen, M.: What Is Powerline Technology? (2015). https://www.tomshardware.com/reviews/network-switch-guide,4047.html
24. Newman, R., Gavette, S., Yonge, L., Anderson, R.: Protecting domestic power-line communications. In: Proceedings of the Second Symposium on Usable Privacy and Security, pp. 122–132. ACM (2006)
25. Newman, R., Yonge, L., Gavette, S., Anderson, R.: HomePlug AV security mechanisms. In: 2007 IEEE International Symposium on Power Line Communications and its Applications, pp. 366–371. IEEE (2007)
26. OWASP: Information exposure through query strings in URL (2017). https://www.owasp.org/index.php/Information_exposure_through_query_strings_in_url
27. Paruchuri, V., Durresi, A., Ramesh, M.: Securing powerline communications. In: 2008 IEEE International Symposium on Power Line Communications and its Applications, pp. 64–69. IEEE (2008)
28. Puppe, A., Vanderauwera, J., Bartels, D.: HomePlug Security (2010)
29. Salem, A., Hamdi, K., Alsusa, E.: Physical layer security over correlated lognormal cooperative power line communication channels. IEEE Access 5, 13909–13921 (2017)
30. Scholz, R., Wressnegger, C.: Security analysis of Devolo HomePlug devices. In: Proceedings of the 12th European Workshop on Systems Security, pp. 7:1–7:6. ACM (2019)
31. Shiflett, C.: Security Corner: Cross-Site Request Forgeries. Shiflett.org (2004). http://shiflett.org/articles/cross-site-request-forgeries
32. Sunguk, L.: Security issues of power line multi-home networks for seamless. Data Transmission (2011)
33. Suomalainen, J., Valkonen, J., Asokan, N.: Standards for security associations in personal networks: a comparative analysis. Int. J. Secur. Netw. 4(1–2), 87–100 (2009)
34. Tasker, B.: Infiltrating a Network via Powerline (HomePlug AV) Adapters (2014). https://www.bentasker.co.uk/documentation/security/282-infiltrating-a-network-via-powerline-homeplugav-adapters
35. Tiwari, A.: Electricity meters' reading comparison: electromechanical, electronic and smart meters (2016)
36. Ur, B., Bees, J., Segreti, S., Bauer, L., Christin, N., Cranor, L.: Do users' perceptions of password security match reality? In: Proceedings of the 2016 CHI Conference on Human Factors in Computing Systems, pp. 3748–3760. ACM (2016)

Watching the Weak Link into Your Home: An Inspection and Monitoring Toolkit for TR-069

Abridged Conference Version

Maximilian Hils$^{(\boxtimes)}$ and Rainer Böhme

University of Innsbruck, Innsbruck, Austria
{maximilian.hils,rainer.boehme}@uibk.ac.at

Abstract. TR-069 is a standard for the remote management of end-user devices by service providers. Despite being implemented in nearly a billion devices, almost no research has been published on the security and privacy aspects of TR-069. The first contribution of this paper is a study of the TR-069 ecosystem and techniques to inspect TR-069 communication. We find that the majority of analyzed providers do not use recommended security measures, such as TLS. Second, we present a TR-069 honeyclient to both analyze TR-069 behavior of providers and test configuration servers for security vulnerabilities. We find that popular open-source configuration servers use insecure methods to authenticate clients. TR-069 implementations based on these servers expose, for instance, their users' internet telephony credentials. Third, we develop components for a distributed system to continuously monitor activities in providers' TR-069 deployments. Our setup consists of inexpensive hardware sensors deployed on customer premises and centralized log collectors. We perform real-world measurements and find that the purported security benefits of TR-069 are not realized as providers' firmware update processes are lacking.

Keywords: TR-069 · CWMP · ACS · Customer Premises Equipment · Remote management · User privacy · Monitoring · Honeyclient

1 Introduction

TR-069 is a technical specification that defines a protocol for the remote management of end-user devices by (internet) service providers. Published by the Broadband Forum, it is also endorsed by a variety of other initiatives (e.g. the DVB Project and the WiMAX Forum). TR-069 is implemented in nearly a billion residential gateways, set-top boxes and other home broadband equipment [31].

Full Version: https://arxiv.org/abs/2001.02564.
Source Code Repository: https://github.com/mhils/tr069.

ⓒ Springer Nature Switzerland AG 2020
M. Conti et al. (Eds.): ACNS 2020, LNCS 12147, pp. 233–253, 2020.
https://doi.org/10.1007/978-3-030-57878-7_12

While TR-069 simplifies device setup for consumers, it provides service providers with unrestricted access to the managed device. This may compromise users' privacy and security expectations in a number of ways: First, service providers can read and write any data on controlled devices. They can query routers for connected devices, obtain television viewing statistics from set-top boxes, or install new firmware. These operations are generally opaque to users and the protocol does not specify a way to seek users' consent. Second, a configuration server can identify connected users and provide tailored firmware to individuals of interest. Providers may be coerced to help authorities to pivot into otherwise protected networks. Third, the configuration server used by a service provider to control TR-069 clients is a single point of failure. If compromised, an attacker gains control over all connected devices. Fourth, TR-069 devices accept HTTP requests on port 7547 in order to initiate sessions. This exposes them to direct attacks.

Arguably, TR-069's ubiquity and opaqueness make it an attractive platform for privacy-infringing data collection, attacks by criminals, or targeted surveillance. For example, attacks on TR-069 devices have contributed to the quick growth of the Mirai botnet and caused widespread internet outages in Germany in 2016 [3]. Even though internet-wide scanning has shown that port 7547 is the third most exposed port on the internet [4,9], very little research has been published on the protocol's security. So far, researchers have primarily pointed out specific implementation vulnerabilities in clients and configuration servers [27,29]. This paper takes a broader look at the TR-069 ecosystem from a security and privacy perspective.

We will first give a security-centric overview of TR-069 in Sect. 2. As the first contribution of this paper, we discuss different methods to inspect TR-069 connections and compare their practical feasibility in Sect. 3. We extract TR-069 configurations from firmware update packages and search them for TR-069 credentials. We find that the majority of providers do not follow recommended security practices.

In Sect. 4, we introduce an open-source TR-069 client that can be used to analyze configuration servers. By emulating a real TR-069 device, the client can monitor the behavior of different service providers over time. This client can also be used to find security vulnerabilities in configuration servers. To demonstrate this application, we test two open-source configuration servers with our client. We find that both do not authenticate clients securely and can be tricked into exposing other users' credentials. As the issues we uncover are not specific to the individual implementations, our findings point to widespread issues regarding client authentication in the TR-069 landscape.

Looking at the implementation of TR-069 in practice, it is interesting to compare how different service providers make use of the protocol. Section 5 presents a sensor software to monitor individual TR-069 devices for privacy infringements and other undesired actions. We perform measurements of real-world TR-069 traffic over a period of twelve months. We do not observe privacy violations by

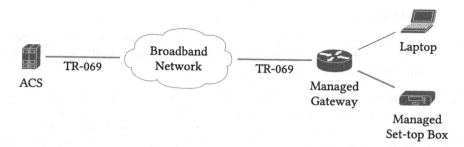

Fig. 1. Basic TR-069 network topology.

providers, but we find that the purported security benefits of TR-069, such as the automated deployment of security updates, are not realized.

We discuss our findings in Sect. 6, review related work in Sect. 7, and conclude in Sect. 8. Given the sensitive nature of TR-069 communications, we document our approach to research ethics and privacy in Appendix A in the full version of this paper.

2 Preliminaries

TR-069 is a technical report that defines an application layer protocol for the remote management of end-user routers, modems, set-top boxes and other Customer Premises Equipment (CPE) [5]. It specifies generic methods that can be applied to manage different types of devices. Additional technical reports specify the data models for concrete device classes or services [30].

TR-069 was initially published in 2004 by the Broadband Forum[1] as a means to configure home routers and business internet gateways, but has since then evolved to cover Voice over IP (VoIP) products, video set-top boxes, network attached storage, femto cells, and other networked products [18]. TR-069 is endorsed by other initiatives, such as the Digital Video Broadcasting consortium and the WiMAX Forum. While the protocol defined in TR-069 is formally entitled *CPE WAN Management Protocol (CWMP)*, both terms are used interchangeably in practice and we will stick with the better known TR-069. Unless otherwise noted, this paper refers to TR-069 Amendment 6 (CWMP Version 1.4) published in April 2018 [5].

In the following, we first describe the goals of TR-069 and then provide a technical introduction to the protocol.

---

[1] The Broadband Forum is a non-profit industry consortium that defines standards for broadband networking. Members include internet and telecommunications service providers as well as device vendors.

2.1 TR-069 Goals

On a functional level, TR-069 covers a wide range of use cases for network providers. We briefly recall the key features to give readers a better understanding of TR-069 usage in practice.

"Zero-Touch" Installation. TR-069 is often used for auto-provisioning of new devices, which simplifies the setup procedure for new customers and thereby reduces support costs. Customers are provided with a modem or router that just needs to be connected to the network. It automatically contacts the provider's Auto Configuration Server (ACS) to receive its configuration (e.g. VoIP credentials).

Firmware Maintenance. Providers can deploy firmware updates to their customers without requiring user interaction.

Diagnostics for Customer Troubleshooting. Customer service agents can remotely access diagnostic information and modify configuration settings of TR-069 devices to help users with troubleshooting their network.

Configuration and Activation of New Services. TR-069 can be used to remotely (de-)activate services or features on a customer's device. For example, some providers charge a monthly fee for activating the router's wireless module. Wireless network functionality is activated remotely via TR-069 when a customer subscribes to the service.

Each of TR-069's use cases comes with its own set of security and privacy challenges. While TR-069 introduces elements that could potentially improve user security (e.g. automated firmware updates), we suppose that its adoption is primarily motivated by prospective reductions in service and support costs.

2.2 TR-069 Protocol

Here we provide a short introduction to the TR-069 protocol. As the official specification counts 276 pages (excluding data models), we do not aim to provide a comprehensive overview but focus on the parts relevant for this paper. We assume the reader to be familiar with TCP/IP, TLS and HTTP.

Fundamentally, TR-069 describes the interaction between an Auto Configuration Server (ACS) and a TR-069 client (hereinafter "client"). Figure 1 shows an example topology: TR-069 communication usually happens only within a provider's network, with the client being located on customer premises and the ACS being part of the service provider's infrastructure. However, some vendors also offer configuration servers as Software-as-a-Service in the cloud

On a high level, connections follow the structure shown in Fig. 2. A TR-069 session is always initiated by the client, which establishes a TCP connection with the ACS. Second, the connection is optionally secured using TLS. Third, the client sends a series of commands to the server. Finally, the ACS sends a series of commands to the client before the connection is terminated. We discuss each step in more detail below.

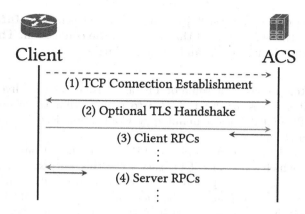

Fig. 2. High-level view on a TR-069 session.

ACS Discovery. Before making first contact with an ACS, a client needs to learn the ACS URL it is supposed to contact. TR-069 defines three mechanisms for this: The use of a preconfigured ACS URL, configuration via a LAN-side protocol (e.g. a router web interface or TR-064 [16]), or configuration via DHCP options 43 and 125 during IP address assignment.

It is noteworthy that the ACS URL determines whether the connection will be secured using TLS. While the TR-069 specification recommends the use of TLS, it is not a mandatory part of the protocol. Therefore, control over the ACS URL can be used to downgrade the security of TR-069 sessions. In particular, the DHCP discovery mechanism is prone to man-in-the-middle attacks unless otherwise secured [5, p. 34].

Connection Establishment. As the first step of a TR-069 session, the client opens a TCP connection to the hostname specified in the configured ACS URL. TR-069 sessions are always initiated by the client as a reaction to one or multiple events. Among others,[2] a connection may be initiated for the following reasons:

- **Bootstrap**: Indicates that the session was established due to first-time client installation or a change to the ACS URL. The ACS transmits initial configuration data to the client.
- **Periodic**: Indicates that the session was established on a periodic interval, e.g., once every 24 h.
- **Value Change**: Indicates that the value of one or more monitored parameters has been modified.
- **Connection Request**: Indicates that the session is a reaction to a Connection Request from the ACS (see below).

---

[2] For a comprehensive listing of non-vendor-specific event types, see [5, p. 65].

After successful connection establishment, the client sends an `Inform` message which indicates the event type(s) that triggered the connection. This allows the ACS to learn the client's intent and act accordingly.

Connection Requests. For some of TR-069's use cases (e.g. live diagnostics, see Sect. 2.1) it is necessary for the ACS to request that the client contacts it immediately. TR-069 defines a mandatory Connection Request mechanism to provide this functionality.

The basic mechanism is a simple HTTP GET request from the ACS to the TR-069 client, which runs an HTTP server for this purpose. The use of TLS for the connection request is prohibited by the specification. To prevent denial-of-service attacks, HTTP digest authentication is used to verify the validity of the request. Connection requests act as a trigger only: The client will connect back to the configured ACS URL, which cannot be modified by the connection request.

A major limitation of the basic connection request mechanism is that the ACS must be able to reach the client over HTTP. While this was negligible when TR-069 was introduced for routers and gateways, it does not work for endpoints which reside behind firewalls or in (IPv4) networks with network address translation. To accommodate for these devices, TR-069 Amendment 5 introduces an XMPP-based mechanism, which supersedes the previously introduced STUN tunneling in TR-069 Annex G [5]. In short, there are multiple methods the ACS can use to instruct the client to contact it immediately. All mechanisms only serve as a trigger for a client-initiated TR-069 session. The client will always connect to the configured ACS URL for the actual TR-069 session.

While all approaches increase the attack surface, the basic connection request mechanism is particularly interesting to attackers for its public facing web server on the client. The connection request server listens on port 7547 by default, which is the third most publicly exposed port in the IPv4 address space (after ports 80 and 443, before port 22) [4,9].

Connection Security. If the ACS URL scheme is HTTPS, the TR-069 session must be secured using TLS before any messages are being sent. However, the specification imposes nonstandard restrictions on the use of TLS, which may raise security concerns:

Hostname Matching. The ACS hostname must be validated against the certificate's Common Name, even though Common Name matching has been deprecated since HTTPS was first introduced in 2000 in favor of Subject Alternative Names [21]. TR-069 describes a simple – yet nonstandard – exact string matching method, which is not available in major TLS libraries and must be implemented manually to fully comply with the specification.

Root Certificate Set. The client must validate the ACS certificate against one or multiple root certificates. TR-069 does not discuss which root certificates should be included on a device. In practice, this allows providers to either limit trust to internal Certificate Authorities (CAs) or to rely on the internet public key infrastructure and use a broader public CA set, such as Mozilla's CA bundle.

The latter approach can lead to degraded security as all major browsers enforce additional constraints on their trusted root certificates (e.g. restricting the certificate issuance date for specific CAs), which are not reflected in the CA file [26]. Additionally, as public CA sets change over time, the provider must update the CA file. TR-069 does not discuss or mandate any form of certificate revocation.

Protocol Downgrades. TR-069 states that "if the ACS does not support the version with which the CPE establishes the connection, it might be necessary to negotiate an earlier TLS 1.x version, or even SSL 3.0" [5, p. 41]. While the specification states that TLS 1.2 *should* be used, it is very possible that some clients will in practice be susceptible to downgrade attacks to SSL 3.0.

Client Certificates. The use of client certificates to identify a client is optional. Client certificates can be unique per device or shared between devices. In the latter case, the specification *recommends* – and does not require – to additionally authenticate the client using HTTP basic or digest authentication.

Notwithstanding these issues, TR-069's major weakness with regard to connection confidentiality and integrity is that the use of TLS is optional. This is particularly severe as the ACS URL can often be reconfigured by various means (see Sect. 2.2), which allows an attacker to downgrade the protocol to plaintext. If TLS is used, the use of nonstandard certificate verification methods, missing guidance on root CA selection, proposed SSL 3.0 support, and shared client certificates may also degrade the security of the connection to a point where man-in-the-middle attacks are feasible.

Authentication and Initial Inform. By definition, the first message of every TR-069 session is an `Inform` command sent by the client (see the extended version of this paper for an example). The initial message identifies the device, lists the events that caused the connection, and informs the ACS about configuration parameters, such as the current public IP address.

If the client has not used a client certificate to authenticate itself during the TLS handshake, TR-069 mandates that the ACS must require HTTP authentication. The specification *recommends* to use a combination of organization identifier and device serial number as the username and states that clients *should* use unique per-device passwords. Clients *must* use HTTP digest authentication for plain HTTP connections, but also *must* support HTTP basic authentication, which is *recommended* if the connection is secured using TLS. If clients erroneously handle basic authentication challenges over unencrypted HTTP, a man-in-the-middle attacker can exfiltrate the client's username and password. We discuss the security of shared credentials in Sect. 3.3.

Commands. After the initial `Inform`, TR-069 defines further commands that can be used for the communication between client and ACS. At the minimum, a conforming ACS must support the `Inform`, `GetRPCMethods` and `Transfer-Complete` commands. For clients, the requirements are more extensive. A client must support `GetRPCMethods`, `GetParameterNames`, `Get-/SetParameter-Values`, `Get-/SetParameterAttributes`, `Add-/DeleteObject`, `Reboot`, and `Download`. Additionally, TR-069 defines optional commands as well as the ability to specify vendor extensions. We describe commands that are interesting from a security and privacy perspective in the extended version of this paper.

Using the `Download` command, an attacker has complete control over devices as new firmware can be uploaded that circumvents any potential access restrictions. Even without a special firmware, TR-069 grants network providers access to valuable data on their customers, ranging from detailed information on devices connected to a router to television viewing statistics. These capabilities for data collection are not an inadvertent byproduct of generic commands. Collection of audience statistics is an explicit part of TR-135, which specifies the TR-069 data model for set-top boxes [17]. Given the sensitivity of the data at hand, it is reasonable to take a look at which parameters providers regularly access. In the next section, we will discuss how TR-069 communication can be intercepted and inspected.

3   TR-069 Inspection

Many TR-069 devices are embedded systems which do not provide immediate means to analyze their inner workings. Our first contribution to research is a systematic exploration of three methods that can be used to inspect TR-069 traffic: man-in-the-middle attacks, client reconfiguration, and client emulation.

3.1   Man-In-The-Middle Attacks

When locked-down devices do not provide any means for inspection, researchers can resort to the analysis of network traffic. If communication is protected with TLS, an analyst needs to mount a man-in-the-middle attack against the client, e.g. by using mitmproxy [8]. While this method relies on the availability of trusted certificate keys or the presence of security vulnerabilities on the device, previous research has shown that this is often the case for non-browser TLS implementations (see Sect. 7). Next, we study the use of TLS by service providers and then discuss the practical traffic interception of internet gateways.

Use of TLS by Service Providers. Recall from Sect. 2.2 that TLS is optional for TR-069. Hence, it is interesting to examine how many providers follow the recommendation to use TLS [5, p. 40] in practice. In search of a data source, we

Country	Provider	Configuration					Firmware			Verification		
		NOHC	TLS	VER	PIN	CRT	2016	2017	2018	PUB	TOR	MAIL
Austria	A1		•	•		•	•	•	•		•	•
	IKB							•	•			•
	UPC								•			•
	highspeed.vol.at	•	•				•	•	•			•
Belgium	BILLI							•	•			•
	Dommel						•	•	•			•
	EDPNET	•					•	•	•			•
	Join Experience		•	•				•	•			•
	TV Vlaanderen		•					•	•	•		•
	Telesat		•						•			•
Croatia	H1 Telekom		•						•			•
Cyprus	Cyta Internet Home	•							•			•
	MTN								•			•
Denmark	Telenor		•				•	•	•			•
Estonia	Elion						•	•	•		•	•
Finland	ANVIA						•	•	•			•
Germany	1&1	•	•				•	•	•	•		•
	BayernDSL	•					•	•	•			•
	Be-Converged						•	•	•	•		•
	EWE (ALL-IP)	•	•	•			•	•	•			•
	EWE (DSL)	•	•				•	•	•			•
	GMX	•	•				•	•	•	•		•
	Kabel Deutschland	•					•	•	•	•		•
	KielNET	•						•	•			•
	M-net	•	•	•	•		•	•	•			•
	NetAachen							•	•			•
	NetCologne								•			•
	QUiX	•					•	•	•			•
	Telekom	•	•	•		•	•	•	•			•
	Vodafone (DSL)	•	•	•			•	•	•		•	•
	Vodafone (LTE)	•	•	•				•	•		•	•
	WOBCOM	•						•	•			•
	htp (DSL)	•					•	•	•			•
	htp (Fiber)	•						•	•			•
	inexio	•					•	•	•			•
	o2	•		•			•	•	•			•
	osnatel (ALL-IP)	•	•	•			•	•	•			•
	osnatel (DSL)	•	•				•	•	•			•
	swb AG (ALL-IP)	•	•	•			•	•	•			•
	swb AG (DSL)	•	•				•	•	•			•
	symbox	•	•				•	•	•			•
Italy	EOLO						•	•	•			•
	Infostrada						•	•	•			•
	Lineacom							•	•	•		•
	Planetel							•	•	•		•
	Raiffeisen							•	•			•
	Telecom Italia	•	•	•	•		•	•	•			•
	Wind Business						•		•			•
	mc-link		•	•				•	•			•
Luxembourg	Join Experience		•	•			•	•	•	•		•
	Luxembourg Online	•	•	•				•	•	•		•
	Orange Luxembourg	•	•	•				•	•			•
	Post Luxembourg							•	•			•
	Tango							•	•			•
	Visual Online		•					•	•			•
Netherlands	EDPNET	•						•	•			•
	Fiber Nederland							•	•	•		•
	Kliksafe (DSL)							•	•			•
	Kliksafe (Fiber)	•						•	•			•
	Scarlet / Stipte		•					•	•			•
	Solcon							•	•			•
	XS4ALL							•	•			•
New Zealand	2degrees		•	•				•	•			•
Poland	Plast-Com							•	•			•
Spain	VozTelecom	•					•	•	•	•		•
Switzerland	Sunrise						•	•	•			•
# Total	60	22	31	16	2	2	37	50	60	11	4	60

NOHC: Firmware does not contain hardcoded credentials; **TLS:** Client should use TLS; **VER:** Client should verify server certificate; **PIN:** The number of trusted root certificates is reduced; **CRT:** Use of a (shared) client certificate; **2016-2018:** Configuration has been found in firmware images released in the respective year; **PUB:** The ACS is reachable from the public internet; **TOR:** The ACS is reachable from selected Tor exit nodes; **MAIL:** Provider has been informed of results and did not rebut findings.

Fig. 3. TR-069 provider configurations

observed that several aftermarket routers sold in Europe[3] prompt users for their provider's name during setup and use this information to configure basic connection parameters of the device, including its TR-069 settings. These settings are also contained in the firmware update packages that many router manufacturers make available on the internet. We systematically downloaded current and outdated firmware images released between 2016 and 2018 for various DSL, cable, and fiber modems as well as routers, extracted the file systems, and searched them for TR-069 credentials. However, as there is substantial overlap between the providers supported by aftermarket routers, we are confident that we have a comprehensive coverage of providers in the relevant markets.

The results of this analysis are shown in Fig. 3. Overall, we obtained 471 TR-069 configurations representing 60 internet service providers. Our sample set likely over-represents European countries (Germany, in particular) as well as larger service providers that are more likely to be included in a router's setup assistant. Strikingly, we found that almost half of the providers do not use TLS at all (29 of 60). Among those who use TLS, almost half do not validate server certificates (15 of 31). Two providers limit the number of trusted CAs to their own authority, whereas all other providers trust the default set of CAs installed on the respective device. Two other providers mandate the use of TLS client certificates. However, they use a shared certificate for all devices, the private key of which can be extracted from the firmware in both cases. While larger providers in our data set seem to use TLS more prudently, we observe that providers often do not adequately protect TR-069 sessions against man-in-the-middle attacks.

We used multiple methods to verify the validity of the provider configurations we found. First, we attempted to establish a TCP connection with all ACSes in our data set to verify their presence. This confirmed the existence of only 11 configuration servers, as many providers block access from external networks. Second, we used the Tor anonymity network to scan for ACSes from within other providers' networks. Even though most Tor exit nodes are not located in residential IP space, this confirmed four additional servers. We presume that we would be able to confirm substantially more ACSes by using "residential proxy services". We did not use these proxies as they are – very similar to DDoS booter services – universally run by criminals [32]. Finally, we informed each provider of our findings and provided them with the opportunity to correct invalid or outdated results in a responsible disclosure process (see extended paper).

Another option to find additional ACSes would have been a scan of the entire IPv4 address space for public instances. As port 7547 is used by both TR-069 clients and configuration servers, we would have needed to interact with these systems to determine their nature. We have refrained from doing this because of the unacceptably high risk of interfering with fragile TR-069 systems in the wild. For example, Weinmann's analysis of an alleged TR-064/069 vulnerability

---

[3] Germany, for example, passed a law establishing freedom of choice for routers in November 2015 [12]. Therefore, Germany has a strong ecosystem of aftermarket routers which are user-friendly to set up. The situation in other European countries is similar.

in 900k routers demonstrated that just probing port 7547 in a specific way can result in an effective DoS attack against routers and large-scale outages [35].

Man-In-The-Middle Attacks on Internet Gateways. A major share of all TR-069 clients are internet gateways. Launching a man-in-the-middle attack against these devices on customer premises can be tricky because it requires – depending on the device type – the interception of copper telephone lines, coaxial cable, or optical fiber. As a workaround, gateways with integrated routers can often be configured to disable the modem and treat a regular LAN port as their (internet) WAN port instead. In this case, the router can be moved into an existing network where it can be monitored. Nonetheless, a "classical" interception of internet gateways remains difficult to implement in general. An oftentimes easier approach is the use of client reconfiguration, which we will discuss in the next section.

3.2 Client Reconfiguration

When analyzing router firmwares for TR-069 configurations, we found that many devices provide means to modify their TR-069 settings. This makes it possible to perform a considerably easier man-in-the-middle attack. Instead of intercepting the connection between gateway and ACS, we place a machine in the local network that acts as a reverse proxy to the original ACS. We then reconfigure the gateway to use this machine as its ACS. This has a number of advantages:

1. Interception can be done with off-the-shelf Ethernet devices.
2. By reconfiguring the ACS URL, one can downgrade the connection between gateway and interception device to plain HTTP (see Sect. 2.2).
3. In contrast to the network setup described in Sect. 3.1, the inspection devices only sees relevant TR-069 communication.

However, client reconfiguration is not free of pitfalls. The ACS may use a TR-069 session to update the server URL, which would override the custom redirection and bypass the proxy. In contrast to a classical man-in-the-middle attack, the local proxy device has limited means to detect and correct this. While regular TR-069 `SetParameterValues` commands can be manipulated on-the-fly, the ACS URL may also be reset by firmware updates. This makes long-term monitoring of reconfigured devices an ongoing challenge.

TR-069 defines multiple mechanisms to configure the ACS URL (see Sect. 2.2). Devices differ widely in what they support. For example, on some TP-Link routers, we were able to configure the ACS URL via the router's web interface. For AVM[4] routers, we found that TR-069 can be configured via TR-064 (the configuration interface available from LAN), or by restoring a forged configuration file. In contrast, we did not find means to reconfigure a Cisco cable modem without intercepting communication on the coaxial cable first. But we were able to reconfigure a Cisco IP phone via DHCP.

---

[4] In 2013, AVM's Fritz!Box series had an estimated market share of 68% in Germany and 18% in Europe [14].

3.3 Emulated Clients

When observing the traffic of a given TR-069 client is impractical, another option is to completely emulate a TR-069 device. This is particularly useful to repeatedly analyze the handling of selected events such as device provisioning.

In contrast to the previously described interception techniques, the major challenge with emulated clients is not intercepting connections, but obtaining valid credentials to communicate with the configuration server. In this section, we discuss how clients can authenticate themselves to existing configuration servers to establish TR-069 sessions. We describe our emulated honeyclient later on in Sect. 4.

To establish a TR-069 session, a client generally needs two pieces of information: the ACS URL and valid credentials for authentication. The difficulty of obtaining these depends on provider and device. If both device manufacturer and provider put a high emphasis on protecting their TR-069 communication against external observers, analysts need to extract credentials by manually reverse-engineering specific devices. However, we find that the use of shared credentials is prevalent in practice. When we analyzed the use of TLS by service providers in Sect. 3.1, 38 of 60 providers had hardcoded authentication credentials in their TR-069 configuration. Next we discuss how this impacts connection security.

Shared Authentication Credentials. Counter-intuitively, hardcoded TR-069 credentials do not necessarily imply a vulnerability. If TR-069 is used for monitoring purposes only and not for the provisioning of, for instance, VoIP credentials, the secure identification of individual devices is less of a concern. Also, a provider may only use hardcoded credentials to provide an initial generic configuration and then update the credentials stored on the device with unique ones using the SetParameterValues command. The TR-069 specification discourages hardcoded credentials, but does not prohibit them. When sharing credentials between devices, providers need to resort to alternative means of identifying individual customers. There are various attributes a provider can use for this purpose:

1. The client's IP address as seen by the server.
2. The client's IP address as reported in the initial Inform command.[5]
3. The device's serial number as reported in the initial Inform command.
4. The router's MAC address, which can be obtained with a GetParameterValues command.
5. User input collected in a custom authentication dialog.

We briefly discuss each option's security properties. For the first four options, we assume that the provider has reliable means to map IP addresses, serial numbers, or MAC addresses to customers.

Option 1 has the major issue that any device in a customer's network can obtain the customer's TR-069 configuration. For example, clients in a public

---

[5] Without taking security concerns into account, a provider may prefer this over option 1 because it works if proxies in the provider's network mask the client's IP.

wireless network (e.g. in cafés) could obtain the owner's VoIP credentials and commit phone fraud.

Options 2–4 have a common problem in that they rely on information which is easily spoofable and should not be considered secret. The IP space of an internet service provider is public knowledge and MAC addresses or serial numbers cannot be assumed to be random nor secret. For example, we found that the serial number of an AVM router can be read by any client in its network without authentication.

Option 5 is the most secure one, but complex to implement correctly. The TR-069 specification does not provide any guidance on possible authentication methods. Moreover, many providers are reluctant to use this option as it conflicts with the stated goal of "Zero-Touch" configuration (cf. Sect. 2.1).

In summary, TR-069 client authentication is a hard problem for service providers in practice. The use of hardcoded credentials comes with unique security challenges, yet the absence of hardcoded TR-069 credentials does not necessarily imply that the provider is using different or better means to identify customers. Previous work has indicated that this problem is not of theoretical nature [20]. The prevalence of hardcoded credentials in practice makes it quite easy to set up emulated clients in many networks.

3.4   Comparison of Inspection Methods

Man-in-the-middle attacks, client reconfiguration, or emulated clients are sufficient to inspect many TR-069 deployments in practice. However, none of the methods is guaranteed to succeed with a specific client and configuration server. As a last resort, interception may require manual reverse-engineering of individual devices. Setting up devices for inspection is a highly manual process.

For researchers and practitioners interested in the analysis of TR-069, we provide practical recommendations in the extended version of this paper.

4   TR-069 Honeyclient

While TR-069 inspection by man-in-the-middle attack or client reconfiguration (cf. Sect. 3.1 and 3.2) can be implemented with standard tools, at the time of writing we are unaware of any existing software that can readily emulate TR-069 clients (cf. Sect. 3.3). Here we introduce an open-source honeyclient we developed to solve this problem. Our honeyclient emulates TR-069 devices and can be used to watch configuration servers and observe their response to certain events. This allows us to assess how different devices are bootstrapped, which parameters a provider accesses, or how fast security updates are rolled out.

The design of the honeyclient is based on three central requirements: full coverage of the TR-069 protocol, usability for the target audience of proficient security analysts, and the capability to perform deliberate protocol violations. We discuss the implementation of these requirements in the extended version of this paper. For an initial exploration, we provide an interactive command line interface that can be used to issue TR-069 commands and observe the provider's response. Alternatively, the honeyclient can be instrumented in Python. Next, we describe the results of using our honeyclient for the automated security testing.

4.1 Analysis of Open-Source TR-069 Servers

To demonstrate that our client is effective at uncovering security vulnerabilities, we have used its scripting capabilities to develop an automated test suite for configuration servers, which we instantiated in a controlled network environment. Our targets are GenieACS [1], the only open-source configuration server in active development, and OpenACS [33]. The latter is still relevant as we found multiple providers with an ACS URL indicating that they likely run OpenACS.

Even though we only performed very limited automated black-box tests with our honeyclient, we found security vulnerabilities in both tested open-source configuration servers (see extended version of this paper). While we note that the vulnerabilities are specific to GenieACS and OpenACS, empirical research has shown that open-source and closed-source software often do not significantly differ with regard to the severity of vulnerabilities [2,23]. We suspect that the use of serial numbers for customer identification might be a widespread issue with configuration servers as the TR-069 specification does not provide any guidance on client authentication. This is critical as it allows attackers to e.g. obtain other user's VoIP credentials for phone fraud [22].

5 TR-069 Infrastructure Monitoring

When looking at TR-069 from a security and privacy standpoint, it is interesting to not only analyze a single client, ACS implementation, or provider in isolation, but to compare how different providers and clients behave over time and in reaction to specific events. For example, how fast are different providers rolling our security updates? How many providers use TR-069 not only for remote management, but also to obtain information on sensitive data such as television viewing statistics? How is TR-069 used in countries with restricted freedoms to implement censorship or surveillance? Monitoring TR-069 infrastructure at a larger scale provides better information on the security and privacy aspects of TR-069 in practice. In this section, we propose how our toolkit can be turned in an infrastructure for monitoring a larger number of TR-069 deployments over longer periods of time. For brevity, we describe the implementation of our individual monitoring sensors based on inexpensive mini routers and our virtual test environment that makes TR-069 more accessible to researchers in the extended version of our paper. Based on our monitoring sensors, we outline the challenges of large-scale TR-069 monitoring and report measurements of twelve months of real-world TR-069 traffic.

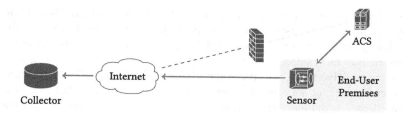

Fig. 4. Data collection setup

5.1 Distributed Monitoring System

Compared to internet monitoring efforts such as Censys [9], collecting data on the TR-069 infrastructure is more challenging because many configuration servers are not reachable from the public internet. To support this with data: among server addresses we obtained in the analysis of Sect. 3.1, we found that 49 out of 60 hosts were shielded off the internet, presumably to reduce the attack surface of the ACS (see Fig. 3). Therefore, a monitoring infrastructure must be distributed with sensors located in each provider's network. Additionally, the installation of sensors requires some expertise and manual configuration: for each deployment, either a suitable inspection method or valid authentication credentials for a honeyclient need to be obtained. For TR-069, this often involves reverse-engineering individual devices and thus limits the scalability of our approach to TR-069 monitoring. However, we believe that a limited network of sensors is still useful to observe basic TR-069 operations in practice.

To collect data from multiple sensors, we have opted for a simple centralized logging infrastructure. Sensors report all TR-069 activity to a dedicated log collector via HTTPS (see Fig. 4). Data is redacted before transmission (cf. Appendix A in the extended paper) and then stored on the collector.

5.2 Real-World Measurement Study

To evaluate our monitoring system, we have conducted a twelve month study where we continuously monitored TR-069 traffic of ten households in Western Europe. Study participants were recruited through the first authors' personal contacts and informed what kind of data will be collected. For each participant, we determined a suitable inspection method for the respective router and configured a monitoring sensor on-site. In total, our measurements cover nine distinct device models and five internet service providers (cable and DSL) starting in March 2018. Our main findings are as follows:

Over the course of our study, three device models received updates from the manufacturer. However, we did not observe any provider deploying these updates to our participants' devices via TR-069. Two devices were manually patched by their owners four and twenty days after firmware release respectively, and one device remains unpatched for ten months as of today (December 2019). A fourth device entered our study in an unpatched state and still remains so. While TR-069 could improve end user security by providing timely firmware updates, we found that providers are not doing their homework as we couldn't observe any evidence of this in practice.

In more positive news, we did not find any "smoking gun" indicating severe privacy violations by service providers. Next to the periodic Inform messages sent by clients, providers sent commands that can all be reasonably linked to regular maintenance work. For example, two providers updated the ACS URL to a new configuration server while a third provider repeatedly queried DSL connection quality parameters for a period of two days to presumably debug connectivity issues. While our findings show no evidence of widespread privacy violations, providers could still target particularly interesting customers individually. Overall, our study validates that the distributed monitoring system works reliably for long-term TR-069 monitoring.

6   Discussion

As the first contribution of this paper, we have discussed man-in-the-middle attacks, client reconfiguration and emulated clients as three methods to inspect TR-069 traffic. Our analysis of provider configurations has shown that providers often neglect to follow the security recommendations made in the TR-069 specification. We hypothesize that this is happening because plain HTTP is still marginally cheaper and simpler to implement while sniffing or man-in-the-middle attacks are not perceived as realistic threats. All devices we analyzed would have supported TLS. From our point of view, allowing plain HTTP is a design mistake of the TR-069 specification which opens the door to a whole class of attacks.

We do want to point out that – notwithstanding our previous point – interception and monitoring of internet gateways can still be difficult to establish when devices are resistant to reconfiguration. There are two reasons why we believe that this is not as much of an issue as one may think: First, TR-069 has moved from being used by internet gateways only to supporting a whole range of devices such as set-top boxes and VoIP phones, which all can be intercepted more easily on Ethernet. Second, the use of emulated clients often is an effective alternative to monitoring real devices.

The second contribution of this paper is an open-source TR-069 honeyclient that can be used to assess TR-069 configuration servers from a security and privacy point of view. As analysts can emulate arbitrary events, we found that it is often more effective to use a honeyclient when analyzing a configuration server than to monitor a real device. We further believe that our client is not only effective at monitoring, but also at offensive security research, as evidenced by the vulnerabilities we found in OpenACS and GenieACS using automated black-box testing. The security of configuration servers is a promising avenue for future research.

With regard to practical TR-069 security, our most important finding is the widespread use of hardcoded credentials. Both GenieACS and OpenACS use the device serial number as the primary means of identification, and the prevalence of hardcoded credentials in provider configurations suggests that this is also the case for a variety of commercial configuration servers. As we discussed in Sect. 3.3, neither the use of IP address-based nor serial number-based authentication can be considered secure. At the same time, the TR-069 specification does not provide any guidance on how clients should be identified. When clients are not authenticated securely, an attacker can impersonate other users to obtain their TR-069 configuration, which includes for example VoIP credentials.

As the third contribution of this paper, we have developed a monitoring sensor and a centralized log collector to monitor TR-069 deployments in practice. We have demonstrated that our sensor can be run on inexpensive routers, but we did not perform a rigorous evaluation of possible hardware alternatives. As our sensor runs on OpenWrt, we believe that it can be easily adapted to work on other hardware platforms. A major concern in the development was the privacy of study participants. The sensitive nature of TR-069 traffic makes it difficult to conduct analyses that are both comprehensive and privacy-preserving. At the very least, the inner workings of our platform are – down to the operating system – open-source software and available for inspection.

An interesting avenue for future work is TR-069 monitoring at high-value endpoints that may be targeted with custom configurations. Here we see two main challenges that need to be addressed in future research. First, our sensor deployment currently has high setup costs. Sensors must be installed on customers' premises, installation is a relatively manual process, and user privacy must be considered appropriately. Second, when asking volunteers to set up sensors and contribute data, the authenticity of our results is at stake as we cannot verify the legitimacy of logs with our current architecture. Nonetheless, we believe that even relatively small sensor deployments can yield interesting insights in practice (see Sect. 5.2). With the growing adoption of TR-069 for devices other than internet gateways, monitoring TR-069 becomes gradually more important and easier to accomplish at the same time.

7   Related Work

Despite the widespread use of TR-069, there is very little public information about the protocol's security and privacy implications. In this section, we first review works on TR-069 security and then discuss publications on man-in-the-middle attacks and honeypots that inspired our work.

TR-069 Security. We are not aware of any academic publications on TR-069 security. Therefore, we deem it also valuable to point to "grey" literature.

One team of security researchers has focused its attention on specific implementation vulnerabilities in TR-069 clients and configuration servers. Most notably, Tal presented a talk on exploiting TR-069 configuration servers at Defcon 22 [27] in 2014. He disclosed vulnerabilities in multiple configuration servers and gained control over 500,000 managed devices in one particular instance.

The respective security advisories are still undisclosed as of December 2019. In a follow-up talk, Tal and Oppenheim demonstrated the "Misfortune Cookie" vulnerability in the RomPager TR-069 connection request server, which is embedded in at least 12 million residential gateways manufactured by ASUS, D-Link, Edimax, Huawei, TP-Link, ZTE, ZyXEL, and others they found exposed to the internet [29]. While RomPager developer AllegroSoft issued a version that fixes the vulnerability in 2005, devices today (2019) still ship with the vulnerable version. This shows that the patch propagation cycle is incredibly slow (sometimes non-existent) for these types of devices [28].

In January 2016, RedTeam Pentesting published an information disclosure vulnerability in o2/Telefonica Germany's configuration server [20]. QA Cafe, a US-based software company specialized in testing broadband gateways, publishes TR-069 security best practices for service providers [19]. We also note Ömer Erdem's master thesis on HoneyThing, a honeypot that emulates three known vulnerabilities in connection request servers [10]. Vetterl and Clayton use firmware images to emulate CPE/IoT devices and run them as honeypots [34].

Man-In-The-Middle Attacks on TLS. Man-in-the-middle attacks are a common technique to learn or modify communication contents that are otherwise protected using Transport Layer Security (TLS) [6]. Previous research has shown that non-browser TLS implementations often implement certificate verification incorrectly and are subject to such attacks [11,13]. For a comprehensive overview of past TLS security issues, we refer to Clark and Van Oorschot [7].

Honeyclients. A honeypot is "a security resource whose value lies in being probed, attacked, or compromised" [25]. One subgroup of honeypots are honeyclients, which mimic the behavior of a network client that actively initiates requests to servers aiming to be attacked [24]. The development of our TR-069 honeyclient was largely inspired by Nazario's PhoneyC, a honeyclient that emulates a web browser to enable the study of malicious websites [15]. Similar to PhoneyC, our honeyclient emulates a TR-069 device and connects to configuration servers to get attacked. In contrast to most existing honeypots, the value of our honeyclient lies not only in the detection of attacks, but also in the logging of events that demonstrate privacy infringements or other unwanted actions by providers.

8   Conclusion

This paper takes a look at the security and privacy aspects of the TR-069 remote management protocol. Although the protocol is used in nearly a billion devices, our work represents (to the best of our knowledge) the first academic publication on the topic.

To facilitate further research, we have first discussed the protocol from a security perspective and presented three methods researchers can use to analyze the TR-069 communication of their devices. None of the approaches is guaranteed to succeed with a specific client or configuration server, but we have shown that man-in-the-middle attacks, client reconfiguration and the use of emulated clients can be used to inspect the majority of networks in practice. To enable analyses that go beyond the monitoring of existing devices, we contribute an open-source honeyclient implementation that can be used to assess configuration servers. Using our client, we were able to obtain information on firmware updates, VoIP credentials, and data access patterns by providers in practice.

While its primary field of use lies in the monitoring of configuration servers, our honeyclient can also be utilized by providers to debug and stress-test their configuration servers, as well as researchers who can instrument it for offensive security research. We have built an automated test suite on top of our client to demonstrate weaknesses in OpenACS and GenieACS, two open-source configuration servers. The vulnerabilities we found provide initial evidence that client authentication could be a systemic issue in the TR-069 landscape. Our findings support the general assertion by Tal and Oppenheim that TR-069 infrastructure is most often inadequately secured [29].

To facilitate the monitoring of providers for privacy infringements and other unwanted behavior conducted over TR-069, we have developed a monitoring sensor based on mitmproxy. Compared to internet-wide scanning studies, the manual work required to deploy individual sensors is a fundamental limitation for large-scale TR-069 measurements. We release both our honeyclient and the sensor software as open source under the MIT license[6].

We have used our monitoring system to conduct real-world measurements of TR-069 traffic for twelve months. While we did not observe any privacy violations by providers, we also found no evidence of providers using TR-069 to push firmware updates released by vendors during our measurement period. The purported security benefits of TR-069 are not realized.

Looking ahead, we hope that our work lays the foundation for more security research on TR-069. We limited our real-world measurements to routers as the most popular TR-069 device type, but we expect research on for example set-top boxes to yield interesting data on potential privacy infringements by providers. Furthermore, we encourage researchers to use our honeyclient for the assessment of TR-069 configuration servers. As these systems effectively have remote execution privileges on all connected devices, they represent high-value targets that would benefit from more throughout security analyses in practice.

References

1. Abdulla, Z.: GenieACS 1.1.3, October 2018. https://genieacs.com/
2. Anderson, R.: Open and closed systems are equivalent (that is. an ideal world). In: Perspectives on Free and Open Source Software, pp. 127–142. MIT Press, Cambridge (2005)
3. Antonakakis, M., et al.: Understanding the Mirai botnet. In: Proceedings of the 26th USENIX Security Symposium, pp. 1093–1110. Vancouver, BC, Canada (2017)
4. Bano, S., et al.: Scanning the Internet for liveness, vol. 48, pp. 2–9. ACM, New York, May 2018

---

[6] https://github.com/mhils/tr069

5. Blackford, J., Digdon, M.: TR-069 Issue 1 Amendment 6. Technical report, The Broadband Forum, April 2018. https://www.broadband-forum.org/technical/download/TR-069_Amendment-6.pdf
6. Callegati, F., Cerroni, W., Ramilli, M.: Man-in-the-middle attack to the HTTPS protocol. IEEE Secur. Priv. **7**(1), 78–81 (2009)
7. Clark, J., van Oorschot, P.C.: SoK: SSL and HTTPS: revisiting past challenges and evaluating certificate trust model enhancements. In: Proceedings of the 2013 IEEE Symposium on Security and Privacy, pp. 511–525. IEEE, Berkeley, May 2013
8. Cortesi, A., Hils, M., Kriechbaumer, T., contributors: mitmproxy: a free and open source interactive HTTPS proxy (2010-). https://mitmproxy.org/, [Version 4.0]
9. Durumeric, Z., Adrian, D., Mirian, A., Bailey, M., Halderman, J.A.: A search engine backed by internet-wide scanning. In: Proceedings of the 22nd ACM Conference on Computer and Communications Security, pp. 542–553. ACM, New York, October 2015
10. Erdem, O.: HoneyThing: Nesnelerin İnterneti için Tuzak Sistem. Master's thesis, Istanbul Şehir University, December 2015. http://earsiv.sehir.edu.tr:8080/xmlui/bitstream/handle/11498/25170/000110615002.pdf
11. Fahl, S., Harbach, M., Muders, T., Baumgärtner, L., Freisleben, B., Smith, M.: Why eve and mallory love Android: an analysis of android SSL (in)security. In: Proceedings of the 2012 ACM Conference on Computer and Communications Security, pp. 50–61. ACM, New York (2012)
12. Free Software Foundation Europe: Timeline of compulsory routers (2016). https://fsfe.org/activities/routers/timeline.en.html
13. Georgiev, M., Iyengar, S., Jana, S., Anubhai, R., Boneh, D., Shmatikov, V.: The most dangerous code in the world: validating SSL certificates in non-browser software. In: Proceedings of the 2012 ACM Conference on Computer and Communications Security, pp. 38–49. ACM, New York, October 2012
14. Koch, R., Stelte, B.: Bot-netz ohne Fritz. In: Sicherheit in vernetzten Systemen: 18. DFN Workshop. Deutsche Forschungsnetz, Berlin, Germany (2013)
15. Nazario, J.: PhoneyC: a virtual client honeypot. In: Proceedings of the 2nd USENIX Conference on Large-scale Exploits and Emergent Threats: Botnets, Spyware, Worms, and More, p. 6. USENIX Association, Berkeley, April 2009
16. Nicolai, S., Stark, B.: TR-064 Issue 2. Technical report, The Broadband Forum, July 2015. https://www.broadband-forum.org/technical/download/TR-064_Issue-2.pdf
17. Ott, J.D.: TR-135 Issue 1 Amendment 3. Technical report, The Broadband Forum, January 2013. https://www.broadband-forum.org/technical/download/TR-135_Amendment-3.pdf
18. QA Cafe: Overview of a TR-069 session, June 2019. https://www.qacafe.com/tr-069-training/session-overview/
19. QA Cafe: Best practices for securing TR-069, January 2020. https://www.qacafe.com/articles/best-practices-for-securing-tr-069/
20. RedTeam Pentesting GmbH: o2/Telefonica Germany: ACS discloses VoIP/SIP credentials, January 2016. https://www.redteam-pentesting.de/en/advisories/rt-sa-2015-005/
21. Rescorla, E.: HTTP Over TLS. RFC **2818**, May 2000
22. Sahin, M., Francillon, A., Gupta, P., Ahamad, M.: SoK: fraud in telephony networks. In: EUROS&P 2017 2nd IEEE European Symposium on Security and Privacy. IEEE, Berkeley, April 2017
23. Schryen, G.: Is open source security a myth? Commun. ACM **54**(5), 130–140 (2011)

24. Seifert, C., Welch, I., Komisarczuk, P.: Taxonomy of honeypots. Technical report, Victoria University of Wellington, June 2006. http://www.mcs.vuw.ac.nz/comp/ Publications/archive/CS-TR-06/CS-TR-06-12.pdf
25. Spitzner, L.: Honeypots: Tracking Hackers. Addison-Wesley, Boston (2002)
26. Stenberg, D.: Lesser HTTPS for non-browsers, January 2017. https://daniel.haxx. se/blog/2017/01/10/lesser-https-for-non-browsers/
27. Tal, S.: I hunt TR-069 admins: Pwning ISPs like a boss. Defcon 22, July 2014. https://defcon.org/images/defcon-22/dc-22-presentations/Tal/DEFCON-22 -Shahar-Tal-I-hunt-TR-069-admins-UPDATED.pdf
28. Tal, S., Oppenheim, L.: Misfortune cookie (2014). http://mis.fortunecook.ie/
29. Tal, S., Oppenheim, L.: Too many cooks - exploiting the Internet-of-TR-069-Things. In: 31th Chaos Communication Congress, December 2014. https://events. ccc.de/congress/2014/Fahrplan/events/6166.html
30. The Broadband Forum: List of technical reports. https://www.broadband-forum. org/technical-reports
31. The Broadband Forum: Global fixed broadband subscribers exceed one billion (2018). https://www.broadband-forum.org/global-fixed-broadband-subscribers-exceed-one-billion
32. Thomas, D.R., Pastrana, S., Hutchings, A., Clayton, R., Beresford, A.R.: Ethical issues in research using datasets of illicit origin. In: Proceedings of the 2017 Internet Measurement Conference, pp. 445–462. ACM (2017)
33. Valunas, A.: OpenACS 0.5.0.3 (2013). https://sourceforge.net/projects/openacs/
34. Vetterl, A., Clayton, R.: Honware: a virtual honeypot framework for capturing CPE and IoT zero days. In: Symposium on Electronic Crime Research (eCrime). IEEE (2019)
35. Weinmann, R.P.: Were 900k Deutsche Telekom routers compromised by Mirai? November 2016. https://comsecuris.com/blog/posts/were_900k_deutsche_telekom_ routers_compromised_by_mirai/

The Naked Sun: Malicious Cooperation Between Benign-Looking Processes

Fabio De Gaspari[1], Dorjan Hitaj[1], Giulio Pagnotta[1], Lorenzo De Carli[2(✉)], and Luigi V. Mancini[1]

[1] Dipartimento di Informatica, Sapienza Università di Roma, Rome, Italy
{degaspari,hitaj.d,pagnotta,mancini}@di.uniroma1.it
[2] Department of Computer Science, Worcester Polytechnic Institute, Worcester, USA
ldecarli@wpi.edu

Abstract. Recent progress in machine learning has generated promising results in behavioral malware detection, which identifies malicious processes via features derived by their runtime behavior. Such features hold great promise as they are intrinsically related to the functioning of each malware, and are therefore difficult to evade. Indeed, while a significant amount of results exists on evasion of static malware features, evasion of dynamic features has seen limited work.

This paper thoroughly examines the robustness of behavioral ransomware detectors to evasion. Ransomware behavior tends to differ significantly from that of benign processes, making it a low-hanging fruit for behavioral detection (and a difficult candidate for evasion). Our analysis identifies a set of novel attacks that distribute the overall malware workload across a small set of cooperating processes to avoid the generation of significant behavioral features. Our most effective attack decreases the accuracy of a state-of-the-art detector from 98.6% to 0% using only 18 cooperating processes. Furthermore, we show our attacks to be effective against commercial ransomware detectors.

Keywords: Malware · Ransomware · Evasion of threat detection

1 Introduction

Malware detection is a difficult problem, with no full solution in sight despite decades of research. The traditional approach—based on analysis of static signatures of the malware binary—is increasingly rendered ineffective by polymorphism and program obfuscation tools [32,34]. Using such tools, malware creators

We thank the authors of RWGuard for sharing their code with us and the authors of ShieldFS for sharing their dataset and helping us re-implement their detector. Fabio De Gaspari, Dorjan Hitaj, Giulio Pagnotta and Luigi V. Mancini are supported in part by the Italian MIUR under grant "Dipartimenti di eccellenza 2018–2022" of the Dipartimento di Informatica of Sapienza University of Rome.

© Springer Nature Switzerland AG 2020
M. Conti et al. (Eds.): ACNS 2020, LNCS 12147, pp. 254–274, 2020.
https://doi.org/10.1007/978-3-030-57878-7_13

can quickly generate thousands of binary variants of functionally identical samples, effectively circumventing signature-based approaches.

As a result, the focus of the community has increasingly shifted towards dynamic, behavior-based analysis techniques. Behavioral approaches sidestep the challenges of obfuscated binary analysis. Instead, they focus on the runtime behavior of malware processes, which is difficult to alter without breaking core functionality. At first sight, these techniques seem to hold great promise: the behavior of malware differs significantly from that of benign processes and this marked difference can be exploited to differentiate between these two classes of processes. In particular, recent improvements in the field of Machine Learning (ML) showed that ML models are extremely effective in distinguishing between different behavioral classes, resulting in very high accuracy [12,29]. Moreover, behavioral-based approaches are also able to correctly detect unseen malware samples, as long as these new samples exhibit some form of anomalous behavior with respect to benign processes as showed by several recent works [12,24,25,29].

Despite the success of ML-based behavioral analysis, a growing body of work has cast a shadow over the robustness of ML in adversarial settings [11,17]. In this work, we assesses the robustness of recently-proposed behavioral-based ransomware detection tools [12,29]. We use ransomware as a case study due to both the gravity of the threat (e.g., [5,7]), and the fact that—given its highly distinctive behavioral profile—ransomware is a nearly ideal target for behavioral-based detection. Our results show that **it is possible to craft ransomware that accomplishes the goal of encrypting all user files, and at the same time avoids generating any significant behavioral features**. Our proposed attacks have fairly low implementation complexity, do not limit ransomware functionality in any significant way, and were found to be effective against a set of academic and commercial anti-ransomware solutions. Moreover, our attacks are successful even in a black-box setting, with no prior knowledge of the tool's inner workings, its training data, or the features used by the ML model. The core of our approach is an algorithm that cleverly distributes the desired set of malware operations across a small set of cooperating processes[1]. While our work has focused on obfuscating ransomware-related features, the underlying principles are general and likely to apply to a wide range of behavioral detectors that analyze the runtime behavior of different types of malware. To the best of our knowledge, this is the first instantiation of an efficient, practical collusion attack in the domain of ransomware.

Our Contributions:

- We perform a comprehensive analysis of characteristic features typically used to detect ransomware, and define techniques and criteria for evasion.
- We assess the robustness of current state-of-the-art behavioral ransomware detectors, showing how it is possible to design ransomware that completely

---

[1] In Isaac Asimov's 1957 novel *The Naked Sun*, a crime is committed by robots which are forbidden, by their programming, to harm humans. Each robot performs an apparently innocuous action, however the combination results in murder.

evades detection. In particular, we analyze three evasion techniques: *process splitting*, *functional splitting*, and *mimicry*.

- We implement and evaluate Cerberus, a proof-of-concept ransomware following our approach, proving that our evasion technique is practical.
- We evaluate the proposed evasion techniques against multiple state-of-the-art behavioral detectors, as well as against a leading commercial behavioral detector. Results show that our techniques are effective and successfully evade detection, even in a black-box setting.
- We evaluate the dependence of our attack on the dataset used. Results show that our evasion techniques are effective even without access to the dataset used to train the target classifiers.
- We discuss the applicability of potential countermeasures.

2   Behavioral Ransomware Detection

The literature presents several recent works on ransomware detection based on behavioral features [9,12,24,29,38]. UNVEIL [9] and its successor Redemption [24] detect suspicious activity by computing a score using a heuristic function over various behavioral features: file entropy changes, writes that cover extended portions of a file, file deletion, processes writing to a large number of user files, processes writing to files of different types, back-to-back writes. Similarly, CryptoDrop [38] maintains a "reputation score"—indicating the trustworthiness of a process—computed based on three main indicators: file type changes, similarity between original and written content, and entropy measurement.

In this paper, we demonstrate (i) heuristics to generate ransomware behavior which goes undetected by behavioral detectors, and (ii) a proof-of-concept ransomware prototype implementing these heuristics. Our attack is motivated by a review of all the approaches cited above; for evaluation we selected two of them, described in greater detail in the following. The selection was based on practical considerations: both approaches were published in highly visible venues, and in both cases the authors kindly provided enough material (code and/or datasets) and support to enable us to run their software. Our evaluation also includes a commercial product from Malwarebytes (discussed at the end of this section).

ShieldFS [12] identifies ransomware processes at file-system level and transparently rolls back file changes performed by processes deemed malicious. Ransomware detection is based on ML models of well- and ill-behaved processes. Detection is performed at the process level, using a hierarchy of random forest classifiers tuned at different temporal resolutions. This approach allows ShieldFS to take into account both short- and long-term process history when performing classification. ShieldFS uses features typically associated with ransomware operation for the classifiers, such as #folder-listing operations, #read operations, #write operations, #rename operations, percentage of file accessed among all those with same extension and average entropy of write operations.

ShieldFS divides the lifetime of each process in up to 28 *ticks*; ticks do not represent fixed interval of times; instead, they define fractions of the overall set

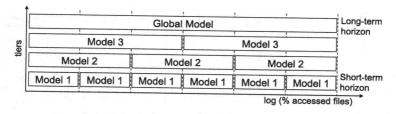

Fig. 1. Incremental models in ShieldFS (reproduced from [12])

of files accessed by a process. Ticks are exponentially spaced; the first tick is reached when a process has accessed 0.1% of the files on the filesystem; the last when a process has accessed 100% of the files. Whenever a certain tick i is reached, ShieldFS computes the features over multiple intervals. The first interval covers operations between ticks $i - 1$ and i. Each of the remaining intervals ends at tick i and begins further in the past compared to the previous one. Features computed over each interval are fed to a dedicated model for classification. Figure 1 (reproduced from [12]) shows the first six ticks in the lifetime of a process, and the various intervals covered by each model. A process is considered malicious if positively detected for $K = 3$ consecutive ticks.

ShieldFS also employs a system-wide classifier that computes feature values across all processes in the system. This is however only used to disambiguate ambiguous results from per-process classifiers. When our attack is successful, individual processes are always classified as benign with high confidence and therefore the system-wide classifier is never triggered.

RWGuard [29] is a ransomware detector which leverages multiple techniques: process behavior, suspicious file changes, use of OS encryption libraries, and changes to decoy files. We do not discuss decoy and library-based detection as it is orthogonal to our work. RWGuard uses a relatively simple detector consisting of a random forest classifier that analyzes process behavior using a 3 s sliding window. The features used by the classifier include the number of various low-level disk operations performed by each process under analysis. The behavioral classifier is complemented by a file monitor component which computes four metrics after each write operation: a similarity score based on similarity-preserving hashing, size difference, file type change and file entropy. Significant changes in any of first three metrics and/or high file entropy are interpreted as a sign of ransomware activity.

The detection process consists of three steps: when the behavioral classifier detects a suspicious process activity, the file monitor component is invoked to validate the detection. If both modules agree that the activity is suspicious, a File Classification module is invoked to further assess if the encryption operation is benign or malicious. Only after all three modules agree on the maliciousness of the suspicion activity, then the responsible process is considered malicious. When our attack is successful, individual processes are classified as benign by the behavioral module, and the remaining modules are not invoked.

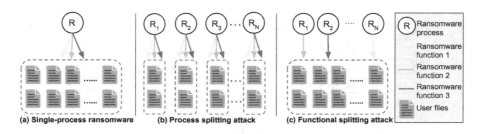

Fig. 2. Process and functional splitting attacks

Malwarebytes. Several commercial anti-ransomware solutions exist; for our work, we chose to evaluate Malwarebytes' Anti-Ransomware [1]. Differently from most other vendors, Malwarebytes distributes the beta versions of their ransomware detector as a discrete component, i.e., one which is not integrated with other types of anti-virus technology. This enables us to evaluate ransomware detection performance without having to account for interference from other malware/virus detection modules. Malwarebytes does not provide details on the inner workings of their product; the company however states that their product "does not rely on signatures or heuristics" [1] and leverages machine learning [8]. These indications suggest some type of behavioral classifier. For our evaluation, we use version 0.9.18.807 beta.

3   Evading Behavioral Detectors

Behavioral classifiers use features that are considered inextricably linked with malicious behavior and generally not present in benign applications. Our approach is based on the insight that behavioral detectors collect these features on a per-process basis. For instance, ransomware detectors profile processes based on features such as entropy of write operations or number of read/write/directory listing operations. We exploit this by devising an evasion technique based on distributing the malware operations across multiple *independent* processes: each process individually appears to have a benign behavior. However, the aggregated action of all these processes results in the intended malicious behavior. It is important to note that this is not just a limitation of current behavioral classifiers, but it is rather an inherent restriction of process behavioral modeling, as there is no straightforward way to identify a set of unrelated processes working independently to achieve a common goal [23]. While communication among coordinating processes could be used to infer cooperation, such communication can be limited and/or hidden using covert channels. Moreover, it is possible to employ techniques to avoid hierarchical relationships between processes (e.g., parent-child) [23]. We omit a full discussion of inter-process covert channels as it is outside the scope of this paper. The remainder of this section describes our three proposed attacks.

3.1 Process Splitting

In process splitting (depicted in Fig. 2b), the ransomware behavior is distributed over N processes, each performing $1/N$ of the total ransomware operations. Effectively, this approach implements a form of data parallelism: each individual process performs all the ransomware operations on a subset of the user files. The intuition is that ransomware classifiers are trained on traditional, single-process ransomware, which exhibits extremely high number of operations such as directory listing, read and write. Splitting the ransomware over N independent processes allows to reduce the number of such operations performed by each individual processes. If we split the original ransomware enough times, the number of operations performed by each individual *process-split ransomware process* becomes low enough that the classifier is unable to detect the ransomware.

While this technique is simple, our experiments (Sect. 6) show it can be extremely effective. Given a target classifier, the number of ransomware processes can be arbitrarily increased until the desired evasion rate is achieved.

3.2 Functional Splitting

While process splitting is very effective in reducing the accuracy of ransomware classifiers, completely evading detection can be challenging. Indeed, process splitting might require creating a very large number of processes, which in turn could be used to detect the presence of ransomware. A more well-rounded approach to classifier evasion is *Functional Splitting* (Fig. 2c). Ransomware processes perform a set of operations (or *functions*) to encrypt user files, such as reading, writing or directory listing. In functional splitting, we separate each of these ransomware functions in a process group: each process within the group (called *functional split ransomware process*) performs only that specific ransomware function. Within each group, we can further apply process splitting to reduce the number of operations performed by each individual process. The intuition behind the functional splitting approach is that classifiers use groups of features to classify processes. If a process only exhibits a small subset of these features, then it will not be classified as malicious. Functional splitting ensures that each functional split ransomware process only exhibit a single ransomware feature.

3.3 Mimicry

Functional splitting is extremely effective against current state-of-the-art ransomware classifiers. Moreover, it does not suffer from the process explosion issue that affects process splitting. However, it could be feasible to train an ML model to recognize this particular attack. Typical benign processes perform several different types of functions, therefore an ML model could be trained to differentiate between benign processes and functional split ransomware processes.

To avoid this potential drawback, we propose a third evasion attack: *Mimicry*. Rather than splitting ransomware processes into individual functional groups, each ransomware process is designed to have the same functional behavior as a benign process, effectively making it indistinguishable from other benign applications. The intuition behind the mimicry approach is that behavioral ML models classify samples based on the expression of a given set of features. Ransomware processes exhibit some characteristic features, while different benign applications exhibit different sets of features to different degrees. By splitting ransomware into multiple processes—and having each individual process exhibit only features displayed by benign processes—it becomes impossible for a classifier to distinguish between the runtime behavior of *mimicry ransomware processes* and benign processes. Effectively, mimicry ransomware processes are modeled after benign processes and exhibit only features that benign processes exhibit. Moreover, the degree to which each feature is exhibited by each mimicry process (e.g., how many read/write operations are performed) is kept consistent with that of benign processes.

The end result of the mimicry approach are ransomware processes that act exactly like benign processes. However, the collective behavior of all the mimicry processes results in the desired malicious goal. Section 4 discusses which features are characteristic of ransomware processes, and how we can limit the occurrence of each of these features in order to mimic benign processes.

4   Features Discussion

Behavioral classifiers exploit the marked behavioral differences between benign programs and malware in order to detect malicious samples. In the context of ransomware, such classifiers rely on a wide range of features that all ransomware programs must exhibit in order to reach their goal. This section discusses these features and analyze their robustness to evasion. Many of the features described here are also displayed by benign processes, and each feature by itself does not provide strong evidence for or against ransomware behavior. However, when considered together, these features highlight a very unique program behavior proper of ransomware processes.

Due to space limitations, in this section we limit the discussion to what we found to be the most used and robust features employed by current ransomware behavioral classifiers. Other file access-based features exist, but they can be evaded using techniques similar to those detailed below.

4.1   Write Entropy

The end goal of ransomware is to encrypt users' files and collect a ransom payment in exchange for the decryption key. Typical encrypted data is a pseudorandom string with no structure, and exhibits maximum entropy [29], while structured data written by benign programs is assumed to have considerably lower entropy. Consequently, entropy of write operations appears to be a useful feature to differentiate ransomware from benign processes. All state-of-the-art ML ransomware detectors use entropy of write operations as a feature [12,24,25,29].

Evasion: Entropy as a feature for ransomware detection can be used at different levels of granularity: (1) overall file entropy [29], (2) average read-write operations difference [24,25], and (3) individual write operations [12]. Feature (1) does not allow accurate differentiation between ransomware and benign processes, as nowadays most common file types are compressed for efficiency, including pdf, docx, xlsx, video and image files. Consequently, the overall estimate of Shannon entropy [26] for these file types is comparable to an encrypted file. For what concerns feature (2), in our research we analyzed several file types with their associated programs, and found out that in general benign processes working on compressed formats exhibit numerous very high entropy reads and writes.

It is worth pointing out, however, that despite the considerations above our dataset (see Sect. 6.1) also shows a non-negligible difference in the average entropy of individual file *write operations*. Such averages are 0.4825 for benign processes vs 0.88 for ransomware, with range [0–1]. Despite this somewhat counter-intuitive result, it is still straightforward to evade feature (3). Average write entropy can be skewed simply by introducing artificial, low-entropy write operations that lower the average write entropy for a ransomware process.

4.2   File Overwrite

One feature that is common across ransomware families is that original user files are fully overwritten, either with the encrypted data or with random data to perform a secure delete [25]. On the other hand, benign processes rarely overwrite user files completely. Therefore, file overwrite is a valuable feature that can be exploited to classify between ransomware and benign processes.

Evasion involves limiting the percentage of a file overwritten by a single ransomware process. Maintaining this percentage within the range exhibited by benign processes can be easily achieved with our proposed multi-process ransomware. It is sufficient to distribute write operations to a given file over multiple processes. Each individual process does not show any suspicious behavior, but the aggregated action of all the processes still overwrites the whole file.

4.3   Read/Write/Open/Create/Close Operations

Ransomware tends to access and encrypt as many files as possible on a victim machine to maximize the damage. This behavior results in an abnormally large amount of file operations such as *read, write, open, close* and, for some ransomware families, *create*. Typical benign processes rarely access so many files in a single run, except for some particular cases (e.g., files indexer).

Evasion: By using multiple coordinated processes to encrypt user files, each individual process only needs to access a subset of all user files. By varying the number of ransomware processes used, it is possible to limit how many file operations each individual ransomware process performs.

Table 1. Notation

DL: Directory listing operation	CL: Close operation
RD: Read operation	FRD: Fast read operation
WT: Write operation	FWT: Fast write operation
RN: Rename operation	FOP: Fast open operation
OP: Open operation	FCL: Fast close operation
{X,Y}: Functional group of processes performing op. X and Y	

Table 2. Most represented behavioral profiles exhibited by benign processes

DL	RD	WT	RN	% of processes
✓	✓	✓	✓	19.07
✓	✓	–	–	18.37
–	✓	✓	✓	16.35
–	✓	–	–	11.44
✓	✓	✓	–	7.60
–	✓	–	✓	6.85
–	–	–	✓	6.21
–	✓	✓	–	5.61

4.4   File Similarity

Ransomware always completely changes the content of a file by encrypting it. Conversely, benign processes rarely perform whole-file alterations. Therefore, overall file similarity before and after write operations from a given process is a strong feature to detect ransomware operation [38].

Evasion: This feature can be evaded similarly to the file overwrite feature. By having each ransomware process encrypt only a portion of any given user file, we preserve the overall file similarity after each individual write operation, and no individual process changes the whole file content.

5   Implementation: The Cerberus Prototype

Here, we briefly describe Cerberus, a new ransomware prototype for Windows developed to demonstrate the feasibility of our evasion techniques. Cerberus implements both *functional splitting* and *mimicry*. Functional splitting separates ransomware functions in different *functional groups*: a process in any given group performs only the specific ransomware functions assigned to that group. For instance, ransomware processes in the read-write functional group only perform read and write operations. Cerberus implements functional splitting by separating ransomware operations in three groups: (1) directory list, (2) write

Table 3. Dataset details

Type	Benign	Ransomware
#Unique applications	2245	383
#Applications training set	2074	341
#Applications testing set	171	42
#IRPs [Millions]	1763	663.6

and (3) read-rename. Read and rename are performed in the same functional group mainly for implementation convenience. We could have considered additional features for the implementation of functional splitting. However, since the goal of Cerberus is merely to prove the feasibility of our evasion techniques, we considered only the most important features exhibited by every ransomware family.

To implement the mimicry attack in Cerberus, we performed a statistical analysis on the behavior of benign processes from the ShieldFS dataset (ref. Sect. 6.1). Table 2 shows that we can identify a few behavioral classes that represent most benign processes in the dataset (notation in Table 1). For our implementation, we chose the 2nd and 3rd most represented classes: directory listing-read and read-write-rename. We chose these because they are highly represented in the dataset of benign processes, as well as because no ransomware process belongs to any of these two classes. Within each class, we strive to maintain the same ratio between operations as exhibited by benign processes. To achieve this, we introduce dummy operations, such as null reads or empty writes, to maintain the exact operation ratio of benign processes. As creating a large number of processes at the same time could be used to detect our evasion technique, Cerberus' ransomware processes are generated in a sequential fashion. It is worth noting that this is not required, and that in general few ransomware processes can be generated at a time in order to improve throughput.

6 Evaluation

This section presents the experimental evaluation of our evasion techniques. In particular, we aim at answering the following research questions: **(1)** Is our theoretical attack technique effective in avoiding detection? (Sect. 6.2); **(2)** Can our theoretical attack evade detection when implemented in a real-world setting? (Sect. 6.3); **(3)** Do our evasion techniques generalize, evading classifiers trained on different datasets? (Sect. 6.3); **(4)** Is our attack effective in a black-box setting against commercial behavioral ransomware detectors? (Sect. 6.4).

6.1 Dataset and Experimental Setup

Our trace-based evaluation leverages a dataset provided to us by the authors of ShieldFS. Table 3 summarizes this dataset; further details can be found in [12].

To train our classifiers, we divided the data on benign processes from the 11 machines comprising the dataset into: 10 machines for the training set and one for the testing set. For the 383 ransomware samples, which include different ransomware families, we use 341 for training and 42 for testing.

In order to test Cerberus, we created a realistic virtual machine testbed, consisting of a VirtualBox-based Windows-10 VM. We based the VM user directory structure and file types on the disk image of an actual office user. File contents were extracted from our own machines and replicated as needed. Our VM is comprised of 33625 files for a total of ~10 GB, distributed over 150 folders.

6.2 Trace-Based Evaluation

This section presents the trace-based evaluation of process splitting, functional splitting and mimicry attacks. This evaluation uses the I/O Request Packets (IRP) traces [3] of real ransomware from the ShieldFS dataset [12]. For each ransomware, the IRP trace contains the complete list of I/O operations performed by the ransomware process. Both ShieldFS and RWGuard extract the ransomware features used for detection, such as number of read/write operations, directly from the IRP Traces.

Our evaluation simulates multiple processes by splitting the IRP trace of a single ransomware in multiple traces, based on each evasion technique. Successively, we compute the feature vector for each individual trace as if it were an individual ransomware process. Finally, we query the classifier and compute the percentage of feature vectors classified as belonging to a ransomware. Table 1 introduces the notations that we will use in the remainder of this section.

ShieldFS - Process Splitting: As mentioned in Sect. 3.1, process splitting evenly splits the operations performed by a ransomware process over N processes. In a process-split ransomware, all processes exhibit almost identical behavior and characteristics. We begin our evaluation by splitting the original ransomware trace in multiple traces, querying the classifier in each trace. We increase the number of traces until complete evasion is achieved. We evaluate process splitting with 42 unique ransomware traces, which include different ransomware families. We compute the feature vector for each process-split ransomware, query the classifier and compute the percentage of feature vectors flagged as malicious. Figure 3a illustrates our results. ShieldFS accuracy decreases already after a single split, going from single-process 98.6% accuracy down to 65.5% on a two-process ransomware[2]. Further splitting incurs diminishing returns. Completely evading the ShieldFS classifier requires approximately 11000 processes. The requirement of such a large number of processes to achieve full evasion is a

---

[2] Our experiments only consider the ability of detectors to correctly classify ransomware processes. Since we do not consider benign processes, there can be no false positives nor true negatives. Therefore, for all our experiments accuracy is equivalent to true positive rate.

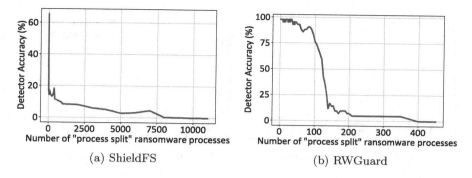

(a) ShieldFS

(b) RWGuard

Fig. 3. Evaluation of the process splitting evasion technique

clear drawback of this simplistic approach. It is reasonable to imagine a countermeasure that can detect process-split ransomware by monitoring the process creation behavior at a system-level.

ShieldFS - Functional Splitting: The ShieldFS classifier is trained on six features: #folder listing (DL), #file reads (RD), #file write (WT), #file rename (RN), file type coverage and write entropy. Our evaluation focuses on the four main operations performed by ransomware—DL, RD, WT, RN—and split ransomware processes based on these four functional groups. Finally, we assess how each functional split ransomware process performs against the detector. Note that focusing only on these 4 features makes it harder to evade the detector, since we make no attempt to evade the remaining 2 features.

First we evaluate single functional splitting, where each functional split process performs only one type of operation, resulting in four functional groups (DL, RD, WT and RN process groups). Within each functional group, we iteratively apply our process splitting technique until complete evasion is achieved. Figure 4a shows that we are able to completely evade ShieldFS by using 20 functional split processes, 5 for each of the four functional groups. Note the contrast between Fig. 4a and Fig. 3a. With single functional splitting, 4 processes (one for each functional group) are enough to drop the detector accuracy down to ~2.5%, compared to the ~7500 processes required with process splitting.

The effectiveness of functional splitting can be explained by analyzing the dataset. There is a significant difference in behavior, in terms of types of operations performed, between benign and ransomware processes over their lifetime. All of the ransomware processes in the dataset perform DL, RD, WT and RN types of operations, while only approximately 19% of benign processes have a similar behavior. Since the feature expression profile between traditional and functional split ransomware is so different, with the latter being closer to benign processes than traditional ransomware, the accuracy of the classifier is heavily affected. To validate this hypothesis, we further study how different functional groups affect the performance of the detector. In particular, using combined functional groups (i.e. processes performing RD and WT, or DL and RN), rather

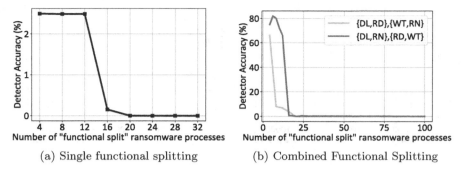

(a) Single functional splitting   (b) Combined Functional Splitting

Fig. 4. Evaluation of the functional splitting evasion technique against ShieldFS

than single functional groups, should result in higher detection accuracy as the behavioral profile of the functional split ransomware gets closer to that of a traditional ransomware. Figure 4b illustrates our results. This experiment evaluates the accuracy of ShieldFS considering two different implementations of functional split ransomware. In the first implementation, the operations are divided into the two functional groups {DL, RD}, {WT, RN}, while in the second implementation the two functional groups are {DL, RN}, {RD, WT}. We chose these groups of operations due to their frequent combined appearance in our dataset (see Table 2). Figure 4b shows that the initial accuracy of the classifier is much higher when compared to single functional splitting, hovering around 80% for {DL, RN}, {RD, WT} and around 70% for {DL, RD}, {WT, RN}. However, the accuracy quickly drops as we apply process splitting within each functional group, reaching ∼0% at 20 processes (10 for each functional group). The high initial detection accuracy for Fig. 4b is due to the fact that in the first ransomware implementation we have the {RD, WT} functional group and in the second implementation we have the {WT, RN} functional group. Both these functional groups are always present in traditional ransomware, therefore the model is more likely to classify processes that heavily exhibit these features as malicious. Indeed, we can see that after process splitting is applied in each functional group—and therefore the number of operations per functional split ransomware process decreases—the accuracy for both functional splitting implementations quickly falls towards zero.

ShieldFS - Mimicry: In the mimicry attack, we model ransomware features so that, on average, they are identical to those of benign processes. We build our model of a typical benign process by statistical analysis of the behavior of benign processes in the ShieldFS dataset [12], which comprises observations of well above one month of data from 2245 unique benign applications and ∼1.7 billion IRPs. We compute the average value for the main features used to profile ransomware and we extract the ratios between different types of I/O operations performed by benign processes. Finally, we split the ransomware activity into multiple processes, based on average feature values and ratios.

We focus on modeling the four main operations performed by ransomware and benign processes—DL, RD, WT, RN—together with the number of file accessed. Note that we could easily consider more features in our modeling, up to all features described in Sect. 4. However, since the goal of this evaluation is to prove the effectiveness of our techniques, it is sufficient to consider the most representative features. Table 2 shows the different behavioral profiles exhibited by benign process, along with how represented that behavior is in the dataset. As can be seen, the most represented functional group of benign processes exhibits all four main operations {DL, RD, WT, RN}, with the functional groups {DL, RD} and {RD, WT, RN} being a close second and third. On the other hand, if we consider the behavioral profile of ransomware processes, all 383 ransomware samples perform all four main operations. Given that the first three process behavior groups in Table 2 are all highly represented, any of them would be a suitable target for mimicry. For this evaluation, we decided to use the {DL, RD, WT, RN} functional group. While this functional group is also representative of most benign processes, the average number and ratio of operations is completely different when compared to ransomware. This functional group seems to be the worst-case scenario for our mimicry evasion technique. As illustrated in Table 4, for benign processes in the {DL, RD, WT, RN} group, the ratio between operations is 1:16:13:1. This means that for each DL operation, there are 16 RD, 13 WT and 1 RN operations respectively. Moreover, processes in this functional group access on average about 0.83% of the total number of user files in the system. We split our ransomware traces in the test set by following these averages and ratios, resulting in 170 mimicry ransomware processes, and successively query the classifier with each of them. We replicate this experiment for each of the 42 ransomware sample in our test set. None of the mimicry processes for any of the 42 ransomware are detected by the ShieldFS classifier.

- **Discussion:** It is worth noting the huge improvement gained with mimicry with respect to process splitting. In both mimicry and process splitting, each process performs all ransomware operations and therefore exhibits all the features used by ShieldFS for classification. However, mimicry requires almost two orders of magnitude less processes to achieve full evasion (170 vs 11000).

RWGuard - Process Splitting: We implement process splitting as in the evaluation against ShieldFS. As illustrated in Fig. 3b, the detection accuracy for RWGuard follows a curve similar to that of ShieldFS: the accuracy of the classifier initially remains stable around the original 99.4%, until a critical point, after which it quickly decreases to ~10%. Afterwards, both curves exhibit a long tail, with RWGuard detection accuracy decreasing to zero after 400 processes.

RWGuard - Functional Splitting: The RWGuard detector uses eight features to classify benign and malicious processes: RD, WT, OP, CL, FRD, FWT, FOP and FCL. In this evaluation, we split the ransomware traces based on all eight features, and assess how each functional split ransomware process performs against the detector. We begin the evaluation with each functional split process performing only one type of operation, resulting in eight functional groups (one for each

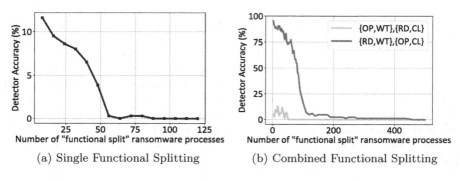

(a) Single Functional Splitting   (b) Combined Functional Splitting

Fig. 5. Evaluation of the functional splitting evasion technique against RWGuard

feature). Within each functional group, we apply process splitting until complete evasion is achieved. As shown in Fig. 5a, to fully evade the RWGuard classifier we need 64 functional split processes – 8 for each functional group.

We further study how different functional groupings affect accuracy. In particular, we evaluate the accuracy of RWGuard against two different implementations of functional split. In the first, the operations are divided into the two functional groups {OP, WT}, {RD, CL}. For the second implementation, we use the {RD, WT}, {OP, CL} functional groups. For the purpose of grouping, we make no distinction between normal and fast operations in this experiment. As shown in Fig. 5b and consistently with our ShieldFS evaluation (Fig. 4b), we see that the initial accuracy for {RD, WT}, {OP, CL} is much higher than in the single functional splitting case, starting at approximately 95% for two processes (one per functional group). This behavior is to be expected since RD and WT, two of the features with the highest importance for both detectors, are performed in the same functional group. When we split these operations in two separate functional groups the accuracy of RWGuard is much lower, starting at ~4% with only 2 processes ({OP, WT}, {RD, CL} in Fig. 5b).

RWGuard - Mimicry: As for the ShieldFS mimicry evaluation, we model ransomware features so they are, on average, identical to those of benign processes. In particular, we model the main features used by RWGuard: RD, WT, OP, CL, FRD, FWT, FOP and FCL. We split the ransomware traces in the test set by following the average operation number and operation ratio performed by benign processes, which resulted in 10 mimicry ransomware processes, and queried the classifier with each individual split trace. None of the 42 ransomware samples in our test set were detected by RWGuard.

6.3   Cerberus Evaluation

This section evaluates our Cerberus prototype, demonstrating that our attacks are effective in practical settings. Furthermore, we show that our techniques can

Table 4. Ratio between different operations for various types of benign processes

Combination	DL	RD	WT	RN	RD Entropy	WT Entropy	File Access
RD, RN	0	2	0	1	0.53	0	0.02%
WT	0	0	1	0	0	0.42	0.60%
DL, RD, WT, RN	1	16	13	1	0.59	0.46	0.83%
RD	0	1	0	0	0.46	0	0.03%
WT, RN	0	0	5	1	0	0.47	0.02%
RD, WT	0	5	1	0	0.29	0.57	1.33%
DL, RD, RN	8	39	0	1	0.42	0	0.09%
DL, WT	2	0	1	0	0	0.51	0.01%
RD, WT, RN	0	6	20	1	0.53	0.28	0.22%
DL, RD, WT	3	52	1	0	0.57	0.77	0.17%
DL	1	0	0	0	0	0	0.00%
DL, RD	1	2	0	0	0.52	0	0.17%
DL, WT, RN	1	0	8	2	0	0.39	0.03%
DL, RN	45	0	0	1	0	0	0.06%
RN	0	0	0	1	0	0	0.03%

generalize to the case where the benign process model is derived from a surrogate dataset (i.e. a dataset different from the one used to train the classifier).

ShieldFS. We evaluate Cerberus against ShieldFS in our virtual machine, both in the functional split and mimicry modes. Cerberus implements functional splitting with the following three functional groups: {DL}, {WT}, {RD, RN}. By setting Cerberus to use 6 processes per functional group (18 processes total, which is the closest to the 20 processes suggested by our trace-based evaluation), we were able to fully evade the detector.

We also evaluate Cerberus in mimicry mode (ref. Sect. 5). The number of processes in mimicry mode depends on the average number of files accessed by the mimicked benign process group in our dataset. Table 4 shows that {DL, RD} processes access on average ~0.17% of the total files, while {RD, WT, RN} processes access ~0.22%. In our VM, this results in a Cerberus run with 470 mimicry processes, which were all able to evade the ShieldFS detector, fully encrypting the VM files. Thus our attacks are practical in realistic settings.

RWGuard. An important difference compared to the RWGuard evaluation in Sect. 6.2 is that functional splitting in Cerberus considers only three functional group, that is: {DL}, {WT} and {RD, RN}. Cerberus does not split RWGuard-specific features (i.e., OP, CL, FOP, FCL, FRD, FWT). Regardless of this fact, we are able to fully evade RWGuard with Cerberus set to use 18 functional split processes in total (6 per functional group), as in the ShieldFS case.

For the mimicry attack, Cerberus is trained with the model of benign processes obtained from the ShieldFS dataset, while the RWGuard model is trained on the original dataset used by the authors in [29]. As before, in our VM evaluation Cerberus runs with 470 mimicry ransomware processes, which are all able to evade RWGuard, fully encrypting the VM files. This evaluation shows that our evasion techniques can generalize to classifiers trained on different datasets.

6.4 Evaluation Against Malwarebytes Anti-ransomware

In previous experiments, the features used by the detectors (ShieldFS and RWGuard) were known. However, in a real attack scenario this white-box setting assumption might not hold true. The last part of our experimental evaluation focuses on black-box settings where details of the detectors are not known. In particular, we pitch Cerberus against a leading commercial ransomware detector: Malwarebytes Anti-Ransomware. Malwarebytes states that their Anti-Ransomware tool "does not rely on signatures or heuristics" [1], but rather leverages machine learning techniques [8]. We have no knowledge of the internal workings of the Malwarebytes classifier, such as which features it uses for classification, nor of its dataset. This makes Malwarebytes an ideal detector to test the viability of our evasion techniques in a black-box setting. We evaluate Cerberus against Malwarebytes in both the functional split and mimicry modes. For the functional splitting approach, we continue to set Cerberus to use a total of 18 functional split processes (6 per functional group). All 18 functional split processes successfully evade Malwarebytes, fully encrypting the VM files.

For the mimicry attack, the mimicry behavior of Cerberus processes is modeled on the ShieldFS benign process dataset. Therefore, Cerberus runs with the usual 470 mimicry ransomware processes, which all successfully evade Malwarebytes and fully encrypt the VM files. This last experiment shows that our evasion techniques are general, are effective on commercial detectors and work in a black-box setting where we have no information on the classifier.

7   Countermeasures

Graph-based approaches work by building a *provenance graph*, which represent data and control flow relationships between processes and operating system entities (files, sockets, memory) on a given machine. Such graphs are then analyzed to detect suspicious behavior using either rules [30] or unsupervised anomaly detection [20,27]. These techniques have been successfully applied to the detection of APTs across long timescales and different machines. While in principle we believe that information-flow correlation between processes is an interesting direction for a countermeasure, current proposals have limitations. While these techniques are successful in detecting APTs, they typically do so only after multiple (or all) stages of the APT have completed. While this is acceptable for APTs since the goal is to eventually reveal their presence, ransomware requires immediate detection and swift remediation *before* the ransomware encrypts user data. Moreover, unsupervised approaches tend to have low accuracy on machines with unpredictable, varied workloads—such as user workstations [20], which are often ransomware targets. Therefore, we believe further work is necessary to adapt graph-based threat detection to the class of attacks described here.

Another approach entails identifying *synchronized process behavior* across applications running concurrently in different machines. This approach leverages the insight that a ransomware infection typically involves an entire network. Similar approaches, although based on network traffic, have proven effective for botnet nodes detection [19]. We note that both the functional splitting and mimicry attack can, by design, split operations in arbitrarily different ways. This would enable randomizing the attack behavior across different machines.

8   Related Work

Ransomware Detection. For a review of behavioral ransomware detection techniques [1,9,12,24,29,38], the reader is referred to Sect. 2. Other proposals [28,35] focus specifically on entropy of written data to identify encrypted content. Depending exclusively on entropy is dangerous for reasons pointed out in Sect. 4.1. The use of *decoy files* has also been proposed for ransomware detection [16,31,33]. Decoys are a promising strategy, but they raise usability concerns, and their evasion is outside the scope of our work. Finally, for a discussion of relevant graph-based detection approaches [20,27,30] see Sect. 7.

Multiprocessing Malware. Several ransomware families use multi-processing. This happens for example in WannaCry and Petya [4,6]. Encryption is still performed by one process, while the others perform non encryption-related auxiliary tasks. The CERBER ransomware (not to be confused with our *Cerberus* prototype), despite its name, does not appear to perform multi-process encryption. Instead, it focuses on obfuscation of static payload features [2]. MalWASH [23] and its successor D-TIME [36] split the malware code into chunks and inject an emulator to execute them across a set of benign processes. This approach would generate a significant overhead for compute-intensive ransomware activity. Conversely, we found that multi-process splitting, combined with mimicry, generates near-zero overhead and suffices to avoid detection.

Evasion of Ransomware Detectors. The work closest in spirit to ours is the critical analysis of ransomware defenses by Genç et al. [15]. Their work is more limited in scope than ours, considers a smaller set of features, and does not incorporate the notion of mimicry (focusing on simple feature obfuscation).

Adversarial Sample Generation. Generation of adversarial samples for various classes of malicious programs has been studied. This include generation of mobile [18] and conventional [10,22,37] malware binaries, and PDF-based file exploits [11,13,39,40]. All the works above focus on static features, i.e., they alter the appearance of a malicious file object, but not its run-time behavior.

There is limited work on attacking dynamic (behavioral) features—i.e., features generated by actions performed by a process at run-time.Existing works [21,37] aim at defeating malware detectors trained on dynamically-generated sequences of API calls. These proposals chiefly work by inserting dummy calls. Besides dummy calls, we also leverage a broader set of capabilities such as distributing calls across processes. This give our technique the ability to decrease per-process frequencies/counts of certain calls (necessary to defeat the detectors in our evaluation) without slowing down the attack, or to obfuscate data dependencies between calls (such dependencies are used by some detectors, e.g. [14]).

9   Conclusions

We demonstrated a novel practical attack against behavioral ransomware detectors. Our attack splits ransomware operations across a set of cooperating processes in such a way that no individual process behavior is flagged as suspicious by a behavioral process classifier. However, the combined behavior of all the processes still successfully accomplishes a malicious goal.

We proposed three attacks, *process splitting*, *functional splitting*, and *mimicry*. Evaluation shows that our methods evade state-of-the-art detectors without limiting the capabilities of ransomware. To the best of our knowledge, this is the first comprehensive evaluation of this attack model in the ransomware domain.

References

1. Introducing the malwarebytes anti-ransomware beta (2016). https://blog.malwarebytes.com/malwarebytes-news/2016/01/introducing-the-malwarebytes-anti-ransomware-beta/
2. Cerber starts evading machine learning (2017). https://blog.trendmicro.com/trendlabs-security-intelligence/cerber-starts-evading-machine-learning/
3. I/o request packets (2017). https://docs.microsoft.com/en-us/windows-hardware/drivers/gettingstarted/i-o-request-packets
4. "Petya-like" Ransomware Analysis, June 2017. https://www.nyotron.com/wp-content/uploads/2017/06/NARC-Report-Petya-like-062017-for-Web.pdf
5. Atlanta spent $2.6m to recover from a $52,000 ransomware scare (2018). https://www.wired.com/story/atlanta-spent-26m-recover-from-ransomware-scare/
6. Wannacry analysis and cracking, November 2018. https://medium.com/@codingkarma/wannacry-analysis-and-cracking-6175b8cd47d4
7. Wannacry cyber attack cost the nhs £92m as 19,000 appointments cancelled (2018). https://www.telegraph.co.uk/technology/2018/10/11/wannacry-cyber-attack-cost-nhs-92m-19000-appointments-cancelled/
8. Malwarebytes anti-ransomware for business (2019). https://www.malwarebytes.com/business/solutions/ransomware/
9. Kharraz, A., Arshad, S., Mulliner, C., Robertson, W., Kirda, E.: UNVEIL: a large-scale, automated approach to detecting ransomware. In: USENIX Security Symposium (2016)

10. Anderson, H.S., Kharkar, A., Filar, B.: Evading Machine Learning Malware Detection, p. 6 (2017)
11. Biggio, B., et al.: Evasion attacks against machine learning at test time. In: Blockeel, H., Kersting, K., Nijssen, S., Železný, F. (eds.) ECML PKDD 2013. LNCS (LNAI), vol. 8190, pp. 387–402. Springer, Heidelberg (2013). https://doi.org/10.1007/978-3-642-40994-3_25
12. Continella, A., et al.: Shieldfs: a self-healing, ransomware-aware filesystem. In: ACSAC (2016)
13. Dang, H., Huang, Y., Chang, E.C.: Evading classifiers by morphing in the dark. In: CCS (2017)
14. Fredrikson, M., Jha, S., Christodorescu, M., Sailer, R., Yan, X.: Synthesizing near-optimal malware specifications from suspicious behaviors. In: IEEE S&P (2010)
15. Genç, Z.A., Lenzini, G., Ryan, P.Y.A.: Next generation cryptographic ransomware. In: Gruschka, N. (ed.) NordSec 2018. LNCS, vol. 11252, pp. 385–401. Springer, Cham (2018). https://doi.org/10.1007/978-3-030-03638-6_24
16. Genç, Z.A., Lenzini, G., Sgandurra, D.: On deception-based protection against cryptographic ransomware. In: Perdisci, R., Maurice, C., Giacinto, G., Almgren, M. (eds.) DIMVA 2019. LNCS, vol. 11543, pp. 219–239. Springer, Cham (2019). https://doi.org/10.1007/978-3-030-22038-9_11
17. Goodfellow, I.J., Shlens, J., Szegedy, C.: Explaining and harnessing adversarial examples. Computing Research Repository, ArXiv (2014)
18. Grosse, K., Papernot, N., Manoharan, P., Backes, M., McDaniel, P.: Adversarial examples for malware detection. In: Foley, S.N., Gollmann, D., Snekkenes, E. (eds.) ESORICS 2017. LNCS, vol. 10493, pp. 62–79. Springer, Cham (2017). https://doi.org/10.1007/978-3-319-66399-9_4
19. Gu, G., Porras, P.A., Yegneswaran, V., Fong, M.W., Lee, W.: BotHunter: detecting malware infection through IDS-driven dialog correlation. In: USENIX (2007)
20. Han, X., Pasquier, T., Bates, A., Mickens, J., Seltzer, M.: Babar: runtime provenance-based detector for advanced persistent threats. In: NDSS (2020)
21. Hu, W., Tan, Y.: Black-box attacks against RNN based malware detection algorithms. arXiv:1705.08131 [cs], May 2017
22. Hu, W., Tan, Y.: Generating Adversarial Malware Examples for Black-Box Attacks Based on GAN. arXiv:1702.05983 [cs], February 2017
23. Ispoglou, K.K., Payer, M.: Malwash: washing malware to evade dynamic analysis. In: USENIX WOOT (2016)
24. Kharraz, A., Kirda, E.: Redemption: real-time protection against ransomware at end-hosts. In: RAID (2017)
25. Kirda, E.: Unveil: a large-scale, automated approach to detecting ransomware (keynote). In: SANER (2017)
26. Lin, J.: Divergence measures based on the Shannon entropy. IEEE Trans. Inf. Theory **37**(1), 145–151 (1991)
27. Manzoor, E., Milajerdi, S.M., Akoglu, L.: Fast memory-efficient anomaly detection in streaming heterogeneous graphs. In: KDD (2016)
28. Mbol, F., Robert, J.-M., Sadighian, A.: An efficient approach to detect torrent-locker ransomware in computer systems. In: Foresti, S., Persiano, G. (eds.) CANS 2016. LNCS, vol. 10052, pp. 532–541. Springer, Cham (2016). https://doi.org/10.1007/978-3-319-48965-0_32
29. Mehnaz, S., Mudgerikar, A., Bertino, E.: RWGuard: a real-time detection system against cryptographic ransomware. In: Bailey, M., Holz, T., Stamatogiannakis, M., Ioannidis, S. (eds.) RAID 2018. LNCS, vol. 11050, pp. 114–136. Springer, Cham (2018). https://doi.org/10.1007/978-3-030-00470-5_6

30. Milajerdi, S.M., Gjomemo, R., Eshete, B., Sekar, R., Venkatakrishnan, V.: HOLMES: real-time APT detection through correlation of suspicious information flows. In: IEEE S&P (2019)
31. Moore, C.: Detecting ransomware with honeypot techniques. In: CCC (2016)
32. Moser, A., Kruegel, C., Kirda, E.: Limits of static analysis for malware detection. In: ACSAC (2007)
33. Moussaileb, R., Bouget, B., Palisse, A., Le Bouder, H., Cuppens, N., Lanet, J.L.: Ransomware's early mitigation mechanisms. In: ARES (2018)
34. OKane, P., Sezer, S., McLaughlin, K.: Obfuscation: the hidden malware. In: IEEE S&P (2011)
35. Palisse, A., Durand, A., Le Bouder, H., Le Guernic, C., Lanet, J.-L.: Data aware defense (DaD): towards a generic and practical ransomware countermeasure. In: Lipmaa, H., Mitrokotsa, A., Matulevičius, R. (eds.) NordSec 2017. LNCS, vol. 10674, pp. 192–208. Springer, Cham (2017). https://doi.org/10.1007/978-3-319-70290-2_12
36. Pavithran, J., Patnaik, M., Rebeiro, C.: D-time: distributed threadless independent malware execution for runtime obfuscation. In: USENIX WOOT (2019)
37. Rosenberg, I., Shabtai, A., Rokach, L., Elovici, Y.: Generic black-box end-to-end attack against state of the art API call based malware classifiers. In: RAID (2018)
38. Scaife, N., Carter, H., Traynor, P., Butler, K.R.B.: CryptoLock (and drop it): stopping ransomware attacks on user data. In: ICDCS (2016)
39. Šrndic, N., Laskov, P.: Practical evasion of a learning-based classifier: a case study. In: IEEE S&P (2014)
40. Xu, W., Qi, Y., Evans, D.: Automatically evading classifiers: a case study on pdf malware classifiers. In: Networks and Distributed Systems Symposium (2016)

Intrusion Detection

Quality Evaluation of Cyber Threat Intelligence Feeds

Harm Griffioen[✉], Tim Booij, and Christian Doerr

Cyber Security Group, TU Delft, Delft, The Netherlands
{h.j.griffioen,c.doerr}@tudelft.nl, t.m.booij@student.tudelft.nl

Abstract. In order to mount an effective defense, information about likely adversaries, as well as their techniques, tactics and procedures is needed. This so-called *cyber threat intelligence* helps an organization to better understand its threat profile. Next to this understanding, specialized feeds of indicators about these threats downloaded into a firewall or intrusion detection system allow for a timely reaction to emerging threats.

These feeds however only provide an actual benefit if they are of high quality. In other words, if they provide relevant, complete information in a timely manner. Incorrect and incomplete information may even cause harm, for example if it leads an organization to block legitimate clients or if the information is too unspecific and results in an excessive amount of collateral damage.

In this paper, we evaluate the quality of 17 open source cyber threat intelligence feeds over a period of 14 months, and 7 additional feeds over 7 months. Our analysis shows that the majority of indicators are active for at least 20 days before they are listed. Additionally, we have found that many list have biases towards certain countries. Finally, we also show that blocking listed IP addresses can yield large amounts of collateral damage.

Keywords: Cyber threat intelligence · Blocklist

1 Introduction

In order to effectively protect a system, one needs information. This includes information about possible attackers, their capabilities, their commonly used tactics and techniques as well as feasible countermeasures. This information can be gathered by a company itself, or obtained from providers specialized in providing this information. At a first glance, the idea of gaining a head start and an upper hand to combat the activities of malicious adversaries seems like an oxymoron. After all, if an intelligence provider distributes information about the activities, used tools or domains and IP addresses from which attacks are being carried out to a wide public, adversaries would immediate recognize having been uncovered and correspondingly change their activities, thereby negating the

© Springer Nature Switzerland AG 2020
M. Conti et al. (Eds.): ACNS 2020, LNCS 12147, pp. 277–296, 2020.
https://doi.org/10.1007/978-3-030-57878-7_14

benefits a defender would have from this information in the first place. The use of cyber threat intelligence is thus a race against the clock, where published information is prone to soon lose its value. This means that the distribution of information about adversarial activities as soon as possible is key. While it is in principle possible for organizations to assemble and grow such a body of knowledge, most shy away from the associated costs and complexity in building such *cyber threat intelligence* (CTI) themselves, but rather turn to commercial and open source threat intelligence providers for help.

In the very recent past, this shift to intelligence-driven defense has led to the emergence of a plethora of companies providing CTI feeds, often at a heavy price tag. Threat intelligence feeds range from complex sitreps, sector analysis and trend reports in essay formats, to machine-readable lists of indicators of compromise such as traffic signatures or malicious IP addresses that organizations can download and install into their firewall, thereby catering to the entire spectrum of organizational cyber security maturity levels. In addition to such for-profit services, a variety of open source alternatives have sprung up, which are provided by security companies as a marketing instrument or driven by a community effort of aggregating information across defenders. While commercial feeds may add unique results for example from internal forensic investigation, many commercial providers have been known to repackage, curate and resell other (open source) lists [5].

By definition, cyber threat intelligence is however a highly perishable good, since as soon as it is discovered and distributed to clients, also adversaries will know that one of their tools or assets has been discovered and would try to replace this "burnt" artifact as soon as possible. Thus, in order to be effective, threat intelligence has to be timely, but also highly accurate. With inaccurate listings, automatic download and application of indicator information could lead to undesired effects such as blocking traffic from benign clients. This collateral damage may overall do more harm than good, which leads to the question how effective these feeds actually are.

In this paper, we aim to answer the question *How effective are open source Cyber Threat Intelligence feeds, and how can we measure their quality?* To do this, we create suitable metrics to evaluate the quality of 24 open source cyber threat intelligence feeds, and estimate the utility and risk each of these services provides to an organization. With our work, we make the following three contributions:

- We introduce a taxonomy to evaluate the quality of cyber threat intelligence feeds aiming to assess the utility the user may gain from such a feed.
- We evaluate the indicators reported on 24 open source threat intelligence feeds across four dimensions, and benchmark using NetFlow data and zone transfers the timeliness, sensitivity, originality and impact of these feeds.
- We empirically analyze the impact, a listing of an indicator on an intelligence feed has, on its activity thereafter. This allows us to evaluate the adoption of these feeds in practice and estimate whether a feed is in practice able to "save" clients and networks from future harm.

The remainder of this paper is structured as follows: Sect. 2 discusses existing work into cyber threat intelligence and its evaluation. In Sect. 3, we develop evaluation criteria for a quality assessment of cyber threat intelligence that will be used within this paper. Section 4 describes open source intelligence feeds collected for the analysis, while Sect. 5 describes their utility in terms of relevance, timeliness, completeness and accuracy. Section 6 evaluates the adoption of these sources in practice and the benefit they bring to networks. Section 7 summarizes our findings and concludes our work.

2   Related Work

Cyber threat intelligence feeds are widely used in industry, and are relied on as a useful tool to mitigate attacks. Despite major commercial interest in these feeds, initial surveys indicate that the quality of these feeds might not be as high as one would like. In a study in 2015 [3], authors state that most intelligence was not specific enough. Additionally, 66% of respondents state that the information is not timely.

On the same note, Tounsi et al. [12] states that there are still many limitations when it comes to threat intelligence. One of the limitations is that there is too much information, with 250 million indicators per day. Another finding in this paper, is that threat intelligence available to enterprises is often out of date due to the short lifespan, and therefore not always useful. Limitations of blocklists are also apparent in [9], in which the authors show the incompleteness of the evaluated blacklists. To further measure the shortcomings, several works have been focused on empirical evaluation of these feeds [7,10,11], as well as test suites with specific goals in testing blocklists [8].

In 2014, Kührer et al. published a paper in which multiple blacklists are empirically analyzed [7]. In this paper, the authors identify for a number of domain lists the active, parked and sinkholed domains. The analysis in the paper gives insight into domain blacklists, measuring their accuracy, completeness and estimating the timeliness of the blacklists. As the goal of the study was not to create metrics to generalize the evaluation of cyber threat intelligence feeds, no metrics have been created and evaluated in this topic.

A Defcon presentation by Pinto and Maxwell [2] aims to measure the effectiveness of threat intelligence feeds in two dimensions. In this presentation, the authors show evaluations for the scope and accuracy of these feeds. Their research has been further complemented by Pawliński and Kompanek [1], which state that there are eight criteria in which the quality of a threat intelligence feed can be measured. These metrics are however not evaluated on a large number of CTI feeds, and some of these metrics are hard to evaluate automatically.

In this paper, we propose four quality metrics for CTI feeds that can be automatically analyzed, and analyze 24 different open source CTI feeds using these metrics.

3   Quality Criteria for Threat Intelligence

In this section, we will describe four different criteria, which we will use in the following to evaluate the quality of open source threat intelligence feeds. As discussed in the related work, Pawliński and Kompanek [1] have proposed at an industry forum a taxonomy to benchmark threat intelligence along the dimensions of (a) relevance, (b) accuracy, (c) completeness, (d) timeliness, and (e) ingestibility. We find this classification however problematic, as several of the criteria are entangled: for example, in the machine learning and pattern recognition domains, relevance is usually measured by precision and recall. In other words, how many of the selected items in a dataset are correctly identified, and how many of the relevant items are found in the dataset, respectively. Recall however also partially assesses similar aspects as completeness, so quantification results would contain some degree of correlation. Along the same lines, accuracy is also widely used concept in machine learning, and in binary classification measures the ratio of true results to all examined data, or $\frac{TP+TN}{TP+TN+FP+FN}$. While threat intelligence is a classification task, classifying activity as either malicious or non-malicious, threat intelligence *feeds* are not classification tasks, but should mainly contain information from one label. Therefore, a binary accuracy characterization does not work well due to imbalance of the data present in the feeds. For these reasons, we propose complementary metrics to measure the quality of these feeds.

A Taxonomy for CTI Quality

In order to evaluate the quality of cyber threat intelligence, we therefore propose a set of four metrics: timeliness, sensitivity, originality and impact, which we will describe in further detail in the following:

1. *Timeliness.* The goal of subscribing to a threat intelligence feed is to obtain early warning of some emergent malicious activity, so that infections in the local area network can be stopped in time before significant losses are incurred. Hence, the earlier indicators such as IP addresses or domain names are flagged, the higher the utility of the feed is to the subscriber, and in turn we can also conclude the better the quality of the provided information. One essential quality criteria of a threat intelligence feed is thus the timeliness of the information posted, in other words how soon a domain or IP address is included in such lists after it has started malicious activities. A high timeliness will minimize the amount of damage that could be incurred as part of a compromise, as it shortens the time window during which hosts may be under adversarial control and the time an adversary may for example exfiltrate data or abuse the infected client.

2. *Sensitivity.* In order to be included into a feed, the threat intelligence provider has to observe some malicious activity in the first place. This is typically done using a variety of sensors, recording network traffic patterns, DNS lookups, as well as for example based on the forensic analysis of malware samples. If

a particular malware instance, C&C server, or maliciously acting host shows only low, sporadic activity, there is a high likelihood that it would not be seen by a provider and thereby go by unmitigated until the problem grows above a certain threshold.

With sensitivity, we therefore assess what volume is necessary for the intelligence provider to take notice of a malicious activity, in other words what is the average and typical minimum threshold at which detection will take place. In addition to quantifying the overall per-feed threshold, we can also measure the sensitivity of a threat intelligence feed with respect to a geographical focus: if a provider predominantly has sensors in a specific region, detection will be biased against threats emerging or deployed in this particular area, while comparatively insensitive towards threats originating outside of the measurement coverage. As Internet threats by definition operate worldwide, heavy geographical biases therefore introduce a significant risk of getting hit unprepared.

3. *Originality.* In practice, an organization would likely subscribe to several threat intelligence feeds, as CTI providers often specialize towards a particular type of threats. We also see this behavior in threat intelligence providers themselves, who – as we have said earlier – are also often aggregating, curating and repacking other sources to be marketed as their own service. An essential metric of a cyber threat intelligence feed is therefore originality, in other words the amount of information that is unique to this particular source and that could not be obtained otherwise.

While originality measure the contribution made by one specific feed, it can also be used as a metric to quantify an ecosystem of intelligence feeds as a whole. Consider a number of k feeds which all report malware C&C servers. If all indicators provided by these feeds are highly unique, in other words there is no or only limited overlap between them, this also means that even their union provides only an insufficient peak at the population of C&C servers. We can thus say that in case of high ecosystem-wide originality each feed only draws for samples from a large problem space, and in these cases the set of intelligence feeds is unsuited to provide sufficient defense against this particular type of threat.

4. *Impact.* When an organization applies the information obtained from the threat intelligence feeds, this should lead to a mitigation of a particular threat, as connections to and from a malicious host are suppressed and no command & control activity or an initial infection should happen anymore. Based this positive impact, an application of the threat information can also have negative consequences, especially if the information is not specific enough or contains false positives.

The former is particularly of concern if feeds only provide IP address information, such as the IP address a command & control server is currently hosted at. While in times of domain-generation algorithms (DGAs) indicators such as domain names have an extremely short lifetime, in many circumstances an actor will not host malicious infrastructure on a dedicated machine, but rather employ the services of commercial vendors as this offer much higher flexibility and incurs no loss (expect for the forfeiture of prepaid service) such as the seizure of own hardware. This however also means that at particular IP address that is flagged as malicious other services may be present which are then also blocked as collateral damage.

Our metric impact measures the consequences to an organization if the information from a threat intelligence feed is applied, for example by blocking IP addresses in the firewall. This can have both positive and negative consequences, and we care whether all of the malicious activity will be suppressed given the feed's data, and whether it *only* covers malicious activity or the application will also cause harm to benign services. For example, if a malware communicates with its C&C server using 10 IP addresses, the blockage is only really successful and useful if all 10 addresses are included in the feed as otherwise the activity simply continues using an alternative channel, and only these 10 addresses are blocked.

4   Datasets

Goal of this paper is to evaluate the quality of cyber threat intelligence feeds, which we will do based on the criteria described in the previous section. For this purpose, we have monitored a total of 24 open source feeds which blacklist domain names as well as IP addresses based on detected malicious activities, annotated into major categories such as botnet C&C server activity, usage as a phishing domains etc. These feeds were continuously monitored over a period of 7 months from August 1, 2018 until February 28, 2019, and when available also all historical records back until January 1, 2018. This yielded a total of 1,383,040 indicators that we are going to use for this evaluation.

For our analysis, we monitored 17 threat intelligence feeds over a period of 14 months, and 7 feeds over a period of 7 months. In Table 1, we will briefly enumerate each of the feeds included in this analysis.

In order to evaluate the available cyber threat intelligence feeds with respect to timeliness, accuracy, completeness and relevance, we make use of two auxiliary datasets:

- **Active domain crawls** Based on zone transfers on registered domains from ICANN and national domain registries, we have crawled approximately 277 million unique domains across 1151 generic and country code top level domains on a daily basis. This data shows which IP address was connected to which domain at any given day.
- **NetFlows of a tier 1 operator** To detect whether an IP address is actually receiving traffic or not, and to investigate the response of networks to a blacklisting, we leverage NetFlow data collected at the backbone of a tier 1 network operator. These NetFlows were recorded at each of the operator's core routers at a sampling rate of 8192:1 and thus allowed the reconstruction of activity towards specific IP addresses. We provided a list of IP addresses flagged as malicious by the threat intelligence feeds, and received an anonymized list of

IP addresses that connected to the suspicious targets. In order to preserve the privacy of the customers, the IP addresses of the clients were anonymized by the ISP using the technique described in [6] and obfuscated at the level of autonomous systems. This allowed to quantify the activity of malicious endpoints without learning anything of about identity of the actual users.

4.1 Anonymization

In order to preserve the privacy of users in the NetFlow dataset, the IP addresses of senders and receivers are randomized to mask their identity. While for Net-Flow datasets only a deterministic, random one-to-one mapping of original to anonymized IP addresses is necessary to match outgoing requests with returning answers, in such blind randomization the relationship information of networks is lost. Thus, it is not possible to preserve information locality information such as a C&C activity realized by several hosts in the same /24 subnet, as these hosts would be scattered across the entire IPv4 space.

In this paper, we use the method introduced by Xu et al. [13], who introduce a random one-to-one mapping while preserving network information. If we represent network addresses in a binary tree which each bit of the IP address when read left to right will result in a transition to the left or right subtree under a node, an IP block under a shared prefix will be expressed as an entire subtree under one specific node. Consider the example in Fig. 1(a), all IP addresses in the prefix P_1 start with the digits "00" in their address, while IP addresses in the adjacent address block begin with "01". Under each leaf node – which are marked in grey – are then all IP addresses associated with this particular IP allocation.

In Xu et al.'s "Cryptography-based Prefix-preserving Anonymization" (Crypto-PAn) [13] scheme, the bit value of every non-leaf node is flipped randomly. This means that if two IP addresses shared a k-bit prefix, also the anonymized IP addresses will share an identical, but now randomized k-bit prefix. Within each netblock, IP addresses can now be scrambled without loosing

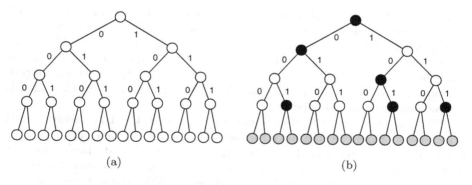

(a)   (b)

Fig. 1. Prefix-preserving randomization after Xu et al. [13]

Table 1. List of evaluated open source feeds

TI Feed	Automated	Period	Amount of IPs
Badips	Yes	14 months	95
Bambenek	Yes	14 months	1,796
Blocklist.de	Hybrid	14 months	944,622
BotScout Bot List	No	14 months	1,564
Botvrij	No	14 months	95
BruteForceBlocker	No	14 months	4,663
CI Army IP	Hybrid	14 months	181,439
CINSscore	Hybrid	14 months	250,153
Charles the Haleys	No	7 months	38,999
Cruzit	No	7 months	49,911
Danger.rulez	No	7 months	3,099
Dshield	No	14 months	106
Emerging Threats	No	14 months	10,464
Greensnow	No	14 months	116,748
MalwareConfig	Yes	14 months	19
Malwaredomainlist	Yes	14 months	1,011
Myip	No	7 months	55,936
Nothink	Yes	7 months	42
Phishtank	Yes	14 months	2,708
Ransomwaretracker	Hybrid	14 months	383
Rutgers	Yes	14 months	112,898
Talos	Hybrid	7 months	2683
Tech. Blogs and Reports	Yes	14 months	6,151
Zeustracker	Yes	7 months	112

information about the logical coherence of the addresses to one provider, and prefix-preserving anonymization comes in handy for the evaluation of threat intelligence feeds as related activity is often located in adjacent IP addresses or subnet blocks as we will show later. The randomness in Crypto-PAn is drawn from the AES block cipher, and a short encryption key is thus sufficient to provide an effective IP randomization function. The authors prove in [13] that this scheme delivers semantic security.

The anonymization of NetFlows was done on site of the Tier1 operator using a secret key chosen by the operator, so that only obfuscated data was analyzed within the context of this project, thus preserving the identity of Internet users. In order to match the information on malicious activity from the threat intelligence feeds to the traffic patterns in the NetFlow dataset, the operator additionally provided us with a lookup table of the malicious IP addresses from the feeds to the anonymized counterpart in the dataset to enable the analysis presented in the remainder of this paper.

5   Quality Evaluation of Feeds

Based on the criteria introduced in Sect. 3, in this section we discuss the results of the quality evaluation of the 24 tested cyber threat intelligence feeds. The following subsections will first review their performance in terms of timeliness, sensitivity, originality and impact, before in Sect. 6 we will in further detail analyze the question of their overall utility and adoption in practice.

5.1   Timeliness

In this section, we are assessing the timeliness of cyber threat intelligence feeds based on the amount of traffic a particular destination has received, prior and after it was included in the analyzed feeds.

To visualize the process, Fig. 2 depicts connections within the Tier1 network to seven example destination IP addresses between July 2018 and January 2019 that were in the second half of 2018 flagged as malicious. For each day, we aggregated flows from distinct clients towards each destination, the size of each circle shows in logarithmic scale the total number of recorded flows. Note that the IP addresses are anonymized as discussed in Sect. 4: while the anonymization protocol matched the feed indicators to the IP addresses, the shown IP addresses are randomized at the level of prefixes. Thus, no conclusion can be taken about the concrete IP addresses at hand or their location in the world.

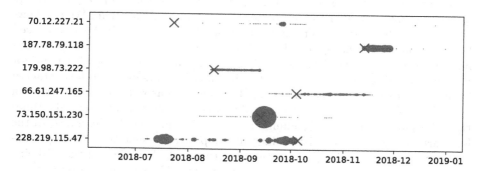

Fig. 2. Scatter plot of netflow activity. The size of the line shows the amount of traffic observed. Crosses denote when the IP address was blacklisted.

As we see in the graph, we find that activity on IP addresses and their appearance in intelligence feeds frequently diverges significantly in practice. The first three IP addresses in the figure are examples of a very timely detection – the IP addresses are reported as soon as the first activity arises, and in the first case

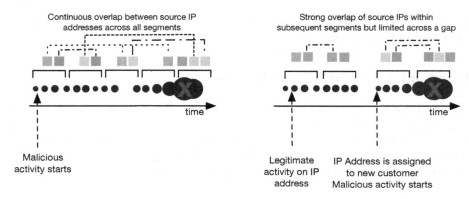

Fig. 3. By comparing the set of IP addresses that are connecting to an IP address flagged as malicious, we can approximate the start of the malicious activity.

even months before significant botnet traffic appears towards this C&C server. Not every intelligence report is however as successful. In the fourth and fifth case, the IP addresses are active for several weeks prior to reporting, and in case of 73.150.151.230 it is only marked as malicious after a significant traffic volume emerges. An even worse outcome is shown just below in case of 228.219.115.47: while after the including of the IP address in the threat feeds activity abruptly stops, the IP address had been active for almost 3 months prior, and been engaged in thousands of connections with clients.

While we could simply mark the onset of a significant number of flows to a flagged IP as the beginning of the illicit activity, this procedure would result in overestimations for example when IP addressed used legitimately before are reallocated by a provider to a customer that starts to abuse them. We can however identify the starting point and transition phases such as IP churn or hacked hosts by comparing the sets of client IP addresses that connect to a flagged destination. Intuitively, we exploit here that a server running as a reporting point for ransomware or as a command & control instance for bots or would be contacted in regular intervals by infected clients [4], while regular website would attract a more diverse group of visitors that would make a connection at unspecific times than the same set of clients coming back in the similar regular intervals. In the left part of Fig. 3, there exists a large overlap of the client IP addresses making contact for the entire period beginning the start of traffic and the IP being reported malicious. In the right part, we can identify a break in this pattern, with a consecutive sequence of windows showing significant overlap until being marked, while earlier activity shows only insignificant overlap with this period. When doing this analysis for the IP addresses flagged as malicious by the feeds, we can thereby obtain a conservative lower rather than a loose upper bound for the start of the malicious activity.

We conducted the analysis of timeliness for all 1,383,040 indicators across the 24 threat intelligence feeds and counted the number of consecutive days

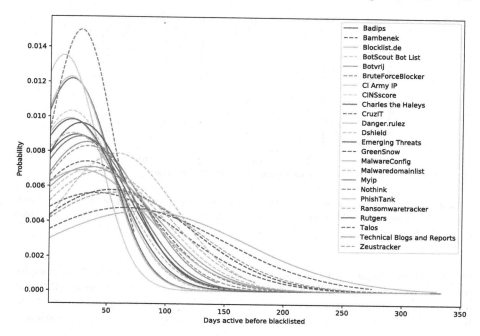

Fig. 4. PDF of the times it takes a list to blacklist a host after it became active. From the plot can be seen that hosts are routinely active for multiple weeks before a destination is marked as malicious by threat intelligence feeds.

IP addresses have received activity from clients before they were included in a particular list. Based on this analysis, we find that the first examples of successful indication in Fig. 2 are the exception rather than the norm, surprisingly we find that it takes on average 21 days before indicators are included in a list.

Figure 4 splits this analysis out, where each curve shows in a probability density function the number of active days until listed by an individual provider. As can be seen in the graph, a handful of feeds are clearly leading the pack, with the response time of CI Army being about 50% better than the overall average. In the bulk of the feeds, we find surprisingly high homogeneity and overall slow inclusion of malicious sources into the feeds, with turn around times of on average approximately one month. Even lists commonly praised by practitioners as "high quality" or "industry standards", such as the widely used *Emerging Threats* score surprisingly average in this respect. At the lower end of the scale, we have already observed activity for on average 65 to 80 days, before the slowest to respond feeds – Talos and PhishTank – include these IP address in their reports as malicious.

This lag between the emergence of malicious activity and the inclusion in the threat intelligence feeds might be due to a slow update frequency. To investigate this hypothesis, we analyzed the inter-arrival time when information was included across the 24 feeds, Fig. 5 shows a cumulative density function of the time in between list updates. As we can see from the graph, information is pushed

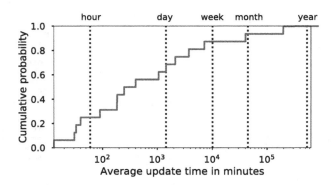

Fig. 5. CDF of update frequency of the evaluated lists. Two thirds of the threat intelligence feeds are updated a least once a day, one thirds even includes new indicators in hourly intervals.

at a very high frequency to the portfolio of lists, in one third of the cases updates occur at least hourly, while approximately two thirds of items are updated at a granularity of at least once per day. Thus, it is not the processing of the lists where reporting latency occurs, but during the selection and preparation of indicators.

5.2 Sensitivity

As we have already seen above, there seems to be a significant deviation between feeds in how soon indicators are included after the first sign of network activity. Figure 6 lists a cumulative density function of the number of connections we observe before an address is included in a particular intelligence feed as malicious. While the majority of lists is surprisingly homogeneous in their sensitivity – we see that the bulk of them triggers with 50% likelihood if at least 6*8192–10*8192 flows are recorded –, also here many drastic outliers emerge. Dshield's sensitivity is across the board 1.5–2 orders of magnitude lower than the rest, here indicators are almost exclusively listed only when they show major activity. When we refer back to Fig. 4, we notice this feed to also perform sub-average with respect to timeliness. Other feeds that are also not very sensitive, like Danger.rulez, have better timeliness.

Sensitivity is however not only dependent on the types of sensors a threat intelligence provider utilizes, but also where these sensors are located. Threats emerging a specific geographic areas might hence be under- or overestimated, leading to an overall bias in sensitivity. As there is no ground truth on where in the world threats are actually located, we can only do a relative evaluation on the position of the listed indicators – based on their IP prefix information – for each individual intelligence feed. Figure 7 shows this relative geographical distribution of indicator per feed, which clearly reveal major differences in reporting between the providers and likely the location of their sensor infrastructure. For instance,

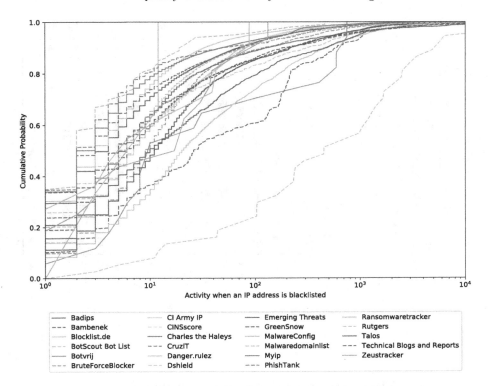

Fig. 6. Cumulative density function of the minimum activity before an IP addresses is included in a threat intelligence feed.

more than 40% of all reports made by Bambenek are located in the United States, whereas more than 40% of reports on MalwareConfig originate from Turkey and around 40% of the data provided by GreenSnow relates to the China.

These biases become even more apparent when we normalize the IP addresses reported as malicious by the number of IP addresses allocated within that region. Assuming that malicious activity is not strongly concentrated within individual countries, we thus obtain a normalized geographical reporting as shown in Fig. 8, this shows that for example CI Army and CINSscore are heavily leaning towards reports from Turkmenistan, which is nearly entirely absent in the reports from all the other threat intelligence providers.

On a positive note, the distribution of reports by Emerging Threats, Badips, Blocklist.de, BruteForceBlocker, CruzIT and Myip show no clear geographical preference, and which seems to lend to the conclusion that their measurement infrastructure is sufficiently diverse.

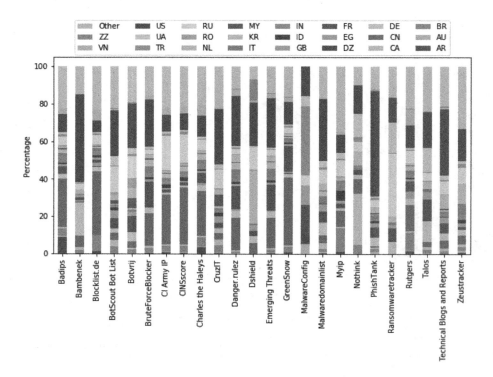

Fig. 7. Geographical distribution of indicators per list.

5.3   Originality

To investigate the uniqueness of the provided information, we traced for each of the 1.38 million indicators when it was first emerging on a particular list and whether individual indicators were afterwards also included on other lists. Besides the result of independent original research, such reuse might also indicate that a particular feed would important the data provided by others. Figure 9 shows the later reuse of indicator information across lists, where an arrow indicates that information first originated at the source of the arrow and was later included in the list its points to. The thickness of the arrow and the corresponding label corresponds with the percentage of information on the receiving list, that earlier appeared somewhere else. For readability, only flows where more than 5% potentially originated from a different list are shown.

While commercial threat intelligence providers often only consolidate and curate information as discussed above, we see also some repackaging – although at highly varying degrees – in case of open source feeds. The indicators first appearing on the feed Blocklist.de routinely appear on other lists, and in two cases a fifth of all indicators are shared with Blocklist.de where they appear earlier. Similarly, a quarter of the indicators on Danger.rulez previously appeared on Emerging Threats, however at a global scale such repacking is comparatively

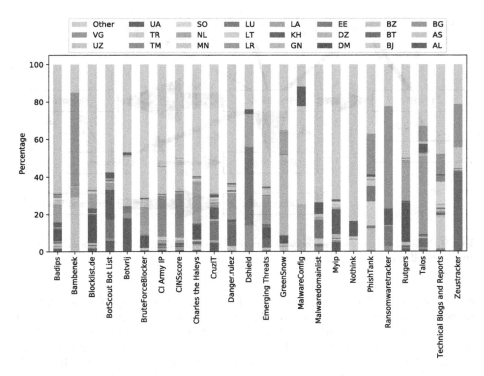

Fig. 8. Relative geographical distribution of indicators, normalized by total number of IP addresses in a country.

seldom and only 11 out of the 24 lists showed such relationships at all. Across the entire dataset, indicators reappear comparatively seldom, in total only 85,906 out of the total 1.38 million entries were also listed on another feed (6.2%).

5.4 Impact

In order to evaluate the level of potential collateral damage, we resolved the IPv4 and IPv6 A records of 277 million domain name across 1151 top-level domain zones that we received from the TLD operators on a daily basis. For every threat intelligence feed, we then analyze how many domain names were pointing to a particular IP address on the day it was marked as malicious, as all of these domain names would no longer be resolvable if a customer would apply the ruleset provided by the threat intelligence provider in for example a firewall. Figure 10 shows the cumulative density function of the number of domain names resolving to the indicated IP addresses by threat feed.

As we can see in the graph, there are drastic differences in the amount of collateral damage between feeds. A homogeneous set of feeds – among them BruteForceBlocker, Talos, CruzIT, CI Army IP, and Rutgers – are comparatively targeted, more than half of their entries are not affected any other domain

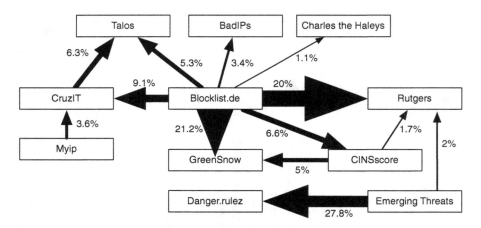

Fig. 9. Indicator reuse across feeds occurs only sporadically, with the expection of two threat intelligence feeds.

names, while the 80% most targeted indicators affect less than 6 other domain names if applying an IP-based block. This is somewhat logical for a list that focuses on bruteforcing, which is typically not happening from servers that host websites or are operated by a shared web hoster, this is however not the case for the information included on CruzIT, CI Army IP or Rutgers, which include IP addresses used to attack or probe certain networks. For Talos we know that it is curated by Cisco, which makes it likely that this is the reason for the low amount of collateral damage.

This is however not true for all of the feeds. In case of Bambenek, only 16% of the best performing indicators will block less than 50 live domains hosted at these websites, where the 50% worst performing indicators even affect 100 or more domains as collateral damage. While some of the blocked domains may certainly also contain malicious activity, some of the instances included large shared hosters, in one case with more than 900,000 domains pointing to the blacklisted IP address. While such issues could be explained due to automatic collection of indicators, we also found a surprisingly poor track record in case of "Technical Blogs and Reports", a curated list of human analyst reports. This indicates that human-made feeds are not necessarily better, or at least suggests that feeds do not filter records that could potentially be harmful to normal system operation.

6   Discussion

After an evaluation of each of the 24 feeds across the four dimensions timeliness, sensitivity, originality and impact, we will take a step back in this section and evaluate the ecosystem of intelligence feeds as a whole. Specifically we will investigate how widely these feeds are adopted by network owners and operators in

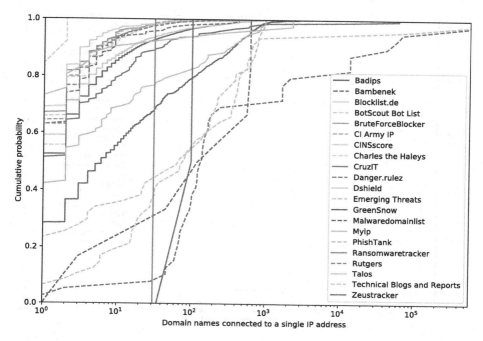

Fig. 10. Cumulative probability function of the domain names associated with the IP addresses indicated as malicious per threat intelligence feed.

practice, and review the issue of the surprisingly high level of originality for the ecosystem as a whole.

6.1   Adoption of Intelligence Feeds

As cyber threat intelligence feeds are meant to alert and empower network owners to block malicious activity, their application should lead to a reduction in network traffic towards the hosts flagged as malicious. This observation provides us with an angle to investigate the adoption of threat intelligence feeds worldwide. After all, as soon as an indicator has appeared on a list we would expect a significant drop of activity – if not the absence of requests – from subscribers.

When networks apply the information provided in cyber threat intelligence feeds at scale, we should ideally see the activity from infected clients to malicious destinations drop and eventually die out. As we have however seen above, intelligence feeds are not universally adopted but have a specific regional footprint and there exists only a marginal overlap between lists; thus, even if a network would subscribe to and apply the information from every single intelligence feed we cannot expect all activity to immediately seize.

Figure 11 shows a probability density function of how long activity towards a particular destination continued after an indicator was listed on a particular intelligence feed. As we see from the graph, the inclusion of indicators on for

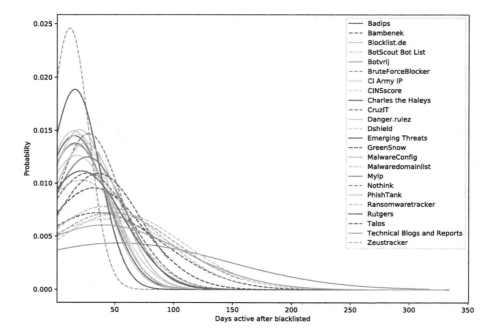

Fig. 11. ontinuation of activity to flagged destinations after listing in a feed.

example BruteForceBlocker seems to be an effective deterrent, as on average activity stops within 2 weeks time. Other lists such as Botvrij are less successful: more than 50% of all hosts reported as malicious by this feed continue their activity for at least 79 days, with an extremely long trail, thus a listing on this block list seems to have almost no impact on the criminal activity itself. Like in case of timeliness until detection (see Sect. 5.1), the threat intelligence feeds are also surprisingly homogeneous with respect to the continuation of activities, and we can clearly see in Fig. 11 two main clusters, with activity termination peaking around 20 days after listing and 60 days after reporting.

6.2 Do We Have Enough Coverage?

There remain however questions about the quality of the ecosystem of cyber threat intelligence providers as a whole. Although it is desirable for a customer that CTI feeds have a large degree of originality as otherwise a customer would subscribe – and pay for – redundant information, we have seen that the amount of overlap between the entire spectrum of analyzed feeds was actually remarkably low. This on the one hand is commendable as it maximizes value of CTI users, on the other hand it also raises questions whether the cyber threat intelligence feeds really provide sufficient information to stop malicious activity in their tracks.

As discussed in Sect. 4, the 24 evaluated open source feeds spanned the entire ecosystem of malicious activity from bruteforcing activity, ransomware and other malware, to botnets. As each type of malicious activity was covered by multiple feeds, we actually would expect *some* overlap in reported indicators. The fact that there is almost no overlap between lists of similar scope could be the result of two reasons: first, all individual lists for example targeting botnets or ransomware rely on orthogonal detection methods and are therefore providing complementary information. Second, the lists monitor malicious activity in comparable ways, but the overall volume of malicious activity is so large that effectively each lists only obtains a tiny sample, and such low rate sampling from a large universe would statistically lead to a very low chance for duplicates.

Conceptually, we can see that we are probably dealing with the latter than the former reason, after all methods to for example detect ransomware C&C servers are limited, and most likely all providers would employ off-the-shelf tools such as an analysis of network activity across malware samples or a forensic analysis thereof. This unfortunately drives us to the conclusion that cyber threat intelligence feeds cover much less of malicious activity than we would expect and require, to apply intelligence feeds and confidently expect that with a very high degree of certainty malicious activity will be stopped through these indicators.

7   Conclusions

Effective protection requires insights into the activities of adversaries, commonly referred to as cyber threat intelligence. In order to protect against evolving threats, networks can subscribe to CTI feeds which list indicators, such as domain names, IP addresses, or hashes, related to malicious activity.

In this paper, we have analyzed 1.38 million indicators provided by 24 open source cyber threat intelligence feeds over a period of 14 months, and analyzed whether the information provided by these lists is timely, original, and estimated how sensitive the detection of the intelligence providers are as well as the positive and negative impacts a utilization of these feeds would have in practice. We find large variations between the performance of these lists, some are providing indicators within a few days while others only report activity months after it has commenced. This variation is surprising as we find all feeds to be relatively homogeneous in sensitivity, in other words the threshold beyond which they pick up undesired activity.

Nearly all of the analyzed lists are able to provide a significant intelligence contribution. Although lists contain a small degree of overlap, these lists are not merely subsets or repackaged versions of each other. This on the one hand is valuable to defenders as each feed does provide benefit with limited redundancy, at the same time the little overlap across all CTI feeds raises the question how much the ecosystem of cyber threat intelligence feeds as a whole really covers, and whether the current feeds will provide defenders with a suitable defense posture if applied.

References

1. Evaluating threat intelligence feeds. https://www.first.org/resources/papers/munich2016/kompanek-pawlinski-evaluating-threat-ntelligence-feeds.pdf
2. Measuring the IQ of your threat intelligence. https://www.slideshare.net/AlexandrePinto10/defcon-22-measuring-the
3. The second annual study on exchanging cyber threat intelligence: there has to be a better way. https://www.ponemon.org/blog/the-second-annual-study-on-exchanging-cyber-threat-intelligence-there-has-to-be-a-better-way
4. Abbink, J., Doerr, C.: Popularity-based detection of domain generation algorithms. In: 2nd International Workshop on Malware Analysis (2017)
5. EclecticIQ: Intelligence-powered defences. https://www.eclecticiq.com/dss
6. Foukarakis, M., Antoniades, D., Antonatos, S., Markato, E.P.: Flexible and high-performance anonymization of NetFlow records using anontool. In: Third International Conference on Security and Privacy in Communications Networks and the Workshops (2007)
7. Kührer, M., Rossow, C., Holz, T.: Paint it black: evaluating the effectiveness of malware blacklists. In: Stavrou, A., Bos, H., Portokalidis, G. (eds.) RAID 2014. LNCS, vol. 8688, pp. 1–21. Springer, Cham (2014). https://doi.org/10.1007/978-3-319-11379-1_1
8. Oest, A., Safaei, Y., Doupé, A., Ahn, G.J., Wardman, B., Tyers, K.: PhishFarm: a scalable framework for measuring the effectiveness of evasion techniques against browser phishing blacklists. IEEE (2019)
9. Ramachandran, A., Feamster, N., Vempala, S.: Filtering spam with behavioral blacklisting. In: Proceedings of the 14th ACM Conference on Computer and communications Security, pp. 342–351. ACM (2007)
10. Sheng, S., Wardman, B., Warner, G., Cranor, L.F., Hong, J., Zhang, C.: An empirical analysis of phishing blacklists. In: Sixth Conference on Email and Anti-Spam (CEAS), California, USA (2009)
11. Sinha, S., Bailey, M., Jahanian, F.: Shades of grey: on the effectiveness of reputation-based "blacklists". In: 2008 3rd International Conference on Malicious and Unwanted Software (MALWARE), pp. 57–64. IEEE (2008)
12. Tounsi, W., Rais, H.: A survey on technical threat intelligence in the age of sophisticated cyber attacks. Comput. Secur. **72**, 212–233 (2018)
13. Xu, J., Fan, J., Ammar, M., Moon, S.B.: On the design and performance of prefix-preserving IP traffic trace anonymization. In: Proceedings of the 1st ACM SIGCOMM Workshop on Internet Measurement, IMW 2001 (2001)

Game Theory-Based Approach for Defense Against APTs

Juan E. Rubio, Cristina Alcaraz$^{(\boxtimes)}$, and Javier Lopez

Department of Computer Science, University of Malaga,
Campus de Teatinos s/n, 29071 Malaga, Spain
{rubio,alcaraz,jlm}@lcc.uma.es

Abstract. The sophistication of Advanced Persistent Threats (APTs) targeting industrial ecosystems has increased dramatically in recent years. This makes mandatory to develop advanced security services beyond traditional solutions, being Opinion Dynamics one of them. This novel approach proposes a multi-agent collaborative framework that permits to trace an APT throughout its entire life-cycle, as formerly analyzed. In this paper, we introduce TI&TO, a two-player game between an attacker and defender that represents a realistic scenario where both compete for the control of the resources within a modern industrial architecture. By validating this technique using game theory, we demonstrate that Opinion Dynamics consists in an effective first measure to deter and minimize the impact of an APT against the infrastructure in most cases. To achieve this, both attacker and defense models are formalized and an equitable score system is applied, to latter run several simulation test cases with different strategies and network configurations.

Keywords: Opinion Dynamics · Advanced Persistent Threat · Detection · Response · Defense · Game theory

1 Introduction

There is an evident growth in the number of cyber-security attacks that worldwide companies have to face, which generates a huge economic loss due to the investment performed in terms of cyber-security [1]. This situation becomes more critical when it comes to critical infrastructures (i.e., nuclear plants, electricity grids, transport and manufacturing systems), whose industrial control systems must be kept working under all conditions. Here, we are dealing with SCADA (Supervisory Control and Data Acquisition) systems that have been working in isolation from external networks for decades; nowadays, in turn, they are increasingly integrating novel technologies such as Internet of Things (IoT) or Cloud Computing to outsource diverse services while cutting costs. As a consequence, a greater effort is needed to keep up with such advancement, as to cope with the newest attack vectors and exploitable vulnerabilities that these systems may pose.

© Springer Nature Switzerland AG 2020
M. Conti et al. (Eds.): ACNS 2020, LNCS 12147, pp. 297–320, 2020.
https://doi.org/10.1007/978-3-030-57878-7_15

One of the most critical issue in recent years is the Advanced Persistent Threats (APTs), which are sophisticated attacks that are especially tailored to a target infrastructure, perpetrated by a well-resource organization. They are characterized for leveraging zero-day vulnerabilities and employ stealthy techniques that make the threat undetectable for a long period of time within the victim network. Stuxnet was the first reported threat of this nature [2], but many others were detected afterwards, usually months after the attack had been completely executed [3]. On the cyber-security side, just some mechanisms have been proposed to address this issue from a holistic perspective, beyond traditional mechanisms (e.g., firewalls, Intrusion Prevention Systems (IPS), Intrusion Detection Systems (IDS), antivirus) that only represent a punctual protection against APTs in their first stages [4].

Among the novel mechanisms, Opinion Dynamics [5] consists in a multi-agent collaborative system that enables the traceability of the attack throughout its entire life-cycle, by means of a distributed anomaly correlation. In this paper, we propose a theoretical but realistic scenario to prove the effectiveness of that approach under different types of attack model, using concepts supported by the structural controllability field [6] and game theory [7]. For that goal, we develop TI&TO, a two-player game where attacker and defender compete for the control of the resources within a modern industrial architecture. Both players have their own movements and associated scores, according to the behavior of an APT and a detection system based on Opinion Dynamics, respectively. This game is ultimately run in different simulations that aim to show the algorithm capabilities, while also suggesting the optimal configuration of the technique in conjunction with other defense solutions. Therefore, we can summarize our contributions as:

- Formal definition of the TI&TO game, specifying the game board, each player's goal and the score rules.
- Design of an attacker model in form of a set of stages that flexibly represents the phases of an APT, to represent the movements of the attacker, which are subject to a determined score.
- Design of a defender model based on the use of Opinion Dynamics and response techniques (i.e., local detection, redundant links, honeypots) to reduce the impact of the APT within the network, which also implies an associated score in the game.
- Experiments carried out to validate the algorithm and recommend the configuration of the defender that returns the best result.

The remainder of this paper is organized as follows: Sect. 2 introduces the concept of Opinion Dynamics and highlights other proposals that apply game theory for the detection of cyber-attacks. In Sect. 3 the game is defined, including the rules as well as the attack and defense models. Then, several simulations are carried out and a discussion is offered in Sect. 4. Lastly, the conclusions and future work are presented in Sect. 5.

2   Preliminaries

In this section, the main concepts that are needed to understand the basics of TI&TO are introduced from a theoretical perspective. Firstly, we explain the aspects of the Opinion Dynamics detection and its benefits, to later set the background with respect to game theory.

2.1   Opinion Dynamics

The Opinion Dynamics approach proposes to aggregate the coverage of multiple detection systems that are strategically deployed over an infrastructure, under a common distributed framework that permanently correlates and learns from all the malware patterns and anomalies detected. This way, various detection solutions can be combined at all levels to anticipate the new technology scenarios of Industry 4.0 in terms of security, by easing the traceability of attacks and the application of effective response procedures. Under a theoretical perspective, it was introduced in [5], and then its authors demonstrated the effectiveness of the approach with an enhanced attack model [8] and an improved correlation of events [9]. Concerning a practical applicability, its authors demonstrated its capabilities to detect and monitor attacks in a real industrial testbed [10], and also showed its contributions to the Smart Grid scenario [11], where it can help to prevent against intrusions and blackouts.

As its name suggests, this correlation algorithm conceptually models the opinion fluctuation in a society. It is one of the most popular consensus models to obtain the accurate polarization of opinions in certain population [12]. In our case, if we assume a set of agents (i.e., that monitor each device of the network) which are connected according to a graph $G(V, E)$ (where V is the set of agents and E the intermediate communication links between resources), each one holds a certain opinion (in our case, about the level of anomaly detected in its surroundings) and influences those of the agents who are closer in their posture. Eventually, once this correlation of opinion has been performed among all the individual agents, this 'society' (i.e., the network) is fragmented into different clusters of opinions that correspondingly identify the areas of the network that experience the same degree of anomaly (potentially caused by an attack focused on that zone).

The formalization of this correlation is the following: Opinion Dynamics is an iterative algorithm which assumes that there is a 1:1 relationship between devices in the control network (modelled with graph $G(V, E)$) and individual agents that are permanently monitoring their security state, so that we have a set of agents $A = \{a_1, a_2, \ldots a_{|V|}\}$. The opinion of an agent a_i at iteration t is represented by $x_i(t)$. Initially, prior to execute the Opinion Dynamics correlation, $x_i(0)$ contains the level of anomaly sensed by agent i, which is a float number that ranges from 0 to 1 (being 1 the highest anomaly). On the other hand, the influence between agents (to determine the new opinions in next iterations) is represented by a weight given by each agent a_i to the opinion of each neighbour a_j in A (i.e., there exists an edge (v_i, v_j) in E), which is denoted by w_{ij}. For each agent a_i in

A, we have that $\sum_{k=1}^{|V|} w_{ik} = 1$. This way, every agent i also takes its own opinion into account and weighs the influence of surrounding agents depending on the closeness of their opinions, as explained in [8]. Finally, the new opinion of the agent i in the iteration $t + 1$ is generated according to the following expression:

$$x_i(t+1) = \sum_{j=1}^{n} w_{ij} x_j(t)$$

Therefore, the correlation of opinion for a given agent is performed as a weighted sum of the other opinions. If this algorithm is executed with enough number of iterations (something trivial due to the lower complexity of calculations), the resulting opinions of all agents can be grouped into clusters with the same anomaly value. Consequently, after the execution of Opinion Dynamics, the more affected areas after an attack will be those that expose a high opinion value.

Due to the flexible characterization of each agent opinion, this algorithm can be conceived as a framework, since multiple detection mechanisms can be orchestrated to analyze each host and its network activity to finally output a single anomaly value to represent $x_i(0)$ in the algorithm. As an example, the original authors suggest the use of anomaly detection mechanisms, vulnerability scanners or Security Information and Event Management systems, as well as ad-hoc machine learning techniques. These systems could be applied in a distributed way, and their outputs would be retrieved by a central correlator that features enough computational capabilities as to execute the Opinion Dynamics algorithm. This centralized entity is put into practice in [10], where other functionalities such as the evolution of anomalies over time and the persistence of resources are also studied.

Here, we leverage game theory to assess the utility of this mechanism when deploying response techniques that use the information provided by Opinion Dynamics in multiple scenarios. For such goal, we base our game on the detection approach and the attacker model presented in the aforementioned publications, to study the optimal configuration of different response procedures that ultimately aim to deter and eradicate the effect of an APT.

2.2 Game Theory: Related Work

In the context of industrial networks defense, researchers have been extensively exploring the applicability of game theory [7]. In these networks, it is common to cope with many levels of criticality, different network sizes, interconnectivity and access control policies. Therefore, decisions in terms of security frequently fluctuate, which is harder in Industry 4.0 scenarios, where many heterogeneous devices interact with each other and organizations exchange information using the Cloud, Fog Computing or Distributed Ledger Technologies. In this sense, game theory offers the capability of analyzing hundreds of scenarios, thereby enhancing the decision making. At the same time, it also allows to validate the effectiveness of a given technique (e.g., Opinion Dynamics in our case) if we analyze different strategies of use for all the scenarios examined.

Based on the information that each player has, there are different types of games: on the one hand, in a *perfect information* game both players are aware of the actions taken by their adversary at all times; on the other hand, a *complete information* game assumes that every player always knows the strategy and payoffs of the opponent. As explained further in Sect. 3, the approach presented in this paper (TI&TO) represents a two-player game with imperfect and incomplete information, since no player (i.e., attacker and defender) knows the location of the adversary within the network topology or his/her score. According to a second level of classification, this game can be considered as dynamic and stochastic, as both players take their actions based on the state of the network and being exposed to events that affect them in a probabilistic way.

There are multiple researches in the literature that fall under these classifications. Concerning complete perfect information games, Lye et al. [13] proposes a two-player game that simulates the security of a network composed by four nodes that can be in 18 potential states, on which both players can take up to 3 actions, that are observable at all times by the opponent. With respect to complete imperfect information games, Nguyen et al. [14] propose 'fictitious play (FP)', a game that considers the network security as a sequence of nonzero-sum games were both players cannot make perfect observations of the adversary's previous actions. On the other hand, Patcha et al. [15] propose a incomplete perfect information approach, for the detection of intrusions in mobile ad-hoc networks. Whereas the attacker's objective is to send a malicious message and compromise a target node, the defender tries to detect it using a host-based IDS. Another related work based on imperfect information is [16], where van Dijk et al. propose a simple game where two players compete for the stealthy control of a resource without knowing the actual identity of the owner until a player actually moves.

Many of these solutions have been successfully applied to the detection of threats. However, most of the models are based on either static games or dealing with perfect and complete information, aiming to find an optimal strategy when a steady state of the game is reached (being the Nash equilibrium the most famous one) [7]. In contrast, a real control system faces a dynamic interaction game with incomplete and imperfect information about the attacker, and the proposed models of this category do not specify a realistic scenario with an extensive attack model [16,17]. This lays the base and inspiration for the design and implementation of our proposed scheme. With TI&TO, we aim to get insight about how to effectively implement and configure a defense strategy based on the use of Opinion Dynamics, under such stochastic conditions.

3   The Game: Attack and Defense Models

Once the problematic has been introduced and the Opinion Dynamics has been explained, this section presents TI&TO from a theoretical perspective, prior to execute simulations in Sect. 4. Firstly, we introduce the board, the rules and the overall objective for both players: attacker and defender. Then, each one is individually addressed and their attack model formalized.

3.1   The Board: Proposed Network Architecture

As defined in next subsection, TI&TO focuses on a game where both attacker and defender fight for the control of an infrastructure. The attacker tries to break into the network in a stealthy way by taking over as many nodes as to complete the predefined kill chain of a specific APT. With respect to the defender, he/she must recover those nodes until he/she completely eradicates the threat from the network. Thus, this network infrastructure plays the role of the game board, and must be designed realistically as to represent the topology of a modern industrial ecosystem.

For this reason, the network used in the game embodies cyber-physical resources of different nature, ranging from operational devices (OT) (e.g., sensors/actuators, Programmable Logic Controllers (PLCs), SCADA systems, etc.) to Information Technology (IT) devices from the managerial point of view (e.g., customer-end systems). Following the Opinion Dynamics solution [8], the board will be an infrastructure composed by two sections with the same number of nodes: OT and IT, connected via firewalls to secure the traffic. Let the network be represented with graph $G(V, E)$, so that V refers to the nodes connected with each other based on links contained in the E set. Thus, OT and IT sections are represented with $G(V_{OT}, E_{OT})$ and $G(V_{IT}, E_{IT})$, respectively (having $V = V_{IT} \cup V_{OT}$ and $E = E_{IT} \cup E_{OT}$). Both sections are randomly generated following a different network distribution, which enables us to simulate different infrastructure setups. On the one hand, the IT section follows a small-world network distribution, that models the traditional topology of TCP/IP networks [18]. In turn, $G(V_{OT}, E_{OT})$ is based on a power-law distribution of type $y \propto x^{-\alpha}$, that is commonly used for the modelling of industrial control systems [19].

Once generated, both sections are connected by means of a set of intermediate firewalls V_{FW}, so that $V = V_{IT} \cup V_{OT} \cup V_{FW}$, in the following way: as for the IT section, we want devices to be able to access the OT section, since they are computationally capable nodes that commonly control the production chain from the corporate network. This means that all nodes in V_{IT} are connected to V_{FW}. However, on the OT side, only SCADA systems and other high-level servers can access external networks, whereas the majority of them are sensors, PLCs and devices with a restricted functionality. Consequently, the connected nodes will be those that have a maximum connectivity (i.e., dominance in graph theory) within the power-law distribution network of the OT section, given the concepts of structural controllability stated in [20] and [21]. According to these, the Dominating Set (DS) of a graph conforms the subset of nodes ($\mathbf{D_N}$ henceforth, also called 'driver nodes') for which every node not in $\mathbf{D_N}$ is adjacent to at least one member of $\mathbf{D_N}$. On the other hand, if we further restrict this condition, the Power Dominating Set (PDS) of a graph is defined as the subset of nodes for which every edge in E is adjacent to at least one node of the PDS. Therefore, for our concerned network infrastructure, this subset of nodes of the OT section will be connected to the firewalls that also connect to the IT nodes. In our simulations, we consider that the 5% of the total number of nodes in V are firewalls, to restrict the traffic between both sections in a realistic way.

In order to characterize the types of nodes within the architecture and enrich the network model, it is also necessary to define some related concepts that will be useful to understand the game dynamics:

Criticality of Nodes. We define the criticality of a resource as the risk subject to that type of device within the organization, and determines the impact of a given threat if the attack is perpetrated at that point. For example, the criticality of a sensor is negligible compared to that of the SCADA system, which implies dramatic consequences on the infrastructure in the event it is disrupted. Likewise, resources in the OT section are also deemed as more critical than the IT ones to ensure the continuity of the production chain. This will be also used by the defender to assess which nodes should be healed in order to minimize the impact of an APT. We formally define this concept taking into account the graph $G(V, E)$ introduced before. Firstly, let $CRIT : V \mapsto \mathbb{R}(0, 1)$ be a function that assigns a criticality degree to all nodes of the network. In order to distinguish which devices present a higher hierarchy within the topology, we leverage the concept of DS and PDS introduced in Sect. 3.1. At the same time, since the OT section is considered as especially critical, its devices will have to be associated with a higher value. As a result, we define Ψ as an *ordered set of criticality values of size d*, where $\Psi = \psi_1, ..., \psi_d$ and $\psi_i = [0, 1]$, such that $\forall \psi_i, \psi_i < \psi_{i+1}$.

Table 1. Map of V to Ψ

$V_{IT} - DS_{IT} - PDS_{IT}$	ψ_1
$V_{OT} - DS_{OT} - PDS_{OT}$	ψ_2
DS_{IT}	ψ_3
DS_{OT}	ψ_4
PDS_{IT}	ψ_5
$PDS_{OT} \cup FW$	ψ_6

Once Ψ is defined, we can create a model that maps every element of the network (i.e., its nodes) to the elements of Ψ. Such model, where $d = 6$ and $\Psi = \psi_1, \psi_2, \psi_3, \psi_4, \psi_5, \psi_6$ to consider all elements of both network sections (i.e., the OT and IT section, including its nodes and the DS and PDS subsets), is described in Table 1.

Vulnerability of Nodes. Besides the criticality, the concept of vulnerability involves the ease of a node to be compromised by the attacker. In this case, we will assume that this value is opposed to the criticality, in the sense that field devices will be commonly equipped with lower security protection measures, whereas high-level systems that control the industrial process will embody advanced security services. Correspondingly, we can define $VULN : V \mapsto \mathbb{R}(0, 1)$ as the function that assigns a vulnerability degree to all nodes of the network. In the same way as criticality, Υ is an ordered set that represents the vulnerability of each node type, where $\Upsilon = v_1, ..., v_d$ and $v_i = 1 - \psi_i$. The particular instantiation of these values for the simulations is carried out when the network represented by $G(V, E)$ is created. This is further addressed in Appendix A.

Redundancy of Links. In order for the OT subnetwork to be resilient against Denial of Service attacks located on their links, and due to the criticality of its resources, we also consider that this section presents redundancy on its edges. This is a solution that was also proposed in [5] as a response technique to enable the reachability of messages across the network. In our case, with the use of auxiliary edges in E (referred to as E_R, so that $E_R \subset E$), we ensure that the detection algorithm exchanges the opinion among agents even when some links are down as consequence of an APT. This may occur in the game when the attacker attempts the defender to lose track of the anomalies in the affected nodes. This way, all nodes in V_{OT} count on an additional channel that interconnects them with another node, based on the strategy explained in [5]. It is worthy to note that these redundant edges are just logical connections that only serve to transfer the anomaly values between agents.

Altogether, Fig. 1 conceptually shows an example of network topology based on these assumptions together with the integration of the Opinion Dynamics correlator. In the diagram, the redundant edges in the OT section are represented with dashed lines.

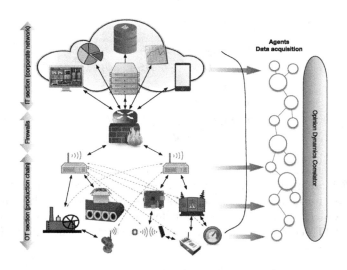

Fig. 1. Example of network topology used in TI&TO

3.2   Rules and Scoring System

We now describe the game dynamics for both players and how each of their movements is measured in quantitative terms. Since the final objective of this research is to assess the effectiveness of the Opinion Dynamics, we aim to analyze the best behavior of the defender for a realistic attack model. Therefore, it becomes necessary to utilize a formal representation of the results while following a fair methodology for both players, which have equivalent costs and rewards assigned to their movements in the game.

We start by defining TI&TO in an informal way. As introduced before, both compete for the control of the game board. The base of the scoring system works as follows: *whereas the attacker earns points as it spreads the threat across the infrastructure, the defender increases the score when those infected nodes are recovered.* However, this is just the number of points scored, which serves as a reference of the throughput achieved by each player. There is a termination condition that regulates who wins a given game: *as for the attacker, the game is over when he/she manages to successfully complete all the phases of the APT kill chain.* Concerning the defender, *the victory is achieved when all nodes infected by the adversary return to their originally uncompromised state.* In the following, we give a formal definition of all the elements involved in TI&TO and the notation used along this manuscript:

Players. There are two players: the attacker and the defender. For simplicity, they are denoted by A and D, respectively.

Time. In our approach, time is split into discrete ticks for the interest of the analysis. The game begins at time $t = 0$ and continues indefinitely as $t \to \infty$. At a given t, A and then D has a turn to play. They act sequentially adopting a Stackelberg game [22], where the attacker is the leader and the defender acts depending on the resulting state of the board.

Movement. It is performed by A or D and changes the board at time t according to their respective attack and defense models. In brief, both players take actions to either take over healthy nodes of the network (in the case of the attacker) or heal a compromised node (by the defender). Therefore, every movement can alter the state of a node. It is denoted by $M^p(t)$.

Node State. It is a time-dependent variable $N = N(t)$ that determines whether a node in V is compromised (i.e., the attacker has reached it) or remains safe from the APT. For a given node i (belonging to the IT or OT section), $N_i(t)$ is equals to one if it is compromised at time t, and zero otherwise. We assume that $\forall v \in V, N_v(0) = 0$.

Reward. Every movement performed by A or D generates a reward depending on the ultimate goal that both of them chase, which determines the score. In this case, A receives one point when a new node is compromised, whereas D obtains the same reward once a previously compromised node has been successfully recovered. A reward for a player p at a time t is denoted by $R^p(t)$.

Cost. Besides a reward, every movement also implies a cost C for the player. This represents the fact that the attacker can exploit vulnerabilities that in turn may cause its detection, while the defender may stop the production chain to recover the security state of a critical resource. It is formalized with $C^p(t)$.

Utility. It is the total number of points scored by a player p at time t. It is calculated as the reward minus the cost of the movement made by p, which is denoted by $U^p(t)$. The overall goal for both players is to maximize the utility as $t \to \infty$, until the game is over.

Strategy. We define a strategy S for a player p as the sequence of movements $M(t)$ along time for a given instance of game, represented by $S^p = \{M^p(0), M^p(1), ..., M^p(t)\}$. As explained later on, this strategy changes as the game evolves: whereas the attacker seeks vulnerable nodes throughout the network while avoiding its detection, the defender follows an adaptive strategy based on the last movement of A (more specifically, on the new state of the affected nodes).

Whereas we consider the utility as a reference for the performance of both players in a given game instance, we define three different termination states:

(TS_1) **Attacker wins.** It is reached when he/she successfully completes all the movements of the strategy S^A, where $S^A = \{M^A(0), M^A(1), ..., M^A(n)\}$. We assume there exists at least one last node v that is compromised, so that $N_v(n) = 1$.

(TS_2) **Defender wins.** It is accomplished when the defender manages to heal all nodes and hence eradicate the effect of the attacker over the entire network, before the succession of movements in S^A are completed. In other words, for a given attacker strategy $S^A = \{M^A(0), M^A(1), ..., M^A(n)\}$, there exists $t' < n$ such that for all $v \in V, N_v(t') = 0$.

(TS_3) **Draw.** For the interest of the analysis, we define an additional third termination condition that occurs when the attacker completes the strategy $S^A = \{M^A(0), M^A(1), ..., M^A(n)\}$ but the defender also performs a last movement that ultimately heals all nodes. In this case, we have that for all $v \in V, N_v(n) = 0$. Even though this may be considered as an attacker win (since he/she succeeds in the disruption of resources), the defender still finds the trace to the threat in the end, which shows the accuracy of the detection technique going after the infection.

With this, the dynamics of the game and the basic rules have been presented. However, we have to describe the precise specification of the players' movements. Whereas the intruder puts into practice a set of individual attack stages that represent an APT (i.e., a strategy of n movements), the defender leverages the Opinion Dynamics algorithm to flexibly adapt to the threat propagation over the network. In both cases, they can apply different actions to change the state of nodes and obtain a score based on different conditions.

3.3 Attacker Model: Succession of APT Stages

As introduced before, we aim to find a formal representation of an APT for the attacker model. In TI&TO, the same authors' methodology in [8] will be used. After an extensive review of the most important APTs reported in recent years, it is possible to specify one of these threats as a finite succession of attack stages perpetrated against an industrial control network defined by the graph $G(V, E)$, so that $attackStages = \{attack\ stage_1, attack\ stage_2, ..., attack\ stage_n\}$. This way, each attack stage corresponds to a different movement performed by the attacker. In the following, we describe the different types of stages and explain their effect on the game board. Then, the reward and cost generated for this player are calculated. Lastly, the strategy creation is explained:

- **initialIntrusion**$_{(IT,OT,FW)}$. After a phase of reconnaissance, the attacker breaks into the network through a 'patient zero' $v_0 \in V$, that can be a node from the IT or OT section. It is the first movement of the attacker ($M^A(0)$), so that $N_{v_0}(0) = 1$.
- **LateralMovement**$_{(IT,OT,FW)}$. Once a node v_i has been compromised, the adversary chooses a FW (if it is accessible), IT, or OT node v_j from the set $neighbours(v_i)$ (i.e., those nodes for which there exists one edge $e = (v_i, v_j)$ such that $e \in E$). For the election of the node to take over, we assume that the attacker scans the network in the seek for the most vulnerable device (according to the $VULN$ function). We assume A can compromise a node that has been previously healed by the defender, but its $VULN$ value is then reduced by half.
- **LinkRemoval**. Once the attacker has perpetrated a lateral movement from v_i towards v_j, that communication channel can be disrupted to decoy the defender (and hence avoid the Opinion Dynamics detection). As a result, the defender cannot exchange the opinion of the agents assigned to v_i and v_j, since no anomaly information is transferred through that link, as explained in the next Section.
- **Exfiltration of information and Destruction**. It represents the final movement of the attacker. The adversary destroys the node that has been previously compromised, after possibly extracting information that is sent to an external Command&Control network.

Each of these movements results in a different cost and reward for the attacker, who determines his or her utility after each turn of the game, so that the score can be compared with the defender. As for the reward, and aiming to hold the symmetry between both players, they will receive one point every time they gain control of a given node that previously belonged to the adversary. For the attacker, it means that there exists one node $v \in V$ at a time t such that $N_v(t-1) = 0$ and $N_v(t) = 1$ after $M^A(t)$, resulting in $R^A(t) = 1$. For simplicity, we consider that all stages have the same reward.

With respect to the cost of every attack stage, we have to recall the Opinion Dynamics algorithm in relationship with the defender goals. We assume all the network resources are monitored by anomaly detection mechanisms, outputs of which are retrieved by a Opinion Dynamics correlation system. This allows the defender to potentially trace the movement of the attacker along the network, since the different attack stages will generate various security alerts that increase the probability of detection, so it can be conceived as a cost. In [8], authors propose a taxonomy of detection probabilities in form of an ordered set associated with each attack stage. Following the same procedure, here we define Θ as the ordered set of detection probabilities, where $\Theta = \{\theta_1, ..., \theta_n\}$ and $\theta_i = [0, 1]$, such that $\forall \theta_i, \theta_i < \theta_{i+1}$. This model, which is illustrated in Table 2, maps every attack stage to the elements of Θ to represent their cost. The precise election of this taxonomy and quantitative instantiation of the θ values is further explained in Appendix A.

As for the strategy applied for the attacker in TI&TO, S^A will vary depending on the state of surroundings nodes that are vulnerable at every time t of the game. The precise behavior to define the chain of attack stages is the following: S^A always starts with an ***initialIntrusion***, which is randomly chosen from the IT or OT section (hence representing multiple kinds of APTs[3]). Then, A attempts to make a ***LateralMovement***$_{FW}$ movement to compromise a firewall. This movement is straightforward on the IT section as every node is connected to them. However, in case of the OT section, the attacker needs to escalate over the hierarchy of nodes until reaching a PDS node and then the firewall, as explained in Sect. 3.1. Once there, A penetrates the other section, where we assume he/she must complete a minimum succession of $\sigma = 3$ ***LateralMovements*** (choosing the most vulnerable nodes) before finally executing the ***Destruction*** of a resource. In that case, the game terminates complying with TS_1 or TS_3, depending on the movements of D. In this sense, the defender can prevent this chain from completing if he/she detects the attacker and successfully eradicates the infection from all nodes (complying with TS_2). In order for the attacker to avoid that situation, a ***LinkRemoval*** can be executed. In TI&TO, D makes this movement when the defender manages to heal $\beta = 3$ nodes in a row, which represents the situation where D is close behind the attacker on the board, as explained in the next Section.

This procedure to define the attacker strategy as the game evolves is formalized in Algorithm 1. Note that the attacker can always follow this chain of stages as long as he/she posses at least one node. In case one is healed, another node is chosen and the APT continues. Otherwise, if the defender manages to heal all victim nodes, the game ends complying with TS_2 or TS_3.

3.4   Defender Model: Detection and Response

As discussed before, the ultimate goal of this paper is the analysis of the Opinion Dynamics technique against the effects of a realistically-defined APT. As such,

Table 2. Map of *attackStages* to Θ

$initialIntrusion(v_0)$	θ_3
$*LateralMovement_{IT,FW}(v_i \rightarrow v_j), neighbours(v_i)$	$\theta_4 \rightarrow \theta_2, \theta_1$
$*LateralMovement_{OT}(v_i \rightarrow v_j), neighbours(v_i)$	$\theta_5 \rightarrow \theta_2, \theta_1$
$*LinkRemoval_{(}v_i \rightarrow v_j)$	$\theta_5 \rightarrow \theta_5$
$destruction(v_i)$	θ_6

we assume that the set of movements that the defender can leverage is summarized in the execution of the algorithm at every turn of the game, followed by an optional node reparation, as described in Sect. 3.2. Therefore, the defender adopts a dynamic behavior which allows us to analyze the effectiveness of different protection strategies.

We start with the basics. As mentioned in Sect. 3.2, the defender aims to locate the attacker position across the whole network, keeping track of the anomalies suffered and their persistence over each area of the network as the game evolves. This is enabled by the Opinion Dynamics traceability, as proposed in [8]. Thus, the status of the network is checked by the defender at each turn: then, the most affected node is selected and, based on the

---

Algorithm 1. Attacker strategy creation

---

output: S^A representing the attacker strategy
local: Graph $G(V, E)$ representing the network, where $V = V_{IT} \cup V_{OT} \cup V_{FW}$, $gameState = 0$ representing initial game state

$S^A \leftarrow \{\}$, $Victims \leftarrow \{\}$, $numSteps \leftarrow 0$
$attackedNode \leftarrow random\ node\ in\ V_{IT} \cup V_{OT}$
$S^A \leftarrow S^A \cup initialIntrusion(attackedNode)$, $Victims \leftarrow Victims \cup attackedNode$
while $gameState == 0$ **do**
    if $defender\ healed\ \beta\ nodes\ in\ a\ row$ **and** $numSteps < \sigma$ **then**
        $S^A \leftarrow S^A \cup LinkRemoval$
    else if $attackedNode\ is\ in\ first\ section\ attacked$ **then**
        $S^A \leftarrow S^A \cup LateralMovement_{FW}(nextAttackedNode)$
        $Victims \leftarrow Victims \cup nextAttackedNode$
        $attackedNode \leftarrow nextAttackedNode$
    else if $attackedNode\ is\ in\ second\ section\ attacked$ **and** $numSteps < \sigma$ **then**
        $S^A \leftarrow S^A \cup LateralMovement_{(IT,OT)}(nextAttackedNode)$
        $Victims \leftarrow Victims \cup nextAttackedNode$
        $attackedNode \leftarrow nextAttackedNode$, $numSteps \leftarrow numSteps + 1$
    else
        $S^A \leftarrow S^A \cup Destruction(attackedNode)$, $gameState \leftarrow TS_1$
    end if

    if $defender\ healed\ attackedNode$ **then**
        $Victims \leftarrow Victims \setminus attackedNode$, $numSteps \leftarrow 0$
        if $Victims\ is\ empty$ **then**
            if $gameState == TS_1$ **then** $gameState == TS_3$
            else
                $gameState \leftarrow TS_2$
            end if
        else
            $attackedNode \leftarrow random\ node\ in\ Victims$
        end if
    end if
end while

---

severity of the anomaly, he/she finally decides to heal the node. Depending on the accuracy of this action, the defender receives a determined utility. This process, which is henceforth referred to as 'reparation', is described in Algorithm 2. It is repeated successively in each turn of the defender, until all compromised nodes are repaired, complying with the defender-win condition (so that the complexity of the defensive approach is linear) or the attacker completes its set of attack stages. There are some aspects to point out here: firstly, the defender can decide whether to repair the most affected node or stay idle during each turn, which depends on a predefined threshold. Namely, if the opinion given by the agent that monitors that node surpasses it, then the defender opts to heal it. After executing the experiments, and since Opinion Dynamics is calculated as a sum of weighted sum of opinions, this threshold is set to 0.5, which returns the best outcome for the defender.

On the other hand, the reward is one as long as the defender succeeds at healing a node that was in fact compromised; otherwise, the reward is zero. With respect to the cost, it is equivalent to the criticality of the node that is healed (regulated with the $CRIT$ function), in such a way that high-level resources are subject to a potential stop in the production chain and usually need a greater effort in terms of security.

Algorithm 2. Reparation of nodes at time t

---

output: $U^D(t)$ *representing the utility*
local: *Graph* $G(V, E)$ *representing the network, where* $V = V_{IT} \cup V_{OT} \cup V_{FW}$
input: X *representing the opinion vector of the network agents*

$candidateNode \leftarrow$ *node in* V *with maximum* $x(t)$
$OldNodeState \leftarrow N_{candidateNode}(t), healThreshold \leftarrow 0.5$
if $x_{candidateNode} > healThreshold$ **then**
     REPAIRNODE($candidateNode$)
end if
if $OldNodeState == 1$ **then**
     $N_{candidateNode}(t) \leftarrow 0, R^D(t) \leftarrow 1$
else
     $N_{candidateNode}(t) \leftarrow 0, R^D(t) \leftarrow 0$
end if
$C^D(t) \leftarrow CRIT(candidateNode), U^D(t) \leftarrow R^D(t) - C^D(t)$

The reparation procedure is the main movement of the defender. However, this reparation strategy can also be influenced by three different configurations:

– *Local Opinion Dynamics.* In practice, a global correlation of the Opinion Dynamics agents in a synchronous way may not be feasible in a real industrial environment. Concretely, we aim to demonstrate that the execution of the aforementioned correlation, but considering a subset of nodes of the original network, is effective enough for the defender. Let $G'(V', E')$ be the subgraph of $G(V, E)$ so that $V' \subset V$ and $E' \subset E$. This subgraph is built including a *candidateNode* and all its child nodes within graph G located at a distance of certain number of hops (in our tests, a distance of one or two hops will be used). The graph G' is used for the computation of the Opinion Dynamics, as usually performed in the original approach. The first election of *candidateNode* is established after $M^A(0)$, considering the highest anomaly measured by the agents over the network. Afterwards, the defender is able to locally compute the correlation and heal nodes in subsequent movements. Thus, at every turn, the *candidateNode* is updated to the node in V' with the greatest opinion, which implies moving the Opinion Dynamics detection zone.

– **Redundancy of links.** In Sect. 3.3 section, the link removal stage was introduced, that allows the attacker to potentially remove links from the topology that make the defender lose track of the threat position, by fooling the local Opinion Dynamics. At this point, we must recall the subset of redundant links $E_R \subset E$ introduced in Sect. 3.1. These channels will be used by the defender whenever the attacker destroys a link in E, so that opinions will be transmitted using those links only in that case. Despite this may seem as an advantage for the defender, those links can randomly cover pairs of nodes that may not be affected by a link removal. Additionally, the disruption of a link from v_i to v_j in E' does not make v_j inaccessible for the local Opinion Dynamics at all times, since there could be a third node v_k covered by the defender that has another connection $(v_k, v_j) \in E'$.

– **Honeypots.** For the interest of the analysis, the defender lastly features the possibility of establishing honeypots. It implies modifying the network from the beginning to assign the role of honeypot to specific nodes, which will be randomly chosen in the simulations. These are used as a bait to lure the attacker to compromise them by exposing a higher degree of vulnerability (which was regulated with the $VULN$ function). If the attacker attempts to compromise it, then a higher anomaly will be generated by that agent, which would help the defender to rapidly find the position of the threat, eradicate the threat at a given turn t and hence update the area of the local Opinion Dynamics detection. For our tests, 5% of the total number of nodes have been considered as honeypots, which is a minimal value to show the effectiveness of this response technique.

Table 3 summarizes the set of movements eligible for each player, indicating their reward and cost. Note that the game approach itself is validated from a theoretical point of view in Appendix C. In the following, we run simulations with different configurations for the defender to assess the Opinion Dynamics detection technique.

4   Experimental Simulations and Discussions

Once both attacker and defender have been described, this section presents the results of playing games under different parameters of TI&TO. As explained,

Table 3. Summary of movements leveraged by attacker and defender

Player	Movements	Reward	Cost
Attacker	Initial Intrusion	1	θ_3
	Lateral Movement $(v_i \rightarrow v_j)$	1	θ_4 or $\theta_5 + \theta_1{}^*\|neighbours(v_i)\|$
	Link Removal $(v_i \rightarrow v_j)$	1	$2 * \theta_5$
	Destruction (v_i)	1	θ_6
Defender	Node reparation (v_i)	1	$CRIT(v_i)$

the aim of these experiments is to find the best strategy for the defender given an APT perpetrated by attacker.

In specific, four test cases of games are conducted to assess incremental configurations for the defender' strategy: (1) a local Opinion Dynamics detection around 1 hop of distance from the observed node; (2) local detection with 2 hops of distance: (3) the addition of redundant edges in V_{OT}; and (4) the integration of honeypots within the topology. On the other hand, the attacker follows the model explained in Sect. 3.3. Each test case is composed by 10 sets of 100 games, where each set is based on a new generated board, following the network architecture introduced in Sect. 3.1. At the same time, different sizes of network are considered in each test case: 100, 200 and 500 nodes. The instantiation values for their criticality and vulnerability are presented in Appendix A.

For each board and game set, the percentage of victories achieved by each player (in addition to the ratio of draws) is calculated. These are shown in form of a boxplot, where each box represents the quartiles for each player given the different configurations of size in each case. Different conclusions can be drawn from these simulations, which are discussed in the following.

Test Case 1: local Op. Dynamics with 1 hop, no redundancy, no honeypots. In this case (Fig. 2), the attacker clearly experiences a high rate of victories as he/she easily escapes from the defender detection, which only encompasses one hop of distance from the affected node. Therefore, the best-case scenario for D occurs when he/she just manages to follow the infection until it is eradicated in the last turn, resulting in a draw.

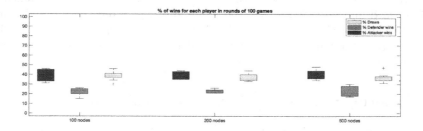

Fig. 2. Test-case 1: Percentage of victories and draws

Test Case 2: local Op. Dynamics with 2 hops, no redundancy, no honeypots. With the introduction of more nodes covered by the local detection (whose number is approximately squared with respect to Test case 1), the percentage of defender wins increases significantly, which shows the importance of applying Opinion Dynamics on a wide area, as shown in Fig. 3. However, the number of attacker victories and draws still remain moderate, since the defender has not sufficient accuracy as to keep track of A when the removal of links is performed and the detection is eluded.

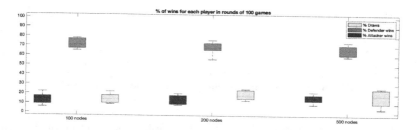

Fig. 3. Test-case 2: Percentage of victories and draws

Test Case 3: local Op. Dynamics with 2 hops, redundancy, no honeypots. The implementation of more defensive aids results in a higher number of wins for the defender (Fig. 4). Here, the redundancy makes D able to trace most of the attacker movements, including when that player wants to get rid of the detection, which is more evident in smaller networks. And yet, the defender must successfully heal all the compromised nodes across the network that may continue the attack and be far away from the current detection focus, which still returns a mild number of attacker victories and draws.

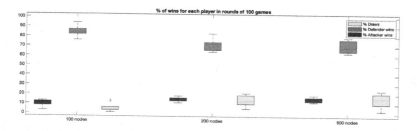

Fig. 4. Test-case 3: Percentage of victories and draws

Test Case 4: local Op. Dynamics with 2 hops, redundancy, honeypots. Lastly, the addition of honeypots are a secure way for the defender to ensure the highest number of victories, as shown in Fig. 5. The presence of these devices triggers severe anomalies when the attacker tries to compromise then. They are sensed by the defender to rapidly locate the current affected node, as long as D covers a wide area that contains the position of the attacker at that time. This situation is illustrated through an example of game instance in Appendix B.

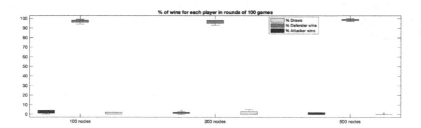

Fig. 5. Test-case 4: Percentage of victories and draws

In general, we can deduce that solely by implementing Opinion Dynamics, the defender can benefit from its detection to reduce the impact of the attacker over the network. The protection improves with the introduction of additional measures such as redundancy or honeypots, and the same results are obtained for different sizes of network.

We can also draw some analysis on the overall score in these test cases: Fig. 6 plots the average score of the defender and attacker for the four test cases presented before. At a glance, we can see how D shows a superior throughput in all cases, and a slightly higher score when using low-size networks, since he/she experiences greater accuracy in the reparation of nodes. Also, the score decreases as test cases implement additional defense measures: on the one hand, the attacker generates more anomalies (and hence more costs) due to the link removal attacks in the attempt to dodge the detection. On the other hand, the

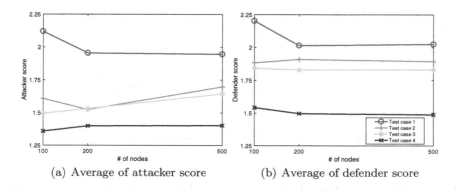

(a) Average of attacker score   (b) Average of defender score

Fig. 6. Percentage of victories for each player in each test case

defender has more candidates to heal due to the increased number of anomalies, and does not always have a high accuracy in choosing them.

To sum up, by means of game theory we have demonstrated that local Opinion Dynamics is still valid for catching the compromised nodes of the attacker when it is applied with a minimally wide detection area (i.e., two hops of distance from the observed node) and it is paired with effective response techniques (i.e., where honeypots pose an effective measure) that precisely make use of the provided detection information.

5   Conclusions

The increasing impact of APTs on modern critical infrastructures demands the development of advanced detection techniques. Opinion Dynamics paves the way towards the effective traceability of sophisticated attacks, as described in this paper. We have leveraged game theory through the design of TI&TO, a two-player game based on a realistic attack and defense model that serves as test-bench for the deployment of response procedures that make use of the information provided by the Opinion Dynamics solution. Based on the execution of multiple games under different configurations, we have extracted guidelines for the correct parametrization of Opinion Dynamics, while we validate the accuracy of the detection technique. Our ongoing work is currently revolving around the reproduction of these test cases on a real environment and the design of an enhanced multi-player game definition that also comprises more than one threat taking place simultaneously. The precise analysis of the optimal parameters for the defender approach (e.g., number of honeypots or thresholds for the Opinion Dynamics detection) will be also carried out.

Acknowledgments. This work has been partially supported by the EU H2020-SU-ICT-03-2018 Project No. 830929 CyberSec4Europe (cybersec4europe.eu), the EU H2020-MSCA-RISE-2017 Project No. 777996 (SealedGRID), and by a 2019 Leonardo Grant for Researchers and Cultural Creators of the BBVA Foundation. Likewise, the work of the first author has been partially financed by the Spanish Ministry of Education under the FPU program (FPU15/03213).

A   Instantiation of Ψ, Υ and Θ Values

In Sect. 3.3 we have presented an ordered set of probabilities Θ that are mapped to the different attack stages to represent the cost that every movement of the attacker implies, which is summarized in Table 2. There are multiple reasons behing this mapping, that are summarized as follows:

1. We assign the lowest level of detection probability (θ_1) only to the devices in the neighbourhood of the affected node in a lateral movement, since some discovery queries will normally raise subtle network alerts.

2. The second lowest probability of detection (θ_2) is linked to the elements that are the target of a lateral movement, because these connections usually leverage stealthy techniques to go unnoticed.
3. An initial intrusion causes a mild detection probability θ_3, since the attacker either makes use of zero-day vulnerabilities or social engineering techniques, which is a crucial stage for the attacker to be successful at breaking into the network through the 'patient zero'.
4. θ_4 and θ_5 are assigned to devices (from the IT and OT section, respectively) causing the delivery of malware to establish a connection to an uncompromised node in a lateral movement. In specific, since the heterogeneity of traffic is lower and the criticality of the resources in that segment is greater, anomalies are likely to be detected when compared to the IT section. On the other hand, θ_5 is also assigned to the involved nodes in a link removal stage, since it is an evident anomaly sensed by both agents.
5. The highest probability of detection (θ_6) is assigned to the last stage of the APT, as it usually causes major disruption in the functionality of a device or the attacker manages to connect to an external network to exfiltrate information, which is easily detected.

Considering a realistic scenario and according to the methodology explained in [8], we have assigned values for this ordered set and also for Ψ and Υ sets, which regulate the criticality and vulnerability of resources in our simulations. This instantiation of values is shown in Table 4. For the interest of realism and to represent a certain level of randomness in the accuracy of the detection mechanisms that every agent embodies, these values will also include a random deviation in the experiments, with a maximum value of ± 0.1.

Table 4. Instances of the Ψ, Υ, Θ ordered sets used in the simulations

i	1	2	3	4	5	6
ψ_i	0.2	0.3	0.4	0.5	0.6	0.8
v_i	0.8	0.7	0.6	0.5	0.4	0.2
θ_i	0.1	0.3	0.4	0.5	0.6	0.9

B   Example of Game Instance with Defender Victory

We have seen that the best results for the defender are achieved when two hops of distance are considered and honeypots are also introduced. In this case, the use of these two tools (besides the redundancy) are enough as to win most of the games. The rationale behind this result is simple: when the attacker attempts to compromise one of this fake nodes, a great anomaly is generated which is detected by the defender, as long as he or she manages to cover a wide area that contains the current position of the attacker (i.e., when 2 or more hops of distance are leveraged by the local Opinion Dynamics). This behavior is shown in Fig. 7: in this network, the attacker traverses the nodes and then they are immediately healed (they are labeled with an 'X' when they are attacked and 'H' when they are healed, along with the anomaly measured by Opinion Dynamics). In the last movement, the attacker attempts to compromise a honeypot (depicted with a diamond shape) and the defender manages to locate and eradicate the infection. Since the defender does not possess any other compromised node, the game is over.

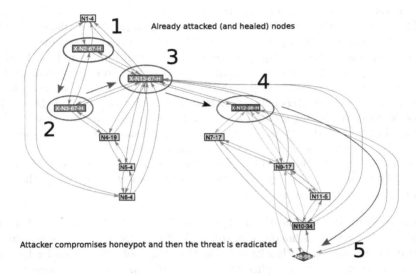

Fig. 7. Example of defender-win after the attacker compromises a honeypot

C   Correctness Proof of TI&TO

This section presents the correctness proof of TI&TO for the different cases that may occur during a certain game instance. This problem is solved when these conditions are met:

1. The attacker can find an IT/OT device to compromise within the infrastructure.
2. The defender is able to trace the threat and heal a node, thanks to the Opinion Dynamics detection.
3. The game system is able to properly finish in a finite time (termination condition).

The first requirement is satisfied since we assume that the attacker can perform different attack stages to define his/her strategy over the game board (assuming $V \neq \oslash$), such as lateral movements, links removal or destruction. The modus operandi of the attacker is systematic, beginning with a random node $v_0 \in V_{IT} \cup V_{OT}$ at $t = 0$ which is compromised (see Algorithm 1). Then, A penetrates the infrastructure to ultimately gain control of the operational or corporate network, where a certain node is finally disrupted (V_{OT}) after a set of σ lateral movements. In an intermediate time t of the game, the attacker can execute a new stage as long as there is at least one node v_a such that $N_{v_a}(t) = 1$, which becomes the new *attackedNode* in Algorithm 1. When the state of all nodes is set to zero, the game terminates.

The second requirement is also met with the inclusion of intrusion detection solutions on every agent $a_i \in A$ that facilitate the correlation of events. With the local execution of the Opinion Dynamics correlation from $t = 1$ on the node that presents the greatest anomaly (using one or two hops of distance), we ensure that the agents associated with the resulting subgraph of nodes will have an opinion $x_i(t) \geq 0$. According to Algorithm 2, this means that D will heal the node with maximum opinion if that value surpasses the threshold (0.5, as explained in Sect. 3.4), setting its state back to zero and updating the detection area. Otherwise, he/she will remain idle during that turn.

We can demonstrate the third requirement (corresponding to the termination of the approach) through induction. More precisely, we specify the initial conditions and the base case, namely:

Precondition: We assume the attacker models an APT perpetrated against the infrastructure defined by graph $G(V, E)$ where $V \neq \oslash$, following the strategy explained in Algorithm 1. On the other side, the defender leverages Opinion Dynamics to visualize the threat evolution across the infrastructure and eventually repair nodes, following the procedure described in Algorithm 2.

Postcondition: The attacker reaches the network $G(V, E)$ and compromises at least one node in V such that $S^A \neq \oslash$ and continues to compromise more devices in the loop in Algorithm 1, to achieve $numSteps = \sigma$. Player D executes Opinion Dynamics to detect and heal the most affected nodes after executing the correlation. The game evolves until any of the termination states (see Sect. 3.2) are reached.

Case 1: $numSteps = \sigma$, but $gameState$ is still set to zero. In this case, player A has successfully traversed the network having $Victims \neq \oslash$. Therefore, he/she needs to launch the Destruction movement over the *attackedNode*. This makes $gameState$ comply with TS_1 temporarily until the defender moves. If D manages to heal *attackedNode* and $Victims = \oslash$, then the game also terminates, with TS_3.

Case 2: $numSteps < \sigma$. In this case, the next stage in S^A implies a lateral movement. If the attacker is still in the first section where the first intrusion took place (whether IT or OT), he/she must locate a firewall to perpetrate the other section before increasing $numSteps$. After this, the defender can make his/her movement and potentially heal a node, which can make the attacker remove a link in the following iteration. If the node healed is $attackedNode$, the attacker must choose another node in $Victims$, resetting $numSteps = 0$. In the event that $Victims = \oslash$, then the game terminates with state TS_2.

Induction: If we assume that we are in step t ($t \geq 1$) in the loop in Algorithm 1, then Case 1 is going to be considered until A completes his/her strategy (TS_1 or TS_3). In any other case, Case 2 applies until achieving $numSteps = \sigma$ (hence applying Case 1 again) or $Victims = \oslash$. In this last case, the game finishes with TS_2.

References

1. Kaspersky Lab ICS CERT. Threat landscape for industrial automation systems. H2 2018 (2019). https://ics-cert.kaspersky.com/reports/2019/03/27/threat-landscape-for-industrial-automation-systems-h2-2018/. Accessed Sept 2019
2. Langner, R.: Stuxnet: dissecting a cyberwarfare weapon. IEEE Secur. Priv. **9**(3), 49–51 (2011)
3. Lemay, A., Calvet, J., Menet, F., Fernandez, J.M.: Survey of publicly available reports on advanced persistent threat actors. Comput. Secur. **72**, 26–59 (2018)
4. Virvilis, N., Gritzalis, D.: The big four-what we did wrong in advanced persistent threat detection? In: 2013 International Conference on Availability, Reliability and Security, pp. 248–254. IEEE (2013)
5. Rubio, J.E., Alcaraz, C., Lopez, J.: Preventing advanced persistent threats in complex control networks. In: Foley, S.N., Gollmann, D., Snekkenes, E. (eds.) ESORICS 2017. LNCS, vol. 10493, pp. 402–418. Springer, Cham (2017). https://doi.org/10.1007/978-3-319-66399-9_22
6. Lin, C.-T.: Structural controllability. IEEE Trans. Autom. Control **19**(3), 201–208 (1974)
7. Roy, S., Ellis, C., Shiva, S., Dasgupta, D., Shandilya, V., Wu, Q.: A survey of game theory as applied to network security. In: 2010 43rd Hawaii International Conference on System Sciences, pp. 1–10. IEEE (2010)
8. Rubio, J.E., Roman, R., Alcaraz, C., Zhang, Y.: Tracking advanced persistent threats in critical infrastructures through opinion dynamics. In: Lopez, J., Zhou, J., Soriano, M. (eds.) ESORICS 2018. LNCS, vol. 11098, pp. 555–574. Springer, Cham (2018). https://doi.org/10.1007/978-3-319-99073-6_27
9. Rubio, J.E., Manulis, M., Alcaraz, C., Lopez, J.: Enhancing security and dependability of industrial networks with opinion dynamics. In: Sako, K., Schneider, S., Ryan, P.Y.A. (eds.) ESORICS 2019. LNCS, vol. 11736, pp. 263–280. Springer, Cham (2019). https://doi.org/10.1007/978-3-030-29962-0_13
10. Rubio, J.E., Roman, R., Alcaraz, C., Zhang, Y.: Tracking APTs in industrial ecosystems: a proof of concept. J. Comput. Secur. **27**, 521–546 (2019)
11. Lopez, J., Rubio, J.E., Alcaraz, C.: A resilient architecture for the smart grid. IEEE Trans. Ind. Inf. **14**, 3745–3753 (2018)
12. Hegselmann, R., Krause, U., et al.: Opinion dynamics and bounded confidence models, analysis, and simulation. J. Artif. Soc. Soc. Simul. **5**(3) (2002)
13. Lye, K., Wing, J.M.: Game strategies in network security. Int. J. Inf. Secur. **4**(1–2), 71–86 (2005)
14. Nguyen, K.C., Alpcan, T., Basar, T.: Security games with incomplete information. In: 2009 IEEE International Conference on Communications, pp. 1–6. IEEE (2009)

15. Patcha, A., Park, J.-M.: A game theoretic approach to modeling intrusion detection in mobile ad hoc networks. In: Proceedings from the Fifth Annual IEEE SMC Information Assurance Workshop, pp. 280–284. IEEE (2004)
16. Van Dijk, M., Juels, A., Oprea, A., Rivest, R.L.: Flipit: the game of "stealthy takeover". J. Cryptol. **26**(4), 655–713 (2013)
17. Alpcan, T., Basar, T.: A game theoretic analysis of intrusion detection in access control systems. In: 2004 43rd IEEE Conference on Decision and Control (CDC) (IEEE Cat. No. 04CH37601), vol. 2, pp. 1568–1573. IEEE (2004)
18. Watts, D.J., Strogatz, S.H.: Collective dynamics of 'small-world' networks. Nature **393**(6684), 440 (1998)
19. Pagani, G.A., Aiello, M.: The power grid as a complex network: a survey. Physica A **392**(11), 2688–2700 (2013)
20. Haynes, T.W., Hedetniemi, S.M., Hedetniemi, S.T., Henning, M.A.: Domination in graphs applied to electric power networks. SIAM J. Discret. Math. **15**(4), 519–529 (2002)
21. Kneis, J., Mölle, D., Richter, S., Rossmanith, P.: Parameterized power domination complexity. Inf. Process. Lett. **98**(4), 145–149 (2006)
22. Simaan, M., Cruz, J.B.: On the stackelberg strategy in nonzero-sum games. J. Optim. Theory Appl. **11**(5), 533–555 (1973)

Software and System Security

MemShield: GPU-Assisted Software Memory Encryption

Pierpaolo Santucci[1], Emiliano Ingrassia[1], Giulio Picierro[2]([✉]),
and Marco Cesati[2]

[1] Epigenesys s.r.l., Rome, Italy
{santucci,ingrassia}@epigenesys.com
[2] University of Rome Tor Vergata, Rome, Italy
{giulio.picierro,cesati}@uniroma2.it

Abstract. Cryptographic algorithm implementations are vulnerable to Cold Boot attacks, which consist in exploiting the persistence of RAM cells across reboots or power down cycles to read the memory contents and recover precious sensitive data. The principal defensive weapon against Cold Boot attacks is memory encryption. In this work we propose MemShield, a memory encryption framework for user space applications that exploits a GPU to safely store the master key and perform the encryption/decryption operations. We developed a prototype that is completely transparent to existing applications and does not require changes to the OS kernel. We discuss the design, the related works, the implementation, the security analysis, and the performances of MemShield.

Keywords: Data security · Memory encryption · Cryptography on GPU

1 Introduction

Strong cryptographic algorithms rely on sensitive data that must be kept hidden and confidential. Nowadays, the most practical attacks against data encryption programs, full disk encryption layers (FDEs), authentication protocols, or secure communication channels are based on memory disclosure techniques that extract keys, hidden configurations, or unencrypted data directly from the RAM memory cells of the running systems. Consider, for an example, the (in)famous OpenSSL's Heartbleed vulnerability [13] that in 2014 allowed a remote attacker to extract secret keys of X.509 certificates used for SSL/TLS secure network protocols. Even worse, also properly implemented cryptographic programs are usually vulnerable to the class of *Cold Boot attacks* [54]. Basically, cryptographic programs rely on memory protection mechanisms implemented by the operating system kernel to hide the sensitive data from any unauthorized user or process in the system. The underlying assumptions, however, are that (1) overriding the operating system control implies rebooting the system, and (2) rebooting the

© Springer Nature Switzerland AG 2020
M. Conti et al. (Eds.): ACNS 2020, LNCS 12147, pp. 323–343, 2020.
https://doi.org/10.1007/978-3-030-57878-7_16

system implies disrupting the contents of all RAM cells. While assumption (1) is correct if the operating system is bug-free, unfortunately assumption (2) does not generally hold. Modern RAM technologies, such as dynamic RAM (DRAM) and static RAM (SRAM), are based on electric charges stored in small capacitors that could retain the charge for several seconds, or even minutes, after power off. The typical Cold Boot attack, therefore, consists of power cycling the system using the reset button and quickly rebooting from a removable device into a program that extracts the RAM contents [21]. Cold Boot attacks are so effective that they are nowadays adopted even in digital forensic activities [5,51].

Many possible mitigations of Cold Boot attacks have been proposed in the past few years, however there still does not exist a full, practical solution. In fact, some proposals are based on cryptographic hardware circuits integrated in the system, which are still not widely adopted [10,27,28]. Other proposals are bound to specific hardware architectures [20,22,36,55]. Moreover, many solutions are not completely transparent to the applications [39,53,55]. Finally, almost all proposed solutions require changes to the operating system kernel [7,17,25,26, 40].

In this work we introduce *MemShield*, a framework based on a general-purpose Graphic Processing Unit (GPU) that encrypts the system memory so as to mitigate the effects of Cold Boot attacks. GPUs benefits of widespread adoption and their massive parallelism may satisfy real-time demands of transparent encryption systems, providing that communication overheads are reasonable.

MemShield is designed so as to overcome most limitations of the previous proposals. In particular, MemShield (i) relies on a vanilla Linux kernel and does not require kernel patches; (ii) it is not bound to a specific hardware architecture; (iii) it does not require specific cryptographic hardware, and uses widely adopted GPUs as secure encryption key store and cryptographic processor; (iv) it can run on legacy systems; (v) it stores encrypted data in system RAM, thus not limiting the amount of protected pages; (vi) it allows users to select the applications to be protected; (vii) it does not require source code changes in the protected applications; (viii) it exploits dynamic linking and does not require program recompilation; (ix) it achieves transparent memory accesses without code instrumentation; (x) it uses a modular software architecture for the cryptographic components, thus permitting to easily change, enhance, or upgrade the encryption cipher; (xi) it is an open-source project, available at: https://gitlab.com/memshield/memshield/.

We developed a prototype based on the GNU/Linux operating system and CUDA GPUs. It provides transparent memory encryption in user mode by using the userfaultfd Linux kernel framework. This prototype is a proof-of-concept aimed at testing the validity of MemShield's design, as well as assessing both security aspects and performances. As far as we know, MemShield is the first framework that achieves system memory encryption by using a GPU. Moreover, while it relies on a vanilla Linux kernel, it does not require patches to the kernel: this is also a novelty for this kind of frameworks.

The article is organized as follows: in Sect. 2 we compare MemShield with other solutions proposed in literature. In Sects. 3 and 4 we describe design and implementation of MemShield. In Sect. 5 we discuss a security analysis, while in Sect. 6 we illustrate how MemShield impairs the overall performances of the protected applications. Finally, in Sect. 7, we draw some conclusions.

2   Related Works

Memory disclosure attacks, and in particular Cold Boot attacks [2,21,54], are nowadays a real menace that might expose sensible information and precious data to unauthorized use or abuse. Therefore, many researchers have proposed technical solutions to mitigate the effects of this kind of attacks.

Some proposals are based on the assumption that the attacker might be interested in a small portion of sensitive data, like the FDE master key used for encrypting a physical disk partition, or the private key of an open SSL connection. In these cases, an effective solution might be storing these data outside RAM, that is, in volatile hardware registers. For example, an AES encryption key could be stored in special CPU registers, such as x86_64 SSE registers (paranoix [35], AESSE [33]), debug registers (TRESOR [36]), profiling registers (Loop-Amnesia [42]), or ARM NEON registers (ARMORED [20]). Another approach is storing sensitive data in locked-down static-RAM caches or hardware transactional memories [19,31,46]. However, storing sensitive data outside system RAM does not scale up, so this solution is unfeasible when the data to be protected have size larger than the storage provided by the available volatile hardware registers.

An easy-to-implement mitigation for Cold Boot attacks aimed at large portions of sensitive data might be based on the power-on firmware of the system. For instance, during the initialization sequence the firmware might ask for a user password, or it might erase the contents of all RAM cells [45]. However, these protections can be overridden, because it is generally possible to change the firmware settings by resetting them to a default configuration, for instance by inserting a jumper on the board or removing the CMOS battery [18]. Even more crucially, the Cold Boot attack might be executed by transplanting the memory chips in a suitable system with a custom firmware [50,51]. It has been shown [18] that cooling down the memory chips to approximately 5 Celsius degree before transplanting them allows an attacker to recover about 99% of the original bits.

Thus, even if Cold Boot attacks can be mitigated, they cannot completely ruled out: if resourceful attackers gains access to the physical RAM chips of a running system, they are able to access the system memory contents. Therefore, the most effective protection against Cold Boot attacks is based on *memory encryption*, where the contents of some (or, possibly, all) memory cells are encrypted by using one or more random keys stored in volatile hardware registers outside of the RAM chips. In order to get meaningful information from the memory dump, the attacker must either recover the encryption key(s) from the volatile hardware registers, or break the encryption cipher. Henson et al. [23] present a survey of hardware enhancements to support memory encryption at memory controller, bus, and caches level, protecting data transfers against eavesdropping.

Ideally, memory encryption could be implemented at hardware level so as to be completely transparent to user mode applications and, in some cases, even to the operating system kernel. Nowadays, major chip manufacturers design processors with MMU-based memory encryption. For instance, Intel Software Guard Extensions (SGX) [28] allows user applications to create an encrypted memory area, called *enclave*, for both code and data. Encrypted pages are stored in a page cache of limited size. Confidentiality and integrity are guaranteed even when the OS kernel is compromised. However, SGX is not designed for full memory encryption and legacy applications cannot use it without source code changes. In 2017 Intel announced Total Memory Encryption (TME) [27], a hardware extension to encrypt all RAM cells with either a global key or multiple keys; in any case, the encryption key cannot be retrieved by software. TME is currently under development. AMD's proposed solution is named Secure Memory Encryption (SME) [10]: it encrypts and decrypts pages of memory if a specific flag in the page table entries is set. The encryption key is randomly generated by the hardware and loaded at boot time into the memory controller. An extension called TSME allows the hardware to perform memory encryption transparently to the OS and the user software. Mofrad et al. [34] analyze features, security attacks, and performances of both Intel SGX and AMD SME solutions.

While there is a raising interest to add support for MMU-based memory encryption solutions in the operating system kernels [41], these systems are still not widespread, because this technology is rather expensive and operating system support is scarce. Thus, in the past years several researchers have proposed to encrypt the memory by using frameworks exploiting either common-of-the-shelf (COTS) hardware components or custom devices. Because the MMUs lack circuits aimed at encryption, all these solutions must rely on procedures included in hypervisors or operating system kernels, so they can be collectively named *software-assisted memory encryption* frameworks. In this work we propose MemShield, an innovative software solution based on COTS hardware.

In software-assisted memory encryption, a typical access to a protected page triggers a chain of events like the following: (i) the ordinary MMU circuits generate a hardware event (e.g., a missing page fault); (ii) the user application that made the access is suspended and an OS kernel/hypervisor handler schedules the execution of a cryptographic procedure (either on a CPU, or on some custom device like a FPGA or a GPU); (iii) the cryptographic procedure encrypts or decrypts the data in the accessed page; (iv) the OS kernel/hypervisor resumes the execution of the user application. A crucial point of this mechanism is that the encryption keys used by cryptographic ciphers must not be stored "in clear" on the system memory, otherwise an attacker might retrieve them and decrypt all RAM contents. Hence, software-assisted memory encryption proposals generally include, as a component, one of the already mentioned solutions for storing a limited amount of sensitive data outside of system RAM [19,31,35,36,42,46].

We can reasonably expect that the performances of software-assisted memory encryption are significantly worse than those of MMU-based memory encryption. However, software-assisted memory encryption has potentially several advantages over MMU-based memory encryption: (i) it can be used on legacy systems, as well as in low-level and mid-level modern systems without dedicated circuits in the MMU; (ii) it might be less expensive, because CPU/MMU circuits without cryptographic support are smaller and simpler; (iii) it is much easier to scrutiny its design and implementation in order to look for vulnerabilities and trapdoors; (iv) it is much easier to fix vulnerabilities and trapdoors, or to enhance the cryptographic procedures if the need arises.

One of the first proposal for software-assisted memory encryption, although motivated by avoiding bus snooping rather than Cold Boot attacks, is in Chen et al. [7]: this framework uses locked-down static cache areas or special scratchpad memories (usually found in embedded hardware) as a reserved area for encrypted data. This solution requires changes in the operating system kernel to support memory access detection and to avoid that data in the static cache are leaked into system RAM. The authors, however, do not discuss how to protect the memory encryption key from disclosure. A similar idea was explored in [53]: the authors describe a FPGA prototype named Exzess that implements a PCIe board acting as a transparent memory proxy aimed at encryption. The encrypted data are stored on the Exzess device itself: device memory is mapped on the address space of a process, so that read and write accesses on those pages trigger decryption and encryption operations on the device, respectively. A drawback of this approach is that the size of the "encrypted RAM" is limited in practice by the capacity of the FPGA board. MemShield is quite different than these solutions because it stores the encrypted data on the system RAM.

CryptKeeper [40] is a closed-source extension to the Linux kernel swapping mechanism: user pages can be flagged as "encrypted" and, when their number in RAM raises above a given threshold, removed from RAM and stored in encrypted form in a swap area. However, CryptKeeper is fragile versus Cold Boot attacks because it stores the encryption key in RAM. A related idea is in Huber et al. [26]: the authors suggest to perform encryption of user space processes memory at suspend time, using the same key used for Full Disk Encryption (FDE). Yet another variant of this idea is presented in [25], where the system memory of portable devices, like notebooks and smartphones, is encrypted by means of the "freezer" infrastructure of the Linux kernel. MemShield is aimed at protecting against Cold Boot attacks possibly performed when the system is up and running, so it has a rather different design.

Henson and Taylor [22] describe a solution based on ARM architecture that implements a microkernel exploiting a cryptographic microprocessor to handle encrypted data either in a scratchpad memory or in the system RAM. An improvement of this idea is in [55], where the ARM TrustZone ensures that unencrypted data never leak to system RAM. The authors use the ARM Trusted Execution Environment to execute a microkernel that loads encrypted program from RAM, decrypt them, and run them safely. The framework requires patches to the general-purpose OS kernel, Linux, that handles the non-trusted programs.

RamCrypt [17] is an open-source Linux kernel extension aimed at encrypting memory at page-level granularity. It is transparent to the user applications because the decryption is automatically triggered by the page fault handler whenever an user access is attempted. RamCrypt protects anonymous pages and non-shared mapped pages of the applications. In order to ensure acceptable performances, a small number of the last recently accessed pages is kept in clear in a "sliding window" data structure. RamCrypt also takes care to avoid key leaks in RAM by using a slightly modified AES implementation from TRESOR [36]. Even if TRESOR has been shown to be vulnerable to some classes of attacks [4], RamCrypt is still an effective mitigation against Cold Boot attacks. MemShield adopts some ideas from RamCrypt, mainly the encryption at page level triggered by page faults and the sliding window mechanism; however, MemShield does not require patches to operating system kernel, and it makes use of a GPU as a safe store and processor for the cryptographic operations.

HyperCrypt [16] is similar to RamCrypt, however memory encryption is handled by a hypervisor (BitVisor) rather than a kernel program; this allows Hyper-Crypt to also protect kernel pages. Like RamCrypt, HyperCrypt is based on TRESOR [36]. TransCrypt [24] is similar to HyperCrypt, yet it relies on ARM Virtualization Extensions to implement a tiny encryption hypervisor.

Papadopoulos et al. [39] proposed a framework for software-assisted memory encryption that can protect either part of, or the whole system memory; the master key is kept in CPU debug registers, like in [36]. The framework relies on code instrumentation to intercept load/store instructions that access memory, and it requires some patches to the operating system kernel.

Finally, EncExec [8] makes use of static caches as storage units for encryption keys and unencrypted data. Whenever a user application accesses an encrypted page, EncExec decrypts the data and locks them in the static cache so that the application can transparently get the unencrypted data. EncExec adopts an interesting approach, however it requires patches to the operating system kernel.

Concerning the usage of the GPU for safely executing cryptographic routines, the seminal work is PixelVault [48], which implements AES and RSA algorithms on the GPU by carefully storing the cryptographic keys inside the GPU registers. The main goal of that work is to implement a more secure version of the OpenSSL library in order to mitigate memory disclosure attacks. PixelVault is based on a GPU kernel that runs forever waiting for crypto operation requests submitted via a memory regions shared between CPU and GPU. As discussed in [56], PixelVault is actually vulnerable to unprivileged attackers, however several authors suggested ways to enhance its approach. For instance, the authors in [52] propose to run CUDA cryptographic applications inside guest VMs by using a virtualized GPU; no privileged attacker on guest VMs is able to retrieve the encryption keys, because they are never stored in the guest VM memory. In [49] the authors suggest to modify the GPU hardware to prevent the device driver from directly accessing GPU critical internal resources. In [29] the authors propose to use a custom interface between GPU and CPU and to extend the Intel SGX technology to execute the GPU device driver in a trusted environment that a privileged attacker cannot access. MemShield mitigates Cold Boot attacks, so it assumes that privileged users are trusted (consider that a privileged user might easily get a full memory dump without a Cold Boot attack). Therefore, MemShield just ensures that unprivileged users cannot access the GPU, thus avoiding the original PixelVault vulnerabilities.

3   Design Overview

MemShield is designed to mitigate Cold Boot attacks perpetrated by malicious actors with physical access to the machine. We assume trusted privileged users and processes, as well as safe operating system and base programs.

The rationale behind MemShield's design was to provide memory encryption services to multiple concurrent users logged on the same machine, using a COTS GPU as secure key store and cryptographic processor. Thus, MemShield does not rely on custom cryptographic circuits or specific hardware architectures.

GPUs are massively parallel accelerators consisting in thousand of cores typically grouped in several *compute units*. Cores in the same compute unit can communicate via *shared memory*, typically implemented as a fast user programmable cache memory. Different compute units can communicate each other via *global memory*, that is, the GPU's RAM. In GPU programming terminology, CPU and system RAM are referred as *host*, while GPU and its RAM are referred as *device*. Device code is written in special functions called *kernels*. Those functions, once invoked from the host, can trigger multiple parallel executions of the same kernel function over the input, depending on how the kernel is launched.

MemShield transparently encrypts user-space memory at page granularity and decrypts them on-demand whenever an access is attempted. There is no need to change or rebuild the source code of the protected applications. Moreover, users may select the programs to be protected, so that applications that do not handle sensitive data do not suffer any slowdown.

By design, for each process and at any time, MemShield enforces a bounded number of pages in clear, while keeping most of them encrypted. This mechanism is based on a *sliding window* and it is an effective solution against Cold Boot attacks, as already proved in [17]. Encrypted data are stored in system RAM, hence there is virtually no limit on the amount of pages that can be protected.

MemShield's core is a daemon that is in charge of encrypting and decrypting memory on behalf of clients. We define as *client* any process interested in memory encryption services. Because GPU programming is supported by user mode tools and libraries, MemShield daemon runs in user mode.

To support transparent memory encryption, the client that attempts to access an encrypted page must be suspended and decrypted contents for that page must be provided. In order to achieve transparent memory encryption, MemShield must be able to detect clients' attempts to access encrypted memory and provide decrypted contents. As a matter of fact, detection of memory accesses represents one of the most challenging aspects of the project. We chose to address this issue by using userfaultfd [47], a framework recently added to the Linux kernel aimed at efficient page fault handling in user space. Thanks to userfaultfd, no changes are required to the operating system kernel. Currently userfaultfd is used by applications that implement memory checkpoint/restore functionality [15] and live migration of both containers [43] and virtual machines [44]. MemShield is the first project that uses userfaultfd for memory encryption, as far as we know.

In systems with a Memory Management Unit (MMU), the *logical addresses* appearing in CPU instructions must be translated in *physical addresses* to be used for RAM's chips programming. Translations are described by means of the *page tables*, usually a per-process data structure kept by the OS kernel. Each page table entry contains a page's virtual-to-physical mapping and attributes such as protection bits (Read, Write, eXecute). A *page fault* is generated by the MMU hardware if a translation is not found (*missing fault*) or the wrong access type is attempted (*protection fault*). This mechanism is actually used by operating systems to isolate process address spaces. In all POSIX-compliant systems there exists an established technique to detect memory accesses in user space: it consists of changing the page permissions so as to forbid any access, then executing a custom handler for the SIGSEGV signal sent by the kernel to the process at any access attempt [6,14]. However, this mechanism may significantly impair the performances of the clients compared to userfaultfd.

A crucial design goal of MemShield is transparency with respect to its clients: no change to the source code of the clients is required, and no recompilation is needed. In order to achieve this goal, we assume that clients are dynamically linked to the C library (*libc*); in practice, this is almost always true. The idea is to intercept calls to the memory management functions typically provided by the *libc* implementation, in order to register the client's memory areas to userfaultfd. The custom handlers of the memory management functions are collected in a user-mode library called *libMemShield*. This library can be loaded in the client's process before the C library using the LD_PRELOAD technique, so that the custom handlers override the original library symbols.

Because MemShield must handle several concurrent clients with a single GPU, userfaultfd works in non-cooperative mode: a single user-mode process is notified of any page fault events occurring in registered clients. We call this process the MemShield's *server*.

The server does not perform cryptographic operations directly, because it cannot access the encryption keys stored in the GPU registers. The most straightforward way to implement this mechanism is to launch on the GPU an always-running kernel that implements a safe cipher.

3.1   Design Limitations

By design, MemShield handles only private anonymous memory: it is not concerned with memory areas backed by files or shared among different processes. It is also based on userfaultfd, which has some constraints of its own: mainly, it cannot protect the memory area handled by brk() or sbrk(). However, MemShield can handle the client's stack, any memory area obtained by `malloc()`, `calloc()`, `realloc()`, as well as the anonymous memory obtained by `mmap()` and `remap()`: typically, sensitive data end up being stored in such pages.

4   Implementation Details

The main activities performed by MemShield are: (i) memory area registration to userfaultfd, (ii) page fault handling, (iii) sliding window management, and (iv) GPU cryptographic operations.

4.1   Memory Area Registration

When a client allocates a memory area to be protected, MemShield must register the corresponding set of virtual addresses to userfaultfd. In order to achieve this, libMemShield overrides some C library functions.

For allocations performed by anonymous memory mapping (`mmap()` and analog functions), the custom wrapper just performs the original procedure and registers the obtained virtual address to userfaultfd.

On the other hand, handling memory areas obtained by `malloc()` and similar functions is more demanding, because the C library might use the `brk()`/`sbrk()` system calls to perform the allocation. MemShield forces the C library to always use anonymous memory mapping when allocating memory by means of the `mallopt()` tuning function.

The userfaultfd framework does not handle stack pages. To overcome this problem, libMemShield replaces original stack pages with memory allocated with `mmap()` using `sigaltstack()`. Since stack encryption could have a significant impact on overall performances of MemShield, encrypting stack pages can be selectively enabled or disabled by means of an environment variable.

libMemShield also overrides the `free()` and `munmap()` functions, because it ensures that any page is filled with zeros before releasing it to the system. Of course, this is crucial to avoid leaking sensitive data in RAM.

4.2   Page Fault Handling

At the core of MemShield there is the virtual address space mechanism implemented by the operating system. Any client is allowed to access a given number of anonymous pages "in clear", that is, in unencrypted form. These pages belong to the address space of the client and the corresponding physical page frames are referenced in the page tables. On the other hand, the page table entries associated with encrypted pages denote missing physical pages. The physical pages storing the encrypted data belong to the server's address space, and are referenced in a per-client red-black tree sorted by virtual addresses.

When a client accesses an encrypted page, the MMU raises a page fault because of the missing physical page in the client's page table. Since the corresponding virtual address has been registered to userfaultfd, the server is notified about the event. As a consequence, the server looks for the virtual address of the missing page in the client's red-black tree and retrieves the physical page containing the encrypted data. Then, the server sends the encrypted data to the GPU, which performs the decryption operation. Subsequently, the server relies on userfaultfd to resolve the client's page fault by providing a physical page containing the decrypted data.

If the server does not find a virtual address in a client's red-black tree, the page is missing because it has never been accessed earlier. Therefore, the server allocates a new red-black tree node and resolves the client's page fault by providing a physical page containing all zeros.

4.3   Sliding Window Management

The server keeps a per-client data structure called sliding window, which is a list of virtual addresses corresponding to unencrypted anonymous pages of the client. The sliding window maximum size is configurable. When the server is going to resolve a page fault, it adds the corresponding virtual address to the sliding window. It also checks whether its size has become greater than a preconfigured maximum. In this case, it takes away the oldest unencrypted page in the sliding window, which is thus removed from the client's page tables.

The server cannot operate on the address space of the client. Therefore, libMemShield creates at initialization time a thread called *data thread*, which acts on the client's address space on behalf of the server. Correspondingly, a thread is created in the server to handle the requests of the client concurrently with those of the other clients.

Server and data thread exchange information by means of a Unix socket and a shared memory area. The Unix socket is used only to transmit open file descriptors and control messages. MemShield does not send sensitive data with this socket, because the Linux implementation makes use of a kernel memory buffer which could be vulnerable to Cold Boot attacks. The shared memory area, instead, is safe, because it is composed by a single page frame in RAM, which is explicitly filled with zeros by the server as soon as a transfer is completed.

When the server must drop a page from a sliding window, it sends the corresponding virtual address to the data thread. The latter provides the contents of the page, that is, the unencrypted data, to the server; then, it clears the physical pages and invokes the MADV_DONTNEED command of the madvise() system call to remove the physical page from the page tables. The server encrypts the data by means of the GPU, and adds the encrypted page to the client's red-black tree.

4.4   GPU Encryption

MemShield cryptographic module services the requests coming from the server using the GPU both as a secure key store and a secure processor. Any cryptographic procedure operates on a single page of 4096 bytes.

The data are encrypted by using the cipher ChaCha [3]. This choice was motivated by the need for a cipher that is, at the same time, (i) secure, (ii) suitable for GPU computation, and (iii) simple enough so that the computation can be performed completely in GPU registers. MemShield implements the strongest variant ChaCha20, which can be regarded as cryptographically safe [9,11,32].

The actual encryption/decryption of a 4096-byte page is performed by XORing the data with several keystream blocks. ChaCha20 computes a 512-bit block of keystream starting from a 384-bit seed composed by a 256-bit key and a 128-bit value. In MemShield the 256-bit key is unique and it is generated by a cryptographically secure pseudo-random number generator provided by the operating system. This key is sent to the GPU and stored only in GPU registers, afterwards it is purged out of the server memory.

The 128-bit value of the seed, which can be used both as a counter in stream ciphering and as a predefined nonce, is composed by the virtual address of the page, the process identifier (PID) of the client, and a counter ranging from 0 to 63 that corresponds to the index of the 512-bit block inside the page. Observe that the keystream blocks could be generated and XORed independently with the plaintext blocks. The ciphertext construction is thus embarrassingly parallel, which is a highly desirable feature in a GPU implementation. Another useful property is that encryption and decryption are performed with the same operations, hence the GPU kernel can use the same function for both.

MemShield cryptographic module makes use of a NVIDIA GPU programmed by means of the CUDA toolchain [37,38]. The GPU is reserved to MemShield, which means that unprivileged users cannot access the device. In practice, because the communication channel between user space and the CUDA driver is based on device files, the permissions of these device files are changed so that access is only allowed to privileged users.

The GPU kernel consists of several CUDA blocks; each block acts as a *worker* whose job is to extract pages from a queue and process them using 32 CUDA threads (one *warp*). Each CUDA thread generates two ChaCha20 keystream blocks (128 bytes), which are then XORed with the same amount of plaintext. The number of CUDA blocks in the GPU kernel is dynamically computed at run time according to the features of the GPU board. Using more than one block allows the server to submit requests for several concurrent clients.

Because the 256-bit encryption key is created at initialization time and stored inside the GPU registers, the GPU kernel cannot be terminated, otherwise the key would be lost. MemShield uses a mapped memory between host and device to implement a shared data structure that controls the GPU operations. The data transfer between host (server) and device (GPU) is realized through a circular buffer implementing a multiple-producer, single-consumer queue: multiple host threads can submit concurrent pages to the same queue, while those will be processed by a single worker on the GPU. Each worker has its own queue, thus the workers runs independently and concurrently.

An important aspect of the implementation is that the encryption key and the internal state of the cipher are never stored in GPU local memory, otherwise

MemShield would be vulnerable to GPU memory disclosure attacks. We verified that the current implementation of the GPU kernel never does register spilling.

4.5 Prototype Limitations

The current implementation of MemShield is a prototype, thus it has some limitations. First of all, any protected application must be single process. There is no major obstacle to enhance MemShield so as to overcome this limit.

Protected applications must also be single thread. It would be possible to extend MemShield to support multi-threaded processes whenever userfaultfd becomes capable of handling write-protect page faults. Work is in progress to integrate this feature in the vanilla Linux kernel [1].

MemShield protects all private anonymous pages. In order to have better performances, it could be preferable to selectively encrypt only the subset of pages containing sensitive data.

Finally, the ChaCha20 implementation is prototypal and could be improved.

5   Security Analysis

MemShield is an effective mitigation against Cold Boot attacks. In fact, RamCrypt's authors already proved [17] that the sliding window mechanism is an effective technique that could drastically reduce the probability to find meaningful encryption keys or other sensitive data in memory dumps. Like RamCrypt, MemShield makes use of one sliding window per each protected application.

MemShield is also inspired by how PixelVault [48] makes use of the GPU to safely store encryption keys and run cryptographic procedures. However, PixelVault is nowadays assumed to be vulnerable [12,56]. The reported attack vectors to PixelVault were based on launching malicious kernel functions on the GPU, or running a CUDA debugger on the running GPU kernels. MemShield avoids these vulnerabilities because it restricts access to the GPU to privileged users. Recall that, in our threat model, privileged users and privileged processes are always regarded as trusted. MemShield also takes care of avoiding GPU register spilling, so that Cold Boot attacks against the GPU memory would not retrieve any sensitive data of the cryptographic procedure.

Memory dumps obtained by Cold Boot attacks might expose data included in the kernel buffers associated to Unix sockets, pipes, or other process communication channels. Actually, we verified that the Linux implementation of Unix sockets is vulnerable, because the kernel never erases the associated buffers. MemShield carefully avoids sending sensitive data by means of Unix sockets. Rather, it makes use of shared memory, whose contents can be explicitly cleared by MemShield at the end of the sensitive data transmission.

MemShield does not weaken the operating system isolation guarantees at runtime, thus the confidentiality of users' data against malicious users logged on the same system is preserved. In particular, observe that a unprivileged user cannot tamper with the server daemon, because we assumed that the operating system is safe and the server is a privileged process.

A malicious user could try to interfere with MemShield's communication channels. The daemon listens on a Unix socket waiting for connection requests from clients; hence, unprivileged processes must have write permissions on this socket. However, an attacker cannot replace the socket (in order to mount a man-in-the-middle attack), because the socket interface file is placed in a directory owned by root and not writable by unprivileged users.

A malicious user cannot even tamper with the shared memory area used to exchange data between client and daemon: in fact, this area is created by means of file descriptors exchanged privately through the Unix socket; the area is then mapped in the address spaces of both daemon and client.

MemShield is not designed to protect sensitive data against DMA attacks or other side channel attacks; just consider that a successful DMA attack might break the whole operating system guarantees, while in our threat model the operating system is assumed to be sound.

6   Performance Evaluation

In order to establish the performance impact of MemShield prototype on protected applications, we ran some benchmarks. All tests have been executed on a workstation equipped with a 3.5 GHz Intel Core i7 4771 CPU having 4 physical and 8 logical cores, 32 GiB RAM, and a GPU NVIDIA GeForce GTX 970 (compute capability 5.2) with 4 GiB of device memory. The workstation used Slackware 14.2 as Linux distribution with kernel 4.14, *glibc* version 2.23, NVIDIA driver version 418.67 and CUDA 10.1. CPU power-saving was disabled.

Two benchmarks (*crypt*, and *qsort*) belong to the stress-ng [30] test suite, version 0.09.48. *crypt* consists of multiple invocations of the C library `crypt_r()` function on data placed onto the stack. The test is executed by:

```
$ stress-ng --crypt 1 --crypt-ops 1000
```

qsort performs multiple sorts of an array of elements allocated with `calloc()`. To sort the array, the C library function `qsort()` is used:

Table 1. Wall-clock execution times of single-instance benchmarks, with different sliding window sizes and without MemShield protection ("Baseline"). Average times and standard deviations are in seconds. Sliding window sizes are in pages. MemShield encrypts all private anonymous pages, including the stack.

		aes	sha512	qsort	crypt
Baseline		0.30 ± 0.03	0.44 ± 0.01	4.67 ± 0.03	4.76 ± 0.02
Sliding window	**32**	1.76 ± 0.02	0.47 ± 0.01	6.07 ± 0.02	12.53 ± 0.08
	16	1.94 ± 0.01	0.48 ± 0.00	6.08 ± 0.04	12.56 ± 0.09
	8	16.64 ± 0.09	4.39 ± 0.02	6.10 ± 0.03	12.56 ± 0.10
	4	35.23 ± 0.22	4.58 ± 0.03	64.35 ± 1.62	12.52 ± 0.08

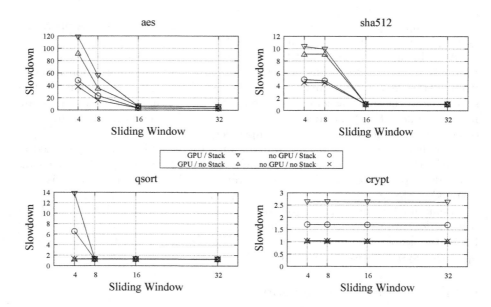

Fig. 1. Slowdowns of a single instance of the benchmarks relative to baseline (no MemShield) varying the sliding window size. MemShield protects all private anonymous pages including the stack ("Stack") or excluding it ("no Stack"). Encryption is performed by the GPU ("GPU") or not done at all ("no GPU").

```
$ stress-ng --qsort 1 --qsort-size 2048 --qsort-opts 10000
```

The third benchmark is *aes* from *OpenSSL* suite version 1.0.2s, which operates on data structures stored in pages allocated with several calls to `malloc()` interleaved with calls to `free()`. The test consists of encrypting the Linux kernel 5.0 source archive, placed in a RAM-based filesystem, using AES-256 in CBC mode:

```
$ openssl enc -aes-256-cbc -in linux-5.0.tar.gz -out /dev/null -k pass
```

Finally, the fourth benchmark is *sha512* from *GNU Coreutils* 1.25: it invokes `malloc()` to allocate a single buffer storing file data, then it computes the digest by storing cryptographic internal state on the stack. The test was launched on the Linux kernel 5.0 source archive placed in a RAM-based filesystem:

```
$ sha512sum linux-5.0.tar.gz
```

In every test run we collected the execution times by using GNU *time* 1.7; each specific test has been repeated 10 times, then average values and standard deviations have been computed.

Table 1 reports how MemShield affects the average execution times of the four benchmarks with different sliding window configurations. Figure 1 shows the slowdowns of the four benchmarks with respect to the baseline, which is the running time without MemShield protection. In order to better understand how the different components of MemShield contribute to the overhead, any plot has four lines, which correspond to the following cases: (i) encryption on GPU of all private anonymous pages, including the stack ("GPU, Stack"), (ii) encryption on GPU of all private anonymous pages, excluding the stack ("GPU, no Stack"), (iii) no encryption at all (the GPU is not involved in handling the protected pages, thus MemShield server stores the pages in clear), but handling of all private anonymous pages, including the stack ("no GPU, Stack"), and finally (iv) no encryption at all, for all private anonymous pages, excluding the stack ("no GPU, no Stack"). Distinguishing between "Stack" and "no Stack" slowdowns is important because, when an application does not have sensitive data stored on the stack, disabling stack encryption significantly improves the performances of MemShield. Distinguishing between "GPU" and "no GPU" slowdowns is useful in order to understand how much the userfaultfd-based mechanism impairs, by itself, the performances of the protected applications. Note that, even if the GPU kernel is a component that can be easily replaced, for instance by an implementation of another, more efficient cipher, transferring the data of the protected pages between system RAM and GPU has an intrinsic cost that could not be easily reduced in the current MemShield implementation.

The *aes* benchmark has a very large slowdown for sliding window size less than 16. A typical AES implementation makes use of very large tables, which are continuously and randomly accessed. The plot shows that the accesses fall both into many `malloc()`ed pages and, to a lesser extent, into the stack. Reducing the sliding window size from eight to four significantly increases the slowdown, which means that the accesses to the encrypted pages are quite random. GPU encryption roughly doubles the slowdown values.

Table 2. Wall-clock execution times of concurrent instances of the benchmarks, without MemShield ("Baseline") and with MemShield using a sliding window of four pages. Average times and standard deviations are in seconds. "Inst." denotes the number of concurrent benchmark instances. MemShield encrypts all private anonymous pages, including the stack.

aes	Baseline	MemShield
Inst. 1	0.30 ± 0.03	35.23 ± 0.22
Inst. 2	0.30 ± 0.01	36.77 ± 0.16
Inst. 4	0.31 ± 0.01	39.91 ± 0.47

sha512	Baseline	MemShield
Inst. 1	0.44 ± 0.01	4.58 ± 0.03
Inst. 2	0.46 ± 0.01	4.82 ± 0.03
Inst. 4	0.48 ± 0.01	5.28 ± 0.06

qsort	Baseline	MemShield
Inst. 1	4.67 ± 0.03	64.35 ± 1.62
Inst. 2	4.74 ± 0.03	67.26 ± 1.23
Inst. 4	4.94 ± 0.01	73.37 ± 1.26

crypt	Baseline	MemShield
Inst. 1	4.76 ± 0.02	12.52 ± 0.08
Inst. 2	4.81 ± 0.04	13.15 ± 0.14
Inst. 4	5.03 ± 0.02	15.04 ± 0.10

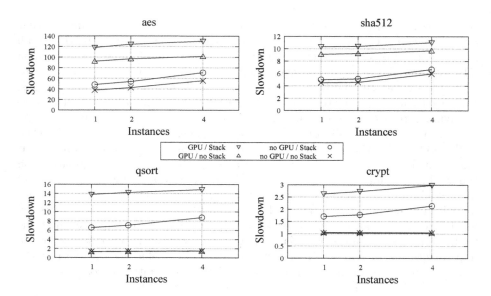

Fig. 2. Slowdowns relative to baseline (no MemShield) varying the number of bench-mark instances. MemShield protects all private anonymous pages including the stack ("Stack") or excluding it ("no Stack"), with a sliding window of 4 pages. Encryption is performed by the GPU ("GPU") or not done at all ("no GPU").

The *sha512* benchmark has negligible slowdown for sliding window sizes greater than eight. The plot shows that the overhead is due mainly to anony-mous private pages not included in the stack, that is, stack handling does not contribute a lot to the slowdown. In fact, the program uses several `malloc()`ed pages as a buffer for data read from file, while it uses the stack to store a small data structure for the digest inner state. Decreasing the sliding window size from eight to four does not significantly change the slowdown, which means that the replacement policy of the sliding window is working fine: actually, the program tends to read sequentially the pages in the buffer. GPU encryption doubles the slowdown values.

The *qsort* benchmark has been selected so to emphasize the effects of stack encryption in some types of protected applications. The program sorts 2048 integers eventually using the C library function `qsort()`. This function avoids recursion by storing on the stack some pointers to the array partitions still to be sorted. Using a sliding window of four pages, page fault handling causes a slowdown roughly seven when the stack is protected, and the GPU encryption doubles this value. On the other hand, if stack is not included in the protected pages, the slowdown is always negligible.

Similarly, the *crypt* benchmark has a significant slowdown only when the stack is encrypted. In fact, the `crypt_r()` function is invoked on data placed on the stack. The slowdown caused by GPU encryption, by itself, is roughly equal to the slowdown caused by page fault handling. The overhead of MemShield is quite small, for every sliding window size.

We also run another set of benchmarks to verify how MemShield scales up when the number of protected clients increases. Each benchmark launches one, two, or four instances of the program at the same time; observe that our test machine has only four physical cores. As shown in Table 2, average execution times have been collected with and without MemShield protection, with sliding window size equal to four pages and stack encryption enabled. Figure 2 shows the slowdowns of the average execution times with respect to the baseline, that is, execution without MemShield protection. According to the plots, there is a limited increase of the slowdown when the number of concurrent instances grows, both for page fault handling and for GPU encryption.

7 Conclusions

Memory encryption is an effective solution against memory disclosure attacks, in which an attacker could access and dump system RAM contents, in order to extract any sort of sensitive data. In this article we presented MemShield, which is a novel approach to software memory encryption for user-mode applications that uses a GPU as a secure key store and crypto processor. By ensuring that the key and the internal state of the cipher are stored into GPU hardware registers, MemShield guarantees that this sensitive information are never leaked to system RAM; therefore, the attacker cannot get meaningful data from a system dump unless the encryption cipher is broken.

Compared to all other proposals for memory encryption frameworks, MemShield is implemented by a user-mode daemon and does not require patches to the operating system kernel. Moreover, user applications do not require source code changes, recompilation, or code instrumentation, hence MemShield can protect even applications for which only the executable code is available.

Functional tests and security analysis suggest that MemShield is an effective mitigation of Cold Boot attacks aimed at system RAM. Performance measures on a prototype implementation show how the MemShield overhead heavily depends on the chosen configuration and clients' memory access patterns. Moreover, the current implementation can be significantly improved, for instance by implementing selective page encryption, by optimizing the GPU kernel implementation, or by introducing some mechanisms that start encrypting pages in the sliding window "in background" as the number of free slots becomes lower than a predefined threshold.

Acknowledgments. We gratefully thank Emiliano Betti for his valuable suggestions, support, and encouragements. The material presented in this paper is based upon work partially supported by Epigenesys s.r.l.. Any opinions, findings, and conclusions or recommendations expressed in this publication are those of the authors and do not necessarily reflect the view of Epigenesys s.r.l..

References

1. Arcangeli, A.: aa.git repository. https://git.kernel.org/pub/scm/linux/kernel/git/andrea/aa.git/. Accessed 17 Sept 2019
2. Bauer, J., Gruhn, M., Freiling, F.C.: Lest we forget: cold-boot attacks on scrambled DDR3 memory. Digit. Invest. **16**, S65–S74 (2016)
3. Bernstein, D.J.: ChaCha, a variant of Salsa20. In: Workshop Record of SASC, vol. 8, pp. 3–5 (2008)
4. Blass, E.O., Robertson, W.: TRESOR-HUNT: attacking CPU-bound encryption. In: Proceedings of the 28th Annual Computer Security Applications Conference, ACSAC 2012, pp. 71–78. ACM, New York (2012)
5. Carbone, R., Bean, C., Salois, M.: An in-depth analysis of the Cold Boot attack: can it be used for sound forensic memory acquisition? Technical report DRDC Valcartier TM 2010–296, Defence R&D Canada - Valcartier, January 2011
6. Cesati, M., Mancuso, R., Betti, E., Caccamo, M.: A memory access detection methodology for accurate workload characterization. In: 2015 IEEE 21st International Conference on Embedded and Real-Time Computing Systems and Applications (RTCSA), pp. 141–148, August 2015
7. Chen, X., Dick, R.P., Choudhary, A.: Operating system controlled processor-memory bus encryption. In: 2008 Design, Automation and Test in Europe, pp. 1154–1159, March 2008
8. Chen, Y., Khandaker, M., Wang, Z.: Secure in-cache execution. In: Dacier, M., Bailey, M., Polychronakis, M., Antonakakis, M. (eds.) RAID 2017. LNCS, vol. 10453, pp. 381–402. Springer, Cham (2017). https://doi.org/10.1007/978-3-319-66332-6_17
9. Choudhuri, A.R., Maitra, S.: Differential cryptanalysis of Salsa and ChaCha–an evaluation with a hybrid model. IACR Cryptology ePrint Archive 2016, 377 (2016)
10. Kaplan, D., Powell, J., Woller, T.: AMD memory encryption whitepaper (2016)
11. Dey, S., Sarkar, S.: Improved analysis for reduced round Salsa and Chacha. Discret. Appl. Math. **227**, 58–69 (2017)
12. Di Pietro, R., Lombardi, F., Villani, A.: CUDA leaks: a detailed hack for CUDA and a (partial) fix. ACM Trans. Embed. Comput. Syst. **15**(1), 15:1–15:25 (2016)
13. Durumeric, Z., et al.: The matter of Heartbleed. In: Proceedings of the 2014 Conference on Internet Measurement Conference, IMC 2014, pp. 475–488. ACM, New York (2014)
14. Edelson, D.: Fault interpretation: fine-grain monitoring of page accesses. Technical report, University of California at Santa Cruz (1992)
15. Emelyanov, P.: CRIU: Checkpoint/restore in userspace, July 2011. https://criu.org
16. Götzfried, J., Dörr, N., Palutke, R., Müller, T.: HyperCrypt: hypervisor-based encryption of kernel and user space. In: 2016 11th International Conference on Availability, Reliability and Security (ARES), pp. 79–87, August 2016
17. Götzfried, J., Müller, T., Drescher, G., Nürnberger, S., Backes, M.: RamCrypt: kernel-based address space encryption for user-mode processes. In: Proceedings of the 11th ACM on Asia Conference on Computer and Communications Security, ASIA CCS 2016, pp. 919–924. ACM, New York (2016)
18. Gruhn, M.: Forensically sound data acquisition in the age of anti-forensic innocence, Ph.D. thesis, Der Technischen Fakultät der Friedrich-Alexander-Universität Erlangen-Nürnberg, November 2016

19. Guan, L., et al.: Protecting mobile devices from physical memory attacks with targeted encryption. In: Proceedings of the 12th Conference on Security and Privacy in Wireless and Mobile Networks, WiSec 2019, pp. 34–44. ACM (2019)

20. Götzfried, J., Müller, T.: ARMORED: CPU-bound encryption for Android-driven ARM devices. In: 2013 International Conference on Availability, Reliability and Security, pp. 161–168, September 2013

21. Halderman, J.A., et al.: Lest we remember: cold-boot attacks on encryption keys. Commun. ACM **52**(5), 91–98 (2009)

22. Henson, M., Taylor, S.: Beyond full disk encryption: protection on security-enhanced commodity processors. In: Jacobson, M., Locasto, M., Mohassel, P., Safavi-Naini, R. (eds.) ACNS 2013. LNCS, vol. 7954, pp. 307–321. Springer, Heidelberg (2013). https://doi.org/10.1007/978-3-642-38980-1_19

23. Henson, M., Taylor, S.: Memory encryption: a survey of existing techniques. ACM Comput. Surv. **46**(4), 53:1–53:26 (2014)

24. Horsch, J., Huber, M., Wessel, S.: TransCrypt: transparent main memory encryption using a minimal ARM hypervisor. In: 2017 IEEE Trustcom/BigDataSE/ICESS, pp. 152–161, August 2017

25. Huber, M., Horsch, J., Ali, J., Wessel, S.: Freeze and Crypt: Linux kernel support for main memory encryption. Comput. Secur. **86**, 420–436 (2019)

26. Huber, M., Horsch, J., Wessel, S.: Protecting suspended devices from memory attacks. In: Proceedings of the 10th European Workshop on Systems Security, EuroSec 2017, pp. 10:1–10:6. ACM, New York (2017)

27. Intel®: Memory encryption technologies specification. Technical report, Intel Corp., April 2019

28. Intel®: Software Guard Extensions. Accessed 9 Sept 2019

29. Jang, I., Tang, A., Kim, T., Sethumadhavan, S., Huh, J.: Heterogeneous isolated execution for commodity GPUs. In: Proceedings of the Twenty-Fourth International Conference on Architectural Support for Programming Languages and Operating Systems, ASPLOS 2019, pp. 455–468. ACM (2019)

30. King, C.: Stress-NG test suite (2011). https://kernel.ubuntu.com/~cking/stress-ng

31. Lin, J., Guan, L., Ma, Z., Luo, B., Xia, L., Jing, J.: Copker: a cryptographic engine against cold-boot attacks. IEEE Trans. Dependable Secure Comput. **15**, 742–754 (2016)

32. Maitra, S.: Chosen IV cryptanalysis on reduced round ChaCha and Salsa. Discret. Appl. Math. **208**, 88–97 (2016)

33. Müler, T., Dewald, A., Freiling, F.: AESSE: a cold-boot resistant implementation of AES. In: Proceedings of the Third European Workshop on System Security, EUROSEC 2010, pp. 42–47 (2010)

34. Mofrad, S., Zhang, F., Lu, S., Shi, W.: A comparison study of Intel SGX and AMD memory encryption technology. In: Proceedings of the 7th International Workshop on Hardware and Architectural Support for Security and Privacy, HASP 2018, pp. 9:1–9:8. ACM, New York (2018)

35. Müller, T.: Cold-Boot resistant implementation of AES in the Linux kernel. Master thesis, RWTH Aachen University, May 2010

36. Müler, T., Freiling, F.C., Dewald, A.: TRESOR runs encryption securely outside RAM. In: USENIX Security Symposium, vol. 17 (2011)

37. Nickolls, J., Buck, I., Garland, M., Skadron, K.: Scalable parallel programming with CUDA. Queue **6**(2), 40–53 (2008)

38. NVIDIA®: CUDA toolkit. https://developer.nvidia.com/cuda-toolkit

39. Papadopoulos, P., Vasiliadis, G., Christou, G., Markatos, E., Ioannidis, S.: No sugar but all the taste! Memory encryption without architectural support. In: Foley, S.N., Gollmann, D., Snekkenes, E. (eds.) ESORICS 2017. LNCS, vol. 10493, pp. 362–380. Springer, Cham (2017). https://doi.org/10.1007/978-3-319-66399-9_20
40. Peterson, P.A.H.: CryptKeeper: improving security with encrypted RAM. In: 2010 IEEE International Conference on Technologies for Homeland Security (HST), pp. 120–126, November 2010
41. Rybczyńska, M.: A proposed API for full-memory encryption, January 2019. https://lwn.net/Articles/776688
42. Simmons, P.: Security through Amnesia: a software-based solution to the Cold Boot attack on disk encryption. Computing Research Repository - CORR, April 2011
43. Stoyanov, R., Kollingbaum, M.J.: Efficient live migration of Linux containers. In: Yokota, R., Weiland, M., Shalf, J., Alam, S. (eds.) ISC High Performance 2018. LNCS, vol. 11203, pp. 184–193. Springer, Cham (2018). https://doi.org/10.1007/978-3-030-02465-9_13
44. Suetake, M., Kizu, H., Kourai, K.: Split migration of large memory virtual machines. In: Proceedings of the 7th ACM SIGOPS Asia-Pacific Workshop on Systems, APSys 2016, pp. 4:1–4:8. ACM, New York (2016)
45. TCG platform reset attack mitigation specification. Technical report, Trusted Computing Group (2008). https://www.trustedcomputinggroup.org/wp-content/uploads/Platform-Reset-Attack-Mitigation-Specification.pdf
46. Tews, E.: Frozencache-mitigating cold-boot attacks for full-disk-encryption software. In: 27th Chaos Communication Congress, December 2010
47. Userfaultfd. Man page on kernel.org. https://www.kernel.org/doc/Documentation/vm/userfaultfd.txt. Accessed 30 Aug 2019
48. Vasiliadis, G., Athanasopoulos, E., Polychronakis, M., Ioannidis, S.: Pixelvault: using GPUs for securing cryptographic operations. In: Proceedings of the 2014 ACM SIGSAC Conference on Computer and Communications Security, pp. 1131–1142. ACM (2014)
49. Volos, S., Vaswani, K., Bruno, R.: Graviton: trusted execution environments on GPUs. In: 13th USENIX Symposium on Operating Systems Design and Implementation (OSDI 2018), pp. 681–696. USENIX Association, Carlsbad, October 2018
50. Vömel, S., Freiling, F.C.: A survey of main memory acquisition and analysis techniques for the Windows operating system. Digit. Invest. 8, 3–22 (2011)
51. Vömel, S., Freiling, F.C.: Correctness, atomicity, and integrity: defining criteria for forensically-sound memory acquisition. Digit. Invest. 9, 125–137 (2012)
52. Wang, Z., Zheng, F., Lin, J., Dong, J.: Utilizing GPU virtualization to protect the private keys of GPU cryptographic computation. In: Naccache, D., et al. (eds.) ICICS 2018. LNCS, vol. 11149, pp. 142–157. Springer, Cham (2018). https://doi.org/10.1007/978-3-030-01950-1_9
53. Würstlein, A., Gernoth, M., Götzfried, J., Müller, T.: Exzess: hardware-based RAM encryption against physical memory disclosure. In: Hannig, F., Cardoso, J.M.P., Pionteck, T., Fey, D., Schröder-Preikschat, W., Teich, J. (eds.) ARCS 2016. LNCS, vol. 9637, pp. 60–71. Springer, Cham (2016). https://doi.org/10.1007/978-3-319-30695-7_5
54. Yitbarek, S.F., Aga, M.T., Das, R., Austin, T.: Cold Boot attacks are still hot: security analysis of memory scramblers in modern processors. In: 2017 IEEE International Symposium on High Performance Computer Architecture (HPCA), pp. 313–324, February 2017

55. Zhang, M., Zhang, Q., Zhao, S., Shi, Z., Guan, Y.: Softme: a software-based memory protection approach for tee system to resist physical attacks. Secur. Commun. Netw. **2019**, 1–12 (2019)
56. Zhu, Z., Kim, S., Rozhanski, Y., Hu, Y., Witchel, E., Silberstein, M.: Understanding the security of discrete GPUs. In: Proceedings of the General Purpose GPUs, GPGPU 2010, pp. 1–11. ACM, New York (2017)

Super Root: A New Stealthy Rooting Technique on ARM Devices

Zhangkai Zhang[1], Yueqiang Cheng[2(✉)], and Zhoujun Li[1]

[1] Beihang University, 37 Xueyuan Road, Haidian District, Beijing, China
zhangzhangkai315@gmail.com, lizj@buaa.edu.cn
[2] Baidu Security, 1195 Bordeaux Dr, Sunnyvale, CA 94089, USA
chengyueqiang@baidu.com

Abstract. Root attack is an unauthorized process of gaining the highest privilege by exploiting the vulnerabilities of a system. After that, attackers can fully control the system, arbitrarily access system resources, and steal private and sensitive information. Fortunately, such root attacks are traceable and detectable by system detection tools as they cannot wholly remove the fingerprints, such as `UID` and `setuid` files. In this paper, we propose a new powerful and stealthy root attack, named **super root**. Comparing to traditional root that grants a user process root privilege, our super root technique can escalate a piece of code to the hypervisor privilege, which is typically left unoccupied in real ARM devices with virtualization support. The super root can do whatever traditional root does, and also can efficiently do Virtual Machine Introspection (VMI) based attacks, such as monitoring system events or steal credential information. The super root can remove the memory fingerprints and thus makes itself stealthy to both kernel and all user detection tools. We implement two VMI-based super root attacks on Pi-top, a *Raspberry pi* powered machine. We measure their performance overheads using two existing benchmark tools and do the security evaluations using root detection tools. The results show that the overhead of the super root is negligible, and the root detection tools cannot detect the existence of the super root.

Keywords: Root attack · ARM virtualization

1 Introduction

ARM devices are widely used in IoT (Internet of Things) markets and mobile products due to the low power consumption and cost [4]. Due to the diversity of applications and the large code base of the monolithic OS, there are numerous security vulnerabilities identified every year. To make the exploit harder, providers forbid the root privilege to all user-installed applications. Moreover, various access control systems [5,24] are added to prevent unprivileged applications from accessing user's private information. To win the arms race, users have to leverage rooting techniques to break the access control system and get

M. Conti et al. (Eds.): ACNS 2020, LNCS 12147, pp. 344–363, 2020.
https://doi.org/10.1007/978-3-030-57878-7_17

the root privilege back. Such (traditional) root attacks [3,9,26] are popular in the current ecosystem. They typically have four main steps to gain the root privilege. First, the attacker identifies specific exploitable kernel vulnerabilities. Second, the attacker selects an application and sets its UID to 0 through the above-identified kernel vulnerabilities. In fact, after this step, the selected application has already obtained the root privilege. Third, the attacker removes its fingerprints from the kernel space, the user space, and the file systems. The primary purpose of the third step is to hide from detection tools to make the rooting procedure stealthy. At last, the attacker obtains the sensitive resources by directly accessing or event interceptions [3,30].

Some detection techniques [8,12,17,25,27] have been proposed. They typically collect root fingerprints from UID values, the presence of particular files, the build setting, and the weird changes of the file permissions. Fortunately, *none* existing traditional root technique can completely remove the fingerprints [27], e.g., malicious files in the file systems, debug build setting, or writable file systems that should be read-only. At least, the detection tools can always identify an unauthorized application with UID equal to 0 [27]. It implies that all traditional root techniques have poor stealthiness. On the other hand, we observed that the hardware-assisted virtualization mechanism had been widely available in the commodity ARM devices. According to the ARM manual, PL2/EL2 is always on, and no mechanism can disable it [2]. Even worse, the entry of PL2/EL2 may be software *writable* and guessable (e.g., Raspberry Pi2). All these observations indicate that an attacker can exploit kernel vulnerabilities to illicitly modify the entry of PL2/EL2 to launch and execute a pre-prepared code as a malicious hypervisor.

Based on the above observations, in this paper, we propose a novel powerful root technique, named *Super Root*, which escalates the privilege of the selected application to the hypervisor privilege and allows the malicious application to efficiently and stealthily monitor system events and steal confidential information. Specifically, the attacker from the hypervisor space can completely remove the fingerprints remained in the kernel and the user space, as well as the file systems, which makes the super root undetectable to all kernel and user root-detection tools. Note that, the super root relies on the hypervisor privilege, and does not require UID of the malicious application to be 0. Thus, checking UID cannot detect the existence of the super root. With hypervisor privilege, the super root is allowed to do whatever the traditional root does, i.e., hook-based monitoring and interception. Besides, it can launch Virtual Machine Introspection (VMI) based attacks wit an advantage that it does not need to modify the binary code of the kernel and userspace libraries. Thus, the super root never introduces fingerprints due to the integrity break.

We have demonstrated two VMI-based super root attacks (VMI-based binder transaction attack and VMI-based Keylogger attack) on Raspberry Pi2 development board running ARM Cortex-A7 processors equipped with Android 5.1.1 system. VMI-based binder transaction attack and VMI-based Keylogger attack adds 238 and 442 SLOC of assembly code and C code into the hypervisor space, respectively. The result of the experiment shows that VMI-based binder transaction attack filtered binder system calls and recoded binder transaction data and VMI-based Keylogger attack recorded all the user input keys. We performed security evaluation on the Raspberry Pi2, the result is a traditional root attack can be detected through the conventional root detection methods, including check UID value, check the presence of special files, check the build setting and check file permissions, but none of these methods can detect super root attack. We also ran two existing benchmark tools to measure the performance overhead of the super root attack from three aspects: install malicious hypervisor, launch VMI-based binder transaction attack, and launch VMI-based Keylogger attack. The performance overhead due to the additional hypervisor layer is 1.5% on average. In the VMI-based binder transaction attack, the performance overhead is about 2.5%, and in the VMI-based Keylogger attack, the overhead is about 1.5%. The overhead of VMI-based super root attacks is significantly small. We discussed the countermeasures of super root attacks such as disable hypercall, protect the HYP vector table, and reduce kernel vulnerabilities.

2   Background

ARM Virtualization Extensions. ARM hardware virtualization extensions provide the CPU virtualization technique via introducing a new CPU mode called HYP mode [2] at privilege level 2 (PL2/EL2) in the Non-secure world. The standard method to enter HYP mode is issuing hypercall (i.e., using HVC instruction) at privilege level 1 (PL1/EL1). The memory virtualization technique is an essential part of virtualization extensions. Before memory virtualization, memory address translation is from a virtual address (VA) to a physical address (PA). With memory virtualization, the virtual address is translated to intermediate physical address (IPA) at first and then translated to PA using a Stage-2 page table.

Hypercall and ERET. The Hypercall Enable bit is in Secure Configuration Register (SCR.HCE). When SCR.HCE is 1, HVC instruction is enabled in PL1/EL1 mode [2]. When hypercall is issued in PL1/EL1, the Current Program Status Register (CPSR) is banked to SPSR_HVC register, and the CPU mode is changed from SVC mode(PL1/EL1) to HYP mode(PL2/EL2). At the same time, the return address of the hypercall is stored in ELR_HYP register. ERET instruction is used to return from HYP mode to SVC mode. When it is executed, CPSR is restored from SPSR_HVC, and CPU mode is changed to SVC mode. PC register (the return address) is restored from ELR_HYP. The hypercall entry is stored in the HYP vector table at offset 0x14, and the base address of the HYP vector table is stored in the HYP Vector Base Address Register (HVBAR).

Stage-2 Translation. Stage-2 translation is a crucial part of memory virtualization on the ARM platform. Guest OS configures and controls the Stage-1 translation (VA to IPA), while the hypervisor controls the Stage-2 translation (IPA to PA). The Stage-2 control registers include Virtualization Translation Control Register (VTCR), Virtualization Translation Table Base Register (VTTBR), and HYP Configuration Register (HCR). All of them can only be accessible in HYP mode. The last bit of the HCR register is the virtualization MMU enable bit, i.e., Stage-2 translation is active when this bit is set to 1 [2]. The attribute bits on the Stage-2 page table descriptors define the access permissions of physical memory pages. The access-permission violations will trigger Stage-2 page fault, and the context will switch into the HYP mode.

Virtual Machine Introspection (VMI). The technology of virtual machine introspection is introduced to enforce security policies on the untrustworthy OS [16]. The typical VMI scenario is that an attacker is inside a virtual machine, and the hypervisor as a system monitor is outside the virtual machine. Thus the hypervisor can use VMI to trace the behavior of the attacker to detect potential threatens. This technology is usually utilized to perform system security protection [10,11,15,19,29]. However, we propose a concept of VMI-based attack that leverages VMI technology to intercept sensitive events and steal private data of the victim in the VM (e.g., VMI-based binder transaction attack, VMI-based Keylogger attack in Sect. 5).

3 Traditional Root Attack

Root attack as one kind of privilege escalation attacks is a popular topic. Traditional root attack leverages user space or kernel space vulnerabilities to obtain root privilege.

3.1 Procedure of Traditional Root

The traditional root attacks typically has four main steps (illustrated in Fig. 1):

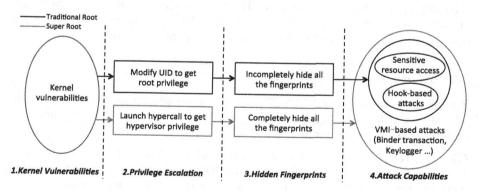

Fig. 1. Root steps and capabilities. The same precondition, different capabilities of fingerprints remove and different attack capabilities between traditional root and super root.

1. **Identify kernel vulnerabilities:** the vulnerabilities could be zero-day or widely known;
2. **Get root privilege:** modify UID to 0 to get root privilege through the above identified vulnerabilities;
3. **Hide attack fingerprints:** remove fingerprints remained in the system;
4. **Launch attacks:** launch attacks with root privilege, e.g., directly access sensitive private resources.

Identify Kernel Privilege (Step 1). The attacker can collect existing kernel vulnerabilities from the CVE list, and test if the target system has patched these bugs. Many users do not patch their systems in time, and thus the attacker usually has a time window to root such systems. Besides, the attacker can identify zero-day vulnerabilities using existing fuzzing tools.

Get Root Privilege (Step 2). There are two typical methods: one is directly modifying the value of process UID to 0 (root privilege) [14]. The other is inserting a set of *su*-like tools to the system partition and issuing *su* shell command to get root privilege. The latter one is relatively popular [26].

Hide Attack Fingerprints (Step 3). To make the traditional root attack hard to detect, the attacker will remove or hide the root fingerprints remained on the operating system. For example, the attacker can remount the access permission of system partition as read-only and remove the *su*. Nevertheless, for such traditional roots, the fingerprints can not be completely hidden, since the UID of the attack process must be 0 for holding the root privilege.

Launch Attacks (Step 4). Root privilege can assist the attacker to access sensitive private resources directly (e.g., contact, photo, GPS) and launch hook-based attacks. The typical hook approach is leveraging root privilege to call the *ptrace* function to attach the target process and modify the control flow to run the pre-prepared code on the memory. Hook-based attacks can perform keylogger attacks, steal SMS data, modify app-internal data [3], and so on. However, it also inevitably introduces fingerprints into the operating system.

3.2   Root Detection Methods

The previous works [8,12,17,25,27] have proposed several root detection methods based on the root fingerprints (e.g., UID and special files) on the operating system, which are summarized as follows:

Check UID. The target of root attack is to set the process UID to 0, and thus, the checking process UID is the most straightforward and efficient root detection method. The traditional root attacks cannot remove these fingerprints.

Check Special Files. The traditional root often relies on special tools (e.g., *su*, BusyBox). With these tools, the attacker can issue *su* shell command to get root privilege. Checking the presence of *su* on the "/system/sbin/" or "/system/xbin/" of the system is a typical method to perform root detection.

Check File Permissions. To perform universal root attack [26], the attacker is used to inserting an executable binary *su* into the system partition. However, the access permissions of system partition are read-only by default. In order to insert *su*, the attacker needs to remount the system partition as writable. Therefore, checking the access permissions of the system partition is also a method for root detection.

Check Build Setting. Checking build setting is a special root detection method on the Android system. Usually, the Android system is built with tags of release-keys [8,12,25] from Google. However, the custom Android system may be accidentally built with the tags of test-keys, facilitating root attacks.

4   Super Root Attack

4.1   Super Root Prerequisites

Super root attack leverages kernel vulnerabilities to escalate the process privilege to hypervisor privilege. There are four prerequisites for the super root attack on target devices:

1. **R1**: ARM CPU should supports hardware virtualization (ARMv7 or newer CPUs);
2. **R2**: PL2/EL2 should not be used (i.e., no hypervisor there);
3. **R3**: Hypercall should be allowed by hardware;
4. **R4**: Hypercall entry should be guessable and writable.

ARM CPUs from ARMv7 start to support both TrustZone and hypervisor. Now the architecture of ARM CPUs equipped on most mobile phones is ARMv8 (satisfy R1), and only one operating system (e.g., Android or iOS) is running on the mobile phones, leaving the hypervisor space empty (satisfy R2). When the SCR.HCE bit is set to 1, hypercall is allowed in the PL1/EL1 (satisfy R3). Based on our observations, this prerequisite is available on most devices. The empty PL2/EL2 will leave all the hypervisor control registers (e.g., HVBAR register) holding the default values. For example, when the value of the HVBAR register is addr_x. The start address of the HYP vector table will be at physical memory address addr_x. The default values are different for different ARM devices, but they are guessable due to the limited entropy (e.g., on our Raspberry Pi device, it is 0x0). Also, a physical address (if it is not ROM memory) is usually writable for the operating system. For example, the first physical page is writable on Raspberry Pi[1] (satisfy R4).

---

[1] Raspberry Pi is the world's third best-selling general-purpose computer. https://www.raspberrypi.org/magpi/raspberry-pi-sales/.

4.2 Super Root Steps

Super root attack aims at gaining the hypervisor privilege on a virtualization-supported ARM device, which has similar steps to traditional root attack (Fig. 1):

1. **Identify kernel vulnerabilities:** find expected kernel vulnerabilities using the method from the transitional root attacks (see details in Sect. 3.1).
2. **Get hypervisor privilege:** modify hypercall entry of the HVC vector table and trigger a hypercall to escalate the privilege of the selected process to the hypervisor privilege.
3. **Hide attack fingerprints:** restore the HVC vector table and completely remove all other fingerprints from the kernel and the user spaces.
4. **Launch attacks:** launch hook-based attacks (as the traditional root attacks) or VMI-based attacks using the hypervisor functionalities.

Identify Kernel Vulnerabilities (Step 1). In this step, we target two kinds of kernel vulnerabilities: (1) a kernel-memory-write vulnerability that is used to modify the HYP vector table and prepare the malicious hypervisor; and (2) a control flow hijacking vulnerability that is used to launch the hypercall. If the first memory-write vulnerability can modify kernel stack (i.e., return address), one vulnerability is also enough.

Get Hypervisor Privilege (Step 2). Based on the identified kernel vulnerabilities, the attacker will do the following two things. First, the attacker locates the address of the HYP vector table. The base address of the HYP vector table could be at 0x0 or a random location. Fortunately, based on our observations, the entropy of the randomness is low, and thus the attacker can easily guess and try all possible locations. Second, the attacker modifies the hypercall entry of the HYP vector table (at offset 0x14) to point to a prepared malicious code. Third, the attacker hijacks the control flow of the kernel to issue a hypercall using the HVC instruction. Once the processor receives the HVC instruction, it will fetch the modified hypercall entry from the HYP vector table and start to execute the prepared malicious code with the hypervisor privilege. Note that, on ARM architecture, the hypercall can only be issued from the kernel space, which is different from X86 architecture.

Hide Attack Fingerprints (Step 3). The purpose of this step is the same as the corresponding one in the traditional root attacks, but the super root can completely remove all detectable fingerprints from the system. Specifically, In the super root attack, the fingerprints remained on the system are the modified hypercall entry, the malicious hypervisor code, and some temporary data on the memory. Once the malicious hypervisor is active, it has the highest privilege to restore the modified HVC entry and remove temporary data on the memory. To hide the malicious hypervisor code, the attacker could enable the Stage-2 MMU and modifies the Stage-2 translation mappings to make the hypervisor memory space invisible to the victim OS. Comparing to the traditional root attacks, the super root with hypervisor privilege does not require that the value of UID is 0.

Launch Attacks (Step 4). The super root can not only cover all the attack capabilities of the traditional root attack but also perform the VMI-based attacks to monitor system events or steal confidential data. Specifically, the hypervisor can insert hooks in the kernel space and the user space, like the hook-based attacks done by the traditional root. In addition, the hypervisor can transparently intercept system events using the virtualization technique via VMI interface, e.g., logging all user inputs by intercepting the accesses of the keyboard input buffer or stealing binder transaction data by intercepting binder communications.

4.3   Advantages of Super Root Attack

The super root attack has two advantages comparing to the traditional root attacks:

Powerful Attack Capabilities with Highest Privilege. After the super root attack, the prepared code becomes a malicious hypervisor with the highest privilege. Thus, the super root can launch the attacks without relying on any kernel-level or user-level modifications; instead, it relies on the virtualization-based mechanism to intercept events or access confidential data. Besides the VMI-based attacks, the super root can do what the traditional root does, but not the other way around (as illustrated in Fig. 1).

Stealthy and Untraceable Attacks. The traditional root attack inevitably leaves some fingerprints (e.g., executable *su*, UID value) on the victim system [8,25,27], and the most obvious feature is that the UID of the rooted process becomes 0. However, after the super root attack, the UID of the rooted process is not changed (i.e., the same as before). For the fingerprints on the memory and file systems, the super root can also remove them. Thus, the super root can hide all the fingerprints on the victim system to make the attack stealthy and untraceable. Besides, the super root can completely control the system and can prepare a virtual/fake environment for the detection tools to induce them to believe that there is no rooting.

5   Super Root Attack Examples

The super root can do hook-based attacks and VMI-based attacks. There is nothing new in the hook-based attacks, as they have been demonstrated many times by existing traditional root attacks. In this section, we demonstrate two real VMI-based attacks on a famous Raspberry powered Pi-top with the Android system and Linux system, respectively. The two attacks are VMI-based Binder transaction attack (Sect. 5.1) and VMI-based keylogger attack (Sect. 5.2).

5.1   VMI-Based Binder Transaction Attack

Binder is the most important mechanism of Android inter-process communication (i.e., Android IPC) [22]. All the data transactions between different processes on Android go through Binder. The Binder framework consists of four components: Client, Server, Service Manager, and Binder driver. Client, Server, and Service Manager running in the user space communicate with each other through the Binder driver working in the kernel space. Service Manager, as a daemon process, manages the Service on the Android system and provides the information of Service to the Client. The Client, Server, and Service Manager invoke binder driver by *ioctl* system call with a particular parameter to transfer the sensitive data between Client and Server. If the attacker can intercept the *ioctl* system call and understand the binder data structures, she can steal the sensitive data from binder transactions. In the following, we will demonstrate the critical steps of launching a VMI-based binder transaction attack (illustrated in Fig. 2).

1. **Launch super root:** repeat the step 1 to 3 of the super root procedure. After that, a prepared code gets the hypervisor privilege.
2. **Intercept system call:** configures DBGBVR, DBGBCR, and HDCR registers to set a hardware breakpoint on 0xFFFF0008 to intercept all the system call to be tripped into the malicious hypervisor. The address 0x0xFFFF0008 is the entry of all system calls.
3. **Steal binder transaction data:** filter out the binder system calls and let all others bypass. Following the binder data structures, the malicious hypervisor locates and steals the sensitive data.
4. **Return to system call table:** modifies the ELR_HYP register (PC will be restored using this value) to continue the intercepted system call.

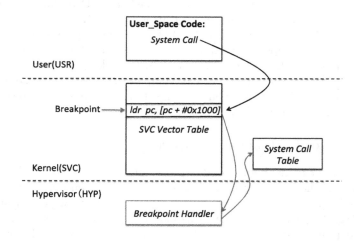

Fig. 2. Hijack control flow without any modification on Android kernel.

Launch Super Root: this step has been introduced in Sect. 4.2.

Intercept System Call: On ARMv7, Breakpoint Control Register (DBGBCR) and Break Value Register (DBGBVR) control the hardware breakpoints. Putting the virtual address of the target instruction into DBGBVR and setting DBG-BCR.E to 1 will enable a breakpoint. When CPU fetches the instruction tagged with the breakpoint, an exception will be generated and handled by the breakpoint handler. However, in the virtualization environment, when the Trap Debug exceptions (TDE) bit in HYP Debug Configuration Register (HDCR) is set to 1, this exception will be routed to HYP mode. On ARMv7, system call entry is at the Kernel Exception Vectors (SVC Vector Table) with the offset 0x8. If the vector bit in System Control Register (SCTLR.V) is 1, the base address of SVC vectors is at the virtual address 0xFFFF0000. When SCTLR.V is 0, Vector Base Address Register (VBAR) holds the SVC Vectors base address. Reading the values of SCTLR and VBAR registers in hypervisor space, the attacker can locate the system call entry and set the breakpoint on it to intercept all the system calls (Fig. 2). The debug configuration registers DBGBCR, and DBGBVR can be accessed from SVC mode. To prevent Android kernel from modifying DBGBVR and DBGBCR registers, the attacker can set HDCR.{TDRA, TDOSA, TDA} to 1 to trap debug OS-related register access [2].

There is another alternative method that sets the hardware breakpoint on the entry of the binder system call handler directly. The advantage of this method is only intercepting the binder system call, rather than all system calls, implying it has a better performance. However, the virtual addresses of the entry of binder system call handlers are different among different kernel versions, which requires additional kernel semantic information. In the current method, the breakpoint is set on the system call entry, which is defined by the hardware (registers) that all kernel versions use the same virtual address for the system call entry on all ARM devices. It is a trade-off between performance efficiency and the solution universality.

Figure 2 depicts the VMI-based binder transaction attack. The system call entry is at virtual address 0xFFFF0008 and the instruction is *ldr pc, [pc + #0x1000]* which indicates the entry address of system call table is stored at the virtual address 0xFFFF1000. When the malicious hypervisor (i.e., the breakpoint handler) collects the binder transaction data, it replaces the value of the ELR_HYP register with the value on 0xFFFF1000 and runs the *ERET* instruction to jump to system call table. This operation can be treated as the malicious hypervisor *emulates* the instruction *ldr pc, [pc + #0x1000]*.

5.2   VMI-Based Keylogger Attack

As described in Sect. 2, the attacker can leverage Stage-2 translation to manage the access control of the physical memory by setting the access permissions of each physical page on the Stage-2 page table. If there is an access violation, a Stage-2 page fault will be generated and trapped by the hypervisor. VMI-based Keylogger attack leverages these features of Stage-2 translation and hardware breakpoints to steal the user input keys.

Correctly, in the VMI-based keylogger attack, we do not choose to intercept the execution of the keyboard driver. Instead, we set the input DMA buffer as non-readable to intercept page fault for each kernel read operation. In the page fault handler, the malicious hypervisor gets the raw data and decodes it into the key. A hardware breakpoint is set on the next instruction of the read instruction, and the input DMA buffer is temporally set readable (Fig. 3). Besides, the interrupt is also temporally disabled to ensure that the read operation and next instruction execution are atomic (i.e., non-interruptible). After the kernel does the read operation, the next instruction tagged with the breakpoint is fetched by CPU. As a consequence, a debug exception is generated to be trapped into hypervisor again. In the breakpoint handler, Stage-2 translation is enabled again to intercept the next access to the key input. At the same time, the breakpoint is disabled, and interrupt is enabled.

The steps (Fig. 3) of launching VMI-based keylogger attack are summarized as follows:

1. **Set input buffer non-readable:** locate the input buffer and set it as non-readable. Note that a dedicated register points the base address of the input buffer.
2. **Intercept page fault:** read operation (*ldr* instruction) triggers a page fault that will be captured by the hypervisor's page fault handler. The page-fault handler will get the raw data and decode it into the input key.
3. **Set breakpoint:** the page fault handler sets the input buffer as readable and enables a hardware breakpoint on the next instruction, i.e., the *mov* instruction
4. **Intercept debug exception:** when the next instruction attempts to execute, a debug exception will trap into the breakpoint handler in the hypervisor space. The handler will set the input buffer non-readable again to wait for the next input key, and disable the breakpoint to make the execution flow continue.

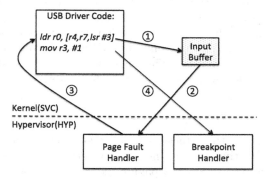

Fig. 3. Key steps of the VMI-based keylogger attack.

6 Implementation

In the implementation, we leverage an installed kernel module (simulating the kernel vulnerabilities) to modify HVC entry located in the first physical memory page. We map the first physical memory page to the virtual address. As a result, we can access the first physical memory page in the user space. The machine code of instruction *mov pc, r0* is written into the hypercall entry (physical memory address 0x14) on the HYP vector table.

The kernel module then performs the following three operations:

1. Allocate memory for Stage-2 page table, the hypervisor code, the hypervisor stack, and the hypervisor heap.
2. Put the prepared malicious code on the allocated memory, and store the start physical address of the malicious code to *R0*
3. Issue a hypercall to execute the malicious code as a hypervisor.

The malicious hypervisor code is written in assembly and C code. It initializes a hypervisor stack to make the *push* and *pop* instructions available. It also sets HCR.VM bit to 1 to enable Stage-2 translation on all of the CPU cores. The physical memory addresses occupied by the malicious hypervisor are configured as non-readable, non-writable, and non-executable for the Android system. In addition, the hypervisor also flushes the TLB (Translation Lookaside Buffer) to make the Stage-2 translation active. The malicious hypervisor sets the HVBAR register to point to a newly prepared HYP exception vector. After these configurations, the malicious hypervisor is installed on Pi-top, and the victim OS is running inside a virtual machine created by the hypervisor. Before *ERET* to the guest kernel, the malicious hypervisor restores the value on the HVC entry to clear the fingerprints of the attack. The hypervisor space is completely hidden through the Stage-2 translation, and all the following operations are transparent for the victim OS.

6.1 VMI-Based Binder Transaction Attack

After the malicious hypervisor is installed, it sets the hardware breakpoint on the system call entry (i.e., virtual address 0xFFFF0008) to intercept all the system calls. When a system call is coming, the malicious hypervisor reads the *R7* register to get the system call number, checking whether it is the *ioctl* system call. If so, the malicious hypervisor obtains the second parameter of the *ioctl* system call. Otherwise, the malicious hypervisor issues *ERET* instruction to return to kernel directly without any operations. For the binder *ioctl* system call, the second parameter is *BINDER_WRITE_READ*, which assists the malicious hypervisor to filter the binder system call.

The critical data structure is the *binder_transaction_data* in the binder transaction, which is located by the third parameter of the binder *ioctl* system call. The *data* field in the *binder_transaction_data* can be utilized to locate the sensitive binder transaction data. However, the malicious hypervisor can not access the virtual address of binder transaction data directly, since PL1/EL1 Stage-1 and Stage-2 MMU translate this virtual address while the memory access in the hypervisor space only walks PL2/EL2 Stage-1 MMU. In order to read the binder transaction data, the malicious hypervisor should explicitly map the target memory into its own space. After the malicious hypervisor successfully reads and saves the sensitive binder transaction data, it will allow the control flow of the intercepted binder *ioctl* to continue, i.e., it replaces the ELR_HYP register with the value on the virtual address of 0xFFFF1000 to *ERET* register.

6.2   VMI-Based Keylogger Attack

In the VMI-based Keylogger attack, the malicious hypervisor locates the DMA input buffer first and then sets it as non-readable in the Stage-2 translation, with the purpose of monitoring the access from the *hid_input* driver. While the Stage-2 page fault is triggered and captured by the malicious hypervisor, the malicious hypervisor configures *HCR* register to disable the Stage-2 translation and tags breakpoint to the next instruction of the current intercepted instruction. At the same time, the hypervisor configures the *SPSR_hyp* register to disable interrupts. When the CPU is switched to the SVC mode, and finishes read operation, the breakpoint will be triggered. In the breakpoint handler, the malicious hypervisor configures *HCR* register to enable Stage-2 translation to wait for the next access, and restores the *SPSR_hyp* to enable interrupts.

In the Stage-2 page fault handler, the malicious hypervisor disables Stage-2 translation instead of setting the input buffer readable. The reason is to avoid missing the interceptions of the keyboard input in a multiple-core system. Correctly, if the Stage-2 page fault happens on core 0 and core 0 configures the input buffer as readable, all other cores will not get any page fault any more due to the shared Stage-2 page table.

7   Evaluation

We implemented our super root work on a Pi-top machine, which is powered by Raspberry Pi2 chipset. Raspberry Pi has been the world's third best-selling general-purpose computer for several years[2], and the commercial products powered by the Raspberry Pi have entered into our lives in many ways[3]. Notably, our pi-top machine is equipped with a Raspberry Pi2 Model B development board, which has a 900 MHz quad-core ARM Cortex-A7 CPU and 1GB RAM on a BCM2836 SoC. The operating system is Android 5.1. The prepared malicious hypervisor contains 55 SLOC assembly and 152 SLOC C code. In our VMI-based attacks, the binder attack includes 77 SLOC assembly and 161 SLOC C code while Keylogger attack includes 188 SLOC assembly and 254 SLOC C code. (Table 1). For each attack, we measured both micro and macro evaluations. For

---

[2] https://www.raspberrypi.org/magpi/raspberry-pi-sales/.
[3] https://www.raspberrypi.org/magpi/gero/.

micro evaluations, we measured the cost of interception operations. For macro evaluations, we measured the system performance overhead using two Android benchmarks tools, i.e., Vellamo (version 3.2.6) and CF-bench (version 1.3).

Table 1. SLOC of super root attacks.

	Assembly code	C code
Malious hypervisor	55	152
Binder attack	77	161
Keylogger attack	188	254

7.1 Micro-evaluation

Both the VMI-based binder transaction attack and the VMI-based Keylogger attack have additional interception operations. Specifically, in the VMI-based binder transaction attack, the hypervisor intercepts every system calls to filter binder transaction. Initially, every system call on ARM devices only has a one-time context switch between USR mode and SVC mode. In the attack scenario, every system call introduces one other context switch between SVC mode and HYP mode triggered by the debug exception. In order to measure the micro-overhead of this attack, we modified the Android kernel source to add a new *null* system call. We inserted a kernel model into the Android kernel to issue this new system call and recorded the time to get the system call latency. The result is shown on the Table 2, the *null* system call takes 1.697 ms on average in the typical case, and it takes 3.815 ms with the virtualization-based interception. The overhead is 2.118 ms.

Table 2. Time for once system call and key input (msec).

	Original	Super root	Overhead
Binder attack	1.697	3.815	2.118
Keylogger attack	62.896	182.659	119.763

In the VMI-based Keylogger attack, when a user touches the screen, the coordinate data of the touchpoints are passed to the DMA input buffer. The input driver reads the data and passes it to the user space. In the attack scenario, the DMA input buffer is set non-readable. Thus a Stage-2 page fault will be triggered when the input driver reads the buffer, which introduces one additional context switch overhead. In the page fault handler, the malicious hypervisor also has some extra delay, i.e., analyzing the coordinates, disabling Stage-2 translation, flushing TLBs, and setting the breakpoint. The breakpoint triggered the second extra context switch, where the malicious hypervisor enables the Stage-2 translation and flushes TLBs in the breakpoint handler. Therefore, the VMI-based Keylogger attack introduces two extra context switches between the kernel and the hypervisor space. We located the read input key operation in the source code of the Android kernel and touched the screen to measure the original performance cost (shown in Table 2). The original read operation takes 62.896 ms on average, while the read operation takes 182.659 ms in the VMI-based Keylogger attack. The overhead, on average, is 119.763 ms for one key input. Note that, such a small delay is imperceptible to users. It is not necessary to enable the interception all the time. Instead, we can only enable it for some particular apps, such as bank apps and other apps with security-sensitive data.

Table 3. Benchmark scores.

	Original	Stage-2 enable	Binder attack	Keylogger
Vellamo:				
Multicore	552.9	548.7(0.8%)	521.3(5.7%)	548.1(0.9%)
Metal	285.2	274.9(3.6%)	276.6(3.0%)	274.2(3.9%)
CF-bench:				
Native	12252.2	12212.1(0.3%)	12171.2(0.7%)	12169.5(0.7%)
Java	3828.1	3831.6(0.0%)	3889.2(-1.6%)	3913.6(-2.2%)
Overall	7237.3	7183.3(0.7%)	7200.3(0.5%)	7218.6(0.3%)

7.2   Macro-evaluation

To measure system-wide performance overhead of the VMI-based binder transaction attack and the VMI-based Keylogger attack, we installed two Android benchmarks (i.e., Vellamo and CF-bench) on Android system. Table 3 depicts the benchmark results (higher scores indicate better performance). The "Original" column represents the running of the benchmarks without hypervisor and VMI-based attacks. "Stage-2 Enable" means Stage-2 translation is enabled, but the hypervisor does not intercept any event. "Binder Attack" is the VMI-based binder transaction attack, and "Keylogger" is the VMI-based Keylogger attack.

When the Stage-2 translation is activated, the performance overhead is introduced by the Stage-2 MMU translation from IPA to PA for every memory address translation. The original one stage memory address translation becomes two-stage translation, which inevitably introduces one more translation overhead. From Table 3, we can find that the overhead of the Stage-2 translation is very small (below 3.6%). The reason is that TLB caches the MMU translations, and the frequency cache hits significantly improve the memory translation performance.

On the VMI-based binder transaction attack, the performance overhead consists of a Stage-2 translation overhead and a system call interception overhead. Every system call needs one extra context switches between the Android kernel and the hypervisor. On a running Android system, system call happens very frequently, and thus the performance overhead could reach 5.7%. On the VMI-based Keylogger attack, the performance overhead contains a Stage-2 translation overhead, two extra context switch overheads, as well as the cost for TLB flush and critical analysis. However, we can find in Table 3, the overhead of Keylogger is almost as the same as the Stage-2 enable-only. The reason is that the screen touches are very infrequent, and thus it is hard to affect the whole system performance.

7.3   Target Devices

The super root technique can be launched no matter what the operating system is, as long as the ARM devices satisfy the following prerequisites: (1) the ARM CPU supports hardware virtualization (ARMv7 or newer CPU), (2) PL2/EL2 is not used; (3) hypercall is allowed; (4) the hypercall entry is guessable and writable (Table 4). Now the architecture of CPUs equipped on most mobile phones is ARMv8 (with virtualization supported), and only one operating system (e.g., Android or ios) is running on the mobile phones (leaving the hypervisor space empty). Thus, any modern ARM devices that satisfy the above prerequisites will potentially suffer from our attacks.

Table 4. Target devices of super root

	CPU version	PL2/EL2	Hypercall	Hypercall entry
Target devices	ARMv7/ARMv8	Empty	Enable	Guessable & Writbale

7.4   Root Detection

We evaluated the stealthiness of super root and traditional root using existing root detection tools on the Android system. We create a new detection tool combining the detection mechanisms from Root Checker [18], Root Detector [23], and one-click root tools (e.g., 360 One-Click Root, Kingo root, Root Master, Root Genius). Specifically, the tool detects rooting attacks from UID, su-like files, system building mode (e.g., test-keys or release-keys), and the access permission of system partition. Figure 4 shows the detection result of one traditional root. In this root application, it uses the terminal (sh) as the target process. When su command is issued, the sh process gets root privilege. The root detection indicates that the UID number is 0, su file exists, the building setting uses test-keys (not release-keys), and the permission of $/system$ partition is read-only. All these imply that the system has been rooted. On the contrary, the root detection tool does not get any rooting features from the system that has been rooted using the super root technique.

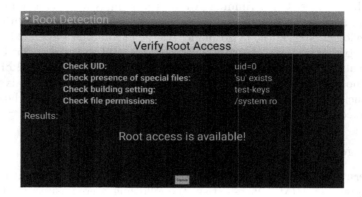

Fig. 4. Traditional root is captured by detection tools.

7.5   Countermeasures of Super Root Attack

Although super root can not only cover all the attack capabilities of the traditional root attack but also perform VMI-based attacks, e.g., monitoring kernel events, intercepting accesses to sensitive resources, stealthily manipulating control flow and data flow, we propose three countermeasures to the super root attack, according to the prerequisites of the super root (mentioned in Sect. 4),

Occupying PL2/EL2. The intuitive idea is to occupy PL2/EL2 by initializing a hypervisor. Specifically, we can configure the HVBAR register to put the HYP vector table into hypervisor space and enable Stage-2 translation to prevent the HYP vector table from malicious modification. This hypervisor does not need to be full-fledged. Instead, it could be a dummy hypervisor with the only propose of occupying PL2/EL2. This countermeasure may introduce some performance overhead due to the additional Stage-2 address translation.

Disabling Hypercall. To launch the super root attack, the attacker has to issue a hypercall with switching to HYP mode. Thus, we can disable the hypercall by configuring the system. The most effective method to disable hypercall is to set SCR.HCE to 0. However, hypercall, as a prevalent method to switch SVC mode to HYP mode, is a critical part of the virtualization technology. Disabling hypercall almost spontaneously disables the virtualization functionalities of an ARM device.

Protecting HYP Vector Table. Protecting the HYP vector table is to prevent the attacker from modifying HVC entry; thus, the attacker can not escalate the malicious code to the hypervisor privilege even if she can issue a hypercall. Generally, there are two methods to achieve this goal. The first one is to add dedicated hardware to protect the HYP vector table, which will inevitably increase the hardware cost and the complexity of the design and implementation. Another solution is to enforce software isolation, e.g., using Stage-2 translation to set the access permission of the HYP vector table as non-writable. An alternative efficient software protection method is setting the HVBAR register to a location out of the physical memory space. All these software protections require some configurations in the hypervisor space, which is not ready on most of the existing ARM devices.

Eliminating 0-day Vulnerabilities. Without 0-day vulnerabilities, Android kernel can be trusted, and the attacker can not hijack kernel control flow to launch the super root attack. Although seL4 already achieved it using several years, it is still hard for commodity operating systems. We suggest the following mitigations to reduce the number of vulnerabilities: (1) remove unnecessary system calls; (2) remove unnecessary kernel modules and drivers; and (3) apply kernel surface reduction techniques, such as KASR [28].

8   Related Work

8.1   Traditional Root and Root Detection

On ARM devices, the motivation of root can divide into two aspects. On the one hand, users have the demand to root their system with total control of the device for convenience. On the other hand, the system privilege model prevents an unprivileged process from accessing the user's private information so that the attacker has to launch a privilege escalation attack (root attack) to bypass the privilege model checks. In the current ecosystem, One-Click root tools [1, 13, 14, 20, 21] are widely available. However, such traditional root attacks are easy to detect, since they inevitably have some non-removable fingerprints, such as UID value, special files, the building setting, and file permissions (Sect. 3.2). UID value is the identifier between root users and normal users. Therefore, the UID value must be 0 for the process with root privilege, which is the most significant fingerprint for traditional root attack. The previous works [8, 12, 17, 25, 27] have proposed some traditional root detection methods, while the super root does not modify UIDs, change file permissions, or relying on special files, which makes it stealthy.

8.2   Hypervisor-Based Rootkits

Robert et al. [6] proposed hypervisor-based Rootkits on the ARM architecture, which leverages implementation bugs of KVM/ARM [7] to hide Rootkits code on the HYP mode (PL2/EL2). As the rootkits have gained the highest privilege of the system, all kernel-level rootkit detection tools cannot detect the existence of such kind of rootkits. However, hypervisor-level rootkit detection still has a chance to detect and remove them. However, for our super root work, we require that the PL2/EL2 layer is empty (i.e., hypervisor is absent). The super root technique will dynamically install a malicious hypervisor and use the VMI technique to monitor system events (e.g., binder operations) or steal information (e.g., keyboard inputs).

9   Conclusion

In this paper, we constructed a new super root attack on virtualization supported ARM devices. The super root attack installs a malicious hypervisor on the ARM devices to stealthily control the victim device and use VMI techniques to monitor system events and steal information. We implemented two VMI-based super root attacks (i.e., binder transaction attack and keylogger). We measured their performance overhead using two existing benchmark tools and evaluated the stealthiness using root detection tools. The experiment results indicated that the overhead of super root is negligible, and all existing root detection tools could not detect the existence of the super root.

Acknowledgement. The authors would like to thank the anonymous reviewers and the shepherd Sudipta Chattopadhyay for their valuable comments and constructive suggestions.

References

1. 360. 360 one-click root. http://root.360.cn
2. ARM. Architecture reference manual ARMv7-a and ARMv7-r edition. Technical report (2014)
3. Artenstein, N., Revivo, I.: Man in the Binder: He Who Controls IPC, Controls the Droid. Black Hat (2014)
4. Blem, E., Menon, J., Sankaralingam, K.: Power struggles: revisiting the RISC vs. CISC debate on contemporary arm and x86 architectures. In: IEEE International Symposium on High PERFORMANCE Computer Architecture, pp. 1–12 (2013)
5. Bugiel, S., Heuser, S., Sadeghi, A.R.: Flexible and fine-grained mandatory access control on android for diverse security and privacy policies. In: Usenix Conference on Security, pp. 131–146 (2013)
6. Buhren, R., Vetter, J., Nordholz, J.: The threat of virtualization: hypervisor-based rootkits on the ARM architecture. In: Lam, K.-Y., Chi, C.-H., Qing, S. (eds.) ICICS 2016. LNCS, vol. 9977, pp. 376–391. Springer, Cham (2016). https://doi.org/10.1007/978-3-319-50011-9_29
7. Dall, C., Nieh, J.: KVM/ARM: the design and implementation of the Linux ARM hypervisor. In: Proceedings of the 19th International Conference on Architectural Support for Programming Languages and Operating Systems, ASPLOS, March 2014
8. Evans, N.S., Benameur, A., Shen, Y.: All your root checks are belong to us: the sad state of root detection. In: The ACM International Symposium, pp. 81–88 (2015)
9. Felt, A.P., Wang, H.J., Moshchuk, A., Hanna, S., Chin, E.: Permission re-delegation: attacks and defenses. In: Usenix Conference on Security, pp. 22–22 (2011)

10. Fu, Y., Lin, Z.: Space traveling across VM: automatically bridging the semantic gap in virtual machine introspection via online kernel data redirection. In: Security and Privacy, pp. 586–600 (2012)
11. Garfinkel, T., Rosenblum, M.: A virtual machine introspection based architecture for intrusion detection. In: Proceedings of the Network & Distributed Systems Security Symposium, pp. 191–206 (2003)
12. Geist, D., Nigmatullin, M., Bierens, R.: Jailbreak/root detection evasion study on iOS and Android. Technical report (2016)
13. Root Genius Team. Root genius. http://www.shuame.com/en/root/
14. Geohot. Towelroot. https://towelroot.cn.uptodown.com/android
15. Sharif, M.I., Lee, W., Cui, W., Lanzi, A.: Secure in-VM monitoring using hardware virtualization. In: ACM Conference on Computer and Communications Security, pp. 477–487 (2009)
16. Jain, B., Baig, M.B., Zhang, D., Porter, D.E., Sion, R.: Sok: introspections on trust and the semantic gap. In: Security and Privacy, pp. 605–620 (2014)
17. Jain, B., Baig, M.B., Zhang, D., Porter, D.E., Sion, R.: Rooting attack detection method on the android-based smart phone. In: International Conference on Computer Science and Network Technology, pp. 477–481 (2011)
18. Joeykrim. Root checker. https://play.google.com/store/apps/details?id=com.joeykrim.rootcheck
19. Liu, Y., Xia, Y., Guan, H., Zang, B., Chen, H.: Concurrent and consistent virtual machine introspection with hardware transactional memory. In: IEEE International Symposium on High PERFORMANCE Computer Architecture, pp. 416–427 (2014)
20. Root Master Team. Root master. https://rootmaster.co
21. Kingo Root. Kingo root. https://www.kingoapp.com/tag/google/
22. Schreiber, T.: Android Binder-Android interprocess communication. Seminar thesis, Ruhr-Universität Bochum (2011)
23. Shin2_D. Root detector. https://play.google.com/store/apps/details?id=shin2.rootdetector
24. Smalley, S., Craig, R.: Security enhanced (SE) android: bringing flexible MAC to android. In: 20th Annual Network and Distributed System Security Symposium, NDSS 2013, San Diego, California, USA, 24–27 February 2013 (2013)
25. Sun, S.T., Cuadros, A., Beznosov, K.: Android rooting: methods, detection, and evasion. In: ACM CCS Workshop on Security and Privacy in Smartphones and Mobile Devices, pp. 3–14 (2015)
26. Xu, W., Fu, Y.: Own your android! yet another universal root. In: Usenix Conference on Offensive Technologies, p. 4 (2015)
27. Zhang, H., She, D., Qian, Z.: Android root and its providers: a double-edged sword. In: ACM SIGSAC Conference on Computer and Communications Security, pp. 1093–1104 (2015)
28. Zhang, Z., Cheng, Y., Nepal, S., Liu, D., Shen, Q., Rabhi, F.: KASR: a reliable and practical approach to attack surface reduction of commodity OS kernels. In: Bailey, M., Holz, T., Stamatogiannakis, M., Ioannidis, S. (eds.) RAID 2018. LNCS, vol. 11050, pp. 691–710. Springer, Cham (2018). https://doi.org/10.1007/978-3-030-00470-5_32
29. Zhao, S., Ding, X., Xu, W., Gu, D.: Seeing through the same lens: introspecting guest address space at native speed. In: Usenix Conference on Security (2017)
30. Zhou, Y., Jiang, X.: Dissecting android malware: characterization and evolution. In: IEEE Symposium on Security and Privacy, pp. 95–109 (2012)

Towards Automated Augmentation and Instrumentation of Legacy Cryptographic Executables

Karim Eldefrawy[1], Michael Locasto[1], Norrathep Rattanavipanon[2(✉)], and Hassen Saidi[1]

[1] SRI International, Menlo Park, USA
{karim.eledefrawy,michael.locasto,hassen.saidi}@sri.com
[2] Prince of Songkla University, Phuket Campus, Phuket, Thailand
norrathep.r@phuket.psu.ac.th

Abstract. Implementation flaws in cryptographic libraries, design flaws in underlying cryptographic primitives, and weaknesses in protocols using both, can all lead to exploitable vulnerabilities in software. Manually fixing such issues is challenging and resource consuming, especially when maintaining legacy software that contains broken or outdated cryptography, and for which source code may not be available. While there is existing work on identifying cryptographic primitives (often in the context of malware analysis), none of this prior work has focused on replacing such primitives with stronger (or more secure ones) after they have been identified. This paper explores feasibility of designing and implementing a toolchain for *Augmentation and Legacy-software Instrumentation of Cryptographic Executables* (ALICE). The key features of ALICE are: (i) automatically detecting and extracting implementations of weak or broken cryptographic primitives from binaries without requiring source code or debugging symbols, (ii) identifying the context and scope in which such primitives are used, and performing program analysis to determine the effects of replacing such implementations with more secure ones, and (iii) replacing implementations of weak primitives with those of stronger or more secure ones. We demonstrate practical feasibility of our approach on cryptographic hash functions with several popular cryptographic libraries and real-world programs of various levels of complexity. Our experimental results show that ALICE can locate and replace insecure hash functions, even in large binaries (we tested ones of size up to 1.5 MB), while preserving existing functionality of the original binaries, and while incurring minimal execution-time overhead in the rewritten binaries. We also open source ALICE's code at https://github.com/SRI-CSL/ALICE.

Keywords: Binary analysis · Cryptographic executables · Software instrumentation

N. Rattanavipanon—Work done partially while at SRI International.

M. Conti et al. (Eds.): ACNS 2020, LNCS 12147, pp. 364–384, 2020.
https://doi.org/10.1007/978-3-030-57878-7_18

1 Introduction

Cryptography is instrumental to implementing security services such as confidentiality, integrity, and authenticity in most software (both, new and legacy). In practice, proper usage and correct implementation of cryptographic primitives are difficult; vulnerabilities often occur due to misuse or erroneous implementations of cryptographic primitives. Example vulnerabilities arising from misuse of cryptography include weak and/or broken random number generators, enabling an adversary to recover servers' private keys [1]. Cryptographic APIs are sometimes misused by software developers, e.g., causing applications to be insecure against specific attacks, such as the chosen plaintext [2], which a typical software developer may be unaware of.

In addition, incorrect implementations of cryptographic primitives can result in leakage of secrets through side-channels [3] or through "dead memory" [4]. Other vulnerabilities in software for embedded and generic systems include implementation flaws in cryptographic libraries (e.g., the HeartBleed [5] and Poodle [6] vulnerabilities in the OpenSSL library), weaknesses in protocol suites (e.g., cryptographic weakness in HTTPS implementations [7,8]), and algorithmic vulnerabilities in cryptographic primitives (e.g., a chosen-prefix collision attack on the MD5 hash function [9] or on the SHA1 hash function [10]). Even after such vulnerabilities are discovered, it may take a while before appropriate fixes are applied to existing software as demonstrated by a recent large-scale empirical study [11] that showed many software projects did not patch cryptography-related vulnerabilities for a full year after their public disclosure. This represents a large window for adversaries to exploit such vulnerabilities.

We argue that (automated) tools that assist software and system designers, and developers, in performing identification, analysis, and replacement in binaries (without requiring source code) can help shorten such vulnerability window, especially for legacy software. While there is existing work on identifying cryptographic primitives (often in the context of malware analysis), none of this prior work has focused on replacing such primitives with more secure ones after they have been identified. To address this issue, we explore feasibility of designing and developing a toolchain for <u>A</u>ugmentation and <u>L</u>egacy-software <u>I</u>nstrumentation of <u>C</u>ryptographic <u>E</u>xecutables (ALICE).

Contributions: Specifically, our goal is to make the following contributions:

1. We design the ALICE framework to automatically augment and instrument executables with broken or insecure cryptographic primitives.
2. We develop heuristics to identify (binary) code segments implementing cryptographic primitives (see the extended version [12] of this work for a list of such primitives).
3. We develop heuristics to determine the scope of the (binary) code segments requiring augmentation if the cryptographic primitives are replaced with stronger ones.

4. We implement ALICE and experimentally evaluate its performance on several executable open source binaries of varying complexity. We also open source ALICE's code at https://github.com/SRI-CSL/ALICE.

Outline: The rest of this paper is organized as follows: Sect. 2 discusses related work. Section 3 overviews the ALICE toolchain, while Sect. 4 contains its design details. Section 5 contains the results of our experimental evaluations. Section 6 discusses ALICE limitations, while Sect. 7 concludes the paper.

Full Paper: Due to space constraints, we refer to the extended version of this paper [12] for more detailed discussion of: challenges in addressing ALICE limitations, ALICE implementation details and full experimental results, as well as background on our evaluation dataset.

2   Related Work

Identifying Cryptographic Primitives. Several publicly available tools [13–15] utilize static analysis to identify cryptographic primitives by detecting known (large) constants used in their operation. Such constants, for example, can be in the form of look-up tables (e.g., S-Boxes in AES) or a fixed initialization vectors/values (e.g., IV in SHA-128/256). Such tools do not always produce accurate results as the detected algorithm may be another function or another cryptographic primitive that uses the same constant values [16]. They are also ineffective when dealing with obfuscated programs [17].

In terms of academic efforts, Lutz [18] detects block ciphers from execution traces based on three heuristics: the presence of loops, high entropy, and integer arithmetic. Grobert et al. [19] introduce an additional heuristic to extract cryptographic parameters from such execution traces and identify primitives by comparing the input-output relationships with those of known cryptographic functions. Lestringant et al. [16] propose a static method based on data flow graph isomorphism to identify symmetric cryptographic primitives. Recently, the CryptoHunt [20] tool develop a new technique called bit-precise symbolic loop mapping to identify cryptographic primitives in obfuscated binaries.

Our work focuses on non-obfuscated programs as we target common (and possibly legacy) software and not malware. We rely on finding known constants to identify cryptographic primitives as our first step. We then improve the accuracy of detection by applying a heuristic based on input-output relationships, similar to the work in [19]. In contrast to [19], our identification algorithm does not require program execution traces.

While there is existing work on identifying executable segments implementing cryptographic primitives, none of such work investigates the problem of replacing an identified weak primitive with a more secure one. Such replacement requires non-trivial operations, even if one can successfully identify executable segments implementing cryptographic primitives. To accomplish such replacement, one has to perform the following: (1) determining all changes throughout the binary necessary for replacing the identified primitive, and (2) rewriting the binary to apply all of the determined changes. *To the best of our knowledge, there is no prior work addressing the first task, as a standalone, or in conjunction with the second.* The second task can be tackled using slight modifications of existing binary rewriting techniques. In this paper, we categorize different types of necessary changes one may require when replacing a cryptographic primitive, and then discuss how to locate and rewrite each category of such changes in Sect. 4.2. In the rest of this section, we overview general binary rewriting techniques.

Rewriting Binaries. Binary rewriting is a technique that transforms a binary executable into another without requiring the original's source code. Typically, the transformed binary must preserve the functionality of the original one while possibly augmenting it with extra functionalities. There are two main categories of binary rewriting: static and dynamic binary rewriting.

In *static binary rewriting* [21–24], the original binary is modified offline without executing it. Static binary rewriting is typically performed by replacing the original instructions with an unconditional jump that redirects the program control flow to the rewritten instructions, stored in a different area of the binary. This relocation can be done at different levels of granularity such as inserting a jump for each modified instruction, for the entire section or for each routine containing modified instructions. Static binary rewriting often requires disassembling the entire binary and thus incurs high overhead during the rewriting phase, but typically results in small runtime overhead in the rewritten binary. This technique is thus well-suited for scenarios where the runtime performance of the rewritten binary is a primary concern. Another approach for static rewriting is to transform the binary into the relocatable disassembled code and directly rewrite instructions in the transformed code. Doing so completely eliminates runtime and size overhead in the rewritten binary. Nonetheless, this approach relies on many heuristics and assumptions for identifying and recovering all relocating symbols and is still subject to the high overhead during the rewriting phase. Some example tools that are based on this approach are `Uroboros` [25] and `Ramblr` [26].

Dynamic binary rewriting (or dynamic instrumentation) [27–30] modifies the binary's behaviors during its execution through the injection of instrumentation code. Due to the need to instrument the code at runtime, this technique may result in higher execution time compared to the original binary. The main advantage of dynamic rewriting is its ability to accurately capture information about a program's states or behaviors, which is much harder when using static rewriting. Example dynamic binary rewriting tools include `Pin` [28] and `DynamoRIO` [29].

In this work, we first leverage the runtime information retrieved from dynamic instrumentation to accurately locate instructions that need to be rewritten. Instruction rewriting is then performed statically in order to minimize the runtime overhead of the rewritten binary.

3   Overview of the ALICE Framework

The most straightforward, and obvious, approach to replace implementations of vulnerable cryptographic primitives requires modifying (and then recompiling) a program's source code. This takes time and effort, and renders it difficult to fix legacy software for which source code may not be available. Instead, we propose ALICE – a toolchain that automatically augments and replaces weak, vulnerable, and/or broken cryptographic primitives at the binary level.

To better illustrate how ALICE works, we start by presenting a simple representative example shown in Fig. 1. This example program first computes an MD5 digest over an input string. The digest is then converted into a human-readable form, which is in turn displayed to the user.

MD5 has been shown to be vulnerable to collision and pre-image attacks [31, 32]. Suppose that a system or software developer would like to manually rewrite parts of the binary in order to support a more secure hash algorithm – e.g., SHA-256. One way to accomplish this task is to perform the following steps:

Step-1: Identify the functions in the binary that implement MD5.
Step-2: Recover the type and order of parameters in the identified functions.
Step-3: Insert an implementation of a SHA-256 function with the same type and order of parameters into the original binary.
Step-4: Redirect all calls to MD5 to the newly added SHA-256 function.
Step-5: Determine all changes throughout the binary affected by an increase in the digest size (MD5's digest size is 128 bits while that of SHA-256 is 256 bits).
Step-6: Rewrite the binary according to changes discovered in step-5.

Goal and Scope: ALICE is designed to automate the aforementioned steps. It targets ELF-based X86/64 binaries generated by compiling C programs. We do not assume any knowledge of, or require, the corresponding source code or debugging symbols. Since ALICE is built as a defensive tool to work on standard and legacy software, it assumes the target programs are not malicious. *Obfuscated or malware binaries are out of scope in this work.* We demonstrate concrete feasibility on cryptographic hash functions, but the design and ideas behind ALICE are general and can be applied to other primitives too.

NOTE: We use *cryptographic hash functions* (or *hash functions*) to denote the algorithmic details behind the implementations/executables. We denote the functions (or methods) in such implementations/executables that realize such hash function(s) as *hash routines*. We use *target* hash functions/routines to refer to the insecure hash functions/routines that need to be identified and replaced.

4   Design Details of ALICE

This section discusses the design details of the ALICE toolchain. The operation of ALICE consists of three main phases: (i) identifying cryptographic primitives, (ii) scoping changes, and (iii) augmenting and rewriting changes.

```
<main_fn_prologue>:
  400629:  push   rbp
  40062a:  mov    rbp,rsp
  40062d:  sub    rsp,0x60
  ...
<call_to_md5>:
  400684:  call   4004c0 <strlen@plt>
  400689:  mov    rcx,rax
  40068c:  lea    rdx,[rbp-0x40]
  400690:  lea    rax,[rbp-0x50]
  400694:  mov    rsi,rcx
  400697:  mov    rdi,rax
  40069a:  call   400616 <MD5>
  ...
<sprintf_loop_body>:
  4006ad:  movzx  eax,BYTE PTR [rbp+rax*1-0x40]
  4006b2:  movzx  eax,al
  4006b5:  mov    edx,DWORD PTR [rbp-0x54]
  4006b8:  add    edx,edx
  4006ba:  movsxd rdx,edx
  4006bd:  lea    rcx,[rbp-0x30]
  4006c1:  add    rcx,rdx
  4006c4:  mov    edx,eax
  4006c6:  mov    esi,0x4007d4
  4006cb:  mov    rdi,rcx
  4006ce:  mov    eax,0x0
  4006d3:  call   400500 <sprintf@plt>
<sprintf_loop_condition>:
  4006d8:  add    DWORD PTR [rbp-0x54],0x1
  4006dc:  cmp    DWORD PTR [rbp-0x54],0xf
  4006e0:  jle    4006a8 <main+0x7f>
  ...
<printf_loop_body>:
  4006eb:  mov    eax,DWORD PTR [rbp-0x54]
  4006ee:  cdqe
  4006f0:  movzx  eax,BYTE PTR [rbp+rax*1-0x40]
  4006f5:  movzx  eax,al
  4006f8:  mov    esi,eax
  4006fa:  mov    edi,0x4007d4
  4006ff:  mov    eax,0x0
  400704:  call   4004e0 <printf@plt>
<printf_loop_condition>:
  400709:  add    DWORD PTR [rbp-0x54],0x1
  40070d:  cmp    DWORD PTR [rbp-0x54],0xf
  400711:  jle    4006eb <main+0xc2>
```

```c
1  void MD5(const unsigned char* input,
     size_t inputlen, unsigned char*
     output) {
2    MD5_CTX ctx;
3    MD5Init(&ctx);
4    MD5Update(&ctx, input, inputlen);
5    MD5Final(output, &ctx);
6  }
7
8  int main(void) {
9    // Initialize input and output buffers
10   char input[] = "Hello, world!";
11   size_t inputlen = strlen(input);
12   unsigned char digest[16];
13   char hexdigest[33] = {0};
14
15   // Compute: output = MD5(input)
16   MD5(input, inputlen, digest);
17
18   // Convert output digest to hex string
19   for(int i=0; i < 16; i++) {
20     sprintf(hexdigest+2*i, "%02x",
       digest[i]);
21   }
22
23   // Print digest in hex format
24   for(int i=0; i < 16; i++) {
25     printf("%02x", digest[i]);
26   }
27
28   // Print hexdigest string
29   printf("\n%s\n", hexdigest);
30   return 0;
31 }
```

(a) Simple program utilizing a cryptographic primitive (the MD5 hash function)

(b) Corresponding disassembly of main function in (a), compiled with O0 flag

Fig. 1. An example of a simple program utilizing a cryptographic primitive (the MD5 hash function in this case)

4.1 Identifying Cryptographic Primitives (Hash Functions)

We designed ALICE to target non-malicious (i.e., unobfuscated) binary programs. The first phase of ALICE leverages this characteristic and identifies hash functions by first detecting static features that are known of the target hash function.

Observation 1 (Constants). *A common design approach for hash functions is to initialize a digest buffer using well-known constants. As an example, MD5 uses 32-bit constant words: $X_1|X_2|X_3|X_4$ with the following hex values:*

$$X_1 = 0x67452301, X_2 = 0xEFCDAB89, X_3 = 0x98BADCFE, X_4 = 0x10325476$$

If we locate such constants in a binary, there is a high chance that a routine enclosing those constants implements part(s) of the MD5 hash function. Our approach starts by scanning a binary program to find the addresses where known constants appear. We then mark a routine in which those constants are enclosed as a candidate implementation of the target hash function.

Observation 2 (Context Initialization). *The example in Fig. 1a illustrates a typical usage of a hash function in practice. An application function – main()* *– calls the MD5() function, which in turn calls MD5Init() to initialize a digest buffer with known constants. Having a dedicated function to setup an initial context (e.g., MD5Init()) is common practice when implementing most crypto-graphic primitives and can be found in several open-source libraries such as the OpenSSL or libgcrypt.*

This observation suggests that the identified candidate implementation will typically correspond to the initialization routine – Init(). However, it is not always the case as Init() could be inlined. For example, MD5Init() in Fig. 1 will be inlined inside MD5() when the program is compiled with the optimization flag O3. In this scenario, the identified routine will instead correspond to the implementation of the target hash function – MD5(). One could use a simple heuristic based on the size of the routine to distinguish between the two scenarios. However, we found this approach to produce a lot of false-negatives in practice. Instead, we adopt a more conservative approach and consider routines produced in both scenarios as candidates. More specifically, ALICE analyzes the program's callgraph and determines all routines that invoke the previously identified routine. It then includes those caller routines into the list of candidates.

Now, ALICE needs a mechanism to eliminate false-positives, which can arise due to two reasons. The first reason is that our approach so far focuses on ensuring no false-negatives by accepting all routines possibly implementing a target hash routine. The second reason is that static features such as a constant vector are not always unique to a single hash function. It is not uncommon for different hash functions to share the same constant vectors. Examples of a pair of hash functions that use the same constant vectors are BLAKE2b – SHA-512 and MD5 – MD4. In Fig. 1, even if we successfully determine that MD5Init() is inlined, we still cannot easily distinguish whether the identified hash routine implements MD4 or MD5 hash function.

Observation 3 (Input/Output Uniqueness). *A cryptographic hash function is deterministic, i.e., for a given input string, it always generates the same digest as output. The input/output pair is usually (in practice) unique to the hash function that produces them.*

With this observation, the best way to test whether a candidate implements the target hash function is to execute the identified routine, and compare the resulting output with the expected output. Since we expect the identification phase to be an offline computation, naturally we would base this step of our approach on an offline dynamic execution technique, which allows us to execute a given routine with any concrete chosen input. This is in contrast with online dynamic execution, which requires running the entire binary program with test cases. To perform offline dynamic execution, it is necessary to setup a call stack with proper parameters that will be passed into that routine.

Observation 4 (Parameters). *An implementation of a cryptographic function generally takes a fixed number of function parameters. For example, in Fig. 1a, MD5() include three parameters: an input string, the input length and an output digest. Some implementations do not mandate the use of input length as it can be inferred from the input string (e.g., via* strlen()). *Thus, a hash routine in such implementations will take only two parameters. It is also worth noting that, even though a number is fixed, the order in which these parameters appear may not be the same for all implementations.*

Based on this observation, ALICE enumerates all possible combinations of a hash routine's parameters and prepares 8 (= 3!+2!) call stacks, each initialized with different combinations of parameters. It then executes a candidate routine on each call stack and observes the output buffer after the execution. The first phase of ALICE finishes by outputting candidates producing the expected output as well as the parameter information obtained from corresponding call stacks.

4.2   Scoping Changes

After locating target hash routines, ALICE must determine changes (throughout the binary) that are required for replacing such routines. We now describe three categories of such changes using the illustrative example in Fig. 1, and later outline how to identify a subset of such changes (at the binary level).

– ⬚C1⬚ **Routine Replacement:** The first category is a change in the hash routine itself. Code/instructions implementing the target hash routine are replaced by code/instructions that implement a more secure hash function. For example, if our goal is to replace the MD5 function with SHA-256 in Fig. 1, instructions corresponding to MD5() (i.e., the ones starting from address 0x400616) need to be replaced by SHA-256 instructions. We will discuss how ALICE augments this type of change into a binary in Sect. 4.3.

– ⬚C2⬚ **Changes in Buffers Sizes:** Depending on the digest size of both the replacement and the target hash functions, other related memory buffers may need to be enlarged to correctly accommodate the new replacement routine. For instance, replacing MD5 with SHA-256 in Fig. 1 would also require enlarging the size of variables storing the output of the hash function (i.e., digest variable) from 16 bytes to 32 bytes. This change in buffer size affects other memory buffers that consume the output digest, e.g., hexdigest also needs to be expanded by 16 bytes. Such changes have to be scoped and propagated throughout the entire binary. We discuss how to identify this type of change in the remaining of this section and how ALICE performs augmentation on such changes in Sect. 4.3.

– ⬚C3⬚ **Changes in Logic:** This category refers to changes that need to be applied to the underlying binary logic in order to have a correct resulting binary function. For example, in Fig. 1, simply replacing MD5() with SHA-256() and enlarging hexdigest and digest variable do not suffice to produce the desired binary. One would have to also edit a loop terminating condition from $i < 16$ to $i < 32$ in line 19 and 24 to reflect the replacement SHA-256. At the binary-level, this change corresponds to modifying the instructions at addresses 0x4006dc and 0x40070d from [cmp DWORD PTR [rbp-0x54],0xf] to [cmp DWORD PTR [rbp-0x54],0x1f]. This requires knowing that the constant 0xf in those instructions is related to the digest size. However, it is hard, in some cases impossible, to locate and augment this type of changes without any prior knowledge of the correct behavior of the resulting binary. Therefore, we do not consider this category of changes in this work.

Of the three categories of changes, $\boxed{\text{C1}}$ is identified in the previous phase of ALICE in Sect. 4.1 while $\boxed{\text{C3}}$ is out of scope in this work. The remainder of this section will focus on how ALICE locates the changes from $\boxed{\text{C2}}$.

ALICE leverages dynamic taint analysis to determine the change in buffer size $\boxed{\text{C2}}$. Typically, dynamic taint analysis starts by marking any data that comes from an untrusted source as tainted. It then observes program execution to keep track of the flow of tainted data in registers and memory. We adapt this idea to identify all *memory buffers* that are affected (or tainted) by the output digest of the target hash routine. In particular, our dynamic taint analysis executes a binary on test inputs with the following taint policies:

Taint Introduction. At the beginning of execution, ALICE initializes all memory locations to be non-tainted. During the execution, whenever entering the target hash routine, ALICE reads the value in the parameter registers to observe the base address of the output digest. Since the digest size is well-known and deterministic for any given hash function, ALICE can also identify the entire address range of the digest buffer. Upon exiting the routine, ALICE then assigns a taint label to all memory locations in the digest buffer. ALICE uses three taint labels to differentiate 3 types of memory allocations:

- **Static allocation.** In our target executables, static memory is allocated at compile time before the program is executed. Thus, the location of this type of memory is usually deterministic, stored in either .data or .bss segment of the associated binary. Detecting whether a given memory location is statically allocated is simply done by checking whether its address lies within the boundaries of those segments.
- **Heap-based allocation.** ALICE traces all heap-based memory allocations by intercepting a call to three well-known C routines: malloc(), calloc() and realloc(). Whenever each of these routines is called, ALICE learns the size of allocated memory by reading values of its parameter registers. Upon exiting the same routine, ALICE then learns the base address of allocated memory via the return value. With this information, ALICE later can determine whether memory at a given location is allocated on the heap.

- **Stack-based allocation.** ALICE maintains stack-related information of the execution via a *shadow* stack. Specifically, after executing any `call` instruction, ALICE pushes into the shadow stack: a pair of the current stack pointer and an address of the function being called. Upon returning from a routine (via a `ret` instruction), ALICE pops the shadow stack. This information allows ALICE to reconstruct stack frames at any point during the execution of dynamic taint analysis. ALICE determines whether memory at a given address is on the stack by checking it against all stack frames.

Taint Propagation. ALICE's taint propagation rules are enforced at the word-level granularity. While we could use a more precise granularity such as the bit-level [33], we did not find such approach to be cost-effective as test inputs may require a timely interaction with a remote server; having a significantly long delay in the dynamic taint analysis can cause the remote server to timeout and consequently the analysis may not be performed as expected.

In addition to the general taint propagation rules, ALICE also considers the *taint-through-pointer* scenario: if a register A is tainted and a register B is assigned with the referenced value of A, i.e., B := *A, then B is considered tainted. Such rule is necessary to accurately capture the data-flow in a common usage of a hash function, where the raw digest value is converted to human-readable format via a look-up table, e.g., the use of `sprintf()` in line 20 of Fig. 1a.

Using these rules, ALICE's dynamic taint analysis can determine, and assign taint labels to, all memory locations affected by the output digest. At the end of the analysis, ALICE aggregates individual tainted memory locations into unified memory buffers. Our aggregation rule is simple: ALICE considers contiguous memory locations to be a memory buffer if their address range is at least as long as the target hash function's digest size. Lastly, in this phase, ALICE outputs the types (i.e., either stack-based, heap-based or static), locations (e.g., a stack offset or global address), and relevant instructions (e.g., an instruction address of a call to `malloc`) of memory buffers that are derived from the output digest.

4.3 Augmenting and Rewriting Changes

ALICE can incorporate several rewriting approaches. Since runtime of rewritten binaries is our primary concern, we mainly use static binary rewriting that has been previously shown to have minimal impact on the runtime [22].

To reduce the size of rewritten binaries, we rewrite at *routine level* rather than at section level[1]. If there is at least one instruction that needs to be edited in a particular routine, we rewrite the binary as follows:

1. Create a new empty section in the binary
2. Apply changes from $\boxed{\text{C1}}$ and $\boxed{\text{C2}}$ to the routine
3. Modify the routine with respect to the placement of the new section

---

[1] We intentionally avoid rewriting at the instruction level as this can potentially incur significant run-time overhead for the rewritten/output binaries.

4. Insert the entire rewritten routine into the new section
5. Insert a `jump` instruction to the new section at original routine's entry point

Steps (1), (4) and (5) are explained in Sect. 2. We focus in this section on steps (2) and (3). We refer to the full version of this paper [12] for implementation details of all steps.

For step (3), we only need to ensure that the rewritten routine maintains the correct control flow targets. Doing so requires editing all instruction operands in the routine that use `rip`-relative addressing. The displacement of such operands is recomputed based on the address of the new location:

$$new\_disp = old\_disp + old\_inst\_addr - new\_inst\_addr$$

In step (2), to apply changes from $\boxed{\text{C1}}$, ALICE generates a patch from a user-supplied C code that implements the replacement hash function, and adds them to the new empty section of the binary. To ensure correctness of the rewritten binaries, implementation of the user-supplied replacement hash function must have the same parameter order as that of the target hash function as well as be self-contained. We also ensure that a call to the target hash routine is redirected to this new code by simply rewriting the first instruction of the target hash routine to: `jmp [new_code_entry_point]`. For each memory buffer identified in $\boxed{\text{C2}}$, ALICE computes the new buffer size based on the ratio of the digest sizes of the target hash function and that of the replacement hash function, i.e., $new\_size = \lceil old\_size \times |digest_{secure}|/|digest_{target}| \rceil$. ALICE rewrites the binary to support the expanded buffers by employing different techniques for each type of buffers:

Static Buffer. As a static buffer is allocated at a fixed address, we expand such buffer by creating another buffer at a new location and modify all instruction operands that access the original buffer to this newly allocated buffer. Specifically, ALICE first allocates a new data segment in the binary, and creates a mapping of the address of the original buffer to the address in the new data segment. To ensure that the rewritten binary uses the new address instead of the original, ALICE scans through all instructions in the original binary and edits the ones that contain an access to the original address by using information obtained from the previously computed address mapping.

Heap-based buffer. Unlike a static buffer, this type of buffer is allocated dynamically through a call to `malloc()`, `alloc()` or `realloc()` routine. Fortunately, ALICE learns when this type of buffer is allocated through the dynamic taint analysis in Sect. 4.2. Thus, expanding a heap-based buffer only requires ALICE to trace back to the instruction allocating such buffer, i.e. a `call` instruction to `malloc()`, `alloc()` or `realloc()`, and update the parameter register value storing the allocation size information to the new buffer size.

Stack-Based Buffer. Figure 2 shows how ALICE modifies the `main` routine in the example from Fig. 1b to support the expansion of stack-based buffers: `digest` and `hexdigest` by 16 and 32 bytes respectively. Intuitively, expanding a buffer

```
<main_fn_prologue>:
  400629:  push   rbp
  40062a:  mov    rbp,rsp
  40062d:  sub    rsp,0x60
  ...
<call_to_md5>:
  400684:  call   4004c0 <strlen@plt>
  400689:  mov    rcx,rax
  40068c:  lea    rdx,[rbp-0x40]
  400690:  lea    rax,[rbp-0x50]
  400694:  mov    rsi,rcx
  400697:  mov    rdi,rax
  40069a:  call   400616 <MD5>
  ...
<sprintf_loop_body>:
  4006ad:  movzx  eax,PTR [rbp+rax*1-0x40]
  4006b2:  movzx  eax,al
  4006b5:  mov    edx,DWORD PTR [rbp-0x54]
  4006b8:  add    edx,edx
  4006ba:  movsxd rdx,edx
  4006bd:  lea    rcx,[rbp-0x30]
  4006c1:  add    rcx,rdx
  ...
  4006d3:  call   400500 <sprintf@plt>
<sprintf_loop_condition>:
  4006d8:  add    DWORD PTR [rbp-0x54],0x1
  4006dc:  cmp    DWORD PTR [rbp-0x54],0xf
  4006e0:  jle    4006a8 <main+0x7f>
  ...
<printf_loop_body>:
  4006eb:  mov    eax,DWORD PTR [rbp-0x54]
  4006ee:  cdqe
  4006f0:  movzx  eax,PTR [rbp+rax*1-0x40]
  4006f5:  movzx  eax,al
  4006f8:  mov    esi,eax
  4006fa:  mov    edi,0x4007d4
  4006ff:  mov    eax,0x0
  400704:  call   4004e0 <printf@plt>
<printf_loop_condition>:
  400709:  add    DWORD PTR [rbp-0x54],0x1
  40070d:  cmp    DWORD PTR [rbp-0x54],0xf
  400711:  jle    4006eb <main+0xc2>
```

(a) Original Binary

```
<main_fn_prologue>:
  400629:  push   rbp
  40062a:  mov    rbp,rsp
  40062d:  sub    rsp,0x90
  ...
<call_to_md5>:
  400684:  call   4004c0 <strlen@plt>
  400689:  mov    rcx,rax
  40068c:  lea    rdx,[rbp-0x70]
  400690:  lea    rax,[rbp-0x80]
  400694:  mov    rsi,rcx
  400697:  mov    rdi,rax
  40069a:  call   400616 <MD5>
  ...
<sprintf_loop_body>:
  4006ad:  movzx  eax,PTR [rbp+rax*1-0x70]
  4006b2:  movzx  eax,al
  4006b5:  mov    edx,DWORD PTR [rbp-0x84]
  4006b8:  add    edx,edx
  4006ba:  movsxd rdx,edx
  4006bd:  lea    rcx,[rbp-0x50]
  4006c1:  add    rcx,rdx
  ...
  4006d3:  call   400500 <sprintf@plt>
<sprintf_loop_condition>:
  4006d8:  add    DWORD PTR [rbp-0x84],0x1
  4006dc:  cmp    DWORD PTR [rbp-0x84],0xf
  4006e0:  jle    4006a8 <main+0x7f>
  ...
<printf_loop_body>:
  4006eb:  mov    eax,DWORD PTR [rbp-0x84]
  4006ee:  cdqe
  4006f0:  movzx  eax,PTR [rbp+rax*1-0x70]
  4006f5:  movzx  eax,al
  4006f8:  mov    esi,eax
  4006fa:  mov    edi,0x4007d4
  4006ff:  mov    eax,0x0
  400704:  call   4004e0 <printf@plt>
<printf_loop_condition>:
  400709:  add    DWORD PTR [rbp-0x84],0x1
  40070d:  cmp    DWORD PTR [rbp-0x84],0xf
  400711:  jle    4006eb <main+0xc2>
```

(b) Rewritten Binary

Fig. 2. Disassembly of **main** before & after increasing **digest** and **hexdigest** buffers by 16 and 32 bytes, respectively. Lines containing rewritten instructions are highlighted in green and changes are in red. (Color figure online)

allocated on the stack at the binary level requires: (i) locating the routine that uses the corresponding stack frame, (ii) enlarging the frame to be large enough to hold the new buffers, and (iii) adjusting every access to memory inside the frame accordingly. ALICE's previous phase, in Sect. 4.2, provides necessary information to satisfy the first requirement (via the shadow stack). To achieve the second requirement, ALICE rewrites the instructions that are responsible for increasing and decreasing the stack pointer in the prologue/epilogue of the located routine, e.g., [40062d: sub rsp,0x60] in Fig. 2a. For the third requirement, ALICE iterates through all instructions in the routine and inspects the ones that use the stack offset, i.e., via rsp or rbp registers. ALICE then recomputes the stack offset with respect to the increased frame size and rewrites those instructions if the newly computed offset differs from the original. In Fig. 2, ALICE identifies all instructions that access a stack element and rewrites the ones highlighted in green.

5 Experimental Evaluation

5.1 Experimental Setup

Goals and Datasets. The goal of this evaluation is two-fold, first, to assess whether ALICE can accurately identify and replace different implementations of hash functions, and second, to measure ALICE's effectiveness on real-world applications. Different implementations may include different hash function structures (e.g., with or without Init()), different parameter orders, or simply different implementation details. We apply ALICE to a dataset that consists of four popular cryptographic libraries: OpenSSL, libgcrypt, mbedTLS, and FreeBL. We compile each library with different optimization levels, including O0, O1, O2, O3 and Os, into a static library. We then create a simple C application (similar to the one in Fig. 1a) that calls exactly one hash function located in the static library. We compile this application without debugging/relocation symbols and link it with each individual static library. We also assess ALICE's effectiveness on 6 real-world applications: smd5_mkpass and ssha_mkpass – github projects for creating LDAP passwords [2], md5sum and sha1sum – string/file checksum programs, lighttpd – a lightweight webserver program, and curl – a webclient command line tool. Similar to the first dataset, each program was compiled without debugging symbols and with various optimization levels, and statically linked to the cryptographic library used within the program.

Insecure Hash Functions. We consider MD2, MD4, MD5, SHA1, and RIPEMD-160 as insecure hash functions to be replaced in our experiments. Our objective is to identify implementations of such hash functions in binaries and replace them with stronger ones, i.e., SHA-256. A list of all (insecure) hash functions in each dataset is shown in Table 1.

Environment. Experiments are performed on a virtual machine with Ubuntu 16.04.5 OS, 4GB of RAM and 2 cores of 3.4 GHz of CPU running on top of an Intel i7-3770 machine. The following versions of required tools are used in the experiments: gcc-5.4.0, angr-7.8.2.21 [34], Triton-0.6 [35] and Pin-2.14.71313 [28].

5.2 Evaluation Results: Cryptographic Libraries

As described in Sect. 4.2, we only consider automated inference of required changes from categories $\boxed{\text{C1}}$ and $\boxed{\text{C2}}$ in this work. In order to properly evaluate ALICE, we perform manual analysis to identify all changes required in $\boxed{\text{C3}}$ and supply them to ALICE. The manually supplied changes for this case (in this dataset) consist of only a couple of instructions that typically specify loop termination condition(s). For example, in the binary from Fig. 1b, we instruct ALICE to modify two instructions at addresses 0x4006dc and 0x40070d from [cmp DWORD PTR [rbp-0x54],0xf] to [cmp DWORD PTR [rbp-0x54],0x1f].

---

[2] https://github.com/pellucida/ldap-passwords.

Table 1. Hash functions used in our test datasets. ✗ indicates no hash function while ILO, OIL and OI denote a function with the parameter order (input,inputlen,output), (output,input,inputlen) and (output,input).

Dataset	Version	MD2	MD4	MD5	SHA1	RIPEMD160
Crypto libraries	OpenSSL-1.1.1	✗	ILO	ILO	ILO	ILO
	libgcrypt-1.8.4	✗	✗	✗	OIL	OIL
	mbedTLS-2.16.0	ILO	ILO	ILO	ILO	✗
	FreeBL-3.42	OI	✗	OIL,OI	OIL,OI	✗
Real-world programs	smd5_mkpass	✗	✗	OIL	✗	✗
	ssha_mkpass	✗	✗	✗	OIL	✗
	md5sum-5.2.1	✗	✗	ILO	✗	✗
	sha1sum-5.2.1	✗	✗	✗	ILO	✗
	curl-7.56.0	✗	✗	OI	✗	✗
	lighttpd-1.4.49	✗	✗	✗	ILO	✗

Correctness of Rewritten Binary. To simplify illustration, we first describe behaviors of the rewritten binaries that are considered *incorrect* in this dataset. First, if ALICE misidentifies any of necessary changes in the input binary, the resulting binary will not display the *correct* SHA-256 digest of the input variable. For instance, it may display nonsensical data, a digest produced by the original hash function or an incomplete version of the SHA-256 digest. Second, if ALICE's rewriting phase does not function properly (e.g., it expands the buffer size by a different amount or adjusts memory access to the stack incorrectly), it likely results in a runtime error for the output binary. We consider the correctness of the rewritten binaries from this dataset to be the converse of the aforementioned behaviors, i.e., execution of the output binary must terminate without any errors and it must result in displaying the correct SHA-256 digest of the input variable. All binaries produced by ALICE in this dataset work as expected.

Binary Size and Execution Overhead. ALICE adds around 3-13KB to the output binaries. On further inspection, we found two main reasons for this overhead. First, ALICE statically adds a patch implementing the replacement SHA-256 hash function, which contributes around 3KB to the output binary. Second, our underlying binary rewriter, patchkit [36], expects code and data of this patch to be aligned to a page size (i.e., 4KB in our testing machine), which can add up to another 8KB to the output binary.

In terms of execution overhead, we implement a simple Pintool [28] to count the number of instructions executed by the output binaries. We then compare the result with the baseline, where manual editing is performed on the original binary's source code in order to replace the insecure hash function and the modified source-code is properly optimized by the standard gcc compiler. The results in Fig. 3a show that the binaries produced by ALICE have low execution overhead with an average of 300 added instructions, or only an increase of 0.3%, compared to the baseline. We also did not observe any noticeable increase in execution-time for the output binaries.

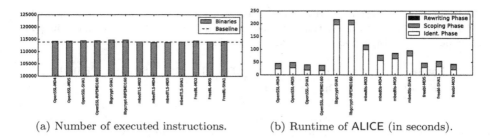

(a) Number of executed instructions.   (b) Runtime of ALICE (in seconds).

Fig. 3. Evaluation results of ALICE on cryptographic libraries. Original binaries are compiled with 02. Results for binaries with different optimization flags are similar and thus omitted.

Toolchain Runtime. Figure 3b shows runtime of ALICE to produce the output binaries. The total runtime heavily depends on the size of input binaries, and is dominated by the runtime of the identification phase. This bottleneck happens because the identification phase involves heavy-weight analysis such as disassembling the entire binary and/or recovering the binary call graph. It is also worth noting that such analysis is performed only once and ALICE re-uses the analysis results in latter phases; this leads to lower runtimes in the latter phases.

5.3   Evaluation Results: Real-World Binaries

Similar to the previous dataset, we manually inspect the binaries in this dataset to identify changes required in $\boxed{\text{C3}}$, then supply them to ALICE. Such changes are mainly related to the digest size that is hard-coded in the source code.

Correctness of Rewritten Binary. We consider rewritten binaries to be correct if changes performed by ALICE: (1) correctly implement new functionalities with respect to the target SHA-256 hash function and (2) do not interfere with the remaining functionalities. For instance, the former enforces the rewritten binary of md5sum to be able to perform sha256sum of a given input string. We realize the latter requirement by executing the binaries produced by ALICE with all test cases (except the ones that use insecure hash functions) provided in their original respective project repository. Indeed, our definition of correctness is an approximation. Satisfying this definition does not guarantee that the rewritten/output binaries are truly correct. However, we believe this definition is a good approximation of what is required in practice, especially with access to a dataset with enough test cases that one can evaluate against results produced by the rewritten binaries.

Table 2 shows the correctness of output binaries produced by ALICE in this dataset. All output binaries pass all test cases in their original project repository while only one output binary fails to pass the expected functionality. We

Table 2. Size of original (O) and rewritten (R) binaries of real-world applications.

Program	OFLAG	Binary size			Correctness of output binaries
		O	**R**	Δ	
md5sum	−O0	43.6 KB	51.9 KB	8.3 KB	✓
	−O1	35.4 KB	45.3 KB	9.9 KB	✓
	−O2	35.4 KB	45.0 KB	9.6 KB	✓
	−O3	39.5 KB	49.1 KB	9.6 KB	✓
	−Os	31.3 KB	40.4 KB	9.1 KB	✓
sha1sum	−O0	43.6 KB	51.9 KB	8.3 KB	✓
	−O1	35.4 KB	45.3 KB	9.9 KB	✓
	−O2	35.4 KB	45.0 KB	9.6 KB	✓
	−O3	39.5 KB	49.1 KB	9.6 KB	✓
	−Os	31.3 KB	40.4 KB	9.1 KB	✓
smd5_mkpass	−O0	22.8 KB	29.9 KB	7.1 KB	✓
	−O1	18.7 KB	25.8 KB	7.1 KB	✓
	−O2	18.7 KB	25.8 KB	7.1 KB	✓
	−O3	22.8 KB	29.8 KB	7.0 KB	✓
	−Os	18.7 KB	25.8 KB	7.1 KB	✓
ssha_mkpass	−O0	22.8 KB	29.9 KB	7.1 KB	✓
	−O1	18.7 KB	25.8 KB	7.1 KB	✓
	−O2	18.7 KB	25.8 KB	7.1 KB	✓
	−O3	22.8 KB	29.8 KB	7.0 KB	✓
	−Os	18.7 KB	25.8 KB	7.1 KB	✓
curl	−O0	929.6 KB	937.3 KB	7.7 KB	✓
	−O1	589.6 KB	596.1 KB	6.5 KB	✓
	−O2	614.2 KB	620.7 KB	6.5 KB	✓
	−O3	675.6 KB	N/A	N/A	✗
	−Os	528.1 KB	534.5 KB	6.4 KB	✓
lighttpd	−O0	720.2 KB	724.0 KB	3.8 KB	✓
	−O1	522.1 KB	529.1 KB	7.0 KB	✓
	−O2	534.7 KB	545.8 KB	11.2 KB	✓
	−O3	584.7 KB	592.0 KB	7.4 KB	✓
	−Os	466.4 KB	473.1 KB	6.6 KB	✓

manually examined the failed binary and found that ALICE misidentified an inse-cure hash routine. Our further inspection reveals that the main culprit appears to be our underlying dynamic concrete executor, which fails to output the expected MD5 digest even if ALICE sets up a proper call stack. As a result, ALICE's identification phase did not detect this insecure hash function in the input binary, and the output binary remained unchanged.

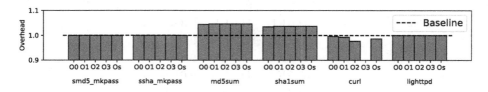

Fig. 4. Overhead in terms of executed instructions of real-world binaries.

Binary Size and Execution Overhead. Table 2 shows the increase in binary size in this dataset. ALICE adds around 4 to 11 KB to the original binary. As mentioned in Sect. 5.2, up to 8 KB of this overhead is caused by the underlying binary rewriter performing a patch alignment. The remaining overhead stems from rewritten functions that are appended at the end of the new binary. We note that we excluded the result for the curl binary compiled with 03 in Table 2 (and subsequent figures) as ALICE could not produce the correct output binary in that case.

We did not observe any noticeable execution overhead in terms of execution-time when running the output binary against the provided test cases from the project's repository. In addition, we measure the number of executed instructions for the output binary to perform the expected functionality with respect to the SHA-256 function and compare it to the baseline, where we manually edit the source code to replace the insecure hash function. The result, shown in Fig. 4, also indicates negligible (< 5%) increase in execution-time in this case. Note that even though execution of the rewritten curl binaries becomes faster (requires 2% fewer instructions), this improvement is still negligible. As such, we do not claim that ALICE helps producing a more efficient output binary.

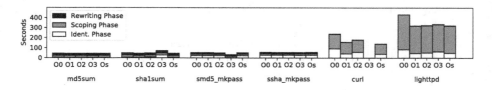

Fig. 5. Runtime of the ALICE toolchain on real-world binaries.

Toolchain Runtime. Figure 5 illustrates ALICE's runtime to produce each output binary. In simpler programs (e.g., md5sum or smd5_mkpass), ALICE identifies and replaces weak primitives in less than a minute. For more complex programs (e.g., lighttpd), ALICE's runtime can be a bit slower – up to 5 min. Most of the runtime overhead comes from the scoping phase because it needs to instrument a large number of instructions (e.g, $\approx$ 500k instructions for `lighttpd`) while execution of simpler programs contains significantly fewer instructions. We consider ALICE's runtime to be acceptable since the entire process only needs to be performed once, making the toolchain runtime not a primary concern.

Table 3. Number of rewritten instructions required for each category of changes.

Program		md5sum	sha1sum	smd5_mkpass	ssha_mkpass	curl	lighttpd	Avg.
Changes:	C1	1024	1806	932	1676	424	1712	1262
	C2	1	1	3	9	8	2	4
	C3	1	1	2	3	1	2	1.7
(C1+C2)/Total		99.9%	99.94%	99.79%	99.85%	99.78%	99.88%	99.87%
C2/(C2+C3)		50%	50%	60%	75%	87.5%	50%	70.17%

Reduction in Manual Efforts. While ALICE currently does not automatically identify changes from the [C3] class, it still saves considerable manual effort. We quantify such savings in Table 3 as the number of instructions required to be rewritten in order to implement changes for each category. On average, ALICE automatically identifies and rewrites 1,266 instructions, which translates into 99.87% reduction in manual efforts. However, we acknowledge that it may be possible to use existing cryptographic identification tools (with some modifications) to locate changes from [C1]. Even when such tools exist, our toolchain still significantly reduces manual work by 70.17%. It is worth emphasizing again that no existing tools are capable of identifying changes from [C2] and [C3].

6 Limitations and Future Work

The current version of ALICE has limitations. First, ALICE relies on some underlying (open source) building-block tools and inherits their limitations. For example, we encountered instances where the underlying x86-64 assembler, `Keystone` [37], fails to translate uncommon instructions whose operands contain `fs` registers or a `rep` instruction. Whenever we encounter such an issue, we manually fixed it by directly hard-coding the correct behavior into ALICE. Furthermore, the first phase of ALICE relies on the `angr` framework [34] for disassembly of stripped binaries; `angr` does not perform static disassembly with correctness guarantees. In fact, static disassembly of stripped binaries with correctness guarantees is still an open problem [38]. Thus, `angr` may produce incorrect results in ALICE's first phase, which affects outcomes of output binaries.

ALICE also assumes that the routine implementing an insecure hash function and necessary changes are statically included in the main application. ALICE does not currently support identifying and replacing insecure cryptographic primitives located in a dynamic library. Expanding ALICE's functionalities to dynamic libraries is possible since most of our underlying tools are capable of locating and analyzing dynamic libraries used by the main application.

ALICE does not automatically identify nor rewrite changes from $\boxed{\textbf{C3}}$ and relies on the user to supply them to the toolchain. In practice, some manual effort is required to locate changes in binary logic for a large binary. Automating this process is a challenging problem and is an interesting avenue for future work.

Finally, we design ALICE to target non-malicious legacy binaries and assume that such binaries are not obfuscated. In practice, even legitimate software may make use of obfuscation techniques, e.g., to protect intellectual property. Extending ALICE to support obfuscated but non-malicious binaries is also an interesting future direction.

7   Conclusion

We have developed ALICE, a toolchain for identifying weak or broken cryptographic primitives and replacing them with secure ones without relying on source code or debugging symbols. We have implemented a prototype of ALICE that can detect several cryptographic primitives while only requiring access to the binaries containing them. Our implementation of ALICE can also automatically replace weak and/or broken implementations of cryptographic hash functions in ELF-based x86-64 binaries. We have demonstrated ALICE's effectiveness on various open-source cryptographic libraries and real-world applications utilizing cryptographic hash functions. Our experimental results show that ALICE can successfully locate and replace insecure hash functions while preserving existing functionalities in the original binaries.

Acknowledgments. This work was sponsored by the U.S. Department of Homeland Security (DHS) Science and Technology (S&T) Directorate under Contract No. HSHQDC-16-C-00034. Any opinions, findings, and conclusions or recommendations expressed in this material are those of the authors and do not necessarily reflect the views of DHS and should not be interpreted as necessarily representing the official policies or endorsements, either expressed or implied, of DHS or the U.S. government. The authors thank the anonymous reviewers for their valuable comments.

References

1. Heninger, N., Durumeric, Z., Wustrow, E., Halderman, J.A.: Mining your Ps and Qs: detection of widespread weak keys in network devices. In: USENIX Security Symposium (2012)
2. Egele, M., Brumley, D., Fratantonio, Y., Kruegel, C.: An empirical study of cryptographic misuse in android applications. In: ACM Conference on Computer and Communications Security (2013)
3. Smart, N.P.: Physical side-channel attacks on cryptographic systems. Softw. Focus **1**(2), 6–13 (2000)
4. Li, J., Lin, Z., Caballero, J., Zhang, Y., Gu, D.: K-Hunt: pinpointing insecure cryptographic keys from execution traces. In: ACM Conference on Computer and Communications Security (2018)

5. US-CERT: Openssl 'heartbleed' vulnerability (cve-2014-0160) (2014). https://www.us-cert.gov/ncas/alerts/TA14-098A
6. US-CERT: Ssl 3.0 protocol vulnerability and padding oracle on downgraded legacy encryption(poodle) attack (2014). https://www.us-cert.gov/ncas/alerts/TA14-290A
7. Calzavara, S., Focardi, R., Nemec, M., Rabitti, A., Squarcina, M.: Postcards from the post-HTTP world: amplification of https vulnerabilities in the web ecosystem. In: IEEE Symposium on Security and Privacy (2019)
8. Adrian, D., et al.: Imperfect forward secrecy: how Diffie-Hellman fails in practice. In: ACM Conference on Computer and Communications Security (2015)
9. Stevens, M.: Counter-cryptanalysis. In: Annual Cryptology Conference (2013)
10. Leurent, G., Peyrin, T.: SHA-1 is a shambles - first chosen-prefix collision on SHA-1 and application to the PGP web of trust (2020). https://eprint.iacr.org/2020/014
11. Li, F., Paxson, V.: A large-scale empirical study of security patches. In: ACM Conference on Computer and Communications Security (2017)
12. Eldefrawy, K., Locasto, M., Rattanavipanon, N., Saidi, H.: Towards automated augmentation and instrumentation of legacy cryptographic executables: extended version. https://arxiv.org/abs/2004.09713
13. aldeid: Ida-pro/plugins/findcrypt2 (2019). https://www.aldeid.com/wiki/IDA-Pro/plugins/FindCrypt2
14. igNorAMUS, snaker, Maxx, and pusher, "Kanal - krypto analyzer for peid" (2019). http://www.dcs.fmph.uniba.sk/zri/6.prednaska/tools/PEiD/plugins/kanal.htm
15. apponic: Hash & Crypto detector (2019). https://hash-crypto-detector.apponic.com/
16. Lestringant, P., Guihéry, F., Fouque, P.-A.: Automated identification of cryptographic primitives in binary code with data flow graph isomorphism. In: ACM ASIA Conference on Computer and Communications Security (2015)
17. Calvet, J., Fernandez, J.M., Marion, J.-Y.: Aligot: cryptographic function identification in obfuscated binary programs. In: ACM Conference on Computer and Communications Security (2012)
18. Lutz, N.: Towards revealing attacker's intent by automatically decrypting network traffic. Mémoire de maıtrise, ETH Zürich, Switzerland (2008)
19. Gröbert, F., Willems, C., Holz, T.: Automated identification of cryptographic primitives in binary programs. In: Sommer, R., Balzarotti, D., Maier, G. (eds.) RAID 2011. LNCS, vol. 6961, pp. 41–60. Springer, Heidelberg (2011). https://doi.org/10.1007/978-3-642-23644-0_3
20. Xu, D., Ming, J., Wu, D.: Cryptographic function detection in obfuscated binaries via bit-precise symbolic loop mapping. In: 2017 IEEE Symposium on Security and Privacy, May 2017
21. Hunt, G., Brubacher, D.: Detours: binary interception of Win32 functions. In: 3rd USENIX Windows NT Symposium (1999)
22. Bauman, E., Lin, Z., et al.: Superset disassembly: statically rewriting x86 binaries without heuristics. In: Network and Distributed System Security Symposium (2018)
23. Anand, K., Smithson, M., et al.: A compiler-level intermediate representation based binary analysis and rewriting system. In: ACM European Conference on Computer Systems (2013)
24. Edwards, A., Vo, H., Srivastava, A., Srivastava, A.: Vulcan binary transformation in a distributed environment. Technical report, Microsoft Research (2001)

25. Wang, S., Wang, P., Wu, D.: Reassembleable disassembling. In: USENIX Security Symposium, pp. 627–642 (2015)
26. Wang, R., et al.: Ramblr: making reassembly great again. In: Network and Distributed System Security Symposium (2017)
27. Nethercote, N., Seward, J.: Valgrind: a program supervision framework. Electron. Notes Theor. Comput. Sci. **89**(2), 44–66 (2003)
28. Luk, C.-K., Cohn, R., et al.: Pin: building customized program analysis tools with dynamic instrumentation. ACM SIGPLAN Not. **40**, 190–200 (2005)
29. Dynamic instrumentation tool platform (2017). http://www.dynamorio.org/
30. Perkins, J.H., Kim, S., et al.: Automatically patching errors in deployed software. In: ACM SIGOPS (2009)
31. Klima, V.: Tunnels in hash functions: Md5 collisions within a minute. IACR Cryptology ePrint Archive 2006/105 (2006)
32. Sasaki, Yu., Aoki, K.: Finding preimages in full MD5 faster than exhaustive search. In: Joux, A. (ed.) EUROCRYPT 2009. LNCS, vol. 5479, pp. 134–152. Springer, Heidelberg (2009). https://doi.org/10.1007/978-3-642-01001-9_8
33. Yadegari, B., Debray, S.: Bit-level taint analysis. In: 2014 IEEE 14th International Working Conference on Source Code Analysis and Manipulation (SCAM). IEEE, pp. 255–264 (2014)
34. Shoshitaishvili, Y., et al.: Sok:(state of) the art of war: offensive techniques in binary analysis. In: 2016 IEEE Symposium on Security and Privacy. IEEE, pp. 138–157 (2016)
35. Saudel, F., Salwan, J.: Triton: a dynamic symbolic execution framework. In: Symposium sur la sécurité des technologies de l'information et des communications, SSTIC, SSTIC 2015, France, Rennes, 3–5 June, pp. 31–54 (2015)
36. Hileman, R.: Binary patching from Python (2018). https://github.com/lunixbochs/patchkit
37. Quynh, N.A.: Keystone - the ultimate assembler (2019). http://www.keystone-engine.org/
38. Andriesse, D., Chen, X., et al.: An in-depth analysis of disassembly on full-scale x86/x64 binaries. In: USENIX Security Symposium (2016)

Web Security

When TLS Meets Proxy on Mobile

Joyanta Debnath[1]([✉]), Sze Yiu Chau[2], and Omar Chowdhury[1]

[1] The University of Iowa, Iowa City, USA
{joyanta-debnath,omar-chowdhury}@uiowa.edu
[2] The Chinese University of Hong Kong, Sha Tin, Hong Kong
sychau@ie.cuhk.edu.hk

Abstract. Increasingly more mobile browsers are developed to use proxies for traffic compression and censorship circumvention. While these browsers can offer such desirable features, their security implications are, however, not well understood, especially when tangled with TLS in the mix. Apart from vendor-specific proprietary designs, there are mainly 2 models of using proxies with browsers: TLS interception and HTTP tunneling. To understand the current practices employed by proxy-based mobile browsers, we analyze 34 Android browser apps that are representative of the ecosystem, and examine how their deployments are affecting communication security. Though the impacts of TLS interception on security was studied before in other contexts, proxy-based mobile browsers were not considered previously. In addition, the tunneling model requires the browser itself to enforce certain desired security policies (*e.g.*, validating certificates and avoiding the use of weak cipher suites), and it is preferable to have such enforcement matching the security level of conventional desktop browsers. Our evaluation shows that many proxy-based mobile browsers downgrade the overall quality of TLS sessions, by for example allowing old versions of TLS (*e.g.*, SSLv3.0 and TLSv1.0) and accepting weak cryptographic algorithms (*e.g.*, 3DES and RC4) as well as unsatisfactory certificates (*e.g.*, revoked or signed by untrusted CAs), thus exposing their users to potential security and privacy threats. We have reported our findings to the vendors of vulnerable proxy-based browsers and are waiting for their response.

Keywords: TLS interception · HTTP tunneling · Proxy-based browsers

1 Introduction

Smartphones have proliferated in the last decade, and consequently there has been a strong growth in Internet traffic powered by mobile devices. The high portability and mobility, however, often comes at a cost, in terms of limitations on bandwidth and latency. Unlike conventional Internet access, mobile data is typically *metered*, and services offer limited capacity within a specific period. Because of this, increasingly there are more browsers offering a so-called "data-saving" feature, which leverage a proxy to help cache and compress objects that

© Springer Nature Switzerland AG 2020
M. Conti et al. (Eds.): ACNS 2020, LNCS 12147, pp. 387–407, 2020.
https://doi.org/10.1007/978-3-030-57878-7_19

need to be sent to the mobile browser, with the aim of reducing mobile data consumption and in some cases lowering the latency as well.

There are other reasons for using proxy-based browser apps on mobile platforms. For example, some use the proxy to conceal their own IP addresses for privacy protection against potentially malicious Web servers. Some would use these apps to bypass *geo-blocking*, a technology commonly used to adjust and restrict contents based on estimations of the users' geolocation. Others rely on these apps to circumvent various forms of censorship [15, 22, 24, 35, 38].

Despite their desirable features, the use of proxy-based browsers is not without its complications, especially when the users' security and privacy are taken into considerations. In this paper, we set out to investigate the implications on security when using these browsers, specifically the scenario where they are entangled with TLS. As we will explain later, based on our investigations, there are primarily two ways of deploying proxies with mobile browsers, along with some other proprietary technologies. The first way follows the TLS interception model, where the proxy acts as an active man-in-the-middle (MITM) and establishes 2 TLS connections (one with the browser, one with the actual Web server). We note that the impact of TLS interception on security has been examined before in the context of anti-virus and parental control software [11], as well as network middleboxes in enterprise environments [14, 37]. However, proxy-based browsers that follow the TLS interception model constitute another class of TLS-intercepting appliances that was not considered by previous work. In this model, the proxy is in charge of enforcing security policies (*e.g.*, avoiding the use of weak ciphers, and validating certificates). It is also desirable to have the two TLS connections exhibit some degree of symmetry in terms of the strength of their corresponding security parameters. Adapting some of the metrics proposed by previous work, we design experiments to evaluate the quality of the TLS connections established by these browsers. Another common way of deploying proxies with mobile browsers is through HTTP tunneling. In this model, the end-to-end nature of a TLS connection is preserved, and the proxy merely helps to relay traffic. Thus the browser apps themselves need to carefully enforce security policies, and ideally they should be as robust as their desktop counterparts. Given that major desktop browsers have gone through years of scrutiny from the security research community, we distillate some of the best practices and design experiments to determine whether the tunneling browser apps are offering adequate protection to their users.

To our surprise, we found that many proxy-based browsers accept weak ciphers, weak TLS versions, and vulnerable certificates offered by a Web server. One notable example is the UC Mini - Best Tube Mate & Fast Video Downloader app, which has more than a hundred million downloads, accepts legacy TLS versions (*e.g.*, TLSv1.0, SSLv3.0, and SSLv2.0), and broken ciphers (*e.g.*, RC4, and 3DES). These findings are worrisome, particularly when one takes into consideration that many users rely on these apps to circumvent censorship. When these apps do not provide an adequate level of security, an oppressive censor can tamper with the TLS connections to attack the users. We believe this research is beneficial in helping the community understand the risks associated with the current practices embraced by vendors of proxy-based mobile browsers, and we have shared our findings with the browser vendors so that they can and improve the overall security of proxy-based browsers.

2 Background

Here we explain technical details of the TLS interception and HTTP tunneling models, using TLSv1.2 handshake messages, employed by most of the proxy-based browsers studied in this paper. However, as we will explain later, some might use a proprietary protocol that is slightly different from these two models.

2.1 TLS Interception

TLS interception [19] is a common technique used to defeat the end-to-end security of TLS and allows the MITM to inspect contents transmitted between the client and the Web server. In this model, the proxy acts as an active MITM, so that some of the contents sent by the Web server could be cached and compressed before sending to the client. The cached objects might be reused later for other clients as well. In a typical setup of TLS interception, a trusted Certificate Authority (CA) certificate of the MITM is installed on the client's machine, so that any MITM-signed certificates will be accepted by the certificate validation procedure. As shown in Fig. 1a, the whole process starts with the client initiating a TLS handshake with a `ClientHello` sent to remote Web server. The proxy however captures and blocks this, and sends its own `ClientHello` to the Web server. The Web server replies back with `ServerHello`, `Certificates`, and `ServerHelloDone` handshake messages to the proxy. The proxy server should then validate the received certificate chain, and if the validation is successful, then it sends back to the client its own `ServerHello`, MITM-signed `Certificates`, and `ServerHelloDone` handshake messages. The MITM-signed certificate chain will then be validated by the client, and the rest of the handshake (*i.e.*, `ClientKeyExchange`, `ChangeCipherSpec`, `Finished`) happens for the two TLS sessions. Hence, through the proxy, two related TLS sessions (*i.e.*, TLS_{CP}, TLS_{PS}) are established between the client and the remote Web server, instead of one. The proxy server can now decrypt any incoming data (*i.e.*, `Application data`) from the client or the server, inspect, or even modify the data before encrypting again to forward it.

2.2 HTTP Tunneling

In HTTP tunneling, the client requests the proxy to relay a TCP connection to the Web server. In most cases, the tunnel is established using the `HTTP CONNECT` [RFC7231], though other HTTP methods can also be used depending on the setup. As shown in Fig. 1b, the client initiates by requesting a tunnel with `HTTP CONNECT`, and specify the port and the Web server that it wants to communicate

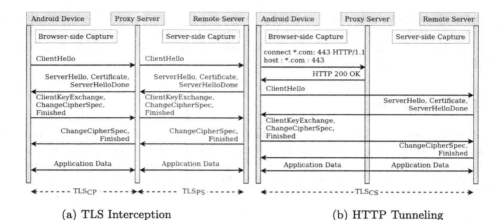

Fig. 1. Comparison of the two proxy deployment models. The yellow boxes illustrate our measurement setup. (Color figure online)

with. After receiving the request, the proxy server tries to establish a TCP connection with the Web server specified by the client. If the TCP connection is successful, the proxy server sends back to the client an HTTP 200 OK, indicating success. The client can then start communicating with the Web server, and the proxy server relays all the subsequent TCP stream between the client and the remote Web server, including the TLS handshake messages between the two sides, as well as the encrypted records. Because of this, the proxy cannot decrypt, read, or modify the contents of these messages, assuming proper cryptographic algorithms are being used. However, from the perspective of the Web server, it would appear that the proxy is the client, as the proxy's IP address would be used in the IP header. Compared to the TLS interception model, though there are also two TCP connections, only one TLS session (i.e., TLS_{CS}) is established.

3   Scopes and Methodologies

In this section, we define the scope of our study. We first discuss how we selected proxy-based mobile browsers apps, and then we describe the experiments used to evaluate their security.

3.1   Selection of Proxy-Based Mobile Browsers

We initially select a total of 36 proxy-based mobile browsers on *Android*; the full list is available at our website [12]. We focus on Android because it is currently the most popular operating system. As discussed before, proxy-based browsers are typically motivated by reduced mobile data consumption, privacy protection, and censorship circumvention. We thus looked for mobile browsers that are advertised with these keywords on app stores like Google Play and AppBrain. In addition to the popular ones, we also consider some relatively lesser known ones, in order to get a more comprehensive picture of the entire landscape.

3.2 Test Environment

Our experiment setup consists of three major components controlled by us: an Android device, a Linux laptop acting as a Wi-Fi access point (AP), and a TLS enabled test website. The goal of this test environment is to analyze all traffic between a proxy-based browser installed on the Android device, and the test website visited by the browser. In general, we refer the traffic between browser and proxy as *browser-side* and the traffic between proxy and test website as *server-side*. We configure the Android device to connect to the Wi-Fi AP provided by the Linux laptop, which allows us to capture browser-side traffic using common network analyzer tools (*e.g.*, Wirehark , and tshark). To capture server-side traffic, we run tshark on the Web server hosting the test website. The yellow boxes with blue borders in Fig. 1 illustrate this idea.

In some of the apps, the proxy-based mode (*e.g.* data-saving feature) is optional and not turned on by default. Hence for these apps, we switch on the relevant options prior to any of the experiments.

3.3 Identification and Classification of Proxy

Now we describe our approach for identifying the (IP address of) proxy server which is necessary to carry out our security evaluations. We also classify the browsers according to the model of their proxy deployment. We have written a Python program to automatically find out these information by analyzing the traffic captured from both browser-side and server-side.

Determining Proxy Server Address. A browser can automatically generate or receive extra traffic from different websites without user interaction. For instance, when a browser uses Google as its default search engine, additional traffic may be present due to auto-complete. Therefore, browser-side traffic tends to be noisy. To filter out the extra traffic and facilitate subsequent analysis, it is useful to know the IP address of the proxy server. Hence, we obtain this information by matching the browser-side and server-side traffic with some heuristics.

Since the server-side traces tend to be cleaner (highly unlikely to have additional visitors beyond our experiments), we can use the Unix epoch time to help match the traffic between the two sides. We use the following steps to automatically identify the proxy server address.

1. We find out the epoch times of the first (let this be $fTime$) and last (let this be $lTime$) frames of the server-side trace.
2. Since browser initiates the communication to server, and server sends data back to the browser, traffic of browser-side begins before the first frame of server-side, and traffic of browser-side ends after the last frame of server-side. We also find client-server communication tends to happen very quickly,

and empirically a 1-second threshold is enough to handle most cases. So we subtract 1 second from $fTime$ and add 1 second with $lTime$ to estimate the corresponding epoch time range for the client-side traffic.

3. Then, we separate destination addresses of the browser-side's trace and source addresses of the server-side's trace into two different sets.
4. If we find any common IP address in both of these sets, this IP address is the address of the proxy server. Otherwise, we know the IP addresses of the proxy server are different in these two traces. So, we go to step 5.
5. Since we have not found any exact match yet, we check whether any two IP addresses from these sets are from same network. In this step, we start matching with a 31-bit netmask and continue till a 28-bit netmask is used. When there is no match, we go to step 6.
6. In this step, we consider a 27-bit netmask down to a 20-bit netmask. In addition, we find out the locations of an IP address using the netaddr Python api. We match the ASN number, city name, region name, and country name from the locations of each pair of IP addresses. If this step still cannot find any match, we go to step 7.
7. Here, we consider netmask 19 to netmask 16 and location matching just like step 6. In addition to these two checkings, we consider the volume of traffic generated per IP address. If two IP addresses from our two sets have almost similar volume (for a particular TCP stream), we conclude both of these IP addresses belong to the same proxy server. Otherwise, we go to step 8.
8. If none of our above heuristics works, we manually analyze the two traces to determine what happened.

Identifying Two Models of Proxy. We classify these proxy-based browsers into two categories according to the role of their proxy servers : HT browser and TI browser, where 'HT' stands for **HTTP tunneling**, and 'TI' stands for **TLS interception**. Proxy server of an HT browser uses HTTP tunneling to create a TLS session between the browser and the website. As shown in Fig. 1b, these browsers most commonly use the HTTP CONNECT method to initiate the tunnel.

Moreover, our Python program looks at the certificate chain received from the identified proxy server in browser-side traffic. In the HT model, the proxy would forward the server's certificate chain to the browser without any modifications. Therefore, if the certificate chain received on the browser-side is exactly the same as the one that server sent, we classify the browser as an HT browser. If the certificate chain is different from the server's original certificate chain, then we classify the browser as a TI browser. From our list of browser applications, we found 18 to be HT browsers, and 16 to be TI-like browsers. We note that some TI-like browsers use a slightly unorthodox approach for TLS_{CP} (*i.e.*, TLS session between browser and proxy server). For example, we found 3 browsers are performing relaxed variants of TI: BROXY Browser and X Web Proxy establish TLS connections only for server-side traffic, and no TLS is used for browser-side; Unblock Sites forces HTTP on both sides and sends all data in plaintext, even if the user explicitly requests HTTPS (*i.e.*, by typing https:// in the URI). Therefore, these browsers are listed as variants of TI browsers [12].

Finally, we categorize 1 browser as *Unidentified* since we cannot observe its proxy-based traffic. The 'Turbo Mode' of Yandex Browser is supposed to leverage proxy servers for data compression, however, we were unable to activate this feature even when we downgrade our uplink and downlink bandwidth to 10kbps. For this reason, we exclude Yandex Browser from our subsequent security evaluations and focus on the remaining 34 apps.

3.4   Security Evaluations

We run multiple experiments to evaluate the strength of overall TLS session between a proxy-based browser and our test website. To do so, we capture traffic from both browser-side and server-side, and perform automatic analysis with a Python program that performs the following security evaluations. The first three security evaluations focuses on TI browsers whereas the last three are applicable for both TI and HT browsers.

Evaluation 1 : Maintaining Strength of Certificate Parameters. The strength of a TLS session depends highly on important certificate parameters such as signature key length and signature hash algorithm. The use of short key length (*e.g.*, RSA-512) and deprecated hash algorithms (*e.g.*, MD5) can pose serious threats to a TLS session [RFC6151]. Therefore, it is recommended that the proxy server use strong parameters in its MITM-signed certificates for browser-side TLS session, or at least it should maintain the same strength as the server's certificates. This is primarily a requirement for TI but not HT browsers.

To evaluate this property, we consider different signature hash algorithms (*e.g.*, SHA256, SHA384, and SHA512), and different certificate key lengths (*e.g.*, RSA-2048, RSA-3072, and RSA-4096). Then, we consider all possible combinations of these certificate parameters to obtain 9 valid certificates from different trusted commercial CAs. For each of these 9 certificates, we load a certificate chain and its corresponding private key to the test Web server and visit the test website from each of the TI browsers. We find out the signature hash algorithms and signature key lengths used in the MITM-signed certificates and investigate whether the proxy server mirrors or downgrades the signature hash algorithms and certificate key lengths with respect to the test Web server's certificates.

In addition to signature hash algorithm and signature key length, we also analyze the validation level of the MITM-signed leaf certificate. We check whether the MITM-signed leaf certificate is Extended Validated (EV), Organizational Validated (OV), or Domain Validated (DV). EV certificates are the most trus-ted ones, as CAs are supposed to issue this type of certificate only after thorough validation of Web server's identity. On the other hand, DV certificates are issued very quickly after some basic validation process, and it offers the least amount of trust among these three. It is preferable that the proxy server should not downgrade the trust level in the MITM-signed certificate compared to the server certificate. For instance, if the server-signed certificate is EV certificate, the MITM-signed certificate should also be EV. For this experiment, we visit Twitter's website (https://mobile.twitter.com/) to explore the validation level of the MITM-signed certificate with respect to Twitter's EV certificate. The validation level of a certificate can be found by inspecting the policy identifier value of the policy extension.

Evaluation 2 : Mirroring TLS Version and Strength of Cipher Suites. This is another desirable property for TI class browsers. The TLS version used by the browser-side TLS_{CP} should not be weaker than that of the server-side TLS_{PS}. This property is necessary to ensure that the proxy is not downgrading the protocol version. We enumerate different versions of TLS (and SSL) and see if the TLS versions negotiation observed in the `ClientHello` and `ServerHello` pairs from both sides match with each other and determine whether the proxy mirrors, upgrades, or downgrades the TLS version.

In addition to the TLS version, when the proxy receives a set of cipher suites proposed by the browser through `ClientHello`, the `ClientHello` sent by the proxy to the remote Web server should offer a comparable set of cipher suites, or it should at least ensure no weak or insecure cipher suites are being offered. Similarly, after the Web server chose a particular cipher suite to use for TLS_{PS}, the proxy should choose one with similar strength, if not exactly the same, for TLS_{CP}. This property is important to ensure similar strength of key exchange algorithms, ciphers, and message authentication code are used in both sides of the proxy (*i.e.*, TLS_{CP} and TLS_{PS}). We find out the sets of cipher suites being negotiated by monitoring the pairs of `ClientHello` and `ServerHello` in TLS_{CP} and TLS_{PS}. Then, we can investigate whether the proxy offers better/weaker cipher suites to the Web server.

Evaluation 3 : Validation of Proxy Certificates. For TI browsers, they need to properly validate certificates coming from their proxies, unless they employ other means for authenticating the proxy servers. Without a robust certificate chain validation, it might be possible for an MITM to perform impersonation attacks against TLS_{CP} and intercept the data exchanged between the browser and its proxy. For this evaluation, we deploy the open source mitmproxy on our Linux wireless AP, to inject invalid certificates to TLS_{CP} when it gets established and see if any of the TI browsers would accept such certificates. Considering the certificate chains of the proxies, we are also interested in seeing the length of the chains and for how long would they be valid for.

Evaluation 4 : Avoiding Weak Cipher Suites. If a Web server is configured to only use weak cipher suites (*e.g.*, those using flawed ciphers like RC4, 3DES and other export-grade ciphers), the proxy (TI browsers) or browser (HT browsers) should not establish a TLS session with it, or some warning messages should be shown to the users. This property is required to provide some basic guarantees on the strength of the overall TLS session between the browser and the remote website. The users might be misled into a false sense of security if the apps silently establish TLS sessions with weak ciphers being used.

In HT browsers, weak cipher suites should be avoided by the browser application itself since the proxy does not actively interfere with the communication with the Web server. However, for TI browsers, the proxy needs to enforce policies regarding weak ciphers. In this experiment, we initially configure the test website with different cipher suite parameters (*e.g.*, OpenSSL's HIGH, MEDIUM, LOW, or EXPORT). LOW and EXPORT level cipher suites are expected to be blocked by the proxy server or the browser because these cipher suites should not be used due to their weaknesses. We also try some additional weak cipher suites involving vulnerable ciphers (*i.e.*, RC4 and 3DES) and modes that are known to be tricky to implement (*i.e.*, block cipher in CBC mode with HMAC-SHA1 and HMAC-MD5) in the test Web server to see if any of the HT and TI browsers consider these acceptable.

Evaluation 5 : Validation of Server's Certificate Chain. In TLS handshake, server sends a certificate chain with ServerHello message as a reply to Client's ClientHello message. The leaf certificate of this certificate chain contains server's public key which is signed by some trusted CA. The client after receiving this certificate chain verifies it to make sure that the client is communicating with the correct server, not an impersonator. The validation process should check the trustworthiness of issuers on the chain, the cryptographic signatures, hostname, revocation status, and validity period. Otherwise, an attacker can exploit some of the missing checks for potential attacks.

The browser (in the HT model) or its proxy (in the TI model) has to perform the aforementioned checks on the received certificate chain, and if the validation fails, it should decline to establish a TLS session, or show appropriate warning messages to the user. To check whether the apps adequately perform such validations, we use the following types of certificates in our experiments: **self-signed** certificates, certificates signed by an untrusted issuer (**Custom CA**), certificates with **invalid signatures** and **incorrect common names**, **revoked** certificates, and **expired** certificates. We configure our test Web server to use these certificates, one at a time, and visit the test website from each of the browsers to determine the robustness of their certificate chain validation process.

Unlike previous work [11], for TI browsers, we cannot install a custom trusted CA to the proxy servers to enable fine-grained experiments. Instead, we have to rely on common trusted commercial CAs to issue our test certificates, and hence the combination of certificate issues that we can experiment with, especially regarding X.509v3 extensions, are restricted by the certificate issuance policies of the commercial CAs. While certificates with incorrect common name was easily obtainable from commercial CAs, we manually modify the signature of a valid certificate to obtain test certificates with invalid signatures. For revoked certificates, we have waited for 2 months to allow the revocation information to get properly disseminated before testing. Considering HT browsers, we also attempt to install a trusted CA certificate on the Android test device, and if the browsers trust the system CA store, additional fine-grained experiments regarding problematic certificate can be performed.

Evaluation 6 : Avoiding Weak TLS Versions. If a remote website only accepts legacy TLS (*e.g.*, versions older than TLSv1.1), the browser or its proxy server should prevent the TLS session from being established, or show appropriate warning message to the user. This is useful in providing the user some guarantees on the overall strength of the TLS sessions. Historic versions of TLS often lack support for modern ciphersuites, and might be susceptible to different kinds of MITM and downgrade attacks [RFC7568, RFC6176].

For the same reason explained in Evaluation 4, this should be performed by the browser application (in case of HT browsers), or by the proxy server (in case of TI browsers). We perform this experiment by configuring the aforementioned weak TLS versions one-by-one in our test Web server. Then, for each of these TLS versions, we visit the test website from each of the browsers and see if the TLS sessions can be successfully established despite the weak TLS versions. This is more reliable than simply monitoring the `ClientHello` messages for protocol version numbers, as the browser/proxies might have fallback/retry mechanisms upon encountering a server with incompatible versions.

4   Findings

4.1   Commercial CA Certificate Issuance Policy

The variety of experiments regarding problematic certificates that we can perform depends on the issuance policy of the trusted issuers. Hence, we set out to explore the possibility of obtaining certificates with weak algorithms and/or bad parameters through commercial CAs. We examined the certificate issuance policies of 11 well-known CAs listed in online surveys[1] and encyclopedia (e.g., Wikipedia). We found that none of the CAs agreed to issue certificates with weak signature hash algorithms (e.g., SHA1, MD5) or short RSA keys (e.g., 512 bits, 1024 bits). At minimum, the issuance policies of these CAs require certificates to use SHA256 with a RSA modulus of at least 2048-bit long, which is coherent with the baseline requirements published by the CA/Browser Forum [1]. While it is fortunate that the commercial CAs we considered all have a somewhat high bar in terms of what kind of certificates they are willing to issue, this also means that for Evaluation 5 (Validation of Server's Certificate Chain), we are unable to perform fine-grained analysis of how the certificate validation performed by the TI proxies behave under different problematic certificates.

4.2   Maintaining Strength of Certificate Parameters

We found that the certificates issued by the proxies of the 11 TI browsers all use a fixed signature hash algorithm and RSA key length, even when the Web server itself uses certificates of longer hashes/keys. See columns 2 & 3 of Table 1 for the results. Our experiments include different certificates with varying signature hash algorithms (i.e., SHA-256/384/512) and different key lengths (RSA with 2048/3072/4096-bit modulus). However, all of these TI browsers use SHA256 as the signature hash algorithm, and nine of these use 2048-bit RSA modulus in their MITM certificates. The remaining one, Upx Browser uses a 1024-bit RSA

---

[1] https://w3techs.com/technologies/overview/ssl_certificate/all.

Table 1. Results of security evaluations 1–3.

Columns 2–4 show the fixed parameters of proxy certificates, irrespective of the server certificates. Column 5 shows the TLS version of TLS_{CP}, irrespective of TLS_{PS}. Columns 6–7 show results of Security Evaluation 2.
HA = Hash Algorithm SPK = Size of Public Key TL = Trust Level Ver = Version
CSD = Cipher Suites Different CV = Certificate Validity MCV = MITM Certificate Validation

Bro wser Name	HA in TLS_{CP}.cert	SPK in TLS_{CP}.cert	TL of TLS_{CP}.cert	Ver of TLS_{CP}	CSD	Pro xy Selected Cipher Suite ‡	Issuer CV †	Leaf CV	MCV
Aloha Browser	SHA256	RSA-2048	OV /DV	TLSv1.2	Yes	0xc030	—	10 yrs	B
Aloha Browser Lite	SHA256	RSA-2048	OV /DV	TLSv1.2	Yes	0xc030	—	10 yrs	B
Go ogle Chrome	SHA256	RSA-2048	OV	GQUIC46	Yes	#	4.5 yrs	3 mths	B
Op era	SHA256	RSA-2048	OV /DV	TLSv1.2	Yes	0xc02f	—	1 mth	W
Op era Beta	SHA256	RSA-2048	OV /DV	TLSv1.2	Yes	0xc02f	—	1 mth	W
Private Browser	SHA256	RSA-2048	OV /DV	TLSv1.2	Yes	0xc030	5 yrs	3 mths	B
Puffin Browser	SHA256	RSA-2048	DV	TLSv1.2	Yes	0xc030	20 yrs	2 mths	B
Tenta Browser	SHA256	RSA-2048	DV	TLSv1.2	Yes	0xc030	—	1 mth	B
Tunnel Browser	SHA256	RSA-2048	DV	TLSv1.2	Yes	0xc02f	5 yrs	1 mth	W
Unblo ck Website..	SHA256	RSA-2048	DV	TLSv1.2	Yes	0xc02f	5 yrs	1 mth	W
UPX Browser	SHA256	RSA-1024	OV /DV	TLSv1.3	Yes	0x1301	10 yrs	2 mths	B

‡ 0xc030 = TLS-ECDHE-RSA-WITH-AES256-GCM-SHA384;
0xc02f = TLS-ECDHE-RSA-WITH-AES128-GCM-SHA256;
0x1301 = TLS-AES128-GCM-SHA256
# = Curve25519 for key exchange, and AES-GCM for authenticated encryption
† '—' means no issuer certificates were sent.

modulus. All in all, **none of the these apps mirrored the strength of the certificate parameters offered by the Web server.**

We also evaluated whether the MITM certificates maintain the trust level of server certificates. In our findings (column 4 of Table 1), the proxies of Puffin Browser, Unblock Website Browser, Tenta Browser, and Tunnel Browser send DV certificates to the browser even though the remote website (https://mobile.twitter.com) sends an EV certificate to the proxy. Google Chrome's proxy use an OV certificate. For rest of the TI browsers, MITM certificates do not have any policy extension fields. Hence, we can only confirm that these certificates are not EV, but cannot determine whether they are OV or DV. According to our findings, **none of the proxy servers use the most trusted EV certificates for** TLS_{CP}; additionally, users are not warned about such discrepancies.

4.3   Mirroring TLS Version and Strength of Cipher Suites

We found that the TLS version of TLS_{CP} for 10 TI browsers is fixed at TLSv1.2, regardless of the version used by TLS_{PS}. Google Chrome uses GQUIC to replace TLS_{CP}. To our pleasant surprise, UPX Browser, uses TLSv1.3 for its TLS_{CP}. Similarly, the cipher suite selected for TLS_{CP} also appears to be fixed, irrespective of what is chosen for TLS_{PS}, though different browsers have different preferences over possible cipher suites. Fortunately, the cipher suites chosen are all reasonably strong and with the property of forward secrecy. These results can be found in columns 5–7 of Table 1.

4.4   Validation of Proxy Certificates

Regarding certificate validation during the establishment of TLS_{CP}, we found that none of the 11 TI browsers silently accept the MITM-signed certificates injected by mitmproxy; 8 of them outright reject the certificates, and the remaining three (Opera, Opera Beta and Tunnel Browser) display warning messages prompting the user to decide whether to continue or not. See column 10 of Table 1 for the results. Moreover, columns 8–9 of Table 1 present the findings on the certificate chain used by the TI proxies. Five of the TI proxies send only a single certificate for authentication purposes, and the others send a chain of two certificates. Most of the proxy certificates (leaf of the chain) have a short validity period of a few months, and the only exceptions are Aloha Browser and Aloha Browser Lite, where the proxy certificates are valid for 10 years (column 9 of Table 1). For the proxies that sent a chain of two certificates, all of the issuer certificates are valid for more than a few years, with Puffin Browser having the longest validity period of 20 years (column 8 of Table 1).

4.5   Avoiding Weak Cipher Suites

For this evaluation, we configure our test Web server with different cipher suites as described in Sect. 3.4. When we use OpenSSL's HIGH and MEDIUM level cipher suites (consisting of key lengths greater than or equal to 128 bits), all TI and HT browsers successfully established TLS sessions. On the other hand, none of the browsers were willing to established TLS sessions with the test Web server when it is using OpenSSL's LOW and EXPORT level cipher suites (consisting of key length less or equal to 64 bits). See columns 2–5 of Table 2 for the results.

Interestingly, a more fine-grained experiment with cipher suites revealed some subtle issues that are worth considering. When we configure the test Web server with cipher suites involving the use of algorithms like **SHA1** and **3DES** that are considered to be weak, **all of the 34 browsers tested turn out to be willing to establish TLS sessions with the remote website**, without showing any warnings to their users warning. Moreover, we found that Tunnel Browser, and the proxy servers of UC Mini and Unblock Website Browser, are willing to **accept without warning cipher suites involving weak algorithms like RC4 and MD5**. These behaviors are consistent with the ClientHello requests observed on the Web server side. See columns 6–9 of Table 2 for the results. RC4 has irreparable weaknesses that can open door to a variety of attacks [3,16,36], 3DES is susceptible to birthday attacks due to its small block size [7], and cipher suites using MD5 and SHA1 are either using the flawed RC4 stream cipher, or block ciphers in CBC mode which has proven to be tricky to implement and are continuously haunted by padding oracle attacks [2,18,28].

4.6   Validation of Server's Certificate Chain

Certificate chain validation ensures that a TLS session was established with the intended entity, given that the claimed identity was verified and vouched by some trusted authorities. The results of this evaluation can be found in Table 2.

Table 2. Results of security evaluation 4–5.

Left half of the table shows actions taken by the browsers (HT browsers) or proxies (TI browsers) on different strengths of cipher suites configured in the Web server.
Right half of the table shows actions taken by the browsers (HT browsers) or proxies (TI browsers) when various invalid certificates are sent from the remote server.
A = Allowed B = Blocked W = Warnings H = HIGH M = MEDIUM L = LOW ET = EXPORT
SS = Self-Signed SM = Signature-Mismatch WCN = Wrong Common Name RV = Revoked
EX = Expired CCA = Custom CA   Undesirable actions are marked in red.

Browser Name	H	M	L	ET	RC4	MD5	3DES	SHA1	SS	SM	WCN	RV	EX	CCA
Aloha Browser	A	A	B	B	B	B	A	A	W	W	W	A	W	W
Aloha Browser Lite	A	A	B	B	B	B	A	A	W	W	W	A	W	W
Arvin Browser	A	A	B	B	B	B	A	A	B	B	B	A	B	B
Blue Proxy Browser	A	A	B	B	B	B	A	A	B	B	B	A	B	B
Browser for Android	A	A	B	B	B	B	A	A	W	W	W	A	W	W
BROXY Browser	A	A	B	B	B	B	A	A	A	A	A	A	A	A
Unblock Smart..	A	A	B	B	B	B	A	A	B	B	B	A	B	B
Ghost Browser	A	A	B	B	B	B	A	A	W	W	W	A	W	W
Google Chrome	A	A	B	B	B	B	A	A	W*	W*	W*	A	W*	W*
Hola Browser	A	A	B	B	B	B	A	A	W	W	A	A	B	W
JAV pekob	A	A	B	B	B	B	A	A	W	W	W	A	W	W
Opera Mini	A	A	B	B	B	B	A	A	W	B	W	B	B	W
Opera Mini Beta	A	A	B	B	B	B	A	A	W	B	W	B	B	W
Opera	A	A	B	B	B	B	A	A	W	W	W	A	W	W
Opera Beta	A	A	B	B	B	B	A	A	W	W	W	A	W	W
Private Browser	A	A	B	B	B	B	A	A	B	B	W	A	W	B
Proxy Browser	A	A	B	B	B	B	A	A	B	B	B	A	B	B
Proxybro	A	A	B	B	B	B	A	A	W	W	W	A	W	W
Proxyfox Browser	A	A	B	B	B	B	A	A	W	W	W	A	W	W
Proxynel Browser	A	A	B	B	B	B	A	A	W	W	W	A	W	W
Puffin Browser	A	A	B	B	B	B	A	A	W	W	W	A	W	W
Super Browser	A	A	B	B	B	B	A	A	W	W	A	A	A	W
Tenta Browser	A	A	B	B	B	B	A	A	B	B	B	A	B	B
Tunnel Browser	A	A	B	B	A	A	A	A	A	A	A	A	A	A
UC Mini	A	A	B	B	A	A	A	A	B	B	B	A	B	B
Unblock Site Browser	A	A	B	B	B	B	A	A	W	W	A	A	A	W
Unblock VPN Browser	A	A	B	B	B	B	A	A	W	W	A	A	A	W
Unblock Website..	A	A	B	B	A	A	A	A	A	A	A	A	A	A
Unblock Websites	A	A	B	B	B	B	A	A	B	B	B	A	B	B
Unlocker Sites	A	A	B	B	B	B	A	A	B	B	B	A	B	B
UPX Browser	A	A	B	B	B	B	A	A	B	B	B	A	B	B
VPN Proxy Browser	A	A	B	B	B	B	A	A	B	B	B	A	B	B
Web Proxy Browser	A	A	B	B	B	B	A	A	W	W	W	A	W	W
X Web Proxy	A	A	B	B	B	B	A	A	A	A	A	A	A	A

* In this case, proxy gets inactive, and TLS session is continued directly between browser and remote server.

When the server certificate is *self-signed*, signed by an *untrusted issuers (Custom CA)*, or has an *invalid signature*, we found that all the HT browsers would either reject it and terminate the TLS connection, or show warning messages to the user before continuing. However, we noticed that four HT browsers (Hola Browser, Super Browser, Unblock Site Browser, and Unblock VPN Browser) would **accept server certificates with an** *incorrect common name* without showing any warnings to the users. The rest of the HT browsers all reject certificates with incorrect common name. Additionally, Super Browser, Unblock Site Browser, and Unblock VPN Browser also **appear to accept** *expired certificates*.

Table 3. Results of security evaluation 6.

Actions of the browsers (HT browsers) or their proxy servers (TI browsers) when different TLS versions are forced on the remote server.
A = Allowed B = Blocked W = Warnings. Undesirable actions are marked in red.

Browser Name	TLS 1.3	TLS 1.2	TLS 1.1	TLS 1.0	SSL 3.0	SSL 2.0	Browser Name	TLS 1.3	TLS 1.2	TLS 1.1	TLS 1.0	SSL 3.0	SSL 2.0
Aloha Browser	A	A	A	A	B	B	Proxyfox Browser	A	A	A	A	B	B
Aloha Browser Lite	A	A	A	A	B	B	Proxynel Browser	A	A	A	A	B	B
Arvin Browser	A	A	A	A	B	B	Puffin Browser	B	A	A	A	B	B
Blue Proxy Browser	A	A	A	A	B	B	Super Browser	A	A	A	A	B	B
Browser for Android	A	A	A	A	B	B	Tenta Browser	B	A	A	A	B	B
							Tunnel Browser	B	A	A	A	B	B
BROXY Browser	B	A	A	A	B	B	UC Mini	B	B	B	A	A	A
Unblock Smart Browser	A	A	A	A	B	B	Unblock Smart Browser	A	A	A	A	B	B
Ghost Browser	A	A	A	A	B	B	Unblock VPN Browser	A	A	A	A	B	B
Google Chrome	A	A	A	A	B	B	Unblock Website Browser	B	A	A	A	A	B
Hola Browser	A	A	A	A	B	B							
JAV pekob	A	A	A	A	B	B	Unblock Websites	A	A	A	A	B	B
Opera Mini	B	A	A	A	B	B	Unlocker Sites	A	A	A	A	B	B
Opera Mini Beta	B	A	A	A	B	B	UPX Browser	A	A	A	A	B	B
Opera	B	A	A	A	B	B	VPN Proxy Browser	A	A	A	A	B	B
Opera Beta	B	A	A	A	B	B	Web Proxy Browser	A	A	A	A	B	B
Private Browser	A	A	A	A	B	B							
Proxy Browser	A	A	A	A	B	B	X Web Proxy	B	A	A	A	B	B
Proxybro	A	A	A	A	B	B							

For all the TI browsers except for Unblock Website Browser and Tunnel Browser, these 5 types of invalid certificates are either outright rejected by their corresponding proxies, or a warning is displayed to their users.

For revoked certificates, we found that out of all the browsers tested, only Opera Mini and Opera Mini Beta would take the revocation status of certificates into consideration, and reject revoked certificates. This is particularly interesting because Opera and Opera Beta, which are from the same vendor and are supposed to be more full-featured, **do not seem to reject revoked certificates**.

Finally, for the two TI-O browsers (BROXY Browser and X Web Proxy), which uses TLS only for server-side traffic but not for browser-side, their certificate chain validation also appears to be very weak, as the proxy servers do not reject any of the 6 types of invalid certificates.

4.7 Avoiding Weak TLS Versions

For this evaluation, when the test server is configured to use TLSv1.2 or TLSv1.1, only UC Mini declined to communicate, while all the other browsers established TLS sessions without errors. Additionally, we noticed that quite **a few proxy-based browsers are still reluctant to support TLSv1.3**. See column 2–4 of Table 3 for the detailed results.

We have also found that **all the browsers continue to support the twenty year old TLSv1.0**. On the other hand, **SSLv3.0 is blocked by all the browsers except UC Mini and Unblock Website Browser**. This is interesting since UC Mini's proxy server does not support TLSv1.2 and TLSv1.1, but instead supports much older and weaker SSLv3.0 and TLSv1.0. We suspect that this is due to a lack of software upgrade and maintenance for these proxies.

Since SSLv2.0 is not supported by any reasonably recent versions of Apache Web server, we have not performed similar experiments with SSLv2.0. Instead, we used the Qualys SSL Client Test[2] to check the list of TLS versions that are supported by the proxy-based browsers. For HT browsers, such a test would reflect the configuration of the browser itself, and for TI browsers, this would effectively be testing the proxies. Through this additional experiment, we found that the **proxy server of UC Mini also supports SSLv2.0**, the usage of which is deprecated since 2011 [RFC6176].

5   Discussions

In this section, we discuss the implications of our findings, as well as some of the limitations of our experiments.

5.1   Browsers with No/Broken TLS

First of all, some proxy-based browsers are **effectively not benefiting from TLS at all**. For example, Unblock Sites strips TLS, and for the two TI-O browsers (Broxy Browser and X Web Proxy), they do not use TLS between the browser and the proxy, and certificate validation for TLS_{PS} is so weak that an impersonation+MITM attack can be mounted against it, which basically renders the TLS useless. Some other problematic browsers in this category include the Unblock Website Browser and Tunnel Browser, both of which have a fairly good TLS_{CP} that uses TLSv1.2 and a reasonably strong ephemeral cipher suite providing forward secrecy, but the TLS_{PS} certificate validation is abysmal and susceptible to impersonation+MITM attacks. Notice that these apps have hundreds to several hundred thousands of downloads. If users of these apps rely on them to exchange confidential data, there could be serious repercussions.

5.2   Leniency in Certificate Validation

Additionally, our experiments have revealed some other subtle unwarranted leniencies in how the browser apps (and their proxies) validate server certificates. Some of them **do not check for common names, opening doors to potential impersonation attacks**. One of the offenders, Hola Browser, had more than 50 million downloads, leaving a large number of users potentially vulnerable.

Moreover, some of the browsers, including ones that have garnered more than hundred thousand downloads (*e.g.*, Super Browser), do not reject expired certificates. While this does not seem immediately alarming, skipping the expiration

---

[2] https://www.ssllabs.com/ssltest/viewMyClient.html.

check is less than ideal for following reasons. First, accepting expired certificates means old certificates whose private keys might have been leaked and exposed (*e.g.*, through OpenSSL heartbleed bug) can still be used by an attacker. Second, given the support for revocation checks remains questionable, a phenomenon also observed by our experiments, there is a new trend of favoring short-lived certificates [25, 34] instead of conventional revocation mechanisms (*e.g.*, CRLs and OCSP) that are considered to be heavyweight and not scaling well. In such a case, the ability to prevent certificates with leaked private keys from functioning again critically hinges on the browsers rejecting expired certificates, and hence we recommend browser vendors to **properly implement expiration checks**.

5.3   Weak Cipher Suites, TLS Versions and RSA Parameters

We have also noticed that **usage of weak cipher suites is not universally banned** in the 34 browsers we have studied. For example, 3 of them still support usage of RC4. RC4 is a stream cipher found to exhibit undesirable statistical biases in its key stream, which leads to a variety of attacks [3, 16, 36]. Major desktop browser vendors have disabled usage of RC4 for some years, and usage of RC4 have since been deprecated [RFC7465]. Moreover, 3DES is also considered weak, especially after the emergence of SWEET32 [7], a birthday attack exploiting its relatively short (64-bit) block size. NIST has since updated its guidelines to restrict the use of 3DES to encrypting not more than 2^{20} blocks (8 MB) of data under one key bundle (made of 3 unique 56-bit keys) [4], which is well within reach of a Web session involving a large amount of multimedia contents. Recently, NIST has announced usage of 3DES is deprecated and will be disallowed after year 2023 [5]. Interestingly, at the time of writing, we have seen that all the tested proxy-based browsers still support 3DES. **We hence recommend browser vendors to consider disabling support for RC4 as soon as possible, and follow the NIST guidelines on phasing out support for 3DES in the near future.**

On the other hand, there exists a series of research on reducing the complexity and monetary costs for finding SHA1 and MD5 collisions to within reach of resourceful adversaries [20, 29–32, 39, 40], and vendors of major desktop browsers have already been rejecting SHA1 and MD5 certificates. However, their use as HMAC in TLS is not immediately problematic [RFC6151], as the security argument for HMAC does not depend on the collision resistance of the hash function [6]. The problem of cipher suites involving HMAC-SHA1 and HMAC-MD5 is that all of them involve either the irreparably flawed RC4 cipher, or block ciphers under the CBC mode, which when paired with the MAC-then-encrypt design choice embraced by TLS, has proven to be tricky to implement and leads to a variety of attacks [2, 18, 28]. TLSv1.2 has since introduced new cipher suites with authenticated encryption (*e.g.*, AES under GCM) [RFC5288], and TLSv1.3 has dropped all CBC-mode ciphers [RFC8446]. It is **advisable to consider removing support for such cipher suites** in the future, or **at least display warnings to the users** regarding these problematic cipher suites.

Apart from the issues related to problematic ciphers, historic versions of TLS like TLSv1.0 and TLSv1.1 are also found to have design flaws, for example, the SLOTH attack [8] demonstrates how to exploit transcript collision, resulted from the hash collision due to SHA1 and MD5, for breaking authentication in TLSv1.0 and TLSv1.1. On top of that, TLSv1.0 deployments can also be vulnerable to the BEAST attack [13], especially if the $1/1 - n$ split client-side mitigation is not being implemented. As the result of which, vendors of major desktop browsers have all agreed to phase out support for TLSv1.0 and TLSv1.1 in 2020 [9,33], and some industry standardization body has already deprecated the use of TLSv1.0 [26]. There is also an IETF draft proposing to deprecate the use of TLSv1.0 and TLSv1.1 [23]. Consequently, we recommend vendors of proxy-based browsers to **consider following suite in phasing out support for TLSv1.0 soon, and TLSv1.1 as well in the near future.** For SSLv3.0 and SSLv2.0, both of them have already been deprecated due to numerous issues [RFC7568, RFC6176] and we recommend UC Mini and Unblock Website Browser to **stop supporting SSLv3.0 and SSLv2.0.**

In the context of TI class proxy-based browsers, this class of offense is particularly worrisome, as the use of historic versions of TLS and weak cipher suites for TLS_{PS} is transparent to the users, especially when TLS_{CP} itself is using reasonably good algorithms, which can potentially lead to a false sense of security. To the very least, **there should be warning messages delivered to the users when the quality of** TLS_{PS} **is subpar.**

Additionally, while UPX Browser is using TLSv1.3 with a reasonably strong cipher suit for TLS_{CP}, its proxy certificate has only a 1024-bit long RSA modulus. NIST has already recommended against usage of RSA modulus shorter than 2048 bits [5], and browsers like Firefox have already been phasing out support for certificates with 1024-bit RSA modulus [41]. Hence, **we recommend UPX Browser to upgrade its proxy certificate to use a longer RSA modulus.**

5.4   Asymmetry of TI Browsers

Finally, we note that for TI browsers, strength of the certificates (in terms of size of RSA modulus and hash algorithms) and cipher suites used by their TLS_{CP} and TLS_{PS} are often not mirrored. This can lead to two contrasting problems. First, as discussed in Sect. 5.3, a good quality TLS_{CP} without any warning messages could potentially mask the problem of a low quality TLS_{PS} (*e.g.*, bad certificates or broken ciphers), leading to a **false sense of security.** On the other hand, if a Web server is configured to use strong cipher suites and certificates with long RSA modulus, the fixed parameters for TLS_{CP} as presented in Table 1 can be seen as downgrading the overall quality of the TLS sessions. **A potentially better approach is to choose matching parameters for** TLS_{CP} **based on the outcome of** TLS_{PS}, but it remains to be seen whether the vendors are willing to deploy such a dynamic negotiation logic on their proxies.

5.5   Limitations

During our experiments in this research, we faced a few technical challenges. We could not locate IP addresses of the proxy servers for Opera Mini, Opera Mini Beta, Opera, Opera Beta, and UC Mini automatically using our heuristic-based approach, since the network addresses as well as the location of the proxy servers appears to be completely different in the browser-side and server-side traffic. Even the volume of traffic in both directions cannot be easily matched, since these browsers compress data in TLS_{CP} which reduces the volume significantly. Therefore, we had to resort to manual analysis for those traces, and tried to fully or partially match the **organization name** field from the locations of the proxy servers to determine the addresses of proxy servers.

As discussed in Sect. 3.4, another limitation of our experiments is that unlike previous work [11, 37], we cannot install a custom CA certificate on the proxy servers of TI class browsers, and we found that *none of the HT class browsers trust the Android system CA store*. Consequently, we were not able to perform a fine-grained analysis of their certificate validation procedures, as we have to resort to obtaining certificates from commercial CAs, and they are quite restrictive in what to issue (Sect. 4.1).

6   Related Work

TLS interception and its effects on security was studied before, where Xavier et al. [11] designed a framework to test TLS proxies used in some antivirus and parental control software, Waked et al. [37] developed a framework for analyzing TLS interception performed by enterprise-grade network appliances, and Zakir et al. [14] presented a comprehensive study on the prevalence and security impact of HTTPS interception made by middleboxes and antivirus software. Previous research has also identified TLS intercepting antivirus and content filtering software are the main contributors of forged certificates [17]. These studies have shown that many TLS intercepting products are negatively impacting security, and their proxy implementations are often problematic.

This paper makes new contributions in two directions. First, we note that proxy-based mobile browsers is another class of appliances that performs TLS interception but not studied before by previous work, and second we include in our study browsers that use an alternative model of HTTP tunneling, which comes with its own security trade-offs and considerations.

Orthogonal to this line of research, researchers have studied the affects of TLS vulnerabilities on Web security [10]. Moreover, there have been studies on whether general Web security mechanisms (e.g., HSTS, CSP, Referrer Policy, etc.) are being supported by mobile browsers [21], and some Android banking apps were also found to have weaknesses regarding certificate validation [27], along with other issues in the choice of cipher suites, signature algorithms and TLS versions, which resonate greatly with our findings presented in this paper.

7   Conclusion

In this paper, we explore the security implications of proxy-based mobile browsers on Android, and found that many of these browsers do not provide adequate security guarantees to their users. Problems include the willingness to support weak ciphers and insecure TLS versions, as well as unwarranted leniency in certificate validation, which can open door to a variety of attacks. In many cases, the proxies' transparent leniency towards subpar TLS connections with the remote server and resulting asymmetry in strength of TLS parameters could potentially lead to a false sense of security. Apart from reducing bandwidth consumption, part of the reason why proxy-based browsers are gaining popularity is their supposed ability to protect user privacy and circumvent censorship. However, the findings of our study suggest that users should be cautions and make informed decisions on which browser to use, or risk serious repercussions.

Acknowledgement. We thank the anonymous reviewers for their comments. This work is supported by NSF grant CNS-1657124.

References

1. Baseline requirements for the issuance and management of publicly-trusted certificates (2019). https://cabforum.org/wp-content/uploads/CA-Browser-Forum-BR-1.6.6.pdf
2. Al Fardan, N.J., Paterson, K.G.: Lucky thirteen: breaking the TLS and DTLS record protocols. In: IEEE S&P (2013)
3. AlFardan, N., Bernstein, D.J., Paterson, K.G., Poettering, B., Schuldt, J.C.: On the security of RC4 in TLS. In: USENIX Security (2013)
4. Barker, E., Mouha, N.: Recommendation for triple data encryption algorithm (TDEA) block cipher. NIST special publication 800–67 Rev. 2 (2017)
5. Barker, E., Roginsk, A.: Transitioning the use of cryptographic algorithms and key lengths. NIST special publication 800–131A Rev. 2 (2019)
6. Bellare, M.: New proofs for NMAC and HMAC: security without collision-resistance. In: Annual International Cryptology Conference (2006)
7. Bhargavan, K., Leurent, G.: On the practical (in-) security of 64-bit block ciphers: collision attacks on http over TLS and openVPN. In: ACM CCS (2016)
8. Bhargavan, K., Leurent, G.: Transcript collision attacks: breaking authentication in TLS, IKE, and SSH. In: NDSS (2016)
9. Bright, P.: Apple, google, microsoft, and mozilla come together to end TLS 1.0 (2018). https://arstechnica.com/gadgets/2018/10/browser-vendors-unite-to-end-support-for-20-year-old-tls-1-0/
10. Calzavara, S., Focardi, R., Nemec, M., Rabitti, A., Squarcina, M.: Postcards from the post-http world: amplification of https vulnerabilities in the web ecosystem. In: IEEE S&P (2019)
11. de Carnavalet, X.D.C., Mannan, M.: Killed by proxy: analyzing client-end TLS interception software. In: NDSS (2016)
12. Debnath, J.: When TLS meets proxy on mobile (2020). https://sites.google.com/view/joyantadebnath/when-tls-meets-proxy-on-mobile
13. Duong, T., Rizzo, J.: Here come the ⊕ ninjas. Technical report (2011)

14. Durumeric, Z., et al.: The security impact of https interception. In: NDSS (2017)
15. Ensafi, R., Fifield, D., Winter, P., Feamster, N., Weaver, N., Paxson, V.: Examining how the great firewall discovers hidden circumvention servers. In: ACM IMC (2015)
16. Garman, C., Paterson, K.G., Van der Merwe, T.: Attacks only get better: password recovery attacks against RC4 in TLS. In: USENIX Security (2015)
17. Huang, L.S., Rice, A., Ellingsen, E., Jackson, C.: Analyzing forged SSL certificates in the wild. In: IEEE S&P (2014)
18. Irazoqui, G., Inci, M.S., Eisenbarth, T., Sunar, B.: Lucky 13 strikes back. In: ACM Symposium on Information, Computer and Communications Security (2015)
19. Jarmoc, J., Unit, D.: SSL/TLS interception proxies and transitive trust. Black Hat Europe (2012)
20. Lenstra, A., De Weger, B.: On the possibility of constructing meaningful hash collisions for public keys. In: Australasian Conference on Information Security and Privacy (2005)
21. Luo, M., Laperdrix, P., Honarmand, N., Nikiforakis, N.: Time does not heal all wounds: a longitudinal analysis of security-mechanism support in mobile browsers. In: NDSS (2019)
22. McDonald, A., et al.: 403 forbidden: a global view of CDN geoblocking. In: ACM IMC (2018)
23. Moriarty, K., Farrell, S.: Deprecating TLSV1.0 and TLSV1.1 (2019). https://tools. ietf.org/html/draft-ietf-tls-oldversions-deprecate-05
24. Niaki, A.A., et al.: IClab: a global, longitudinal internet censorship measurement platform. In: IEEE S&P (2019)
25. Payne, B.: PKI at scale using short-lived certificates. In: USENIX Enigma (2016)
26. PCI Security Standards Council: Migrating from SSL and early TLS. Technical report (2015)
27. Reaves, B., et al.: Mo (bile) money, mo (bile) problems: analysis of branchless banking applications. ACM Trans. Priv. Secur. **20**(3), 1–31 (2017)
28. Ronen, E., Paterson, K.G., Shamir, A.: Pseudo constant time implementations of TLS are only pseudo secure. In: ACM CCS (2018)
29. Sotirov, A., et al.: MD5 considered harmful today, creating a rogue CA certificate. In: Annual Chaos Communication Congress (2008)
30. Stevens, M., Bursztein, E., Karpman, P., Albertini, A., Markov, Y.: The first collision for full sha-1. In: Annual International Cryptology Conference (2017)
31. Stevens, M., Karpman, P., Peyrin, T.: Freestart collision for full sha-1. In: Annual International Conference on the Theory and Applications of Cryptographic Techniques (2016)
32. Stevens, M., Lenstra, A., Weger, B.: Chosen-prefix collisions for md5 and colliding x.509 certificates for different identities. In: Annual International Conference on Advances in Cryptology (2007)
33. Taylor, M.: Tls 1.0 and 1.1 removal update (2019). https://hacks.mozilla.org/2019/ 05/tls-1-0-and-1-1-removal-update/
34. Topalovic, E., Saeta, B., Huang, L.S., Jackson, C., Boneh, D.: Towards short-lived certificates. Web 2.0 Secur. Priv. (2012)
35. VanderSloot, B., McDonald, A., Scott, W., Halderman, J.A., Ensafi, R.: Quack: scalable remote measurement of application-layer censorship. In: USENIX Security (2018)
36. Vanhoef, M., Piessens, F.: All your biases belong to us: Breaking RC4 in wpa-tkip and TLS. In: USENIX Security (2015)
37. Waked, L., Mannan, M., Youssef, A.: To intercept or not to intercept: analyzing TLS interception in network appliances. In: ACM AsiaCCS (2018)

38. Wang, Q., Gong, X., Nguyen, G.T., Houmansadr, A., Borisov, N.: Censorspoofer: asymmetric communication using IP spoofing for censorship-resistant web browsing. In: ACM CCS (2012)
39. Wang, X., Feng, D., Lai, X., Yu, H.: Collisions for hash functions MD4, MD5, HAVAL-128 and RIPEMD. IACR Cryptology ePrint Archive (2004)
40. Wang, X., Yin, Y.L., Yu, H.: Finding collisions in the full SHA-1. In: Annual International Cryptology Conference (2005)
41. Wilson, K.: Phasing out certificates with 1024-bit RSA keys (2014). https://blog.mozilla.org/security/2014/09/08/phasing-out-certificates-with-1024-bit-rsa-keys/

Human Factors in Homograph Attack Recognition

Tran Phuong Thao[1]([✉]), Yukiko Sawaya[2], Hoang-Quoc Nguyen-Son[2],
Akira Yamada[2], Ayumu Kubota[2], Tran Van Sang[1],
and Rie Shigetomi Yamaguchi[1]

[1] The University of Tokyo, Tokyo, Japan
tpthao@yamagula.ic.i.u-tokyo.ac.jp, 4040961653@g.ecc.u-tokyo.ac.jp,
yamaguchi.rie@i.u-tokyo.ac.jp
[2] KDDI Research Inc., Fujimino, Japan
{yu-sawaya,ho-nguyen,ai-yamada,kubota}@kddi-research.jp

Abstract. Homograph attack is a way that attackers deceive victims about which website domain name they are communicating with by exploiting the fact that many characters look alike. The attack becomes serious and is raising broad attention when recently many brand domains have been attacked such as Apple Inc., Adobe Inc., Lloyds Bank, etc. We first design a survey of human demographics, brand familiarity, and security backgrounds and apply it to 2,067 participants. We build a regression model to study which factors affect participants' ability in recognizing homograph domains. We find that for different levels of visual similarity, the participants exhibit different abilities. 13.95% of participants can recognize non-homographs while 16.60% of participants can recognize homographs whose the visual similarity with the target brand domains is under 99.9%; but when the similarity increases to 99.9%, the number of participants who can recognize homographs significantly drops down to only 0.19%; and for the homographs with 100% of visual similarity, there is no way for the participants to recognize. We also find that female participants tend to recognize homographs better the male but male participants tend to able to recognize non-homographs better than females. Security knowledge is a significant factor affecting both homographs and non-homographs; surprisingly, people who have strong security knowledge tend to be able to recognize homographs but not non-homographs. Furthermore, people who work or are educated in computer science or computer engineering do not appear as a factor affecting the ability in recognizing homographs; however, interestingly, right after they are explained about the homograph attack, people who work or are educated in computer science or computer engineering are the ones who can capture the situation the most quickly.

Keywords: Human factors in security · Homograph domain ·
International Domain Name (IDN) · Linear regression model · Student
t-test statistics

M. Conti et al. (Eds.): ACNS 2020, LNCS 12147, pp. 408–435, 2020.
https://doi.org/10.1007/978-3-030-57878-7_20

1 Introduction

Homograph attack is first described by E. Gabrilovic et al. [1] in 2002. To demonstrate the feasibility of the attack, the authors registered a homograph targeting to the brand domain `microsoft.com` using the Russian letters 'c' (U+0421) and 'o' (U+041E). The homograph contains the two non-ASCII characters and has an ASCII converted form as `xn--mirsft-yqfbx.com`.[1] However, the attack was not much attracted at that time. Until 2017, the attack had raised broad attention when the famous brand domain `apple.com` (Apple Inc.) is attacked by the homograph that appears under the Punycode form [2] such as `xn--pple-43d.com`, which uses the Cyrillic 'a' (U+0430) instead of the ASCII 'a' (U+0061). Thereafter, many homograph attacks targeting other famous brand domains have been found such as Adobe Inc. [3], LLoyds Bank [4], Google Analytics [5], etc. A recent large-scale analysis [6] about International Domain Names (IDNs) in 2018 shows that, just for the first 1,000 brand domains in top Alexa ranking, more than 1,516 homograph domains were already registered. Furthermore, the attack becomes more progressive and sophisticated today.

Motivation. Many defensive approaches have been proposed such as applying machine learning to some features (e.g., visual similarity metrics, HTML content, and optical character recognition (OCR)) [7–10], using empirical analysis based on registered databases (e.g., Whois, DNS, blacklists, confusable Unicode) [6,11], or blocking International Domain Names (IDNs) (e.g., disabling the automatic IDN conversion on browsers) [12–15]. So, we ask the question: *how to design an approach that focuses on pro-active defense which can control the attack rather than just responding to it after it has really happened; and is it possible if the approach is based on ergonomics rather than machine engineering?* We therefore in this paper, aim to propose a system that analyzes human factors in the ability of homograph domain identification. This, in turn, allows for various security training courses against the attack aiming to appropriate participants.

Contribution. To the best of our knowledge, our work is the first to devise a system that predicts if human demographics, brand familiarity, and security backgrounds can influence the ability of homograph recognition. To do so, we designed a survey and applied it to 2067 participants who are Internet users in Japan. We subsequently build a regression model to study which factors affect the ability. As a result, we find that for different levels of visual similarity, the participants exhibit different abilities. 13.95% of participants can recognize non-homographs while 16.60% of participants can recognize homographs whose visual similarity with the target brand domains is under 99.9%; but when the similarity

---

[1] International Domain Names (IDNs) contain non-ASCII characters (e.g., Arabic, Chinese, Cyrillic alphabet). Therefore, they are encoded to ASCII strings using Punycode transcription known as IDNA encoding and appear under ASCII strings starting with "`xn--`". For example, the domain `xn--ggle-0qaa.com` is displayed as `gо̃о̃gle.com`.

increases to 99.9%, the number of participants who can recognize homographs significantly drops down to only 0.19%; and for the homographs with 100% of visual similarity, there is no way for the participants to recognize. We also find that while female participants tend to be able to recognize homographs, male participants tend to able to recognize non-homographs. The result also shows that security knowledge is a significant factor affecting both homographs and non-homographs. We hypothesized that people who have strong security knowledge can recognize both homograph and non-homograph; but surprisingly, it is only true for the case of homographs but not for the case of non-homographs. Another interesting result is that people who work or are educated in computer science or computer engineering do not appear as a factor affecting the ability of homograph recognition. However, right after they are explained about what the homograph attack is, people who work or are educated in computer science or computer engineering are the ones who can capture the situation the most quickly (i.e, from not an affecting factor to become an affecting factor the most quickly). We believe that it opens avenues to help users reduce their presumptuousness and improve knowledge and carefulness about security threats.

Roadmap. The rest of this paper is organized as follows. The related work is described in Sect. 2. The procedure for preparing the survey is presented in Sect. 3. The methodology is given in Sect. 4. The experiment is analyzed in Sect. 5. The discussion is mentioned in Sect. 6. Finally, the conclusion is drawn in Sect. 7.

2   Related Work

In this section, we introduce related work about defending homograph approaches and related work about factor analysis of the brand familiarity, and security background in computer security-related issues.

2.1   Disabling the Automatic IDN Conversion

In this approach, the feature of automatic IDN conversion is disabled in the web browser. Instead of showing the converted form of the domain such as gōōgle.com, the browsers only display the original IDN form such as xn--ggle-0qaa.com in the address bar. In reality, some popular web browsers applied this approach including Chrome and Firefox [12], Safari [13], Internet Explorer [14], and Opera [15]. However, there is a big trade-off when the browsers stop supporting the automatic IDN conversion because a large number of Internet users are using non-English languages with non-Latin alphabets through over 7.5 million registered IDNs in all over the world (by December 2017) [16]. Furthermore, the homograph attack exploits not only look-alike Punycode characters in IDNs, but also look-alike Latin characters in non-IDNs. For instance, the homograph bl0gsp0t.com targeted to the brand domain blogspot.com by replacing the 'o' by the '0'; or the homograph wlklpedia.org targeted to the brand domain `wikipedia.com` by replacing the 'i' by the 'l'. Also, if the homographs can deceive users before appearing in the address bar of browsers (e.g., the homographs are given from an email or a document under hyper-links) without the users' awareness of the browsers, disabling IDN conversion is not meant to prevent users from accessing the homographs.

2.2 Detecting Homographs

Several methods have been proposed to detect homographs. K. Tian et al. [7] scanned five types of squatting domains over DNS records and identified domains that are likely impersonating popular brands. They then build a machine learning classifier to detect homographs using page behaviors, visual analysis and optical character recognition (OCR). L. Baojun et al. [6] made a large-scale analysis on IDNs using correlating data from auxiliary sources such as Whois, passive DNS and URL blacklist. They found that 1.4 million IDNs were actively registered in which 6000 IDNs were determined as homographs by URL blacklists. They also identified 1,516 IDNs showing high visual similarity to reputable brand domains. S. Yuta et al. [8] applies machine learning on optical character recognition (OCR) feature of a huge 1.92 million actual registered IDNs and over 10,000 malicious IDNs. A. Pieter et al. [9] collected data about the typosquatting homographs of the 500 most popular websites for seven months. They reveal that 95% of the popular domains they investigated are actively targeted by typosquatters, only few brand owners protect themselves against this practice by proactively registering their own typosquatting domains. The study also reveals that a large of typosquatting homographs can be traced back to a small group of typosquatting page hosters and that certain top-level domains are much more prone to typosquatting than others. T. Thao et al. [10] constructed a classification model for homographs and potential homographs registered by attackers using machine learning on feasible and novel features which are the visual similarity on each character and selected information from Whois. Several tools [17–23] generate permutations of homographs from a defined subset of lookalike characters from Confusable Unicode table defined by Unicode Inc. [11], then look up Whois and DNS to check whether the homographs are registered and active. Compared to the approach of disabling the automatic IDN conversion, the homograph detection is more attractive to the research community.

2.3 Brand Familiarity and Security Backgrounds in Computer Security

In this section, we present work related to web familiarity and security backgrounds including security warnings, security knowledge, security behavior, and security self-confidence that affect human decisions on security threats. Since some previous papers analyzed both brand familiarity and security backgrounds, we do not separate them into two different sections.

T. Kelley et al. [24] simulate several secure non-spoof and insecure spoof domains with different authentication levels such as extended validation, standard validation, or partial encryption. A logistic model is then applied to participants' respondents to compare how encryption level, web familiarity, security knowledge, and mouse tracking influence the participant accuracy in identifying spoof and non-spoof websites. Their result shows that user behavior derived from mouse tracking recordings leads to higher accuracy in identifying spoof and non-spoof websites than the other factors. Y. Sawaya et al. [25] apply the Security Behavior Intentions Scale (SeBIS) [26] to participants from seven countries and build a regression model to study which factors affect participants' security behavior using a cross-cultural survey. The work concluded that self-confidence in computer security has a larger positive effect on security behavior compared to actual knowledge about computer security. I. Kirlappos et al. [27] show that users do not focus on security warnings (or not understand what they are) rather than looking for signs to confirm whether a site is trustworthy. The study reveals that advice given in some current user educations about phishing is largely ignored. It, therefore, suggests that rather than flooding users with information, we need to consider how users make decisions both in business and personal settings for the user education. M. Sharif et al. [28] design a survey of security warnings, user behavior, knowledge and self-confidence about security to evaluate the utility of self-reported questionnaire for predicting exposure to malicious content. Their result confirms that the self-reported data can help forecast exposure risk over long periods of time but is not as crucial as behavioral measurements to accurately predict exposure. S. Das et al. [29] find that social processes played a major role in security behavior. Furthermore, conversations about security are often driven by the desire to warn or protect others from immediate novel threats observed or experienced. C. Erika et al. [30] study user confidence toward security and privacy for smartphone and find that participants are apprehensive about running privacy- and financially-sensitive tasks on their phones as four factors: fear of theft and data loss, misconceptions about the security of their network communications, worries about accidentally touching or clicking, and mistrust of smartphone applications. I. Iulia et al. [31] compare security behaviors between expert and non-expert and find that while experts frequently report installing software updates, using two-factor authentication and using a password manager, non-experts report using antivirus software, visiting only known websites, and changing passwords frequently. A. Felt et al. [32] examine whether security warnings from the Android permission system is effective to users. Their result shows that only 17% of participants paid attention to permissions during installation, and only 3% of Internet survey respondents could correctly answer all permission comprehension questions. This indicates that current Android security warnings do not help most users make correct security decisions.

3   Procedure

In this section, we present how the survey is designed and distributed to the participants. The survey is created in the Japanese and is embedded to a webpage. The webpage is then distributed to 2,067 participants who are Internet users in Japan.[2] The participants cannot submit their responses if any of the questions is not answered. There are three question parts about the human factors (including demographics, brand familiarity, and security backgrounds), and the final part about the participants' ability in distinguishing homographs. The following sections describe the design of each part.

3.1   Demographics

For the human demographics, the survey consists of the following seven questions:

1. Gender (male: 1 and female: 0).
2. Age (the inputs are integers).
3. Having a job (having a full-time job: 1, freelancer or part-time job: 0.5, and not have a job: 0).
4. Whether the participant has studied so far the languages including English, Spanish, French, Russian, Portuguese, German, Vietnamese, Turkish, Italian, Greek, and Dutch. The languages chosen are the common languages that use Punycode (i.e., confusable letters with the English alphabet). For each language, there are two answer options (yes:1 and no: 0). Thereafter, we calculate the number of languages that the participants answer 'yes'.
5. Knowing only Japanese (yes: 1, and no: 0). Although there is a variable related to the number of languages that the participants have studied so far, we hypothezied that knowing only Japanese or not is probably an affecting factor because the survey is done in Japan. Thereby knowing only Japanese is chosen as a variable that needs to be measured.
6. Whether the participant graduated or enrolled in computer science or computer engineering (yes: 1 and no: 0).
7. Whether the participant worked (or is working) in computer science or computer engineering (yes: 1 and no: 0).

3.2   Brand Familiarity

For the brand familiarity, the nine famous brands are chosen including Amazon, Google, Coinbase, Wiki, Booking, Expedia, Paypal, Sex.com and Facebook. For each of the brands, the participants respond to how they are familiar with the brands with 4-point Likert-scale answer options (do not know: 1, know but never

---

[2] The Appendix in this paper describes the questions in English but the survey is designed in Japanese language and distributed to Japanese, so there is no translation problem for the preservation of the survey's reliability and structure validity.

use: 2, occasionally use: 3, and often use: 4). The brands may have multiple authentic domains (i.e., the domains that the brands themselves registered), and thus the logos and the names of the brands are used to represent the brands and showed in the questions instead of listing all their domains.

3.3 Security Backgrounds

For the security backgrounds, the survey consists of the following five questions:

1. Anti-virus software installation on PCs or mobile devices: (yes: 1 and no: 0).
2. Security warning: When browsing a website, a browser or anti-virus software issues a warning, whether the participants continue browsing or not (yes: 1 and no: 0).
3. Security behavior: that consists of sixteen sub-questions as described in Appendix A. For each of the sub-questions, the participants choose 5-point Likert-scale answer options (not at all: 1, rarely: 2, sometimes: 3, often: 4, and always: 5). The summation of all the sixteen answers is then calculated and used as the variable in the model instead of each separated answer.
4. Security knowledge: that consists of eighteen sub-questions as described in Appendix B. For each of the sub-questions, the participants have two answer options (true: 1 and false: 0). Then, based on the actual correct answers given at the end of the appendix, we count the number of correct answers of the participants.
5. Security self-confidence: that consists of six sub-questions as described in Appendix C. The participants have 5-point Likert-scale answer options (not at all: 1, not applicable: 2, neither agree nor disagree: 3, applicable: 4, and very applicable: 5). Similar to the security behavior, the summation of the six answers is calculated and used for the model.

For the security behaviors, security knowledge, and security self-confidence, we use the design from the paper [25]. The paper aims to analyze factors that affect security behavior and thus uses security behavior in the target function. Meanwhile, our work aims to analyze factors (including security behavior) that affect the ability of homograph recognition, and thus security behavior is just one of the features, not used in the target function.

3.4 Homograph Recognition

This part is used for calculating the values of the target function. The eighteen sample domains mixed between homographs and non-homographs are showed in Fig. 1 and explained in Appendix D. The domains target to the nine brands mentioned in the brand familiarity. The domains are chosen for different purposes. For example, the domain #2 (amazonaws.com) is chosen because participants probably only know amazon.com and think amazonaws.com is a homograph but actually it is not. Another example is the domain #16 (sex.com) which is a pornographic domain, and thus the participants probably think it is homograph

No	Domains	Target Brand	No	Domains	Target Brand
#1	amazon.com	Amazon	#10	booking.com	Booking
#2	amazonaws.com	Amazon	#11	jbooking.jp	Booking
#3	amazon.com	Amazon	#12	expedîa.com	Expedia
#4	google.com	Google	#13	expedia.co.jp	Expedia
#5	google.com.vn	Google	#14	paypâl.com	Paypal
#6	goole.co.jp	Google	#15	paypal.com	Paypal
#7	coinbasė.com	Coinbase	#16	sex.com	Sex.com
#8	wikimedia.org	Wiki	#17	faeceb0ok.com	Facebook
#9	wikipédia.org	Wiki	#18	vi-vn.facebook.com	Facebook

Fig. 1. Sample domains used for testing the ability in distinguishing homographs

(unsafe) but actually it is not. For each of the eighteen domains, the participants answer whether it is safe or not. Based on the correct answers described in the Appendix D, we extract whether the participants have a correct answer for each domain (true: 1, and false: 0). The reason we choose the number of domains as 18 but not 30, 40 or even more is that the participants will tend to randomly choose the answer options instead of actually answering if a survey contains too many questions, and 18 questions are a good limit for our design.

4   Methodology

This section describes the pre-process on the raw data of the participants' responses, determine the target function and define the model.

4.1   Domain Grouping

The eighteen sample domains are grouped based on the visual similarity with the brand domains. In this paper, the Structural Similarity Index (SSIM) [33] is chosen for the visual similarity metric. SSIM is commonly used since it outperforms the traditional methods such as Peak Signal-To-Noise Ratio (PSNR) and Mean Squared Error (MSE) which can estimate only the absolute errors. Firstly, the domains are parsed to images in the same size $N \times N$. The SSIM between two images x and y is then calculated as follows:

$$SSIM(x,y) = \frac{(2\mu_x\mu_y + c_1)(2\sigma_{xy} + c_2)}{(\mu_x^2 + \mu_y^2 + c_1)(\sigma_x^2 + \sigma_y^2 + c_2)} \quad (1)$$

The μ_x and μ_y represent the averages of x and y, respectively. The σ_x^2 and σ_y^2 represent the variances of x and y, respectively. $c_1 = (k_1 L)^2$ and $c_2 = (k_2 L)^2$ represent the variables to stabilize the division with weak denominator where L is the dynamic range of the pixel-values and is typically set to $L = 2^{\#bits\_per\_pixel} - 1$

Table 1. The SSIM of eighteen sample domains

Group no	Group name	Domain#	Brand domain	SSIM
Group 1	Homographs with SSIM ≥ 0.999	#3	`amazon.com`	1.000
		#4	`google.com`	1.000
		#10	`booking.com`	0.999
		#15	`paypal.com`	1.000
Group 2	Homographs with SSIM < 0.999	#1	`amazon.com`	0.994
		#6	`google.com`	0.838
		#7	`coinbase.com`	0.996
		#9	`wikipedia.org`	0.994
		#12	`expedia.com`	0.995
		#14	`paypal.com`	0.993
		#17	`facebook.com`	0.845
Group 3	Non-homographs	#2	`amazon.com`	0.865
		#5	`google.com`	0.950
		#8	`wikipedia.org`	0.853
		#11	`booking.com`	0.780
		#13	`expedia.com`	0.950
		#16	`sex.com`	1.000
		#18	`facebook.com`	0.667

and $k_1 = 0.01$, $k_2 = 0.03$ by default. SSIM values $[-1, 1]$ where 1 indicates perfect similarity.

Using the SSIM, the eighteen sample domains are categorized into three groups:

- *Group 1: Homographs with SSIM ≥ 0.999.* This group consists of four homographs including the domains #3, #4, #10 and #15 in Fig. 1. The domains #3, #4 and #15 have SSIM = 1 which means they look completely the same as the brand domains. The domain #10 has SSIM = 0.999 because the look-alike letter 'g' is very difficult to be recognized.
- *Group 2: Homographs with SSIM < 0.999.* This group consists of seven homographs including domains #1, #6, #7, #9, #12, #14, and #17 in Fig. 1. This group considers the homographs whose SSIM scores are lower than those in Group 1, but not so low, i.e., ranging from 0.838 to 0.996. Other homographs with lower SSIM are not considered since it may be trivial to be recognized by the participants.
- *Group 3: Non-homographs.* This group consists of seven non-homographs including the domains #2, #5, #8, #11, #13, #16, and #18 in Fig. 1. The domains #2, #5, #8, #11, #13, and #18 are safe domains that are registered by the brand themselves for different services but have less popularity than the main brand domains. For instance, the domain #2 `amazonaws.com` (Amazon

Web Services (AWS)) is a cloud computing service of Amazon. Many people may be confused with the main service of Amazon which is the selling service amazon.com. The domain #16 sex.com is chosen since we want to know how participants balance their decisions between a domain that is famous and actually safe with a domain that is notorious for its content category (e.g., pornographic, darknet, terrorism).

For each group, the domain numbers, the brand domains, and the corresponding SSIMs are summarized in Table 1.

4.2 Lucky Answers and Neutral Answers

The survey is designed so that for each of the eighteen sample domains, the participants not only answer whether the domain is a homograph but also describe the reasons for their decision. A lucky answer is an answer that has a correct decision but inappropriate reason. A neutral answer is an answer that has a correct decision but unclear reason. For instance, a participant who decides goole.co.jp as a homograph and answers a correct reason such as *"the letter g is missing"* is not considered as a lucky answer. A participant who decides goole.co.jp as a homograph and answers an incorrect reason such as *"Google only has .co.jp as a top-level domain, and thus google.com is unsafe"* is considered as a lucky answer. A participant who decides goole.co.jp as a homograph and answers an unclear reason such as *"I have a feeling that"* is considered as a neutral answer.

The lucky answers are excluded from the dataset since they are completely data outliers. For the neutral answers, we cannot just flip the decision from *true* to *false* because there is a well-known finding from researchers showing that very often, human experts cannot explain why they make a choice that they do, but they are correct far more often than non-experts. Ericsson et al. [34] first found this studying chess experts, and the finding has been replicated and found many times since then by people such as Gerd Gigerenzer et al. [35] and Gary Klein [36]. This means that it is difficult to classify the neutral answers into data bias or actual correct answers. Therefore, in this paper, we decide to just exclude them from the dataset. It is safe rather than adjusting the participant responses like flipping from *true* to *false*. We manually check each of $2,067 \times 18$ answers from the 2,067 participants for the eighteen sample domains to find the lucky answers and neutral answers and summarize in Table 2. In this table, the incorrect answers (column 3) and the correct answers with appropriate reasons (column 4) are used for the model. For group 3 (non-homograph), we do not need to remove lucky and neutral answers because: if the participants answer correctly (i.e., the domains are non-homograph), there is nothing to do; but if they answer incorrectly (the domains are homograph), with any reason, the participant's decisions are wrong.

Table 2. Lucky answers and neutral answers

Group	Domain #	Incorrect answer	Correct answer	
			Appropriate reason	Lucky and neutral answers
Group 1	#3	1411 (68.26%)	0 (0%)	656 (31.74%)
	#4	1432 (69.28%)	0 (0%)	635 (30.72%)
	#10	755 (36.53%)	4 (0.19%)	1308 (63.28%)
	#15	756 (36.57%)	0 (0%)	1311 (63.43%)
Group 2	#1	495 (23.95%)	470 (22.74%)	1102 (53.31%)
	#6	649 (31.40%)	167 (8.08%)	1251 (60.52%)
	#7	173 (08.37%)	302 (14.61%)	1592 (77.01%)
	#9	354 (17.13%)	296 (14.32%)	1417 (68.55%)
	#12	243 (11.76%)	341 (16.50%)	1483 (71.75%)
	#14	171 (08.27%)	354 (17.13%)	1542 (74.60%)
	#17	229 (11.08%)	471 (22.79%)	1367 (66.13%)
Group 3	#2	1796 (86.89%)	271 (13.11%)	
	#5	1823 (88.20%)	244 (11.80%)	
	#8	1827 (88.39%)	240 (11.61%)	
	#11	1832 (88.63%)	235 (11.37%)	
	#13	1397 (67.59%)	670 (32.41%)	
	#16	1841 (89.07%)	226 (10.93%)	
	#18	1935 (93.61%)	132 (6.39%)	

4.3   Model

Let f denote the model for measuring the participants' ability in distinguishing homographs. f is defined as follows:

$$f \sim \mathsf{Demographics} + \mathsf{WebFamiliarity} + \mathsf{SecBackgrounds} \qquad (2)$$

The explanatory variables related to Demographics consist of gender, age, having a job, whether the participants know only Japanese, the number of specific languages that the participant has studied so far, whether the participant is educated in computer science/computer engineering, whether the participant works in computer science or computer engineering. The explanatory variable related to WebFamiliarity is the usage frequency of the brands. The explanatory variables related to SecBackgrounds are anti-virus installation, security warnings, security behaviors, security knowledge, and security self-confidence.

Target Functions. The incorrect answers and the correct answers with appropriate reasons are extracted for the model. For each group, two experiment plans are performed using two different target functions.

– *Integration*: This plan integrates all the domains in the group using the target function:

$$f_1 = \sum_{d_i} \text{SSIM}(d_i, b_i) \times \text{difficult}(d_i) * \text{decision}(d_i) \tag{3}$$

where $\text{decision}(d_i)$ denotes the decision of the participants in distinguishing whether the domain d_i is a homograph. $\text{SSIM}(d_i, b_i)$ denotes the SSIM between the domain d_i and its corresponding brand domain b_i. $\text{difficulty}(d_i)$ denotes the difficulty of the domain d_i and is defined as $(1 - \frac{c_i}{t})$ in which c_i is the number of participants who give correct decisions for d_i and $t = 2,067$ is the total number of participants. For example, there are 10 participants in which 7 participants answer correctly and thus the difficulty of the question is $1 - \frac{7}{10}$. In this plan, the multiple (linear) regression model is applied one time for all the domains, and then the affecting factors for the integration target functions are extracted.

– *Separation*: This plan applies the multiple (linear) regression model for each domain in the group and finds the affecting factors for each domain. The common affecting factors are then extracted. The target function is defined as follows:

$$f_2 = \text{decision}(d_i) \tag{4}$$

Since each domain is considered separately, $\text{SSIM}(d_i, b_i)$ and $\text{difficult}(d_i)$ are not necessary for the target function. After the factors affecting the target function are determined, the common factors for all the domains are extracted.

The SSIM and the difficulty are not used as variables in the features but used as elements in the target functions because the SSIM and the difficulty are not related to human information but domain information, and the goal in this paper is analyzing the human factors. Furthermore, for each domain, the SSIM and the difficulty are the same for all 2,067 participants. If the SSIM and the difficulty are used as the variables, the regression model always results that the SSIM and the difficulty are the affecting factors with $p \leq 0.05$. It is therefore not meant in finding factors.

Factor Determination. Before showing how the factors affecting the target functions are determined, we briefly describe the preliminary of the (student) *t*-test. A *t*-test [37,38] is commonly used to determine whether the mean of a population significantly differs from a specific value (called the hypothesized mean) or from the mean of another population. In other words, the *t*-test can tell if the differences could happen by chance. For the first step, the *t*-test takes the sample from each set and establishes the problem statement by assuming a null hypothesis that the two means are equal. Then, it calculates certain values and compares them with the standard values to determine if the assumed null hypothesis is accepted or rejected. If the null hypothesis is rejected, it indicates that data readings are strong and are not by chance. In the *t*-test, the *t*-value represents a ratio between the difference between the two groups and the difference within the groups. The larger the t-value, the more difference there is between groups (the more likely it is that the results are repeatable). The smaller the t-value, the more similarity there is between groups. If the t-value is negative, it shows a reversal in the directionality of the effect being studied. However, it has no impact on the significance of the difference between groups of data. Every t-value has a corresponding p-value. A p-value is the probability that the results from the sample data occurred by chance. The p-values vary from 0 to 1. The low p-value is good (it indicates the data did not occur by chance). In most cases, a p-value that is ≤ 0.05 is accepted to mean the data is valid. In this paper, the affecting factors have the following p-values:

- $p \leq 0.001$: *significant factors* that strongly affect the target function, marked as (***) in the experiment result.
- $0.001 < p \leq 0.01$: *semi-significant*, marked as (**) in the experiment result.
- $0.01 < p \leq 0.05$: *normal factor* affecting the target function, marked as (*) in the experiment result.

In the experiment result, we also show 95% confidence interval (CI) which is a range of likely of the unknown population parameter. For the first plan (integration), the common samples which contain only incorrect answers and correct answers with appropriate reasons are inputted in the regression model. The factors are then determined based on the t-test's result. For the second plan (separation), the factors affecting the target function in each domain are determined. The common factors are then extracted. The final factors chosen for this plan is the common factors that affect $\geq \lceil \frac{N}{2} \rceil$ domains where N denotes the number of domains in the group, and $\lceil \frac{N}{2} \rceil$ denotes the upper bound of $\frac{N}{2}$.

4.4   Consistency of Integration and Separation Plans

The best case is when both the plans result in the same set of affecting factors. If the case does not happen, we determine the final affecting factor as follows. Let I and S denote the set of affecting factors found in the integration and separation plan, respectively. Let R denote the set of the affecting factors that we are aiming to find.

- All the common affecting factors of both the plans $I \cap S$ are included in R.
- If there exists a factor $x \in I$ such that $x \notin S$, x is included in R if x is an *significant factor* in the integration plan ($p \leq 0.001$).
- If there exists a factor $x \in S$ such that $x \notin I$, x is included in R if the *significant p-values* ($p \leq 0.001$) are dominant in S (i.e., the significant p-values belong to more than $\frac{|S|}{2}$ domains where $|S|$ denotes the number of factors in S).

The consistency of both the plans is the final result used for the conclusion; however, the factors found in each plan still gives a lot of important information and we cannot omit their details.

5   Experiment

The program is written in Python 3.7.4 on a computer MacBook Pro 2.8 GHz Intel Core i7, RAM 16 GB. The multiple (linear) regression model is executed using *scikit-learn* package version 0.21. The *t*-test is computed using *statsmodels* package version 0.10. The SSIM is computed using the *skimage* package version 0.15.dev0.

5.1   Participant Population

Before performing the model, we check if the participant sampling process is valid. First, we analyze whether the participant demographics of gender and age statistically match those of an actual data (e.g., data from government census). Second, we show that the distribution of the age (continuous values) is a normal distribution (Gaussian distribution) (for the gender, the data is binary not continuous values and thus, there is no need for normal distribution test).

Table 3. Participant sampling

Age range	Male	Female
Under 20	52	86
20–29	244	210
30–39	148	148
40–49	148	148
50–59	148	148
60–69	171	236
Over 70	123	57

(a) Age Ranges and Gender

Gender	Male	1034 (50.02%)
	Female	1033 (49.98%)
	Actual male %	50% [39]
Age	Average	44.81
	Median	45
	Min	15
	Max	70
	Actual median	35 to 44 [39]

(b) Matching Actual Statistics

As mentioned in Sect. 3, the 2067 participants are chosen from Internet users in Japan. We match them with a report of the population census from Japanese Internet users [39]. Table 3 describes the age and gender of our samples. Table 3a describes the distribution of gender with different age ranges. Table 3b shows the actual percentage of men within the population of Internet users, and the range in which the actual median age of Internet users lies. The normal distribution test is given in Fig. 2. The bell curve and the skewness (0.005) that is very close to 0 show that the data is valid for a normal distribution.

5.2   Cronbach's Alpha (α) Measurement

We use the Cronbach's α [40,41] to measure the internal consistency (IC) or the reliability of the questions that have multiple Likert-scale sub-questions.

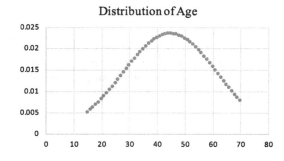

Distribution of Age

Metric	Value
Mean	44.812
Standard Error	0.375
Median	45.000
Standard Deviation	17.072
Sample Variance	291.439
Kurtosis	-1.361
Skewness	0.005
Range	55.000
Confidence Level (95.0 %)	0.736
Count	2067.000

Fig. 2. Distribution curve and distribution summary of the age

Suppose that we measure a quantity which is a sum of K components: $X = Y_1 + Y_2 + \cdots + Y_K$. The Cronbach's α is defined as follows:

$$\alpha = \frac{K}{K-1}(1 - \frac{\sum_{i=1}^{K} \sigma_{Y_i}^2}{\sigma_X^2}), \tag{5}$$

where σ_X^2 denotes the variance of the observed total test scores, and $\sigma_{Y_i}^2$ denotes the variance of the component i for the current sample of persons. We then use the rule of thumb for interpreting α as follows:

- $\alpha \geq 0.9$: *Excellent* IC
- $0.9 > \alpha \geq 0.8$: *Good* IC
- $0.8 > \alpha \geq 0.7$: *Acceptable* IC
- $0.7 > \alpha \geq 0.6$: *Questionable* IC
- $0.6 > \alpha \geq 0.5$: *Poor* IC
- $0.5 > \alpha$: *Unacceptable* IC

In our survey, five questions consist of multiple sub-questions. Three of them include brand familiarity (4-point Likert-scale), security behavior (5-point Likert-scale), and security self-confidence (5-point Likert-scale). For the security knowledge (that contains eighteen binary sub-questions) and the user decision on distinguishing eighteen domains (that contains also eighteen binary sub-questions), we consider them as 2-point Liker-Scale questions. The result of Cronbach's α is showed in Table 4. The internal consistency of all the questions is better than or equal to *acceptable*. This indicates that our survey is reliable.

5.3 Result for Group 1

When distributing the survey to the participants, we hypothezied that nobody can distinguish the homographs because the visual similarity is almost 100%. However, the actual data surprisingly contains a large number of correct answers (over 30% for domain #3 and #4, and even over 60% for domain #10 and #15). Fortunately, the analysis of lucky and neutral answers given in Table 2 indicates

Table 4. Cronbach's α results for Likert-scale questions

Question	No. of sub-questions (K)	Sum of item variances $(\sum_{i=1}^{K} \sigma_{Y_i}^2)$	Variance of total scores (σ_X^2)	Cronbach's α	IC
Brand familiarity	9	4.446	12.167	0.713	Acceptable
Security behavior	16	27.203	163.219	0.889	Good
Security confidence	6	5.699	25.920	0.936	Excellent
Security knowledge	18	3.038	10.109	0.741	Acceptable
Homograph decision	18	2.585	16.095	0.889	Good

that there is no correct answer with appropriate reasons in the case of domains #3, #4 and #15 which have 100% of SSIM, and only 0.19% of correct answers with appropriate reasons in the case of domains #10 which has 99.9% of SSIM. We now can confirm that there is no way for the participants to distinguish such extremely high-SSIM homographs. This raises the seriousness of homograph attacks. For this group, we only did the statistics without the need to apply the regression model.

5.4   Result for Group 2

In the first experiment plan (integration), each domain in this group has a different set of incorrect answers and correct answers with appropriate reasons. Finally, 146 common samples (out of 2067 samples) are filtered. The regression model with the target function f_1 given in Eq. 3 is applied and the result is showed in Table 5. Remind that, (*) represents $0.01 < p \leq 0.05$, (**) represents $0.001 < p \leq 0.01$, and (***) represents $p \leq 0.001$. There are four affecting factors found including:

- Have a job: *normal factor*, the positive coefficient (0.1425) indicates that people who have a job tend to have the ability of homograph recognition.
- Know only Japanese: *semi-significant factor*, the negative coefficient (−0.2636) indicates that people who do not only know the Japanese have the ability of homograph recognition.
- Frequently use the brands: *semi-significant factor*, the positive coefficient (0.0322) indicates that people who are more familiar with the brands have the ability of homograph recognition.
- Have better security knowledge: *significant factor*, the positive coefficient (0.0624) indicates that people who have better security knowledge have the ability of homograph recognition.

For the second experiment plan (separation), the regression model with the target function f_2 given in Eq. 4 is applied on seven different sets of the incorrect answers and correct answers for appropriate reasons of the seven domains in this group. The factors affecting f_2 are found for each domain. The common factors are then extracted. The number of samples in each domain is respectively 965 (#1), 816 (#6), 475 (#7), 650 (#9), 584 (#12), 525 (#14), and 700 (#18).

The result is shown in the last seven columns of Table 5. In this table, only the p-values of the affecting factors are described so that the common factors can be easily observed. (+) represents the positive coefficients. (−) represents the negative coefficients. The factors chosen for this plan is the common factors that affect more than or equal to $\lceil N/2 \rceil = 4$ domains including:

- Sex (male): affecting 6/7 domains, is a *significant factor* of 5 domains (#1, #9, #12, #14, #17) and a *normal factor* of #7. All the coefficients are negative, this indicates that the females tend to recognize homographs better than the males.
- Have a job: affecting 5/7 domains, is a *significant factor* of #9, #17 and a *normal factor* of #7, #12 and #14. All the coefficients are positive; this indicates that the people who have a job tend to be able to recognize the homographs.
- Still browsing the website even if there is a warning from an anti-virus software: affecting 4/7 domains, is a *semi-significant factor* of #1 and a *normal factor* of #12, #14, and #17. All the coefficients are negative; this indicates that people who do not browse the website when there is a warning tend to be able to distinguish the homographs.
- Have more security knowledge: affecting 7/7 domains, is a *significant factor* and has positive coefficients for all the domains. This indicates that the people who have better security knowledge tend to be able to distinguish the homographs.

Consistency. The results of the plans are not the same, so we perform the result consistency as indicated in Sect. 4.4. The final set we are aiming to find (filled with gray color in Table 5) consists of the following affecting factors:

- Sex (female) since all the coefficients are negative for males in the separation plan.
- People who have a job: this is the common factor of both the plans.
- More security knowledge: this is also the common factor of both the plans.

5.5   Result for Group 3

In this group, as explained in Sect. 4.2, the lucky and neutral answers are not necessary to be excluded from the dataset. For the both experiment plans (integration and separation), the regression model is applied on all 2067 samples using the target function f_1 (Eq. 3) in the case of integration and f_2 (Eq. 4) in the case of separation. The results are showed in Table 6.

For the first experiment plan (integration), there are seven affecting factors found including:

- Sex (male): *normal factor*, the positive coefficient (0.1354) indicates that the males tend to be able to distinguish the non-homographs.

Table 5. Experiment result of Group 2 (Homograph with SSIM < 0.999)

No.	Factors	Integration			Separation						
		Coef.	p	95%CI	#1	#6	#7	#9	#12	#14	#17
	Number of Samples	146			965	816	475	650	584	525	700
	(Intercept)	-0.6607	0.007	[-1.134, -0.187]							
1	Sex (male)	-0.0705	0.261	[-0.194, 0.053]	<0.001 (−)***		0.032 (−)*	0.001 (−)***	<0.001 (−)***	<0.001 (−)***	0.001 (−)***
2	Age (older)	-0.0022	0.251	[-0.006, 0.002]					<0.001 (−)***	0.001 (−)***	<0.001 (−)***
3	Have a job	0.1425	0.036 *	[0.009, 0.276]			0.016 (+)*	<0.001 (+)***	0.015 (+)*	0.043 (+)*	<0.001 (+)***
4	Know only Japanese	-0.2636	0.006 **	[-0.451, -0.077]					0.015 (−)*	<0.001 (−)***	0.007 (−)**
5	Number of languages	0.0262	0.519	[-0.054, 0.106]							
6	Install anti-virus	-0.0920	0.189	[-0.230, 0.046]							
7	Browse even warning	-0.0295	0.648	[-0.157, 0.098]	0.010 (−)**				0.018 (−)*	0.042 (−)*	0.044 (−)*
8	Frequently use brands	0.0322	0.004 **	[0.010, 0.054]	0.001 (+)***			0.010 (−)**			
9	Education in CS/CE	-0.0316	0.820	[-0.306, 0.243]							
10	Work in CS/CE	-0.1940	0.093	[-0.421, 0.033]							
11	More sec. behavior	0.0009	0.753	[-0.005, 0.007]	0.043 (+)*						
12	More sec. knowledge	0.0624	<0.001 ***	[0.041, 0.084]	<0.001 (+)***	<0.001 (+)***	<0.001 (+)***	<0.001 (+)***	<0.001 (+)***	<0.001 (+)***	<0.001 (+)***
13	More sec. confidence	-0.0007	0.930	[-0.015, 0.014]							

'*': $0.01 < p \le 0.05$, '**': $0.001 < p \le 0.01$, '***': $p \le 0.001$
(+): coefficient > 0, (−): coefficient < 0

- Age (older): *semi-significant factor*, the negative factor (−0.0052) indicates that the young people tend to be able to distinguish the non-homographs.
- Have a job: *significant factor*, the negative factor (−0.2104) indicates that the people who do not have a job tend to be able to distinguish the non-homographs.
- Browsing the website even if there is a warning from an anti-virus software: *semi-significant factor*, the positive coefficient (0.1484 > 0) indicates that the people who still browse the website even if there is a warning tend to be able to distinguish the non-homographs.
- Education in CS/CE: *normal factor*, the positive coefficient (0.3072) indicates that the people who are educated in computer science or computer engineering tend to be able to distinguish the non-homographs.
- Work in CS/CE: *normal factor*, the positive coefficient (0.2861) indicates that the people who work in computer science or computer engineering tend to be able to distinguish the non-homographs.
- Have better security knowledge: *significant factor*, the negative coefficient (−0.0551) indicates that people who have less security knowledge have better ability in distinguishing the non-homographs.

For the second experiment plan (separation), since this group also has seven domains as the group 2, the factors chosen for this plan are the common factors that affect more than or equal to 4 domains.

- Sex (male): affecting 4/7 domains, *significant factor* of #2, *semi-significant factor* of #8, *normal factor* of #5 and #18. All the coefficients are positive; this indicates that the males tend to be able to distinguish the non-homographs.
- Age (older): affecting 4/7 domains, *significant factor* of #11 and #13, *semi-significant factor* of #8 and #16. All the coefficients are negative; this indicates that the young people tend to be able to distinguish the non-homographs.
- Have a job: affecting 6/7 domains, *semi-significant factor* of #8, #13, and #16, *normal factor* of #2, #11, and #18. All the coefficients are negative; this indicates that the people who do not have a job tend to be able to distinguish the non-homographs.
- Have better security knowledge: affecting 5/7 domains, is a *significant factor* and has negative coefficients for all the domains. This indicates that the people who have less security knowledge tend to be able to distinguish the non-homographs.

Table 6. Experiment result of Group 3 (Non-homograph)

No.	Factors	Integration			Separation						
		Coef.	p	95%CI	#2	#5	#8	#11	#13	#16	#18
	No. of Samples				2067						
	(Intercept)	1.3626	<0.001	[0.934, 1.791]							
1	Sex (male)	0.1354	0.012 *	[0.029, 0.241]	<0.001 (+)***	0.019 (+)*	0.004 (+)**				0.011 (+)*
2	Age (older)	-0.0052	0.002 **	[-0.008, -0.002]			0.002 (−)**	<0.001 (−)***	<0.001 (−)***	0.003 (−)**	
3	Have a job	-0.2104	<0.001 ***	[-0.326, -0.095]	0.011 (−)*		0.007 (−)**	0.020 (−)*	0.009 (−)**	0.007 (−)**	0.027 (−)*
4	Know only Japanese	0.0931	0.258	[-0.068, 0.254]				0.014 (+)*			
5	Number of languages	0.0087	0.830	[-0.071, 0.088]							
6	Install anti-virus	-0.0796	0.211	[-0.204, 0.045]							0.043 (−)*
7	Browse even warning	0.1484	0.009 **	[0.037, 0.259]			0.001 (+)***		0.040 (+)*		
8	Frequently use brands	0.0149	0.138	[-0.005, 0.035]					<0.001 (+)***		
9	Education in CS/CE	0.3072	0.035 *	[0.021, 0.593]	0.016 (+)*						
10	Work in CS/CE	0.2861	0.018 *	[0.049, 0.523]	0.002 (+)**						0.010 (+)**
11	More sec. behavior	-0.0020	0.412	[-0.007, 0.003]							
12	More sec. knowledge	-0.0551	<0.001 ***	[-0.075, -0.035]	<0.001 (−)***	<0.001 (−)***	<0.001 (−)***	0.001 (−)***			<0.001 (−)***
13	More sec. confidence	0.0060	0.322	[-0.006, 0.018]							0.049 (+)*

'*': $0.01 < p \leq 0.05$, '**': $0.001 < p \leq 0.01$, '***': $p \leq 0.001$

(+): coefficient > 0, (−): coefficient < 0

Consistency. Similar to the group 2, the results of the plans in this group are also not the same, so we perform the result consistency as indicated in Sect. 4.4. The final set we are aiming to find (filled with the gray color in Table 6) consists of the following affecting factors. Fortunately, all the factors are the common factors of both the plans.

- Sex (male): since all the coefficients are positive for both the plans.
- Young people: since all the coefficients are negative.
- People who do not have a job: since all the coefficients are negative.
- Less security knowledge: since all the coefficients are negative.

6 Discussion

In this section, we discuss how the factors change when the participants are explained about the homographs. We then discuss some several ideas for improving the result and their challenges for future work.

6.1 Before and After Homograph Explanation/Education

The main result is described in Sect. 5. In this section, we perform an extra analysis of how the factors change when the participants are explained about what the homograph attack is. In the survey, after the participants give their decisions to the eighteen domains, a description of the homograph is displayed (Appendix E). The participants then respond to their decision again to the same eighteen domains. To avoid data outlier in the participants' decisions (for ensuring the independency in their decision before and after the homograph explanation), the web interface of the survey is designed so that the participants cannot go back to previous questions before the homograph explanation from the questions that are displayed after the homograph explanation.

In this analysis, we consider the integration plan for all the eighteen domains with all the 2067 participants[3]. Table 7 shows the experiment result. p_{BE} and p_{AF} denotes the p-values before and after the homograph explanation, respectively. $|\triangle p|$ denotes the change's magnitude of p. The fifth and sixth columns are the change of the coefficient signs and the significane, respectively. N/A in the sixth column means that the factor is not an affecting factor (e.g., ** $\rightarrow$ N/A means the variable is a semi-significant factor before the homograph explanation, but after that, it is no longer an affecting factor). The result shows that there are five factors found in both cases of before and after the homograph explanation. The three factors (anti-virus installation, frequently use brands and more security knowledge) are consistent for both the cases. Sex (male) is no longer an affecting factor after the homograph explanation. Interestingly, working in computer science or computer engineering from not an affecting factor becomes an

---

[3] Although there are lucky and neutral answers, they actually happened (these answers are the actual samples in the dataset) and we would want to know how the factors are in this extra analysis.

affecting factor. Furthermore, $|\triangle p| = 0.061$ is highest compared to other affecting factors. This indicates that people who work in computer science or computer engineering are able to capture the situation quickly after being explained about the homographs.

Table 7. Factors change before and after the homograph explanation

Factors	p_{BE}	p_{AF}	$|\triangle p|$	Coefficient sign	Significancy
Sex (male)	0.018	0.339	0.321	$(+) \rightarrow (-)$	** $\rightarrow$ N/A
Install anti-virus	0.001	0.045	0.044	$(-) \rightarrow (-)$	*** $\rightarrow$ *
Frequently use brands	<0.001	<0.001	<0.001	$(-) \rightarrow (-)$	*** $\rightarrow$ ***
Work in CS/CE	0.083	0.022	0.061	$(+) \rightarrow (+)$	N/A $\rightarrow$ *
More security knowledge	<0.001	< 0.001	<0.001	$(-) \rightarrow (-)$	*** $\rightarrow$ ***

6.2   Future Work and Challenges

Related to the survey itself, there are three ideas that can improve the study. First, in this current work, the survey is applied for local participants (i.e., Japanese). If it can be applied for global participants, the responses would be more objective. In this case, there is a challenge in translating the survey across the languages in different countries. The translation should be appropriately considered while preserving its reliability and structure validity. Second, some features which may affect the ability of homograph recognition including how many hours for using the Internet per day, factors related to participant psychology like emotional state, demands and the environment when answering the questionnaire, etc. Third, if the domains are asked to the participants in an actual simulation rather than in a self-report questionnaire, the bias can be reduced and also other information related to participants can be extracted such as the time of accessing domains, the scenario of accessing domains, and the mouse move.

Related to the model, some promising elements can be included in the target functions. The first is the Alexa ranking. Some domains are very famous (e.g., `amazon.com` or `google.com`), and thus the participants are more familiar with them rather than the domains that are less popular (e.g., `coinbase.com`). The Alexa ranking can be considered in a global scope (if the survey is applied to different countries) or in a local scope (if the survey is applied to a country like this work). The second is the order of the domains in the questionnaire. In fact, the participants tend to carefully answer the first few domains but gradually tend to answers the domains randomly; and therefore there is bias in this case. The domain order in the questions should be added as a component in the target function. Furthermore, there can be another bias when the participants answer all domains as homographs because they perhaps think that it has a high probability for the domains to be homographs in such a security survey, or think that false positive is better than false negative when they are not sure. Designing a survey that can eliminate data bias is a challenge in most of human factor research topics.

7   Conclusions

We designed and ran an online study to explore how user demographics, brand familiarity, and security backgrounds affect the ability in recognizing homographs. We collected 2,067 responses to our survey from participants located in Japan and analyzed them using linear regression. Our results shed light on the differences in the ability of homograph recognition for different kinds of homographs. We find that 13.95% of participants can recognize non-homographs while 16.60% of participants can recognize homographs when the visual similarity with the target brand domains is under 99.9%; but when the similarity increases to 99.9%, the number of participants who can recognize homographs significantly drops down to only 0.19%; and for the homographs with 100% of visual similarity, there is no way for the participants to recognize. We also find that for different levels of visual similarity, the participants exhibit different abilities. Female participants tend to recognize homographs while male participants tend to able to recognize non-homographs. Security knowledge is a significant factor affecting both homographs and non-homographs. Surprisingly, people who have strong security knowledge tend to be able to recognize homographs but not non-homographs. Furthermore, an interesting result is that people who work or are educated in computer science or computer engineering is not an affecting factor for the ability in recognizing homograph as hypothesized; however, right after being explained about homograph attack, they are the ones who can capture the situation the most quickly.

For the implication, first, we want to raise the seriousness of the homograph attack. Second, we want to recommend looking into directions beyond user education to promote more ability in homograph recognition, especially aiming at people who are male, who do not have a job, and who have less security knowledge. Third, we want to emphasize that not all the domains that have high visual similarity with the brand domains are the homographs. User education for non-homographs is also necessary and can be aimed at people especially those who are female, elder, have a job and have good security knowledge.

A   Appendix: Security Behavior

The question of security behavior consists of the following sixteen sub-questions:

1. I set my computer screen to automatically lock if I don't use it for a prolonged period of time.
2. I use a password/passcode to unlock my laptop or tablet.
3. I manually lock my computer screen when I step away from it.
4. I use a PIN or passcode to unlock my mobile phone.

5. I change my passwords even if it is not needed.
6. I use different passwords for different accounts that I have.
7. When I create a new online account, I try to use a password that goes beyond the site's minimum.
8. I include special characters in my password even if it's not required. requirements.
9. When someone sends me a link, I open it only after verifying where it goes.
10. I know what website I'm visiting by looking at the URL bar, rather than by the website's look and feel.
11. I verify that information will be sent securely (e.g., SSL, "https://", a lock icon) before I submit it to websites.
12. When browsing websites, I mouseover links to see where they go, before clicking them.
13. If I discover a security problem, I fix or report it rather than assuming somebody else will.
14. When I'm prompted about a software update, I install it right away.
15. I try to make sure that the programs I use are up-to-date.
16. I verify that my anti-virus software has been regularly updating itself.

Answer Options. There are five answer options for each sub-question. The order numbers are also the actual values used in the experiment.

1. Not at all
2. Not much
3. Sometimes
4. Often
5. Always.

B   Appendix: Security Knowledge

The question of security knowledge consists of the following eighteen sub-questions:

1. My Internet provider and location can be disclosed from my IP address.
2. My telephone number can be disclosed from my IP addresses.
3. The web browser information of my device can be disclosed to the operators of websites.
4. Since Wi-Fi networks in coffee shops are secured by the coffee shop owners, I can use them to send sensitive data such as credit card information.
5. Password comprised of random characters are harder for attackers to guess than passwords comprised of common words and phrases.
6. If I receive an email that tells me to change my password, and links me to the web page, I should change my password immediately.
7. My devices are safe from being infected while browsing the web because web browsers only display information.

8. It is impossible to confirm whether secure communication is being used between my device and a website.
9. My information can be stolen if a website that I visit masquerades as a famous website (e.g., amazon.com).
10. I may suffer from monetary loss if a website that I visit masquerades as a famous website.
11. My devices and accounts may be put at risk if I make a typing mistake while entering the address of a website.
12. My IP address is secret and it is unsafe to share it with anyone.
13. If my web browser does not show a green lock when I visit a website, then I can deduce that the website it is malicious.
14. It is safe to open links that appear in emails in my inbox.
15. It is safe to open attachments received via email.
16. I use private browsing mode to protect my machine from being infected.
17. It is safe to use anti-virus software downloaded through P2P file sharing services.
18. Machines are safe from infections unless participants actively download malware.

Answer Options. There are two answer options for each sub-question. The order numbers are also the actual values used in the experiment.

1. True (the value used in the experiment: 1)
2. False (the value used in the experiment: 0)

Correct Answers. The correct answers for the eighteen sub-questions are: *true* for sub-questions 1, 3, 5, 9, 10, 11, and *false* for the others.

C   Appendix: Security Self-Confidence

The question of security self-confidence consists of the following six sub-questions:

1. I know about countermeasures for keeping the data on my device from being exploited.
2. I know about countermeasures to protect myself from monetary loss when using the Internet.
3. I know about countermeasures to prevent my IDs or Passwords being stolen.
4. I know about countermeasures to prevent my devices from being compromised.
5. I know about countermeasures to protect me from being deceived by fake web sites.
6. I know about countermeasures to prevent my data from being stolen during web browsing.

Answer Options. There are five answer options for each sub-question. The order numbers are also the actual values used in the experiment.

1. Not at all
2. Not applicable
3. Neither agree nor disagree
4. Applicable
5. Very applicable

D   Appendix: Ability of Homograph Recognition

The question of homograph recognition consists of the following eighteen sub-questions:

1. Domain #1: `xn--mazon-zjc.com` (displayed as the sample 1 in Fig. 1).
2. Domain #2: `amazonaws.com`.
3. Domain #3: `xn--mazon-3ve.com` (displayed as the sample 3 in Fig. 1).
4. Domain #4: `xn--gogle-m29a.com` (displayed as the sample 4 in Fig. 1).
5. Domain #5: `google.com.vn`.
6. Domain #6: `goole.co.jp`.
7. Domain #7: `xn--coinbas-z8a.com` (displayed as the sample 7 in Fig. 1).
8. Domain #8: `wikimedia.org`.
9. Domain #9: `xn--wikipdia-f1a.org` (displayed as the sample 9 in Fig. 1).
10. Domain #10: `xn--bookin-n0c.com` (displayed as the sample 10 in Fig. 1).
11. Domain #11: `jbooking.jp`.
12. Domain #12: `xn--expeda-fwa.com` (displayed as the sample 12 in Fig. 1).
13. Domain #13: `expedia.co.jp`.
14. Domain #14: `xn--paypl-6qa.com` (displayed as the sample 14 in Fig. 1).
15. Domain #15: `xn--pypal-4ve.com` (displayed as the sample 15 in Fig. 1).
16. Domain #16: `sex.com`.
17. Domain #17: `faeceb0ok.com`.
18. Domain #18: `vi-vn.facebook.com`.

Answer Questions. There are two answer options for each sub-question. The order numbers are also the actual values used in the experiment.

1. Homograph (the value used in the experiment: 1)
2. Non-homograph (the value used in the experiment: 0)

Correct Answers. The eighteen domains are displayed respectively in Fig. 1. The correct answers for the eighteen domains are as follows:

- Homograph: the domains #1, #3, #4, #6, #7, #9, #10, #12, #14, #15, #17.
- Non-homographs: the others.

The homographs #1 and #3 target to the brand Amazon. The homographs #4 and #6 target to the brand Google. The homograph #7 targets to the brand Coinbase; the homograph #9 targets to the brand Wikipedia. The homograph #10 targets to the brand Booking. The homograph #12 targets to the brand Expedia. The homographs #14 and #15 target to the brand Paypal. The homograph #17 targets to the brand Facebook.

E   Appendix: Homograph Explanation

The description about the homograph attack is given as follows:

"Homograph attack is a way that the attackers deceive victims about what domain they are communicating with by exploiting the fact that many domains look alike. There are several kinds of homographs in the wild, we thus synthesize them into 5 categories. The first is visual homograph which uses different characters but visually look alike, for example: facebook.com and facebôok.com. The second is semantic homograph which use synonyms or contextual similar words, for example: facebook.com and markzuckerbergsocialnetwork.com. The third is TLD homograph which uses the same main domain names, but different the top-level-domain (TLD), for example: facebook.com and facebook.biz. The fourth is typosquatting which relies on mistakes such as typos made by Internet users when typing the domain names, for example: facebook.com and faceboook.com. The last is the combination of the previous 4 categories. Also, note that the homographs in which certain characters are inserted or replaced (known as bit-squatting) in the brand domains are listed in the fourth type (typosquatting homograph); for instance, travelgoogle.com targeting to google.com".

References

1. Evgeniy, G., Alex, G.: The homograph attack. Commun. ACM **45**(2), 128–129 (2002)
2. Zheng, X.: Phishing with unicode domains (2017). https://www.xudongz.com/blog/2017/idn-phishing/?_ga=2.53371112.1302505681.1542677803-1987638994.1542677803
3. Michael, M.: IDN homograph attack spreading betabot backdoor (2017). https://threatpost.com/idn-homograph-attack-spreading-betabot-backdoor/127839/
4. Graham, C.: Lloydsbank, lloydsbank - researcher highlights the homographic phishing problem (2015). https://www.grahamcluley.com/lloydsbank-homographic-phishing-problem/
5. NTT-Security: IDN Homograph Attacks (2017). https://www.solutionary.com/resource-center/blog/2017/01/idn-homograph-attacks/
6. Baojun, L., et al.: A reexamination of internationalized domain names: the good, the bad and the ugly. In: 48th Annual IEEE/IFIP International Conference on Dependable Systems and Networks (DSN 2018) (2018)
7. Tian, K., Steve, J., Hang, H., Danfeng, Y., Gang, W.: Needle in a haystack: tracking down elite phishing domains in the wild. In: Internet Measurement Conference (IMC 2018), pp. 429–442 (2018)

8. Yuta, S., Daiki, C., Mitsuaki, A., Shigeki, G.: Detecting homograph IDNs using OCR. In: 46th Asia Pacific Advanced Network (APAN) (2018)
9. Pieter, A., Wouter, J., Frank, P., Nick, N.: Seven months' worth of mistakes: a longitudinal study of typosquatting abuse. In: Proceedings of the 22nd Network and Distributed System Security Symposium (NDSS 2015). Internet Society (2015)
10. Thao, T.P., Sawaya, Y., Nguyen, S.H.Q., Yamada, A., Omote, K., Kubota, A.: Hunting brand domain forgery: a scalable classification for homograph attack. In: Dhillon, G., Karlsson, F., Hedström, K., Zúquete, A. (eds.) SEC 2019. IAICT, vol. 562, pp. 3–18. Springer, Cham (2019). https://doi.org/10.1007/978-3-030-22312-0_1
11. Unicode-Inc.: Unicode Security Mechanisms for UTS #39 (2018). http://www.unicode.org/Public/security/11.0.0/confusables.txt
12. Mark, M.: Chrome and firefox phishing attack uses domains identical to known safe sites (2017). https://www.wordfence.com/blog/2017/04/chrome-firefox-unicode-phishing/
13. Apple Inc.: About Safari International Domain Name support (2016). https://support.apple.com/kb/TA22996?locale=en_US
14. Microsoft: Changes to IDN in IE7 to now allow mixing of scripts (2006). https://blogs.msdn.microsoft.com/ie/2006/07/31/changes-to-idn-in-ie7-to-now-allow-mixing-of-scripts/
15. Opera: Advisory: Internationalized domain names (IDN) can be used for spoofing (2007). https://web.archive.org/web/20070219070826/www.opera.com/support/search/view/788/
16. IDN World Report: Internationalised domains show negative growth in 2017 (2017). https://idnworldreport.eu/
17. Marcin, U.: Dnstwist: domain name permutation engine for detecting typo squatting, phishing and corporate espionage (2018). https://github.com/elceef/dnstwist
18. Timo, F.: IDN Homograph Attack (2017). https://github.com/timofurrer/idn-homograph-attack
19. Alisson, M., Vandre, A.: EvilURL: generate unicode evil domains for IDN homograph attack and detect them (2018). https://github.com/UndeadSec/EvilURL
20. Remco, V.: Homographs: brutefind homographs within a font (2017). https://github.com/dutchcoders/homographs
21. Domain Name Generator. https://instantdomainsearch.com/domain/generator/
22. DNPedia, Search Domain Zones. https://dnpedia.com/tlds/search.php
23. Adrian, C.: Homoglyph Attack Generator. http://www.irongeek.com/homoglyph-attack-generator.php
24. Timothy, K., Mary, J.A., Bennett, B.: Statistical models for predicting threat detection from human behavior. Front Psychol. 9, 466 (2018). https://doi.org/10.3389/fpsyg.2018.00466
25. Yukiko, S., Mahmood, S., Nicolas, C., Ayumu, K., Akihiro, N., Akira, Y.: Self-confidence trumps knowledge: a cross-cultural study of security behavior. In: Conference on Human Factors in Computing Systems, pp. 2202–2214 (2017)
26. Serge, E., Eyal, P.: Scaling the security wall: developing a security behavior intentions scale (SeBIS). In: 33rd Annual ACM Conference on Human Factors in Computing Systems (CHI 2015), pp. 2873–2882 (2015). http://dx.doi.org/10.1145/2702123.2702249
27. Iacovos, K., Angela, S.: Security education against phishing: a modest proposal for a major rethink. IEEE Secur. Priv. 10(2), 24–32 (2012)

28. Mahmood, S., Jumpei, U., Nicolas, C., Ayumu, K., Akira, Y.: Predicting impending exposure to malicious content from user behavior. In: 2018 ACM SIGSAC Conference on Computer and Communications Security (CCS 2018), pp. 1487–1501 (2018)

29. Sauvik, D., Tiffany, H.J.K., Laura, A.D., Jason, I.H.: The effect of social influence on security sensitivity. In: 10th USENIX Conference on Usable Privacy and Security (SOUPS 2014), pp. 143–157 (2014)

30. Erika, C., Adrienne, P.F., Vyas, S., David, W.: Measuring user confidence in smartphone security and privacy. In: Eighth Symposium on Usable Privacy and Security (SOUPS 2012) (2012)

31. Iulia, I., Rob, R., Sunny, C.: No one can hack my mind: comparing expert and non-expert security practices. In: 11th USENIX Conference on Usable Privacy and Security (SOUPS 2015), pp. 327–346 (2015)

32. Adrienne, P.F., Elizabeth, H., Serge, E.: Android permissions: user attention, comprehension, and behavior. In: Eighth Symposium on Usable Privacy and Security (SOUPS 2012) (2012)

33. Zhou, W., Alan, C.B., Hamid, R.S., Eero, S.: Image quality assessment: from error visibility to structural similarity. IEEE Trans. Image Process. **13**(4), 600–612 (2004)

34. Ericsson, K.A., Prietula, M.J., Cokely, E.T.: The making of an expert. Harv. Bus. Rev. **85**(7–8), 114–21 (2007)

35. Gigerenzer, G., Gaissmaier, W.: Heuristic decision making. Annu. Rev. Psychol. **62**(1), 451–482 (2011)

36. Klein, G.: A naturalistic decision making perspective on studying intuitive decision making. J. Appl. Res. Mem. Cogn. **4**(3), 164–168 (2015)

37. Richard, M.: The Story of Mathematics. Princeton University Press, Princeton (2004). ISBN 9780691120461

38. Derrick, B., Toher, D., White, P.: How to compare the means of two samples that include paired observations and independent observations: a companion to Derrick, Russ, Toher and White. Quant. Methods Psychol. **13**(2), 120–126 (2017). https://doi.org/10.20982/tqmp.13.2.p120

39. ComScore: The Japan Digital Audience Report in 2015 (2016). https://www.comscore.com/layout/set/popup/Request/Presentations/015/2015-Japan-Digital-Audience-Report?req=slides&pre=2015+Japan+Digital+Audience+Report

40. Cronbach, L.J.: Coefficient alpha and the internal structure of tests. Psychometrika **16**(3), 297–334 (1951)

41. Jerry, J.V., Beaman, J., Sponarski, C.: Rethinking internal consistency in Cronbach's alpha. Leis. Sci. **39**(2), 163–173 (2016)

Publicly Evaluatable Perceptual Hashing

Rosario Gennaro$^{(\boxtimes)}$, David Hadaller, Tahereh Jafarikhah, Zhuobang Liu,
William E. Skeith, and Anastasiia Timashova

Center for Algorithms and Interactive Scientific Software,
The City College of New York, New York, USA
{rosario,wes}@ccny.cuny.edu, dahadaller@gmail.com, jafarikhah@gmail.com,
zliu001@citymail.cuny.edu, anastimashova@gmail.com

Abstract. Perceptual hashing allows the computation of a robust fingerprint of media files, such that the fingerprint can be used to detect the same object even if it has been modified in perceptually non-significant ways (e.g., compression). The robustness of such functions relies on the use of secret keys both during the computation and the detection phase. We present examples of *publicly evaluatable* perceptual hash functions which allow a user to compute the perceptual hash of an image using a public key, while only the detection algorithm will use the secret key. Our technique can be used to encourage users to submit intimate images to blacklist databases to stop those images from ever being posted online – indeed using a publicly evaluatable perceptual hash function the user can privately submit the fingerprint, without ever revealing the image.

We present formal definitions for the security of perceptual hash, a general theoretical result that uses Fully Homomorphic Encryption, and a specific construction using Paillier's encryption. For the latter we show via extensive implementation tests that the cryptographic overhead can be made minimal, resulting in a very efficient construction.

Keywords: Perceptual hash · Homomorphic encryption · Social media abuse

1 Introduction

1.1 Background and Motivation

Many social media platforms have policies against uploading explicit images of anyone without their consent and will take down such images upon an affected user's request. However, substantial harm may have already occurred by the time a victim finds out that such an image is online. Ideally, these platforms would prevent such images from being uploaded from the beginning, and indeed, efforts in this direction are already underway. This task, however, is a technically challenging one: images (and other types of multimedia files) can be processed and

Supported by Facebook through a 2018 Secure the Internet Award.

manipulated so that while their semantic meaning remains the same (perceptually the images are still the same), their digital representations in bits are entirely different. Therefore, it is challenging to build a blacklist of images using traditional forms of hashing (such as cryptographic collision-resistant hashing) as perceptually similar images will almost certainly produce a completely different hash.

To address the problems outlined above, the concept of *perceptual hashing* has been developed (see e.g., [14, 16]). Perceptual hashing (PH) produces a fingerprint of an image with the property that "similar" images (i.e., perceived as similar by human vision) will produce "similar" fingerprints (i.e., bit-strings which are close under some metric). A sufficiently robust PH will detect if two different files represent perceptually the same image, even in the presence of a malicious user who is attempting to modify the original image in a way to remain perceptually similar, while producing a substantially different PH value.

As one might imagine given the multitude of ways available to modify an image without substantially affecting what the image depicts, it is a difficult task to design a robust PH algorithm, and such algorithms are often carefully guarded to prevent analysis by malicious parties. Not only is the source code for such algorithms kept secret, but also *the input/output behavior* is not made available to the public. For example, Microsoft's *PhotoDNA* [1] algorithm is only available *as an online service*, and furthermore, only specific organizations they deem qualified may access it.

The secrecy of the PH algorithm is not only worrisome from a security point of view (as security by obscurity is never a good design principle) but also raises a very important privacy concern. If users are aware that an explicit image of theirs is in another's possession and want to prevent such an image from being posted, they have to provide the image to the social media platform, so that a PH can be evaluated on it and added to the blacklist. This is, of course, problematic for users who are reluctant (if not outright unwilling) to share such images.

THE FACEBOOK PILOT PROGRAM. In 2017 Facebook developed a pilot program in Australia to combat the diffusion of so-called *Non-Consensual Intimate Images (NCII)* (also inappropriately termed *revenge porn* in the press). In this pilot program, Facebook asked users to voluntarily submit intimate images that they were afraid could be posted on the site by former sexual partners. Facebook would compute a perceptual hash (specifically PhotoDNA) on the image, and add the resulting fingerprint to a blacklist database.

Facebook made it very clear that the NCIIs submitted by users would be used exclusively to compute a PH on them and then would be immediately removed from their servers. The blacklist database would then be used to block future posting of that image, no matter how manipulated, compressed, cropped, etc.

The program was broadly covered even by the popular press (see e.g., [13]). In spite of Facebook's extensive guarantees, the coverage was not always in positive terms. Much of the criticism focused on the need by users to *trust* Facebook with their intimate images. Given Facebook's overall (and often dubious) track record on privacy, the criticism could be seen as well-founded. Apart from intentional misuse of the data (e.g., Facebook using the images for other purposes like training algorithms), even a benign bug in the code could expose data that users had entrusted to the platform *specifically to protect it from exposure* (see [3] for a very cogent discussion on what could possibly go wrong with this approach).

The question raised from many corners was, "why must the users send the NCII to Facebook, instead of just computing and submitting the hashes themselves?" The answer lies precisely on the need to keep the PH algorithm secret.

THE RESEARCH QUESTION. The Facebook pilot program exposed one of the main weaknesses of known PH algorithms: in order to be robust, they have to be secret. An adversary, given a particular image and knowledge of how the algorithm operates, can devise a modified image which looks perceptually similar to the original one and yet maps to a sufficiently far fingerprint. The natural question we therefore asked is whether or not it is possible to have robust and publicly evaluatable perceptual hash functions. Such functions would allow users to register sensitive images into the blacklist without revealing the actual image, but rather just a non-sensitive fingerprint of it.

1.2   Our Contribution

We answer the above question in the affirmative for the case of PH functions that are *keyed* with a secret key, i.e., PH functions for which the algorithm is public, but it requires the use of a secret random key to achieve robustness. For such PH functions, it is possible to construct a cryptographic *public key* version of it that can be evaluated by the user. We show that such public key constructions can be achieved with only modest computational overhead, as exemplified by our extensive implementation test of one such candidate function. More specifically, our contributions can be summarized as follows:

- We introduce formal definitions for perceptual hashing for both the secret and public key versions. As far as we know, this is the first formalization of the concept, and it lays the theoretical foundations on which we analyze the security of our proposed scheme.
- We then present a theoretical result showing that any secret-key PH algorithm can be transformed into a public key one via the use of *Fully Homomorphic Encryption (FHE)* [8]. While the intuition is fairly simple, the full details of the proof of security reveal several interesting technical complications which we resolve via the use of *Zero-Knowledge Proofs* [10].
- We show that for a specific candidate PH function [14], the full power of FHE is not needed and we can instead use any additively homomorphic encryption such as Paillier's [12]. For this particular scheme, we present an optimized (using vectorization) implementation that shows the computational overhead of adding encryption to PH is minimal, resulting in an efficient scheme.

OVERVIEW OF OUR RESULTS. We first present game-based definitions of security for a PH algorithm. The idea is to formally define what the algorithms are (key generation, hash computation, and hash detection) and then parametrize security according to a *similarity* function that determines if two images are perceptually similar or not. We then define the capabilities of the adversary – we allow the adversary to make:

- *Registration Queries* where the adversary submits images to the database at will (in the secret key case by submitting the actual image, and in the public key case by computing and sending the tag)
- *Detection Queries* where the adversary submits images to see if the server detects them as similar to any of the images registered earlier.

The adversary succeeds if it finds two pictures which are perceptually similar (according to the parametrized similarity function) and yet are not detected as such by the PH algorithm. Details appear in Sects. 3.1 and 3.2.

With formal definitions for security in place, we start from the assumption that secure secret-key PH functions exist (e.g., PhotoDNA, or other schemes in the literature which specifically fit the public algorithm/secret key framework [6,14,16]). The basic intuition to construct a public-key version is fairly simple: the server (e.g., the owner of the secret key) publishes an encryption of the secret key under an FHE key. This allows any user to evaluate an encrypted form of the PH fingerprint over a private image and send that to the server. The server then decrypts it and stores. Later, when an image is submitted to the server, the latter can compute the PH and use it for detection.

This basic idea, however, is not sufficient by itself to formally prove security. If we want to prove that the public key version of PH we construct is as secure as the private key one we started with, we need to show a *reduction* from an adversary breaking the public key version to one breaking the secret key one. However, a technical problem arises when the adversary makes *Detection Queries* as it is not immediately clear how we can answer those in the reduction (since we do not know the secret key we are trying to break). We solved this problem by adding a *Zero-Knowledge Proof of Knowledge* of the image submitted during a Registration Query which allows the reduction to build a blacklist database on the secret key server, and to correctly answer Detection Queries, without knowledge of the actual secret key. Details appear in Sect. 3.3.

The above approach works for any PH algorithm, though it is admittedly not feasible in practice due to the high computational cost of implementing FHE. Our next step was to look at concrete PH candidates to see if we can gain better efficiency. We restricted our attention to non-proprietary algorithms which have been published in academic venues and we specifically focused on [14]. For this function, we realized that it is possible to use additively homomorphic encryption such as Paillier's [12], and we show that the result is highly feasible through a complete implementation of a publicly evaluatable version of the scheme in [14]. Details appear in Sects. 4 and 5.

2   Technical Preliminaries

In this section we recall the cryptographic primitives that we are going to need later on.

2.1   Public Key Encryption

A public-key encryption system Π consists of three algorithms (KGen, Enc, Dec), where KGen is a key generation (randomized) algorithm that takes a security parameter 1^n and outputs a public-secret key pair (PK, SK); Enc(PK, m) is the encryption (randomized) algorithm that on an input message m and the public key PK outputs a ciphertext c; and Dec(SK, c) decrypts ciphertext c with secret key SK. Obviously if $(PK, SK) \leftarrow_{\$} \text{KGen}(1^n)$ and $c \leftarrow \text{Enc}(PK, m)$ then $m = \text{Dec}(SK, c)$.

Semantic Security [9] says that no polynomial time adversary can distinguish between the encryption of two messages of its choice. For all PPT $\mathcal{A}$

$$Pr[b' = b : (PK, SK) \leftarrow_{\$} \text{KGen}(1^n), (m_0, m_1) \leftarrow \mathcal{A}(PK),$$

$$b \leftarrow \{0, 1\}, b' \leftarrow \mathcal{A}^{\mathcal{O}_b}(PK)] \leq \frac{1}{2} + \nu(n)$$

where oracle $\mathcal{O}_b$ takes no input and outputs $c \leftarrow \text{Enc}(PK, m_b)$, and $\nu(n)$ is a negligible function.

2.2   Fully Homomorphic Encryption

At a high level, a fully homomorphic encryption (FHE) scheme [8] is an encryption scheme that allows the computation of arbitrary functions over encrypted inputs. More specifically given ciphertexts that encrypt $\pi_1, \ldots, \pi_t$, fully homomorphic encryption should allow anyone (not just the key-holder) to output a ciphertext that encrypts $f(\pi_1, \ldots, \pi_t)$ for any desired function f, as long as the function can be efficiently computed. No information about $\pi_1, \ldots, \pi_t$, or any other intermediate plaintext value should leak; the input, output, and intermediate values are always encrypted. Formally, a public key encryption scheme $\mathcal{E} = [\text{KGen}_{\mathcal{E}}, \text{Enc}_{\mathcal{E}}, \text{Dec}_{\mathcal{E}}]$, is fully homomorphic if there is an additional algorithm Eval$_{\mathcal{E}}$ that takes as input the public key PK, a circuit C from a permitted set $C_{\mathcal{E}}$ of circuits, and a tuple of ciphertexts $\Psi = <\psi_1, \ldots, \psi_t>$; it outputs a ciphertext ψ. The computational complexity of Eval$_{\mathcal{E}}$ must be polynomial in security parameter 1^n and the size of C. The minimal requirement is correctness. $\mathcal{E}$ is correct for circuits in $C_{\mathcal{E}}$ if, for any key-pair (SK, PK) output by KGen$_{\mathcal{E}}(1^n)$, any circuit $C \in C_{\mathcal{E}}$, any plaintexts $\pi_1, ..., \pi_t$, and any ciphertexts $\Psi = <\psi_1, \ldots, \psi_t>$ with $\psi_i \leftarrow \text{Enc}_{\mathcal{E}}(PK, \pi_i)$, it is the case that:

$$\psi \leftarrow \text{Eval}_{\mathcal{E}}(PK, C, \Psi) \Rightarrow C(\pi_1, \ldots, \pi_t) = \text{Dec}_{\mathcal{E}}(SK, \psi)$$

2.3   Paillier Encryption

An encryption scheme is said additively homomorphic if it allows computation of affine functions over encrypted inputs. Examples include [9], where the plaintext values are elements of $\mathbb{Z}_2$, Paillier [12], with plaintext set $\mathbb{Z}_N$ for an RSA modulus N, and the generalizations by Damgård and Jurik [5,11] which work over $\mathbb{Z}_{N^s}$ for any positive integer s. As Paillier is most appropriate for our implementation, we describe briefly below.

Let N be an RSA modulus, i.e. $N = pq$ where p, q are primes. A number z is said to be an N-th residue modulo N^2 if there exists a number $y \in \mathbb{Z}_{N^2}^{\times}$ such that $z = y^N \mod N^2$. We assume that there exists no polynomial time distinguisher for N-th residues mod N^2. We will refer to this hypothesis as the *Decisional Composite Residuosity Assumption* (DCRA). More formally, we assume that there exists a randomized RSA key generation algorithm KGen_{RSA} that on input a security parameter 1^n selects two n-bit primes. Then we say that the DCRA holds if for all PPT $\mathcal{A}$ there exists a negligible function $\nu(n)$, such that

$$Pr[b' = b : (p, q) \leftarrow \mathsf{KGen}_{RSA}(n), N = pq, b \leftarrow \{0, 1\},$$

$$b' \leftarrow \mathcal{A}^{\mathcal{O}_b}(N)] \leq \frac{1}{2} + \nu(n)$$

where oracle $\mathcal{O}_b$ takes no input, selects y uniformly at random in $\mathbb{Z}_{N^2}^{\times}$ and outputs z such that $z = y$ if $b = 0$, and $z = y^N$ if $b = 1$.

The Paillier encryption scheme [5,11,12], whose security is based on DCRA is defined as follows. The key generation algorithm $\mathsf{KGen}_{Paillier}(1^n)$ picks two n-bit prime numbers p and q such that $N = pq$ satisfies $(N, \varphi(N)) = 1$ (which will hold with high probability for such n), computes $\lambda = \varphi(N) / \gcd(p-1, q-1)$ (the least common multiple of $p - 1$ and $q - 1$) and outputs (PK, SK) for $PK = N$ and $SK = \lambda$. The encryption algorithm for a message $m \in \mathbb{Z}_N$ is defined by

$$\mathsf{Enc}_{Paillier}(PK, m) = (1 + N)^m \cdot r^N \mod N^2$$

and the decryption algorithm for $c < N^2$ is defined by

$$\mathsf{Dec}_{Paillier}(SK, c) = \frac{L(c^\lambda \mod N^2)}{L((1 + N)^\lambda \mod N^2)} \mod N$$

$$\text{where } L(u) = \frac{u - 1}{N}$$

Note that this scheme is additively homomorphic: given only the public-key and $c_i = \mathsf{Enc}_{Paillier}(m_i)$ then

$$c_1 \cdot c_2 \mod N^2 = \mathsf{Enc}_{Paillier}(m_1 + m_2 \mod N).$$

2.4   Proofs of Knowledge

Let $Q(\cdot, \cdot)$ be a polynomial time computable predicate over two inputs. On a public input x a party (usually called the Prover) wants to prove to a Verifier that he knows a "witness" w, i.e., a string such that $Q(x, w) = 1$. He wants to do this without revealing any information about w. The following definition [7,10], captures what we need.

Definition 1. *An interactive protocol* (P, V) *is a* zero-knowledge proof of knowledge *for a relationship* Q *if the following holds:*

- *(Completeness.)* V *running on input* x *accepts when interacting with* P *running on input* x, y *such that* $Q(x, y) = 1$
- *(Soundness.) There exists an efficient program* K, *called knowledge extractor, with the following property. For any* P^* *which makes* V *accept on input* x, *with non-negligible probability,* K *with oracle access to* P^* *will output (with overwhelming probability) a* y *such that* $Q(x, y) = 1$.
- *(Zero-Knowledge) For any PPT verifier* V^* *running on input* x *and any additional auxiliary information* aux *there exists an expected PPT simulator* S *such that* $\forall x \in \mathcal{L}, z \in \{0, 1\}^*$,

$$View_{V^*}[P(x) \leftrightarrow V^*(x, aux)] \approx S(x, aux)$$

The $View$ of the Verifier is defined as the transcript of the interaction with P and the coin tosses used by the Verifier. With $\approx$ we define any of the notions of indistinguishability in [10].

Note that the Soundness condition enforces that we can extract the witness w when using P^* as an oracle (therefore guaranteeing that if P^* convinces V then he must "know" w).

Also the Zero-Knowledge condition guarantees that the interaction is simulatable even without knowing the secret witness w and therefore the verifier (no matter if honest or malicious) learns nothing about w.

3   Perceptual Hashing

3.1   Private-Key Perceptual Hash Definition

Let us recall the typical application scenario for perceptual hashing. The idea is to develop a system where a social media platform (e.g., Facebook) can prevent inappropriate images from being posted. The system is divided in three phases:

- Setup: The platform chooses a secret key for a PH function, and initializes an empty database of forbidden images (the blacklist);
- Image Registration: Users submit images that they do not want posted online. The platform computes a fingerprint on those images via the PH and stores it in the database.
- Image Submission: Users submit images for posting. The platform computes their fingerprint via the PH and blocks them if the fingerprint matches any of the ones stored in the blacklist.

The goal is to prevent an adversary – who has access to the Image Registration and Submission functions – to find two perceptually similar images that will not yield a match via the PH computation.

Our first task therefore is to formally define what a secure secret-key PH function is.

Definition 2. *A private-key perceptual hash scheme* $\mathcal{SPH}$ *consists of three algorithms as follows;*

- *The key generation algorithm* kg *that takes the security parameter* 1^n *and outputs a secret key* k.
- *The keyed perceptual hash function* ph *that takes an image* I *and the secret key* k *and outputs a tag* t.
- *The keyed detection algorithm* det *that takes two tags and the secret key as input and outputs a bit.*

The corresponding Image Registration and Submission procedures are described in Fig. 1.

To clarify the triplet (kg, ph, det) denotes the algorithm that defines a perceptual hash. Image Registration and Image Submission are the procedures by which a client interacts with a server using a perceptual hash.

We define a PH adversary $\mathcal{A}^{DB_k(\cdot)}$ as an efficient program which is allowed to arbitrarily interact with the server using the Image Registration and Submission procedures on a private key k (in other words the adversary has access to the stateful oracle $DB_k(\cdot)$ which it can affect via Image Registration and Submission queries).

Note that $\mathcal{A}$ has no direct access to the secret key k but each time she queries during image registration or submission, she gains partial information about the secret key via the oracle queries to $DB_k(\cdot)$.

Let sim be a predicate defined over pair of images. This function is intended to model "perceptually similar" pictures.

We say that a secret key perceptual hash scheme $\mathcal{SPH}$ is secure with respect to sim if no PH adversary is able to find two images I, I' which are perceptually similar ($\mathsf{sim}(I, I') = 1$) but are not detected as such by $\mathcal{SPH}$ (i.e. if $t = \mathsf{ph}_k(I)$ and $t' = \mathsf{ph}_k(I')$ then $\mathsf{det}_k(t, t') = 0$). More formally for all PH adversaries $\mathcal{A}$

$$Prob[\mathsf{k} \leftarrow \mathsf{kg}(1^n); \ (I, I') \leftarrow \mathcal{A}^{DB_k(\cdot)}; \ \mathsf{sim}(I, I') = 1;$$
$$t \leftarrow \mathsf{ph}_k(I); \ t' \leftarrow \mathsf{ph}_k(I'); \ \mathsf{det}_k(t, t') = 0] = \mathsf{negl}(n)$$

3.2   Public-Key Perceptual Hash Definition

As we discussed earlier, the problem with the private-key ph is that the client during Image Registration must completely trust the platform and reveal her image.

We would like to have a public-key version of a perceptual hash scheme as follows:

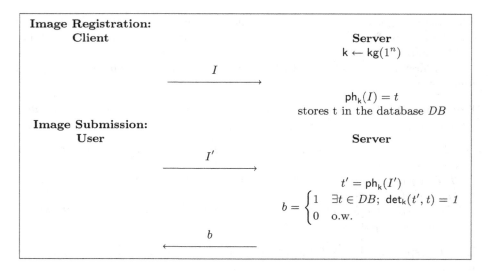

Fig. 1. Private-key perceptual hash $\mathcal{SPH} = (\mathsf{kg}, \mathsf{ph}, \mathsf{sim}, \mathsf{det}))$

- Setup: The platform (e.g., Facebook) generates a pair of secret-public key, and broadcasts only the public key.
- Image Registration: A client produces the tag of her image using the public key then PH algorithm and sends the tag T to the server. The server stores T in the database.
- Image Submission: A user submits an image I, the server computes its tag and compares it with the ones stored in the database.

More formally,

Definition 3. *A public-key perceptual hash scheme $\mathcal{PPH}$ consists of three algorithms as follows,*

- *The key generation algorithm* KG *that takes the security parameter 1^n and outputs a pair of secret key/public key* $(\mathsf{sk}, \mathsf{pk})$.
- *The perceptual hash function* PH *that takes the public key and an image and computes a tag for the image.*
- *The* Det *algorithm that takes the secret key and two tags and decide if their underlying images are similar.*

The steps of the scheme are shown in Fig. 2.

As before we denoted with $\mathcal{A}^{DB_{pk,sk}(\cdot)}$ the adversary who is allowed to interact arbitrarily with the stateful oracle DB via the Image Registration and Submission procedures.

We say that a public key perceptual hash scheme $\mathcal{PPH}$ is secure with respect to Sim if no PH adversary is able to find two images I, I' which are perceptually similar ($\mathsf{Sim}(I, I') = 1$) but are not detected as such by $\mathcal{PPH}$ (i.e. if $T = \mathsf{PH}_k(I)$

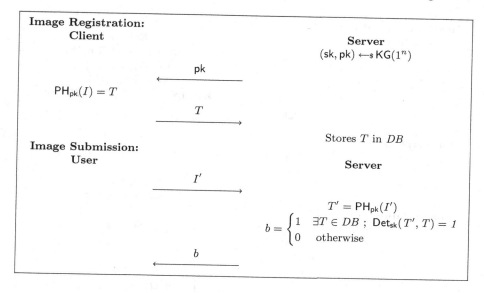

Fig. 2. Public-key PHash $\mathcal{PPH} = (\mathsf{KG}, \mathsf{PH}, \mathsf{Sim}, \mathsf{Det})$

and $T' = \mathsf{PH_k}(I')$ then $\mathsf{Det_k}(T, T') = 0)$. More formally for all PH adversaries $\mathcal{A}^{DB_{pk,sk}(\cdot)}$

$$Prob[(\mathsf{sk}, \mathsf{pk}) \leftarrow \mathsf{KG}(1^n);\ (I, I') \leftarrow \mathcal{A}^{DB_{pk,sk}(\cdot)}(\mathsf{pk});\ \mathsf{Sim}(I, I') = 1;$$
$$T \leftarrow \mathsf{PH_{pk}}(I);\ T' \leftarrow \mathsf{PH_{pk}}(I');\ \mathsf{Det_{sk}}(T, T') = 0] = \mathsf{negl}(n)$$

3.3 The Construction of Public-Key PHash from Private-Key Phash

In this section, we show how to construct a secure public-key perceptual hash scheme based on a secure private-key one.

Our first attempt is to start from a secure private key perceptual hash $\mathcal{SPH} = (\mathsf{kg}, \mathsf{ph}, \mathsf{det})$ and a fully homomorphic encryption scheme $\mathcal{E} = (\mathsf{KGen}, \mathsf{Enc}, \mathsf{Dec}, \mathsf{Eval})$.

Setup. The key generation algorithm KG for the public key PH function will work as follows. First it generates a secret key $\mathsf{k} \leftarrow \mathsf{kg}$ for $\mathcal{SPH}$ and public/secret key pair for the FHE $(PK, SK) \leftarrow \mathsf{KGen}$. It then encrypts k using PK: $\mathsf{ck} \leftarrow \mathsf{Enc}_{PK}(\mathsf{k})$. The public key for the public-key perceptual hash consists of $\mathsf{pk} = [PK, \mathsf{ck}]$. The secret key is set to $\mathsf{sk} = [SK, \mathsf{k}]$.

Image Registration. During the registration phase, the client computes the function PH as follows. It runs the evaluation algorithm Eval on keyed[1] ph,

---

[1] Abusing notation we use ph to refer also to the circuit for the algorithm ph and this is the circuit fed to Eval by the client.

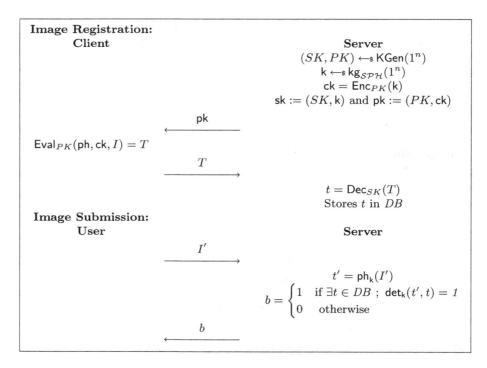

Fig. 3. Public-key PHash $\mathcal{PPH} = (\mathsf{KG}, \mathsf{PH}, \mathsf{Sim}, \mathsf{Det})$

encrypted k and her image I: $T = \mathsf{Eval}_{PK}(\mathsf{ph}, \mathsf{ck}, I)$ which due to the property of FHE is $T = \mathsf{Enc}_{PK}(t = \mathsf{ph}_\mathsf{k}(I))$. The server using the FHE secret key SK, first decrypt the tag T and stores the underlying tag t.

Image Submission. At image submission the Det algorithm works as follows. When a user (possibly an adversary) wants to upload a photo I', the server first computes its tag $t' = \mathsf{ph}_\mathsf{k}(I')$ and compares it with all the keyed tags stored in the database. If it finds t such that $\mathsf{det}_\mathsf{k}(t, t') = 1$ it rejects, otherwise it accepts I'.

The scheme[2] is shown in more details in Fig. 3.

If we try to prove the security of the scheme in Fig. 3, we end up on a dead end. To show the public-key perceptual hash scheme $\mathcal{PPH}$ is secure if the underlying keyed perceptual hash scheme $\mathcal{SPH}$ is secure, we try to build a *reduction*. We assume by contradiction that the public-key scheme $\mathcal{PPH} = (\mathsf{KG}, \mathsf{PH}, \mathsf{Det})$ is not secure and there exists an efficient adversary $\mathcal{A}$ which breaks it for a particular

---

[2] Note that our construction is not exactly conforming to Definition 3; We should technically store the encrypted tag T, and then at image submission, the server would compute PH on I', i.e.another encrypted tag, and then the Det algorithm would decrypt and compare. Our construction is equivalent and is more efficient since it reduces the number of FHE operations.

similarity function Sim. We need to build an efficient adversary $\mathcal{B}$ that breaks the security of the secret-key scheme $\mathcal{SPH} = (\text{kg}, \text{ph}, \text{det}))$.

An attempt to build algorithm $\mathcal{B}$ would work as follows: $\mathcal{B}$ is allowed to interact via Image Registration and Submission with a private key $\text{k} \leftarrow \text{kg}(1^n)$. It can run the public key adversary $\mathcal{A}$ as a subroutine. The first thing that $\mathcal{B}$ has to do is to provide $\mathcal{A}$ with a public key. $\mathcal{B}$ can generate PK for the FHE, but then does not really know what to encrypt for $\text{ck} = \text{Enc}_{PK}(\text{k})$ since it does not know k. So it sets $\text{ck} = \text{Enc}_{PK}(r)$ for some arbitrary value r. It then provides $\mathcal{A}$ with $\text{pk} = [PK, \text{ck}]$, which $\mathcal{A}$ accepts as it looks indistinguishable from a real key due to the semantic security of the FHE.

Now $\mathcal{B}$ has to simulate the Image Registration and Submission public key procedures for $\mathcal{A}$. It can easily simulate the Registration procedure since $\mathcal{B}$ does not have to provide any output here. But $\mathcal{B}$ will get stuck in the simulation of the Image Submission procedures. Here it is not clear how $\mathcal{B}$ can answer in a way consistent with an actual PH algorithm.

If $\mathcal{B}$ set $r = \widehat{\text{k}}$ for a correct secret key for $\mathcal{SPH}$ then it would be able to answer correctly. But the deceptive answer of $\mathcal{A}$ would not be related to the actual key k that $\mathcal{B}$ wants to break. On the other hand if r is arbitrary the simulation will not be indistinguishable at all, as there may not even be a way to answer consistently.

The problem is that we need $\mathcal{B}$ to simulate an environment for $\mathcal{A}$ which implements the PH with secret key k. But $\mathcal{B}$ has no information about k, though he is allowed to query its own Image Registration and Submission with that key.

THE CORRECT APPROACH. To solve that problem we require the user during the Image Registration phase to prove in a zero-knowledge way that he knows the image is registered. The zero-knowledge part is required to preserve the privacy of the user (she still reveals nothing about the image being registered). The proof of knowledge is needed to build a successful reduction.

The scheme is described in Fig. 4. Setup and Image Submission are identical to the ones from the flawed scheme described above. Image Registration proceeds as before but after the user submits T, the user and the server engage in a zero-knowledge proof of knowledge of the image I such that $T = \text{Enc}_{PK}(t = \text{ph}_\text{k}(I))$.

Moving to the proof of security, the adversary $\mathcal{B}$ runs the adversary $\mathcal{A}$ on $\text{pk} = [PK, \text{ck}]$, where $\text{ck} = \text{Enc}_{PK}(r)$ for some arbitrary value r.

At Image Registration, the adversary $\mathcal{B}$ extracts the image I being registered by $\mathcal{A}$ and submits it via its own Image Registration oracle to the secret key $\mathcal{SPH}$ running under key k that he is trying to break.

At Image Submission, when $\mathcal{A}$ submits I', the simulator $\mathcal{B}$ submits I' to its own Image Submission oracle and relies its answer to $\mathcal{A}$.

We note that the simulation produced by $\mathcal{B}$ is indistinguishable from a real execution in which $\mathcal{A}$ ran against a $\mathcal{PPH}$ with secret key k. Indeed all the oracle queries are consistent with k since $\mathcal{B}$ relies them to its own oracles (that use k), and the only difference between a real execution and $\mathcal{B}$'s simulation is in the public key. In a real execution $\text{ck} = \text{Enc}_{PK}(\text{k})$, while in the simulation $\text{ck} = \text{Enc}_{PK}(r)$

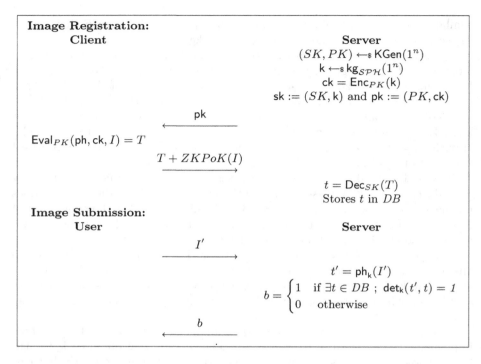

Fig. 4. Public-key PHash $\mathcal{PPH} = (\mathsf{KG}, \mathsf{PH}, \mathsf{Sim}, \mathsf{Det})$

for some arbitrary value r. But this is easily shown to be indistinguishable under the semantic security of the FHE scheme $\mathcal{E}$.

The above basically proves the following

Theorem 1. *Assuming* $\mathcal{E} = (\mathsf{KGen}, \mathsf{Enc}, \mathsf{Dec}, \mathsf{Eval})$ *is a semantically secure FHE scheme, and* $\mathcal{SPH} = (\mathsf{kg}, \mathsf{ph}, \mathsf{det})$ *a secure private-key perceptual hash scheme with respect to the similarity function* sim, *then the public-key perceptual hash scheme described in Fig. 4 is a secure public-key perceptual hash scheme with respect to the same similarity function* sim.

4   An Efficient Construction

We now show a particular example of PH function for which the above transformation can be efficiently carried out, using only additively homomorphic encryption rather than FHE. We first summarize the private-key perceptual hashing construction from [14], and then show that it can be easily transformed into a public-key one.

4.1 Outline of the Algorithm

We refer the reader to [14] for a complete description and empirical analysis of the hash function. Here, we summarize their method. For now we leave all the algorithm parameters unspecified and discuss how to set them in Sect. 5. Their algorithm (specifically the more robust "Scheme 2" in [14]) consists of the following steps. On input image I:

1. *Preprocessing.* After low-pass filtering, downsampling to a fixed size (512 × 512, as suggested by [14]), and histogram equalization, a pixel matrix $i(x, y)$ is obtained. A Fourier transform is then applied. Let $I(\rho, \theta)$ denote the Fourier-transformed $i(x, y)$, in polar coordinates.
2. *Feature Generation.* The algorithm chooses m sets $\{\Gamma_j\}_{j \in [m]}$, where each $\rho \in \Gamma_j$ is uniformly chosen (without repetition) from the set of possible radii (determined by the size of the downsampled image). Each ρ is also associated with a random number β_ρ (chosen according to a Gaussian distribution). The secret key is used for the random selections of $\rho \in \Gamma_j$ and β_ρ.
   The algorithm then takes a β_ρ-weighted combination for $\rho \in \Gamma_j$ of summations of the magnitude of I along the θ-axis at the points $\left\{ \left(\rho, \frac{(2i+1)\pi}{K} \right) \right\}_{i=0}^{K-1}$, i.e.,

$$h_j = \sum_{\rho \in \Gamma_j} \beta_\rho \sum_{i=0}^{K-1} \left| I(\rho, \frac{(2i+1)\pi}{K}) \right| \tag{1}$$

   yielding a feature vector $[h_1, \ldots, h_m]$.
3. *Post Processing.* Quantization and compression are performed on the feature vector obtained above, and a permutation (derived from the key) is applied to the compressed result.

4.2 Evaluation on an Encrypted Key

We first point out that the Preprocessing Step does not involve any use of the secret key, so we assume that the client performs it before any interaction with the Server.

To implement our transformation, the Server has to provide an encryption of the secret key. As we pointed out above, during Feature Generation the secret key is used to generate the β_ρ values and to select which $\rho \in \Gamma_j$. Therefore these are the only values we need to hide in the computation of our public key. Let

$$\beta_{\rho,j} = \begin{cases} \beta_\rho & \text{if } \rho \in \Gamma_j \\ 0 & \text{else.} \end{cases}$$

The public key of the scheme will be a Paillier public key together with Paillier encryptions $\widehat{\beta}_{\rho,j}$ of $\beta_{\rho,j}$ for each radius ρ and each $j \in [m]$.

Setting $c_\rho = \sum_{i=0}^{K-1} \left| I(\rho, \frac{(2i+1)\pi}{K}) \right|$, the client's computation is then expressed as

$$\widehat{h}_j = \hat{c}_0 \prod_{\rho=1}^{u} (\widehat{\beta}_{\rho,j})^{c_\rho} \bmod N^2 \tag{2}$$

where $\widehat{h}_j$ is a Paillier encryption of the j-th entry of the feature vector $[h_j]$ and $\hat{c}_0$ is an encryption of 0.

The client sends the encrypted vector $[\widehat{h}_j]$ to the Server together with a ZKPoK of the values c_ρ (described below).

The server can now decrypt the feature vector and proceed with the Post Processing phase (which might include other components of the secret key, but can be done without interacting with the client).

THE ZKPOK PROOF. Dropping the index j, the client has to prove that he knows a vector $[c_\rho] \in \mathbb{Z}_N$ (for $\rho = 1\ldots, u$) such that

$$\hat{h} = \prod_{\rho=1}^{u} (\hat{\beta}_\rho)^{c_\rho} \bmod N^2$$

This is a standard proof of knowledge of the representation of $\hat{h}$ with respect to basis $[\hat{\beta}_\rho]$ which can be performed as follows

- The Client computes $\hat{R} = \prod_{\rho=1}^{u} (\hat{\beta}_\rho)^{r_\rho} \bmod N^2$ for values $r_\rho \in_R \mathbb{Z}_N$.
- The Server sends a random challenge $e \in_R \mathbb{Z}_N$.
- The Client answers with $s_\rho = r_\rho + ec_\rho \bmod N$.
- The Server checks that $\prod_{\rho=1}^{u} (\hat{\beta}_\rho)^{s_\rho} = \hat{R}\hat{h}^e \bmod N^2$.

The proof of security of this scheme immediately follows from the security of the generalized FHE scheme[3].

5   Implementation and Analysis

In this section we explore the efficiency of the scheme in Sect. 4 through implementation tests. As we show below, with some careful optimization much of the computation on encrypted values can be vectorized, making the cryptographic overhead of transforming the algorithm in [14] from private-key to public-key rather modest. This yields a highly efficient scheme in practice.

---

[3] The ZK proof described above is only honest-verifier ZK, which is sufficient in our scenario since we assume honest but curious players (see Sect. 6) but it can be turned into a full ZK proof by standard techniques.

5.1 Parameter Settings

In our implementation we had to decide how to set the parameters in [14] where many of them had been left unspecified[4].

The only parameter set in [14] was $K = 360$. For the value m (the length of the feature vector) we chose $m = 23$ (the reason for this choice is explained below). Somewhat arbitrarily we set the size of every Γ_j to 3 and chose the distribution of the β_ρ as a Gaussian with mean $\mu = 50$ and variance $\sigma = 10$.

We have no way of guaranteeing that with this choice of parameters the algorithm in [14] will display the remarkable robustness properties shown in the implementation tests of [14]. However in our implementation tests the algorithm performed reasonably well against many image manipulations.

We stress however that the goal of our experiments was to quantify the cost of the cryptographic overhead of the "private to public key" transformation. On that front, the choice of parameters has a minimal effect and we are confident that our timings are valid regardless of how one chooses the parameters above.

The only difference would be if we need to increase the length of the feature vector. We point out that the final hash in [14] was 400 bits long. This implies an extraction of about 18 bits from each feature of the vector if $m = 23$ which we believe is reasonable. In any case the timings reported below can be adjusted by a multiplicative factor of λ for a feature vector of length 23λ.

5.2 Optimizations

Perhaps the most important optimization from the basic description in Sect. 4 comes from the observation that there is a lot of extra "space" in each ciphertext. This allows us to vectorize the computation, thereby reducing the work by a substantial factor. The plaintext group for Paillier is $\mathbb{Z}_N$, where N is an integer of at least 1024 bits, which as we will show is much larger than the values β_ρ and h_j to be encoded in ciphertexts. Let us compute bounds on h_j. First note that with high probability, $\beta_\rho \leq 128 \stackrel{\text{def}}{=} M_\beta$ for each ρ (these values were normally distributed with $\mu = 50, \sigma = 10$), and thus we can force $\beta_\rho \leq 128$ via rejection sampling without noticeably impacting the performance or security of the hash function. Let s denote the width of the scaled image. Then from Parseval's formula and the Cauchy inequality, we have the bound

$$c_\rho \leq \sum_{\rho,\theta} |I(\rho,\theta)| \leq s^2 \left(\sum_{x,y\in[s]} |i(x,y)|^2 \right)^{1/2}$$
$$\leq s^3 \sup_{x,y\in[s]} |i(x,y)|. \qquad (3)$$

---

[4] We repeatedly contacted the authors of [14] to inquire about how they had set those parameters in their implementation but received no answer. We were not able to locate the code used in [14] for their experiments either.

Given the maximal (grayscale) pixel value of 255, and given that the image is scaled to 512×512 during preprocessing, we have $c_\rho \leq 255 \cdot 512^3 = 34225520640 \overset{\text{def}}{=} M_c$, which we note is independent of K.[5] Now let $B = M_\beta \cdot M_c \cdot |\Gamma_j| + 1$ so that for all $j \in [m]$, we have

$$h_j = \sum_{\rho \in \Gamma_j} \beta_\rho c_\rho \leq M_\beta \cdot M_c \cdot |\Gamma_j| < B. \tag{4}$$

Let $\ell = \lfloor \log_B(N) \rfloor$ so that $B^\ell \leq N$ (this ensures that any base B, ℓ-digit number will be smaller than N). Concretely, we would have $\ell = 23$ for any 1024 bit modulus, given our setting of $|\Gamma_j| = 3$ and thus $B = 13142599925761$. We can now modify the scheme as follows: suppose for simplicity that the number of features m is equal to ℓ, and define values

$$\eta_\rho = \sum_{j=0}^{\ell-1} B^j \beta_{\rho,j}. \tag{5}$$

Letting $\widehat{\eta}_\rho$ be an encryption of η_ρ, the client could then compute and return to the server

$$\widehat{h} = \prod_{\rho=1}^{u} (\widehat{\eta}_\rho)^{c_\rho}. \tag{6}$$

Note that upon decryption of $\widehat{h}$, the server will find a feature vector of length ℓ encoded in the base B digits of the result. The bound in (4) ensures that no "carries" occur in any of the base B digits. This provides a factor of ℓ speedup, which is substantial. As mentioned, for our settings $\ell = 23$, but even for large values of $|\Gamma_j|$, we would still have $\ell \geq 20$. Lastly, we note that the proof of knowledge in § 4.2 works identically in this situation, just using $\widehat{\eta}_\rho$ in place of $\widehat{\beta}_\rho$.

Depending on the parameters, some additional optimizations are also possible. If m is large (and hence the product in (6) must be computed repeatedly), addition chains can be precomputed for the exponents c_ρ, reducing the number of multiplications required for each exponentiation. Furthermore, to compute the long sequence of multiplications in the product, intermediate values could be kept in Montgomery form until the end. Also note that for small values of ρ, the sum c_ρ is "degenerate" in the sense that there will be far fewer than K distinct pixel values at radius ρ. Thus it may be sensible for the server to *publicly* constrain the range of radii that will be used so that each $\Gamma_j \subset [l, u]$ for $l = \lceil K/2\pi \rceil$, thereby improving the client's efficiency. This somewhat increases an adversary's ability to find images with colliding hashes, however in our main applications we are far more concerned with the opposite problem of an adversary producing non-colliding hashes from similar images.

---

[5] We note that the seemingly crude estimate $c_\rho \leq K \cdot s^2 \cdot 255$ is actually better if $K \leq s$.

5.3 Analysis and Benchmarks

We consider here the cost of our scheme relative to the original work of [14], which must be privately evaluated by the server. As the image preprocessing (the computation of c_ρ) is identical for our scheme as that of [14], we focus our analysis on the additional work performed by our client, which is essentially the work to compute the product in (6). Lastly, we compare this additional work to the total cost of computing the perceptual hash.

Analysis. We begin with an asymptotic analysis of the cost in terms of the security parameter and the size of the downsampled image. Let s denote the width in pixels of the scaled image (which we take to be square). For the unoptimized version, a client in our scheme must compute $\widehat{h}_j$ for $j \in [m]$ as in (2). Since $c_\rho = \mathcal{O}(\mathsf{poly}(s))$ as shown in (3), we see that an upper bound on the number of modular multiplications would be $\mathcal{O}(ms\log(c_\rho)) = \mathcal{O}(ms\log(s))$, using any efficient algorithm for modular exponentiation (e.g., square and multiply). Applying the main optimization from Sect. 5.2, m effectively drops out of the equation,[6] as we now compute the single product in (6). Letting $\lambda = \log N$, where N is the modulus used by Paillier, then the cost of our optimized scheme is now $\mathcal{O}(s\log(s)\lambda^2)$, even with a naive $\mathcal{O}(\lambda^2)$ method for multiplication of long integers. The proof of knowledge is a similar computation to that of $\widehat{h}$, however the exponents are much larger (random elements of $\mathbb{Z}_N$). Since λ certainly upper bounds $\log(s)$, the cost of the overhead for the full scheme (including the PoK)

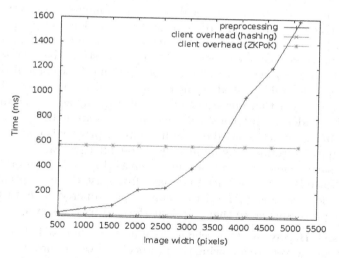

Fig. 5. Pre-processing cost (grayscale; gaussian blur; histogram equalization; FFT) vs additional work for computing on encrypted data (client's overhead).

---

[6] We can think of m in this case as being determined by the security parameter of the encryption scheme.

is $\mathcal{O}(s\lambda^3)$. As for the size of keys, the server's private key can simply be the seed for a pseudorandom function. However, the public key will be $\mathcal{O}(ms\lambda)$ bits. With our concrete setting of parameters, public keys are approximately 65 KB.

Benchmarks. For benchmarking we wrote a C/C++ prototype of the algorithm, making use of the CImg library [15] for the image pre-processing phase, and libpaillier [2] for handling Paillier encryption. For our settings of parameters (and indeed for most reasonable settings), we found that the scheme (with optimizations) does not dramatically increase the cost of computing the hash. By far, the most expensive element of our computation is the proof of knowledge, but even this takes less than 600ms on our test machine (a 2011 laptop). The preprocessing phase of an image of around 3500 pixels wide equals the cost of the overhead of our scheme. These results are summarized in Fig. 5.

6   Remarks

Is the Image Hidden? Can we claim that the image is hidden in our public key scheme? The answer is not that simple. If we take the standard definition of semantic security [9] as our notion of hiding, then this is clearly impossible. Remember that semantic security means that the adversary (in our case the server) cannot distinguish between two pictures. But our system is exactly designed to recognize pictures!

What we would like to say is that whatever information is leaked about the image by the underlying secret key scheme, then our simulation argument shows that our public key scheme leaks the same amount. But even this is not necessarily true since the standard definition of FHE does not guarantee *circuit privacy* (i.e. hiding the function which is applied to the encrypted data – which in our case depends on the image being hashed). If we strengthen the requirement on FHE to be circuit private (i.e. that no information is leaked about the function except what is inevitably leaked by the result of the computation itself), then we obtain our statement that our scheme does not leak any additional information. We refer the reader to [4] for a survey on circuit-private FHE.

In our efficient scheme based on Paillier, circuit privacy is guaranteed by the additional noise introduced by adding the zero-ciphertext $\hat{c}_0$.

We can safely conjecture that schemes such as [14] are at least one-way meaning it is infeasible to reconstruct the image from just the perceptual hash tag. For our efficient scheme we need to assume this property holds to the scheme before post-processing since that step is performed by the server[7].

Semi-honest Behavior. Our scheme assumes semi-honest behavior in which both client and server are following the protocol and we are protecting only from un-necessary leaking of information. In other words the Server (e.g. Facebook) is not maliciously trying to learn the images submitted by the Client.

---

[7]   This notion of one-wayness can be strengthened by using the similarity predicate and assuming that it infeasible to reconstruct an image that is perceptually similar to the one submitted by the client.

One could strengthen the model by enforcing a proof of correctness for the generation of the public key by the Server, that would guarantee to the Client that the evaluation is performed correctly.

7   Conclusions

Our work shows that constructing publicly evaluatable perceptual hash schemes can be feasible. We hope that our work will lead to the design of systems that help reining in online abuse over social media, and encourage users to participate in the creation of blacklist databases to stop the spread of non-consensual intimate imagery. On that front, important future directions are to apply our techniques to other perceptual hash schemes used in practice (such as PhotoDNA) and deploy such systems in the real world.

References

1. Photodna, May 2019. https://www.microsoft.com/en-us/photodna
2. Bethencourt, J.: Paillier library (2006). http://acsc.cs.utexas.edu/libpaillier/
3. Bloom, D.: Facebook Wants Your Nude Photos; What Could Possibly Go Wrong? (2018)
4. Bourse, F., Del Pino, R., Minelli, M., Wee, H.: FHE circuit privacy almost for free. In: Robshaw, M., Katz, J. (eds.) CRYPTO 2016. LNCS, vol. 9815, pp. 62–89. Springer, Heidelberg (2016). https://doi.org/10.1007/978-3-662-53008-5_3
5. Damgård, I., Jurik, M.: A generalisation, a simplification and some Applications of Paillier's probabilistic public-key system. In: Kim, K. (ed.) PKC 2001. LNCS, vol. 1992, pp. 119–136. Springer, Heidelberg (2001). https://doi.org/10.1007/3-540-44586-2_9
6. Farid, H.: Reining in online abuses. Technol. Innov. **19**(3), 593–599 (2018)
7. Feige, U., Fiat, A., Shamir, A.: Zero-knowledge proofs of identity. J. Cryptol. **1**(2), 77–94 (1988). https://doi.org/10.1007/BF02351717
8. Gentry, C.: Fully homomorphic encryption using ideal lattices. In: STOC 2009: Proceedings of the 41st Annual ACM Symposium on Theory of Computing, pp. 169–178. ACM, New York (2009)
9. Goldwasser, S., Micali, S.: Probabilistic encryption. JCSS **28**(2), 270–299 (1984)
10. Goldwasser, S., Micali, S., Rackoff, C.: The knowledge complexity of interactive proof systems. SIAM J. Comput. **18**(1), 186–208 (1989)
11. Jurik, M.J.: Extensions to the Paillier cryptosystem with applications to cryptological protocols. BRICS (2003)
12. Paillier, P.: Public-key cryptosystems based on composite degree residuosity classes. In: Stern, J. (ed.) EUROCRYPT 1999. LNCS, vol. 1592, pp. 223–238. Springer, Heidelberg (1999). https://doi.org/10.1007/3-540-48910-X_16
13. Solon, O.: Facebook asks users for nude photos in project to combat revenge porn (2017)
14. Swaminathan, A., Mao, Y., Wu, M.: Robust and secure image hashing. IEEE Trans. Inf. Forensics Secur. **1**(2), 215–230 (2006)
15. Tschumperle, D.: Cimg library, May 2019. http://cimg.eu/
16. Venkatesan, R., Koon, S.-M., Jakubowski, M.H., Moulin, P.: Robust image hashing. In: Proceedings 2000 International Conference on Image Processing (Cat. No. 00CH37101), vol. 3, pp. 664–666. IEEE (2000)

TrollThrottle—Raising the Cost of Astroturfing

Ilkan Esiyok[1(✉)], Lucjan Hanzlik[2], Robert Künnemann[1], Lena Marie Budde[3], and Michael Backes[1]

[1] CISPA Helmholtz Center for Information Security, Saarbrücken, Germany
ilkan.esiyok@cispa.saarland
[2] CISPA Helmholtz Center for Information Security, Stanford University, Stanford, USA
[3] Saarland University, Saarbrücken, Germany

Abstract. Astroturfing, i.e., the fabrication of public discourse by private or state-controlled sponsors via the creation of fake online accounts, has become incredibly widespread in recent years. It gives a disproportionally strong voice to wealthy and technology-savvy actors, permits targeted attacks on public forums and could in the long run harm the trust users have in the internet as a communication platform.

Countering these efforts without deanonymising the participants has not yet proven effective; however, we can raise the cost of astroturfing. Following the principle 'one person, one voice', we introduce TrollThrottle, a protocol that limits the number of comments a single person can post on participating websites. Using direct anonymous attestation and a public ledger, the user is free to choose any nickname, but the number of comments is aggregated over all posts on all websites, no matter which nickname was used. We demonstrate the deployability of TrollThrottle by retrofitting it to the popular news aggregator website Reddit and by evaluating the cost of deployment for the scenario of a national newspaper (168k comments per day), an international newspaper (268k c/d) and Reddit itself (4.9M c/d).

Keywords: Anonymous communications · Unlinkability · Censorship

1 Introduction

Astroturfing describes the practice of masking the sponsor of a message in order to give it the credibility of a message that originates from 'grassroots' participants (hence the name). Classic astroturfing involves paid agents fabricating false public opinion surroundings, e.g., some product. The anonymity of the cyberspace makes astroturfing very inexpensive; now, it can even be mechanised [22]. This form of astroturfing, also called 'cyberturfing', is a Sybil attack that exploits a useful, but sometimes fallible heuristic strategy in human cognition: roughly speaking, the more people claim something, the improved judgement of credibility [32,33]. In the wake of the 2016 US elections, Twitter identified, '3,814 [..] accounts' that could be linked to the Internet Research Agency

© Springer Nature Switzerland AG 2020
M. Conti et al. (Eds.): ACNS 2020, LNCS 12147, pp. 456–476, 2020.
https://doi.org/10.1007/978-3-030-57878-7_22

(IRA), a purported Russian 'troll factory'. These accounts 'posted 175,993 Tweets, approximately 8.4% of which were election-related' [44], which is likely only a fraction of the overall activity. This influence comes at a modest price, as the IRA had a \$1.25M budget in the run-up to the 2016 presidential election [3] and only 90 members of staff producing comments [16].

The everyday political discourse has also suffered. Many newspapers have succumbed under the weight of moderation, e.g., the New York Times [21]. Some newspapers decided to move discussion to social media [48], where they only moderate a couple of stories each day and leave out sensitive topics such as migration altogether [39]. Kumar et al. show that many popular news pages have hundreds of active sock puppets, i.e., accounts controlled by individuals with at least one other account [31]. The New York Times, one of the largest newspapers worldwide, has put serious effort and technological skills into moderating discussion, but ultimately, they had to give up. In mid-2017, they reported how they employ modern text analysis techniques to cluster similar comments and moderate them in one go. At that point in time, they had 12 members of staff dedicated to moderation, handling a daily average of 12,000 comments [35]. Despite the effort and expertise put into this, they had to give up three months later, deactivating the commenting function on controversial topics [21].

In this paper, we propose a cryptographic protocol that permits throttling the number of comments that a single user can post on all participating websites *in total*. The goal is raising the cost of astroturfing: if the threshold is τ, the cost of posting n comments is the cost of acquiring $\lceil \frac{n}{\tau} \rceil$ identities, be it by employing personnel, by bribery or by identity theft. Our proposal retains the anonymity of users and provides accountability for censorship, i.e., if a user believes her comment ought to appear on the website, she can provide evidence that can be evaluated by the public to confirm misbehaviour on the part of the website. Part of this system is a pseudo-random audit process to ensure honest behaviour, which we have formally verified.

We show that this protocol, TrollThrottle, can be retrofitted to existing websites. We set up a forum[1] on Reddit that demonstrates our proposal. We also compute the additional cost of operation incurred by our protocol by simulating user interaction for three real-life scenarios: an international newspaper, a nationwide publication and all comments posted on Reddit in one day. In the newspaper case, the computational overhead incurs a cost of about \$1.20; for the whole of Reddit, \$3.60 is sufficient.

As a by-product and second contribution, we extend the notion of direct anonymous attestation (DAA) by proposing two features with applications outside our protocol. Both are already supported by an existing DAA scheme by Brickell and Li [13]. First, updatability, which means that the issuer can non-interactively update the users' credentials. This allows for easy key rollover in the mobile setting and for implicit revocation of credentials by not updating them (old credentials invalidated). Second, instant linkability, which means that each signature contains a message-independent pseudonym that determines whether

---

[1] https://old.reddit.com/r/trollthrottle/.

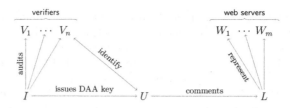

Fig. 1. Approach

two signatures can be linked. This allows to efficiently determine whether a signature can be linked to any existing signature within a given set (Fig. 1).

2   TrollThrottle

Despite text analysis techniques that can facilitate moderation, e.g., clustering [35], many local and international newspaper websites gave up on moderating and disabled commenting sections [21,48]. Even if troll detection could be automated, e.g., via machine learning, as soon as the detection algorithm becomes available to attackers, numerous techniques permit the creation of adversarial examples [34] to evade classifiers. Fundamentally, astroturfing does not even rely on automated content generation and can be conducted by paid authors in countries with low labour cost: e.g., the so-called 50-cent party, a group of propagandists sponsored by China, was named after the remuneration they receive per comment [36].

Our approach is orthogonal to detection by content. If we can limit the number of messages to a certain threshold τ that each physical person can send per day, bots become largely useless, and troll farms need to pay, bribe or steal identities from sufficiently many actual people to send messages in their name. Besides raising the cost, this also raises the probability of detecting larger operations.

We built our approach on direct anonymous attestation (DAA [11]). In DAA, an issuing party distributes membership credentials to signers (in our case users) that it considers legitimate. Each signer can prove membership by signing data: a valid DAA signature guarantees that a valid signer signed this data, but does not reveal the signer's identity. DAA schemes can also be seen as group signature schemes that prevent the issuing party to identify the signer of the message, a feature known as *opening*.

To avoid a single point of trust, the identification of the user is not only a matter of the issuer, who is likely to be the provider of this service. Instead, an agreed upon set of verifiers establishes the legitimacy of users, i.e., that they are real people and that they have not received a DAA key before. We will discuss how the issuer and the verifiers keep each other honest in the full version [20]. To provide accountability, a public ledger keeps records about the comments that websites ought to publish.

Thus, the following parties cooperate in TrollThrottle: an issuer I, who issues DAA keys, a set of verifiers V, who verify the users' identities, a set of users U, who create DAA signatures of their comments, a public append-only ledger L, who records these signatures, and a set of websites, who verify these signatures and are bound to publish comments whose signatures exist on the ledger.

In DAA, a signature can be created and verified with respect to a so-called *basename*. Signatures created by the same user with the same basename can be linked. This is the key feature to achieve throttling. Within a commenting period t, e.g., a day, only signatures with a basename of the form (t, seq) are accepted, where seq is a sequence number between 1 and the desired threshold τ. If a user signs two messages with the same basename, they can be linked and discarded by the website. Hence a user can create at most τ signatures that are unlinkable to each other. A valid DAA signature assures the website that a valid user signed this comment, but neither the website, nor the issuer or the verifier learns who created the comment, or which other comments they created.

By storing the signatures on the ledger L, the websites (a) can enforce a global bound, and (b) provide accountability for censorship by promising to represent all comments addressed to this website that appear in the ledger. If a website does not publish a user's comment, it must have sufficient grounds for censorship.

We build on Brickell and Li's DAA scheme [13] for its efficiency, but extend it with various features to make TrollThrottle more efficient (see the full version [20, Appendix A]), more secure (Sect. 3), more practical (Sect. 4), and more resistant against compromise (Sect. 4).

We assume the issuer I is known to all users and websites; the verifiers V are known to the issuer and all websites; and the public ledger L is known to all participants in the protocol. The ledger can be implemented using a consensus mechanism between the websites and some trusted representatives of civil society (e.g., via Tendermint [24] or PBFT [17]) or open consensus mechanisms like blockchains. We will formalise our approach in terms of PPT algorithms and an interactive protocol.

Definition 1 (Accountable Commenting Scheme). *An accountable commenting scheme consists of a tuple of algorithms* (Setup, KeyGen, Comment, Verify, Claim, VerifyClaim) *and an interactive protocol* (Join − Issue). *The algorithms and the protocol are specified as follows.*

Setup(1^λ) models the generation of a setup parameter ρ used by all participants from the security parameter 1^λ. This parameter is an implicit argument for the other algorithms, but we omit it for brevity. The issuer I invokes KeyGen(ρ) to generate its secret key sk_I and public key pk_I from this parameter.

The issuing procedure $\langle$Join(pk_I, U) $\leftrightarrow$ Issue(sk_I, ver, U)$\rangle$ is an interactive protocol between I and a new user (identified with U) that has not registered so far. At the end of the protocol, the user receives a credential $cred_U$ and a secret key sk_U. For now, we abstract away from the verifiers by giving the issuer access to a read-only database ver such that ver[V, U] $\in \{0, 1\}$ is 1 iff the verifier

V confirms the identity of a user. In Sect. 4, we present and verify a protocol to implement and audit this verification step.

The commenting procedure is split into four PPT algorithms, Comment for U to generate comments that she sends to the ledger, Verify for W to verify that a comment on the ledger should be displayed, Claim for U to generate a claim that a valid comment on the ledger ought to be published, and VerifyClaim for the public to verify that said claim is valid.

Comment($pk_I, sk_U, cred_U, dom, m$) is executed by U, who knows the issuer's public key pk_I, its own secret key sk_U and credentials $cred_U$. U chooses a basename $dom \in \{0,1\}^*$ and a message $m \in \{0,1\}^*$ and obtains a signed comment γ and a pseudonym nym, both of which she stores on the ledger. The basename determines a user's nym, so that anyone can check whether two comments were submitted with the same basename by checking their respective nyms for equality. This is a key feature: in TrollThrottle, all basenames have to be of the form $\langle t, i \rangle$ for a commenting period t and an integer $i \in \{1, \ldots, \tau\}$. Hence there are at most τ unique basenames within t, and thus at most τ nyms per sk_U and t.

Verify($pk_I, nym, dom, m, \gamma$) can be computed by any website that has access to the issuer's public key pk_I, the comment on the ledger γ, pseudonym nym, domain dom (which can be determined by trial and error) and a message $m \in \{0,1\}^*$ received from the user. If the output is 1 and γ is valid w.r.t. m, the website W must display m. If W fails to do that, the user computes Claim($pk_I, sk_U, cred_U, dom, m, \gamma$) on the same data as before. The output *evidence* can be publicly verified using the VerifyClaim($pk_I, dom, m, \gamma, evidence$) algorithm. It outputs 1 iff *evidence* and the ledger entry γ prove that m ought to be displayed during the commenting period indicated by dom.

3   Protocol Definition

Before we present TrollThrottle as an instance of an accountable commenting scheme, we introduce the necessary cryptographic notions.

We follow the DAA definition proposed in [13]. A DAA scheme consists of four PPT algorithms (Setup$_{DAA}$, Sign$_{DAA}$, Verify$_{DAA}$, Link$_{DAA}$) and an interactive protocol (Join − Issue$_{DAA}$), between parties: an issuer I, a verifier V and a signer S. In our case, the websites take the role of the verifiers, and the users the role of the signer.

Setup$_{DAA}(1^\lambda)$ is run by I; based on the security parameter 1^λ, it computes the issuer's secret key sk_I and public key pk_I, including global public parameters. Join − Issue$_{DAA}$ is an interactive protocol between I and S to provide credentials issued by I to S. It consists of sub-algorithms Join$_{DAA}$ and Issue$_{DAA}$. S executes Join$_{DAA}(pk_I, sk_S)$ on input pk_I and sk_S to obtain the commitment com.[2] I executes Issue$_{DAA}(sk_I, com)$ to create a credential $cred_S$ that is associated with sk_S and sent to S. Note the key of S remains hidden from I.

---

[2] We slightly alter the original definition and assume that instead of sampling this key inside the algorithm, S provides the key as an input.

$\mathsf{Sign}_{\mathsf{DAA}}(sk_S, creds_S, dom, m)$ is executed by S to create a signature σ for a message m w.r.t. a basename dom, which is optionally provided by V. If $dom \neq \bot$, signatures created by the same signer can be linked.

$\mathsf{Verify}_{\mathsf{DAA}}(pk_I, m, dom, \sigma, RL)$ is a deterministic algorithm run by V on a message m, a basename dom, a signature σ, and a revocation list RL to determine if a signature σ is valid. In [13], I stores revoked secret keys in the revocation list RL; signatures created with a revoked secret key are not valid.

$\mathsf{Link}_{\mathsf{DAA}}(\sigma_0, \sigma_1)$ is a deterministic algorithm that determines with overwhelming probability whether signatures σ_0 and σ_1 were created by the same signer with the same basename $dom \neq \bot$. It outputs 1 if the signatures are linked, 0 for unlinked and $\bot$ for invalid ones.

DAA Features. Brickell and Li's DAA scheme [13] has the following security properties (formally stated in the full version [20, Appendix F]).

Correctness: If an honest signer's secret key is not in the revocation list RL, then, with overwhelming probability, signatures created by the signer are accepted and correctly linked by an honest verifier.

User-Controlled-Anonymity: A PPT adversary has a negligible advantage over guessing in a game where she has to distinguish whether two given signatures associated with different basenames were created by the same signer or two different signers.

User-Controlled-Traceability: No PPT adversary can forge a non-traceable yet valid signature with $dom \neq \bot$[3] without knowing the secret key that was used to create the signature, or if her key is in the revocation list RL.

We add the following property (formally stated in the full version [20, Appendix A]):

Instant-Linkability: There is a deterministic poly-time algorithm NymGen s.t. $\mathsf{NymGen}(sk_S, dom)$ generates a nym that is otherwise contained in the signature, and two nyms are equal iff the corresponding signatures are linkable.

Zero-Knowledge: The user creates non-interactive proofs of knowledge to show that her key was honestly generated. We highlight the notation here and refer to the full version [20, Appendix C.1] for the full security definitions. Let $\mathcal{R}$ be an efficiently computable binary relation. For $(x, w) \in \mathcal{R}$, we call x a *statement* and w a *witness*. Moreover, $L_{\mathcal{R}}$ denotes the language consisting of statements in $\mathcal{R}$, i.e., $L_{\mathcal{R}} = \{x \mid \exists w : (x, w) \in \mathcal{R}\}$.

Definition 2. *A non-interactive proof of knowledge system Π consists of the following three algorithms* ($\mathsf{Setup}, \mathsf{CreateProof}, \mathsf{VerifyProof}$). $\mathsf{Setup}(1^\lambda)$: *on input security parameter* 1^λ, *this algorithm outputs a common reference string* ρ. $\mathsf{CreateProof}(\rho, x, w)$: *on input common reference string* ρ, *statement* x *and witness* w; *this algorithm outputs a proof* π. $\mathsf{VerifyProof}(\rho, x, \pi)$: *on input common reference string* ρ, *statement* x *and proof* π; *this algorithm outputs either* 1 *or* 0.

---

[3] Note that basenames in TrollThrottle are always different from $\bot$, see Sect. 3.

TrollThrottle: We will now present TrollThrottle in terms of an accountable commenting scheme (see Definition 1). Besides an instantly linkable DAA scheme, we assume a collision-resistant hash function h and a non-interactive proof of knowledge system for the relation:

$$((\mathsf{com}, pk_{I,\mathsf{DAA}}), (sk_{S,\mathsf{DAA}})) \in \mathcal{R}_{\mathsf{Join}} \iff \mathsf{com} \xleftarrow{\$} \mathsf{Join}_{\mathsf{DAA}}(pk_{I,\mathsf{DAA}}, sk_{S,\mathsf{DAA}}).$$

We assume that the witness for the statement $(\mathsf{com}, pk_{I,\mathsf{DAA}})$ contains the random coins used in $\mathsf{Join}_{\mathsf{DAA}}$.

Definition 3. *TrollThrottle Protocol*

$\mathsf{Setup}(1^\lambda)$ - *compute the parameters for the zero-knowledge proof of knowledge* $\rho_{\mathsf{Join}} \xleftarrow{\$} \mathsf{Setup}_{\mathsf{ZK}}(1^\lambda)$ *and output* $\rho = (1^\lambda, \rho_{\mathsf{Join}})$.

$\mathsf{KeyGen}(\rho)$ - *execute* $(pk_{I,\mathsf{DAA}}, sk_{I,\mathsf{DAA}}) \xleftarrow{\$} \mathsf{Setup}_{\mathsf{DAA}}(1^\lambda)$, *set and return* $pk_I = pk_{I,\mathsf{DAA}}$ *and* $sk_I = (pk_{I,\mathsf{DAA}}, sk_{I,\mathsf{DAA}})$.

$\mathsf{Join}(pk_I, sk_U, U)$ - *let* $pk_I = pk_{I,\mathsf{DAA}}$ *and* $sk_U = sk_{S,\mathsf{DAA}}$. *Run* $\mathsf{com} \xleftarrow{\$} \mathsf{Join}_{\mathsf{DAA}}$ $(pk_{I,\mathsf{DAA}}, sk_{S,\mathsf{DAA}})$ *and compute proof* $\Pi_{\mathsf{Join}} = \mathsf{CreateProof}(\rho_{\mathsf{Join}}, (\mathsf{com}, pk_{I,\mathsf{DAA}}), sk_{S,\mathsf{DAA}})$. *Send* $(\mathsf{com}, \Pi_{\mathsf{Join}})$ *to the issuer and receive* $cred_U$. *Return* $(cred_U, sk_U)$.

$\mathsf{Issue}(sk_I, \mathsf{ver}, U)$ - *parse* $sk_I = (pk_{I,\mathsf{DAA}}, sk_{I,\mathsf{DAA}})$. *Receive* $(\mathsf{com}, \Pi_{\mathsf{Join}})$ *from the User. Abort if the proof is invalid, i.e.,* $\mathsf{VerifyProof}(\rho_{\mathsf{Join}}, (\mathsf{com}, pk_{I,\mathsf{DAA}}), \Pi_{\mathsf{Join}}) = 0$. *Otherwise, execute the* $\mathsf{Issue}_{\mathsf{DAA}}$ *protocol with input* $(\mathsf{com}, sk_{I,\mathsf{DAA}})$, *receiving credentials* $cred_U$. *Send* $cred_U$ *to the user.*

$\mathsf{Comment}(pk_I, sk_U, cred_U, dom, m)$ - *set and return* $\gamma = (\sigma, nym, dom, h(m))$ *where* $\sigma \xleftarrow{\$} \mathsf{Sign}_{\mathsf{DAA}}(sk_U, cred_U, dom, h(m))$ *and* $nym \xleftarrow{\$} \mathsf{NymGen}(sk_U, dom) = \mathsf{NymExtract}(\sigma)$.

$\mathsf{Verify}(pk_I, nym, dom, m, \gamma)$ - *Parse* $\gamma = (\sigma, nym, dom, h^*)$ *and* $pk_I = pk_{I,\mathsf{DAA}}$. *Output* 1 *iff* $\mathsf{Verify}_{\mathsf{DAA}}(pk_{I,\mathsf{DAA}}, h^*, dom, \sigma, RL_\emptyset) = 1$, $h(m) = h^*$, $\mathsf{NymExtract}(\sigma) = nym$, *and* $\mathsf{VerifyBsn}(\sigma, dom) = 1$.

$\mathsf{Claim}(pk_I, sk_U, cred_U, dom, m, \gamma)$ - *return evidence* $= \gamma$.

$\mathsf{VerifyClaim}(pk_I, dom, m, \gamma, evidence)$ - *Parse* $\gamma = (\sigma, nym, dom, h)$ *and output* 1 *iff* $\mathsf{Verify}(pk_I, nym, dom, m, \gamma) = 1$.

The algorithms Setup and KeyGen generate the issuer's DAA keys and parameters for the non-interactive zero-knowledge proof of knowledge for the relation $\mathcal{R}_{\mathsf{Join}}$. The $\mathsf{Join} - \mathsf{Issue}$ protocol closely resembles the $\mathsf{Join} - \mathsf{Issue}_{\mathsf{DAA}}$ protocol of the DAA scheme with two main differences. Firstly, the user provides her secret key as input to the Join algorithm. This is for practical reasons: in Sect. 4, we explain how this key can be recomputed from a pair of login and password using a key derivation function when a user switches machines. The second difference is the Π_{Join} proof created by the user to ensure honestly generated secret keys and allow the security reduction to extract secret keys generated by the adversary. We remark that during the $\mathsf{Join} - \mathsf{Issue}$ protocol, the user communicates with a publicly known verifier who validates her identity and confirms it to I. In Sect. 4, we present a protocol for obtaining this confirmation and running a pseudo-probabilistic audit of V by I.

Comment creates the information that U stores on the ledger, consisting of the signed comment γ and pseudonym nym. To provide accountability for censorship, U sends the signature to the ledger, which notifies the website W. At this point, W must publish the comment $\gamma = (\sigma, nym, dom, m)$ as long as the signature σ, message and dom are deemed valid, and nym appears exactly once on the ledger.

With the validity requirement on the basename dom and the ability to detect repeated basenames in the ledger, we can easily implement the desired throttling mechanism. Let τ be a threshold for some time frame (e.g., a day) and let t mark the current period. Then, a valid dom is of the form (t, seq) with $seq \in \{1, \ldots, t\}$. The sequence number seq in dom is allowed to arrive out-of-order, but it cannot be larger than τ. The throttling is ensured because there exist only τ valid basenames per commenting period and thus only τ valid nym per (sk_U, dom).

If W refuses to publish the comment, then U can use Claim to claim censorship and provide the entry on the ledger γ and m as evidence to the public that m ought to be displayed. The public checks the same conditions that W should have applied. Part of this check is to interpret a common agreement for moderation, which we discuss in more detail in Sect. 4, but do not model explicitly. We show the security of this protocol in the cryptographic model, see the full version [20, Appendix B].

4   Practical Implementation

A deployable system needs more than just a cryptographic specification, but a system of incentives and checks. First, we discuss what methods for identity verification are available. We detail how to identity verification can be deferred to the verifiers and misbehaviour can be detected using pseudo-probabilistic audits. A realistic system also has to deal with revocation, which we solve by exploiting a novel property called *updatability*. Finally, we discuss questions related to the end user: how moderation is handled and where to store credentials. Table 1 summarises the protocol components and their security analysis.

Table 1. Overview: security analysis.

Components	Security analysis
Base protocol	Cryptographic proof [20, App. B]
Encrypted ledger	Strictly weakens the attacker
Identity verification	Formally verified [20, App. 4]
Revocation	Simple hybrid argument using [20, App. F]
Extended protocol	Cryptographic proof [20, App. C]
Storing credentials	Trivial modification

Table 2. Time periods used in protocol.

Name	Symbol	Purpose	Typical duration
Epoch	t_e	Implicit revocation	One week
Billing period	t_b	Billing	One month
Commenting period	t	Throttling	One day

Identity Providers: The verifiers need to attest that only real people receive digital identities and each person obtains only one. We discuss multiple competing solutions to this problem, none perfect by itself. In combination, however, they cover a fair share of the users for our primary target, news websites.

Identity Verification Services (IVS): Banks, insurers and other online-only services already rely on so-called identity verification services, e.g., to comply with banking or anti-money laundering regulations. Usually, IVS providers verify the authenticity of claims using physical identity documents, authoritative sources, or by performing ID checks via video chat or post-ID. McKinsey anticipates the market for IVS to reach $16B-20B by 2022 [46]. The business model of these companies revolves around their trustworthiness.

Subscriber Lists: Newspaper websites are the main targets of our proposal, because of their political and societal relevance and the moderation cost they are currently facing. It is in their interest to provide easy access to their subscribers. Insofar as bills are being paid, they do have some assurance of the identity of their subscribers, so they can use their existing relationship to bootstrap the system by giving access to their customers right away.

Biometric Passports and Identification Documents: Biometric passports are traditional passports that have an embedded electronic microprocessor chip containing information for authenticating the identity of the passport holder. The chip was introduced to enable additional protection against counterfeiting and identity theft. This authentication process can be performed locally (as part of e.g., border control) or against a remote server. Biometric passports are standardised by the International Civil Aviation Organization (ICAO) [27] and issued by around 150 countries [23].

Encrypting Comments on the Ledger: We distinguish a billing period t_b that is distinct from the commenting period t (see Table 2). Assume a CCA-secure public key encryption scheme ($\mathsf{KG_{enc}}$, enc, dec), a collision-resistant hash function h and a standard existentially unforgeable digital signature scheme ($\mathsf{KG_{sig}}$, sig, ver). We apply the accountable commenting scheme from Definition 3. The output of Comment is encrypted with a public key pk_{W,t_b} distributed to all websites participating in the current billing period t_b. Claims need to include the randomness used to encrypt. See Fig. 2 for the complete message flow.

Deferring Identity Verification with Pseudo-probabilistic Auditing: Our security model in he full version [20, Appendix B] abstracts away from the communication between verifier and issuer. We propose a protocol to implement this step and formally verify it in the symbolic setting, which is better suited for reasoning about complex interactions. The protocol (Fig. 3) improves privacy by hiding the identity verification process from the issuer and improves accountability by providing a pseudo-random audit.

We assume a collision-resistant one-way hash function h to instantiate a binding commitment scheme. When a user wants to register, the website directs

0. U can restore sk_U from $login$ and pw,
   and download $h(login)$, $cred_{t_e}$ from L:
   $$sk_U := kdf(login, pw)$$
   $$L \rightarrow U : \{h(login), cred_{t_e}\}$$
1. U computes the basename from date and sequence:
   $$dom := (t, seq)$$
2. U computes the nym from sk_U and dom:
   $$nym := \mathsf{NymGen}(sk_U, dom))$$
3. U signs the hash of his comment:
   $$\sigma := \mathsf{Sign}(sk_U, cred, dom, h(m), W)$$
4. U encrypts σ, attaches metadata and sends it to L:
   $$\gamma := \{enc(pk_{W, t_b}, (\sigma, nym); r), h(m), W, dom\}$$
   $$U \rightarrow L : \gamma$$
5. L notifies W and U sends the raw comment to W:
   $$L \rightarrow W : \gamma$$
   $$U \rightarrow W : m$$
6. W decrypts γ and verifies the following:
   σ valid, $\mathsf{VerifyBsn}(\sigma, dom) = 1$, $seq \leq \tau$, m acceptable.
7. W queries L with nym:
   $$nym := \mathsf{NymExtract}(\sigma)$$
   $$W \rightarrow L : nym$$
8. W publishes m if nym fresh and m acceptable.
9. U claims censorship to public, if m not published:
   $$claim_U := \{\sigma, nym, r, m\}$$
   $$U \rightarrow public : claim_U$$

1. U creates a secure channel with I, with session id sid:
   $$I \rightarrow U : sid$$
2. U chooses $login$, pw and random r_U, sends to I:
   $$r_U \leftarrow_\$ \{0, 1\}$$
   $$U \rightarrow I : login, h(r_U, nbd, 1)$$
3. I chooses random nonce r_I, creates a commitment c_I,
   signs it and sends it to U:
   $$r_I \leftarrow_\$ \{0, 1\}$$
   $$c_I := h(r_I, sid, h(r_U, nbd, 1))$$
   $$I \rightarrow U : sig(sk_I, c_I)$$
4. U creates a secret key from his $login$ and pw:
   $$sk_U := kdf(login, pw)$$
5. U creates a secure channel with V and sends:
   $$U \rightarrow V : \{nbd, c_I, r_U, sig(sk_I, c_I)\}$$
6. V verifies U's identity with evidence E,
   signs the commitment and sends it to U:
   $$\psi := sig(sk_V, c_I)$$
   $$V \rightarrow U : \psi$$
7. U recreates the secure session with the previous sid,
   and sends the commitment (signed by V) to I:
   $$U \rightarrow I : \psi$$
** U and I run Join $-$ Issue protocol (Fig. 4)
** I use ψ to start auditing with V (Fig. 6)

Fig. 2. Message flow for commenting. In step-0, the user's secret DAA key is restored using a password, see Sect. 4, and the entries in the ledger are encrypted. Also, we identify the comment m by its hash to save space on the ledger.

Fig. 3. Identity verification protocol specification

her to the issuer. They run an authentication protocol akin to the ASW protocol for fair exchange where, in the end, U gets V's signature on a commitment c_I generated by I. Only with this signature, the issuer runs the Join $-$ Issue procedure from Definition 3 (repeated in Fig. 4 for completeness). Note that the ledger distributes the issuer's public key and public parameters. In Sect. 4, we explain a revocation mechanism that is based on updating the issuer's public key every epoch and publishing the fresh key in the ledger. U also makes use of the ledger by storing its credentials in case it needs to recover its state (see Sect. 4).

After verification, I may trigger a pseudo-random audit by sending the previously hidden values sid, r_I in the commitment c_I of the identity verification protocol to V (see Fig. 6). If the hash of these values matches the hash of V's signed commitments, an audit is triggered. If we consider a random oracle in place of the hash function, the probability of an audit is $\Pr[\text{audit}] = 2^{-L}$, where L is the number of bits both parties compare. L is agreed upon in advance, to define this probability. Since the nonce r_I has been revealed to V before, I cannot modify the second hash (s') to avoid audit. As the digital signature scheme is

1. U downloads pk_I from L :
   $$L \to U : pk_I$$
2. U and I run Join $-$ Issue$_{\text{DAA}}$ proto. using sk_U and pk_I for epoch t_e, and U gains $cred_{t_e}$ and w_{t_e}.
3. U inserts $h(login)$ and $cred_{t_e}$ into L :
   $$U \to L : h(login), cred_{t_e}$$
4. I inserts $h(login)$ and w_{t_e} into L :
   $$I \to L : h(login), w_{t_e}$$

Fig. 4. Join $-$ Issue protocol specification

1. I announces new epoch t'_e and updates her pk_{I,t'_e} :
   $$I \to L : t'_e$$
2. I asks all Vs, to report all valid $logins$ to be updated :
   $$V \to I : \text{sig}(sk_V, (\text{'update'}, c_I))$$
3. I obtains $update\ message\ u$ for all valid $logins$ from L :
   $$L \to I : h(login, u)$$
4. I creates new credentials for each $login$:
   $$cred_{t'_e} := \text{Issuer}_{\text{DAA}}(sk_I, pk_I, u)$$
5. I stores new credentials for each $login$ in L :
   $$I \to L : h(login, cred_{t'_e}, t'_e)$$

Fig. 5. Certificate update protocol specification

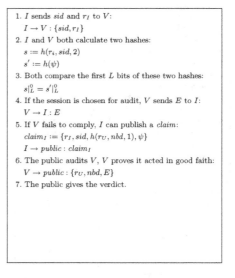

1. I sends sid and r_I to V :
   $$I \to V : \{sid, r_I\}$$
2. I and V both calculate two hashes:
   $$s := h(r_i, sid, 2)$$
   $$s' := h(\psi)$$
3. Both compare the first L bits of these two hashes:
   $$s|_L^0 = s'|_L^0$$
4. If the session is chosen for audit, V sends E to I :
   $$V \to I : E$$
5. If V fails to comply, I can publish a $claim$:
   $$claim_I := \{r_I, sid, h(r_U, nbd, 1), \psi\}$$
   $$I \to public : claim_I$$
6. The public audits V, V proves it acted in good faith:
   $$V \to public : \{r_U, nbd, E\}$$
7. The public gives the verdict.

Fig. 6. Auditing protocol specification

existentially unforgeable, I cannot fabricate a valid signature to raise the probability of an audit and to learn something about U. If the session is chosen for audit, V has to hand over the evidence $\{E\}$ it collected for identification—this is a standard procedure for IVS. If V fails to comply, then I can publish a $claim$ and the public can determine whether to audit V.

Presuming that I is honest, the probability that colluding U and V can create n usable fake identities is thus bound by $(1 - \text{Pr}[\text{audit}])^n + \text{negl}(\lambda)$ for some negligible function $\text{negl}(\lambda)$.

The auditing protocol is very simple cryptographically, but has many possible message interleaving. It is well known that pen-and-paper proofs for such protocols are not only tedious, but also prone to errors. We analyse the protocol in the symbolic model, using the SAPIC process calculus [30] and Tamarin protocol verifier [40]. We formally verify that:

1. Whenever I accepts to run the Join $-$ Issue protocol with a user, V has validated her identity, unless I or V are dishonest.
2. When determining the need for an audit, neither a dishonest I, nor a dishonest V can predict the value of the other party, unless both are dishonest. Therefore, they cannot trigger or avoid the audit.
3. If the public accepts a claim, then V did indeed receive the values r_I and sid and send out ψ (unless V is dishonest and tricks itself into the obligation of an audit). As these values determine both hashes, the public can now decide if an audit was justified.

The verification takes about 10 sec on a 3.1 GHz Intel Core i7 and 16 GB RAM computer.[4]

Revocation: In case U runs the identification protocol a second time with a different V, or simply forgets her password and needs to re-identify, her previous DAA key $sk_{U,DAA}$ needs to be revoked. But how can U revoke her DAA key if she forgets her password? We circumvent this problem by *implicit revocation*: DAA keys are short-lived by default, but the system can issue new keys without interacting with the user. Keys that are not issued are thus implicitly revoked by the end of their lifetime, which we call the *epoch* (see Table 2).

At the start of each epoch t_e, I defines a new public key pk_{I,t'_e} which is chosen so that I can recompute all credentials $cred_{t'_e}$ for the new epoch by itself (see Fig. 5). At this point, only those DAA keys remain valid, for which such a $cred$ is computed, all others are implicitly revoked. If a user forgets her password, she reports to the verifier, who confirms (by means of the commitment c_I) that her old key is invalidated. Starting from the next epoch, she can use her new key. To allow for such mechanism, the DAA scheme has to be structured in a way that I can update her public key and all users 'credentials without any interaction.

Brickell and Li's scheme with a minor modification possess these features (see the full version [20, Appendix F] for a formal proof).

Updatability is interesting on its own: it allows for regular, non-interactive key rollovers in DAA. I can create each user's credential offline, so the user can fetch this credential (in encrypted form) at later point, even if I is offline.

Holding the Issuer Accountable: In TrollThrottle, a corrupt issuer and verifier can collude to introduce arbitrarily many valid credentials into the system. This form of Sybil attack is difficult to counter while retaining the user's privacy: Without trust in either the verifiers or the issuer, the only way of determining whether a user is legitimate is to have another entity (e.g., the websites, or the public) check this identity—otherwise, the adversary controls all parties involved. Even if done in a pseudo-random manner similar to the auditing procedure in Sect. 4, the loss of individual privacy would be considerable.

In the full version [20, Appendix C] we present the extended TrollThrottle protocol to mitigate this issue to the extent possible. Here, for every user that joins, a *genesis block* is added to the ledger. This block is signed by the verifier, which allows the public to tell how many credentials were validated by each verifier. Large-scale fraud could thus be detected through an unusual number of participants coming from a single verifier. This information is public and can be computed by any participant at any time.

During the commenting phase, U downloads a subset of genesis tuples[5] and computes a zero-knowledge proof that her genesis tuple is part of this set. She includes this proof along with the time point at which she queried the list in her

---

[4] See the full version [20, Appendix E] for the model code.

[5] To achieve, e.g., anonymity among 100 users, about 49 KB of data is downloaded once per commenting period.

DAA signature. In the full version [20, Appendix C.5], we show that for Brickell and Li's scheme [13], we can instantiate a non-interactive proof of knowledge system with proofs that are logarithmic in the number of genesis tuples in the ledger. We show that, in addition to the security properties in the full version [20, Appendix B], no adversary can create comments that cannot be attributed.

Other Considerations: News websites need to moderate comments (see step 8 in Fig. 2). This decision is ultimately a human decision, but it should be based on a binding agreement between the websites and applying laws.

Also, many users expect a system where they can log in from any platform. We, therefore, allow users to restore their identities, by making the users' secret keys e.g., sk_U derivable from their login and password chosen by themselves in the identification process. Hence, we assume there exists an efficient key-derivation function *kdf* that maps to the space of secret keys. Such a function exists for the scheme we use, where the secret key is just an element in $\mathbb{Z}_q^*$. The secret key sk_U can be recomputed with the *kdf* and the DAA credentials *cred* can be recovered from the ledger by querying with the hash of the login. Note that the login should not identify the user on other platforms, otherwise an attacker can use it to check if the user is participating in TrollThrottle. The last value of *seq* can be recovered by using bisection to discover the largest *seq* s.t. $\mathsf{NymGen}(sk_U, (t, seq))$ is on the ledger.

5   Evaluation

We evaluate TrollThrottle in terms of how easy it is to deploy, and how much performance overhead it incurs. To demonstrate the former, we retrofit it to an existing website, without any modification to the server-side code—in fact, without the website being aware of this. To demonstrate that it incurs only modest costs, we simulate realistic traffic patterns using a recorded message stream and measure computational overhead and latency.

Deployability: We demonstrate that the protocol can be deployed easily by retrofitting it, without any server-side changes, to Reddit.com, the most visited news website in the world [7] and an alleged target for large-scale astroturfing and propaganda efforts [43].

On Reddit, we created a forum as a testing ground. We implemented signature creation and verification in a JavaScript library and used a simple browser extension [5] to load this library when entering the forum. In an actual deployment, this library would be loaded via JavaScript inclusions. We point out, however, the known problem that there is no guarantee the website W is transmitting the correct script. This is a well-known issue for all web-based services that claim end-to-end security and sometimes mitigated by offering optional plugins (e.g., mega.co.nz). We also present the cryptographic implementation details of the simulation [6] in the full version.

Any comment posted in this subreddit is transmitted according to the protocol (see Fig. 2). As the server side is not validating the comments in this instance,

Fig. 7. Screenshot of Reddit deployment, for identity creation and commenting scenarios, see Retrofitting sub reddit

Table 3. Evaluation of Reddit case (3 cores).

Measure		Mean	Median	Variance
Issuing (on U)[1]	δ_U^{Issue}	0.038	0.036	0.069
Issuing (on W)[1]	δ_I^{Issue}	0.010	0.009	0.0006
Commenting[2]	δ^{Comment}	0.036	0.032	0.0003
Verification	δ^{Verify}	0.021	0.018	0.0002
Latency[3]	$t_f - t$	0.022	0.019	0.0002
Commenting (on U)[4]	$\delta_U^{\text{Comment}}$	0.058	0.057	0.01

(1) over all new users. (2) computation overhead w/ pre-computed signatures. (3) shows server-side total processing time. (4) on 1000 samples, single-threaded.

this task is performed by the JS library as well. It communicates with a simple HTTP server implementing the public ledger. Comments that do not pass are greyed out by using a subreddit-specific stylesheet (see Fig. 7).

Performance: To evaluate TrollThrottle's performance, we compiled three realistic datasets [2] to represent plausible scenarios. Our focus is on traditional news outlets that want to establish a close relation with their readership. We thus examine two scenarios in this domain, and a third, representing an extreme case: the entirety of Reddit, the largest website categorised as 'News' by Alexa [7]. We use Reddit to retrieve realistic commenting patterns for the following scenarios (more details in the full version [20]): (1) Scenario I: nationwide news source News websites operating on national scale have sharp traffic patterns, e.g., the users in the same time zone. We take Germany as an example and simulate the traffic patterns of the German-speaking r/de subreddit with a volume of 168k comments. (2) Scenario II: international newspaper We collect all comments on submitted links to nytimes.com over two months to reach 268k comments and aggregate them to a 24 h period. (3) Scenario III: Number of comments per day on Reddit From a 10-year dataset that includes all comments ever posted on Reddit, we pick the recent busiest day, which is 27 June 2019 with 4 913 934 comments.

Performance Measures: We focus on the performance requirements from the perspective of the news outlet that has to serve users within a given latency and compute the additional cost due to the new computations. To get a precise measure of the overhead incurred, our experiment only simulates the cryptographic operations and does not display the comments or use network communication. The computation is performed separately for the server and the client. We assume the issuer is trusted and thus disregard the extension in the full version [20, Appendix C].

Table 4. Scenarios for performance evaluation, including the number of comments, source of the data stream, number of Intel E5 2.6 GHz cores, operating cost per day, maximum latency, percentage of queries answered within 0.1 s, number of genesis tuples computed (i.e., number of distinct nicknames), and total ledger size.

Scenario	#comments	#cores	Daily cost	Max. latency	Latency < 0.1 s	#genesis tuples	Ledger size (MB)
Nationwide newspaper (r/de)	168k	1	$1.20	0.166 s	99,99%	13,975	204
International news. (url:nytimes)	268k	1	$1.20	0.391 s	99.99%	87,223	633
Reddit (r/all)	4.9M	3	$3.60	1.011 s	99.99%	1,217,761	10628

As for the other datasets, we collected the comments annotated with their author's nickname and the time point they were posted. The dataset is thus a sequence of tuples (t, u, m) ordered by the time point t at which u posted comment m. We assume each nickname corresponds to a different actual person, thus over-approximating the effort for key generation. For each (t, u, m), we (1) simulate the issuing protocol, if u comes out in the entire (10 years) dataset for the first time, (2) simulate the commenting protocol to produce a signature for the comment, and finally (3) simulate the server side signature verification.

Step (1) and (2) can be done in a pre-processing step, as they are computed by the user and issuer. We measure the time for commenting ($\delta^{\mathsf{Comment}}$) and issuing ($\delta_I^{\mathsf{Issue}}$ and $\delta_U^{\mathsf{Issue}}$, for the issuer and the user, respectively). For step (3), we simulate the load of the server side on a Ruby-on-Rails application with Nginx load balancer.

For each point (t, u, m) in the database, we simulate the arrival of the encrypted signature (γ, nym) resulting from pre-processing m, at time $t + \delta^{\mathsf{Comment}} + \delta_I^{\mathsf{Issue}} + \delta_U^{\mathsf{Issue}}$. We run Verify on the signature and measure the finishing time t_f, as well as the actual processing time δ^{Verify}. We report the results in seconds for the largest dataset in Table 3.

In Table 4, we report the number of cores needed and the cost incurred by the computations just described, i.e., the overhead compared to normal website operations. The number of cores to meet the latency requirement was estimated as described above and used in the simulation. To account for the cost, we employ the core hours metric, which is the product of the number of cores and the total running time on the server. We take Amazon on Demand EC2 pricing [1] as an example and assume $0.05 per core hour. We also report on the maximal latency encountered in the simulation and the percentage of comments that met the target latency of ≤ 0.1 s. Finally, we report the number of genesis tuples created in the ledger, i.e., the number of nicknames in the dataset, and the total size of the ledger, representing an over-approximation of the storage requirements of a single day of operation.

Since comments are hashed before signing, the communication overhead is approximately 2.4 KB, independent of the comment size. To evaluate the storage requirements on a consensus-based public ledger, we chose Tendermint [24] as an example. Tendermint employs a modified AVL tree to store key-value pairs. Values are kept in leaf nodes and keys in non-leaf nodes. The overhead is about 100 bytes per non-leaf node [4]. For the largest dataset, each participant in Tendermint would thus require approximately 12 GB of space. Once the current commenting period is over, the signed comments and hence most of the data can be purged. To allow accountability for censorship over the last month, the data of the last thirty commenting periods can be stored on less than 0.5 TB.

In summary, the additional cost on the websites is modest compared to the moderation effort saved.

6 Limitations

Despite the auditing by the issuer and the limited accountability for colluding issuer and verifiers in the extended protocol, we have centralised trusted authorities. One way to remove these is to introduce protocols that can recognise Sybils. This could relieve the issuer from the responsibility of auditing the verifiers and potentially allow for a protocol with accountability features to deter misbehaviour. As this topic is orthogonal to our protocol, we leave it for future work, but remark that, theoretically, Sybil-detection is possible without user identification. A potential approach is to combine biometric methods [8, 41] with captchas. Uzun and Chung proposed such a protocol to show liveness. Here, the user's response to a captcha involves physical actions (smiling, blinking) that she captures in a selfie video [45] within a 5 s time limit. Their approach is based on the fact that automated captcha-solving takes considerable time, and face reenactment (e.g., [42]) is difficult to do at scale. Building on the same assumptions, a Sybil-detection scheme could be built by pseudo-randomly defining sets of users that need to show liveness *at the same time*.

TrollThrottle aims to provide a similar user experience to website logins. Hence, all client-side secrets are derived from the login and password of the user and thus vulnerable to password-guessing attacks. This can be mitigated by incorporating a two-factor authentication into the protocol, or by setting up the key generation to require a password of sufficient length and entropy, as to enforce the use of password managers.

Finally, the client-side code is loaded by the website, which could potentially include a different script albeit this behaviour would leave traces. As previously discussed (see Sect. 5), this is a well-known problem for web-based apps, and usually mitigated by offering optional plugins.

7 Related Work

The detection of astroturfing has been tackled using reputation systems (e.g., [37]), crowdsourcing (e.g., [47]) and text analysis (e.g., [38]). Fundamentally, the posting profile of a politically motivated high-effort user is not very different from a state-sponsored propagandist [29], hence we focus on prevention instead of detection. The detection and prevention approaches could be combined, but detection approaches either come at a loss of accountability, or they need to explain their decisions, although many of them rely on the fact that the bot is not adapting to the mechanism (e.g., via adversarial machine learning).

Our approach is similar to anonymity protocols in which we specify a way of exchanging messages without revealing identities. In contrast to anonymity protocols, TrollThrottle provides anonymity with respect to the ledger, but presumes the communication channels to provide sufficient anonymity. By itself, TrollThrottle is not resistant against traffic analysis—here anonymity protocols come into play. One might ask whether anonymity protocols already do what TrollThrottle proposes to do. To the best of our knowledge, Dissent [18] is the only anonymity protocol that provides explicit accountability guarantees, but these pertain to the type of communication, not to sending more messages than allowed. Furthermore, unlinkability is not achieved within the group, but towards outsiders.

Pseudonymity systems like Nym [25] or Nymble [28] provide anonymous, yet authenticated access to services, but some allow resource owners to block access at their discretion. By using a ledger and a common set of rules, TrollThrottle users can claim and prove censorship, but have to trust the ledger. This is in contrast to p2p-protocols, where censors may be sidestepped, but cannot be forced to publish the content themselves. Dingledine et al. advocate for the transaction of reputation/credit between pseudonyms [19]. By contrast, the credit in our scheme is essentially the number of nyms. This simplifies the system and ensures unlinkability, at the cost of inherent limitations: the 'credit' is the same for every participant (τ for each commenting period) and cannot be transferred.

One of the main cryptographic components of TrollThrottle is a specific DAA scheme with additional properties (instant-linkability and updatability). DAA was introduced as a way to address privacy issues of the remote attestation protocol proposed for TPMs. We focused on the scheme by Brickell and Li [13], because it supports these properties, produces short signatures and because a reference implementation was available. Other DAA schemes(e.g., [11,12]) may also provide these properties.

There are building blocks besides DAA that are compatible with TrollThrottle. Anonymous Credentials (AC) allow users to prove (a set of) attributes about themselves to third parties, usually via an interactive protocol (but there are non-interactive schemes).

Single-show schemes (e.g., [9]), would require a fresh credential for each comment the user would like to post in the future. Multi-show schemes (e.g., [14]) mitigate this issue, but a user would still need a unique *attribute* per day and sequence number – this would allow the issuer to link comments. Therefore, lightweight AC schemes are not suitable – a fitting AC scheme needs to support domain-specific pseudonyms with a secret-key based attribute. Indeed, DAA can be viewed such a credential system with the DAA key as the attribute.

The most similar credential system to the DAA scheme, that we used, was proposed by Camenisch et al. [15]. In this system, an issuer creates and distributes so-called dispensers. Dispensers are used to create a pre-defined number of one-time credentials valid for a given date. This system can be immediately used in TrollThrottle. As an implementation was not available, we perform a qualitative analysis. On the one hand, verification is faster in their scheme, they perform seven multi-exponentiations in a prime order group and one in an RSA group, while Brickell and Li's scheme perform one multi-exponentiation in each group i.e., $\mathbb{G}_1, \mathbb{G}_2, \mathbb{G}_T$, and one pairing computation. On the other hand, the signatures, which consists of a unique serial number (similar to a pseudonym) and a number of proofs of consistency are at least twice as much larger and their size depend on how the proofs are implemented. This produces considerable computation and communication overhead in the ledger. Moreover, the verification of comments is performed by the websites, making verification efficiency less important than the size of the data included in the ledger. Therefore, the DAA scheme represents a preferable tradeoff.

8   Conclusion

The prevalence of social bots and other forms of astroturfing in the web poses a danger to the political discourse. As many newspapers are closing down their commenting functionality despite the availability of sophisticated detection methods, we argue that they should be combined with a more preventive approach.

We presented TrollThrottle, a protocol that raises the cost of astroturfing by limiting the influence of users that emit a large amount of communication, even if using different pseudonyms. TrollThrottle preserves anonymity, provides accountability against censorship, it is easy to deploy and comes at a modest cost. We also discuss its social impact in the full version [20, Appendix D].

By how much do we raise the cost of astroturfing? We shall regard the last week before the 2016 US election for a rough calculation. The computational propaganda project considered around 3.4M election-related tweets to be originating from bots who emit more than 50 messages per day [26]. If we assume a threshold of 20 messages/day and perfect coordination between the bots, 24 178 identities need to be stolen to reach the same target. A lab study [10] finds that users are willing to sell their Facebook accounts for $26 on average, which is only slightly above the black-market value for stolen verified Facebook accounts. Such operation would thus face a cost of $634 501 and a risk of detection.

Acknowledgements. This work has been partially funded by the German Research Foundation (DFG) via the collaborative research center "Methods and Tools for Understanding and Controlling Privacy" (SFB 1223), and via the ERC Synergy Grant IMPACT (Grant agreement 610150). The first author holds the Turkish Ministry of National Education Scholarship. The second author is supported by the German Federal Ministry of Education and Research (BMBF) through funding for the CISPA-Stanford Center for Cybersecurity (FKZ: 16KIS0762).

References

1. Amazon EC2 on-demand pricing. https://aws.amazon.com/ec2/pricing/on-demand/
2. Big query reddit dataset. https://bigquery.cloud.google.com/dataset/fh-bigquery: reddit_comments
3. Department of justice: Charges in case 1:18-cr-00032-dlf. https://www.justice.gov/file/1035477/download
4. Tendermint avl performance and benchmarks. https://github.com/tendermint/iavl/blob/master/PERFORMANCE.md
5. Trollthrottle Browser Extension. https://github.com/iesiyok/trollthrottle_chrome
6. Trollthrottle Simulation. https://github.com/iesiyok/trollthrottle
7. Alexa News (2019). https://www.alexa.com/topsites/category/Top/News
8. Azimpourkivi, M., Topkara, U., Carbunar, B.: A secure mobile authentication alternative to biometrics. In: Proceedings of the 33rd ACSAC. ACSAC 2017, pp. 28–41. ACM, New York (2017). https://doi.org/10.1145/3134600.3134619
9. Baldimtsi, F., Lysyanskaya, A.: Anonymous credentials light. In: CCS 2013, pp. 1087–1098. ACM (2013)
10. Benndorf, V., Normann, H.T.: The willingness to sell personal data. Scand. J. Econ. **120**(4), 1260–1278 (2018)
11. Brickell, E.F., Camenisch, J., Chen, L.: Direct anonymous attestation. In: CCS 2004, pp. 132–145. ACM (2004)
12. Brickell, E., Chen, L., Li, J.: A new direct anonymous attestation scheme from bilinear maps. In: Lipp, P., Sadeghi, A.-R., Koch, K.-M. (eds.) Trust 2008. LNCS, vol. 4968, pp. 166–178. Springer, Heidelberg (2008). https://doi.org/10.1007/978-3-540-68979-9_13
13. Brickell, E., Li, J.: A pairing-based DAA scheme further reducing TPM resources. In: Acquisti, A., Smith, S.W., Sadeghi, A.-R. (eds.) Trust 2010. LNCS, vol. 6101, pp. 181–195. Springer, Heidelberg (2010). https://doi.org/10.1007/978-3-642-13869-0_12
14. Camenisch, J., Drijvers, M., Dzurenda, P., Hajny, J.: Fast keyed-verification anonymous credentials on standard smart cards. In: Dhillon, G., Karlsson, F., Hedström, K., Zúquete, A. (eds.) SEC 2019. IAICT, vol. 562, pp. 286–298. Springer, Cham (2019). https://doi.org/10.1007/978-3-030-22312-0_20
15. Camenisch, J., Hohenberger, S., Kohlweiss, M., Lysyanskaya, A., Meyerovich, M.: How to win the clone wars: efficient periodic n-times anonymous authentication. In: CCS 2006, pp. 201–210. ACM (2006)
16. Carroll, O.: St. Petersburg troll farm to influence US election campaign. https://www.independent.co.uk/news/world/europe/russia-us-election-donald-trump-st-petersburg-troll-farm-hillary-clinton-a8005276.html
17. Castro, M., Liskov, B., et al.: Practical byzantine fault tolerance. In: OSDI 1999, pp. 173–186 (1999)
18. Corrigan-Gibbs, H., Ford, B.: Dissent: accountable anonymous group messaging. In: CCS 2010, pp. 340–350. ACM (2010)
19. Dingledine, R., Mathewson, N., Syverson, P.: Reputation in P2P anonymity systems. In: Workshop on Economics of Peer-to-Peer Systems. vol. 92 (2003)
20. Esiyok, I., Hanzlik, L., Kuennemann, R., Budde, L.M., Backes, M.: Trollthrottle - raising the cost of astroturfing (2020). https://arxiv.org/abs/2004.08836
21. Etim, B.: Why no comments? it's a matter of resources. https://www.nytimes.com/2017/09/27/reader-center/comments-moderation.html

22. Ferrara, E., Varol, O., Davis, C., Menczer, F., Flammini, A.: The rise of social bots. Commun. ACM **59**(7), 96–104 (2016). https://doi.org/10.1145/2818717
23. Gemalto: The electronic passport in 2018 and beyond, Jun 2018. https://www.gemalto.com/govt/travel/electronic-passport-trends
24. Herlihy, M., Moir, M.: Enhancing accountability and trust in distributed ledgers, June 2016
25. Holt, J.E., Seamons, K.E.: Nym: practical pseudonymity for anonymous networks. Internet Security Research Lab Technical Report 4, pp. 1–12 (2006)
26. Howard, P., Kollanyi, B., Woolley, S.C.: Bots and automation over twitter during the second us presidential debate. Technical report, Political Bots (2016)
27. ICAO: Machine Readable Travel Documents - Part 11: Security Mechanism for MRTDs. Doc 9303 (2015)
28. Johnson, P.C., Kapadia, A., Tsang, P.P., Smith, S.W.: Nymble: anonymous IP-address blocking. In: Borisov, N., Golle, P. (eds.) PET 2007. LNCS, vol. 4776, pp. 113–133. Springer, Heidelberg (2007). https://doi.org/10.1007/978-3-540-75551-7_8
29. Kreil, M.: Social bots, fake news und filterblasen (2017). https://en.wikipedia.org/wiki/List_of_newspapers_by_circulation
30. Kremer, S., Künnemann, R.: Automated analysis of security protocols with global state. In: S&P 2014, pp. 163–178. IEEE Computer Society (2014). https://doi.org/10.1109/SP.2014.18
31. Kumar, S., Cheng, J., Leskovec, J., Subrahmanian, V.: An army of me: Sockpuppets in online discussion communities. In: Proceedings of the 26th International Conference on WWW, pp. 857–866 (2017)
32. Kuran, T., Sunstein, C.R.: Availability cascades and risk regulation. Stan. L. Rev. **51**, 683 (1998)
33. Leiser, M.: Astroturfing, cyberTurfing and other online persuasion campaigns. EJLT **7**(1) (2016). http://ejlt.org/article/view/501
34. Li, Y., Ye, J.: Learning adversarial networks for semi-supervised text classification via policy gradient. In: Proceedings of the 24th ACM SIGKDD. KDD 2018, pp. 1715–1723. ACM, New York (2018). https://doi.org/10.1145/3219819.3219956
35. Long, K.: Keeping the times civil, 16 million comments and counting. https://www.nytimes.com/2017/07/01/insider/times-comments.html
36. Bristow, M., BBC News: China's internet 'spin doctors' (2008). http://news.bbc.co.uk/2/hi/7783640.stm
37. Ortega, F.J., Troyano, J.A., Cruz, F.L., Vallejo, C.G., Enríquez, F.:Propagation of trust and distrust for the detection of trolls in a social network. Comput. Netw. **56**(12), 2884 – 2895 (2012).https://doi.org/10.1016/j.comnet.2012.05.002, http://www.sciencedirect.com/science/article/pii/S138912861200179X
38. Peng, J., Choo, R.K., Ashman, H.: Astroturfing detection in social media: Using binary n-gram analysis for authorship attribution. In: 2016 IEEE Trustcom/BigDataSE/ISPA, pp. 121–128, Aug 2016. https://doi.org/10.1109/TrustCom.2016.0054
39. Reuter, M., Dachwitz, I.: Moderation bleibt handarbeit: Wie große online-medien leserkommentare moderieren. https://netzpolitik.org/2016/moderation-bleibt-handarbeit-wie-tageszeitungen-leserkommentare-moderieren
40. Meier, S., Schmidt, B., Cremers, C., Basin, D.: The TAMARIN prover for the symbolic analysis of security protocols. In: Sharygina, N., Veith, H. (eds.) CAV 2013. LNCS, vol. 8044, pp. 696–701. Springer, Heidelberg (2013). https://doi.org/10.1007/978-3-642-39799-8_48

41. Sluganovic, I., Roeschlin, M., Rasmussen, K.B., Martinovic, I.: Using reflexive eye movements for fast challenge-response authentication. In: Proceedings of the 2016 ACM SIGSAC CCS, pp. 1056–1067. ACM (2016)
42. Thies, J., Zollhofer, M., Stamminger, M., Theobalt, C., Nießner, M.: Face2Face: real-time face capture and reenactment of RGB videos. In: Proceedings of the IEEE CVPR, pp. 2387–2395 (2016)
43. Tony Romm, W.P.: Senate investigators want answers from reddit and tumblr on Russia meddling (2018)
44. Twitter, I.: Update on twitter's review of the 2016 US election. https://blog.twitter.com/official/en_us/topics/company/2018/2016-election-update.html
45. Uzun, E., Chung, S.P.H., Essa, I., Lee, W.: rtCaptcha: a real-time captcha based liveness detection system. In: NDSS. Georgia Institute of Technology (2018)
46. Vikram Iyer, M.C.: The next $20 billion digital market – id verification as a service (2018). https://fuelbymckinsey.com/article/the-next-20-billion-digital-market-id-verification-as-a-service
47. Wang, G., et al.: Social turing tests: Crowdsourcing sybil detection. arXiv preprint arXiv:1205.3856 (2012)
48. Wullner, D.: Lassen sie uns diskutieren. https://www.sueddeutsche.de/kolumne/ihre-sz-lassen-sie-uns-diskutieren-1.2095271

Author Index

Printed in the United States
By Bookmasters